Advance Praise for
Diversity in Couple and Family Therapy

"Shalonda Kelly brings a fresh perspective on diversity to the treatment of families and couples. Structural oppression is an overarching concept, different for each group, but pernicious nevertheless, in its effects on people engendered through stereotypes, intergenerational trauma, discrimination, and disparities. Building on earlier approaches calling attention to therapist self-awareness and knowledge, this book introduces and emphasizes a process approach to cultural competence which focuses on interactional processes—going beyond the therapist-client dyad to the exchange among families, couples, and therapists. It is how the complexity of social identities and their intersection influence the therapeutic process that needs attention. Shared history and experiences related to race, ethnicity, sexual orientation, gender and religion are all in the room. Hence, the concept of dynamic sizing—the ability to be flexible in individualizing knowledge of a client underscores the important balance between knowing the client and generalizing cultural-specific knowledge and world-views of the group to which the client belongs. It is a book worth reading with key concepts and practical tools for culturally competent practice."

Jean Lau Chin, EdD, ABPP
Professor, Adelphi University

"This outstanding book will make a major contribution to the field of couple and family therapy by providing experienced and beginning therapists with a comprehensive, in-depth view of multicultural and diversity issues. All chapters and case examples are exceptionally well written and include areas such as race, ethnicity, gender, sexual orientation, religion, spirituality, different socioeconomic levels and intersecting identities. It will be an excellent textbook for introductory as well as graduate-level courses in all programs training mental health professionals."

Nancy Boyd-Franklin, PhD
Distinguished Professor, Rutgers University
Author of *Black Families in Therapy: Understanding the African American Experience*

Diversity in Couple and Family Therapy

Diversity in Couple and Family Therapy

Ethnicities, Sexualities, and Socioeconomics

SHALONDA KELLY, PhD,
EDITOR

Race and Ethnicity in Psychology
Jean Lau Chin, Series Editor

 PRAEGER™

An Imprint of ABC-CLIO, LLC
Santa Barbara, California • Denver, Colorado

Library of Congress Cataloging-in-Publication Data

Names: Kelly, Shalonda.
Title: Diversity in couple and family therapy : ethnicities, sexualities, and
    socioeconomics / Shalonda Kelly, PhD, editor.
Description: Santa Barbara, California : Praeger, an Imprint of ABC-CLIO, LLC,
    [2017] | Series: Race and ethnicity in psychology | Includes bibliographical
    references and index.
Identifiers: LCCN 2016032095 (print) | LCCN 2016035272 (ebook) |
    ISBN 9781440833632 (alk. paper) | ISBN 9781440833649 (ebook)
Subjects: LCSH: African Americans—Counseling of. | African American
    families. | Family psychotherapy.
Classification: LCC RC451.5.N4 D58 2017 (print) | LCC RC451.5.N4 (ebook) |
    DDC 616.89/156—dc23
LC record available at https://lccn.loc.gov/2016032095

ISBN: 978-1-4408-3363-2
EISBN: 978-1-4408-3364-9

21 20 19 18 17   1 2 3 4 5

This book is also available as an eBook.

Praeger
An Imprint of ABC-CLIO, LLC
ABC-CLIO, LLC

130 Cremona Drive, P.O. Box 1911
Santa Barbara, California 93116-1911
www.abc-clio.com

This book is printed on acid-free paper ∞
Manufactured in the United States of America

Contents

Part III   Religious and Spiritual Identities

Part IV   Identity Intersections and Diverse Family Forms

Part V   Identity Models and Structural Systems

Part VI   Cross-Cultural Assessment, Research, and Practice on Health and Pathology

Acknowledgments

I thank everyone at Praeger/ABC-CLIO for helping me the entire way along. Alicia Merritt, the Consulting Acquisitions Editor, interested me in doing this volume; Dr. Jean Chin graciously allowed it into her Psychology, Race, and Ethnicity series; and Debbie Carvalko, the Senior Acquisitions editor, helped me gather information and graciously gave me time to produce the book. Thanks to the Praeger/ABC-CLIO staff who brought the book to fruition from behind the scenes.

Thanks to my family for their support and encouragement, especially my husband Ken who gave a listening ear and was my cheerleader all along the way. His daily actions show me the importance of couples and families.

I thank all of my academic colleagues and friends who gave pointers and support. I extensively thank Dr. Nancy Boyd-Franklin, my close friend and colleague, who advised me at every step and linked me to a great editor, Hazel Staloff. She and Drs. Daniela Blei and Traci Maynigo made the wisdom of various authors shine clearly and brightly. Special thanks to Dr. Maynigo for her organizational charts that created continuity across chapters and helped me reflect on the entire book.

I thank the Graduate School of Applied & Professional Psychology at Rutgers University, my academic home, which houses colleagues who truly value scholarship on diversity. Thanks to my graduate students whom I supervise in working with diverse couples and families, and my undergraduate students who I hope will join my field. I especially thank Simone Humphrey who assisted with my book proposal, and Brittani Hudson who assisted me in working with reviewers and in all things needed to bring the book to fruition.

Thanks to the chapter reviewers who assisted me in giving feedback to the authors: Nicholas A. Culp, Wei-Chun Vivi Hua, Gayle Iwamasa, Jaslean LaTaillade, Terry Lerma, Corinne Lykins, Jeffrey Mio, Barbara Streets, and Vivian Tamkin. You contributed significantly to the quality of the book.

I am deeply indebted to all authors in this book; you gave me chapters full of wisdom and experience. Individually and collectively, you show the wide range of diversity in couples and families. I also appreciate your willingness to work extensively with me to produce excellent chapters, all of which are essential to this book. Every couple and family member likely can find some aspect of themselves in your vignettes and descriptions of experiences that are too important to leave out. I'm saddened by the loss of Dr. Karen Haboush, a friend and colleague who passed away before she could see this book in print, but I am happy to have her chapter as a lasting memory of her knowledge of and passion for Muslim couples and families.

Finally, I thank all of the couples and families whom I have treated and with whom I have conducted research. You teach me daily about your struggles and strengths, and I hope that this book does justice to you and all of the diverse couples and families who have the courage to seek treatment or be part of a study.

Introduction

My private practice work as a licensed psychologist and experiences with research and training as a professor at Rutgers for 18 years have shown me big gaps in the field. As an African American therapist with a diverse caseload, I noticed that theoretical orientations tend to erroneously assume that everyone adheres to Eurocentric values and that non-European groups often struggle with dilemmas of acculturation and assimilation. Also, many potential clients lack financial and physical access to therapy. As a researcher, I noticed that findings on studies conducted on middle-class Whites still are viewed as universally applicable, they are most frequently recruited into studies, and researchers commonly use instruments normed on Whites for every group. In class, students commonly lack a contextual understanding of challenges faced by diverse groups, and the literature often omits this information. As a supervisor, I must balance teaching my supervisees treatment-as-usual factors such as applying a theoretical orientation and conducting assessment, diagnosis, and treatment, with the need to teach them cultural competence. I realized that these gaps could be filled by contributions to the literature by experts on these populations, which led to this edited book.

For the average professional, these gaps are not due to malice. Structural oppression involves social norms, laws, and policies across many contexts, systematically disenfranchising and marginalizing diverse groups. Thus, the average person, even one from a very diverse background, can be oblivious about and contribute to oppression. Thus, every chapter in this book includes vignettes that illustrate these issues and provides effective methods of coping with issues such as stereotypes, intergenerational trauma, discrimination, and disparities, and ways to assess for strengths and empower couples and families.

A major goal is to enlighten readers, build their cultural competence with clients, and engender a desire to continue addressing diversity. The focus is on couples and families as a key context for individual development. In this regard, this book identifies cultural competence that includes areas of diversity-related knowledge, dynamic sizing or the ability to generalize or individualize this knowledge, the skills to address diversity issues, and therapist awareness about their own identities, biases, and structural oppression. I present a model of using cultural competence to bridge differences in worldviews and values, experiences and contexts, power, and felt distance between the therapist and family members.

A second goal is for *all* readers to see themselves within this book, as it covers key factors involved in establishing all of our identities. These include race and ethnicity, gender and sexual orientation, religion and spirituality, varying family structures, and identities embedded within contexts and systems. Everyone has multiple intersecting identities, some dominant and some marginalized, which powerfully shape our experiences. Thus diversity encompasses us all. For example, this book includes experiences and traditions of subgroups that receive little attention from being seen as too common or the norm, such as White and Christian families, or from being seen as too uncommon, such as Native American and multiracial couples and families. As such, this book includes the curriculum needed to master the diversity found in the United States.

With this book, I have amassed a team of experts in addressing contemporary elements of diversity within couples and families in the United States. Every chapter that discusses an identity group also has at least one author who is from that group, *and* who is a culturally competent expert in working with that group. This does not negate the fact that we can and should conduct effective cross-cultural treatment and research. Rather, this book marries both professional and group member perspectives.

All authors were asked to be comprehensive in covering their area of diversity from multiple perspectives. Everyone was asked to (1) present the shared history and common experiences of group members, (2) explicitly attend to couples and families, (3) discuss similarities and differences across the main subgroups within the group, (4) discuss intersections of identities, (5) provide specifics for working with clients from that group, (6) present a case vignette demonstrating the success of that work, (7) provide conclusions, (8) provide a chapter review section, and (9) provide references. The chapter review section is an innovation that helps readers to immediately take away key points, key terms, distinctions between myths and realities, and tools and tips for cultural competence.

The book is divided into six sections. Part I focuses on racial and ethnic identities and includes chapters on African Americans, Asian Americans, Latinos, Native Americans and Whites. Part II provides chapters on gender and sexual orientation. Part III focuses on religious and spiritual identities, with chapters covering Christians, Jews, and Muslims. Part IV focuses on identity intersections and diverse family forms. It includes chapters on multiracial and intercultural couples and families, and a third chapter on diverse family forms, such as surrogate and extended families. Part V focuses on overarching factors of identity models and structural disparities. Part VI focuses on cross-cultural assessment, research, and practice. The final practice chapter presents insights gained from the contributors, toward informing my model of how to bridge differences with diverse couples and families.

In sum, this book offers a holistic perspective on diverse couples and families that is consistent with prominent models that transcend individual conceptualizations to include social factors and context. Theory, prevention, policy, service provision, and research considerations are included in each chapter. The book covers a wide breadth of groups with depth that includes attention to subgroups, such as African American and Caribbean couples and families, as well as intersectionality, such as with an intercultural family with a biracial gay son. Additionally, the chapter review sections summarize key take-away points regarding knowledge, dynamic sizing, skills, and awareness, the major components of cultural competence. This volume will prepare students, therapists, scholars/researchers, and policy makers in psychology and allied fields to understand and address the unique issues faced by diverse couples and families.

PART I

Racial and Ethnic Identities

CHAPTER 1

African American Couples and Families and the Context of Structural Oppression

Shalonda Kelly
Brittani N. Hudson

African American couples and families have unique concerns and over-looked strengths useful for therapists who work with them. As one of the largest minority groups in the country, African Americans constitute 14 percent of the U.S. population (United States Census Bureau, 2013). Despite significant contributions to the United States, African Americans have experienced **oppression,** or systematic unjust treatment from slavery to the present. African Americans also face **structural racism,** oppression due to their race that confers widespread disadvantages on their group (Wallace, Mendola, Liu, & Grantz, 2015), which is widely misunderstood and underestimated (e.g., Nelson, Adams, & Salter, 2013). Data show that structural racism has a negative impact on African Americans' physical and mental health (e.g., Wallace et al., 2015), and couple and family relationships (e.g., Bryant et al., 2010). Thus, one purpose of this chapter is to facilitate understanding of African Americans within their full context. We also seek to help clinicians address contextual adversities, respect the culture and values of African American couples and families, and harness their strengths.

THE INTERLOCKING ASPECTS OF STRUCTURAL OPPRESSION

Since slavery, views and practices toward African Americans have coalesced to form a system of structural racism and oppression that we detail using Bronfenbrenner and Evans's (2000) **bioecological model,** which highlights key life contexts: (1) the microsystem, or environments with which individuals interact regularly, such as the family and schools;

(2) the mesosystem, or interactions among microsystems; (3) the exosystem, or settings that indirectly impact individuals, such as the influence of parents' jobs on their children; (4) the macrosystem, representing cultures, subcultures, and extended social structures whose members share beliefs, resources, life hazards, and the like; and (5) time, or the chronosystem, representing constancy and change of individuals and systems across their histories.

We will show that African Americans experience oppression at each contextual level of the bioecological model, and we will start with the chronosystem to put oppression into historical context. Importantly, often factors at one level of context have corresponding and supporting factors at other levels, and so we present them together for ease of understanding. Key features of these contexts will illustrate how their impacts are manifest in African American couples and families.

Shared Historical Experiences of African American Couples, Families, and Communities

Data show that historical knowledge helps in understanding structural racism better (Nelson et al., 2012), such as the ongoing, cumulative oppression of African Americans since slavery (Black & Jackson, 2005). Unlike popular stereotypes, Africa had advanced agricultural kingdoms such as Timbuktu and Mali before slavery. Millions of Africans lost their lives in the **Middle Passage**, being brutally transported to America and legally abused and killed for disobedience because they were seen as **chattel** or property, consistent with portrayals of them as less than human. Their forced labor built the cotton industry, which established the economic infrastructure of the United States (Coates, 2014). After slavery, Jim Crow laws sanctioned enforced segregation and unprovoked violence toward African Americans such as lynching until segregation was banned in 1954. Extreme racism in the South prompted the **Great Migration** of many African Americans to the north, and many ascended from poverty into the lower middle class. They still were denied basic rights until the Civil and Voting Rights Acts of the 1960s. We detail next the structural racism and oppression that remain.

Multilevel Impacts on African American Couples and Families

Stereotypes, Discrimination, Microaggressions, and Internalized Racism

At a macrosystemic level, stereotypes legitimize society-wide negative treatment of African Americans (e.g., Goff, Eberhardt, Williams, & Jackson, 2008). For example, African Americans are typically assumed to be low in competence, consistent with corresponding stereotypes (Fiske, 2012). Sampson and Raudenbush's (2004) review of theory and data on **implicit racial bias** suggests that due to segregation and socioeconomic stratification, African Americans are observed to be in disproportionately low socioeconomic and adverse situations on average. This facilitates stereotyping and bias against African Americans by all racial groups, including by African Americans themselves, and persons without negative intent toward the group, as their skin color itself becomes a marker for poverty, pathology, and automatic negative stereotypes.

These beliefs often lead to discrimination at exo- to microsystemic levels. For example, in 2014, 62.7 percent of racially motivated hate crimes were motivated by their offenders' anti-Black bias (United States Federal Bureau of Investigation, 2015). The pervasive criminal stereotype of African Americans in the media is consistent with data on **racial profiling** (Goff et al., 2008). In this discriminatory practice, law enforcement officers use race as a decision-making factor in conducting stops, searches, and investigations (Goff & Kahn, 2012). This results in a disproportionate number of African Americans in the criminal justice system, rendering them unavailable to their families. In addition to major acts, there are **microaggressions**, or discrimination in the form of daily intentional or unintentional racial slights and insults toward people of color (Sue et al., 2007).

At the microsystemic level, African Americans may internalize negative stereotypes of themselves, which may result in viewing one's partner as inferior or undesirable. Data show that on self-report measures, some African Americans endorse items representing African American women as lazy and nonworking mothers and both genders as lazy and weak, and hypersexual, consistent with long-standing oppression-justifying stereotypes (Welfare queens, Coons, and Jezebels or Bucks, respectively; Wesley, Kelly, & Chestnut, 2017). In another study of 221 African American men, almost half endorsed that African American women fit the Jezebel promiscuous stereotype, and almost three-quarters reported that African American women fit the controlling, emasculating matriarch stereotype. Moreover, the men who endorsed the most negative stereotypes about African American women were least likely to have successful relationships (Gillum, 2007).

Structural racial oppression in the form of cumulative, multilevel prejudice is harmful to African American individuals, couples, and families. Many studies show that African Americans' reports of racism are associated with poor mental health (e.g., Williams, Neighbors, & Jackson, 2003) and poor relationship quality (e.g., Murry et al., 2008). Similarly, African Americans' negative views about their own racial group are positively associated with both partners' individual distress (Kelly, 2004) and poorer trust and relationship quality for African American men (Kelly & Floyd, 2006).

The power of negative stereotypes is notable in the case of Terrence and Renee, an African American couple in their thirties seeking treatment to help them progress to marriage. A genogram revealed that both parents grew up in single-parent homes without models of a viable couple relationship other than fairy tales and movies. Terrence's hard upbringing in low-income housing projects fueled his desire to better himself and distance himself from perceived negative influences of his family of origin. As Renee grew up, her mother warned her frequently not to depend on men, suggesting that African American men were unreliable, and that Renee could take care of herself as a strong Black woman. She loved that Terrence "broke the mold" with a great relationship with her son Brian, born 10 years earlier out of wedlock, and she fervently did not want to expose Brian to relationship instability. In transitioning to a blended family, Terrence began staying over at her home, but sometimes he chose to stay at his own home to cut down on his work commute. In Renee's eyes, such behaviors signified relationship reluctance, and she would become hostile and tell Terrence that she was not a woman who leaves dresser drawers empty, waiting in vain for a man to come. Terrence responded by balking, stating that they were not ready for marriage and their relationship needed work. This pattern reinforced Renee's beliefs that as a Black man, Terrence did not want to be tied down in marriage and reinforced Terrence's beliefs that as a Black woman, Renee wanted to control him. Contrary to these internalized stereotypes, the therapist's interviews and experience confirmed their strong desire to marry each other. Clearly, behavior that even remotely touched their stereotypes triggered their fears and protection behaviors and prevented them from noticing these desires in each other.

Socioeconomic Status and Interlocking Adversities across Major Life Areas

Since African Americans were granted civil rights, the structural nature of poverty and wealth at all contextual levels has prevented the group from catching up to their White counterparts, irrespective of individual achievements, thus disproportionately harming their families. At the chronosystem level, African Americans have been among the poorest racial/ethnic groups since poverty and race were first measured by the U.S. Census (e.g., Wickrama, Noh, and Bryant, 2005). Poverty is durable and self-reinforcing, such that poverty levels in 1970, when African Americans had just been granted civil rights toward equality, is correlated .90 with poverty in 2000 (Sampson, 2009). The intersection of race and poverty matters, as some of the poorest White neighborhoods are richer than the poorest African American neighborhoods, making it impossible to remove the racial confound with socioeconomic status (SES) (Sampson, 2009). Also, unlike their White counterparts, African American adults tend to financially assist older family members, and irrespective of age, middle-class African Americans are expected to assist their poorer relatives financially (Bryant et al., 2010). Per the **Family Stress Model** and supporting data (Conger et al., 2002), financial strain felt within the family is associated with parental emotional distress, and hostile couple and family co-caregiver interactions, which in turn are associated with emotional and behavioral disorders in their children. On the other end of the SES spectrum, African Americans lack wealth; at the same income levels, they have much lower net financial assets than their White counterparts. These poverty and wealth gaps render significantly less wealth and resources than Whites for each generation of African Americans to pass on to their children (Saegert, Fields, & Libman, 2011).

Community factors exacerbate the SES gap. Nationally representative data show that communities of African American adolescents have greater poverty and diversity as compared to their White counterparts (Wickrama et al., 2005). Even nonpoor African American youth are exposed to more community poverty than their White counterparts (Wickrama et al., 2005). Both community poverty and family poverty are associated with African American adolescents' distress. However, nonpoor African American youth's distress levels are less adversely affected by community poverty than their poor African American counterparts (Wickrama et al., 2005). Moreover, longitudinal exosystemic and mesosystemic-level data from Chicago reveal that community factors such as stigma and crime reproduce poverty significantly more than income (Sampson, 2009). For example, data show that predominately African American neighborhoods are stereotyped and stigmatized in being perceived as disordered even when no disorder exists, and perceptions of neighborhood disorder are associated with neighborhood decline (Sampson & Raudenbush, 2004). These neighborhoods then become characterized by poverty, welfare recipients, unemployment, female-headed households, and more children (Sampson, 2009).

The systemic, long-term disparities faced by African Americans in many life areas go beyond SES, and we highlight three of them. Wesley (Chapter 15, this volume) details historic and current systemic inequalities between African Americans and their White counterparts in mental and physical health, such that the Institute of Medicine deems them to be a public health issue. For example, African American patients are significantly more likely than White patients to receive an inappropriate and poorer-quality health care procedure across many health and mental health conditions. In the educational arena, African Americans tend to be segregated into poorer-quality schools that spend less than half of the money per child, have many more children with special needs, and have teachers who are poorly trained with high turnover, as compared to schools with few African Americans (Blanchett, 2006). In addition, African Americans receive disproportionately higher rates of disciplinary actions for nebulous infractions as compared to children of other racial groups (Gregory, Cornell, & Fan, 2011). Systemic and ongoing disparities in homeownership exist between African Americans and their White counterparts. Examples are **redlining**, wherein banks declined loans to those in predominately African American neighborhoods (Edsall & Edsall, 1991), and the disproportionate selling of predatory subprime loans to African Americans as compared to their White counterparts at similar demographic levels in the past decade (see Wesley, Chapter 15, this volume).

Models of Structural Impacts on African American Couples and Families

Race-specific models of couple and family functioning advance our ability to understand micro- and mesosystemic factors uniquely affecting African American couples and families. When longitudinally and prospectively sampling 345 African Americans, Simons, Simons, Landor, Bryant, and Beach (2014) found that harsh and supportive parenting in childhood had the expected direct and indirect effects on their early adult romantic relationships. These findings are consistent with general couple models that include the role of individual and couple stressors, vulnerabilities, and resources on relationship quality (e.g., Randall & Bodenmann 2009). Yet Bryant et al.'s (2010) race-related model is more comprehensive in showing how many proximal contexts and stressors disproportionately encountered by African Americans interact with individual characteristics and psychosocial resources to impact couple relationships. Consistent with such a model, Simons, Simons, Lei, and Landor (2012) examined data from the same sample of African Americans, albeit from an earlier data collection wave. Together, family instability, discrimination, criminal victimization, and financial hardship, along with harsh parenting, all disproportionately experienced by African Americans, robustly increased the probability of distrustful relational schemas. This increased the probability of conflict-ridden early romantic relationships, and in turn increased the probability of negative views of marriage. Similarly, within a sample of 540 African American newlyweds, Wickrama, Bryant, and Wickrama (2010) found that African American husbands' perceptions of community disorder were associated with hostility in their marriages and both spouses' physical and mental health.

The studies that examine additional race-related disparities faced by African Americans reveal that African Americans' disproportionately adverse contexts essentially tax every variable within general models of couple and family functioning, across life-cycle phases. Also, they go beyond the wear-and-tear of daily hassles and cumulative adversities considered in general models (Randall & Bodenmann, 2009). Clearly, without race-specific models, professionals may not understand the "what, where, and how" of the adversities faced by African Americans. Moreover, our review suggests that *all* existing models need inclusion of variables representing macro- and chronosystemic race-related factors as well.

As clinicians, we observe that for many African Americans of all SES, being "tough" helped them handle growing up with adversity, yet those coping skills do not translate into relationship intimacy or closeness. The tough approach to life may result in using treatment like an Emergency Room visit, where the family comes in only during crisis. Reluctance to attend sessions also can relate to financial problems that require time for extra shifts and second jobs to feed their families. Many African Americans tell us that they are tough on their children so that they adjust to a world that is harsh on people of color. The tough approach also may result in a preference for blunt or harsh language with each other and the therapist. We find that often these clients are unaware that their family relationships can be better. In discussing family warmth, one African American husband said, "I never saw that."

Many African Americans also may cope with adversity or stigma by being close to perfect. They do not want to let down their extended families and communities, and try hard not to represent any stereotypes. Yet this coping method can constrict their own freedom to express their thoughts, feelings, and needs, even with family members.

The Impact of Interlocking Oppressions on Couples and Families

Dixon's (2009) literature review found that economic factors, particularly African American men's economic instability, make both genders reluctant to marry. Some African Americans may have economic marital prerequisites, such as educational achievement and the type of wedding desired; these can be social indicators of financial stability and future marital success (Chaney & Monroe, 2011).

Economic barriers to marriage mean that cohabitation and nonmarital births occur disproportionately among African Americans, which are risk factors for relationship dissolution. While half of African American adults formalize relationships and begin families through cohabitation (Chaney & Monroe, 2011), cohabitation carries risk. Compared to their White and Latino counterparts, African American cohabiting relationships are less likely to lead to marriage, more likely to lead to single parenthood, and more likely to dissolve (Chaney, 2014; Kamp Dush, 2011). Moreover, cohabiting often relates to another risk factor of nonmarital birth (e.g., Tach & Halpern-Meekin, 2012). For example, as compared to White and Hispanic mothers, Black mothers are significantly less likely to cohabit or marry post-conception, including during nonmarital childbirth, and are more than twice as likely to experience the dissolution of their relationships between conception and childbirth (Lichter, Sassler, & Turner, 2014).

Harknett and McLanahan (2004) longitudinally examined 2,205 unmarried heterosexual couples regarding factors impacting likelihood of marriage after conceiving a child. They found a small impact of multipartnered fertility, or having children with another partner, and aspects of the couples' relationship quality. More importantly, they found a large impact of African Americans being less likely to cohabit at the time of the child's birth, a lower ratio of African American men to women overall (0.82), a lower ratio of nonincarcerated African American men to women, and a lower ratio of employed African American men to women. Their data show the interlocking nature of structural oppression, as the African Americans' adverse **marriage market**, measured by the men's incarceration and employment rates and lower male-to-female ratios, is associated with nonmarital births (Harknett & McLanahan, 2004), which themselves adversely affect relationship stability (Lichter et al., 2014).

Aliya and Chris's marriage represents a common example of how SES impacts African American couples. After six months, the therapist found out from an individual session with Aliya that Chris had lost his job years ago, making her the sole breadwinner. Aliya did not mind the breadwinner role, given her job as the marketing director for a Fortune 500 company. Yet Chris's difficulty adjusting to his job loss and his desire to no longer work for corporate America led to his depression, and he had been unsuccessfully trying to start a business for several years. He began taking financial risks like failing entrepreneurial endeavors (or for others, gambling, or making money illegally) that caused marital discord, particularly when his actions and inactions led to their lights being turned off and narrowly averting foreclosure. He also withdrew from his husband role and became less motivated to become a father. He eventually confessed to feeling emasculated by focusing on the home, given his perceived work failures. Chris's reluctance led to Aliya's distress about her biological clock, navigating maternity time off from work as the sole breadwinner, and their inability to move into a bigger home as originally planned. She secretly worried that perhaps Chris no longer saw her as soft, submissive, and warm, given her breadwinner role, and that it might lead him to cheat. These SES aftereffects of structural oppression led to fears that the spouses couldn't share, which led to extensive discord, and then treatment.

AFRICAN AMERICANS' SHARED VALUES AND STRENGTHS

Despite oppression, African Americans have many values and strengths that help them to overcome hardships and thrive. Because they are not a monolithic group, a variety of values and strengths have been observed (e.g., Hill, 1999). Hence, only some treatment- and family-relevant values and strengths are discussed.

Values

Individualism and Collectivism

Compared to other Americans, African Americans tend to be high on both **individualism and collectivism** (Komarraju & Cokley, 2008). Mainstream influences and survival needs likely resulted in individualism for many, often manifested in a tendency toward self-reliance and the belief of some that turning to others indicates weakness. It may manifest in a desire for personal distinctiveness or uniqueness, particularly in a society that erects barriers to African Americans' achievement. Additionally, threads of their collectivist African heritage remain part of African American culture and aid survival, such as turning to their communities for support (Hines & Boyd-Franklin, 2005). For example, they may join African American–oriented groups, such as fraternities and sororities, Jack and Jill, Black Masons, and Eastern Stars. These groups help them to provide mutual aid and support, give back to their communities, and balance out their experiences of living in predominately White communities or having jobs where they are the only or one of few African Americans.

Expressiveness, Authenticity, and Related Values

Some therapists may be surprised by some nontraditional presentations of African American couples and families in treatment. First, perhaps due to mistrust of "the system" and structural oppression, many African Americans trust their lived experience and the "vibes" that they get from the therapist over therapists' credentials and seek therapists who are authentic and not phony (e.g., Boyd-Franklin, 2003). When African American clients have this kind of trust and feel safe and at home within the therapy sessions, cultural values and informality may manifest. Examples are expressiveness involving emotions and nonverbal gestures, taking one's shoes off, bringing food into the session when hungry, asking personal questions about the therapist's life, and the like.

Family Values

African Americans often express a value for the **extended family**, wherein some have multiple generations living within one household, sometimes children are sent down South to stay with relatives during the summer, and family members and/or their children may move back into the homes of their families of origin during tough times (Hines & Boyd-Franklin, 2005). Other family values are the beliefs that children should be obedient and that elders should be respected (Dixon, Graber, & Brooks-Gunn, 2008). These family values go hand in hand with their strengths.

Strengths

Religion and Spirituality

Spirituality and religion are important strengths for African Americans. African Americans are markedly more religious than other American citizens in their reported belief in God, frequency of prayer, and attendance at religious services (Pew Charitable Trust Forum, 2009a). Also, 87 percent of African Americans report a religious affiliation; 78 percent are Protestant, with 59 percent belonging to historically Black Protestant churches (Pew Charitable Trust Forum, 2009b). African American churches support African Americans in providing leadership roles and status, community support programs, and doctrines that positively socialize African Americans toward marriage and family (Boyd-Franklin, 2003). Many African Americans turn to the church for mental health and family support, rather than mental health professionals (Chatters, Taylor, Bullard, & Jackson, 2008). Cutrona, Russell, Burzette, Wesner, and Bryant (2011) found that African American religiosity fosters relationship stability through its association with marriage, biological family status, and women's relationship quality. African American spouses' spirituality is positively associated with husbands and wives' positive marital quality, as well as their own and their spouses' marital satisfaction (Fincham, Ajayi, & Beach, 2011). Further, culturally sensitive prayer-focused marital enrichment produces positive change for African American married couples (Beach et al., 2011).

Racial and Ethnic Identity

Cross's (1971) seminal **racial identity model** proposed that under U.S. oppression, African Americans undergo stages ranging from perceiving blackness as something to be degraded to having a positive sense of their own blackness. Cross's updated model (Vandiver, Cross, Worrell, & Fhagen-Smith, 2002) posits that African Americans initially undergo a "prediscovery" phase adhering to Whites' standards, values, and beliefs and espousing society's anti-Black views. It comprises pre-encounter attitudes ranging from *assimilation*, wherein race is less salient, to *miseducation* regarding negative stereotypical beliefs about African Americans, to *self-hatred* of one's African American identity. They may have upsetting racial experiences that lead them to consider a new Black identity in the "discovery" phase. They reactively develop *immersion* attitudes characterized by intense Black involvement and an anti-White stance. Finally, they develop *internalization* attitudes, where they have a pro-Black frame of reference that may take on African-centered or multiculturalist overtones. Jernigan, Green, and Helms (Chapter 14, this volume) detail the role of racial identity in mental health, relationships, and treatment. Similarly, Phinney has outlined **ethnic identity** stages (Phinney & Ong, 2007).

As with racial identity, ethnic identity is more salient for African Americans than for their White counterparts (Gray-Little & Hafdahl, 2000).

Racial and ethnic identities are important for mental health and family adjustment. The prediscovery phase of a negative racial identity and other anti-Black attitudes are positively associated with psychological distress (e.g., Kelly, 2004), while a positive racial or ethnic identity is associated with better well-being, self-esteem, and less psychological distress (Franklin-Jackson & Carter, 2007; Gray-Little & Hafdahl, 2000). Meta-analytic findings show that African Americans have higher self-esteem relative to other groups and that this may be linked to the positivity and centrality of ethnic and racial identities (Gray-Little & Hafdahl, 2000). Within couples, discussing racial stress and discrimination with one's partner may elicit support and externalize the experience (Murry, Brown, Brody, Cutrona, & Simons, 2001). Within families, preparation for overcoming racist barriers may buffer African Americans from the effects of racism on their own mental health (Fischer & Shaw, 1999), and such preparation and discussion of their cultural heritage with one's children is called **racial socialization**. Indeed, African American youth's appropriate vigilance for the level of discrimination that they face is associated with positive adjustment (Quintana, 2007).

Flexible and Egalitarian Gender and Family Roles

Partly to overcome structural oppression, African Americans engage in many nontraditional healthy behaviors to support their families. For example, while women in the United States do significantly more housework and child care than men, African American men support the home by doing it significantly more than their White counterparts (Orbuch & Eyster, 1997). This **role flexibility** has led to more **egalitarian relationships** or role equality for some African American couples (e.g., Boyd-Franklin, 2003). Role flexibility includes grandparents helping to raise children. Also, we observe that there tends to be clear roles, shared repertoires, and less concern about achieving mainstream standards, within this healthy and viable alternative approach to family life.

Chaney and Monroe (2011) interviewed 30 low-income cohabitating African American couples and found that economic impediments do not always mean relationship dissolution, particularly for happy relationships. These couples indicate desirable relationship characteristics including stability, longevity, and cooperative parenting. They reported basing their commitment on their investment in the relationship, confidence in its permanence, and a lack of desire to start a new relationship, rather than on their marital status. Couples who cohabited the longest reported a value for growing old together as a couple, more than marriage. Many couples reported unwillingness to pay for a wedding when they were content with stable, committed, and functional relationships. Some viewed legal marriage as a government ploy for money and as a socially imposed construct and vacillated between a desire for and an indifference toward marriage. Perhaps these couples focus more on relationship success than mainstream standards.

VARIATIONS WITHIN THE AFRICAN AMERICAN COMMUNITY

West Indian Couples and Families

Those of African descent in the United States vary in their ethnic backgrounds, and here we focus on immigrants from the West Indies or the Caribbean. These two terms often are used interchangeably; however, the West Indies also includes the Bahamas and Turks and Caicos. Some West Indians identify themselves as Black American, some prefer a hyphenated American identity derived from their country of origin, and still some prefer solely the specific ethnic identity label of their home country (Hall & Carter, 2006). Some of the most salient differences between West Indians and their African American counterparts are related to their nationality, better economic prospects, communal family structure, and common cross-generational immigrant issues, as discussed next.

While they recognize common African ancestry with United States–born African Americans and shared history with the slave trade, nationality is more salient than racial identity for Black immigrants (Foner, 2005), at least in the first generation. This means that the Black immigrant populations typically do not strongly identify with experiences of racial oppression. Rather, they tend to be proud of their cultural heritage, national identity, and being the racial majority in their islands of origin (Brooks, 2013).

As a group, West Indians and other recent Black immigrants surpass African Americans in SES. They have higher household incomes, hold more prestigious jobs, and report higher levels of educational achievement, as well as higher employment levels and lower poverty rates (Thornton, Taylor, & Chatters, 2013). Brooks' (2013) literature review revealed that even among those with the lowest levels of education, West Indians have high rates of labor force participation and are highly represented in skilled, white-collar, and professional occupations. Some attributions are that West Indians' majority status in the Caribbean fostered a strong belief that all is possible through hard work and effort and a value for trying one's best (Brooks, 2013).

West Indians' higher SES may be partially assisted by their communal family values, which are similar to those of African Americans. This is exemplified by their common economic practice of pooling resources to establish a rotating credit union, known as the "partner" for Jamaicans, or the "susu" for other Caribbean immigrants. This is usually a form of enforced savings among an informal group of 15 to 20 individuals, where trusted members deposit a specific sum of money weekly and one member serves as the banker who is responsible for distributing the week's contributions to a selected group member. This process repeats until every group member has had a chance to receive money from the banker (Vickerman, 2007).

West Indians' communal family structure also is manifest in the flexibility in support and caregiving provided by the extended family. Extended family members, often grandparents, tend to care for children left behind by their parents who have emigrated to the United States for better life prospects. This is part of **serial migration**, where one family member migrates in advance of others, as the parents tend to send for their children after they are established in the United States (Brooks, 2013). West Indians in the United States also report advantages in their ability to return to their parents' countries of birth and establish relationships with their relatives there, such as being sent to live with these relatives and be educated there (Brooks, 2013).

Caribbeans' advantages as compared to African Americans may extend into their mental health and marital adjustment. West Indians and other recent Black immigrants report higher levels of physical and emotional well-being than their African American counterparts (Thornton et al., 2013). Also, in one study, Caribbean men and women who were married for longer reported higher satisfaction than their African American counterparts. Higher satisfaction also was reported by men who immigrated, and immigrant women from Jamaica had higher levels of satisfaction than their African American counterparts and those from the Spanish Caribbean and Haiti (Bryant, Taylor, Lincoln, Chatters, & Jackson, 2008). The authors speculate from these findings that Caribbean women in the United States may have higher marital satisfaction because the United States espouses greater egalitarian roles and family time than in the Caribbean.

Cultural differences between African Americans and West Indians such as the foregoing can act as interethnic barriers to intraracial marriage between the two groups (Batson, Qian, & Lichter, 2006). However, when West Indians marry outside of their culture, they tend to marry more African Americans than Whites (Batson et al., 2008). Perhaps this is due to the prominence of racial categorization in the United States, such that shared skin color can lead to West Indians and African Americans occupying the same spaces (Batson et al., 2008).

Data show that the longer that West Indians live in the United States, the more their racial views approximate those of African Americans (Phinney & Onwughalu, 1996). These changes also extend into the second generation, as their children may share common childhood experiences with African Americans and have difficulty separating themselves culturally from African Americans. At times, West Indian parents view their children as rejecting their culture when they **acculturate** or take in the host culture of the United States. These children may become frustrated with their parents' higher expectations and lesser acknowledgment of racial and ethnic stressors (Brooks, 2013).

Intersectionality

Low SES, being phenotypically African, and being part of the LGBTQI (lesbian, gay, bisexual, transgender, queer or questioning and intersex) community are several common ways that African Americans can suffer from double or triple oppression related to the intersection of having several minority identities at once. First, being African American and having a low SES is one of the most common and pernicious examples of dual oppression, and the adversity of lower SES has been noted previously (e.g., Sampson, 2009). Second, African Americans have many shapes and skin tones, but having a phenotype that is associated with being African can lead to oppression. For example, White and African American participants view darker-skinned African Americans more negatively and stereotypically than their lighter-skinned counterparts (Maddox & Gray, 2002). This may be more difficult to navigate for African American women who may not fit mainstream standards of beauty. For example, a positive association between habitual monitoring of skin tone and general body image disturbance was found in a sample of 117 African American women (Buchanan, Fischer, Tokar, & Yoder, 2008). Finally, African Americans in the LGBTQI community face issues of nonacceptance within their racial group. For example, 40 percent of the larger society believe that homosexuality should be discouraged, whereas 46 percent of African Americans hold such a view (Pew Charitable Trust Forum, 2009b). Thus, this group faces double stigma from within and outside the community.

CASE CONSIDERATIONS FOR WORKING WITH AFRICAN AMERICAN COUPLES AND FAMILIES

A Principle-Based Approach to Treatment That Includes Cultural Competence

Our treatment approach adheres to a principle-based integrative therapy (PBIT) model asserting that abiding principles underlie theoretical orientations and their variants. Treatment is tailored to how those principles manifest within each person, couple, or family. We believe in the social learning principles that underlie a cognitive behavioral orientation; systems principles conceptualizing aspects of the whole family system and its subsystems that are not reducible to the individual parts of a family system; a multicultural approach that builds cultural competence in bridging differences in worldviews, experiences, power, and the felt distance in the therapy room; and attachment principles that underlie emotionally focused couple and family therapy. Kelly et al. (2013) provide details on this principle-based approach, and Kelly, Bhagwat, Maynigo, and Moses (2014) provide details on the principles and techniques of these orientations.

For the purposes of this chapter, we detail aspects of our multicultural approach. There is broad consensus on the elements of **cultural competence** (e.g., Sue, 2006). These are: 1) knowledge about diversity within the couple or family, 2) dynamic sizing or the understanding of when to generalize the knowledge gained to the family and when to individualize their experiences, 3) treatment skills, and 4) therapists' awareness about their own identities, biases, and how they fit with structural oppression. Kelly et al. (2014) theorize that cultural competence works through four potential mechanisms that bridge differences in areas often overlooked by treatment as usual. These are: (1) differences in worldviews and values between the therapist and family members, (2) differences in their experiences and contexts, (3) differences in the power they wield in and out of the therapy session, and (4) the felt distance experienced by the therapist or family members because of the foregoing differences. Thus, the following case considerations use cultural competence to bridge those four potential areas of difference in therapy.

Five Areas for Therapists to Address in Treatment

We identify five areas for clinicians to assess and address with African Americans. First, data on African Americans' higher treatment dropout rates than their White counterparts (e.g., King & Canada, 2004) and therapist observations regarding negative vibes and inexperience with treatment suggest that therapists need to join with African American couple and family members and orient them to treatment (e.g., Boyd-Franklin, 2003). Second, structural oppression can result in multiple additional stressors and SES concerns and a lack of role models. Third, data cited in our foregoing review suggest that treatment tailored to African American couples should develop components to reduce stigma and racial shame (e.g., Kelly, 2004; Kelly & Floyd, 2006) and work with common coping methods. Fourth, many African American values and strengths can be utilized by the therapist in treatment. Fifth, therapists need awareness of their own stimulus value and biases related to their own race, as discussed next.

*Joining with and Orienting African American Couples
and Families to Treatment*

It is important to **join** with and orient African American couples and families to treatment. This consists of being authentic as the therapist, while also being as warm and inviting as possible, so that the clients overtly understand that the therapist is not phony, cares about them, and wants to work with them. It may include matching the family on their level of formality or informality, such as asking if they want to be called by their first names or not, to let them know that the therapist cares about their treatment preferences (Boyd-Franklin, 2003). It also includes using measures normed on African Americans and minimizing formal assessments and questionnaires prior to joining to prevent dropout. **Orienting clients to treatment** consists of providing a treatment overview and clarifying the roles of the therapist and the client to prevent misunderstandings for those naive to treatment. These interventions help to bridge differences by decreasing potential feelings of distance in the room between the therapist and family members.

Stressors, Traumas, SES Concerns, and a Lack of Role Models

Our genograms of African Americans often reveal many family stressors, including racial traumas (Franklin, Boyd-Franklin, & Kelly 2006), community violence (e.g., Cedeno, Elias, Kelly, & Chu, 2010), and poverty (Saegert et al., 2007). For example, one genogram revealed a family where three sons were lost to the ills of structural oppression. One innocently died from a stray bullet, the second was alive and imprisoned, and the third had the family's hopes pinned on him, which led him to significant achievements, but also distance from his family of procreation and an early death from cirrhosis of the liver. Therapists need to learn how to bridge these experiences and contexts, as they may not encounter such situations in their own lives and may be at a loss for how to respond. This is reasonable, as the magnitude of the issues requires preventive multilevel interventions. Empathy, validation, and increasing self-efficacy are crucial, including the labeling of racism and other "isms" in the clients' lives and validation that they are unfair. For low-SES families, therapists can increase access to treatment, such as with home-based services and multifamily groups, and decrease attrition with addressing needs like child care (e.g., Snell-Johns, Mendez, & Smith, 2004). Also, therapists need to know that such stressors *and* their accumulations adversely affect individuals and families (e.g., Bryant et al., 2008). Treatment may necessitate advocating with organizations and larger system-level responses to better help to meet African Americans' needs, such as increasing institutions' ability to reduce discrimination and increase their sense of belonging and having a voice (Cedeno et al., 2010). Therapists should shore up support for family members, including linking them to any underutilized strengths of positive community role models, particularly those who successfully deal with similar issues. This helps family members to have their experiences and contexts acknowledged and addressed and empowers them to use their own strengths, which also are also valued by the therapist.

Racial Stigma and Shame, and Coping via Toughness or Perfection

Disproportionate stressors may lead to acting on in-group stereotypes and negative family interactions, which can be detected with genograms. With genograms, therapists explore family members' histories and views of their own group. It also can be used for **dynamic sizing**, such as determining if in-group stereotypes and strengths apply with a given family, such as if family members feel racial, ethnic, or cultural shame or pride (Hardy & Laszloffy, 1995), or make race-based criticisms of each other. Therapists can then ask about how family members cope with adversity, racism, and racial shame, such as being tough or a perfect representative of the group.

Therapist skills can empower family members who experience internalized racism and a lack of power in society, even when they have achieved personally. First, therapists can label the issues between the couple as being related to racism and discrimination and normalize their varying reactions regarding dilemmas often unique to people of color. Therapists can provide psychoeducation about stigma with case vignettes like we have provided to show how it adversely affects African Americans. This externalizes it by acknowledging the structural context and protecting the couple, to the extent of reframing the issue by telling them "don't let racism win." Therapists can validate toughness and perfection as common methods of coping, and also highlight the need to find space within the family to be free to be themselves and let their guards down. Therapists can also reinforce positive views of the group and support a positive racial and ethnic identity to counter identification with stereotypes or to at least frame behavior accurately as responses to adverse contexts. As a **cultural broker**, the therapist can help family members to share with each other how they learned to cope and help them to negotiate how to address such issues in culturally syntonic ways that don't conflict between the members and which can include gaining community support and help.

Identifying and Supporting Cultural Values and Strengths

Throughout the foregoing interventions, African American strengths and values have been identified and used, such as with finding positive community role models and fostering a positive racial and ethnic identity. Religious and spiritual strengths can help to unify family members, and praying for each other, engaging in spirituality, or finding a "church home" helps, particularly for those who are isolated. Therapists can also take often overlooked opportunities to appreciate and utilize African Americans' creativity in overcoming structural racism, such as persisting in education and use of their role flexibility to handle various challenges (e.g., Hill, 1999).

Therapist Self-Awareness

Therapists working with African American couples and families need awareness about biases of those in the helping professions and need to understand their own stimulus value so as to address them in treatment. Common biases include a Eurocentric orientation that prioritizes values such as logic and individualism and a deficit view of African Americans (e.g., Hines & Boyd-Franklin, 2005). This helps therapists to understand the impact of structural racism and oppression even with positive intent and in the absence of an individual act of discrimination. It can also help therapists to be vigilant for microaggressions, prioritizing Eurocentric values over other equally valid worldviews and approaches, and to confront automatic thoughts regarding superiority and inferiority of groups. For example, sometimes therapist reflection can reveal that some client tendencies assumed to be "negative traits" may be viable alternative views and adaptive coping with structural racism.

Race and how the therapist uses himself or herself matter in treatment (Boyd-Franklin, 2003). White therapists may need vigilance for a tendency to minimize racial factors to the point of not assessing them just as they would assess other background factors of their clients. Many African American clients may need therapists to raise and label racial issues, given that therapists set the tone about what is appropriate to discuss in treatment. White therapists may feel overwhelmed or inadequate in addressing racial factors, and thus err in approaching clients and raising racial factors in an overly tentative manner that gives off vibes that they are not sure that they can help. Therapists of color need to be vigilant against overidentifying with African American clients, to the point of not assessing racial and other structural factors in believing that they know them, thus forgetting the variation within the group. Finally, therapists of all racial backgrounds may need to assess for being seen as representatives of "the system" that might create felt distance in the room and necessitate stronger efforts to join. We suggest that therapists authentically be themselves, while simultaneously using overt positive gestures that convey enthusiasm and warmth and confidence in one's ability to bond and work with the family members. While many African Americans may assume that an African American therapist is needed to help them, it is not always feasible, and we have found that culturally competent therapists of all backgrounds have the ability to do great work with this population.

CASE EXAMPLE

Andrew, a massage therapist, and Hazel, a nurse, were in their early thirties and had cohabited for a year, along with Andrew's three-year-old daughter from his previous marriage. They sought treatment for poor communication, Andrew's drinking and childhood loss of his parents, and his lack of support, per Hazel. She reported that Andrew couldn't stop drinking, so she asked his sister to intervene. Andrew admitted to social drinking and sometimes overdoing it. He said that it helps to vent, and sometimes he does try to cut down. She said that he drank to address his demons, and when drunk he would say things like if he was older, he'd have been the one to kill his stepfather, and that he never thought he'd see adulthood. She also reported resentment that though he attended some doctor appointments with her, he did not support her through her recent fibroid surgery. She reported that he withdraws and doesn't let her get close. He replied that everyone is dealt a different hand of cards, and that Hazel makes things big when they are not. He also stated that Hazel would throw things in his face later on, judge him, and tell others. Hazel admitted to hurting Andrew sometimes by getting hot and mean after no success in confronting problems together.

The couple met through a mutual friend. Andrew reported attraction to Hazel's beauty, self-sufficiency, "wifely and mother abilities," and her depth, unlike his ex-wife. Hazel was attracted to Andrew's physique and said he was calm, chivalrous, and originally was interested in knowing her. They began living together upon Andrew's request, after Hazel got a job offer in another state.

Their genogram revealed important family contexts. Andrew was raised by his Southern maternal grandmother who emphasized manners and respect, within a family that spoke little about itself. When he was four, Andrew's mother was imprisoned for killing his abusive stepfather and died in prison under unknown circumstances. The family assumed that he didn't remember his mother, so it wasn't discussed. He reported family histories of alcoholism and a childhood filled with hardship, and he was not close to his family since his grandmother died. He acknowledged his much older sister as a role model, as from a distance she seemed to have a good relationship with her husband. He divorced his distant ex-wife after she cheated on him. He loved Hazel, but reported that her family had lots of drama and conflict. Andrew started his job in college and took a full-time position once he got his associate degree.

Hazel's half of the genogram revealed that her Jamaican family confronted problems together, yet also had conflicting factions related to things like money and infidelity. She was the youngest of three children and grew up with a strong grandmother and aunt; her aunt came to the United States first and through serial migration brought her mother, siblings, and herself as a teen, enabling them to leave her abusive father. She was closest to and missed her eldest sister, who had moved back to Jamaica. Her most vivid recollections involved her mother's motto of "sacrifice to see you through," always having multiple jobs and bitterness over having loaned money to her family that they never returned, stating, "I need someone to be there for me."

Andrew wanted to turn to Hazel, but in having a family that dealt silently with their adversity, he didn't know how to raise it, so he would drink and then vent. Then Hazel would get alarmed, and like her family, she sought to confront "his demons" together. Then Andrew would withdraw, and Hazel would try harder to open him up and not be alone. Andrew experienced Hazel as twisting his words, blaming him, or telling their problems, so he would minimize issues, withdraw, and drink. Hazel typically wanted to "get him to see my problems as his own," which would overwhelm Andrew. Then he would not know how to respond, or he'd comply and then shut down in feeling controlled, or label her as being dramatic or controlling. She then felt rejected and turned to other family members and then treatment for help.

A PBIT approach was used. Alcohol behavioral couple therapy (McCrady, 2012) addressed Andrew's alcohol use disorder. Hazel's intimacy-seeking approach involved criticism that functioned to punish Andrew's sharing and negatively reinforce his escape by shutting down or drinking. Andrew thought that his daily presence should be enough for Hazel, so his withdrawal functioned to protect himself by keeping her at a distance, but it also positively reinforced her panic and doubt and led to her increasingly dysregulated approach and help seeking. As a new couple, rather than have a joint method of problem solving, they also unsatisfactorily alternated between the preferred methods of each. From an emotionally focused therapy (EFT) perspective, the foregoing interactions comprised their negative cycle, with Hazel as the pursuer and Andrew as the withdrawer. The EFT goal was to develop a secure attachment by catching their negative cycle and replacing it with one wherein they met each other's needs. From a systems perspective, this new couple needed to prioritize their relationship with permeable boundaries and decrease their either-or polarization process that resulted in triangles with extended family.

Culturally, Andrew was more individualistic and Hazel was more collectivist. Both had traditional gender role preferences that worked for the household. They were egalitarian regarding finances and decision-making; despite both wanting Andrew to decide and initiate more, Hazel was more educated and decisive. Andrew reported that giving her the reins with decisions to make her happy did not help. Conversely, Hazel viewed Andrew as pacifying her and not caring about their future. As an African American man, Andrew coped with life adversity by being tough and stoic, and he sometimes stereotyped Black women as controlling. Neither consistently had access to positive family role models.

This couple called to interview their therapist prior to treatment, when the therapist joined with them, answered questions, and explained her approach. Aware of her stimulus value as an African American therapist, she told them that she wanted to support their values and strengths. After an assessment yielding the foregoing information, the therapist instituted dates and caring days to show mutual appreciation. This was tough, as they worked opposite shifts, had revolving schedules, and picked up extra shifts for money. But they reported that it helped them to connect. They also agreed to track Andrew's alcohol use.

The therapist provided psychoeducation about the disproportionate adversity they faced, and their normal but different individualistic and collectivist coping responses were validated as important within their communities. Hazel reported noticing how African American men were treated in the United States, and how she was proud of his accomplishments and financial stability, though she wanted him to join a saving partnership like her family taught her. The therapist raised Hazel's role as a Black Jamaican woman who went the extra mile in forging a new life in the United States and helping family members here and back home. Andrew then noted how he saw her positive energy and striving as fuel when they dated, such that he sought and obtained a raise at work. The therapist magnified that powerful positive memory to decrease racial stigma and increase racial pride that his woman had achieved so much. She also asked him to consider if the times he felt controlled related to her having to overcome and achieve. He was able to believe that, and he took in her desire to have him show his strength in being there for her. He said he wanted to be her rock, and they reaffirmed that they wanted to be best friends and make their home of three a haven. The therapist also taught them joint problem solving to support the egalitarian aspects of their relationship.

In one poignant session, they discussed that work needed to be done in the relationship, and both used increasingly vague, anxious, and dire language, such as "we need to figure out what this relationship is, and where we are going." This polarization led the therapist to recall how they lacked positive role models, and how she had seen Black couples with viable foundations flounder in getting to marriage. She stopped the interaction and clarified with Andrew that it was *both* a fact that work was needed to strengthen the relationship, *and* a fact that he had told her that marriage was the goal. He said yes. She asked Andrew what made that hard to say, and he said that they always get caught up on the steps to it. The therapist affirmed that it is hard to jump to marriage, and that they want to have the foundation set and the confidence to fix what comes when they get there. Hazel responded: "I still don't know—a lot has happened." The therapist affirmed that it gets cloudy and hard, even though she wants it, differentiating between uncertainties about their ability to make it versus her desire to marry him. Hazel replied that she wanted the relationship, and thought that Andrew did too. The therapist affirmed that uncertainty is normal and okay, that she could help them reach the end goal and clarify how they can make each other happy. In the next session, the couple reported that they went shopping for wedding rings, and the therapist helped them build on their foundation by spending time with other couples to crystalize their sense of being a unit.

The therapist then used EFT and cognitive behavioral therapy (CBT) to help the couple to identify and address their negative cycle. They found that Hazel would get very anxious when Andrew did anything unexpected, which led her to searching for answers, and his shutdowns led her to feel abandoned. Conversely, Andrew felt like he failed in meeting Hazel's needs and that he was the problem and reacted by putting up a wall and going numb, yearning for a simple and fun life with Hazel. Treatment helped Hazel to be less critical through sharing her anxiety, to take in that Andrew's presence, gentlemanliness, and daily considerations of her were demonstrations of his care and commitment, and to share when she needed his comfort and reassurance. Teaching her to express specific emotional and instrumental needs clearly led to Andrew feeling pride in his ability to consistently meet them. Andrew learned to catch the cycle by reacting to Hazel's emotions with approach and reassurance and turning to her when not drinking. The therapist also did more behavioral couple interventions for alcoholism, such as developing stimulus control plans to control drinking and clarifying Hazel's role in situations with alcohol.

As the couple's lives became hectic, they raised termination, and the therapist agreed, just as she agreed to shorter sessions and alcohol moderation rather than abstinence as reasonable treatment preferences. They reviewed their gains, including how they caught their cycle, asked for and met each other's attachment needs, came together to moderate his alcohol use, and supported each other as a strong Black couple.

CONCLUSIONS

While African Americans' history of slavery is well known, many remain unaware of its ongoing legacy of structural racism and how it affects most contextual levels in their lives. Despite the harm of oppression, African Americans' common coping methods, values, and strengths continue to help protect them. Therapists need to develop cultural competence to understand the challenges that these couples and families face, including where, how, and why they apply. This will enable them to harness African Americans' abilities to enhance their couple and family relationships in culturally syntonic ways.

CHAPTER REVIEW

Key Points

1. African Americans' status in society and couple and family relationships are heavily intertwined with the context of structural racism and oppression, which are key factors in fully understanding and helping them.
2. People of African heritage are not monolithic. African Americans, West Indians, and Africans have important differences and similarities. Also, skin

tone, sexual orientation, and SES are important to consider as areas of potential double oppression.

3. Joining and orienting African Americans to treatment, addressing stigma and common coping methods, understanding and advocating regarding common stressors and traumas, making use of common values and strengths, and being aware of biases and structural oppression are ways that therapists can further strengthen African American families.

Key Terms

acculturate, bioecological model, chattel, cultural broker, cultural competence, dynamic sizing, egalitarian relationships, ethnic identity, extended family, Family Stress Model, Great Migration, implicit racial bias, individualism and collectivism, join, marriage market, microaggressions, Middle Passage, oppression, orienting clients to treatment, racial identity model, racial profiling, racial socialization, redlining, role flexibility, serial migration, structural racism

Myths and Realities

- It is a myth that African Americans are inferior and without strengths. The reality is that structural racism and oppression prevent a level playing field, and African Americans have utilized many strengths in achieving positive relationships in the face of oppression.
- It is a myth that race does not matter unless the client tells you that it does. Many African American clients need signals from the therapist that it is okay to discuss racism and oppression. Some who have internalized racism may need to be educated about the impact of the contexts and stressors that they face. Some can benefit from reconnecting with cultural strengths in addressing such issues.

Tools and Tips

Knowledge

Boyd-Franklin, N. (2003). *Black families in therapy: Understanding the African American experience* (2nd ed.). New York, NY: Guilford Press.

Bryant, C. M., Wickrama, K. A. S., Bolland, J., Bryant, B. M., Cutrona, C. E., & Stanik, C. E. (2010). Race matters, even in marriage: Identifying factors linked to marital outcomes for African Americans. *Journal of Family Theory & Review, 2,* 157–174. doi: 10.1111/j.1756-2589.2010.00051

The movie *Crash* has a scene in which an affluent African American couple gets pulled over and then the spouses argue at home regarding how to perceive and cope with the trauma they just experienced from the police officer. Their argument provides examples of conflicting perceptions and coping approaches, as well as internalized racism in the form of stereotypical race-based criticisms of each other.

Dynamic Sizing

It is helpful for therapists to conduct a genogram during which they ask about the important factors highlighted in this chapter, such as religious and spiritual beliefs and practices, socioeconomic factors, racism experienced by family members, and their varying coping responses. This knowledge will enable therapists to know when to generalize their knowledge to the family members sitting in their offices.

Skills

Theory. There is a need to utilize race-specific or diversity-specific models that include examination of all ecological levels to have a more comprehensive understanding of contexts that impact African American couples and families.

Prevention. There is a need to implement large system-level responses to increase institutions' abilities to reduce discrimination, increase African Americans' sense of belonging, and provide avenues to empower their voices.

Service Provision. Service providers need to develop cultural competence to enable them to bridge differences they may have with their African American clients' worldviews and values, experiences and contexts, levels of power, and felt distance experienced in the therapy room.

Policy. There is a need to target policies and laws that confer structural disadvantage to African Americans, such as in the areas of housing, education, criminal justice, and jobs.

Research. There is a need to go beyond general research constructs like warmth and hostility to examine the race-specific interactions within African American couples and families that provide mutual support to overcome racial stress and internalized racism.

Awareness

All service providers need to take workshops, classes, and/or consultations to help them to learn about their own racial/ethnic heritage, White supremacy, privilege, and oppression, overcome biases, and develop openness to alternative non-Eurocentric perspectives.

REFERENCES

Batson, C. D., Qian, Z., & Lichter, D. T. (2006). Interracial and intraracial patterns of mate selection among America's diverse Black populations. *Journal of Marriage and Family, 68,* 658–672. doi: 10.1111/j.1741-3737.2006.00281

Beach, S. R. H., Hunt, T. R., Fincham, F. D., Franklin, K. J., McNair, L. M., & Stanley, S. M. (2011). Enhancing marital enrichment through spirituality: Efficacy data for prayer focused relationship enhancement. *Psychology of Religion and Spirituality, 3,* 201–216. doi: 10.1037/a0022207

Black, L., & Jackson, V. (2005). Families of African origin: An overview. In M. McGoldrick, J. Giordano, & N. Garcia-Preto (Eds.), *Ethnicity and family therapy* (pp. 77–86). New York, NY: Guilford Press.

Blanchett, W. J. (2006). Disproportionate representation of African American students in special education: Acknowledging the role of white privilege and racism. *Educational Researcher, 35*(6), 24–28. doi: 10.3102/0013189X035006024

Boyd-Franklin, N. (2003). *Black families in therapy: Understanding the African American experience* (2nd ed.). New York, NY: Guilford Press.

Bronfenbrenner, U., & Evans, G. W. (2000). Developmental science in the 21st century: Emerging questions, theoretical models, research designs and empirical findings. *Social Development, 9*, 115–125. doi: 10.1111/1467-9507.00114

Brooks, L. J. (2013). The Black survivors: Courage, strength, creativity and resilience in the cultural traditions of West Indian immigrants. In J. Sinnott (Ed.), *Positive psychology* (pp. 121–134). New York, NY: Springer.

Bryant, C. M., Taylor, R. J., Lincoln, K. D., Chatters, L. M., & Jackson, J. S. (2008). Marital satisfaction among African Americans and West Indians: Findings from the National Survey of American Life. *Family Relations, 57*, 239–253. doi: 10.1111/j.1741-3729.2008.00497

Bryant, C. M., Wickrama, K. A. S., Bolland, J., Bryant, B. M., Cutrona, C. E., & Stanik, C. E. (2010). Race matters, even in marriage: Identifying factors linked to marital outcomes for African Americans. *Journal of Family Theory & Review, 2*, 157–174. doi: 10.1111/j.1756-2589.2010.00051

Buchanan, T. S., Fischer, A. R., Tokar, D. M., & Yoder, J. D. (2008). Testing a culture-specific extension of objectification theory regarding African American women's body image. *The Counseling Psychologist, 36*, 697–718. doi: 10.1177/0011000008316322

Cedeno, L., Elias, M. E., Kelly, S. & Chu, B.C. (2010). School violence, adjustment, and the influence of hope in low-income, African American youth. *The American Journal of Orthopsychiatry, 80*, 213–226. doi: 10.1111/j.1939-0025.2010.01025

Chaney, C. (2014). "No matter what, good or bad, love is still there": Motivations for romantic commitment among Black cohabiting couples. *Marriage & Family Review, 50*, 216–245. doi: 10.1080/01494929.2013.851056

Chaney, C., & Monroe, P. (2011). Transitions to engagement among low-income, cohabiting African American couples: A family perspective for policy. *Journal of Family Issues, 30*, 653–678. doi: 10.1177/0192513X10390860

Chatters, L. M., Taylor, R. J., Bullard, K. M., & Jackson, J. S. (2008). Spirituality and subjective religiosity among African Americans, West Indians and Whites. *Journal for Scientific Study of Religion, 47*, 725–737. doi: 10.1111/j.1468-5906.2008.00437

Coates, T. (2014, June). The case for reparations. *The Atlantic*. Retrieved from http://www.theatlantic.com/magazine/archive/2014/06/the-case-for-reparations/361631/

Conger, R. D., Wallace, L. E., Sun, Y., Simons, R. L., McLoyd, V. C., & Brody, G. H. (2002). Economic pressure in African American families: A replication and extension of the family stress model. *Developmental Psychology, 38*, 179–193. doi: 10.1037/0012-1649.38.2.179

Cross, W. E., (1971). The Negro-to-Black conversion experience. *Black World, 20*(9), 13–27.

Cutrona, C. E., Russell, D. W., Burzette, R. G., Wesner, K. A., & Bryant, C. M. (2011). Predicting relationship stability among midlife African American couples.

Journal of Consulting and Clinical Psychology, 79, 814–825. doi: 10.1037/a0025874

Dixon, P. (2009). Marriage among African Americans: What does the research reveal? *Journal of African American Studies, 13*, 29–46. doi: 10.1007/s12111-008-9062-5

Dixon, S. V., Graber, J. A., & Brooks-Gunn, J. (2008). The roles of respect for parental authority and parenting practices in parent-child conflict among African American, Latino, and European American families. *Journal of Family Psychology, 22*, 1–10. doi: 10.1037/0893-3200.22.1.1

Edsall, T. B. & Edsall, M. D. (1991). *Chain reaction: The impact of race, rights, and taxes on American politics.* New York, NY: W.W. Norton & Company.

Fincham, F. D., Ajayi, C., & Beach, S. R. (2011). Spirituality and marital satisfaction in African American couples. *Psychology of Religion and Spirituality, 3*, 259–268. doi: 10.1037/a0023909

Fischer, A. R., & Shaw, C. M. (1999). African Americans' mental health and perceptions of racist discrimination: The moderating effects of racial socialization experiences and self-esteem. *Journal of Counseling Psychology, 46*, 395–407. doi: 10.1037/0022-0167.46.3.395

Fiske, S. T. (2012). Managing ambivalent prejudices smart-but-cold and warm-but-dumb stereotypes. *The Annals of the American Academy of Political and Social Science, 639*, 33–48. doi: 10.1177/0002716211418444

Foner, N. (2005). *In a new land: A comparative view of immigration.* New York, NY: New York University Press.

Franklin, A. J., Boyd-Franklin, N., & Kelly, S. (2006). Racism and invisibility: Race-related stress, emotional abuse and psychological trauma for people of color. *Journal of Emotional Abuse, 6*, 9–30. doi: 10.1300/J135v06n02_02

Franklin-Jackson, D., & Carter, R. T. (2007). The relationships between race-related stress, racial identity, and mental health for Black Americans. *Journal of Black Psychology, 33*, 5–26. doi: 10.1177/0095798406295092

Goff, P. A., Eberhardt, J. L., Williams, M. J., & Jackson, M. C. (2008). Not yet human: Implicit knowledge, historical dehumanization, and contemporary consequences. *Journal of Personality and Social Psychology, 94*, 292–306. doi: 10.1037/0022-3514.94.2.292

Goff, P. A., & Kahn, K. B. (2012). Racial bias in policing: Why we know less than we should. *Social Issues and Policy Review, 6*, 177–210. doi: 10.1111/j.1751-2409.2011.01039

Gillum, T. L. (2007). "How do I view my sister?" Stereotypic views of African American women and their potential to impact intimate partnerships. *Journal of Human Behavior in the Social Environment, 15*, 347–366. doi: 10.1300/J137v15n02_20

Gray-Little, B., & Hafdahl, A. R. (2000). Factors influencing racial comparisons of self-esteem: A quantitative review. *Psychological Bulletin, 126*, 26–54. doi: 10.1037/0033-2909.126.1.26

Gregory, A., Cornell, D., & Fan, X. (2011). The relationship of school structure and support to suspension rates for Black and White high school students. *American Educational Research Journal, 48*, 904–934. doi: 10.3102/0002831211398531

Hall, S. P., & Carter, R. T. (2006). The relationship between racial identity, ethnic identity, and perceptions of racial discrimination in an Afro-Caribbean descent sample. *Journal of Black Psychology, 32,* 155–175. doi: 10.1177/0095798406287071

Hardy, K. V., & Laszloffy, T. A. (1995). The cultural genogram: Key to training culturally competent family therapists. *Journal of Marital and Family Therapy, 21,* 227–237. doi: 10.1111/j.1752-0606.1995.tb00158

Harknett, K., & McLanahan, S. S. (2004). Racial and ethnic differences in marriage after the birth of a child. *American Sociological Review, 69,* 790–811. doi: 10.1177/000312240406900603

Hill, R. (1999). *The strengths of African American families: Twenty-five years later.* Lanham, MD: University Press of America.

Hines, P.M., & Boyd-Franklin, N. (2005). African American families. In M. McGoldrick, J. Giordano, & N. Garcia-Preto (Eds.), *Ethnicity and family therapy* (pp. 87–100). New York, NY: Guilford Press.

Jernigan, M. M., Green, C. E., & Helms, J. E. (this volume). Identity models. In S. Kelly (Ed.) *Diversity in couple and family therapy: Ethnicities, sexualities, and socioeconomics* (pp. 363–392). Santa Barbara, CA: Praeger.

Kamp Dush, C.M. (2011). Relationship-specific investments, family chaos, and cohabitation dissolution following a nonmarital birth. *Family Relations, 60,* 586–601. doi: 10.1111/j.1741-3729.2011.00672

Kelly, S. (2004). Underlying components of scores assessing African Americans' racial perspectives. *Measurement and Evaluation in Counseling and Development, 37,* 28–40.

Kelly, S., Bhagwat, R., Maynigo, T., & Moses, E. (2014). Couple and marital therapy: The complement and expansion provided by multicultural approaches. In F. Leong, L. Comas-Diaz, G. Hall, V. McLloyd, & J. Trimble (Eds.), *American psychological association handbook of multicultural psychology, vol. 2: Applications and training.* Washington, DC: American Psychological Association.

Kelly, S., & Floyd, F.J. (2006). Impact of racial perspectives and contextual variables on marital trust and adjustment for African American couples. *Journal of Family Psychology, 20,* 79–87. doi: 10.1037/0893-3200.20.1.79

Kelly, S., Maynigo, P., Wesley, K., & Durham, J. (2013). African American communities and family systems: Relevance and challenges. *Couple and Family Psychology: Research and Practice, 2,* 264–277. doi: 10.1037/cfp0000014

King, A. C., & Canada, S. A. (2004). Client-related predictors of early drop-out in a substance abuse clinic. *Journal of Substance Abuse Treatment, 26,* 189–195. doi: 10.1016/S0740-5472(03)00210-1

Komarraju, M., & Cokley, K. O. (2008). Horizontal and vertical dimensions of individualism-collectivism: A comparison of African Americans and European Americans. *Cultural Diversity and Ethnic Minority Psychology, 14,* 336–343. doi: 10.1037/1099-9809.14.4.336

Lichter, D. T., Sassler, S., & Turner, R. N. (2014). Cohabitation, post-conception unions, and the rise in nonmarital fertility. *Social Science Research, 47,* 134–147. doi: 10.1016/j.ssresearch.2014.04.002

Maddox, K. B., & Gray, S. A. (2002). Cognitive representations of black Americans: Reexploring the role of skin tone. *Personality and Social Psychology Bulletin, 28,* 250–259. doi: 10.1177/0146167202282010

McCrady, B. S. (2012). Treating alcohol problems with couple therapy. *Journal of Clinical Psychology, 68,* 514–525. doi: 10.1002/jclp.21854

Murry, V. M., Brown, P. A., Brody, G. H., Cutrona, C. E., & Simons, R. L. (2001). Racial discrimination as a moderator of the links among stress, maternal psychological functioning, and family relationships. *Journal of Marriage and Family, 63*, 915–926. doi: 10.1111/j.1741-3737.2001.00915

Murry, V. M., Harrell, A. W., Brody, G. H., Chen, Y. F., Simons, R. L., Black, A. R., . . . & Gibbons, F. X. (2008). Long-term effects of stressors on relationship well-being and parenting among rural African American women. *Family Relations, 57*, 117–127. doi: 10.1111/j.1741-3729.2008.00488

Nelson, J. C., Adams, G., & Salter, P. S. (2013). The Marley hypothesis: Denial of racism reflects ignorance of history. *Psychological Science, 24*, 213–218. doi: 10.1177/0956797612451466

Orbuch, T. L., & Eyster, S. L. (1997). Division of household labor among Black couples and White couples. *Social Forces, 76*, 301–332. doi: 10.1093/sf/76.1.301

Pew Charitable Trust Forum (2009a). African-Americans and religion. Retrieved from Pew Research Religion and Public Life Project website: http://www.pewforum.org/2009/01/30/african-americans-and-religion/

Pew Charitable Trust Forum (2009b). A religious portrait of African Americans. Retrieved from Pew Research Religion and Public Life Project website: http://www.pewforum.org/2009/01/30/a-religious-portrait-of-african-americans/

Phinney, J. S., & Ong, A. D. (2007). Conceptualization and measurement of ethnic identity: Current status and future directions. *Journal of Counseling Psychology, 54*, 271–281. doi: 10.1037/0022-0167.54.3.271

Phinney, J. S., & Onwughalu, M. (1996). Racial identity and perception of American ideals among African American and African students in the United States. *International Journal of Intercultural Relations, 20*, 127–140. doi: 10.1016/0147-1767(95)00040-2

Quintana, S. M. (2007). Racial and ethnic identity: Developmental perspectives and research. *Journal of Counseling Psychology, 54*, 259–270. doi: 10.1037/0022-0167.54.3.259

Randall, A. K., & Bodenmann, G. (2009). The role of stress on close relationships and marital satisfaction. *Clinical Psychology Review, 29*, 105–115. doi: 10.1016/j.cpr.2008.10.004

Saegert, S. C., Adler, N. E., Bullock, H. E., Cauce, A. M., Liu, W. M., & Wyche, K. F. (2007). Report of the APA Task Force on socioeconomic status. Washington, DC: American Psychological Association.

Saegert, S., Fields, D., & Libman, K. (2011). Mortgage foreclosure and health disparities: Serial displacement as asset extraction in African American populations. *Journal of Urban Health, 88*, 390–402. doi: 10.1007/s11524-011-9584-3

Sampson, R. J. (2009). Racial stratification and the durable tangle of neighborhood inequality. *The Annals of the American Academy of Political and Social Science, 621*, 260–280. doi: 10.1177/0002716208324803

Sampson, R. J., & Raudenbush, S. W. (2004). Seeing disorder: Neighborhood stigma and the social construction of "broken windows". *Social Psychology Quarterly, 67*, 319–342. doi: 10.1177/019027250406700401

Simons, L. G., Simons, R. L., Landor, A. M., Bryant, C. M., & Beach, S. R. (2014). Factors linking childhood experiences to adult romantic relationships among

African Americans. *Journal of Family Psychology, 28,* 368–379. doi: 10.1037/a0036393

Simons, R. L., Simons, L. G., Lei, M. K., & Landor, A. M. (2012). Relational schemas, hostile romantic relationships, and beliefs about marriage among young African American adults. *Journal of Social and Personal Relationships, 29,* 77–101. doi: 10.1177/0265407511406897

Snell-Johns, J., Mendez, J. L., & Smith, B. H. (2004). Evidence-based solutions for overcoming access barriers, decreasing attrition, and promoting change with underserved families. *Journal of Family Psychology, 18,* 19. doi: 10.1037/0893-3200.18.1.19

Sue, S. (2006). Cultural competency: From philosophy to research and practice. *Journal of Community Psychology, 34,* 237–245. doi: 10.1002/jcop.20095

Sue, D. W., Capodilupo, C. M., Torino, G. C., Bucceri, J. M., Holder, A., Nadal, K. L., & Esquilin, M. (2007). Racial microaggressions in everyday life: Implications for clinical practice. *American Psychologist, 62,* 271–286. doi: 10.1037/0003-066X.62.4.271

Tach, L. M., & Halpern-Meekin, S. (2012). Marital quality and divorce decisions: How do premarital cohabitation and nonmarital childbearing matter? *Family Relations, 61,* 571–585. doi: 10.1111/j.1741-3729.2012.00724

Thornton, M. C., Taylor, R. J., & Chatters, L. M. (2013). African American and West Indian mutual feelings of closeness: Findings from a National Probability Survey. *Journal of Black Studies, 44,* 798–828. doi: 10.1177/0021934713516978

United States Census Bureau. (2013). Annual social and economic supplement to the current population survey (black population) [Data file]. Retrieved from http://www.census.gov/population/race/data/black.html

United States Federal Bureau of Investigation. (2015). Uniform crime report hate crime statistics 2014. Retrieved from https://www.fbi.gov/about-us/cjis/ucr/hate-crime/2014/topic-pages/victims_final.pdf

Vandiver, B. J., Cross, W. E., Jr., Worrell, F. C., & Fhagen-Smith, P. E. (2002). Validating the Cross Racial Identity Scale. *Journal of Counseling Psychology, 49,* 71–85. doi: 10.1037/0022-0167.49.1.71

Vickerman, M. (2007). Jamaica. In M. C. Waters & R. Udea (Eds.), *The new Americans: A guide to immigration since 1965* (pp. 479–490). Cambridge, MA: Harvard University Press.

Wallace, M. E., Mendola, P., Liu, D., & Grantz, K. L. (2015). Joint effects of structural racism and income inequality on small-for-gestational-age birth. *American Journal of Public Health, 105,* 1681–1688. doi: 10.2105/AJPH.2015.302613

Wesley, K. (this volume). Disparities in mental health care and homeownership for African Americans and Latinos in the United States. In S. Kelly (Ed.) *Diversity in couple and family therapy: Ethnicities, sexualities, and socioeconomics* (pp. 393–419). Santa Barbara, CA: Praeger.

Wesley, K., Kelly, S., Chestnut, C. (2017). *Exploratory factor analysis of stereotype scale scores.* Manuscript submitted for publication.

Wickrama, K. A. S., Bryant, C. M., & Wickrama, T. K. (2010). Perceived community disorder, hostile marital interactions, and self-reported health of African American couples: An interdyadic process. *Personal Relationships, 17,* 515–531. doi: 10.1111/j.1475-6811.2010.01299

Wickrama, K. A. S., Noh, S., & Bryant, C. M. (2005). Racial differences in adolescent distress: Differential effects of the family and community for blacks and whites. *Journal of Community Psychology, 33,* 261–282. doi: 10.1002/jcop.20053

Williams, D. R., Neighbors, H. W., & Jackson, J. S. (2003). Racial/ethnic discrimination and health: Findings from community studies. *American Journal of Public Health, 93,* 200–208. doi: 10.2105/AJPH.93.2.200

CHAPTER 2

Asian American Couples and Families

Lisa A. Suzuki
Grace Wong
Masako Mori
Kyoko M. Toyama

Asian American couples and families are comprised of individuals from diverse backgrounds. The U.S. Census defines "Asian American" as the original peoples of the Far East, Southeast Asia, and the Indian subcontinent. There are over 40 countries in Asia and many contain more than one ethnic group; for example: Central Asians (e.g., Afghani, Armenian, Mongolian), East Asians (e.g., Chinese, Japanese, Korean, Taiwanese), Southeast Asians (e.g., Burmese, Cambodian, Filipino, Hmong, Singaporean, Vietnamese), South Asians (e.g., Indian, Pakistani, Sri Lankan), and West Asians (a contested category referring to peoples from the Middle East; Asian Pacific Islander Institute of Domestic Violence, n.d.). Each ethnic and national identity carries with it complex political, social, and familial meanings. Therefore, clinicians working with Asian American clients must recognize the complex array of social locations that individuals from these communities bring with them to therapeutic context.

It is critical to recognize that Asian Americans are a heterogeneous grouping of communities; therefore, generalizations as presented in the literature cannot be uniformly applied to individual clients. Thus, dynamic sizing must be applied in clinical context with Asian Americans. **Dynamic sizing** refers to "knowing when to generalize and be inclusive and when to individualize and be exclusive" (Sue, 1998, p. 446). Using this knowledge, the clinician avoids stereotypes and takes into consideration the unique contexts of the couple or family members. This chapter

Authors' Note: Special thanks to Anna Cho for her assistance in conducting literature searches to facilitate the writing of this chapter.

highlights aspects of the historical contexts, religious and cultural foundations, current demographic characteristics, mental health utilization, and other considerations in working with Asian American couples and families. Clinical vignettes are used to illustrate various features of clinical intervention.

HISTORICAL CONTEXT OF ASIAN AMERICANS

Understanding the social context of Asian Americans includes attention to immigration history and the laws that have governed the process of arrival and adaptation in the United States. Hundreds of thousands of Chinese, Japanese, South Asians, Koreans, Filipinos, and Southeast Asians arrived in the United States during the 19th and 20th centuries (Liu, Murakami, Eap, & Hall, 2009). It is beyond the scope of this chapter to provide a comprehensive examination of critical historical events and policies that have impacted Asian communities in the United States. Instead we provide a few examples of how historical context has impacted the formation of couples and families in the United States.

Various laws governed the immigration and naturalization of particular Asian ethnic groups. Examples are the Chinese Exclusion Act (1882) that suspended immigration of Chinese laborers for a decade and the National Origins Act (1924) that prohibited Asian immigration with the exception of Filipinos. Quotas also were instituted to limit the number of immigrants from particular countries, such as with the Luce-Cellar Bill that allowed naturalization and immigration quotas of 100 to Asian Indians and Filipinos in 1946 (cited in Liu et al., 2009).

Immigration policies also impacted the formation of marital relationships and formation of family life. Between 1850 and 1930, Asian immigrants were primarily single male and unaccompanied married men, as they provided a source of cheap labor on plantations and in mining and construction (Fujino, 2000). Most males came in search of economic opportunities in the United States and the American government did not want to support children and families nor allow permanent residency or citizenship. Anti-miscegenation laws made it illegal for Asian males to marry White women. Military occupation and wartime also impacted the formation of intimate relationships. During WWII, the Korean War, and the Vietnam War, American servicemen married Asian women and brought them back to the United States following the passage of various legislative actions, including the War Brides Act (Shinagawa & Pang, 1996).

Model Minority and Foreigner Stereotypes

The most prevalent stereotypes pertaining to Asian Americans are that of the **model minority** and **perpetual foreigner** (Lee, Wong, & Alvarez, 2009). The cultural emphasis placed upon hard work and achievement led to the academic and economic success of Asian Americans. However, the model minority stereotype promotes the idea that given these indicators of success, Asian Americans no longer face economic, social, or political barriers. This is misleading given that a number of Asian American communities (e.g., Hmong, Cambodian) live in poverty and students from these communities are not faring well educationally. The perpetual foreigner stereotype promotes the perception that Asians are not genuinely American. A related stereotype promoted during WWII after the attack on Pearl Harbor was the view of Asians as "dangerous" and not to be trusted. Another stereotype and myth is that all Asians within the same region speak the same language, such as in the case of East Asians (Japanese, Chinese and Koreans) and South Asians (Indians, Bangladeshes and Sri Lankans). These stereotypes are misleading and mask the diversity that exists within the Asian American community (Lee et al., 2009).

Pan-Asian Identity and Solidarity

Despite similarities in cultural values and historical oppression, the existence of a pan-Asian identity has been viewed as controversial, given the great diversity that exists under the Asian American label in terms of ethnicity, history, culture, religion, socioeconomic indicators, and so forth (e.g., Suzuki, Ahluwalia, & Alimchandani, 2012). Those who are supportive of a pan-Asian identity note the importance of a communal sociopolitical identity to obtain economic resources and political representation (Espiritu, 1993). Advocating a unified Asian American identity, however, has created a sense of homogeneity that does not exist in reality. Scholars have noted the political, historical, economic, and religious differences between countries of origin that comprise a pan-ethnic Asian American identity. Challenges have been raised regarding the extent to which experiences and perspectives of particular groups (e.g., South Asian Americans) are included in the Asian American discourse (Shankar & Srikanth, 1998).

RELIGIOUS ROOTS OF ASIAN COMMUNITIES

Confucianism, Buddhism, Hinduism, Islam, and Christianity all have influenced many Asian societies. Asian-born faiths and practices influence conceptualization of psychology and spirituality in the United States (Ai, Bjork, Appel, & Huang, 2013). Religious affiliation varies among Asian Americans. According to the Pew Report (2012), "about half of Chinese are unaffiliated, most Filipinos are Catholic, about half of Indians are Hindu, most Koreans are Protestant, and a plurality of Vietnamese are Buddhist ... Overall, 39% of Asian Americans say religion is very important in their lives, compared to 58% of the U.S. general public" (p. 8). Religious communities provide support in the adaptation process to the

United States as well as spiritually based counseling services. For example, Korean and Chinese churches may provide services including English language instruction, social events, and music programs for children to ease adaption to the American culture. We describe briefly aspects of Confucianism, Buddhism, and Hinduism, as these have been identified in the literature as potentially impacting the formation of family relationships, role functioning, and therapeutic change processes for Asian Americans.

Confucianism established **filial piety** as the cultural norm characterized by respect for parents, elders, and ancestors (Hsu, 1971). The Confucian concept of filial piety set the stage for a number of East Asian countries such as China, Japan, Korea, and Vietnam to establish the duty of the child, especially the eldest male, to parents and grandparents.

South Asian families also maintain strong ties to the clan or extended family rather than just the nuclear family (e.g., Shariff, 2009). The care of parents may fall on the eldest male or on a dutiful daughter. Sometimes practical needs like child care also dictate the role and residence of the grandparents. Most couples depend on a dual income, and reliable child care offered by grandparents is highly valued. Among South Asian families, Indian families have been greatly influenced by a patriarchal, interdependent family system, with parents, grandparents, and other elders playing a significant role in socializing young children into culturally expected behaviors. Family obligation and loyalty, as well as self-sacrifice and obedience toward one's elders, are paramount for Indian families (Shariff, 2009).

Buddhism is a religious tradition born in India that spread to many countries in Asia. Buddhism is based upon four noble truths illuminating how the "individual causes his/her own suffering through creation and identification with illusion, and the way to begin dissolving these illusions" (Daya, 2000, p. 270). A review by Daya (2000) indicates the four noble truths as the following: (a) acknowledgment that life consists of suffering and disease (e.g., dissatisfactions) due to old age, sickness, death, and not getting what one desires; (b) "suffering is caused by the individual's belief in a persistent, unchanging self" (p. 259); (c) release from disease is accomplished through seeing things as they truly are—deconstructing boundaries without judgment or evaluation; and (d) truth requires the presence of eight factors: understanding, thought, speech, action, livelihood, effort, mindfulness, and concentration. These four noble truths translate well in societies and social relationships where living closely together necessitates peaceful coexistence.

Right speech, right action, and right occupation mean living in harmony with the unity of life, speaking kindly, and earning livelihood in a way that is not harmful or at the expense of others. (pp. 260–261)

Mindfulness and meditation are emphasized to address five hindrances or emotional states that "make thoughts unwholesome" (Daya, 2000, p. 262).

They are overexuberance and remorse, vindictiveness, gloominess, attachment, and indecision. The principles of Buddhist religion relevant to therapy include (a) flexibility of self, (b) being in the present, (c) experiencing without evaluation, (d) compassion, (e) openness, (f) interdependency, and (g) sitting with suffering. Following these principles can serve as a psychological comfort by providing the religious narrative to help reinterpret life events (Suh, 2011).

Hinduism is an ancient religion referred to as *Sanatana Dharma* meaning "ancient and eternal moral duty" (Ano, Mathew, & Fukuyama, 2009, p. 136). Hindu Indians believe in the principles of dharma or appropriate conduct at every level of social life, wherein natural laws are believed to operate according to context-dependent moral obligations (Menon, 2003). In their review of this religion in relation to psychological tenets, Ano, Mathew, and Fukuyama report central beliefs including a soul in all beings; the continuous flow of birth, death, and rebirth; devotion to duty; and all actions have consequences or karma. The goal of life is to reach the ultimate reality of the Brahma (the creator) and to no longer return to the cycle of birth and death. Belief in reincarnation can instill hope in a better future life, and karma can be linked to assuming personal responsibility and control.

Christianity was brought to Asia by missionaries primarily from Europe as early as the 14th century. Christianity was cultivated in Asia over the centuries. Many Asians who immigrate to the United States are Christians, and today Christianity makes up the largest religious group (42%) among Asian Americans. More Asian Christians attend worship services than other Christians (Pew Research Center, 2012). The interconnectedness between the role of the individual and community in the Christian life may create a conflict with the Eastern-influenced values of Asian Americans. The conflicts between these cultural differences also can lead to the unique blending of values in Asian Americans as they try to integrate opposing influences (Hung, 2006). For example, the worship of ancestors may be seen as idolatry for Christian converts. In order to show respect to ancestors, these Christians may find a compromise to demonstrate their respect for the dead, for example, by saying special prayers.

Islam means "peace" and "submission to the will of God" (Ano et al., 2009, p. 142). Beliefs of this religion include (a) unity of God in all things, (b) Mohammed the prophet, (c) innate goodness in humankind, (d) importance of faith community, and (e) living a righteous life to achieve peace and harmony (Altareb, 1996; cited in Ano et al., 2009). Obligations of faith, prayer, charity, fasting, and pilgrimage to Mecca are considered the five pillars. Islamic teachings are conservative and strict in comparison to liberal American practices, though similar values are placed on benevolence, forgiveness, and personal development. Ano et al. (2009) cite literature indicating that mental health services may be viewed negatively because they are perceived to reflect inherent Western values and therefore result in low utilization rates among Muslims.

Being aware of the potential impact of Confucian, Buddhist, Hindu, Islamic, and Christian beliefs can assist the clinician in understanding the nature of family relationships and perceptions of mental illness, as well as the process of change for members of the Asian American community. Mindfulness, as noted in Buddhism, translates well to family and couples therapy, where harmony contributes to reduction of stress in relationships. Depending upon their religious/spiritual affiliation, Asian American couples and families may approach their issues differently, and the alleviation of distress may take different forms. For example, clients may seek services from a Buddhist Monk to help them "sit with suffering" and let go or release the pain in their lives over time rather than speaking about it in a traditional Western approach to therapy.

CURRENT DEMOGRAPHICS ON ASIAN AMERICANS IN THE UNITED STATES

In 2012, a nationally representative survey of 3,511 Asian adults was conducted in the United States, focusing on the six largest subgroups—namely, Chinese, Filipino, Indian, Japanese, Korean, and Vietnamese (Pew Research Center, 2013). According to the report, Asians comprise the largest group of new immigrants to the United States and are the most highly educated. Asians value marriage, creation of families and becoming parents, and maintaining a strong sense of filial respect. In comparison to other racial and ethnic groups, Asian Americans are more likely to intermarry across racial lines and live in mixed neighborhoods.

There also is variability within the Asian American community with respect to family structure, values, roles, child-rearing goals, and parenting style across different Asian subgroups. For example, Asian Americans who are third generation or greater in the United States may identify strongly with mainstream Western cultural values, practices, and communication styles. The **family structure** may be more focused, for example, on the nuclear rather than on extended family. Rather than adopting traditional male and female roles, marriage and parenting practices may reflect a more egalitarian relationship as both husband and wife make decisions collaboratively (Del Carmen, 1990). On the other hand, Asian families who recently immigrated may be more likely to retain traditional Asian family structure, values, roles, child-rearing goals, and parenting practices.

VARIABLES IMPACTING MENTAL HEALTH SERVICE UTILIZATION AMONG ASIAN AMERICANS

Numerous culturally related factors can impact the understanding of the mental health issues of Asian Americans. These include somatization, acculturation, generational status, ethnic identity, geographic location, discrimination, and language. Note that many of these factors are inter-related as highlighted in the following sections.

Expression of Feelings and Psychosomatic Symptoms

In many traditional Asian communities, overt expression of feelings is considered to reflect a lack of maturity and self-control, especially by males (Shimizu & Devine, 2001). Thus, feelings are almost never discussed directly. Mental illness or psychological problems of a family member are seen as a failure of the family functioning or even genetics, which brings shame to the family. Strong **stigma** and guilt are associated with receiving mental health professionals' services (Mathur, Ann, Kumar, & Menon, 2014; Sanchez & Gaw, 2007). Affective concerns may be represented in terms of physical complaints or psychosomatic symptoms like headaches and stomach ailments. Psychoeducational interventions provided in a nonjudgmental atmosphere can help the individual to understand that he or she is not alone. Mental health professionals can provide support and encouragement to the family for what they have been doing on behalf of the client. This can be helpful in enabling the counselor to "join" with the family in creating a sense of hope and future direction.

Interrelated Variables: Acculturation, Generational Status, Ethnic Identity, and Discrimination

Assessment of the client's level of acculturation and ethnic identity may be helpful in contextualizing the couple's or family's commitment and engagement in mental health services. Acculturation has been measured through proxies such as length of stay in the host country or generational status. However, these do not necessarily indicate stronger acculturation or ethnic identification as some individuals still live in ethnic enclaves (e.g., Chinatown) where they may not be required to adapt to mainstream American cultural values and practices. In recent years, though, most Asian Americans tend to live in mixed neighborhoods (Pew Research Center, 2013).

Attitudes and beliefs regarding mental health treatment vary among Asians living in the United States. Those Asians who are highly acculturated to the Western culture may be more open and willing to seek psychological treatment for their emotional problems. Others who are more strongly identified with traditional Asian culture may have less inclination to receive psychotherapy because of less exposure to mental health services and its efficacy. However, new immigrants do use psychiatric services for the chronically and persistently mentally ill when the symptoms become more severe (Okazaki, 2000).

A content analysis of 62 studies examining the relationship between racial discrimination and health indicated that most studies found that racial discrimination is related to poorer health and the most consistent findings were for mental health problems (Gee, Ro, Shariff-Marco, & Chae, 2009). As noted in previously cited studies, ethnic identity was also noted to be a moderator of discrimination. Yet the direction of moderation is mixed; some studies found that ethnic identity buffers associations between discrimination and health outcomes, while others found that a strong ethnic identity exacerbates those associations. The reasons for these different findings may be linked to culture and dimensions of social context, as described next.

Associations between discrimination and poor health were weaker for those with high levels of social support. Another key context is immigration; studies indicate that "immigrants are healthier than nonimmigrants but, the relationship is complex, given findings that this 'immigrant advantage' erodes with time in the United States" due to acculturation or cultural change and experience of discrimination (Gee et al., 2009, p. 17). For example, colorism or prejudice against persons with darker skin tones was found to be a factor, as Asian groups with darker skin may experience greater discrimination than those who are lighter. Familiarity was also reported to "breed liking" as "less common groups," that is, those with a shorter history in the United States, encounter more discrimination (p. 17). Factors such as these may impact the role of ethnic identity.

Connections between ethnic identity, discrimination, and mental health have also been noted in a National Latino and Asian American study (Yip, Gee, & Takeuchi, 2008). Results indicate developmental differences. For U.S. born individuals aged 41–50, a strong/positive ethnic identity was found to buffer the association between discrimination and poor mental health. For those between 31 and 40 years of age and 51 and 75 years of age, ethnic identity exacerbated the negative effects of discrimination on mental health. The authors note that life span research indicates that individuals in the age group of 41–50 years cope more effectively with stress and are better able to regulate their emotional responses. As individuals age, they may actively try to minimize negative interactions, thus experiencing discrimination may be viewed as particularly noxious. The authors conclude that "although levels of ethnic identity do not seem to vary across age groups, but its role with respect to mental health might" (Yip et al., 2008, p. 797). Thus, the relationship between ethnic identity, discrimination, and well-being among Asians in the United States must take into consideration age, immigrant status, and other contextual and sociocultural factors.

Literature on **microaggressions**, or subtle acts of discrimination, includes the often subtle automatic exchanges that "put down" (Sue, Bucceri, Lin, Nadal, & Torino, 2009, p. 89) or denigrate members of Asian American communities. Microaggressions against Asian Americans include beliefs that all Asian Americans are "aliens" even for those of whom America is their own land of birth, ascriptions of greater achievement and intelligence, exoticization of Asian women, invalidation of interethnic differences, denial of oppressive racial realities, pathologizing Asian American cultural values/communication styles, and treating them as second-class citizens or as if they are invisible (Sue, et al., 2009).

Language

Knowledge of the English language varies between Asian subgroups arriving in the United States (Ahmad-Stout & Nath, 2013). Many South Asian Indians and Filipinos arrive in the United States with proficient skills in English based upon the educational experiences in their homeland, whereas most other immigrants often struggle to learn a new language, creating acculturative stress and difficulties in adapting to the United States. Access to employment, education, and health services is much easier for those proficient in English.

WORKING WITH ASIAN AMERICAN COUPLES

The complexity of working with Asian American couples may be increased, given that Asians are more likely than other ethnic groups to intermarry outside of their race. From 2008 to 2010, 29 percent of all Asian newlyweds married outside of their race. Asian women were found to be twice as likely, in comparison to Asian men, to marry out (Pew Research Center, 2012). Ethnic group differences, however, are noted as Japanese have the highest rates of intermarriage in comparison to South Indians who were found to have the lowest. The Japanese American community suffered during WWII through internment and being treated as "outsiders" despite being naturalized citizens. Intermarrying with White Americans led to greater assimilation into the U.S. mainstream culture. In addition, Japanese Americans have a longer history in the United States in comparison to South Indians.

Acculturation issues, gender roles, the impact of the intergenerational/extended family, and parental patterns of behavior must be considered in working with Asian American couples (Dupree et al., 2013). Indeed, the role of the extended family is crucial to consider, as the couple is a unit within the larger clan and family is formed by an obligation to the care of one another. The process of acculturation tests couple and familial bonds as old and new values jockey for viability in new world. Traditional gender roles may be challenged because of the practical necessity to break out of traditional role arrangements, such as when the husband no longer is the sole breadwinner for educational and financial reasons.

A mixed-method study on the marital happiness of 91 Hindu Indian urban couples from three socioeconomic classes revealed that happy couples in comparison to unhappy couples reported higher levels of agreement, empathy, validation, support, and fulfilled expectations (Sandhya, 2009). Couples' experience and expression of intimacy, affected by social context, predicted enhanced levels of happiness in marriage. The majority of couples in this study reported being "very" or "perfectly happy" and 71 percent noted that they would marry again. Gender differences were also noted as Indian wives reported less intimacy and lower levels of attention and help in daily affairs from their spouses than reported by husbands. Interestingly, the number and quality of reported "good times" of one spouse with the other were important correlates to marital happiness beyond the effects of conflict. This finding indicates that conflict may be a stable feature of fulfilling relationships.

Findings of a national study of Asian Americans found that the positive effects of marriage on well-being were indicated primarily for women and the foreign born. Women and foreign-born individuals who were not married were more likely to experience psychological distress (Walton & Takeuchi, 2009). No relationship between mental and physical health was noted for men and the U.S. born. The authors note that traditional Asian immigrant families often adhere to gender-role differentiation in which women are responsible for caretaking; thus their well-being is often connected to the emotional makeup of the marriage.

A study examined the concept of assertiveness, involving courage, authenticity, and autonomy, in marital relationships among Asian Indians residing in a metropolitan area located in the Southwestern region of the United States (Abbassi & Singh, 2006). Findings suggest gender differences as female respondents were found to possess a higher level of authenticity while males expressed a greater sense of autonomy. The male participants in the study were identified as the primary breadwinner in the family. No gender differences were noted in degrees of courage. Age and level of communication were also found to be significantly related to assertiveness as older persons and those who had been married for longer periods expressed a greater sense of autonomy and those who reported more effective communication with their spouses reported higher levels of courage and authenticity.

Division of labor among couples has also been addressed in studies examining marital satisfaction among diverse ethnic and racial communities in the United States. With respect to housework, Asian and Hispanic women do more cooking and cleaning compared to White and Black women (Sayer & Fine, 2011). Across many cultures (including Asian) where both partners work, women who have a higher percentage of household work express greater complaints and reported higher degrees of dissatisfaction with the division of labor (Stohs, 2000).

Traditionally, Asian women have been disadvantaged in these historically male-dominated societies (Hyun, 2001) that often follow mores based upon Confucian values. Asian men are responsible for the financial security of the family. Values, however, change with exposure to Western ideas. For example, Hyun found "Korean women who have been historically disadvantaged by the Confucian value system, endorse traditional values less strongly than Korean men regardless of sociocultural contexts," challenging the characterization of Asian women as subservient (p. 223).

Intimate Partner Violence

A content analysis of 60 empirical publications on domestic violence among Asians and Asian Americans revealed that the most frequently studied groups were Asian Indians and Chinese, and over 50 percent of the articles focused on Asian subgroups abroad from India, China, Korea, etc. (Yick & Oomen-Early, 2008). The authors note that research on domestic violence within a cultural context is multifaceted, requiring an understanding of the unique implications of historical, political, and economic forces in context. Thus, 90 percent of the empirical studies examined specific Asian ethnic subgroups rather than conducting a general analysis on Asian Americans and **intimate partner violence** (IPV).

According to the first study to yield national estimates of IPV in Asian American communities, Chang, Shen, and Takeuchi (2009) reported low overall rates in comparison to other racial and ethnic groups. This finding was based on their examination of 1,470 Asian Americans interviewed for the National Latino and Asian American Study. Ten percent of Asian American women and 12 percent of Asian American men reported minor incidents of IPV. A greater proportion of participants admitted to having perpetrated IPV than being a victim. Predictors of IPV included younger age, higher socioeconomic status, alcohol and substance use disorders, depression, ethnicity, and being born in the United States. Vietnamese Americans were found to be less likely than other Asian American respondents to report IPV. The authors also suggest that cultural traditions may play a role in the data gathered. Tjaden and Thoennes (2000) found that traditional Asian values regarding family ties and maintenance of harmony may prevent Asian women from disclosing physical and emotional abuse from partners. For example, Confucian values emphasize the family obligation and filial piety.

Interethnic differences are also supported in a study of 78 Indian and Pakistani immigrant women in Illinois. Findings indicate a greater frequency of IPV among women who were raised in India or Pakistan, as 77 percent of the women reported experiencing domestic violence in their lifetime and 71 percent reported domestic violence within the past year (Adam & Schewe, 2007). In addition, women were found to be at greater risk when violence was evident in their immediate and extended families.

Cultural beliefs in male domination were also found to be a contributory factor in these communities.

WORKING WITH ASIAN AMERICAN FAMILIES

With few exceptions, traditional Asian family structure is patriarchal and hierarchical (Sue & Sue, 2008; Yamamoto & Iga, 1983; Yamamoto & Kubota, 1983). Being male and older is associated with a higher status. The father is the head of the household, holding the most power. The first son is the successor of the family lineage who is valued most among siblings. Clear gender roles exist in marriage. The role of the father is to provide for the family, while the mother is responsible for all domestic matters including household and child-rearing issues. The father is the decision maker of important family matters.

In many Asian communities, family is the basic unit of the society (Shimizu & Devine, 2001), and parent–child relationships differ from those within Western culture. In the Western culture, a child is perceived as being separate from parents, whereas in the traditional Asian culture, a child is perceived as an extension of the parents themselves. The parent–child psychological boundary in a traditional Asian family is more blurred, given roles depicted within the family (Azuma, Hakuta, & Stevenson, 1986). These cultural differences have important implication for parent–child relationship, child-rearing goals, and parenting practices.

Asian culture is more collectivist than Western culture. Western cultures emphasize an individualistic orientation, and thus cultivating independence and individuality is a primary child-rearing goal. In contrast, traditional Asian families emphasize a more collectivistic orientation, and thus cultivating interdependency and conformity is a primary child-rearing goal (Azuma et al., 1986; Shimizu & Devine, 2001). Western parents foster such qualities as self-assertion, verbal competence, creativity, and assertiveness in their children so they will stand out in a crowd (Rubin & Chung, 2006; Shimizu & Devine, 2001). By contrast, traditional Asian parents foster conformity, self-restraint, and empathy to maintain harmonious interpersonal relationships within the family and community (Berry, 1997; Yamamoto & Iga, 1983; Yamamoto & Kubota, 1983). Parents often guide their children to become aware of how others might think and feel in a given situation and behave in a way to be sensitive to the feelings and needs of others. Shaming is occasionally used as a method of disciplining a child (Azuma et al., 1986; Shimizu & Devine, 2001). A child growing up in a traditional Asian family is socialized to conform and be mindful of others in the group.

Parenting styles in traditional Asian culture tend to be authoritarian and protective (Lee et al., 2014; Sue & Sue, 2008; Xia, Do, & Xie, 2013), as compared to authoritative Western parenting. While this is not true across the board, some trends are noted. Authoritarian parents tend to believe they know what is best for their child and take responsibility to make decisions for the child, including daily matters such as curfews, dating, and chores, as well as important life decisions such as college, occupation, and spousal choices. Focus is not on the interests or needs of the child, and the child is expected to obey without questioning (Baumrind, 1996; Maccoby & Martin, 1983). When the child breaks a rule or disobeys parents, he.or she is corrected sometimes through guilt or shaming practices (Sue & Sue, 2008). Also, authoritarian parents do not overtly express their warmth and nurturance (Baumrind, 1996; Maccoby & Martin, 1983). Emphasis is placed upon the child understanding the value placed upon humility. Conversely, in the Western culture, authoritative parenting is more common (Baumrind, 1996; Lee et al., 2014; Maccoby & Martin, 1983; Xia et al., 2013), in which parents attempt to encourage the child's independence in a more democratic manner. When making decisions about the child, they listen to the child's opinions. It is the parents who make a final decision, but they consider the child's needs in the process. Parents set firm limits, and if a child violates a rule, consistent and fair consequences are implemented. Authoritative parents express warmth and nurturance more overtly (Baumrind, 1996; Maccoby & Martin, 1983).

Treatment of children's behavior and qualities also differ in traditional Asian and Western cultures. In Western parenting practice, parents actively acknowledge a child's positive aspects, good behavior, and achievement, even if they are small, with verbal praise and positive reinforcement. On the contrary, in traditional Asian parenting practice, parents tend to point out a child's weak points, problem behavior, or incompetency in an attempt to "correct" through criticism. The child's positive qualities or behavior are not overtly acknowledged or praised (Del Carmen, 1990; Wu & Chao, 2011).

Western and traditional Asian parents express their love for the child differently (Del Carmen, 1990). Western parents convey their love more overtly through words and physical affection such as hugs and kisses. On the other hand, traditional Asian parents tend to express their love for the child by attending to their physical needs, for example, by preparing nutritious meals and providing instrumental support (Cheah, Leung, & Zhou, 2013; Wu & Chao, 2011).

Guiding a child to academic and professional success is an extremely important aspect in Asian parenting practices as success brings honor and a sense of pride to the family. Asian parents commonly invest a great deal of time, energy, and emotional commitment to educational and professional pursuits. Traditional Asian mothers may strictly and rigidly structure the child's life by scheduling study sessions with tutors and other academic programs. The child's play time, sport and leisure time, and sometimes sleep are sacrificed. This is an extension of the belief in education noted in some Asian countries such as Japan, where the prestige of the university a child graduates from has life-long influence over his or her professional life (Qin, 2009). Admission to Japanese universities is largely determined by the results of the entrance examination. As a result, parents send their children to "Jyuken Jyuku" ("Entrance examination preparatory cram school") that demands extremely high academic performances and time commitment from their students and parents. The child's academic success is regarded as the mother's success, as she is responsible for child-rearing and education, meaning at the same time that she is the one responsible if the child fails. This creates an enormous psychological pressure for both the mother and the child (Qin, 2009).

Acculturation Conflicts

Given the individualism and other differences of mainstream American culture, immigration and practicality in the new world can challenge the order of traditional Asian family structures. For example, *acculturation conflicts* arise as Asian children and adolescents are exposed to American culture in school and social relationships with peers. This can create concern and stress for traditional Asian parents who worry that their offspring are becoming too "Westernized" or "Americanized." Parents may associate this with a loosening of family values, leading to misunderstandings, miscommunication, and conflicts (Sue & Sue, 2008). Studies indicate that Chinese American youth reported greater respect for parental authority and less autonomy than European American students (e.g., Chang & Greenberger, 2012). Chang and Greenberger examined parenting satisfaction among mothers with college-age children. Seventy-two Chinese American mothers reported lower parenting satisfaction, less positive relationship quality, and poorer perceived college performance of their young adult child in comparison to 68 European American mothers. Findings of a regression analysis indicated that mutual warmth and acceptance were independent contributors to maternal satisfaction, and when included in the analysis, these contributors reduced ethnic differences in parenting satisfaction to nonsignificant levels.

Bicultural Adaptation

Asian adolescents living in the United States face the challenge of managing the complex developmental task of identity formation and group affiliation, while being exposed to very different cultures of Asia and the West (Yamaguchi Williams et al., 2005). This can create confusion and anxiety, and affect Asian adolescents' self-esteem negatively (Kim & Omizo, 2010; Lorenzo, Fronst, & Reinherz, 2000). What is valued at home, such as conformity, self-restraint, and obedience, are not valued in an American school. Rather, the ability to assert one's opinion even if they are different from others, think independently, and assume leadership roles is highly valued and defines "good students" (Russell, Crockett, & Chao, 2010).

These qualities are not likely to be fostered in schools in Asia where a direct, didactic teaching style is common. Students are expected to sit quietly in a classroom, absorb information, and do well on examinations. For those Asian children who come to the United States as school-age children, language barrier is a major obstacle to attain academic success and social adjustment (Yeh et al., 2003).

Living in a bicultural world impacts the formation of ethnic identity. For example, Inman, Howard, Beaumont, and Walker (2007) revealed that Indian ethnic identity retention was influenced by "engagement in cultural celebrations and activities, a need to hold onto tradition and upbringing, family ties, social support, and a rejection of perceived Western values" (p. 93). Environmental obstacles and barriers in American society that challenge these practices and beliefs include "loss of familial support, lack of cultural continuity," and an inability to experience positive benefits of living fully in both worlds (p. 93).

Intergenerational Conflict

Research indicates the intergenerational parent–child cultural gap could be a major stressor to Asian adolescents, which could affect the child's psychological health negatively (Ying & Han, 2008). Parent–child conflict is more likely in Asian American families in which parents' ethnic identification with traditional Asian culture is strong, while their adolescent child is highly acculturated to Euro-American culture (Lim, Yeh, Liang, Lau, & McCabe, 2009; Serafica, 1990). During adolescence in mainstream American culture, a child's psychological autonomy is often encouraged. This may result in parent–child conflict with more traditional authoritarian parents. The adolescent child may develop negative feelings like anger and frustration, and oppose parental demands and control. The intensity of such conflict is likely to be greater between parents and children whose cultural gap is larger (Ying & Han, 2008). Asian adolescents' reported open parent–child communication, family cohesion, and parental warmth are related to better psychological adjustment, whereas reported parent–child conflict, authoritarian parenting, and excessive academic pressure are related to negative psychological outcomes in both American and Asian samples abroad (Costigan, Hua, & Sue, 2010; Hwang & Wood, 2008; Kordi & Baharudin, 2010; Lim et al., 2009; Rhee, Chang, & Rhee, 2003; Shek, 2007; Wu & Chao, 2005).

INTERSECTING IDENTITIES

Understanding the multiple intersecting identities for any individual is a complex process. As Hays (2008) highlights in her ADDRESSING model, numerous facets of identity can and should be considered when working with any client. The model's ADDRESSING acronym stresses the importance of Age, Developmental and acquired Disabilities, Religion, Ethnicity, Socioeconomic status, Sexual orientation, Indigenous heritage, National origin, and Gender. While it is beyond the scope of this chapter to examine all of these important identity constructs, we provide highlights of the growing literature examining lesbian and gay individuals in Asian American communities.

Studies on lesbian and gay Asian Americans often center on East Asian Americans (Korean, Japanese, and Chinese), leaving out other ethnic subgroups. Despite this limitation, findings are often applied to all Asian Americans (Horton, 2014; Nadal & Corpus, 2013). Therefore, care must be taken when considering the applicability and generalizability of findings within the heterogeneous Asian American ethnic groups.

As research about the different gay and lesbian groups in ethnic communities emerge, studies have identified challenges faced in different cultural contexts. Horton (2014) and Nadal and Corpus (2013) are two examples from Vietnamese and Filipino American communities that highlight the need to address unique cultural specificities while also recognizing that similar questions can be asked of each culture's population. A third study (Hom, 1994) addresses parental response to the coming out process with their parents of lesbian and gay students.

Horton (2014) focuses on the political issue of the invisibility of gay individuals in Vietnam. The society's misrecognition and non-recognition have had adverse effects on the community, which can go so far as inflicting what Taylor (1994) describes as a "wounding" that contributes to suicidal ideation and existential anxiety. Horton (2014) highlights how the heteronormative pressure in the Vietnamese context can render significant action, such as a gay couple registering for marriage, remaining invisible by not bringing up the topic or legislating laws forbidding same-sex marriage. This is done through the raising of heterosexuality as the norm for society while homosexuality is devalued, and discussed as a disease to be cured. In such a context, lesbian and gay individuals and couples are identified as abnormal.

In a study of Filipino Americans in the United States, Nadal and Corpus (2013) attempt to describe issues unique to gay Filipino Americans. The first is religious influence on sexual and gender identity. In the Philippines, Catholicism is a powerful religion. Cultural beliefs regarding sexual and gender identity are known to most individuals who grew up in the Philippines, and the impact of Catholicism is personal and social. Some individuals initially respond to their homosexual feelings by turning to religion to dispel the unacceptable desires. Family and social disapproval add additional pressures. Thus, homophobia comes from internalized as well as externalized sources found in family and society. Many family members themselves struggle to accept their gay family members coming out to them. Some have dealt with prescribed prohibition by using denial. Members coming out have reported that family members fail to absorb what is being shared, forcing individuals to tell their relatives several times before the information is accepted.

Hom (1994), a classroom teacher, was moved to write about the "10% of her students" who are gay because she witnessed the negative responses of Asian parents toward their gay children. Recognizing that sexuality, let alone homosexuality, is not often talked about among Asian parents with their children, she decided to conduct a group interview with 13 parents from Chinese, Japanese Vietnamese, Korean, and Filipino descent. The themes that emerged pertained to attitudes before disclosure/discovery, attitudes and reactions after disclosure/discovery, disclosure to friends and their community, and advice to other parents. Hom indicated that the parents did not associate homosexuality with Westernization; however, they did note that there is more room to express homosexuality in the United States in comparison to Asian countries. Many parents associate gay characteristics as "reversal of gender roles" (feminine men, masculine women) and might have homophobic opinions about gays, but the general attitude is to leave the sexual orientation issue alone. Once parents discover their child's homosexuality, they sometimes report a period of prolonged shock, and strong emotions are eventually followed by tolerance if they realize their child is happy. Often there is concern about social judgment and whether they have raised a "bad child," stemming from internalized homophobia. Given that concern, some parents' agreement to participate in Hom's study was an indication of how they had come to accept their children's sexual orientation. The advice that many parents shared was telling other parents to just love their child.

CASE VIGNETTES

In the following sections we provide case examples to highlight some of the clinical issues that can arise when working with Asian American couples and families. Each case is followed by a discussion of clinical implications. The reader should consider the formulation of these two cases in reference to (1) presenting problems/symptoms, (2) precipitating events/stressors, and (3) predisposing factors (e.g., vulnerability and environmental stressors). Note the interaction of these three areas in understanding what maintains the problems and symptoms within the individual, couple, and family system.

Bon-Hwa and Cho

Dr. Bon-Hwa Yong and his wife Cho came to a mental health clinic seeking couples counseling. They were matched with an experienced clinician who had some knowledge of East Asian cultural issues. Their presenting problem pertained to making a decision about caring for Bon-Hwa's parents who were becoming more dependent and unable to care for themselves. The family had been very poor when they first emigrated to the United States from Korea, and Bon-Hwa's parents worked hard to support their son through medical school, often sacrificing their own needs, such as buying a house or car. It was expected that Bon-Hwa would care for his aging parents. Now that he is financially successful, living in a big house in a suburban neighborhood, Cho is dreading the thought of living with her mother-in-law, whom she perceives to be emotionally needy and egocentric.

Bon-Hwa's mother communicates her needs silently or through indirect complaints. During meal times, when her rice bowl is empty, she would stop eating and place her empty rice bowl on the table, looking sad and hurt rather than ask for more or get up and fill her own bowl. She would not suggest going shopping for new clothing but would pine about her ragged clothing. While Cho did not mind helping her mother-in-law, she eventually experienced the silence as passive-aggressive behavior and was becoming increasingly annoyed. Rather than helping Cho with her three young grandchildren, Bon-Hwa's mother would talk incessantly about her somatic concerns.

Bon-Hwa's father was more helpful with the children, driving them around and sometimes picking them up from preschool and kindergarten. He has learned to ignore his wife by avoiding her, doing hours of garden work or helping out an old friend at the store.

Cho has protested having them move in, as she was already overwhelmed caring for their three children while holding a part-time position as a nurse at a nearby hospital. As a medical doctor, Bon-Hwa was frequently "on call" and she would have to take care of her husband's parents by herself while managing their three children. While Cho understands filial duty and loves her husband, the thought of living with her mother-in-law is too much and the couple has had numerous arguments over the care of Bon-Hwa's parents. Bon-Hwa feels very guilty about not caring for his parents, as they have truly sacrificed in order to make it possible for him to be a doctor; yet he feels torn as he worries about his wife as well and becomes defensive and silent when he thinks she is criticizing his parents.

Clinical Implications

Many couples come into therapy to deal with issues related to managing their extended family obligations. In many Asian families, the extended family and nuclear family boundaries are less defined. Confucian ideals reinforce some of the notions of obligation, but even without Confucian "filial piety" dictating these social obligations, family support has been a crucial aspect in the survival of the clan for generations. Bon-Hwa feels guilty that he is not caring for his parents himself and repaying them for sacrificing for him, but he is sensitive to his wife's feelings and needs as their relationship is representative of a more egalitarian relationship rather than traditional. He would not dictate what must happen within his household. Hence, Bon-Hwa is caught between his sensitivity to his wife, and the guilt he feels about not taking his parents in to live in his house.

The therapist must take into consideration the dilemma that this couple is facing given their filial responsibilities and their feelings regarding taking on additional caretaking of Bon-Hwa's aging parents. In the supportive environment of couples therapy, Cho was able to express to her husband her love and devotion to him but also articulate why she was frustrated with her mother-in-law's way of relating. She was also able to explore that silence may not necessarily be passive-aggressiveness and that her mother-in-law may be dependent and unable to articulate her own needs. Bon-Hwa's whole physical posture became less defensive and he began to acknowledge and verbalize his own dilemma, recognizing that his mother is not easy to live with. He was able to express the cultural pressure he feels about his responsibility as the eldest son toward his parents. To reconcile these different values, Bon-Hwa and Cho agreed during a session to rent a separate residence nearby for his parents where they can easily visit and to hire an assistant to help around the apartment and drive them to church and other activities. Bon-Hwa and his wife and children can visit his parents several times a week, and since they are both medical professionals, they can be watchful of the health of Bon-Hwa's parents.

Chanda and Her Family

Chanda is a 15-year-old South Asian American adolescent who was born and raised in New York City. She was referred due to depressed mood, anxiety, and passive suicidal ideation, associated with excessive academic pressure and family conflict. She is an only child and was often described by teachers as "bright, diligent, and emotionally sensitive." Her parents immigrated to the United States in hope of better work for her father and educational opportunities for their child. Her father currently drives a taxi in NYC and her mother does child care for families in the rent-controlled apartment building where they reside. Chanda's father works long hours and is often absent from home. Chanda's parents believe in traditional Asian family values supporting the belief that they know what is best for their daughter with expectations that Chanda will obey unconditionally. Her mother is responsible for all household matters, including Chanda's school and discipline issues. Chanda has attended public schools and up until recently excelled academically. Her parents have always valued higher education and expect their only daughter to attain high academic achievement. Chanda's mother wishes that Chanda would pursue a higher degree and eventually obtain a professional career, which she herself wanted as a young girl but was unable to attain. Chanda's falling grades have been a major source of conflict in the family as Chanda's parents feel that she is becoming too "Westernized," texting at all hours and being on the computer.

Chanda's mother does not speak English fluently and she relies upon her daughter's assistance to translate when she goes to the grocery store, doctor, and school, and negotiating with neighbors; thus Chanda is parentified, or taking on parental duties as a youth, within her family. Recently, her mother has been so stressed that she began to complain of headaches and stomach aches though doctors have not been able to determine the cause of her discomfort. Her mother misses the extended family support system she had in her home country.

In high school, Chanda has found it difficult to form lasting friendships with peers in her school that is predominantly made up of Latino/a and Black/African American students. Socially somewhat shy, Chanda feels invisible as girls in her school seem uninterested in forming a friendship with her. She feels socially isolated and lonely at school. Increasing academic demands in high school serve as an additional stressor. Chanda has become depressed and her energy level and concentration have declined. Chanda engages in internet surfing for long hours to escape from feeling depressed and pressured. Subsequently her grades have dropped.

Clinical Implications

Therapy with Chanda was started by providing her with a safe place to express her feelings freely without fear of being judged as a "bad" child by her parents. Chanda was overwhelmed with feelings of frustration and sadness, as she felt unaccepted and criticized by her parents. Chanda also felt tremendous guilt about disappointing her parents and making them worry. She blamed herself for her mother's physical symptoms. The therapist empathized with Chanda's struggles and communicated acceptance, something that Chanda did not experience at home with her parents.

Psychoeducational information was provided regarding cultural differences in parenting styles, and parental expectations were discussed as a potential cause of the conflict in her family. This helped Chanda feel less guilty. The therapist also worked with Chanda's parents, highlighting cultural differences in parenting style and the emotional consequences for Chanda. During one session, Chanda's parents confessed they were worried that if they did not criticize their daughter she would not work harder and that they would be seen as irresponsible parents by members of the community. Chanda was able to express to them how much she appreciated their sacrifices, and with the therapist's support, she was able to tell them that the criticism was emotionally hard on her. Much to her surprise, her parents understood her pain and told her how important she was to them. The therapist helped Chanda learn effective ways of communicating her needs to her parents. Subsequent sessions focused on ways to help Chanda explore her overall identity, in particular her ethnic identity. Her feelings and thoughts about what aspects of South Asian culture, as well as American culture (language, custom, practice, people, communication style, nature of interpersonal style, pop culture, etc.), she liked/disliked and felt comfortable/uncomfortable with were discussed. The therapist also assisted in finding a place for her to meet other South Asian girls and feel a sense of belonging. Chanda became involved in a South Asian culture center where she went once a week to learn traditional dance with peers of same ethnic roots.

Over the course of the treatment, Chanda and her parents increased their understanding of each other. They were better able to communicate and learned to negotiate some of the issues at home, such as the time she is allowed to spend at the computer and cell phone at home. As Chanda felt better and gained peer support, her sense of self-acceptance and confidence increased, her depressed and anxious mood decreased, and she no longer experienced suicidal ideation. She was able to become more active in seeking friendships with her peers at school and felt less invisible and more happy. Her grades also improved, leading to greater parental support. As Chanda's mother became less worried about her daughter's well-being, her somatic stress-related physical symptoms also abated.

CONCLUSIONS

Counseling and other forms of mental health treatment may be a foreign concept to many Asian American couples and families (Sue & Sue, 2008). Given the stigma associated with mental health problems, Asian American clients may present to health care providers with **somatic complaints** including headaches, stomach aches, fatigue, and other physical symptoms (Meyer, Dhindsa, Gabriel, & Sue, 2009).

Explaining the process of therapy, the role of the client, assessment procedures, and the expectations of potential outcome is critical. It is important to provide information to Asian couples and families regarding the collaborative and co-constructed nature of the therapeutic relationship (Hwang, 2006). It is respectful to provide clients with information about the structure of therapy and how it works from the clinician's theoretical orientation. For example, if the clinician comes from a psychoanalytic tradition, then starting with an explanation of the process will help the client. "In therapy, it is important and helpful to understand and discuss your feelings. Let us try. I am going to be silent for a while so you can find your own words to describe how you feel, ok?." In addition, Western-based psychotherapies should be culturally modified and/or adapted to become more effective (Hwang, 2006). For example, in the case of Chanda, the therapist adapted treatment to enable Chanda a safe place to express herself without concern for violating filial piety.

   Understanding the values of family members in cultural context must be taken into consideration during the therapeutic process. Each member of the family may integrate a balance between the old traditional values and those that emerge in their interaction with the new culture. For example, how much do children follow the dictates of their parents versus asserting their own feelings/behaviors based upon the norms they have adopted from interactions with others, including their peers?

   Working with Asian couples and families requires an assessment of acculturation, level of English proficiency, ethnic identity, and an understanding of how family members negotiate individual differences. Note that in Asian families, the emphasis is placed upon indirect communication and collectivism, and this will impact how negotiation is communicated. Clinicians need to be sensitive to nonverbal communication patterns as in the case of Cho's understanding of Bon-Hwa's mother's behavior.

   When working with families, it is critical to assess the parents as well as the children to gain an understanding of the degree of parent–child differences in their levels of acculturation and identity. Psychoeducational approaches can again be used to highlight differences in parenting style between traditional Asian culture in comparison to U.S. parenting norms (e.g., authoritarian versus authoritative). Parent–child conflict may arise as rates of acculturation differ because children and adolescents are Westernized at a faster rate than their parents. The clinician may serve as a cultural bridge to facilitate the families' understanding of generational differences and the process of negotiating change.

   When working with parents, it is important to facilitate their understanding of the possible emotional consequences of strictly adhering to an authoritarian parenting style and lack of overt expression of warmth and affection. In addition, information regarding the positive emotional impact of authoritative parenting could be helpful, allowing parents opportunities to reflect on their own parenting traditions and find helpful ways to integrate the two styles of parenting. A mother may perceive her child's emotional symptoms and/or behavior problems as a failure of her parenting. The clinician can address this self-criticism in a supportive manner, recognizing the cultural pressures put on the mother to raise the children to be "successful" while working to alleviate the level of responsibility. Understanding the cultural and generational context that is affecting the child's emotional state may be helpful. Normalizing developmental and social concerns that occur during adolescence could help reduce the parental sense of guilt and shame.

   Providing information regarding possible acculturative stressors for adolescents and parents, symptoms of stress and effective stress management strategies, and preventive strategies (e.g., avoid excessive academic pressure, adjust daily schedule according to the child's level of stress, seeking support from school) is useful. When providing psychological intervention, it may help to begin the treatment by highlighting that lowering stress may increase motivation, concentration, and productivity to attain academic success.

CHAPTER REVIEW

Key Points

1. Asian American couples and families comprise individuals from diverse ethnic backgrounds.
2. Every Asian ethnic and national identity carries with it complex political, social, and familial meanings.
3. Immigration laws and other legislative actions have impacted the historical formation of Asian American marital relations and family life.
4. Various religious traditions have influenced Asian American communities.
5. Immigration stress is one of many risk factors that may include experience of discrimination and chronic microaggressions. These stressors increase the likelihood of domestic violence, suicide, and mental health concerns.
6. Stigma remains as major contributor to lack of acceptance and stress for Asian American LGBTQ community members.
7. Parenting practices in the Asian American ethnic communities may be more authoritarian.
8. Mothers, in particular, may blame themselves if they perceive their child as failing academically or experiencing emotional and behavioral problems.
9. Psychoeducational interventions may be helpful in addressing and normalizing developmental issues among children and adolescents.
10. Clinicians should inform couples and families about the process of psychological treatment based upon their theoretical orientation.
11. Cultural beliefs and values will impact the understanding of presenting problems and should be taken into consideration in adapting treatment modalities and interventions.

Key Terms

acculturation conflicts, bicultural adaptation, Christianity, Confucianism, dynamic sizing, family structure, filial piety, Hinduism, intimate partner violence, Islam, microaggressions, model minority, Pan-Asian identity and solidarity, parenting style, perpetual foreigner, somatic complaints, stigma

Myths and Realities

- It is a myth that Asian Americans do not experience mental illness. In reality, there may be cultural differences in the presentation of signs and symptoms—that is, they may report more somatic symptoms or choose not to report symptoms at all.
- It is a myth that Asian Americans are the model minority. In reality there are over 40 different Asian American ethnic groups, each with a different history and context in the United States.

- Academic success of some Asian Americans overshadows the reality that those who do not fit the stereotype can "fall through the cracks."
- Low utilization of mental health services may be reflective of stigma rather than less need for mental health services.

Tools and Tips

Knowledge

Asian American Journal of Psychology.
Chin, J. L. (2005). *Working with Asian American clients* [DVD]. APA.
Huang, K. Y., Calzada, E., Kamboukos, D., Rhule, D., Sharma, K. C., Cheng, S., & Brotman, L. M. (2014). Applying public health frameworks to advance the promotion of mental health among Asian American children. *Asian American Journal of Psychology, 5,* 145–152.
Jacob, J., Gray, B., & Johnson, A. (2013). The Asian American family and mental health: Implications for child health professionals. *Journal of Pediatric Health Care, 27,* 180–188.
Kim-Goh, M., Choi, H., & Yoon, M. S. (2015). Culturally responsive counseling for Asian Americans: Clinician perspectives. *International Journal for the Advancement of Counseling, 37,* 63–76.
Tewari, N., & Alvarez, A. N. (2009). *Asian American Psychology: Current Perspectives.* New York, NY: Lawrence Erlbaum.

Dynamic Sizing

Knowing the potential impact of religion, immigration generation, and other contextual factors such as whether not a particular Asian American couple or family lives in an ethnic enclave means that one cannot apply general information (e.g., stereotypes) about Asian Americans to particular couples or families that are being treated. Values, beliefs, behaviors, etc. must be understood in relation to the unique cultural context of the client(s). It is not a one-size-fits all!

Skills

Theory. Numerous theories have emerged in the literature to address to explain the impact of cultural context in understanding various psychological constructs in relation to members of the Asian American community. Important figures include theories of acculturation (e.g., John Berry); microaggressions (e.g., Derald Sue); intersecting identities (e.g., Pamela Hays), etc.

Prevention. Prevent *by* knowing—get to know your client communities and their needs to anticipate potential counseling concerns.

Service Provision. Make efforts to learn about the Asian American communities in relation to therapeutic interventions and culturally adapted methods for working and establishing a therapeutic relationship. In addition, clinicians should integrate their knowledge of culturally based practices and theoretical understanding (e.g., ethnic identity, racial identity), values, and so forth into treatment.

Policy. Remember to advocate for the underserved and avoid stereotyping members of diverse Asian American communities.

Research. Research needs to address the multiple intersecting identities of Asian Americans.

Awareness

Students should explore their own family-of-origin relationships.

Tools include a genogram and family history to explore one's own ancestry.

Study the historical, political, economic, and social context that your extended family has lived in over time. Document the history. How has that context changed?

Examine what possible effects your ancestors have on you (e.g., Your parents are refugees from war and grew up deprived and traumatized). What is the transgenerational impact of these events or historical periods?

Explore your values and beliefs regarding dating and marriage. Do you want to marry within your own race, ethnic group, religion, and so on? Are you aware of historical events that have impacted the formation of intimate relationships and families in your community?

How did your parents' parenting style impact you?

REFERENCES

Abbassi, A., & Singh, R.N. (2006). Assertiveness in marital relationships among Asian Indians in the United States. *The Family Journal: Counseling and Therapy for Couples and Families, 14*, 392–399.

Adam, N., & Schewe, P. (2007). A multilevel framework exploring domestic violence against immigrant Indian and Pakistani women in the United States. *Journal of Muslim Mental Health, 2*, 5–20.

Ahmad-Stout, D.J., & Nath, S.R. (2013). South Asians in college counseling. *Journal of College Student Psychotherapy, 27*, 43–61.

Ai, A., Bjork, J., Appel, H., & Huang, B. (2013). APA Asian American spirituality and religion: Inherent diversity, uniqueness, and long-lasting psychological influences. In K. Pargament, J.J. Exline, & J.W. Jones (Eds.), *Handbook of psychology, religion, and spirituality, vol. 1: Context, theory, and research* (pp. 581–598). Washington, DC: American Psychological Association.

Ano, G. G., Mathew, E.S., & Fukuyama, M. A. (2009). Religion and spirituality. In N. Tewari & A.N. Alvarez (Eds.), *Asian American psychology: Current perspectives* (pp. 135–152). New York, NY: Taylor & Francis.

Asian Pacific Islander Institute on Domestic Violence. (n.d.). API ethnicities and regional groupings. Retrieved from http://www.apiidv.org/resources/census-date-api-identities.php on January 17, 2015.

Azuma, H., Hakuta, K., & Stevenson, H. (1986). *Child development and education in Japan*. New York, NY: W. H. Freeman.

Baumrind, D. (1996). Parenting: The discipline controversy revisited. *Family Relations, 45,* 405–414.

Berry, J. W. (1997). Immigration, acculturation, and adaptation. *Applied Psychology: International Review, 46,* 5–34.

Chan, C. (1989). Issues of identity development among Asian-American lesbians and gay men. *Journal of Counseling and Development, 68,* 16–20.

Chang, E. S., & Greenberger, E. (2012). Parenting satisfaction at midlife among European- and Chinese-American mothers with a college-enrolled child. *Asian American Journal of Psychology, 3,* 263–274.

Chang, D. F., Shen, B.-J., & Takeuchi, D. T. (2009). Prevalence and demographic correlates of intimate partner violence in Asian Americans. *International Journal of Law and Psychiatry, 32,* 167–175.

Cheah, C. S. L., Leung, C. Y. Y., & Zhou, N. (2013). Understanding "tiger parenting" through the perceptions of Chinese immigrant mothers: Can Chinese and U.S. parenting coexist? *Asian American Journal of Psychology, 4,* 30–40.

Costigan, C. L., Hua, J. M., & Su, T. F. (2010). Living up to expectations: The strengths and challenges experienced by Chinese Canadian students. *Canadian Journal of School Psychology, 25,* 223–245.

Daya, R. (2000). Buddhist psychology, a theory of change processes: Implications for counselors. *International Journal for the Advancement of Counseling, 22,* 257–271.

Del Carmen, R. (1990). Assessment of Asian-Americans for family therapy. In F. C. Serafica, A. I. Schwebel, R. K. Russell, P. D. Isaac, & L. B. Myers (Eds.), *Mental health of ethnic minorities* (pp. 139–166). New York, NY: Praeger.

DuPree, W. J., Bhakta, K. A., Patel, P. S., & DuPree, D. J. (2013). Developing culturally competent marriage and family therapists: Guidelines for working with Asian Indian American Couples. *The American Journal of Family Therapy, 41,* 311–329.

Espiritu, Y. L. (1993). *Asian American pan ethnicity: Bridging institutions and identities.* Philadelphia, PA: Temple University Press.

Fujino, D. C. (2000). Structural and individual influences affecting racialized dating relationships among Asian Americans. In J. L. Chin (Ed.), *Relationships among Asian American women* (pp. 181–209). Washington, DC: American Psychological Association.

Gee, G. C., Ro, A., Shariff-Marco, S., & Chae, D. (2009). Racial discrimination and health among Asian Americans: Evidence assessment, and directions for future research. *Epidemiologic Reviews, 31,* 130–151.

Hays, P. A. (2008). Addressing cultural complexities in practice: Assessment, diagnosis, and therapy (2nd ed.). Washington, DC: American Psychological Association.

Hom, D. C. (1994). Stories from the homefront: Perspectives of Asian-American parents with lesbian daughters and gay sons. *Amerasia Journal, 20,* 19–32.

Horton, P. (2014). "I thought I was the only one": The misrecognition of LGBT youth in contemporary Vietnam. *Culture, Health, and Sexuality, 16,* 960–973.

Hsu, F. L. K. (1971). Filial piety in Japan and China: Borrowing, variation and significance. *Journal of Comparative Family Studies, 2,* 67–74.

Hung, A. H (2006). Concept of differentiated oneness and implications for Asian American families. *Journal of Psychology and Christianity, 25,* 226–239.

Hwang, W.C. (2006). The psychotherapy adaptation and modification framework: Application to Asian Americans. *American Psychologist, 61,* 702–715.

Hwang, W. C., & Wood, J. J. (2008). Acculturative family distancing: Links with self-reported symptomatology among Asian American and Latinos. *Child Psychiatry & Human Development, 40,* 123–138.

Hyun, K. J (2001). Sociocultural change and traditional values: Confucian values among Koreans and Korean Americans. *International Journal of Intercultural Relations, 25,* 203–229.

Inman, A.G., Howard, E.E., Beaumont, R. L., and Walker, J.A. (2007). Cultural transmission: Influence of contextual factors in Asian Indian immigrant parents' experiences. *Journal of Counseling Psychology, 52,* 93–100.

Kim, B.S.K., & Omizo, M. M. (2010). Behavioral enculturation and acculturation, psychological functioning, and help-seeking attitude among Asian Americans. *Asian American Journal of Psychology, 1,* 175–185.

Kordi, R., & Baharudin, A. (2010). Parenting attitude and style and its effect on children's school achievements. *International Journal of Psychological Studies, 2,* 217–222.

Lee, S.J., Wong, N.-W.A., & Alvarez, A. (2009). The model minority and the perpetual foreigner: Stereotypes of Asian Americans. In N. Tewari & A.N. Alvarez (Eds.), *Asian American psychology: Current perspectives* (pp. 69–84). New York, NY: Taylor & Francis.

Lee, E.H., Zhou, Q., Ly, J., Main, A., Tao, A., & Chen, S. H. (2014). Neighborhood characteristics, parenting styles, and children's behavioral problems in Chinese American immigrant families. *Cultural Diversity and Ethnic Minority Psychology, 20,* 202–212.

Lim, S.L., Yeh, M., Liang, J., Lau, A.S., & McCabe, K. (2009). Acculturation gap, intergenerational conflict, parenting style, and youth distress in immigrant Chinese American families. *Marriage & Family Review, 45,* 84–106.

Liu, C.H., Murakami, J., Eap, S., & Nagayama Hall, G.C. (2009). Who are Asian Americans?: An overview of history. In N. Tewari & A.N. Alvarez (Eds.), *Asian American psychology: Current perspectives* (pp. 1–30). New York, NY: Lawrence Erlbaum Associates.

Lorenzo, M. K., Fronst, A. K., & Reinherz, H. Z. (2000). Social and emotional functioning of older Asian American adolescents. *Child and Adolescent Social Work Journal, 17,* 289–304.

Maccoby, E.E., & Martin, J.A. (1983). Socialization in the context of the family: Parent–child interaction. In P.H. Mussen (Series Ed.) & E.M. Hetherington (Ed.), *Handbook of child psychology (vol. 4): Socialization, personality, and social development* (pp. 1–101). New York, NY: Wiley.

Mathur, G.S., Ann, S.G., Kumar, R., & Menon, S. (2014). Enhancing mental health literacy in India to reduce stigma: The fountainhead to improve help-seeking behavior. *Journal of Public Mental Health, 13,* 146–158.

Menon, U. (2003). Morality in context: A study of Hindu understandings. In J. Valsiner & K. Connolly (Eds.), *Handbook of developmental psychology* (pp. 431–449). Thousand Oaks, CA: Sage Publications.

Meyer, O., Dhindsa, M., Gabriel, C., & Sue, S. (2009). Psychopathology and clinical issues with Asian American populations. In N. Tewari & A.N. Alvarez (Eds.),

Asian American psychology: Current perspectives (pp. 519–536). New York, NY: Taylor & Francis.

Nadal, K., & Corpus, M. J. H. (2013). "Tomboys" and "Baklas": Experiences of lesbian and gay Filipino Americans. *Asian American Journal of Psychology, 4,* 166–175.

Okazaki, S. (2000). Treatment delay among Asian-American patients with severe mental illness. *American Journal of Orthopsychiatry, 70,* 58–64.

Pew Research Center. (2012). Asian Americans: A mosaic of faiths, in religion and public life, Pew report. Retrieved from http://www.pewsocialtrends .org/files/2013/04/Asian-Americans-new-full-report-04–2013.pdf on February 27, 2015.

Pew Research Center. (2013). The rise of Asian Americans. Retrieved from http:// www.pewsocialtrends.org/2012/06/19/the-rise-of-asian-americans/ on February 15, 2015.

Qin, D. B. (2009). Gendered processes of adaptation: Understanding parent–child relations in Chinese immigrant families. *Sex Roles, 60,* 467–481.

Rhee, S., Chang, J., & Rhee, J. (2003). Acculturation, communication patterns and self-esteem among Asian and Caucasian American Adolescents, *Adolescence, 38,* 749–768.

Rubin, K. H., & Chung, O. B. (2006). *Parenting beliefs, behaviors, and parent–child relations.* New York, NY: Psychology Press.

Russell, S. T., Crockett, L. J., & Chao, R. K. (2010). *Asian American parenting and parent–adolescent relationships: Advancing responsible adolescent development.* New York, NY: Springer.

Sanchez, F., & Gaw, A. (2007). Mental health care of Filipino Americans. *Psychiatric Services, 58,* 810–815.

Sandhya, S. (2009). The social context of marital happiness in urban Indian couples: Interplay of intimacy and conflict. *Journal of Marital and Family Therapy, 35,* 74–96.

Sayer, L. C., & Fine, L. (2011). Racial-ethnic differences in U.S. married women's and men's housework. *Social Indicators Research, 101,* 259–265.

Serafica, F. C. (1990). Counseling Asian-American parents: A cultural-developmental approach. In F. C. Serafica, A. I Schwebel, R. K. Russell, P. D. Isaac, & L. B. Myers (Eds.), *Mental health of ethnic minorities* (pp. 222–244). New York, NY: Praeger Publishers.

Shankar, L. D., & Srikanth, R. (1998). *A part, yet apart: South Asians in Asian America.* Philadelphia, PA: Temple University Press.

Shariff, A. (2009). Ethnic identity and parenting stress in South Asian families: Implications for culturally sensitive counseling, *Canadian Journal of Counselling, 43,* 35–46.

Shek, D. T. L. (2007). A longitudinal study of perceived parental psychological control and psychological well-being in Chinese adolescents in Hong Kong. *Journal of Clinical Psychology, 63,* 1–22.

Shimizu, H., & Devine, R. A. (Eds.). (2001). *Japanese frames of mind: Cultural perspectives on human development.* New York, NY: Cambridge University Press.

Shinagawa, L. H., & Pang, G. Y. (1996). Asian American panethnicity and intermarriage. *Amerasia Journal, 22,* 127–152.

Stohs, J. H. (2000). Multicultural women's experience of household labor, conflicts and equity. *Sex Roles, 42,* 339–361.

Sue, S. (1998). In search of cultural competence in psychotherapy and counseling. *American Psychologist, 53,* 440–448.

Sue, D. W., Bucceri, J., Lin, A. I, Nadal, K. L., & Torino, G. (2009). Racial microaggressions and the Asian American experience. *Asian American Journal of Psychology, 8,* 88–101 (Original work published 2007).

Sue, D. W., & Sue, D. (2008). *Counseling the culturally diverse: Theory and practice* (5th ed.). Hoboken, NJ: John Wiley & Sons.

Suh, S. (2011). A review of Carolyn Chen's getting saved in America: Taiwanese immigration and religious experience. *Pastoral Psychology, 60,* 583–592.

Suzuki, L. A., Ahluwalia, M. K., & Alimchandani, A. (2012). Asian American women's feminism: Sociopolitical history and clinical considerations. In C. Z. Enns & E. N. Williams (Eds.), *The Oxford handbook of feminist multicultural counseling* (pp. 183–198). New York, NY: Oxford University Press.

Taylor, C. (1994). The politics of recognition. In A. Gutman (Ed.), *Multiculturalism: Examining the politics of recognition* (pp. 225–273). Princeton, NJ: Princeton University Press.

Tjaden, P., & Thoennes, N. (2000). Extent, nature, and consequences of intimate partner violence: Findings from the National Violence Against Women survey. Washington, DC: National Institute of Justice and Centers for Disease Control.

Walton, E., & Takeuchi, D. T. (2009). Family structure, family processes, and well-being among Asian Americans: Considering gender and nativity. *Journal of Family Issues, XX(X),* 1–32 (online journal).

Wu, C., & Chao, R. K. (2005). Intergenerational cultural conflicts in norms of parental warmth among Chinese American immigrants. *International Journal of Behavioral Development, 29,* 516–523.

Wu, C., & Chao, R. K. (2011). Intergenerational cultural dissonance in parent–adolescent relationships among Chinese and European Americans. *Developmental Psychology, 47,* 493–508.

Xia, Y. R., Do, K. A., & Xie, X. (2013). The adjustment of Asian American families to the U.S. context: The ecology of strengths and stress. In G. W. Peterson & K. R. Bush (Eds.), *Handbook of marriage and the family* (pp. 705–722). New York, NY: Springer.

Yamamoto, J., & Iga, M. (1983). Emotional growth of Japanese American children. In G. J. Powell, J. Yamamoto, A. Romero, & A. Morales (Eds.), *The psychosocial development of minority group children* (pp. 167–178). New York, NY: Brunner/Mazel.

Yamamoto, J., & Kubota, M. (1983). The Japanese-American family. In G. J. Powell, J. Yamamoto, A. Romero, & A. Morales (Eds.), *The psychosocial development of minority group children* (pp. 237–247). New York, NY: Brunner/Mazel.

Yamaguchi Williams, J. K., Else, I. R. N., Hishinuma, E. S., Goebert, D. A., Chang, J. Y., Andrade, N. N., & Nishimura, S. T. (2005). A confirmatory model for depression among Japanese American and part-Japanese American adolescents. *Cultural Diversity and Ethnic Minority Psychology, 11,* 41–56.

Yeh, C. J., Arora, A., Inose, M., Okubo, Y., Li, R. H., & Greene, P. (2003). The cultural adjustment and mental health of Japanese immigrant youths. *Adolescence, 38,* 481–500.

Yick, A. G., & Oomen-Early, J. (2008). A 16-year examination of domestic violence among Asians and Asian Americans in the empirical knowledge base: A content analysis. *Journal of Interpersonal Violence, 23,* 1075–1094.

Ying, Y., & Han, M. (2008). Variation in the prediction of cross-cultural adjustment by ethnic density: A longitudinal study of Taiwanese students in the United States. *College Student Journal, 42,* 1075–1086.

Yip, T., Gee, G.C., & Takeuchi, D.T. (2008). Racial discrimination and psychological distress: The impact of ethnic identity and age among immigrant and United States-born Asian adults. *Developmental Psychology, 44,* 787–800.

CHAPTER 3

Latino Couples and Families[1]

Melissa Rivera Marano
Emily Roman

Latinos currently constitute a significant portion of the U.S. population. As of 2010, there are approximately 50.5 million Latinos in the United States, or close to one-sixth of the total population. Of those who are foreign-born, Latin Americans represent 55 percent of the total (Ennis, Rios-Vargas, Albert, 2011; U.S. Census Bureau, 2010). Demographic trends are predictive of Latinos forming an increasingly larger proportion of the population by 2050—doubling its present size to 30 percent—when it is projected that there will be no racial or ethnic majority within the United States. Four states—California, Hawaii, New Mexico, and Texas—are currently less than 50 percent White (APA Presidential Task Force on Immigration, 2013), although Hispanics do not constitute a significant proportion of Hawaii's non-White population. More than half (55%) of the U.S. Hispanic population resides in California, Texas, and Florida (Brown & Lopez, 2013). More than 14,400,000, or over one-fourth (28%) of U.S. Hispanics live in California (Brown & Lopez, 2013), the state with the largest Hispanic population.

Given the large and increasing rates of the Latino population, it is crucial for mental health professionals to be knowledgeable about this group in order to provide culturally competent treatment (APA Presidential Task Force on Immigration, 2013; Falicov, 2013; Hernandez, Nesman, Mowery, Acevedo-Polakovich, & Callejas, 2009; Kouyoumdjian, Zamboanga, & Hansen, 2003). This chapter aims to provide a foundation for understanding, assessing, and incorporating Latinos' culture, identity, and socioeconomic and sociopolitical roles in order to improve cultural competency and treatment with Latino couples and families.

Latinos, with origins in the Spanish-speaking Caribbean islands and Central and South America and Spain, are a varied group within the United States with those from Mexico, Cuba, Puerto Rico, El Salvador, and the Dominican Republic forming the five largest subgroups. Despite origins in different countries, the identity of many Latinos in the United States has been shaped by common values and beliefs (Garcia-Preto, 2005; Hernandez, 2005). During the era of colonialism, Spanish conquests introduced the Spanish language, a new set of cultural and religious beliefs, African slaves, and the Spaniards themselves to the indigenous population, resulting in the blends that now constitute the Latino diaspora. Thus, Latino identities are based on a mixture of indigenous, African and European languages, religions, and cultures, and Latino history represents both the oppressors and the oppressed (Garcia-Preto, 2005). This shared history of colonialization and conquest serves as a point of interconnectedness when understanding and working with Latino couples and families. There is also, however, a great deal of variation among Latinos in the United States and the diversity among and within the Latino population needs to be acknowledged. The reality of Latinos in the present day continues to be marked by a history of colonization and conquest and the ongoing pursuit of opportunity for self and family. Each Latino group's history in both its country of origin and the United States tells a different story, its own story.

HISTORY OF THE THREE MOST COMMON LATINO GROUPS IN THE UNITED STATES

Mexico

Latinos were present in the Americas as early as the 1500s. Mexicans lived in the Southwest for several generations prior to the westward expansion of the United States (Falicov, 2005), a situation that can best be summed up by the saying that Mexicans did not cross the border, "the border crossed them." Mexican self-rule was followed in what is now Texas until it was annexed by the United States in 1845. The Mexican government viewed the annexation of Texas as a declaration of war. Mexican interests were defeated and the land comprising Texas, California, and New Mexico was ceded to the United States. The Treaty of Guadalupe Hidalgo promised the following concessions for the Mexican population residing in those areas: (a) U.S. citizenship, (b) freedom of language and religion, and (c) maintenance of their lands. The reality was quite different. Mexicans became strangers in their own land, faced with discrimination and social injustice (Falicov, 2005).

The status of Mexicans in the United States has been further complicated through policies reflective of the country's labor and wartime needs. For example, during wartime, Mexicans were encouraged to come to the United States to work. In addition, the Selective Service Act granted Mexican immigrants, who were otherwise ineligible, the ability to serve in the armed forces. Yet in 1921, after American soldiers returned from abroad after World War I in need of jobs, limits were imposed on immigration from Mexico for the first time, enforceable through the creation of a border patrol in 1925. During the 1930s, as the Depression worsened, deportations of Mexican immigrants began. Despite this curtailment, the Mexican immigrant presence in the United States is striking: one-third of the foreign-born population in the United States is from Mexico and 31,000,000 Mexican Americans represent the largest segment of the Latino population in the United States (U.S. Census Bureau, 2010).

Cuba

Cuban independence from Spain resulted from its cooperation with the United States during the Spanish–American War of 1898. The first migrants to the United States from Cuba, well-educated professionals, were often recipients of noteworthy largesse in the form of aid in securing business loans and being able to transfer professional credentials (Saiz, 2003; Vega & Alegría, 2001). As with any group, economic diversity exists among Cuban Americans; however, of the Latino groups that have emigrated to the United States, Cubans are the most affluent. Socioeconomic status bears some relation to time and circumstance of their migration.

According to Bernal and Shapiro (2005), working with Cuban families must include a political, social, and economic context including an understanding of the migration waves to the United States. The greatest impetus for migration to the United States was the Cuban Revolution, a war that lasted from 1953 to 1959, when more than 1.1 million fled Cuba (Bernal & Shapiro, 2005). As a consequence of the revolution, many Cuban American families had their land and property confiscated. U.S. Immigration policies reflected the view that Cubans arriving in the United States after the Cuban Revolution were fleeing political persecution and thus deserved special status. The second wave occurred in 1965 when the Cuban government allowed those who had relatives in the United States to leave Cuba. Later in the 1980s, after a sharp downturn in the Cuban economy, the Cuban government allowed its citizens to leave the country. This migration wave is known as "the Mariel Boatlift."

The economic situation in Cuba also was reflective of its relationship with the former Soviet Union. The Soviet Union furnished Cuba with considerable financial aid; however, once this entity disbanded in the 1990s, the assistance stopped. The U.S. imposition of an economic blockade of Cuba left the Cuban people facing extreme hardship. Under these circumstances, many Cubans took great risks to reach the United States (Bernal & Shapiro, 2005). As of 2009, the Cuban American population totaled over 1.6 million (Saenz, 2010).

Puerto Rico

Following the Spanish–American War, Puerto Rico became a U.S. commonwealth territory, a status it maintains today. In 1917, Puerto Ricans were granted a form of U.S. citizenship that allows them certain benefits, such as federal social welfare program eligibility, the same military status as Americans, and the ability to move freely from the island to the mainland. However, Puerto Ricans living in Puerto Rico cannot vote for president of the United States. Poor socioeconomic conditions in Puerto Rico often lead to an increased flow of Puerto Ricans to the mainland United States. In 2009, over 4.4 million Puerto Ricans were living in the United States (Saenz, 2010). The unique relationship offered by commonwealth status not only means that U.S. government and economic policy significantly impact the island, but also has the consequence of Puerto Rican culture being dramatically transformed by nearly a century of American dominance (Guarnaccia, 1997). This may be manifested in a variety of contexts, such as a hybrid United States–Puerto Rican cultural identity among members of this group.

When Latino Subgroup Values Clash in Couple and Family Relationships

The foregoing histories of Latino subgroups in the United States comprise one source of within-group differences that may manifest in the treatment of Latino couples and families. Immigration policies are often reflective of the relationship each country's government has with the United States (Guarnaccia, 1997), which affects Latinos themselves. Thus, Latino subgroups may differ with regard to (a) the circumstances of their entry into the United States and their reception upon arrival, (b) their reasons for migration, (c) the relationship of their native country with the United States at the time of entry, and (d) cultural aspects characterizing the areas in which they settled. These factors, among others, influence the availability of opportunities and contribute to differences in mental health functioning within and among Latino groups (Vega & Alegría, 2001). In addition to their historical journeys, the varied emphases that different countries put on values common to Latinos provide a foundation for understanding both the similarities and differences of these subgroups in treatment. The following example illustrates how a married couple, although both Latino, experience conflicts as a result of opposing cultural values arising out of their origins in different countries.

Case Example

Jose was born and raised in Mexico. Consistent with the Latino cultural value of *familismo*, which refers to the strong importance of immediate and extended family bonds, he maintains very close relationships with his mother and brother who immigrated to the United States soon after. In addition, the mother and eldest son dyad is considered to be very strong for Mexicans (Falicov, 2005). Jose's wife, Beatriz, is from Brazil. She shares the Latino value of *familismo*, which also is the most central element of Brazilian culture that serves as an important source of support. After Jose's long layoff from a well-paying job, the couple moved from New York to California so that Jose could work in a relative's landscaping business. It is painful for Beatrix that her family is far away in Brazil while Jose's family is nearby in California and Mexico. She turns to Jose for support, which he generally gives.

As Jose's new job does not pay as well as his former one, the couple experiences financial problems as well as difficulty adjusting to the new state. In dealing with these issues, Jose tries to maintain the Mexican value for harmony by trying not to display his feelings of anger. Rather, he suppresses his feelings and uses *indirectas*, that is, indirect hints or insinuations of one's thoughts and feelings about a topic. *Indirectas*, while not overtly confrontational, can be sarcastic and belittling. Conversely, in Brazil, people are expected to acknowledge others' problems and needs, and to perceive such concerns even when they are not expressed verbally. In Brazil, when others fail to respond with nurturance and support, one's sense of well-being can be harmed (Korin & Petry, 2005). While Beatriz tries to acknowledge Jose's feelings around their problems, Jose tries to maintain harmony. This incompatibility in emotional expression made it harder to solve their differences, which engendered symptoms of depression in Beatriz and led to the couple's decision to seek treatment.

LIVING IN AMERICA: CHALLENGES COMMON TO MANY LATINOS

Education, employment, and poverty rates reveal issues with the economic progress of Latinos in the United States. While the gap is narrowing, Latinos continue to lag behind other racial and ethnic groups in educational attainment (Marotta & Garcia, 2003). High unemployment rates may be explained, in part, by the classification of jobs having a significant Latino presence or the absence of one. For example, many Latinos are employed in jobs impacted during a recession, such as construction and manufacturing (Marotta & Garcia, 2003), and do not have a significant presence in sectors with high growth potential, such as education and health care (Marotta & Garcia, 2003), or enhanced job security, such as the public sector. Latinos who do work in the public sector are especially underrepresented in the senior executive level (Marotta & Garcia, 2003). The combination of lower educational attainment and higher unemployment rates is reflected in recent census data indicating that

23.6 percent of Latinos—over 13 million people—live below the poverty line (DeNavas-Walt & Proctor, 2015).

Access to health and mental health services is more limited for Latinos than other groups, although the gap is narrowing. In 1999, only 66 percent of Latinos had health insurance coverage that met the U.S. Census Bureau standards, as compared to 89 percent of Whites, 79 percent of Asians, and 79 percent of African Americans (Marotta & Garcia, 2003). By 2014, the improvement in coverage was noteworthy despite the continuing lag: 19.9 percent of Latinos, roughly 10.9 million, were uninsured compared to 10.1 percent of Whites, 9.3 percent of Asians, and 11.8 percent of African Americans (Smith & Medalia, 2015). While census data are helpful in indicating the extent to which a lack of health coverage may impede mental health care, they may be misleading in that Latinos who are not citizens or permanent residents may have reason not to participate in data collection and hence not be included in the surveys. Thus, many Latinos not only may lack coverage but also be in great need of services. Whether insured or not, high poverty rates correspond with poorer health quality, and this is a concern for the Latino community (DeNavas-Walt & Proctor, 2015). These significant barriers to health services, including mental health treatment, contribute to the health disparities between Latinos and Whites.

Physical appearance, language, and cultural variables often distinguish Latinos from other Americans, allowing all in this population group to be characterized as "other" (Garcia-Preto, 2005). In addition, Latinos tend to be grouped by the mainstream as immigrants irrespective of their place of birth, and even if they are born in the United States. The emotional impact of the larger culture's stereotyping on self-image and stressors related to Latino identity in the United States are other crucial factors in the overall health and mental health of Latinos.

For many Latinos, cultural differences between their native countries and that of the United States create stress. **Bicultural stress**, the process of negotiating two cultures simultaneously, is a common experience among Latinos. Acculturative stress that occurs when traditional values and beliefs conflict with those prevalent in America may be overwhelming. It may be especially stressful for older Latinos who may be at greater risk of experiencing lack of support, isolation, and language barriers (González, Haan, & Hinton, 2001). Latino youth may find themselves at odds trying to navigate between two opposing cultures. Those who want to blend quickly into the new culture may not find acceptance, however. Bicultural stress may be exacerbated by discrimination and confrontations with negative stereotypes, as well as the necessity to communicate in two languages—English and Spanish—depending on the setting (Romero, Carvajal, Valle, & Orduña, 2007). Latino youth also may experience cultural conflict within their families, who may fear losing their child to a new culture and world that they do not yet trust nor understand (Romero & Roberts, 2003). Conflicts arising out of intergenerational differences in values and beliefs is one example of how acculturative and bicultural stress manifest in family functioning (Romero & Roberts, 2003).

Additional sources of stress for Latino families include the institutions that endorse oppression and erect barriers. According to Dr. Martin J. La Roche, a leading scholar in the field of multicultural psychology, structural racism and xenophobia systematically deny Latinos equal opportunities to advance in American society, resulting in challenging economic realities for many Latino families (Goertz, 2015). Conflicting values and beliefs between the majority U.S. culture and Latinos' culture of origin can be compounded by negative institutional pressures. Together, these factors can impact identity and functioning, contributing to bicultural stress and psychological distress (Pina-Watson, Ojeda, Castellon, & Dornhecker, 2013).

Traditional Cultural Values and Their Influence in Treatment

Cultural values among Latinos are grounded in the importance of relationships, hierarchical and formal, as these connections are often essential to help Latinos navigate the high and low points of life (Arredondo, Gallardo-Cooper, Delgado-Romero, & Zapata, 2014). In addition, cultural factors have considerable implications for clinicians working with Latino couples and families, such as (a) defining the presenting problem, (b) outlining the course of treatment, and (c) influencing treatment outcomes. Understanding how these concepts manifest is essential to cultural competence.

Cultural competence requires assessing the impact of cultural variables on Latinos' understanding of their psychological distress and how adaptation of traditional cultural values can be a factor in successful outcomes (Whaley & Davis, 2007). Clinicians working with Latino couples and families must first determine the level of individual acculturation by ascertaining the following for each: (a) self-identity, (b) language preference, (c) country of origin/family's country of origin, and, if applicable, (d) migration history. Assessing country of origin and journey to the United States when appropriate involves collecting a "migration narrative," an important tool in the initial stages of treatment (Falicov, 2005). This narrative provides (a) a more detailed account of each individual's history and (b) a foundation for understanding what the client has experienced. Obtaining a migration narrative also contributes to rapport building.

Developing rapport is well understood as critical to the treatment of all populations; however, rapport takes on more depth with Latinos as components of rapport are influenced by important cultural concepts, such as *personalismo* (valuing personal relationships), *respeto* (respect), and *humilidad* (humility). The extent to which clinicians can integrate such cultural concepts into their treatment approach may determine whether

Latino couples and families feel understood. As with any group, clinicians need to account for the heterogeneity among Latinos. How much or how little a particular value or concept applies to the presenting issues will vary with individual couple and family members. In order for clinicians to engender a sense of trust and confidence in their ability to help clients, it is important for clinicians to meet clients where they are. In practice, this may lead to a clinician's "use of self" whereby she or he shares superficial personal information such as the country of origin of the clinician's family to connect with Latino couples and families. In addition, given the emphasis that traditional Latino culture places on *personalismo*, limited gestures that generally may not be encouraged in treatment, such as hugs, may enhance rapport with Latino couples and families.

These and other cultural values that are important to Latinos may lead to obstacles in treatment, if not handled sensitively (Garcia-Preto, 2005). *Simpatia*, or "friendliness," is the expectation of being polite and kind to others in all situations. This quality may prove to be an obstacle in treatment when couples and families are hesitant to assert themselves or express disagreement out of concern about being seen as impolite. *Respeto*, or respect, includes deference to authority, which can manifest in the dynamic among couple and family members, and/or in the client–therapist relationship. For example, Latino clients may feel unable to disagree with a treatment plan or conceptualization for risk of disrespecting the "expert" (Santiago-Rivera, Arredondo, & Gallardo-Cooper, 2002). *Personalismo* involves warmth and engagement with others and is considered vital to fostering interpersonal relationships. It is also a quality that is often sought by many Latino clients in their treating clinician. Conflicts may arise within couples and families when individuals who are introverted or have social phobias feel that cultural expectations demand that they seek out and form undesired interpersonal relationships. *Fatalismo*, the belief that one cannot do anything to change the course of events, is commonly associated with a religious principle that God's will is determinative in all life circumstances. This belief can provide comfort when it involves "giving" one's pain and suffering to a higher power to manage, but can also lead to learned helplessness when people relinquish agency in their lives and feel that all negative aspects must be endured as they are destined by God (Miranda & Matheny, 2000).

Research findings have corroborated the importance of cultural congruence, or the fit between the culture and treatment for Latinos. In a study of 272 older Hispanic adults receiving mental health treatment either within a primary care setting or at a specialized mental health facility, researchers found that cultural congruence predicted reduction of symptomology independent of treatment (Costantino, Malgady, & Primavera, 2009). Examples of cultural fit are found in recent pilot studies with the use of culturally sensitive guided imagery (La Roche,

D'Angelo, Gualdron, & Leavell, 2006) and relaxation interventions (La Roche, Batista, & D'Angelo, 2014). Both the guided imagery and relaxation interventions utilize an allocentric approach, viewing self in relation to others. For example, a typical imagery script may have individuals imagine themselves alone in a calming, pleasant location. A culturally adapted imagery script would include individuals imagining themselves surrounded and comforted by those they love. These initial exploratory and pilot studies suggest that the process of adapting existing empirically validated treatments to various cultures may increase their efficacy with Latino clients (Kalibatseva & Leong, 2014).

Gender Roles

Many Latinos consider traditional gender roles to be an important cultural value. The traditional masculine role in Latino culture is called *machismo*. A man who exemplifies this norm would display strong leadership within the home and the community, and have the responsibility for maintaining the family and its honor. In response to the negative connotations of *machismo* as representative of an oppressive ideology of male supremacy and dominance, a more positive term, *caballerismo*, is used to stress the chivalrous and protective nature of the traditional male role (Arciniega, Anderson, Tovar-Blank, & Tracey, 2008). Latino men may engage in either or both aspects of *machismo* (Arciniega et al., 2008). When working with Latino men, it is important to understand the complexities of gender norms and to highlight the positive aspects of *machismo* and address any negative consequences that arise during treatment.

The corresponding traditional gender role for a Latina is termed *marianismo*. The underlying characteristics include sacred duty, self-sacrifice, chastity, care for others, and prioritizing the happiness of others over one's own (Aquino, Machado, & Rodriguez, 2002; Gil & Vasquez, 1996). The reinforcing aspects of this gender role include allowing women to feel revered, respected, and protected. Similar to *machismo*, the *marianismo* or *marianista* gender role has faced criticism in that it is viewed by many as leading to oppression and lack of self-fulfillment when women are expected to ignore their needs and desires for the sake of their husband, children, and family. Gil and Vasquez (1996) expressed this pejorative perspective as the "Ten Commandments" of *marianismo*, which include: don't give up your traditions; don't be independent, or have your own opinions; don't put your needs first; don't ask for help; don't discuss your personal problems outside the house; and don't change.

Adherence to these strictures would present a significant barrier to psychological treatment in that women would feel constrained from discussing their personal problems in a clinician's office, assuming a willingness to even ask for help. As with the male gender role of *machismo*, it is important that therapists highlight the positive components of *marianista* values and address the potential negative ones, and thus help Latinas to decide how, when, and to what degree they are to be governed by traditional gender role expectations. For those Latinas who are foreign-born, clinicians may also assist in helping them to navigate the manner in which their new environment and the larger American culture may challenge or complement this role.

The Stigma of Treatment and Culturally Acceptable Alternatives and Adaptions

Due to the stigma surrounding mental illness, hesitation to seek mental health treatment is common. The U.S. Department of Health and Human Services (1999) characterized stigma as "the most formidable obstacle" to improving mental illness and health. While stigma affects all individuals with mental illness across various ethnic and racial identities, individuals from minority racial and ethnic backgrounds, such as Latinos, may be even more hesitant to seek treatment as the stigma of mental illness is combined with the existing stigma of the minority racial/ethnic group. While an individual may be unable to avoid the stigma associated with his or her racial or cultural identity, the decision not to seek professional mental health treatment may be viewed as a viable way for the individual to avoid the double stigma. A further factor complicating accessing treatment is due to the association of ethnic minority status and mental illness with incarceration. According to Gary (2005), the stigma of being a member of an ethnic minority increases the chances of criminal conviction and a resultant long-term incarceration (Hartwell, 2001). Furthermore, society has historically been unwilling to distinguish between mental illness and criminal behaviors, with the consequence that mentally ill individuals are often imprisoned, frequently without receiving the needed treatment.

Traditional Latino gender roles also can have a negative influence on obtaining treatment. Yousaf, Popat, and Hunter (2015) found that men who endorsed more traditional masculine norms were less likely to seek help for mental health issues. This suggests that women's greater likelihood than men to seek help for mental health issues may be due to the absence of certain cultural expectations for women, such as restrictions on emotionality (Yousaf et al., 2015).

Hesitation to seek treatment from mental health professionals should not be viewed as reluctance to draw on others for support, as there are various culturally favored avenues in which Latinos access help. As presenting with somatic complaints is viewed as a more acceptable expression of distress, many Latinos first approach their primary or family doctors (Barrio et al., 2003; Pina & Silverman, 2004).

Another alternative for help commonly accessed by many Latinos involves consultations with traditional or folk healers. Typically, folk healers are connected with religious practices indigenous to the country of origin, namely, *Santeria* among Cubans, *Espiritismo* among Puerto Ricans, and *Curanderismo* among Mexicans. All of these practices attempt to define the source of physical and mental illness. For example, *Santeria*, which draws on both traditional African and Catholic cultures, holds that certain *orichas* (saints or entities) can influence those on earth. Their healing practices include the use of amulets, expelling of evil spirits, and magic medicines (Baez & Hernandez, 2001). Those who practice *Espiritismo* believe that a person's fluids represent an individual's spirit, the spirits of those close to them, and of those who have passed. When the fluids are disturbed or otherwise negatively influenced, mental and physical illnesses result (Hohmann et al., 1990). Mexican *Curanderos* might employ physical and supernatural healing practices such as *limpias* (spiritual cleansings), herbal preparations, and prayers in response to illness that they believe is caused by a combination of natural and supernatural forces (Luna, 2003). Many of these Latino belief systems commonly use herbs, teas, and other home remedies as the first line of defense for mental health issues. In clinical practice, asking couples and families about previous healing attempts is important, as the combination of psychotropic interventions of Western medicine with certain home remedies may be contraindicated (Comas-Diaz, 2006).

As is common with many other cultures, Latinos often rely on extended family members, community figures, and conventional religious and spiritual leaders as well as other resources within houses of worship for help during a mental health crisis. While such sources may act in positive ways, the danger exists that individuals also may receive messages reinforcing stigmas, resulting in concerns that family and community members may view them as crazy. Stigmas and fears of being perceived as crazy inhibit many Latinos from utilizing community resources and seeking or engaging in treatment, and may cause them to terminate treatment prematurely. In addition, gender differences may exist in the messages conveyed by the support systems of men and women. For example, one study found that the presence of social supports, such as practical, emotional, and informational assistance, led to improved chances of help-seeking in Latinas, but did not increase help-seeking in males (Gagne, Vasiliadis, & Preville, 2014). This finding suggests that Latino males' support network may be likely to view professional help-seeking in males as violating "masculinity norms" within this population.

Generally, Latinos in need of support tend to follow a family-based decision-making process rather than an individual determination (Maly, Umezawa, Ratliff, & Leake, 2006). Thus, when Latinos present for treatment, it may be helpful for the clinician to assess the feasibility of engaging family members as well. Transforming treatment into a family intervention likely will be culturally congruent for many Latinos. This serves as a guide in treatment and merges a family systems approach to working with couples and individuals.

INTERSECTIONALITY: LATINO LGBT COUPLES
AND FAMILIES IN TREATMENT

While individual Latinos may vary in adherence to such values, cultural ideals of familial duty, gender roles, and religious observance may lead to less tolerance of lesbian and gay individuals within the Latino population (Sanabria & Puig, 2015). When the sexual minority status of Latino LGBT (lesbian, gay, bisexual, and transgender) individuals is combined with membership in an ethnic/racial minority group, such individuals— possessing two oppressed identities—face increased challenges (Galarza, 2013). This may result in increased social alienation, lower self-esteem, and significant psychological distress (Diaz, Ayala, Bein, Henne, & Marin, 2001; Meyer, 2003).

When working with LGBT couples and families, it is important that clinicians provide an environment of safety and trust. The therapeutic alliance develops during the course of assessing the role of Latino culture and understanding its effects on LGBT couples and family members. When culturally competent treatment is offered to Latino LGBT couples and families, they are best able to integrate their ethnic and sexual orientation identities. A case example of this is shown next, using a cognitive behavioral approach, employed within a cultural framework.

Case Vignette: Working with the Individual, Couple, and Family

Edwin was a 31-year-old male of Mexican descent who presented for treatment after experiencing the symptoms of a heart attack. The attending physician at the hospital emergency room diagnosed Edwin as suffering from a panic attack. This was Edwin's second such episode and he was advised to seek counseling and possibly psychotropic intervention.

Edwin arrived alone to his intake appointment. He was a tall, imposing man with slightly effeminate facial features. Edwin began speaking in English, but after becoming aware that the therapist was fluent in Spanish, he switched to Spanish. He spoke Spanish for the remainder of the intake and subsequent sessions. Allowing Edwin to switch languages as needed helped to establish the initial rapport and build the therapeutic alliance. Edwin enquired as to how the clinician knew Spanish and the clinician's country of origin. The clinician shared this information with Edwin, which furthered his connection with the clinician and strengthened rapport building, consistent with the cultural value of *personalismo*.

In response to questions on his immigration history during the clinical interview, Edwin reported that he was born and raised in Mexico, and arrived in the United States with a student visa 10 years prior, at the age of 21. None of his family members were in the United States when he arrived. In explaining his reason for leaving his native country, Edwin chronicled a history of oppression and discrimination that began in his elementary school years when he was targeted, harassed, and victimized for showing effeminate traits. His decision to come to the United States was prompted by a severe beating he received at the hands of the local police.

Edwin endorsed immense feelings of guilt about his homosexuality during his years in Mexico, related to both his religious upbringing and the shame he believed that he brought to his family. He explained while in Mexico he immersed himself in religion and dated women in an effort to live a heterosexual lifestyle. However, his attempts at hiding his sexuality only served to increase his isolation, resulting in depressive episodes and anxiety symptoms. He never sought treatment in Mexico.

To determine the feasibility of including his family in his treatment, the therapist explored Edwin's couple and family relationships. Edwin reported that although his family did not address his sexuality directly, his father verbally abused him and made him feel worthless because he was not "macho" enough. His mother attempted but often failed to protect Edwin from his father's abuse. When his parents divorced, Edwin's distant relationship with his father was severed completely and they had had no contact after Edwin's move to the United States. Edwin maintained contact with his mother and sister and sent them money due to his sense of responsibility to aid them financially. Edwin disclosed that he and his male partner, Javier, had recently married. Javier, also of Mexican descent, had been born in the United States. Edwin spoke positively of their relationship and noted that Javier's family had become a significant source of support for him and was accepting of Edwin, the couple's sexual orientation, and their relationship. Edwin also described having supportive friends.

During the assessment phase, it was discovered that Edwin's panic attacks began after his sister mentioned her intentions to visit him. Since that telephone conversation, he had avoided speaking to his sister and mother, fearful that a visit from his family would reveal his sexual orientation and the fact that he was married to another man. This avoidance, however, resulted in feelings of guilt about not speaking to them. Once the therapist enabled Edwin to understand the connection between his anxiety and his worries about his family, a plan to manage the panic attacks could be defined.

Cognitive behavioral treatment with Edwin included educating him about anxiety and introducing him to techniques that would calm both his mind and his body. These included (a) relaxation exercises, (b) identifying the anxiety, and (c) providing himself with alternative thoughts to help him cope with symptoms if they arose. Keeping with Edwin's strong cultural beliefs of *familismo*, alternative positive thoughts that complemented Edwin's values could replace negative perspectives. For example, his thought of failing his family because he is homosexual was reframed, highlighting that by allowing himself to be happy with who he is, he is better able to give to them. In addition, family sessions including Edwin's sister-in-law as well as Javier were integrated into the treatment, thus providing additional support so that Edwin might achieve the goal of discussing his sexuality with his family. In addition, their presence as alternative familial support system helped reduce Edwin's fears regarding potential family rejection.

Together with Javier, Edwin decided to open up to his sister about his sexual orientation and his marriage. Understanding that a break and rejection from his family was possible, Edwin was encouraged to focus on the supports currently in place with Javier's family and his friends. Edwin's eventual disclosure to his sister was received positively and supportively. Edwin's sister helped him speak with his mother. After these disclosures and acceptance of his sexuality by his mother and sister, the panic attacks stopped and his anxiety symptoms significantly decreased.

WORKING WITH LATINO FAMILIES

The Latino family structure, whether a two-parent or single-parent household, traditionally contains an identified individual who is the authority figure. The cultural expectation is that this person is revered and respected. In the absence of such a well-established figure, there is typically conflict and familial stress. This situation often arises when family members immigrate to the United States separately. It is frequently the practice for parents to come to the United States first and leave children in the care of family members in their native country until the parents are in a position to provide a home for the children. In addition to issues of attachment and separation, sometimes the authority of the biological parent has not been established when the family does reunite, often leading to conflict and imbalance. An initial goal becomes to identify this parent as the authority in order to build respect and an agreed-upon family structure.

It is important for clinicians working with Latinos to understand that those who constitute their family may vary among couples and families. For example, clinicians may need to include family support sources who are neither part of the nuclear family nor biological relatives. This can be illustrated by the situation common in many Latino cultures where other adults like a friend or family member may take on the responsibility of caring for the children when the parents are experiencing a crisis. These children, referred to as *hijos de crianza*, may present in family sessions even though their status is intended to be temporary. Understanding their role within the family is important in both guiding the intervention and connecting with the family. In addition, godparents or other trusted adults can have key roles to play with the children and adolescents in the family. When working with the Latino population, family may include not only those related by blood and marriage, but also *compadres* (godparents) and *hijos de crianza* (Garcia-Preto, 2005). The clinician's openness to include such individuals in the treatment process can positively impact adherence and outcomes.

Familismo is one of the most salient and empirically supported characteristics of Latino culture (Vasquez, 1994). It represents a family orientation that includes obligation and support. In essence, the family is believed to come before all else, and its impact extends to most, if not all, aspects of life. It is common among Latinos for individuals to feel compelled to self-sacrifice when they believe it best for family well-being. One example of how the role of *familismo* can impact treatment at the most basic level would be when clients might limit treatment to one monthly session due to concern that having weekly sessions as revealed on insurance statements might cause other family members to become worried. *Familismo* can also contribute to positive outcomes. According to Arredondo (2015), this cultural value may have multiple benefits in that it enables Latino families to maintain strong intergenerational ties, and helps all family members manage (a) lifestyle changes, (b) stress related to acculturation and discrimination, (c) lifespan changes, and (d) life in general. Thus, therapists must understand this value as critical in the mental health of many Latinos (Pina-Watson et al., 2013), and respect the core tendency for many Latinos to turn to their families first.

Traditional Latino collectivist values, such as *familismo*, are in stark contrast to traditional American culture that values independent thinking and individual success rather than the importance of interdependence (Caplan, 2007). Many Latinos are taught and positively reinforced for thinking of the self in relationship to others. Thus, a family member's economic success is an achievement for the family and the community as much as it is a personal accomplishment. Conflicts between this traditional value system and American cultural norms that emphasize individuality may often result in tremendous stress on family members.

For many Latino families, therapy can be very helpful in managing bicultural stress. The difficulty of deciding what parts of the traditional culture to keep, alter, or do away with is a daily concern that impacts individuals, couples, the family, and community. Additional conflicts may arise when family members have opposing views on ways to negotiate the demands of one culture with the other. When healthy communication and flexibility are in place, the family can define together what their hybrid culture might look like. In treatment, the key to success is to guide families struggling with these issues to find balance and a common vision.

Case Example

Ms. Mendoza, a 53-year-old single parent of a teenage daughter Ada, was born and raised in Puerto Rico. She moved to the mainland at the age of 16. Ms. Mendoza presented for treatment as a result of being mandated to family counseling by the state's child protection agency. She explained that the child protection agency intervened as a result of Ada's school truancy and numerous attempts at running away. Ms. Mendoza appeared her stated age and was well groomed and appropriately dressed.

Ms. Mendoza identified as bilingual, but preferred speaking Spanish. Ada, who had been born and spent her life on the mainland, understood Spanish but spoke only English. One of the first issues the clinician addressed was language preference. It was agreed that both Spanish and English would be used in session, allowing both to express themselves comfortably. This also was their first successful joint decision that met both of their needs and set the foundation for improved communication.

Ms. Mendoza reported being overwhelmed with Ada. She spoke of her many sacrifices for her daughter's well-being and future and she could not understand why her daughter was disobeying her rules. In many ways, Ms. Mendoza endorsed values of *marianismo* that corresponded with her role as mother, her primary identity. She believed that her emphasis on self-sacrifice would be met by gratitude and recognition from Ada. When this did not occur, Ms. Mendoza felt unappreciated. Without the reinforcing aspects of *marianismo*, her distress and the negativity between the mother and daughter increased. In contrast, Ada expressed anger toward her mother for having "too many rules," and not allowing her to go out with friends.

In developing a culturally relevant treatment plan, both mother and daughter were asked to provide a wish list for their relationship and for their home life in general. Prior to engaging them in active conversation about changes, it was important to establish a connection with both mother and daughter. The clinician asked Ms. Mendoza to share how her parents managed her teenage years. This introduced traditional cultural expectations related to gender roles and the importance of *respeto*. It also revealed the extent to which the differences in expectations between Ms. Mendoza and Ada were due to cultural influences. Ms. Mendoza maintained a traditional approach to parenting based on her Puerto Rican upbringing, while Ada's view of adolescence was consistent with an American culture that emphasized greater freedom. They were asked to discuss these differing views in treatment, after which the therapist provided psychoeducation surrounding intergenerational conflict and bicultural stress. This process opened both Ms. Mendoza and Ada to active and increased communication. Each being able to listen to and comprehend what the other was experiencing led to a deeper degree of understanding between mother and daughter.

Negotiating areas of compromise followed. Ada expressed the change she desired, and Ms. Mendoza was asked to consider these requests. Also, Ms. Mendoza defined her expectations of Ada. The result was an agreement between mother and daughter that Ms. Mendoza would allow Ada to engage in social activities with peers as long as she complied with the guidelines defined by Ms. Mendoza. Consistent with *marianismo*, identifying ways for Ada to communicate gratitude for Ms. Mendoza as a parent was integrated into the treatment. As Ada felt better understood by her mother, she was able to express more appreciation and affection toward her. In turn, the validation Ms. Mendoza felt in her parental role enhanced her self-image and positively reinforced the parenting changes Ms. Mendoza was implementing.

Working with Latino Couples

Working with Latino couples includes an initial assessment of gender roles. Given the variability as to how much Latino clients will adhere to the traditional roles of *marianismo* and *machismo*, clinicians need to understand the cultural values and behavior comprising the couple's respective roles within the marriage to allow for engagement with their clinician and improve treatment planning and outcome. One study investigating successful Latino marriages found that, with the exception of shared decision-making, the couples typically adhered to traditional gender roles (Skogrand, Hatch, & Singh, 2008).

The impact of American culture on these roles may create additional stress and conflict. Clinicians may encounter Latino couples who appear assimilated yet function more traditionally within the home. For example, a woman might conform to American behavior and norms in the workplace, particularly if she holds a powerful position, yet uphold a traditional *marianismo* role at home, placing the needs of her husband and children before her own. It is common for such women to feel pressure from a workplace where assertiveness is prized, as well as from family members or friends to maintain behaviors and values consistent with enculturation, or norms from her culture of origin (Miville & Constantine, 2006). The opposite also can occur when it is the male in the couple who is most impacted by changes related to the influence of American culture. For example, particularly among new arrivals to the United States, it is not uncommon for women to have an easier entry into the workplace and for the male to confront far more limited work opportunities. This situation creates economic power differentials between them (Maciel, Van Putten, & Knudson-Martin, 2009) and may be a presenting issue in clinical practice.

At this intersection in treatment, in order to make changes within the system, the clinician may experience a pull to address gender roles. It is recommended that the clinician work within the *couple's* definition of roles, other than when issues of abuse exist that must be addressed (Orengo-Aguayo, 2015). Also, therapists should identify treatment goals *with* the couple, not *for* the couple. This approach allows for (a) further trust to develop, (b) strengthening of the therapeutic relationship, and (c) guiding the couple toward achieving positive outcomes.

Addressing the topic of sexuality with Latino couples should be approached with care, as doing so prior to establishing a good therapeutic alliance can be viewed as disrespectful and lead to disengagement by the couple. For many of these couples, an initial attempt to seek help to improve their relationship may have been within a religious context, that is, engaging with their pastoral advisor (priest, pastor, deacon, minister, etc.). The couple's religious identity is also a factor to be considered in the clinician's approach to discussing sexuality, as beliefs related to marital roles, family planning, separation, and divorce may influence the treatment of clients who self-identify as religious. Approaching couples treatment with an understanding of how faith influences the relationship may help the clinician frame the goals and interventions in a manner in which they can both relate and utilize, thereby increasing the likelihood of a couple's engagement in treatment.

Given the importance of familial influence within Latino culture, working with Latino couples often necessitates an understanding of family dynamics. For example, it is not uncommon to treat Latino couples who have identified familial pressure to have children as a source of stress and conflict. When there are children, a clinician can note their importance in the couple's family structure so as to strengthen rapport. Their children also may provide a source of common ground for the couple. In a situation where the extended family influences the couple's decision-making, understanding the family's authority and influence on the couple may be necessary for positive outcomes. Thus, including key family members in select sessions may be indicated. The clinician may also need to guide the couple in developing ways to communicate with their family members who are mindful of familial roles and expectations.

Case Example

Mr. and Mrs. Torres were undocumented immigrants. Mrs. Torres arrived in the United States from Mexico at age 22, and Mr. Torres arrived from Honduras at age 25. The couple met at work and, shortly after meeting, began living together. They were married within a year and had their only child after a year of marriage. Both Mr. and Mrs. Torres described a generally loving and supportive relationship. Their son, aged three, was reported to have normal development and functioning.

The couple began with pastoral counseling due to marital difficulties. When Mrs. Torres began to suffer worsening anxiety symptoms, their pastor recommended that they seek professional psychological treatment. At intake with the therapist, Mrs. Torres presented with depressed mood and slightly anxious affect. Mr. and Mrs. Torres were asked to identify their issues and evaluate their pastoral counseling experience in terms of both positive outcomes and areas with no improvement. Beyond an unremarkable mental status and history, part of the assessment phase included a discussion about their faith and beliefs, especially related to marriage. Mr. and Mrs. Torres expressed their belief that God had a plan for them to stay together, an example of *fatalismo*. The clinician utilized this belief system to highlight how their faith led them to seek support. Integrating their faith by defining it as a strength for the couple helped build initial rapport and also engaged the couple in active participation in the treatment.

Prior to their son's birth, a plan was put in place for Mr. Torres's mother to come and live with them. Mr. Torres explained that his mother offered to help them with child care so that Mrs. Torres could continue to work. Mrs. Torres expressed her hesitancy at this arrangement, having had no contact with her mother-in-law other than phone conversations. Cultural concepts of *respeto* and *familismo* influenced her decision to not communicate these concerns to her husband. Mrs. Torres explained that she did not want to appear disrespectful and ungrateful. Addressing this in session helped to facilitate the first conversation between the couple about expectations and honesty in communication. Reframing communication as integral to their relationship and not counter to *respeto* and *familismo* moved the treatment forward.

As treatment progressed, the mother-in-law's presence was understood to be the catalyst for the couple's discord. Mrs. Torres thought highly of her mother-in-law and expressed appreciation for her help. However, she also felt that her mother-in-law's presence had reduced her own importance in her home. Her son was very attached to his grandmother and, at times, showed a preference toward her over his mother. In addition, Mrs. Torres disclosed that household chores, such as cooking and laundry, were no longer within her sole domain. She had felt revered and valued for what she did for her family and was experiencing her current situation as a loss of that status. In addition, she felt that her husband was no longer as attentive to her as he had been in the past. All these combined to give her a sense that she was powerless and without a clear role in her home. Mrs. Torres's self-identity as mother and wife followed many traditional reinforcing beliefs related to the concept of *marianismo*. Her increasing emotional distress led to arguments with her husband. She began to experience such severe anxiety that she missed work, a circumstance that added to her anxiety because her employer was sponsoring her for citizenship. Her debilitating symptoms prompted her family to care for her and rally around her, and became the new way for her to receive the attention and recognition she sought from home.

The treatment plan for Mr. and Mrs. Torres included increasing their understanding of how changes in their home life affected each family member. The couple engaged easily in this process, as it complemented the value of *familismo*. Time was spent outlining roles and how best to communicate these roles to one another, all within a cultural framework that incorporated the values of *respeto*, *familismo*, and *marianismo*.

In addition, the importance of Mrs. Torres's contribution to household finances was better defined.

Both Mr. and Mrs. Torres expressed concern about informing the mother-in-law of the agreed-upon changes. They worried she might misinterpret them and be offended. After discussing the substance of what they wanted to communicate and the methods of doing so, including brief role-play, the mother-in-law was invited to attend a session. As her inclusion served as a sign of her importance in the family home, she responded positively. In the session, she was incorporated into the discussion about the proposed changes within the household. One of the changes was the designation of days of the week in which Mrs. Torres would cook for the family. The mother-in-law began attending a prayer group on one of these evenings, allowing her to engage in an activity other than attending to her son's family. A bedtime routine, including storytelling and a lullaby, was defined in which Mr. and Mrs. Torres would put their son to bed unless they were unavailable. Additionally, more family outings were planned.

For the Torres family, defined roles with better communication allowed them to make the changes needed to improve their family functioning. Changes in the family systems resulted in the reestablishment of Mrs. Torres's role within the family and better communication between the couple. With increased familial validation, Mrs. Torres felt better, and her anxiety decreased.

Treatment of the Torres family incorporated the clinician's knowledge and understanding of cultural values that were intrinsic to many of the family's thoughts and actions. Identifying the culturally normed concepts of *familismo, respeto, fatalismo,* and *marianismo* as key areas to address in treatment allowed the clinician to guide the couple to maintain the core message of such values while making adjustments so they would better fit the Torres family's situation. Thus, the importance of family was utilized to outline actions that would be in the family's best interests. *Respeto* was the guiding principle in communication between family members in terms of both approach and substance. The couple's belief that God was driving their relationship was integrated into their treatment by defining God to be present in all they do, including treatment. For Mrs. Torres, her role as wife and mother was clearly defined by *marianismo* in terms of her dutiful self-sacrifice, deference to her husband, and the expectation of reverence from her family in return for her loving care of them. When she was unable to fulfill what she perceived to be key caretaking responsibilities, she felt displaced and emotionally deprived. Including her financial assistance to the family as a self-sacrificing behavior was a step in reestablishing her sense of purpose and worth within the family system. By including the mother-in-law in family sessions, the couple was able to move forward in making changes that honored their *respeto* for her and allowed for an easier acceptance of the changes by all family members.

CONCLUSIONS

Providing services to Latino families and couples necessitates an understanding of their cultural beliefs and values, as well as migration and acculturation experiences. The clinician must also be aware of the diversity among and within Latino groups and that each client, whether in individual, couple or family therapy, brings a unique history to treatment.

Culturally competent treatment begins with a culturally competent assessment. Knowing how to approach and what to ask Latino clients begins with culturally driven training, and exposure to culture-specific research and literature. Working with Latino couples and families necessitates the skill of establishing a relationship that (a) follows cultural expectations, (b) is based on a foundation of understanding cultural variables, (c) allows for variability, and (d) reflects the clinician's willingness to adapt interventions to meet the needs of treatment. Accurate assessment will enable the clinician to evaluate the existence and extent to which culture and Latino identity may influence treatment and outcomes.

Additional research is needed in the development and utilization of culturally adapted, empirically validated treatment with the Latino community. While research and dialogue about working with the Latino community in the mental health field have grown, there is a continued lag in evidence-based treatments. A consistent criticism of evidence-based practice is its inattention to cultural considerations. While research exists on cultural adaptations of evidence-based treatment with Latinos (Griner & Smith, 2006), no studies have been conducted utilizing Latino-only samples or developed in accordance with cultural considerations of Latinos (Arredondo et al., 2014). The mental health field needs increased culturally specific research as well as increased utilization of appropriately normed and validated assessment tools.

Overall, meeting the needs of the growing Latino community will be ongoing for mental health providers. The role of culture in both assessment and treatment needs to be incorporated into training programs in addition to course instruction. There is also an increased need for Spanish-speaking clinicians. Furthermore, it is recommended that there be additional support initiatives facilitating access to higher education for Latinos wishing to enter both the academic and applied mental health fields.

CHAPTER REVIEW

Key Points

1. The Latino population is an ever-growing and heterogeneous group comprised of subcultures, which must be considered along with the common cultural values associated with this population.
2. As an ethnic group, Latinos in the United States have a long history filled with various political and socioeconomic intersections, constituting the

basis of common values and beliefs, shaping Latino identities in the United States. The historical journeys of different Latino groups provide a foundation for understanding both the similarities and differences of these groups in treatment.

3. Practical barriers to health services, including mental health treatment, contribute to the increasing health disparities between Latinos and Whites.
4. Acculturative stress relating to pressures to adopt a host culture and bicultural stress relating to the push and pull between culture of origin and host culture are commonly experienced by Latino couples and families.
5. Practitioners should be mindful of the potential influences of cultural values, such as *familismo, marianismo, machismo,* and *respeto,* on the way presenting problems are defined and on the course of treatment, as well as treatment outcomes.
6. It is crucial for clinicians to also account for the heterogeneity among Latinos. The degree to which a particular value or concept applies to the presenting issues will vary with the individual couple or family.

Key Terms

bicultural stress, cultural competence, familismo, machismo, marianismo, personalismo, respeto

Myths and Realities

- It is a myth that Latino culture is homogenous and that understanding common cultural values will make a clinician culturally competent. True cultural competence involves sensitivity to the heterogeneity of the experiences of Latinos.
- It is a myth that traditional Latino gender roles, specifically *machismo* and *marianismo,* are always characterized by sexism and create inequality in relationships. Many Latino couples adhere to these gender norms and view their roles as equal partners who share power in the relationship. There are both positive and negative components of these and other traditional Latino values.

Tools and Tips

Knowledge

Arredondo, P., Gallardo-Cooper, M., Delgado-Romero, E. A., & Zapata, A. L. (2014). *Culturally responsive counseling with Latinas/os.* Alexandria, VA: American Counseling Association.

Falicov, C. J. (2013). *Latino families in therapy.* New York, NY: Guilford Publications.

McGoldrick, M., Giordano, J., & Garcia-Preto, N. (Eds.). (2005). *Ethnicity and family therapy.* New York, NY: Guilford Press.

Paniagua, F. A., & Yamada, A.M. (Eds.). (2013). *Handbook of multicultural mental health: Assessment and treatment of diverse populations.* San Diego, CA: Academic Press.

Santiago-Rivera, A. L., Arredondo, P., & Gallardo-Cooper, M. (2002). *Counseling Latinos and la familia: A practical guide.* Thousand Oaks, CA: Sage Publications.

Dynamic Sizing

Due to the heterogeneous nature of Latino culture, it is important not to overgeneralize and assume that all Latinos will present in the same ways. While the common Latino values and norms described within this chapter can help to guide understanding of Latino cases, their primary value is to increase awareness of potential factors to be assessed, such as acculturation. The individual's manifestation of these values will differ.

Skills

Theory. The cognitive behavioral approaches utilized in the case examples integrate components of family systems. Familial conceptualization is often an integral component of treatment with Latinos not only in family counseling but also in individual and couple treatment.

Prevention. Traditional Latino families revere and respect authority. Establishing this authority may prevent conflict and familial stress. This is particularly relevant with Latino parents separated from their children, then later reunited.

Service Provision. While cultural commonalities can guide successful treatment outcomes, clinicians must also account for variation among Latinos. How much or how little a particular value or concept applies to the presenting issues will vary. There is a history unique to the individual, couple, and family in treatment.

Policy. The experience of discrimination and negative stereotypes increases bicultural stress. Immigration policy that promotes equality and fairness, rather than anti-immigrant sentiment, is necessary to reduce barriers to mental health treatment and decrease emotional distress.

Research. Best practices with Latinos need to include research derived from Latino samples. Evidence-based practice needs to include culturally adapted approaches. Recent studies speak to the identification of treatment interventions that are a cultural fit. Increased sample size can further explore the strength of the study findings and provide further support for the development of culturally congruent, evidence-based treatment.

Awareness

Migration history provides the clinician a road map between point of origin to point of destination, encompassing all parts of the individual's reality and experience. This increased awareness of the variations in Latino clients' journeys to the United States can provide culturally relevant information that can guide treatment and outcome success. For example, clinicians must be aware of how these experiences differ from the assumptions of many Americans that migration involves either a border crossing or a simple application.

NOTE

1. The terms "Latina/o" and "Hispanic" will be used interchangeably in this chapter.

REFERENCES

American Psychological Association, Presidential Task Force on Immigration. (2013). *Working with immigrant-origin clients: An update for mental health professionals.* Washington, DC: American Psychological Association. Retrieved from http://www.apa.org/topics/immigration/immigration-report-professionals.pdf

Aquino, M. P., Machado D. L., & Rodríguez, J. (2002). *A reader in Latina feminist theology: Religion and justice.* Austin, TX: University of Texas Press.

Arciniega, G. M., Anderson, T. C., Tovar-Blank, Z. G., & Tracey, T. J. (2008). Toward a fuller conception of Machismo: Development of a traditional Machismo and Caballerismo Scale. *Journal of Counseling Psychology, 55,* 19–33. doi: 10.1037/0022-0167.55.1.19

Arredondo, P. (2015). The legacy of Latina/o families: Persistence, fuerza, & dreams in the 21st century. *Latina/o Psychology Today, 2*(2), 7–12.

Arredondo, P., Gallardo-Cooper, M., Delgado-Romero, E. A., & Zapata, A. L. (2014). *Culturally responsive counseling with Latinas/os.* Alexandria, VA: American Counseling Association.

Baez, A., & Hernandez, D. (2001). Complementary spiritual beliefs in the Latino community: The interface with psychotherapy. *American Journal Orthopsychiatry, 71,* 408–415. doi: 10.1037/0002-9432.71.4.408

Barrio, C., Yamada, A.M., Atuel, H., Hough, R. L., Yee, S., Berthot, B., & Russo, P. A. (2003). A tri-ethnic examination of symptom expression on the positive and negative syndrome scale in schizophrenia spectrum disorders. *Schizophrenia Research, 60,* 259–269. doi: 10.1016/S0920-9964(02)00223-2

Bernal, G., & Shapiro, E. (2005). Cuban families. In M. McGoldrick, J. Giordano, & N. Garcia-Preto (Eds.), *Ethnicity and family therapy* (3rd ed., pp. 202–215). New York, NY: Guilford Press.

Brown, A., & Lopez, M. H. (2013). Mapping the Latino population, by state, county and city. Pew Research Center's Hispanic Trends Project. Retrieved from http://www.pewhispanic.org/2013/08/29/mapping-the-latino-population-by-state-county-and-city/

Caplan, S. (2007). Latinos, acculturation, and acculturative stress: A dimensional concept analysis. *Policy, Politics, & Nursing Practice, 8,* 93–106.

Comas-Diaz, L. (2006). Latino healing: The integration of ethnic psychology into psychotherapy. *Psychotherapy: Theory, Research, Practice, Training, 43,* 436–453.

Costantino, G., Malgady, R. G., & Primavera, L. H. (2009). Congruence between culturally competent treatment and cultural needs of older Latinos. *Journal of Consulting and Clinical Psychology, 77,* 941–949. doi: 10.1037/a0016341

DeNavas-Walt, C., & Proctor, B. D. (2015). *Income and poverty in the United States: 2014.* Retrieved from https://www.census.gov/content/dam/Census/library/publications/2015/demo/p60-252.pdf

Diaz, R. M., Ayala, G., Bein, E., Henne, J., & Marin, B. V. (2001). The impact of homophobia, poverty, and racism on the mental health of gay and bisexual Latino men: Findings from 3 US cities. *American Journal of Public Health, 91*, 927–932.

Ennis, S. R., Rios-Vargas, M., & Albert, N. G. (2011). *The Hispanic population: 2010* (2010 Census Briefs C2010BR-04). Washington, DC: U.S. Census Bureau. Retrieved from http://www.census.gov/prod/cen2010/briefs/c2010br-04 .pdf

Falicov, C. J. (2005). Mexican families. In M. McGoldrick, J. Giordano, & N. Garcia Preto (Eds.), *Ethnicity and the family in clinical practice* (3rd ed., pp. 229–241). New York, NY: Guilford Press.

Falicov, C. J. (2013). *Latino families in therapy.* New York, NY: Guilford Publications.

Gagne, S., Vasiliadis, H., & Preville, M. (2014). Gender differences in general and specialty outpatient mental health service use for depression. *BMC Psychiatry, 14*, 135–146. doi: 10.1186/1471-244X-14-135

Galarza, J. (2013). Borderland queer: Narrative approaches in clinical work with Latina women who have sex with women (WSW). *Journal of LGBT Issues in Counseling, 7*, 274–291. doi: 10.1080/15538605.2013.812931

Garcia-Preto, N (2005). Latino families: An overview. In M. McGoldrick, J. Giordano, & N. Garcia-Preto (Eds.), *Ethnicity and family therapy* (3rd ed., pp. 153–165). New York, NY: Guilford Press.

Gary, F. A. (2005). Stigma: Barrier to mental health care among ethnic minorities. *Issues in Mental Health Nursing, 26*, 979–999. doi: 10.1080/01612840500280638

Gil, R. M., & Vazquez, C. I. (1996). *The Maria paradox: How Latinas can merge old world traditions with new world self-esteem.* New York, NY: G. P. Putnam's Sons.

Goertz, M. T. (2015). Reflections on being effective providers for Latina/o families: A dialogue with Dr. Martin J. La Roche. *Latina/o Psychology Today, 2*(2), 18–21.

González, H. M., Haan, M. N., Hinton, L. (2001). Acculturation and the prevalence of depression in older Mexican Americans: Baseline results of the Sacramento area Latino study on aging. *Journal of the American Geriatrics Society, 49*, 948–953. doi: 10.1046/j.1532-5415.2001.49186.x

Griner, D., & Smith, T. B. (2006). Culturally adapted mental health interventions: A meta-analytic review. *Psychotherapy Theory Research and Practice, 43*, 531–548. doi: 10.1037/0033-3204.43.4.531.

Guarnaccia, P. J. (1997). Social stress and psychological distress among Latinos in the United States. In Al-Issa & Tousignant (Eds.), *Ethnicity, immigration, and psychopathology* (pp. 71–94). New York, NY: Plenum Publishing Corporation.

Hartwell, S. (2001). An examination of racial differences among mentally ill offenders in Massachusetts. *Psychiatric Services, 52*, 234–236.

Hernandez, M. (2005). Central American families. In M. McGoldrick, J. Giordano, & N. Garcia-Preto (Eds.), *Ethnicity and family therapy* (3rd ed., pp. 178–191). New York, NY: Guilford Press.

Hernandez, M., Nesman, T., Mowery, D., Acevedo-Polakovich, I. D., & Callejas, L. M. (2009). Cultural competence: A literature review and conceptual model for mental health services. *Psychiatric Services, 60*, 1046–1050.

Hohmann, A. A., Richeport, M., Marriott, B. M., Canino, G. J., Rubio-Stipec, M., & Bird, H. (1990). Spiritism in Puerto Rico: Results of an island-wide community study. *British Journal of Psychiatry, 156*, 328–335. doi: 10.1192/bjp. 156.3.328

Kalibatseva, Z., & Leong, F. L. (2014). A critical review of culturally sensitive treatments for depression: Recommendations for intervention and research. *Psychological Services, 11*, 433–450. doi: 10.1037/a0036047

Korin, E. C., & Petry, S. S. (2005). Brazilian families. In M. McGoldrick, J. Giordano, & N. Garcia-Preto (Eds.), *Ethnicity and family therapy* (3rd ed., pp. 166–177). New York, NY: Guilford Press.

Kouyoumdjian, H., Zamboanga, B. L., & Hansen, D. J. (2003). Barriers to community mental health services for Latinos: Treatment considerations. *Clinical Psychology: Science & Practice, 10*, 394–422.

La Roche, M. J., Batista, C., & D'Angelo, E. (2014). A culturally competent relaxation intervention for low-income Latino/as: An exploratory study. *Journal of Latina/o Psychology, 2*, 146–155. doi: 10.1037/lat0000018

La Roche, M. J., D'Angelo, E., Gualdron, L., & Leavell, J. (2006). Culturally sensitive guided imagery for allocentric Latinos: A pilot study. *Psychotherapy: Theory, Research, Practice, Training, 43*, 555. doi: 10.1037/0033-3204.43.4.555

Luna, E. (2003). Las que curan at the heart of Hispanic culture. *Journal of Holistic Nursing, 21*, 326–342. doi: 10.1177/0898010103258574

Maciel, J. A., Van Putten, Z., & Knudson-Martin, C. (2009). Gendered power in cultural contexts: Part I. Immigrant couples. *Family Process, 48*, 9–23. doi: 10.1111/j.1545-5300.2009.01264.x

Maly, R. C., Umezawa, Y., Ratliff, C. T., & Leake, B. (2006). Racial/Ethnic group differences in treatment decision-making and treatment received among older breast carcinoma patients. *Cancer, 106*, 957–965. doi: 10.1002/cncr.21680

Marotta, S. A., & Garcia, J. G. (2003). Latinos in the United States in 2000. *Hispanic Journal of Behavioral Sciences, 25*, 13–34. doi: 10.1177/0739986303251693

Meyer, I. H. (2003). Prejudice, social stress, and mental health in lesbian, gay, and bisexual populations: Conceptual issues and research evidence. *Psychological Bulletin, 129*, 674–697. doi: 10.1037/0033-2909.129.5.674

Miranda, A. O., & Matheny, K. B. (2000). Socio-psychological predictors of acculturative stress among Latino adults. *Journal of Mental Health Counseling, 22*, 306–317.

Miville, M. L., & Constantine, M. G. (2006). Sociocultural predictors of psychological help-seeking attitudes and behavior among Mexican American college students. *Cultural Diversity and Ethnic Minority Psychology, 12*, 420–432. doi: 10.1037/1099-9809.12.3.420

Orengo-Aguayo, R. E. (2015) Mexican American and other Hispanic couples' relationship dynamics: A review to inform interventions aimed at promoting healthy relationships. *Marriage & Family Review, 51*, 633–667, doi: 10.1080/01494929.2015.1068253

Paniagua, F. A., & Yamada, A. M. (Eds.). (2013). *Handbook of multicultural mental health: Assessment and treatment of diverse populations*. San Diego, CA: Academic Press.

Pina, A. A., & Silverman, W. K. (2004). Clinical phenomenology, somatic symptoms, and distress in Hispanic/Latino and European American youths with anxiety disorders. *Journal of Clinical Child and Adolescent Psychology, 33*, 227–236. doi: 10.1207/s15374424jccp3302_3

Pina-Watson, B., Ojeda, L., Castellon, N. E., & Dornhecker, M. (2013). Familismo, ethnic identity, and bicultural stress as predictors of Mexican American adolescents' positive psychological functioning. *Journal of Latina/o Psychology, 1,* 204–217. doi: 10.1037/lat0000006

Romero, A.J., Carvajal, S.C., Valle, F., & Orduña, M. (2007). Adolescent bicultural stress and its impact on mental well-being among Latinos, Asian Americans, and European Americans. *Journal of Community Psychology, 35,* 519–534. doi: 10.1002/jcop.20162

Romero, A.J., & Roberts, R.E. (2003). Stress within a bicultural context for adolescents of Mexican descent. *Cultural Diversity & Ethnic Minority Psychology, 9,* 171–184. doi: 10.1037/1099-9809.9.2.171

Saenz, R. (2010). Latinos in America 2010. *Population Bulletin Update, 2010.* Population Reference Bureau.

Saiz, A. (2003). Room in the kitchen for the melting pot: Immigration and rental prices. *Review of Economics and Statistics, 85,* 502–521.

Sanabria, S., & Puig, A. (2015). Counseling Latin gays and lesbians. In S.H. Dworkin & M. Pope (Eds.), *Casebook for counseling* (pp. 185–196). Alexandria, VA: American Counseling Association.

Santiago-Rivera, A.L., Arredondo, P., & Gallardo-Cooper, M. (2002). *Counseling Latinos and la familia: A practical guide.* Thousand Oaks, CA: Sage Publications.

Skogrand, L., Hatch, D., & Singh, A. (2008). Strong marriages in Latino culture. In R. Dalla, J. DeFrain, J. Johnson, and D. Abbott (Eds.), *Strengths and challenges of new immigrant families: Implications for research, policy, education, and service.* Lexington, MA: Lexington Press.

Smith, J.C., & Medalia, C. (2015). *Health insurance coverage in the United States: 2014.* Retrieved from https://www.census.gov/content/dam/Census/library/publications/2015/demo/p60-253.pdf

U.S. Census Bureau. (2010). *Race and Hispanic or Latino origin: 2010.* Retrieved from: http://factfinder.census.gov/faces/tableservices/jsf/pages/productview.xhtml?src=CF

U.S. Department of Health and Human Services. (1999). Mental health: A report to the Surgeon General. Rockville, MD: Author, Substance Abuse and Mental Health Services Administration, Center for Mental Health Services.

Vasquez, M.J. (1994). Latinas. In L. Comas-Díaz & B. Greene (Eds.), *Women of color: Integrating ethnic and gender identities in psychotherapy* (pp. 114–138). New York, NY: Guilford Press.

Vega, W.A., & Alegría, M. (2001). Latino mental health and treatment in the United States. In M. Aquirre-Molina, C.W. Molina, & R.E. Zambrana (Eds.), *Health issues in the Latino community* (pp. 179–208). San Francisco, CA: John Wiley & Sons.

Whaley, A.L., & Davis, K.E. (2007). Cultural competence and evidence-based practice in mental health services: A complementary perspective. *American Psychologist, 62,* 563–574. doi: 10.1037/0003-066X.62.6.563

Yousaf, O., Popat, A., & Hunter, M.S. (2015). An investigation of masculinity attitudes, gender, and attitudes towards psychological help-seeking. *Psychology of Men & Masculinity, 16,* 234–237. doi: 10.1037/a0036241

Challenges Faced by Native American Couples and Families and a Place-Focused Approach to Treatment

Rockey Robbins
Tahereh Ryland-Neal
Shannon Murphy
Chris Geis

NATIVE AMERICAN COUPLES AND FAMILIES: PLACE-FOCUSED THERAPY

More than 4,000,000 Native Americans, comprising over 530 tribes and 22 different ethnic groups, currently live in the United States, with Alaska Natives constituting approximately one-quarter of that population. Although Native Americans—2 percent of the U.S. population—are dispersed across the country, the states with the highest numbers, in order, are California, Oklahoma, Arizona, Texas, and New Mexico. The largest tribes are the Cherokees, followed by Navahos and Choctaws (Norris, Vines, & Hoeffel, 2012). Of the approximately 44 percent of Native Americans who list more than one race on the census, 63 percent are Native American and White, and 12 percent are Native American and Black.

Native Americans are often overlooked in research studies, possibly due to their small numbers. In this chapter, the available research is reviewed and placed in an historical and culturally relevant context. A case study is then presented, which (a) illustrates issues commonly faced by many Native Americans, (b) highlights the need for a clinician's cultural competence, and (c) offers interventions that may be helpful in working with Native American couples and families.

Historical and Current Conditions Faced
by Native Americans

History

The history of Native Americans has involved repeated trauma since the arrival of Europeans to the continent, first as explorers and then as colonizers. When the Pilgrims arrived almost 500 years ago, they introduced diseases, which proved devastating to the Native American population. Smallpox and measles alone reduced the population of Native Americans by over 90 percent within the first 200 years of European colonialization (Mann, 2005). The smallpox epidemic was exacerbated by the distribution of smallpox-infected blankets to Native Americans (Usner, 1992). Another source of destruction was the importation of European swine. These animals were contaminated with brucellosis, leptospirosis, trichinosis, and tuberculosis. As they roamed the forest, they infected turkeys and deer, staples of the Native Americans diet (Usner, 1992).

A second major trauma involved efforts to strip Native Americans of their independence, land, and culture. Prior to the establishment of the United States, European explorers captured many Southeastern tribal people, transported them to the Caribbean islands, and sold them into slavery (Ehle, 1988; Usner, 1992). Once the United States became a formal entity, expulsion of Native Americans from their land became governmental policy, along with measures to forcibly resettle them. In most cases, they were relegated to virtual imprisonment on reservations. Another policy was to grant families small, isolated pockets of farmland where they would be surrounded by farmland inhabited by non-Native Americans. This offered little appeal to Native Americans, not only due to their isolation, but also because the Western concept of private property was heretofore unknown and contradictory to the communal nature of Native American culture. In an attempt to preserve their traditional ways and values, tribes such as the Cherokees moved further South and west, to Texas and Mexico (Woodward, 1963).

For Native Americans who stayed on reservations, some of their traditional practices and in-group interactions were outlawed. Native American traditions of farming and hunting to provide their families with food became prohibited on reservations, and were replaced by food distributed by charity organizations. Religious rituals, such as Sun Dances or those involving peyote, were viewed as satanic and/or anarchic (Usner, 1992) and banned until the 1978 passage of the Religious Freedom Act (Child, Lomawaima, & Archuleta, 2010). All of these actions, intended to assimilate Native Americans, only served to further isolate them.

Current Living Conditions of Native Americans

Native Americans have a poverty rate in excess of 30 percent. Their median income, approximately $39,000, is comparable to that of African

Americans. These two population groups have the lowest median incomes in the United States (Sarche & Spicer, 2008). Moreover, Native Americans have the lowest levels of homeownership and health insurance in the country (U.S. Census Bureau, 2009). Currently, one-third of all Native American children attend schools in what are characterized as "distant or remote areas" (DeVoe, Darling-Churchill, & Snyder, 2008). Native Americans living in rural areas are more likely to be poor and grow up in two-parent households with parents of the same ethnicity than Native Americans living in urban areas (Sarche & Spicer, 2008).

The impacts of historical trauma cannot be underestimated. They have manifested in symptoms such as guilt, anger, depression, and self-destructive behaviors (Brave Heart, 2005). Native American children have high rates of mental health problems, such as alcohol abuse, and suicide rates (Clayton, Brindis, Hamor, Raiden-Wright, & Fong, 2000). They start drinking at an earlier age, drink more frequently and in higher quantities, and experience more alcohol-related negative consequences than other populations (Oetting & Beauvais, 1989). For adult Native Americans, post-traumatic stress disorder has been found to be two to three times the national rate (Beals et al., 2005).

Historical and Current Conceptions of Native American Identity

Historical Conceptions of Identity

From colonial days, Euro-Americans have sought to define Native American identity in an effort to assimilate Native Americans into Euro-American culture. The Bureau of Indian Affairs was established in 1854 to manage relations with, and to define the political and legal status of, Native Americans (Getches et al., 2004). One component of defining who was Native American involved tracking their **blood quantum,** or the percentage of their ancestry that was Native American. Persons who had no biological ties to other races were deemed to be "full blood," and those with less than one-quarter Native American ancestry were considered not to be Native American. At the same time, Native American children were removed from their homes and cultural contexts and compelled to attend boarding schools where only mainstream American culture and values were taught in an effort to assimilate and "civilize" them (Phinney, 2000).

In the 1960s, government-mandated assimilation practices were replaced with policies of tribal self-determination. Each tribe was allowed to decide for itself the criteria for tribal membership, and consequently define Native American identity (Usner, 1992); however, many tribes differed in how they did so. Many tribes set one-quarter blood quantum as the standard for tribal identity. Others, such as the Cherokee, did not have a blood quantum minimum, but relied on an ancestor's appearance on the **Dawes Roll**. The Dawes Roll, undertaken between 1894 and 1906, was a census of Native American individuals who registered by tribe. Use of the Dawes Roll as the criteria for determining Native American ancestry was problematic. For instance, some tribes limited registration only to those members living in the tribal jurisdiction. Other tribes did not allow persons who were part African American to enroll. Incentives also existed to fraudulently register as a Native American to obtain land made available only to Native Americans with tribal memberships (Usner, 1992).

The blood quantum emphasis remains a central factor in Native American interactions (Pewewardy, 2002). It is important to note that the root cause is a history of forced assimilation and forced designations of who is Native American, which arguably adversely affected group cohesion. Moreover, subsequent policies of self-determination within the context of continuing government oppression and incentives to identify what it means to be Native American in specific divisive ways have ensured continuation of these problems across generations. For instance, tribes may impose a blood quantum requirement for participation in tribal elections, and may curtail the tribal privileges of children when both parents are not Native American. In addition, much of the contention over identity among Native Americans may be attributed to government-granted financial resources that are divided among tribal members. By setting a high blood quantum requirement for certification, fewer members qualify for funds, thus leading to contention and alienation among tribal members (Pewewardy, 2002).

Identification with Native American Culture

Psychological identification with one's Native American culture has been associated with good mental health. In a study with more than 2,000 Native American youth across the United States, Oetting, Donnermeyer, Trimble, and Beauvais (1998) found that the cultural identity of these youth was deeply rooted in the cultural identity of their families. In a sample of 2,000 Native American adolescents, Moran, Fleming, Somervell, and Manson (1999) further found that the highest levels of social competency and self-esteem were associated with those who reported a bicultural identity, which is a high level of identification with both Native American and White culture. The lowest levels of social competency and self-esteem were found in adolescents who reported little identification with either Native American or White culture. Those who identified with one culture, but not the other, represented the middle of the spectrum in terms of social competency and self-esteem. Identification with the Native American culture was found to be a strength, as such identification correlated with higher social competency and self-esteem than those who reported low levels of Native American culture. The correlation between identification with whiteness and high scores for social competency and self-esteem was more attenuated, as those who solely identified as White had only slightly higher scores than those who reported low levels of Native American culture.

In a separate study that corroborated the benefits of a bicultural identity, LaFromboise, Albright, and Harris (2010) found that biculturally competent Native Americans scored lower on hopelessness than those who identified solely with Native American culture. Moreover, in a separate study, LaFromboise et al. (2010) measured enculturation, that is, the acquisition of White culture, and participation in traditional Native American activities, and found both associated with prosocial outcomes and lower rates of drug and alcohol use. Participants who reported no identification with White culture and no participation in Native American ceremonies were found to have the most problems with drugs and alcohol.

Continuities and Discontinuities among Different Tribes

Most Native Americans share a legacy of long-term trauma as a result of European American colonialization, as discussed earlier, which harms Native American individuals, couples, and families. Brave Heart (2005) defined "historical trauma" as "cumulative psychological and emotional wounding across generations, including one's own life span that comes from massive group traumatic events and experiences" (p. 1). In addition to the shared history of oppression, Native American cultural identity includes a shared belief system, spirituality, language, history/stories, worldview/values, and practices (Markstrom, 2011). For many Native Americans, as with other more **collectivist cultures**, the self is often defined in terms of one's relation to family, clan, and tribe. Tribal values stress humility, bravery, a belief in the interconnectedness of everything, and the importance of living in harmony with the earth. Most Native Americans believe that nature should be respected and protected as a source of continued life (Beck, Walters, & Francisco, 1977/1996).

Nonetheless, grouping tribes all together obscures important differences (Sutton, 2000). For instance, when the Choctaw tribe underwent its long walk on the "trail of tears," it became divided into the territories that are now Oklahoma and Mississippi. Many Choctaws continue to speak Muskogean, a language similar to other Southern tribes; they keep grounds where they stomp dance and adeptly play stickball, a game similar to lacrosse that is commonly played by Southern tribes; like most other Southern tribal people, they have intermarried frequently with Whites, although at a later time in history (late 1800s) than surrounding tribes; and they have largely adopted Christian values, although some Choctaws have resisted this stridently. Navajos, a Southwestern tribe, are matrilineal like Choctaws, but differ in many ways. Although the Navajos had been dislocated by their own "long walk" during the mid-1800s (as had the Cherokees in addition to the Choctaws, as discussed earlier), they were able to return to their ancestral lands after a few years, unlike the Choctaws (Sutton, 2000). Conversely, Navajos retain more traditional ceremonies untouched by Christianity, such as puberty and initiation rites, and seasonal ceremonies. Navajo also speak a different language that is a branch of Athapaskan.

Unique colonialization experiences combined with varying levels of acculturation have resulted in different couple and family interactions among the tribes discussed earlier (Calloway, 1999). American colonists in the 19th century influenced Choctaws to become farmers, primarily to grow cotton. They were heavily pressured by evangelical Christians to convert to Christianity and restructure their society to reflect the patriarchal values inherent in evangelical Christianity. Currently, a majority of Choctaws are evangelical Christians, and have high divorce rates, with many single-parent families. Mothers generally assume the majority of child-rearing responsibilities, often with the assistance of the child's grandparents. Many Choctaws have little knowledge of their ceremonies.

The Navajo, influenced by early Spanish colonialization, became a herding society. Although Navajos were Christianized, they had considerably less interaction with Whites, and thus maintained many of their traditions. Today, despite distinct roles in tribal ceremonies, the level of participation of Navajo women and men is equal. Wives and mothers have great power within the home, share the responsibilities to provide for the family by working with livestock, and have the primary responsibility for child-rearing. The degree to which traditional Native American gender roles and ceremonies have been retained has contributed to a greater confidence among Navajos in their cultural identities than many other tribes.

Native American Strength and Resilience

In the face of systematic oppression and efforts to damage the fabric of tribal communities, many Native American families have provided the security, education, material needs, and cultural tutelage that their children need. These families, aided by their tribal community, have demonstrated great resilience, adaptability, and healing (Robbins, Robbins, & Stennerson, 2013). Extended families commonly come together to care for children who have lost parents; they share meals with special honor and offer care and money "giveaways" to the impoverished elderly. Generational transmission of tribal culture is best achieved by healthy families and communities, which are repositories of spiritual rites, naming ceremonies, language acquisition, and celebratory commemorations important for individuals, couples, families, and tribes. In a qualitative study,

Allen et al. (2011) investigated the impact of reintegrating spiritual practices in the lives of Alaska Natives/Native Americans of the Yupiit tribe, and found that such practices were healing to the individuals. Moreover, they served as protective factors for their families and had a positive impact on their community's stability and cohesion. Consistent with the study's findings of the powerful positive influence of traditional culture, Badhand (2002) notes that tribal languages have been retained, and in many cases revived in tribal churches and weekly community gatherings. Also, women elders have resurrected the songs accompanying sweat ceremonies and Sun Dances when it had been thought that these had been lost forever.

Native American Couples

Native American men's and women's roles in couple and family relationships are not uniform among tribes. Such differences influence present-day relationships; however, certain continuities exist (Sutton, 2000). Native American marriages were characterized as affectionate and caring by early missionaries (Newell, 2005). Common to almost all tribes was the tradition of both families exchanging gifts prior to marriage. Polygyny, although rare, was permitted in almost all tribes, but was often only engaged in by wealthy men (Sutton, 2000). In many of the matrilineal tribes, such as the Navaho, Chumash, Cherokee, and Muskogee, women controlled their own sexuality, and, upon marriage, the husband moved to the wife's clan's land, a practice known as **matrilocality** (Sutton, 2000). Among Cherokees and Choctaws, adultery was common and was punished by the women in the community with physical attacks (Sattler, 1995). Among the Cherokees, a divorce could only be initiated by the wife. For other Native Americans, divorce entailed no formality and was often accomplished when a wife cast her husband's belongings out of the family dwelling (Sattler, 1995).

Although roles and interaction expectations may have changed with colonialization, historical patterns and values continue to resonate in the present. For example, Robbins, the lead author of this chapter, worked with two couples from different areas fluent in their tribal languages, who had expressed similar views disparaging of "White peoples' ideas of love," which they and the traditionalists in their tribes considered to be sentimental and suffocating. Both couples independently argued that rather than being sentimental, love among traditional Native Americans was closer to the English concepts of respect and admiration.

One area of continuity in Native American couples and families is the degree of fluidity in tasks performed by women and men, reflective of a lack of dominance and status differentiation (Bonvillain, 1989; Perdue, 1998). Bonvillain (1989) acknowledged that substantive tasks were historically assigned by gender. For example, although everyone participated in communal hunts, in most tribes men were the hunters, providing meat for their families and tribes. Women did most of the gathering and gardening, providing fruits, nuts, and vegetables. Yet Bonvillain (1989) found that women in many tribes accompanied their fathers and husbands in hunting, and, although women had the primary role in child-rearing, especially with young children, men also tended to children's needs and also men assumed more of the caretaking for boys once they reached puberty. Moreover, men and women had equal influence in family and tribal matters, a situation that continues to exist today (Leacock, 1981). For example, Navajo gender relations are egalitarian and autonomous with economic contributions of women and men equally central to household functioning and equally valued. Leadership roles are typically shared jointly. Farmland is worked by both men and women and allocated through matrilineal clans. Husbands and wives own individual sheep, which are pooled as the household's herd. Community networks are based on family bonds. This social valuation of both genders is congruent with mutual interdependence and fluidity of roles (Sutton, 2000).

Intersectionality: Women and LGBT People

Native American Women

Traditional Native American women tend to associate motherhood with status and power in their communities and thus have not been receptive to feminist positions viewing motherhood as the source of women's subjugation (Grande, 2004). In addition, strengths of Native American couple relationships, as discussed earlier, may counteract a sense of oppression experienced by women. Leacock (1981) expressed the unique gender structure common among Native Americans:

Indian women were not categorized as dependents who fell somewhere between men and children in the social hierarchy. Women, men and children were recognized as autonomous beings which held the extended family or clan together within a system of mutual obligation and respect. (p. 202)

Some might argue that women's high status might be attributable to the financial contribution childbearing made to Native American economies; however, it is also undeniably a function of the deep reverence for life and nature, which is intrinsic to Native American culture. In stories and rituals, women's productivity was metaphorically identified with food, nurturing, and life itself (Mann, 2005).

Since the advent of European colonialization efforts to reduce the status and power of Native Americans, White missionaries, policy makers, reformers, and teachers have attempted to restructure Native American extended families into patriarchal nuclear units, and align their gender roles with those of the White culture (Shoemaker, 2014). This assimilation process was overcome, to some extent, by the traditional Native American value for women. By the 1970s, women began to assume more of their lost power in tribal councils (Shoemaker, 2014). Shoemaker hypothesized that the prominence of Native American women in tribal political affairs can be explained as analogous to their power in everyday **extended family** life (Shoemaker, 2014). One highly visible and powerful Native American woman, Wilma Mankiller, held the highest office in the Cherokee Nation, Principal Chief, in the late 20th century.

Native American LGBT and Gender-Variant People

Native American cultures also counteract the stigma experienced by the LGBT (lesbian, gay, bisexual, and transgender) and gender-variant population (Jetzkowitz & Brunzel, 2005). Prevalent among many tribes is the view that as many as seven genders exist, some of which are not aligned with sex. In addition, those who naturally engage in roles tradition-ally ascribed to the opposite gender are referred to as **Two-Spirits**, and instances of men taking Two-Spirits as wives is not uncommon among Native American tribes. Many tribes have been accepting when chil-dren demonstrated preferences for behavior or attire associated with the opposite gender. For example, Pueblos, Cherokees, Tarahumara, Plains, Zuni, and California tribal people supported male children who exhibited interests in cooking and gathering vegetables, and female children who liked hunting and other aggressive activities (Jetzkowitz & Brunzel, 2005). Tribal women who are successful in roles reserved for males in much of mainstream society are referred to as "brave hearted women" by some, a sign of respect and another example of the acceptability of persons with gender-variant behavior.

Current Challenges of Native American Couples

The loss of the strength of their cultural values against dominance and status differentiation has resulted in many challenges to Native Ameri-can couples. In a survey administered to 67 Native American behav-ioral health center therapists, findings demonstrated that couples most frequently presented with issues involving (a) drug and alcohol misuse, (b) affective communication, (c) family history of stress, (d) aggressive-ness, (e) difficulties with problem solving, and (f) power struggles (Hong & Robbins, 2016).

Current data suggest that both Native American men and women experience more interpersonal violence than any other ethnic group (Greenfield & Smith, 1999). In a study with 42 Native American men and 52 Native American women, Robbins and Stoltenberg (2006) adminis-tered the Revised Conflict Tactics Scale (Straus, Hamby, Boney-McCoy, &

Sugarman, 1996) and piloted a Historical Trauma Scale to investigate the role of drug and alcohol use in Native American partner relations. They found that Native American male participants were more likely to engage in interpersonal physical violence, while Native American female participants engaged in more interpersonal psychological violence, relative to each other. Males who had witnessed psychological aggression between their parents were significantly more likely to engage in psychological aggression with their partners. Alcohol misuse, much higher for Native Americans than the national norm, was positively correlated with both forms of aggression exhibited by men and women (Chester, Robin, Koss, Lopez, & Goldman, 1994). Also, the study found that men who reported experiencing **historic trauma** were more likely to engage in both verbal and physical forms of aggression (Robbins & Stoltenberg, 2006), confirming our foregoing assertion that oppression has negatively impacted Native American relationships. Notably, this correlation was not present with women.

A study by Robbins, Stoltenberg, Robbins, and Ross (2002) also suggested that although Native American couples may benefit from treatment, there are issues with assessing their relationships using conventional measures. Robbins et al. (2002) surveyed 162 volunteer Cherokee participants utilizing the Marital Satisfaction Inventory–Revised. In addition to finding elevated levels of global relationship distress and relationship aggression as compared with other groups, scores related to response consistency suggested that words may have different connotations and cultural meanings for Cherokees, thus calling into question the validity of the instrument for this population. Moreover, investigators interpreted high scores on the inventory's conventionalization scale as suggesting that Cherokees may distrust researchers with their personal information.

Family

The erosion of traditional tribal structures and the impact of historical and current oppression, as discussed before, have undermined many Native American families. Tribal communities offered intact nurturing structures with extended family members protecting, supporting, and teaching Native American children traditional values. Today many Native American children are dispersed in communities where such caring persons no longer surround them. An inability to replicate traditional support structures may have significant negative consequences for many Native Americans: findings have indicated that 48 percent of Native American mothers of children enrolled in Early Head Start programs nationwide exhibit clinical symptoms of depression (Administration for Children and Families, 2010).

Depression in parents and other caregivers can negatively influence practices associated with children's healthy development, thus putting children at greater risk for depression, anxiety, behavioral problems, poorer physical health, accidents, and maltreatment (National Research Council and Institute of Medicine, 2009). Poverty is also highly correlated with a mother's depression, and the poverty rate for Native Americans is more than three times that of Euro-Americans: 25 percent versus less than 8 percent (U.S. Census Bureau, 2001).

The quality of the parent–child relationship has been demonstrated to impact the child's mental health in significant ways. Mmari, Blum, and Teufel-Shone (2010) found that stronger parent–child attachments were protective factors against Native American adolescent delinquent behaviors. Gray, Shafer, Limb, and Busby (2013) reported that Native American family-of-origin relationship qualities as perceived by the child comprised (a) the parent's marital relationship and (b) the mother–child relationship as measured by time engaged in affective communication, which influenced the child's later relationship quality (Walters, Evans-Campbell, Simoni, Ronquillo, & Bhuyan, 2006). Poor parent–child relationships resulting from coercive parenting and caretaker rejection have been predictors of Native American suicidality (Walls, Chapple, & Johnson, 2007).

Research suggests the importance of open communication in Native American families. Healthy families are more likely to talk about the effects of past problems and traumas. Walters et al. (2006) found that many Native American children avoided discussing their problems with their parents, reporting that they did not want to present additional burdens to already overwhelmed families. Moreover, these Native American children reported greater disconnection from parents who coped with harsh pasts by silencing them.

In regard to family treatment, a survey with Indian Behavioral Health providers (Hong, Robbins, & McWhirter, 2015) revealed that Native American families are counseled most frequently for (a) lack of parental authority, (b) child neglect, (c) poor boundary problems, and (d) avoidance of feelings. The findings suggest that counselors might support Native American families by (a) giving them the opportunity to express their feelings openly in individual therapy; (b) helping them to explore ways of creating new support systems in areas where they are isolated from other family members and/or other Native Americans, such as in urban areas; (c) empowering adults with culturally appropriate parenting skills; and (d) providing spaces for Native American families to meet and communicate openly with each other.

Extended Family and Grandparents

Grandparents as well as other extended family members, such as aunts and uncles, have played a vital role in raising children within Native American communities. Large families have been the norm with grandparents often being viewed as at the top of the familial hierarchy. Grandparents have assisted parents in passing on knowledge of tribal customs, culture, and language to children (Robbins et al., 2005), often providing them with "Indian names" reflecting their heritage. Today, many children are being raised primarily by grandparents. In fact, Native American grandmothers report a larger share of caregiving responsibility than other racial groups (Cross & Day, 2008). Reasons for such high rates of grandparent custodial roles include parental unemployment, substance abuse, incarceration, and death (Cross & Day, 2008; Hayslip & Kaminski, 2005). Statistics reveal that approximately 48,000 Native American grandparents have the sole responsibility for raising children under the age of 18 (U.S. Census Bureau, 2006–2008). This figure is especially significant in view of the increased challenges faced by Native Americans, which include higher poverty rates, more physical problems, less reliable transportation, and more crowded living situations than other populations (Mutchler, Baker, & Lee, 2007; U.S. Government Accountability Office, 2005).

Many Native American grandparents assume a custodial role without formal adoption proceedings. This absence of a legally sanctioned arrangement may result in grandparents being unable to obtain medical care for their grandchildren, receive financial support on their behalf, or participate in the child's education. Without proper forms on file with school authorities, children's schooling may be in jeopardy (Day & Cross, 2004). Day and Cross (2004) argued that many Native American grandparents may be reluctant to obtain legal custodial status because (a) they hope the biological parents will eventually be able to care for the children, and (b) they have historically based fears that once the legal system becomes involved, the children will be removed from the home and the family will be broken up.

Grandparents raising their grandchildren often experience stress due to difficult relationships with their grandchildren's parents and embarrassment when their family situation is known within the community (Smith & Palmieri, 2007). When raising grandchildren with behavioral and emotional problems, the grandparents are at greater risk for depression, insomnia, hypertension, diabetes (Cross & Day, 2008), and other physical health issues (Hayslip & Kaminski, 2005).

Despite such challenges to grandparents, this arrangement may be beneficial to children, as the traditional beliefs and practices that are typically passed down by grandparents are associated with resilience against risk factors such as violence (Greenfield & Smith, 1999), suicide (Olson & Wahab, 2006), and substance abuse (SAMHSA, 2012). When raised by their grandparents, children are more likely to maintain strong tribal/ cultural identities; remain in contact with their extended family members, including their parents; and are less likely to suffer the trauma that a foster placement might entail. In addition, the benefits to Native American custodial grandparents may also be significant as they may derive satisfaction from direct caregiving (Cross, 2005), and they know that their grandchildren's needs are being met.

Treatment Theory and Interventions: Native American Place-Focused Therapy

A strong sense of place permeates Native American cultural, social, and civic lives across the country (Cajete, 1994, 2000; Doering & Veletsianos, 2008; Semken, 2005). Native Americans have deep connections to their traditional homelands, the source of their cultural traditions and knowledge (Cajete, 1994, 2000). Fogelson (1998) argued that Native American identity is connected to the land as a site of origination in their narratives of ethno-genesis. Native Americans interpret their histories, culture, and natural events according to a belief that they are a part of nature and connected to their place of tribal origin (Cajete, 2000; Semken, 2005). Traditional Native Americans believe in the responsibility to protect and show appreciation for the earth. Thus, many Native Americans are part of the "Idle No More" movement working to protect the land and water from further oil exploration. Locales also often are used as a method by which Native Americans can distinguish authenticity. For example, Robbins's observation is that given that ceremonial grounds are profound elements in the lives of many Native Americans, it is common in Oklahoma to ask people claiming a shared Native American heritage about the location of their ceremonial grounds. If this information is unknown, it is often revelatory that the person claiming a Native American identity does not live in accordance with its culture and values.

Scholars' assertions that a focus on the land is key to understanding and engaging Native Americans (Cejete, 2000; Pewewardy, 2002) have resulted in our development of a unique approach, **Native American Place-Focused Therapy** (NAPFT), to treat couples and families from this population. In addition, NAPFT deals with the displacement issues that many Native Americans experience having been separated from their original home places, and incorporates their beliefs about healing and spirituality. For Native Americans, a specific physical landscape may have been inextricably linked to their tribe's identity for many centuries, and traditional Native Americans believe that spiritual awareness necessitates the convergence of nature and themselves. Moreover, the traditional Native American perspective on healing is that it cannot be accomplished without the reintegration of one's self into one's ancestral land. For example, Silko (1977) related that traditional Native Americans have been taught that a life of balance and centeredness requires one's interior psychological landscape to be in tune with one's physical geography.

Many Native American children are told stories of their tribal place of origin, and often, when they return as adults, they bring herbs to be used in purification ceremonies. Thus, to engage in meaningful conversations with traditional Native Americans, it is vital that therapists make space to talk about places that resonate for these clients. For example, therapists can elicit ways for couples and family members to connect through sharing and addressing the values and needs discussed earlier to aid in their healing.

Core features of NAPFT include the use of **storying,** symbols, and metaphors (Robbins & Harrist, 2004). While such features are common in other treatment approaches, such as Narrative Therapy (Nichols & Schwartz, 2006), NAPFT differs in how these concepts are tailored to Native Americans. Storytelling is a way for many Native Americans to organize and understand the meaning of individual and tribal experiences as well as the meaning of the natural world, and they have long used symbols and metaphors in traditional healing. In a family therapy session, the NAPFT approach may begin with one person telling a story about an incident or to explain an idea. Rather than using that story as the springboard for discussion, the therapist can ask another family member to relate a relevant story. After having listened to the two stories, each is asked to graft on relevant details, feelings, and ideas engendered by the other person's story, consistent with Native American traditions. Greater empathy for the other family member's feelings, as well as an expansion of one's own perspective, may occur. Similarly, therapists may use metaphors in helping clients to describe their problems. In this manner, indefinite feelings are transformed into something more concrete and manageable, and clients are enabled to detach from a destructive mode of being and/or no longer feeling identified with a problem (Nichols & Schwartz, 2006; White, 1991).

NAPFT uses **decolonizing conversations,** which are conversations to help clients to see the linkage between their problems and their tribal history of colonization. These conversations are similar to narrative family therapy approaches that seek to **deconstruct** destructive cultural discourses (Nichols & Schwartz, 2006). Treatment can help clients connect their family disruptions, such as psychological abuse, domestic violence, and substance abuse, to their own dislocation, tribal histories, and oppressive social conditions. Such decolonizing conversations may help Native American clients to (a) become freer to think and act from the liberated verdicts of their own hearts and minds, (b) reconnect with tribal wisdom and places, and (c) become engaged in creating social conditions that promote equality and freedom. For example, as clients attain greater awareness of their interrelatedness to earth and experience empowerment and spiritual growth through NAPFT's decolonizing conversations, they may become involved in enhancing environmental quality.

In the authors' clinical experience, the degree of English language fluency is one indicator of Native American traditionalism. Because English is the second language for some, words may be used in non-mainstream contexts and may carry meanings reflective of the clients' tribal/cultural contexts and values. An advantage of the NAPFT approach is that it acknowledges Native American clients' use of language and thus may help to enable therapists to (a) cultivate the strengths of Native Americans' values and (b) offer referrals to underdeveloped local resources such as informal helpers, namely, tribal elders, tribal mother societies, and ceremonial participants and leaders. Interaction with such resources can encourage clients to utilize tribally appropriate ways to resist the influence of their problems, such as involving the land as a method of healing. For a therapist to fail to consider strengths, healing interventions, and traditional systems within tribal communities is to risk participation in ongoing colonialization. In the following case study, illustrations will include examples of each of the above traditional Native American perspectives and techniques.

CASE STUDY[1]

A married Native American couple, 27-year-old Topaz and 31-year-old Perry, presented for couples therapy, citing the wife's difficulty in adjusting to the couple's state of residence, Oklahoma, and "White society." Topaz indicated on the intake form that she was "lonely for her family, [but] not depressed." The wife, a Navajo from the Southwest, was in graduate school, and the husband, who identified as "one-quarter Choctaw," grew up in Oklahoma and was currently a business executive in Oklahoma City.

Topaz's appearance suggested her heritage, with dark brown skin and coal black long hair. She was conservatively attired in a below-the-knee dress and was visibly pregnant. Her husband Perry looked White, with light skin and brown eyes, and was casually dressed in blue jeans and a T-shirt, which had a picture of Indians accompanied by the phrase "Homeland Security." They said they wished to interview Robbins, the therapist, to see if he was qualified to help them. Having been informed that their therapist was Choctaw, the wife first needed to confirm that the therapist was Native American. They were not interested in whether the therapist identified himself as "Indian," but whether the therapist was tribally/culturally connected, as concerns about a therapist's ability to connect with clients culturally are common in couple therapy. They asked about the therapist's family, ritual grounds, if the therapist spoke his tribal language, how involved the therapist was in his tribe's ceremonies, and if the therapist had worked extensively with Native American clients. When the husband started speaking to the therapist in

Choctaw, the therapist acknowledged his lack of fluency but he conveyed an identification with and understanding of the culture.

The husband said, "I grew up with my grandparents speaking our language at home and in church." The therapist replied, "It is important that I have an understanding of Indian ways, isn't it?" They nodded. The wife, especially concerned that the therapist was familiar with Native American culture, asked whether he had "been around Indians much of his life." The therapist assured her that he had, but added, "I'm sure I could learn a lot from both of you." The wife remained unconvinced that the therapist had the knowledge to treat the couple. "You must have some understanding of my culture in order to help us. I don't want to spend half our sessions teaching you," she stated. During the session, the therapist gained the couple's confidence that he was culturally competent and, with some slight misgivings, decided to work with him.

During the second session, the couple collaborated with the therapist on a plan for their therapy. Topaz commented that the very process of explaining their problems and setting forth concrete goals "seemed very White," reminded her of "White schooling," and was "too organized." When Perry commented that "too organized" described her well, she said that "thinking and acting White has taken the fun out of my life." When the therapist asked her about what way of approaching therapy would be best for her, she agreed that it was "right to start therapy with intention," but she hoped to "break out of the rigidness" later. Consistent with the NAPFT approach, the goals collaboratively reached were (a) to make explicit and reconsider some of the "White" values in their lives, (b) to reconnect to their home places, and (c) to feel more emotionally connected to each other without sacrificing their uniqueness.

Perry had been raised by his grandparents due to his parents' heavy drug involvement, his father's frequent incarceration, and his mother's abandonment. His father, who was half-Choctaw and half-White, was killed in prison. When Perry was six, he saw his mother for the last time when she left him with his paternal grandparents. She made a trip back to their hometown before her death, when Perry was 14, but made no effort to see her son. Perry suggested that distrust issues he had with women in past relationships might have been attributed to the disconnection with his mother, but had not affected his feelings toward Topaz. His grandparents, who had been deceased for five years, taught him the Choctaw language and other traditional knowledge, and attended a Choctaw Baptist church. He acknowledged his great appreciation for them.

Topaz reported that she had enjoyed her early home life until she was sent to live in an Indian boarding school in the fourth grade. Topaz's mother had also attended boarding school. Topaz expressed that her mother had never learned how to raise children as an explanation for why her mother sent Topaz and her two siblings away to be educated at such young ages. Topaz loved her father deeply, saying he had "the most brilliant and strange sense of humor," although she also stated that her father drank constantly and was not supportive of the family. Despite forming close relationships with schoolmates, she hated boarding school life for its "regimentation and lifelessness," blamed it for keeping her separated from her parents, and yearned for the holidays when she was able to return home to Navajo ceremonies, her parents, and the land-scape. She complained about the "Protestant work ethic" that had been instilled in the boarding school, leading to her working long hours while simultaneously attending college. She had many friends from her own tribe at her undergraduate school, a hundred miles from home.

When she met Perry at a Native American conference, he was working with Native American people in a nearby town and intended on return-ing to Oklahoma. They fell in love and had a simple Navajo marriage cer-emony in the mountains. Perry's father wore a traditional Choctaw shirt to the ceremony, which pleased Topaz. Once married, the couple moved to Oklahoma and she worked in an Indian services organization while attending graduate school in human relations. Although Perry's salary at the large business firm where he was currently employed was more than enough to support them, she continued to work, as she would otherwise "feel lazy." She became pregnant soon after establishing their home in Oklahoma.

Topaz felt isolated. She missed her homeland and family and felt an emptiness as she was no longer able to participate in her tribe's spiritual rituals on a regular basis. Her graduate program added to her isolation: "No Native Americans, only a few claiming ancestors. No real cultural connections." Although coworkers at her part-time job in a Native Ameri-can organization shared her heritage, they had "abandoned their tradi-tional ways for a narrow-minded Christianity." When she suggested to them that they begin a workshop she was planning with a traditional cere-mony, she was "shot down" by colleagues who said it would upset Chris-tians. She said at this moment she began to fear that her baby might be "carried away by White ways in Oklahoma." Both of them stated similar concerns throughout therapy. As Topaz expressed it, "White ways were all pervasive." Both indicated that they felt that their spiritual healing was dependent on Native American medicine.

Treatment involved decolonizing conversations starting with what Topaz called her "internalized Protestant work ethic." When the therapist asked her for a metaphor to describe this, she said it looked like a "moun-tain lion pacing back and forth in a cage," unhappy, anxious, and "want-ing to do something, but never being able to." The cage kept her trapped in a world where she could not move freely or relax. She said that because she was so stressed, she sometimes growled at Perry for no reason.

Over the course of several sessions, the therapist used the metaphor to explore Topaz's sense of being trapped by asking questions such as,

"How much time did you stay in the cage this week?" "Who did you see through the bars and how did you feel about them?" and "How did you get in the cage to begin with?" Then the therapist asked her how she might get out of the cage, and what she would do in the outside world. She offered several alternatives, such as attacking the jailer, whom she identified as "the entire white system that dominates everything." But then she said such an approach wouldn't work, since escape would still not free her from a White world. Then, Perry interjected that he might have a key to open the cage—he could accompany her back to the Navajo reservation for a two-week stay. He said that being there might enable him to communicate with her with greater understanding. The therapist asked her if her husband might open the cage with his key, and if it would be all right if he spoke with her more about his idea. The ensuing conversation was emotional and connecting and the first time a cathartic release occurred during a session. After the emotion subsided, the therapist asked them what that moment meant to them. They both said it produced greater trust in each other. The trip was scheduled to occur when Perry had accrued sufficient vacation time, three months later.

Perry initially stated that he also had issues he wanted to work on, but during sessions he deferred to Topaz. However, one incident and its subsequent ramifications were so distressing that Topaz insisted it needed to be discussed in session. Perry related that Topaz's crying had awakened him one night. She had dreamed of running toward the rising morning sun, as she had done many times on her Navajo reservation, and this dream brought out her deep sadness at being away from her homeland. Initially, Perry had snuggled her and offered comforting words, but, when "the sun came up" he became distant. Perry said that since that day, he had "been inside" himself, apart from Topaz. Topaz said that this distancing was uncharacteristic of him, and she had tried to give him space. During the session, Perry commented that he worried sometimes that she might leave him. The therapist asked him if he had ever felt abandoned before. He stated, "Probably." When the therapist asked how he had handled his feelings then, he stated that he dealt with the deep pain he felt when his mother left him by walking alone in the woods behind his house. He explained that he and his grandparents had never talked about this.

The therapist asked him to relate a story about a time when he was young that was associated with his mother's leaving. Without hesitation, he related an incident that occurred when he was in first grade. He walked deep into the woods after school and became lost. He ran around frantically for an hour or two, terrified and afraid. He eventually sat down and sobbed for his "lost" mother to find and save him. Although she never came, he saw two deer and went in the direction they were going, which led him back to his house. This was the first time he told anyone about the incident. When the therapist asked him how he felt as he told the story, he said, "Sad." Then the therapist asked if the plans to go back to the Navajo reservation might have anything to do with his recent experiences. He looked at Topaz and said, "I never want to lose you. I love you with all my heart." She quietly embraced him, and stated that as long as they were emotionally connected, the spirits would always bring them back to their home.

Treatment focused on connecting the couple by helping them see their shared/similar cultural and personal losses and needs. For example, place-focused discussions seemed to help Perry to clarify his own needs to connect with his homeland, and help him to understand Topaz's profound connection with her homeland as well. Perry had spoken frequently about a hill that his grandparents had told him about when he was young, Nynih-vayia. Like other Choctaws in Oklahoma, he believed it was important for him to make that pilgrimage. The therapist discussed with them the value of visiting their tribes' spiritually and historically significant places together. Topaz mentioned her desire to climb a mountain where there were "artifacts that were so sacred they could not even be touched" when they visited her home reservation, as well as wanting to go with Perry to his "special place," Nynih-vayia.

After the visit to Topaz's homeland, Topaz briefly talked about how happy she was to see Perry interacting with her extended family and helping to feed the sheep. He said that he had never seen anything as beautiful as the mountain she "revealed" to him. Much of the session was spent discussing Perry's use of the word "revealed." He explained that the beauty of the mountain was breathtaking even without Topaz's presence, but its meaning was magnified by her stories about her visits with her sisters when she was a child; it also had significance in tribal history, thus he felt connected to her and her people. While there, they sat on a rock and did not speak for 30 minutes to an hour, awestruck by a sight "beyond words." When asked how the experience connected them, Topaz stressed its spiritual aspect. When they left the mountain, she said that she knew her connection to Perry was a spiritual transcendence that overcame tribal differences.

During that session, Topaz stated that they both wanted to honor and appreciate Navajo and Choctaw tribal places and ways and the need to visit Nynih-vayia before she was too far along in her pregnancy. The next three-day weekend they took a trip to Nynih-vayia, described by Perry as the place from which Choctaws were born and which offers up its power to revitalize Choctaws' lives. After they returned, Perry related how he crawled alone up to the dark deep hole in the hill. Overwhelmed with emotion, he curled up in a fetal position and sobbed for a quarter of an hour. He said that he felt totally loved by his mother. Then he walked back down to Topaz, who was waiting for him with a loving embrace. The therapist delved into the emotional aspects of this experience, asking him how it felt when he lay down in the hole, why it was important to go to the hole alone, how the experience related to his feelings of abandonment, and what Topaz's support and embrace meant to him. In exploring how the experience was related to his mother's abandoning him, he said it had helped him to feel accepted and allowed him to love Topaz more deeply.

For the first time in therapy, Perry did not deflect the focus from himself by either changing the subject or redirecting the conversation to Topaz's concerns. He expressed himself freely and explained that both he and Topaz intuitively knew that in order to deal with his feelings associated with his mother's abandonment, he needed to go up the hill alone. He said that he believed that while he was on the hill, mother earth had filled the emptiness he felt for the loss of his mother. When he saw Topaz waiting for him, he viewed her differently. They both said that they felt more "mature" now, having visited "their places," as their trust for themselves as individuals and in each other was greater and thus they felt more prepared to work on problems together.

About a month before Topaz was due to give birth, she was notified by her doctor that there might be some problems with the baby. There was a four-day wait for the results after X-rays were taken. Topaz and Perry were extremely anxious and worried, venting their feelings and leaning heavily upon each other in the session. Topaz said she had never needed to be with her people more than at that moment; however, she was aware that there was a danger that the long trip back to her reservation might put their baby at further risk. Topaz said she needed a ceremony to center herself. When the therapist inquired as to whether there was another place where they might go to meet these needs, Perry suggested going to an old Choctaw church only two hours away to meet with and pray with Choctaw elders. When asked by the therapist, Perry explained the significance of that place for him. Careful to acknowledge tribal and personal differences in beliefs, the therapist turned to Topaz and asked her what it would be like for her to go to such a different "ceremonial place." Although she stressed her continued lack of confidence in Christian healing, she agreed to go to the Choctaw elders with Perry as a way to honor the baby's Choctaw heritage.

In the next session, Topaz stated that their visit to the Choctaw church had been one of the most healing experiences of her life because of the spirituality and culture of the ceremony, which she viewed as separate from theology. She said she was put off at first because there were no women to greet them, only five old Choctaw men. When asked why that was disturbing, she explained that the Navajo custom, given the situation, would have included women. Nonetheless, she tried to approach it without judgment. She sat in the front pew with Perry, with the elders sitting in folding chairs in front of them. The men initially greeted them in English, but never spoke anything other than Choctaw thereafter. They sang Choctaw songs in low guttural voices with a prayer between each song. At the end, they spoke in Choctaw to Perry, shook both their hands, and left.

The therapist asked Topaz to listen to Perry's account of the experience. He said he could understand only portions of what they said and sang, but heard the word "love" throughout. He said he was proud of his culture as the ritual proceeded. He said he had forgotten how low the octave was when male elders sang Choctaw songs and this had put him in an "almost trancelike state." He also affirmed Topaz's initial reaction by disclosing that he would have preferred women to have been involved in the healing ceremony as well.

When Topaz was asked whether Perry's story had impacted her vision of her experience, she said that she too felt she was in a trance during the singing of the songs and elaborated that she liked the way the old men moved and demonstrated compassion, which transcended any specific religious context. The songs and language, however unfamiliar, appeared "somehow related to old Navajo spiritual ways." She said she felt at peace about what might happen to her baby. When the therapist asked her to explain what aspects of the ceremony gave her the positive feelings she described, considering how different this was from where she would normally have sought healing, she acknowledged its contemplative nature. While there, she reflected that many Choctaws had probably translated their spiritual experiences into Christian frameworks and places, but had "kept the spirit of their ways as much as they could." She affirmed her satisfaction: She got what she needed from the experience.

A month later, Perry and Topaz came into the counseling room accompanied by a multitude of Topaz's family members: her mother, her sister, her brother and his wife, a 10-year-old boy . . . and a baby girl in Topaz's arms. The 10-year-old boy was laughing, and his mother had him explain to the therapist that he "had to take an icy bath because the baby came. It is the way for the oldest boy." Everyone laughed. Topaz's brother explained how their whole community pitched in to take care of their sheep so they could visit Oklahoma for a week to see the baby. Each family member participated in the counseling session, expressing their wishes for this new life. Topaz's mother brought up how important it was for the baby to grow up knowledgeable about her Navajo homeland and culture, and requested that as soon as the child was six, she spend an annual visit with Topaz's family for that purpose. She also had several children's books containing Navajo stories and history that she wanted read to the baby. Perry agreed and added that he would teach the baby the Choctaw language. He then brought up another responsibility that he undertook when becoming a father: he vowed that he would never drink alcohol or use drugs. When the therapist asked Topaz what she wanted for her child, she said she wanted everything the others had mentioned, and for her child to be herself.

The therapist sensitively asked the family how they might support the child in coping effectively and possibly even appreciate living in larger American society, careful that this not be constructed as suggesting assimilation. Topaz's brother retorted that that was exactly what Native Americans attempt to do every day. There was a long pause and then Topaz said she had to face this issue herself. She had concluded that Native Americans reap many privileges living in the United States, and gave the example of advanced medical services. She said that she wanted her child to take advantage of the financial and employment opportunities offered to her as a citizen of both the United States and the Navajo Nation. Her brother expressed his view that attempts to become part of the mainstream always exact a cost for Native Americans. When the grandmother was asked for her opinion, she stated that the Navajo traditions were too wise to ignore, but interacting with other cultures was inevitable in today's world and might offer great possibilities for the child.

With that session, Topaz and Perry decided to end therapy, stating that they felt "healed" and that they had reached their goals in treatment. They found ways to live cross-tribally, in connection with their homelands, relatives, and themselves. Even as they were successful in the White world, they were committed to stay connected to their tribal ways, rituals, and places. All the family members shook one of the therapist's hands on their way out.

CONCLUSIONS

Therapists who work with Native American clients must consider the ongoing impact of colonialization and understand how historical losses, including displacement, relate to the problems Native American clients' present today. In its absence, profound healing is not possible. The case example demonstrated how historical losses have present ramifications for many Native Americans, such as dislocation, boarding schools, and the loss of parents to oppression-related societal ills, such as drug and alcohol misuse and imprisonment. Therapists also should be trained in (a) cultural sensitivity with Native American clients, (b) understanding their needs, (c) communicating respect and rapport building, and (d) the healing values, such as a love of the land, that have been a part of tribal traditions for thousands of years. They also should be well informed about the tribal community they will be working with, as well as available tribal and state resources. In addition, because members of different tribes are intermarrying and may be operating at varying acculturation levels, therapists must strive to be knowledgeable and flexible to respond to intragroup differences.

Tribal mental health facilities that fail to include traditional healing approaches are contributing to ongoing colonialization. It is unethical for anyone working with Native American clients to offer only Western approaches, neglecting tribal values, customs, and ways of healing, or neglecting the exploration of the assaults of racism and microaggressions Native Americans experience on a daily basis. Interventions must necessarily build on Native American knowledge about place, traditional parenting beliefs, decolonization strategies, and personal and tribal identity issues.

Garrett and Pichette (2000) observed that bicultural competence is a critical factor of resilience determining a person's ability to negotiate and manage the self in his/her own cultural context as well as in the broader society. Thus, interventions with Native Americans that only address cultural content may also be deficient. Native American clients, just as clients of any other population group, may need to develop additional life skills for coping and managing the complexities of the broader society.

CHAPTER REVIEW

Key Points

1. Although there is great diversity among individuals belonging to the over 500 Native American tribes, they share values, such as love of homeland and the earth, bravery, and the interconnectedness of everything.
2. Boarding schools and other forced assimilation experiences may have resulted in Native Americans having few couple and parenting role models. Research suggests that Native American families who talk openly about their problems and traumas are healthier.
3. Extended family and grandparent support can facilitate more positive functioning in Native American nuclear families, especially in regard to the passing on of traditions.

Key Terms

blood quantum, collectivist culture, Dawes Roll, decolonizing conversations, deconstruct, extended family, historic trauma, matrilocality, Native American Place-Focused Therapy, storying, Two-Spirits

Myths and Realities

- It is a myth that all Native American tribes have identical values, beliefs, and behaviors. In reality, persons who belong to different tribes speak different tribal languages, engage in different tribal ceremonies, and adhere to different beliefs and values regarding gender, power relations, religion, and many other topics.
- It is a myth that persons from different tribes vary so greatly that no generalizations can be made about their beliefs, values, and behaviors. In reality, most Native American tribes share similar values for the land, more egalitarian and varied experiences of gender, and histories of dislocation.

- Many people believe that the most utilized psychological approaches are applicable to all racial and ethnic groups; however, many of the basic epistemological assumptions that undergird Western psychological theoretical perspectives often may not be shared by Native Americans. For instance, telling stories about one's condition may be more valued than Western methods of identifying and solving problems.
- Some people think of the nuclear family as the primary group unit, whereas many Native Americans may think more in terms of the extended family and tribe as their primary group unit.

Tools and Tips

Knowledge

Jim, R. L. (1996). *Encyclopedia of North American Indians: Native American history, culture, and life from Paleo-Indians to the present.* Boston, MA: Houghton Mifflin.
Vogel, V. J. (1972). *This country was ours: A documentary history of the American Indian.* New York, NY: Harper and Row.
White, M. (2007). *Maps of narrative practice.* New York, NY: W.W. Norton.

Dynamic Sizing

Within-group differences among Native Americans are vast. Many are assimilated into mainstream American culture. On the other hand, traditionalists speak their tribal language most of the time and live their lives in accordance with their tribe's ceremonial customs on a day-to-day basis. Therapists must determine the assimilation level of their clients in various spheres of life in order to be effective. Every Native American is different.

There are general differences between tribes. Some are more matriarchal and others more patriarchal. Some tribes teach that traditional stories should be told only during winter; for others, season is not a concern. Therapists must educate themselves about such matters.

Skills

The Native American Place-Focused Approach, which emphasizes psychological connections with the place, is congruent with many Native Americans' values and may address distressors related to dislocation and alienation. It involves storying and questioning that utilizes deconstruction techniques that may facilitate liberation from neocolonial influences.

Awareness

Therapists must overcome any biases related to seeing a focus on the land as unimportant. For many Native American clients, becoming aware of one's inner life's intersection with one's own and one's tribal geographical place expands one's awareness of one's self. Such an expanded awareness bursts the mundane shell of self-absorption and connects one to the natural environment, the past, present, and future, and to others.

NOTE

1. Identifying information has been disguised to protect client confidentiality.

REFERENCES

Administration for Children and Families. (2010). *Head Start Impact Study* (Final report). Washington, DC: U.S. Department of Health and Human Services.

Allen, J., Mohatt, G. V., Rasmus, S. M., Two Dogs, R., Ford T., Two Dogs, E., & Moves Camp, R. (2011). Cultural interventions for American Indian and Alaska Native youth: The Elluam Tungiinun and Nagi Kicopi programs. In M. C. Sarche (Ed.), *American Indian and Alaska Native children and mental health*. Santa Barbara, CA: Praeger.

Badhand, H. P. (2002). *Native American healing*. Taos, NM: Dog Soldier Press.

Beals, J., Manson, S. M., Whitesell, N. R., Spicer, P., Novins, D. K., & Mitchell, C. M. (2005). Prevalence of DSM-IV disorders and attendant help-seeking in 2 American Indian reservation populations. *Archives of General Psychiatry, 62,* 99–108.

Beck, P. V., Walters, A. L., & Francisco, N. (1996). *The sacred: Ways of knowledge, sources of life*. 1977. Reprint. Tsaile, AZ: Navajo Community College Press.

Bonvillain, N. (1989). Gender relations in Native North America. *American Indian Culture and Research Journal, 13*(2), 1–28.

Brave Heart, M. Y. H. (2005). *Substance abuse, co-occurring mental health disorders, and the historical trauma response among American Indians/Alaska Natives* [Research monograph]. Washington, DC: Bureau of Indian Affairs, DASAP.

Cajete, G. (1994). *Look to the mountain: An ecology of indigenous education*. Durango, CO: Kivaki Press.

Cajete, G. (2000). Indigenous knowledge: The Pueblo metaphor of Indigenous education. In M. Battiste (Ed.), *Reclaiming indigenous voice and vision*, Vancover: University of British Colombia Press, 181–191.

Calloway, C. G. (1999). *First peoples: A documentary survey of American Indian history*. New York, NY: Dartmouth College.

Chester, B., Robin, R. W., Koss, M. P., Lopez, J., & Goldman, D. (1994). Grandmother dishonored: Violence against women by male partners in American Indian communities. *Violence and Victims, 9,* 249–258.

Child, B. J., Lomawaima, K. T., & Archuleta, M. L. (Eds.). (2010). *Away from home: American Indian boarding school experiences 1879–2000*. Phoenix, AZ: Heard Museum.

Clayton, S., Brindis, C., Hamor, J., Raiden-Wright H., & Fong, C. (2000). *Investing in adolescent health: A social imperative for California's future*. San Francisco, CA: University of California, National Adolescent Health Information Center.

Cross, S. L. (2005). *American Indian grandparents parenting their grandchildren in Michigan* [Research monograph]. Lansing: Michigan State University School of Social Work.

Cross, S. L., & Day, A. G. (2008). American Indian grandfamilies: Eight adolescent and grandparent dyads share perceptions on various aspects of the kinship care relationship. *Journal of Ethnic & Cultural Diversity in Social Work, 17,* 82–100.

Day, A., & Cross. S. (2004, Spring). Legal options for grandparents raising their grandchildren. *NASW Aging Section Connection,* 6–9.

DeVoe, J., Darling-Churchill, K., Snyder, T. (2008). *Status and trends in the education of American Indians and Alaska Natives: 2008.* Washington, DC: National Center for Education Statistics, U.S. Department of Education.

Doering, A., & Veletsianos, G. (2008). An investigation of the use of real-time, authentic geospatial data in the K-12 classroom [Special issue on Using Geospatial Data in Geographic Education]. *Journal of Geography, 106,* 217–225.

Ehle, J. (1988). *Trail of tears: The rise and fall of the Cherokee Nation.* New York, NY: Anchor Books.

Eleanor Burke Leacock. (1981). *Myths of male dominance: Collected articles on women cross-culturally.* New York, NY: Monthly Review Press.

Fogelson, R. D. (1998). Perspectives on Native American identity. In R. Thornton (Ed.), *Studying Native America: Problems and prospects* (pp. 40–59). Madison, WI: University of Wisconsin Press.

Garrett, M. T., & Pichette, E. F. (2000). Red as an apple: Native American acculturation and counseling with or without reservation. *Journal of Counseling & Development, 78,* 3–13.

Getches, David H., Wilkinson, Charles F., & Williams, Robert A. (2004). *Cases and materials on federal Indian law (American casebook series).* Eagan, MN: West Publishing. ISBN 0–314–14422–6.

Grande, S. (2004). *Red pedagogy: Native American social and political thought.* Lanham, MD: Rowman & Littlefield.

Gray, A. C., Shafer, K., Limb, G. E., & Busby, D. M. (2013). Unique influences on American Indian relationship quality: An American Indian and Caucasian comparison. *Journal of Comparative Family Studies, 44,* 589–607.

Greenfield, L. N., & Smith, S. K. (1999). *American Indians and crime.* Washington, DC: U.S. Department of Justice, Office of Justice Statistics.

Hayslip, B., & Kaminski, P. L. (2005). Grandparents raising their grandchildren: A review of the literature and suggestions for practice. *The Gerontologist, 45,* 262–269.

Hong, J. Y.& Robbins, R. R., (2016). Needs of behavioral health providers working with American Indians within Indian mental health settings. *Native Studies Review, 23,* 121–136.

Jetzkowitz, J., & Brunzel, S. (2005). Transgressing the boundaries: An experimental reconnoitre. *Graduate Journal of Social Science, 2,* 134–147.

LaFromboise, T. D., Albright, K., & Harris, A. (2010). Patterns of hopelessness among American Indian adolescents: Relationships by patterns of acculturation and residence. *Cultural Diversity and Ethnic Minority Psychology, 16,* 68–76.

Mann, C. C. (2005). *1491: New revelations of the Americas before Columbus.* New York, NY: Alfred A. Knopf.

Markstrom, C. A. (2011). Identity formation of American Indian adolescents: Local, national, and global considerations. *Journal of Research on Adolescence, 21,* 519–535.

Mmari, K. N., Blum, R. W., & Teufel-Shone, N. (2010). What increases risk and protection for delinquent behaviors among American Indian youth: Findings from three tribal communities. *Youth & Society, 41,* 382–413.

Moran, J. R., Fleming, C. M., Sommervell, P., & Manson, S. M. (1999). Measuring bicultural ethnic identity among American Indian adolescents: A factor analytic study. *Journal of Adolescent Research, 14,* 405–426.

Mutchler, J. E., Baker, L. A., & Lee, A. (2007). Grandparents responsible for grandchildren in Native-American families. *Social Science Quarterly, 88,* 990–1010.

National Research Council and Institute of Medicine. (2009). Associations between depression in parents and parenting, child health, and child psychological functioning. *Depression in Parents, Parenting, and Children: Opportunities to Improve Identification, Treatment, and Prevention.* doi: 10.17226/12565

Newell, Q. (2005). "The Indians generally love their wives and children": Native American marriage and sexual practices in missions San Francisco, Santa Clara, and San Jose. *The Catholic Historical Review, 91,* 60–82.

Nichols, M. P., and Schwartz, R. C. (2006). *Family therapy: Concepts and methods* (7th ed.). Boston: Pearson Education.

Norris, T., Vines, P. L., & Hoeffel, E. M. (2012). *The American Indian and Alaska Native population: 2010* (pp. 1–32). Washington, DC: U.S. Department of Commerce, Economics and Statistics Administration, U.S. Census Bureau.

Oetting, E. R., & Beauvais, F. (1989). Epidemiology and correlates of alcohol use among Indian adolescents living on reservations. In *Alcohol use among US ethnic minorities* (pp. 239–267). Washington, DC: National Institutes of Health, National Institute of Alcohol Abuse and Alcoholism.

Oetting, E. R., Donnermeyer, J. F., Trimble, J. E., & Beauvais, F. (1998). Primary socialization theory: Culture, ethnicity, and cultural identification. The links between culture and substance abuse. IV. *Substance Use & Misuse, 33,* 2075–2107.

Olson, L. M., & Wahab, S. (2006). American Indians and suicide: A neglected area of research. *Trauma, Violence, & Abuse, 7,* 19–33.

Perdue, T. (1998). *Cherokee women: Gender and culture change, 1700–1835.* Lincoln, NE: University of Nebraska Press.

Pewewardy, C. (2002). Learning styles of American Indian/Alaska Native students: A review of the literature and implications for practice. *Journal of American Indian Education, 41*(3), 22–56.

Phinney, J. S. (2000). Identity formation across cultures: The interaction of personal, societal, and historical change. *Human Development, 43,* 27–31.

Robbins, R., & Harrist, S. (2004). American Indian constructionalist family therapy for acculturative stress. In J. R. Ancis (Ed.), *Culturally responsive interventions: Innovative approaches to working with diverse populations* (pp. 23–47). New York, NY: Taylor & Francis Books.

Robbins, R., Robbins, S., & Stennerson, B. (2013). Native American family resilience. In D. S. Becvar (Ed.), *Handbook of family resilience* (pp. 197–213). New York, NY: Springer Press.

Robbins, R., Stoltenberg, C., Robbins, S., & Ross, M. (2002). Marital satisfaction and Cherokee language fluency. *Measurement and Evaluation in Counseling and Development, 14*, 134–146.

Robbins, R., Sherman, A., Holeman, H., Wilson, J. (2005). Roles of American Indian grandparents in times of culturial crisis. *Journal of Cultural Diversity, I*, 46-56.

Robbins, S., & Stoltenberg, C. (2006). Physical aggression: The effects of alcohol and drug use, influence of parent relationship aggression, and historical trauma in an American Indian sample (Unpublished manuscript, University of Oklahoma).

Sarche, M., & Spicer, P. (2008). Poverty and health disparities for American Indian and Alaska Native children: Current knowledge and future prospects. *Annals of the New York Academy of Sciences, 1136*, 126–136. http://doi.org/10.1196/annals.1425.017

Sattler, R. (1995). Women's status among the Muskogee and Cherokee. In L. F. Klein & L. A. Ackerman (Eds.), *Women and power in Native North America* (pp. 214–229). Norman, OK: University of Oklahoma Press.

Semken, S. (2005). Sense of place and place-based introductory geoscience teaching for American Indian and Alaska Native undergraduates. *Journal of Geoscience Education, 53*, 149–157.

Shoemaker, Nancy. (2014). *Living with whales: Documents and oral histories of native New England whaling history*. Amherst, MA: University of Massachusetts Press.

Silko, L. M. (1977). *Ceremony*. New York, NY: Viking Press.

Smith, G. C., & Palmieri, P. A. (2007). Risk of psychological difficulties among children raised by custodial grandparents. *Psychiatric Services (Washington, D.C.), 58*, 1303–1310. http://doi.org/10.1176/appi.ps.58.10.1303

Straus, M., Hamby, S., Boney-McCoy, S., & Sugarman, D. (1996). The Revised Conflict Tactics Scales (CTS2): Development and preliminary psychometric data. *Journal of Family Issues, 17*, 283–316. doi: 10.1177/019251396017003001

Substance Abuse and Mental Health Services Administration (SAMHSA). (2012). Mental Health, United States, 2010. HHS Publication No. (SMA) 12–4681. Rockville, MD: Substance Abuse and Mental Health Services Administration.

Sutton, M. (2000). *An introduction to Native North America*. Boston, MA: Allyn and Bacon.

U.S. Census Bureau. (2001). *Current Population Reports, P60–219, Poverty in the United States*. Washington, DC: U.S. Government Printing Office.

U.S. Census Bureau. (2009). *2006–2008 American Community Survey*. Retrieved from http://www.census.gov/prod/2003pubs/c2kbr-31.pdf

U.S. Census Bureau. (2009). *Income, poverty, and health insurance coverage in the United States*. Retrieved from https://www.census.gov/prod/2009pubs/p60–236.pdf

U.S. Government Accountability Office. (2005). *Indian Child Welfare Act: Existing information on implementation issues could be used to target guidance and assistance to states*. Retrieved from http://www.gao.gov/new.items.d05290.pdf

Usner, D. H. (1992). *Indians, settlers, and slaves in a frontier exchange economy: The lower Mississippi valley before 1783*. Chapel Hill: University of North Carolina Press.

Walls, M. L., Chapple, C. L., & Johnson, K. D. (2007). Strain, emotion, and suicide among American Indian youth. *Deviant Behavior, 28*, 219–246.

Walters, K. L., Evans-Campbell, T., Simoni, J. M., Ronquillo, T., & Bhuyan, R. (2006). "My spirit in my heart": Identity experiences and challenges among American Indian two-spirit women. *Journal of Lesbian Studies, 10*(1–2), 125–149.

White, M. (1991, December). Deconstruction and therapy. In *Postmodernism and deconstruction in therapy. Dulwich Centre Newsletter,* No. 3, 21–40.

Woodward, G. S. (1963). *The Cherokees.* Norman, OK: University of Oklahoma.

CHAPTER 5

White Racial Identity in Therapy with Couples and Families

Hinda Winawer

WHITE RACIAL IDENTITY IN THERAPY WITH COUPLES AND FAMILIES

In 2010, 72 percent of the U.S. population identified as White. Another 2 percent identified as White in combination with another racial category (U.S. Census Bureau, 2011). White racial identity in therapy, however, has received little attention in the mental health literature (Helms, 2014). White people cannot be unaffected by the racist structure of society, but an introduction of White racial identity into the therapeutic encounter often presents challenges, and such examination may evoke uncomfortable emotions (Helms, 1990; Tatum, 1997). The intention of this chapter is to heighten therapists' understanding of how the various factors related to White racial identity exist in terms of their importance and meaning for White couples and families.

This chapter offers clinical guidelines as to how whiteness may be integrated into an exploration of couples' and families' emotional and interpersonal struggles. It is organized into four sections: (a) the history of whiteness in the United States; (b) the intersection of whiteness with ethnic social identities generally considered White, specifically German Americans and Jewish Americans; (c) a treatment example illustrating how whiteness is addressed as an aspect of the therapeutic process with a couple in therapy; and (d) a chapter review providing key points, key terms, and a list of skills applied in therapy. Suggested relevance to other professional fields and resources for further study are included as well. Given that this chapter is limited in scope and length and that European Americans have the longest history among Whites in the United States, its emphasis is largely Eurocentric. Additional immigrant groups, such as those from Latin America (Haney-Lopez, 2013b) and the Middle East (Ferber, 2014), may be affected by controversies concerning whiteness.

Race is a significant dimension of an individual's identity (Blitz, 2006). It is therefore relevant to present and intergenerational family narratives. Granting whiteness immunity from the scrutiny received by other social identities in treatment not only reinforces the message that whiteness is so privileged and acceptable as a standard that it need not be deconstructed, but also it is complicit in perpetuating what Hardy and Laszloffy (2008) describe as "a generalized belief that espouses and supports the superiority of Whites" (p. 227). This belief is related to internalized dominance for White people. However, as Tappan points out, dominance can be understood in "the relationship between the individual and the social, cultural, historical, and institutional contexts in which the individual lives" (Tappan, 2006, p. 2122). Therefore the objective of this chapter is not to blame White people, nor to minimize the impact of whiteness in a racialized society, but mainly to understand the societal historical phenomena that contribute to the inevitability of White privilege experienced by all White people, even those who value justice. Accordingly, it is important for all therapists working with White couples and families—whether White or of color—to understand the significance of being White in the United States.

Therefore, it may be essential for White couples and families to view their struggles in the context of a racist society insofar as their relationships can be affected by unexamined expectations afforded by White privilege (McIntosh, 2008). Unfortunately, the mental health field has not been responsive to this view. In most scholarly publications, White families are presented as the norm. When race is not explicitly identified, the underlying assumption is that the subjects are White. Additionally, the omission of whiteness in the psychotherapeutic process renders the impact of racism on the inner lives and relationships of White people invisible and disregards the complexity of their identity, thereby potentially narrowing the therapist's understanding of their struggles. Moreover, most clinical literature ignores White racial identity (Helms, 2014), thus privileging and conferring normativity on whiteness.

RACE AS A SOCIAL CONSTRUCT

Race is socially constructed; it is not a biological fact (McDermott & Sampson, 2005; Haney-Lopez, 2013a). This can be most easily illustrated in the context of European immigrant groups who were not considered White upon entry to the United States, suffered discrimination in their early waves of immigration (McDermott & Samson, 2005), and were eventually considered White. For example, people from Ireland were not accepted as White in the late 19th and early 20th centuries (Roediger, 2007). A more current example of an immigrant group categorized as

White yet not considered White by the dominant culture are some people from the Middle East who may face discrimination because they are Muslim in a society that privileges Christian identity (Ferber, 2014). Therapists must be mindful that a family who enters therapy and does not appear stereotypically European may or may not identify as White.

Thus, were race simply a matter of skin color, all who could qualify as "White" by that standard would face no discrimination. However, race is a sociopolitical identity invented in the service of racism (Coates, 2015) in order to sustain domination of one segment of society over others. Additionally, such designations confer degrees of power, marginalization, oppression, and opportunity (Guinier & Torres 2002; Painter, 2010).

Ideas from Europe about Difference, Race, and Superiority

Racism in the United States has its genesis in Europe where ideas about difference and superiority had a long and varied history. Attempts to develop a **"science" of race** were evident in Europe and the U.S. Eighteenth-century Germans attempted to elevate race as a "science" (Painter, 2010) by establishing a hierarchy based on regional origins to determine the "ideal" people. Other theories emerged, such as the superiority of ancient tribal races (i.e., Teutons, Saxons), which gained prominence in the United States. Adherents were among highly regarded Americans, such as Thomas Jefferson, Ralph Waldo Emerson, and Theodore Roosevelt. Their views contributed to a racialized environment into which immigrants entered the United States in the 19th and early 20th centuries. Parallel to discourses of Germanic/Anglo Saxon superiority was the constant ongoing racist oppression of people of color. Efforts to justify color-based racism using "scientific data" to suggest an innate inferiority of people of color were presented in a bestselling book, *The Bell Curve*, written by a psychologist and a political scientist. The book promoted views of racial determinism so extreme as to propose limiting procreation by people of color (Bell, 1995). While such theories have almost no support within the scientific community, the underlying concepts have been part of the national consciousness throughout U.S. history.

Variations in Racism and the Race to Be White and American

During the late 19th and early 20th centuries, two parallel discourses about race in the United States intersected: the White/people of color binary and the relative superiority among Whites. In addition to the color-based racism and ongoing structural oppression long experienced by African Americans and Native Americans, the second race narrative emerged as a consequence of massive waves of immigration, with new immigrants deemed not meeting the standard of "whiteness" by established Whites, regardless of their skin color. The convergence of these two narratives allowed members of the dominant racial group to internalize an ethic of supremacy not only over people of color but also in relation to subordinated groups seeking to identify as White. This phenomenon is epitomized by a dialogue written by Sinclair Lewis in his 1922 novel, *Babbitt*: "We ought to get together and show the black man, yes, and the yellow man, his place. . . . These [derogatory epithets for people of Spanish, Italian, and Eastern European descent] would have to learn that this is a White man's country, and they ain't wanted here" (Lewis, 1922, as cited in Roediger, 2005).

Thus, dominant Whites' hegemony over other minorities impacted all groups considered to be people of color today (African Americans, Native Americans, Asian Americans, and Latin Americans), and it also extended to Europeans who were initially marginalized and experienced discrimination. The impact of efforts to become truly American by gaining entry into the White category, and thus obtaining the social value of whiteness, is part of the history of many families, yet may not be even known by individuals, couples, or families today. Such family histories, including immigrant experiences, may elucidate why many protect their whiteness in ways that may include mistreating people of color.

The Price of the Ticket: Becoming White

The exclusionary practices of the existing White power structure in the face of massive European immigration to the United States in the late 19th and early 20th centuries contributed to the emergence of a category of people referenced by labor historian Roediger (2005, p. 12) as "in-between peoples," neither Black nor White. Irish immigrants, for example, faced extreme prejudice, and many Irish workers were willing to accept very low wages in higher skilled positions in order to be distinguished from African Americans who were given unskilled labor. Other examples of European immigrants' attempts to distinguish themselves as White included participation in anti-Black activism, union activities, and blackface minstrel shows (Roediger, 2007). These efforts to be considered White and achieve "Americanness" (Kolchin, 2002; Roediger, 2007) were not without consequence. As James Baldwin noted, to become American, one had to become White, and inherent in this transition was not only ethnic assimilation, but becoming the oppressor (Baldwin, 1998). In other words, becoming racist was "the price of the ticket." Consider the following example.

A man's father was a Jewish illegal immigrant from Eastern Europe during the Nazi regime. His father was reported to the immigration service and jailed. The man's mother, pregnant with him, frantically ran to relatives and charitable organizations to procure funds to hire a lawyer to prevent her husband's deportation to his Nazi-occupied country. In fact, some of the father's relatives were later murdered by the Nazis.

Procured in crisis and tragedy, the man's American status was hard won and valuable to him. Determined not to be a victim, throughout his life he increasingly adopted mainstream White values and power. His consecutive marriages to two Jewish wives ended in divorce. Married to a White Anglo Saxon woman, he became a wealthy financier, owned multiple homes and a private plane, sent his sons to premium prep schools, and often reviled affirmative action policies. His Brooklyn Jewish parents who worked in the garment industry had been labor-style Democrats. The price of the ticket: in contrast to his Jewish heritage, he became a right-wing Republican and felt that he was indisputably a White American.

Becoming White also can result in intergenerational conflicts in some ethnic groups. For example, a White Italian American Catholic man married a White Jewish woman. They adopted dominant culture practices in which the emotional distance of the nuclear family from the extended family was more pronounced than in the prior generation of Italian and Jewish families. When the couple did not attend the Holy Communion of their twin nephews, the Italian mother of the twins and the Italian grandparents were so profoundly hurt that a deep family conflict ensued.

Exclusionary Immigration Policy: Additional Challenges to Becoming White

Immigration has played, and continues to play, a significant role in U.S. history. As of 2010, 40 million, or 13 percent of the population, was foreign-born (U.S. Census Bureau, 2011). The nation's enduring struggle with racial and ethnic diversity is reflected in changing immigration policies (Falicov, 2015). Immigration laws were often enacted as a response to economic conditions. When great numbers of workers were needed by a growing manufacturing sector and westward expansion, immigration laws were relaxed. However, when the need for labor decreased, immigration laws followed suit. For example, mid-19th-century immigrants from China were extensively employed in mining and railroad construction. A recession in 1882 caused curtailment of those activities, resulting in the passage of the Chinese Exclusion Act, one of the earliest legislative acts limiting entry into the United States. It was not until China became an ally in World War II that Chinese immigrants were once again welcomed (Potocky-Tripodi, 2002). In addition to economic factors, legislation is responsive to public opposition (Gonzalez-Barrera & Krogstad, 2014) and xenophobia (Potocky-Tripodi, 2002), such as with the 1954 initiative, "Operation Wetback" (a derogatory term), in which more than a million Mexicans were deported from the United States (Chomsky, 2014; Hernández, 2006). In short, immigration laws in the United States have been both variable and unequal (Desilver, 2015).

SIMILARITIES AMONG MANY WHITE FAMILIES

Overall, general characteristics of White American families include family loyalty, defined parental roles, and structured and planned activities (McEachern & Kenny, 2002). However, historically, many of these characteristics were a standard to which Americans aspired. For example, only 10 percent of U.S. families actually lived the life that was held out as a model to the nation, depicted in all-White casted television shows of the 1950s such as *Leave It to Beaver* and *Ozzie and Harriet* (Coontz, 1992). The pressure to be a model American family had consequences for family relationships. Accordingly, aspiring to be a dedicated child-rearing, domesticated woman during the day and a highly engaged sex partner at night was a 1950s' concept "that drove many women to psychotherapy, tranquilizers and alcohol" (Coontz, 1992, p. 22).

The post-modern family from 1970 to the present has included increasingly varied roles for White American families. Women's dual role as they increasingly work outside the family has become more accepted. Additionally, family compositions have evolved to include less patriarchal families and greater incidence of single-parent, blended, intercultural, and interracial families (McEachern & Kenny, 2002). White families have become more diverse with respect to sexual orientation and gender identity. Differences in family beliefs and patterns can be influenced as well by ethnicity, as the impact of ethnic heritage can be evident four or five generations after immigration (McGoldrick, Giordano, & Garcia-Preto, 2005). Additionally, socioeconomic status (SES) can have a significant impact on the life cycle trajectory of White families (Kliman, 2015). The White family is therefore diverse, complex, and changing. However, White racial identity and the potential for internalized privilege cannot be overlooked as a common feature for all White families, which can impact family relationships.

White Racial Identity

Racial identity is separate from racial categorization and ethnicity. Helms has contributed significant scholarship about racial identity. The following is an abbreviated account of one aspect of her work (see Jernigan, Green, & Helms, Chapter 14, this volume.) According to Helms "[racial identity] refers to a sense of group or collective identity based on one's perception that he or she shares a common racial heritage with a particular racial group" (Helms, 1990, p. 3). Identity theory had been a realm in which research was conducted primarily with minority populations. Helms (1990) extended the process and developed a theory of **White racial identity** development (WRID). WRID occurs in a society that reinforces notions of White superiority through institutional means, such as with policies that oppress non-Whites and a culture in which White norms are promoted. The progression of White racial identity development starts with the lack of awareness of whiteness and/or of racism. The second stage is the formation of a positive White identity whereby a person moves beyond guilt to *actively* seek to learn from people of other racial identities. The final stage in the evolution is the abandonment of racism. Notably, consistent with the first WRID stage, many White people, living in a society where White is considered "normal," have little reason to give any consideration to their racial identity. Therefore, White people who enter therapy may not be open to the relevance of White racial identity in individual and family life, or discussions about this issue, especially if such discussions make them uncomfortable (Tatum, 1997). Thus, culturally sensitive therapists at times may not directly discuss WRID and instead use WRID to better conceptualize and know how to assist with the struggles of their White clients (Blitz, 2006), and at other times it is discussed in ways that are balanced and supportive, as will be shown in this chapter. A third factor complicating the deconstruction of whiteness in therapy may result from an environment in which White domination derives its power, in part, from legal sanction.

Legal Sanctions Which Support Superiority and Domination

A brief history of the oppression of people of color illustrates how the legal system has codified domination by Whites. An egregious example is the enslavement of people from Africa, followed by Jim Crow laws that mandated discrimination through racial segregation (Alexander, 2012) and lynching until the middle of the 20th century, some with the complicity of White churches (Patterson, 1998). Similarly, Native Americans have been forcibly ejected from their lands (Sutton & Broken Nose, 2005), and Native American children were removed from their families and sent to boarding schools to disconnect them from their language and culture (Tafoya & Del Vecchio, 2005). Additionally, refugees from war-torn countries in Central America were denied entry to the United States (Hernandez, 2005). Racist policies continue in the mass incarceration of people of color (Alexander, 2012), in the detention and deportation of Latin Americans (Gonzalez-Barrera & Krogstad, 2014), and schools of inferior standard in which children of color are treated in a harsh and punitive manner (U.S. Department of Education, 2014; Wetzel & Winawer, 2011/2012). Most White couples and families do not bear these burdens.

Privilege: Invisible to White Children and Families

Despite an increasingly multicultural society, the message of the assumed superiority of whiteness continues to be pervasive, particularly in the media (Giroux, 1998; Sandlin, O'Malley, & Burdick, 2011). White children see films with idealized characters that look like them (Hurley, 2005).

Disney films, for example, have associated white with goodness and happy endings, and black or darkness with bad and evil. These racist images subliminally support White privilege without being explicitly racist and are internalized by children of all backgrounds (Hurley, 2005).

White privilege ensures that emotional and physical safety concerns about racial discrimination and racial disparities are not integral to child-rearing for Whites. White families experience life *without* having to confront a dual identity as a person of color and as an American (Du Bois, 2003), and *without* needing to function in what Hardy (2008) has described as a world with two sets of rules: "one for White folks, and one for everyone else" (p. 462). For example, White families are protected from the burden of social disparities in poverty and incarceration rates, with African Americans and Latinos disproportionately experiencing those injustices (Patten & Krogstad, 2015). When White adults interact with others in a White-dominated world, they are not likely to be the target of **microaggressions**, the subtle verbal or nonverbal put-downs often directed at individuals based on their group membership (Sue, 2006). Moreover, the unearned privilege Whites attain through societal racial oppression may be a factor in their psychosocial development (McIntosh, 2008), and its exploration may be indicated when working with White families insofar as it may have an unexamined impact on relationships. The following clinical example shows how the invisibility and normativity of whiteness operated for one interracial couple.

A White German American man and his Peruvian-born wife who identifies as a woman of color, both cisgendered heterosexual professionals, came to therapy to address differences about raising their 5-year-old son. However, as the intensity of their dispute was explored, she expressed how marginalized she felt at his family's functions. On those occasions he would congregate with his brothers and leave her to her insensitive sisters-in-law. He felt that she was overly emotional and didn't work at "fitting in." The therapeutic process revealed that she was routinely experiencing microaggressions. He considered himself liberal and was taken aback that he was complicit with racist acts against his wife, whom he loved. The White therapist explained that "most of us" commit these inadvertent acts. Beyond listening to his feelings of guilt, she supported him in finding accountability as a productive area of exploration. With suggested reading (Sue, 2010) and further conversations, he began to support his wife at family functions, and their child-rearing exchanges became more focused and less fraught with the underlying pain of racist/sexist injury.

INTERSECTIONALITY

Crenshaw (1991) emphasized the significance of examining **intersectionality,** the intersection of social identities, that is, race, gender, and class, which also pertain to White couples and families. People who are

White may also identify as lesbian, gay, bisexual, transgender, queer, questioning, or intersex (LGBTQI). Such intersections with racial identity become an appropriate aspect of clinical focus. Furthermore, social class, as previously noted, is also a critical factor (Kliman, 2015). Ethnic identity, as well, can impact families for many generations after immigration (McGoldrick et al., 2005).

Notably, intersections with marginalized social identities can catapult a family that benefits from White privilege out of the domain of previously assumed, though not necessarily conscious, privilege. Consider the example wherein affluent parents of German and English heritage suddenly found themselves outside the mainstream of U.S. values. They had sent their daughter to an Ivy League school. On return for winter break their child announced that he was a transgender male. The therapy focused not only on the parents understanding and accepting their child's gender identity, but processing how they would present him to a Christian extended family and their dominant culture social network.

An Ethnic Group Raced White: German Americans

Examination of two ethnic groups, German Americans and Jewish Americans, can highlight subgroup differences among Whites that are important to couple and family dynamics. German Americans have a long history in the United States. Along with the English, they were among the first settlers of the United States from Europe, and currently constitute the largest ethnic group in the United States (Winawer & Wetzel, 2005). While some Germans were in Jamestown in 1607, the arrival of the *Concord*, known as "The German Mayflower," led to the founding of the first German settlement in Pennsylvania, Deutschstadt, in 1683. Germans fought on both sides in the Revolutionary War, and participated in the Continental Congress in 1776 (Winawer & Wetzel, 2005). Carl Schurz, ultimately a Union general who had long opposed slavery, influenced other Germans to support Lincoln after Southern secession. German Americans experienced discrimination during World War I and World War II, when the United States and Germany were on opposing sides (Conzen, 1980). Clients' grandparents may have transmitted intergenerational stories about such experiences. In the postwar years, the strong alliance between Germany and the United States has eliminated incidents of this nature. Overall, German American clients generally take pride in their forebears' contributions to the nation. Accordingly, German American families often welcome questions about their culture, which may be valuable in facilitating therapist–client joining and mutual understanding of each other's social location.

Given their early entry, major contributions, and large numbers in America, some German values seem synonymous with mainstream American values. For example, a strong work ethic and thriftiness, particularly in farming areas, were integral to early family life (Billigmeier, 1974).

While this endures as a source of pride, a disproportionate emphasis on work may be disruptive to family life and thus should be explored in therapy. German American families have roles and relationships that tend to be structured. Traditional German families tend to be patriarchal, with women assuming subservient complementary roles (Winawer & Wetzel, 2005). German American values also include extended families, adult children's responsibility to care for their parents in their old age, and the integration of work and family in rural areas. Germans tend to value emotional restraint, including in response to relationship stress, such as stress experienced during autonomy struggles with children (Winawer & Wetzel, 2005). Other than in geographic areas with large German American populations, there is little widespread recognition of German ethnicity as distinct from being American.

Jewish Couples and Families

There are 5.3 million Jews in the United States (Lipka, 2013). Not all Jews practice the faith; for some, Jewish identity is ethno-cultural (Rosen & Weltman, 2005). Their national origins are primarily European, but include other cultures. Nineteenth- and twentieth-century Jewish immigrants initially were referred to as the "Hebrew race" (Roediger, 2005). However, this population has achieved White status within U.S. society, perhaps because of their cultural emphasis on education and success (Rosen & Weltman, 2005). For example, 58 percent complete college, including 28 percent who have earned a graduate degree (Pew Research Center, 2013), and Jewish Americans have been elected to high political offices. Yet not all Jews are White. Jews of color are not beneficiaries of White privilege in the United States and may experience microaggressions in segments of the European American Jewish community.

Jewish people share a legacy of historical oppression and survival. Expulsions in Biblical times and anti-Semitism from the Middle Ages to modern times are part of the collective memory of Jews (Rosen & Weltman, 2005). In 19th-century Eastern Europe, persecution of Jews was rampant. Comprehensive restrictions were imposed on their land ownership, employment, and educational opportunities. Massive waves of anti-Jewish violence, known as *pogroms*, characterized by mass slaughter, rape, and pillaging of their communities were conducted by non-Jews. The awareness of persecution is significant. The majority (73%) of American Jews report that remembering the Nazi Holocaust in which 6 million Jews were killed is an *essential* part of being Jewish (Desilver, 2013). The Holocaust is also part of the personal history of many Jewish families.

Cultural Beliefs

Principles important to Jewish identity are "leading an ethical and moral life" (69%), "working for justice/equality" (56%), and "being intellectually curious" (49%) (DeSilver, 2013). Education, the importance of family, prioritizing children's well-being, and open expression of feelings are highly valued (Rosen & Weltman, 2005). Within traditional families, the marital couple is heterosexual, and the father is the head of household. Rituals are the bedrock of family life (Imber-Black, Roberts, & Whiting, 2003) and rites of passage are generally communal, including various mourning practices (Mirkin & Okun, 2005; Rosen & Weltman, 2005). Jewish feminism is an established area of study (Heschel, 1995). Within the less traditional Conservative, Reform, and Reconstructionist denominations, it is common for female rabbis to lead congregations.

Jews in Therapy

For therapists of all backgrounds, in the initial phase of therapy, it is important to join Jewish families by understanding the nature of their Jewish identity and its influences on family roles and daily practices. Jews, especially those who see their group as oppressed, may have difficulty owning White privilege.

Families and couples generally begin therapy with interest. The values of education and intellectual curiosity, imparted by Talmudic tradition, contribute to a desire to understand problems in relationships (Rosen & Weltman, 2005). This may not be true, however, for Israeli American Jews due to a more direct communication style, and their high expectation for quick results (Ziv, 2005). Overall, parents are dedicated to their children and will often make sacrifices on their behalf (Zborowski & Herzog, 1995). Children are encouraged to be verbally outgoing and the boundaries between parents and children may be more blurred than with families from other backgrounds. The use of criticism by parents is not uncommon (Rosen & Weltman, 2005). Therapists can help families develop more positive narratives when they deconstruct such critical exchanges, often associated with caring and worry. Worrying about their children is extremely prevalent among Jewish parents (Zborowski & Herzog, 1995).

Intersections of Whiteness with SES, Ethnic, and LGBTQI Identities

Within White families, there is much variation in SES. At times, the experiences and associated values of one's SES can affect relationships, as shown in the following clinical example: The White Anglo American son of a wealthy New England family and a White Chilean woman fell in love in graduate school. They were strongly attracted to one another. Her parents owned a modest business in Chile. She and her brothers understood that advancement came only through academic achievement. The woman became a scientist. He became eligible for income from his trust fund, stopped working, and had various projects of interest. She gained recognition in her field and was energized by her commitment to her work. His laid back demeanor became increasingly frustrating for her. She became out of reach for him; the sexual attraction diminished. The marriage of this White man of privilege to a striving immigrant woman of lower income background began to fail.

Heterosexuality is as much a default category as whiteness. **Heteronormativity,** a belief that a family consists of a conventional heterosexual parental unit with heterosexual children, not only is pervasive in society but also underlies most mental health research, practice, and use of language (Hudak & Giammattei, 2014). Same-sex relationships and people who identify on the queer spectrum as LGBTQI are marginalized in the United States (Green, 2008; Nealy, 2008). In his discussion of LGBT families, Nealy described "multiple layers of stigma" (Nealy, 2008, p. 293) for couples who are gay and interracial. Green (2008) pointed to pervasive anti-gay laws and practices. There have been efforts in recent years to increase the representation of LGBT issues in professional discourse, which had previously marginalized LGBT families and couples. However, publications focusing on LGBT issues comprise only 2 percent of the professional literature, a number far lower than the population of LGBT individuals, couples, or family members would indicate (Addison & Coolhart, 2015). Increased attention to LGBT families, including transgender youth (MacNish & Gold-Peifer, 2014), is particularly crucial as family acceptance can protect LGBTQI children and adolescents from self-destructive behaviors (Ryan, Russell, Huebner, Diaz, & Sanchez, 2010).

Ethnic groups may vary in their support of queerness.[1] Most Jews (Reform, Reconstructionist, and Conservative) support same-sex relationships. However, among Orthodox Jews, heterosexual marriage and procreation are highly valued and same-sex relationships are prohibited (Pew Research Center, 2012). The struggles of Orthodox gay men have been vividly captured in the film *Trembling before G-d* (Mirkin & Okun, 2005).

German Americans are likely to accept same-sex relationships. Acceptance may correspond to religion. For example, 62 percent of mainline Christians accept homosexuality (Masci & Lipka, 2015). Accordingly, depending on their religious affiliation, German American family members of LGBT individuals may vary in their level of acceptance.

ORIENTATION TO THERAPY, INCLUDING CONSIDERATION OF WHITENESS AS A SOCIAL IDENTITY

A Collaborative Context. Therapeutic orientation and stance are crucial in developing a collaborative context. A postmodern therapist's stance is to be a collaborative appreciative ally (Madsen, 2013). Treatment is non-objectifying and does not give primacy to a medical model orientation; collaborative therapy is a bottom–up process (Dickerson, 2010), driven by curiosity, from a position of "not knowing" (Anderson, 2005). The clinical approach applied in the treatment example in this chapter includes consideration of ethnicity and other contextual factors, including politically constructed racial identity. Conceptual underpinnings include social constructionism, systems theory, and a theory of oppression which explores individuals' relationship to oppression along five parameters: including marginalization and powerlessness, among others (Young, 1990). The therapist who employs a collaborative approach in work with families will be prepared to discuss whiteness as a relevant aspect of people's lives.

Therapy as an Intersubjective Experience: Therapy Begins with the Therapist

To develop and enhance racial awareness and sensitivity, many clinical teachers emphasize the importance of the therapist's self-reflection, particularly with regard to race, ethnicity, marginalization, and power disparities (Falicov, 2015; McGoldrick & Hardy, 2008; Watts-Jones, 2010; Winawer-Steiner, 1979). Such awareness should extend to the therapist's professional setting so that the therapist's language and office artwork, as well as dolls and toys convey an endorsement of multiculturalism and racial equity rather than White normativity. Generally, close to the beginning of therapy, therapists who practice cultural humility in combination with cultural competence[2] will share their own social location with clients, regarding race, ethnicity, class, gender, and relevant social identities. Doing so opens a respectful dialogue related to privilege and subjugation in the family's life and in the relationship with the therapist; it sets a tone that these dimensions of people's lives are relevant and will be heard respectfully. The importance of this approach represents an essential way of thinking and relating to families in a therapy that will include sensitive discussions about racial and other identities (Watts-Jones, 2010). In accordance with this approach, the author will share aspects of her social location with respect to whiteness.

Author's Social Location

I am the White **cisgendered** daughter (born with the physical attributes and biological congruence with femaleness) of Jewish parents who emigrated from Poland after World War I, neither of whom finished high school. I did not personally experience anti-Semitism, but I noticed Nazi concentration camp tattoos on the arms of family friends. When I was 10, I remember my parents' horror at the execution of a Jewish couple, the Rosenbergs, for espionage, during the Cold War-McCarthy era. A friend's family changed their name to something "more American." My father's accent embarrassed me as a teen. My brother's goal of becoming a physician was made more difficult by quota systems limiting the number of Jews accepted into medical schools. My parents' wish for me and my sister was to marry "a nice

Jewish boy" and have a family. Motivated to achieve and to escape early domestication, and as my working-class parents could not afford private college, I entered a tuition-free New York City college at 16. I met White Protestants for the first time there, although I had been long acquainted with their existence and considered them to be the "real" Americans.

As a child, I didn't know any African Americans; however, negative stereotypes of Black people were in school textbooks and permeated the media, that is, radio shows, films, and TV, as victims, comic figures, and criminals. I learned that slavery and segregation were wrong, but my knowledge was superficial—I had no idea of the extent and brutality. Much later I realized that the U.S. history I had been taught was selective, so as to omit the strengths, achievements, and contributions of people of color to the United States.

As a young adult I joined Dr. King when he led the March on Washington with 250,000 other citizens on August 28, 1963, which began my conscious education about racism, a commitment that has lasted throughout my lifetime. As an adult, I have learned that it is not the responsibility of people of color to teach me about race relations but I am grateful to friends, colleagues, clients, and acquaintances who have been part of my ongoing learning about racism. I aim to be accountable for White privilege, in a continuing imperfect process. My occasional discomfort is insignificant compared with the suffering racism has engendered. To keep learning I have participated in and led various trainings addressing racism, and work and write cross-culturally.

For Therapists of Color and White Therapists

As a White person, I cannot possibly know the experience of therapists of color. The following commentary is based on conversations with colleagues and students of color, and on various resources. Microaggressions can and do occur in the therapy room. Racist subtexts can challenge the leadership of a therapist of color in encounters with White families. Microaggressions can also occur within the workplace of therapists (Sue, 2010), such as with White supervisors and supervisees (Ali et al., 2005). Given the profession's continued acquiescence to whiteness as the norm, articles about cross-racial therapy are generally focused on White therapists working with families of color (Watts-Jones, 2010). White therapists can perpetuate racism in encounters with White families by failing to respond to racist comments (Hardy & Laszloffy, 2008). Similarly, a silent collusion between White therapists and families can communicate that "race does not matter" (Blitz, 2006, p. 251). In undoing racism, White therapists must listen to colleagues of color and be authentic allies.

Some cross-cultural therapy sources have addressed the difficult experiences of therapists of color in various encounters with Whites (McGoldrick & Hardy, 2008). For example, in training, many therapists of color express anxiety about the possibility of experiencing mistrust from White clients, and being unsure of how to react when they perceive such clients' racism (Kaplan & Small, 2005). Hardy (2008), a therapist of color, wrote a supportive, satirically formulated essay advising colleagues of color in White context: "How to Become a GEMM [Good Effective Mainstream Minority] Therapist."

Several resources on cross-racial therapy note group support as helpful (Kaplan & Small, 2005; Watts-Jones, Ali, Alfaro, & Frederick, 2007). Elements of supportive approaches are community, collegiality, and the courage to embrace honest, difficult dialogues. The readings in the chapter review section, therefore, are suggested for *all* therapists of *all* backgrounds. Overall, some culturally attuned therapists assert that it is essential that racism be addressed within the belief system of therapists themselves irrespective of ethnicity or background (Hardy & Laszloffy, 2008; Kaplan & Small, 2005). Therefore, with adequate self-reflection, all therapists should be able to provide a supportive environment in which to encourage their White clients to reflect both on their White privilege and also upon the areas in which they lack privilege, as will be shown in this chapter.

COLLABORATIVE INQUIRY TO IDENTIFY THE PRIDE STORY WITH WHITE FAMILIES

Early in the clinical encounter, cross-racial discussion can be awkward. Whiteness can have negative associations. Collaborative inquiry is a process in which the therapist learns how the family sees itself, rather than the therapist imposing her/his views (Madsen, 2013). Use of this approach contributes to a context in which a discussion of whiteness, given its sensitive nature, may be more easily negotiated and less awkward when it becomes relevant in the course of therapy. The discussion of race later occurs in a relationship that has begun with mutual respect and appreciation for the complexity experienced by people who come for consultation. Sheinberg and Fraenkel (2001) developed the "pride story" in their work with families with occurrences of incest. The **pride story** is an opportunity to hear family members speak to the couple's/family's individual and interpersonal strengths and talents, thus privileging their knowledge about themselves and providing room for a narrative that is not problem-saturated. The pride story replaces the notion of one single objective truth in favor of the "both-and" of their relationship: They are *both* addressing a problem *and* have experienced pleasure and love in the relationship. The therapist meets them as complex people, not just as bearers of problems. This exchange positions the therapist, early on, as an appreciative ally in a relationship in which they are being seen and experiencing themselves and each other as multidimensional people—the context in which a discussion of whiteness can be grounded. The pride story for couples can include what attracted them to one another and the early history of the relationship.

Developing and Changing Hypotheses in Work with White Families

After setting goals, the therapist develops an initial tentative *systemic cultural hypothesis* in work with all families. This is an initial formulation combining interactional and contextual factors to guide inquiry about how these factors relate to problems or dominant interactional patterns (Sheinberg & Brewster, 2014). The hypothesis privileges the subjective experience of the people in therapy, and can evolve to reflect information gathered during the course of treatment (Anderson, 2005; Freedman & Combs, 1996). Racial identity for Whites is included in the hypothesis in terms of its relationship to the problem and its intersection with multiple social identities, reflecting Sue's (2006) concept of **dynamic sizing**. General knowledge about cultures provides a foundation for more specific inquiry (McGoldrick et al., 2005; Sue, 2006). Rather than be wedded to a set view, it can be revised to integrate greater complexity, adding the intersection of social identities, including whiteness, and its relevance to problematic interactional phenomena.

Understanding White Families Using Migration Narratives and Genograms

Both migration narratives and **genograms,** or family trees constructed by therapists during discussions of family histories with clients, are essential in assessing key contexts for all families, including White families. Falicov (2015) proposes an examination of the **migration narrative,** the story and condition of a family's immigration experience, to understand decisions about relocation, hopes, regrets, choice points, ordeals suffered, and other salient factors that influence troubled family interactions. Migration has been defined as having four major stages: premigration, departure, transit, and resettlement (Drackman, 1992, as cited in Potocky-Tripodi, 2002). An indispensible tool, the genogram has been widely used by family therapists for many years. While there is no one standard approach, it is a graphic representation using symbols to show the structure of a family and family relationships (McGoldrick, 2011). A cultural genogram, or a genogram that focuses on culture, was designed to help therapy trainees examine their cultural identities and beliefs, but can be adapted to use with families in therapy (Hardy & Laszloffy, 1995). Genograms can be constructed in one or two sessions and/or can be woven into the process of therapy as historical/relational information emerges in conversation. Children can be engaged through use of animal figures to represent members or they can draw them. Some have adapted genograms to specific cultures, such as African American families (Watts-Jones, 1997). Similarly, genograms may be adapted to clarify the multigenerational role of whiteness, whether in dominant or in subordinated ethnic groups.

Clinical Example: Elements of Practice with a White Anglo American Couple

Initial Contact

Elizabeth and Owain[3] entered therapy, seeking help for a long history of marital discord. Elizabeth (Liz) is a White, 55-year-old, cisgendered heterosexual female. A nurse with 25 years of experience working in medical practices, she is a nonobservant Protestant of English colonial ancestry. Her maternal grandmother was a member of "Daughters of the American Revolution" (DAR), an organization of women whose ancestors fought for American independence. Until the late 20th century, DAR's policy was to exclude Black women from membership (Nir, 2012). Liz's Southern relatives boast of ancestors who were leaders during the Civil War Confederacy. Owain is a White, 55-year-old, cisgendered heterosexual male. He is a physics professor at a university in a major city and of both maternal and paternal Welsh heritage. The couple has been married for 22 years and they have a 20-year-old heterosexual cisgendered daughter, Gwen, a successful college student, who was not involved in therapy.

Their previous therapy in an affluent suburb consisted of both being treated by the same therapist in separate individual therapies for several years. Liz had been diagnosed bipolar. When she had angry outbursts, her mood-stabilizer and antipsychotic medications were increased, which may have contributed to her tardive dyskinesia. The previous therapist predicted that Liz would never improve. Owain had a brief affair with another woman, which he deeply regretted. He left the marital home at the previous therapist's recommendation. Liz immediately terminated therapy. After two days Owain returned, and stopped therapy as well.

The Pride Story: Creating an Initial Context in Which to Address White Racial Identity

The therapist drew upon literature about the disclosure of **social location** (Watts-Jones, 2010) and the social constructionist attitude of transparency, in which the therapist is forthcoming about the process of therapy (Roberts, 2005). The therapist discussed her ethnic and geographic background and added that she was curious about the relevance of racial identity in therapy, naming her identity as White. Both said they hadn't thought of racial identity before, but found it interesting. The therapist then explained that by beginning with their pride in their relationship strengths, the resources available for addressing problems can be identified, and that therapy will not be concerned exclusively with the negative aspects of their relationship. They enumerated aspects of their life together they enjoyed: exciting travel, support of each other's extended family, parenting, and mutually gratifying sexual activity early in their relationship. Owain loved Liz's beauty and spark and she admired his brilliance and his professional ambition.

Setting Goals and Understanding the Problem Systemically

The couple wanted to save their marriage. The therapist and the couple together began to delineate the dominant problematic interactional pattern. Owain saw Liz as "over-demanding" and insatiably needy. Liz felt she could not trust Owain. She was frustrated when he withdrew from her, most often to his work or to watch sports on TV. Historically, when he had been even less available emotionally, her response would begin with deprecatory remarks and escalate to yelling at him. Crushed by her harshness, he would increase his avoidance of her. They could see the reciprocal nature of their behaviors. They agreed to understand the forces that rendered this long-standing pattern intransigent, and committed to try to change. An initial general hypothesis began to emerge.

The General Relevance of Ethnicity

The couple's backgrounds indicated that the therapist should be familiar with the following: (a) the cultural background of families with European ancestry (Giordano & McGoldrick, 2005), (b) the cultural background of families with English ancestors from the colonial era (McGill & Pearce, 2005), and (c) Welsh culture (Berthoff, 1980).

The couple benefited from White privilege. For Liz, her English ancestry was considered synonymous with American (Roediger, 2005; Painter 2010). Owain's working-class status intersected with whiteness to partially drive his professional ambition. As pertains to Liz's heritage, the general characteristics of English/Southern U.S. culture are individualism, emotional reticence and privacy, and the absence of racial/ethnic discrimination directed toward them. Liz and Owain affirmed and expanded cultural descriptions during the course of therapy. For example, the intersection of whiteness in the South and Liz's family's elevated financial status gave her a sense of security that she felt contributed to her strong social presence.

Initial Hypothesis Including White Racial Identity

The initial hypothesis was formulated as follows: Owain and Liz were a middle-aged White Protestant (nonobservant) couple. Each was raised in a culture where open expression of feelings was not fostered. Raced White, they would unconsciously expect White privilege, and thus when they experienced problems, particularly in regard to any identities that were not privileged (e.g., SES, mental health), they perceived them as personal failings. In Owain, the privilege manifested in whiteness, education, his high societal standing, his previous therapy, and as a man in the couple relationship (Knudson-Martin, 2013; McIntosh, 2008). However, the advantages and consequent expectations inherent in his White privilege intersected with his working-class upbringing to instill an intense drive for achievement that often left him feeling inadequate. Liz's previous therapy made her feel stigmatized, powerless, and marginalized as a mentally ill person, which, combined with her husband's White male power and privilege in the previous therapy, subjugated and disempowered her, reducing her to the status of "an overly emotional woman."

The couple's problematic interaction pattern suggested a "vulnerability cycle" (Scheinkman & Fishbane, 2004) that needed clarification. When Owain felt criticized in the relationship, his survival strategy was to distance; when Liz felt abandoned, hers was to be angry, to pursue, and to protest. The cycle may have been exacerbated by culturally influenced behaviors for dealing with difficult feelings. Both had entered therapy with problem-saturated narratives informed by an adherence to psychopathology that narrowed their views about their relationship. The intersection of whiteness with other factors was initially not clear. The hypothesis was the guide for further inquiry with the goal of understanding the intersection of privilege and lack of it in their relationship and how social identities were related to their pattern of interaction. Guided by the hypothesis, inquiry was conducted about the relationship of their interpersonal and multigenerational cultural and racial experiences to their recurrent painful interactional pattern.

Migration Narrative

The intersection of the migration experience with whiteness often reveals stories of oppression and hardship that impact the lives of couples and families, although this was not the case for Owain or Liz. For Liz, while there was no recent immigration, her childhood moves within the United States included loss of home, school, social life, and daily contact with relatives. These disruptions, which were not discussed with her at the time, contributed to her pronounced need for stability and contact. For Owain, his grandfather discussed how hard work enabled him to rise from the tedious position of "coal breaker" in the mines. Therefore, the mandate to reap the benefits of coming to the United States was strongly imparted to him and contributed to his drive to succeed.

Tracking Their Problematic Cycle across Generations with a Genogram

Follow-up inquiry informed by the original hypothesis and guided by the therapist's curiosity (Cecchin, 1987) constituted a process in which a genogram was constructed linking multigenerational family dynamics, ethnicity, and race. Their genogram revealed two shared factors. Serious mental illness was a powerful element for both families, though it was never discussed. Both identified an emotionally reticent mode of communication as ethnically normative, which confirmed the therapist's global knowledge of their racial and ethnic backgrounds.

The development of a genogram also revealed Liz's profound recurrent childhood loss, starting when her father left the family when Liz was two. When she was five, her younger brother was precipitously sent to live with an aunt. As a result of her mother's long-term psychotic depression, frequent hospitalizations, withdrawal, and electroconvulsive therapy with associated acute memory loss, Liz moved often between the homes of various relatives. A narrative of resilience emerged as she noticed that she had no help processing the trauma, a factor that is linked to optimal child development (Siegel & Bryson, 2011).

Aware of the importance of secrets in families (Imber-Black, 2009), the therapist asked why Liz thought people in her family were silent and secretive. She attributed it to her Southern culture. Her Southern grandmother was the family matriarch. She was "strict" with Liz and didn't discuss feelings. Her grandmother respected Liz for her honesty and, as a financially successful White woman with considerable land holdings, was a powerful role model. Her lifestyle was reflective of the segregation of races codified by the Jim Crow laws, as discussed earlier. Black workers stayed in the barn or the shop, and were never allowed in the house other than to work. Liz was forbidden to share the family pool on hot summer days with "colored" children. Liz deplores racism and, in hindsight, was aware of her privilege in the South. Seeking narratives of strength, the therapist inquired about Liz's childhood resilience, wondering how she coped with traumatic losses with no apparent emotional guidance. She described herself as strong-willed, a quality her husband affirmed. Both were able to redefine her anger as way of surviving trauma. Her White privilege, amplified by a Southern upbringing in which African American people were disempowered, may have resulted in an additional internalized unconscious sense of privilege; it may have contributed an element of power to her ability to confront emotional challenges and expect to be able to make changes. As a nurse, Liz worked side by side with people of color and attended patients of all backgrounds. Like many White people, she does not regularly think about the benefits of privilege.

For Owain, privilege as a White man intersected with his non-privileged experiences being raised in a second-generation immigrant blue-collar family. His father did not talk specifically about non-Whites, but Owain suspected prejudice against African Americans. His father drank excessively, consistently complained about his union, and expressed bitterness often. Toward Owain, he was either silent and distant, or critical. He took Owain on some trips when Owain was young, and they shared interests, but father was profoundly withholding of praise and demeaned his son's achievements, among them the publication of Owain's first book. Upon the therapist's inquiry, Owain confirmed the strong work ethic and emotional reserve as most likely cultural, but viewed his father's bitterness as uncharacteristic of Welsh families. Unlike his father, Owain's mother was supportive, but primarily engaged in caring for his autistic brother. His brother's autism was never discussed in the family.

Owain worked hard, and accustomed to privilege as a White man, he was blindsided by professional competition with people of color and experienced it as a disqualification of his worth. This may have contributed to him being highly sensitive to criticism. Disavowing racist intent, he expressed resentment that foreigners were given more recognition than him in his department. "I am the American," he stated, although, when asked, he acknowledged that his colleagues of various international origins were U.S. citizens. He realized that workplace disappointments contributed to his depression and emotional distancing in his marriage, which exacerbated Liz's fear of abandonment.

The problematic interactional pattern was examined at the intersection of whiteness, ethnic influences, social class, sexism, the stigma of mental illness, and family relationships, toward revising the hypothesis. The revised hypothesis related to their difficult pattern was formulated as follows: being a White male in the United States can impart an unconscious innate sense of privilege (McIntosh, 2008). Whiteness combined with successful academics and an advanced degree had allowed Owain to believe that he could feel: (a) greater self-worth having achieved upward mobility from his social class of birth and (b) more valued than the "not good enough" message from his father. Furthermore, the internalization of the power of meritocracy—the harder one works, the greater the reward (McNamee & Miller, 2014)—was dissonant in his workplace where hard work and whiteness were not equated with recognition of merit. This disappointment reinforced his sense of worthlessness and contributed to his depression and distancing. The circular interactional pattern was becoming more clear to the couple: when Owain distanced, Elizabeth's childhood losses triggered reactivity, which, when expressed in anger and derogatory comments, made him feel worthless and engendered further distancing, leaving her feeling emotionally alone. Coming from ethnic backgrounds that did not support discussion of difficult feelings, and a previous therapy that had privileged him as a man and disqualified her feelings as psychopathology, they were relationally trapped in a multi-generational, socio-politically reinforced cycle of pain and frustration, all of which contributed to eclipsing the relationship's strengths.

The Work of Therapy

Listening to stories of resilience and pain, the spouses developed more compassionate constructs of self and other. A change in roles was apparent in the discussion of Owain's feelings about the workplace. Acknowledging the workplace dynamics as contributing to his depression, he said, "I guess I wasn't very easy to live with." In this conversation, the balance of power began to shift, revealing Elizabeth's capacity as a compassionate partner, competent and willing to be supportive of her husband's struggles. Owain experienced Liz as an empathic listener to whom he could confide his disappointment as a White man. This perspective allowed him to be increasingly available to her emotionally. The benefits to each individually and as a couple were notable: (a) Liz became asymptomatic without medication, (b) Owain became more open (c) conflict was very minimal, and (d) they were able to more fully enjoy each other.

CONCLUSIONS

This chapter has offered a beginning conversation about an often-missing element in the treatment of White families, namely, rendering White racial identity visible and accessible for integration into systemic treatment. For all therapists, clinical hypothesizing that includes whiteness as it intersects with other privileged and unprivileged dimensions of identity, as well as how it is revealed in family stories, ethnicity, and context, can support the emergence of new meanings and narratives of empowerment.

To afford more comprehensive attention to the lives of White couples and families, White racial identity requires visibility in professional discourses, in conferences, in the classroom, and in publications. Epistemologically and ethically, how do we justify the absence of whiteness from mental health discourse? Thus, studies investigating whether therapists are integrating discourses of whiteness into therapy are indicated. Furthermore, it could be useful to explore if there is an association between a positive White racial identity and satisfying relationships.

CHAPTER REVIEW

Key Points

1. Whiteness is a social construct, invisible to White people, and has been the standard for being "American." It affords unearned, unacknowledged societal privilege, and is part of people's identities and family relationships, even though the discussion of whiteness is underrepresented in the mental health literature.
2. White people are a heterogeneous racial identity group. Their White identity may intersect with a history of oppression regarding other marginalized identities that they may hold (e.g., low SES, a non-Christian religion). These intersections can present challenges that can reduce the advantages of White privilege, at times resulting in individual and relational distress.
3. Exploration of White families' history of anti-immigrant discrimination in the United States can yield relevant information about family dynamics and the importance of whiteness.
4. Therapists' collaborative, meaning-based, curiosity-driven inquiry will include construction of a hypothesis that connects whiteness to interactional patterns, history, and role expectations within the couple or family.

5. Therapists of all backgrounds who understand racism as a system of hierarchy and power and who have worked toward their own positive racial identity will be able to ethically and relevantly deconstruct whiteness in treatment with couples and families.

Key Terms

cisgendered, collaborative context, dynamic sizing, genograms, heteronormativity, intersectionality, microaggressions, migration narrative, pride story, "science" of race, social location, systemic cultural hypothesis, White racial identity

Myths and Realities

- It is a myth that U.S. laws and attitudes have always welcomed all immigrants. In reality, many groups, including those now considered White, entered the United States and experienced xenophobia from the dominant groups, in addition to having experienced how the immigration laws are not uniformly or fairly applied.
- It is a myth that societally perpetuated White privilege cannot lead to unconsciously internalized domination and the assumption of superiority, even among well-meaning and loving liberal people.
- It is a myth that White racial identity and the expectation of privilege cannot impact intimate relationships among White people.
- It is a myth that those who are considered to be White today were always considered White. In reality, many historically were not accepted as White by the dominant culture and experienced discrimination and marginalization. Some asserted their whiteness, on occasion discriminating against African Americans and others not considered "White" to become Americans.

Tools and Tips

Knowledge

McGoldrick, M., Giordano, J., & Garcia-Preto, N. (Eds.). (2005). *Ethnicity and family therapy* (3rd ed.). New York, NY: Guilford Press.

McGoldrick, M., & Hardy, K.V. (Eds.). (2008). *Re-visioning family therapy: Race, culture, and gender in clinical practice* (2nd ed.). New York, NY: Guilford Press.

Rastogi, M., & Wieling, E. (Eds.). (2005). *Voices of color: First-person accounts of ethnic minority therapists*. Thousand Oaks, CA: Sage Publications.

Roediger, D. (2005). *Working toward whiteness*. Cambridge: Basic.

Watts-Jones, T.D. (2010). Location of self: Opening the door to dialogue on intersectionality in the therapy process. *Family Process, 49*, 405–420.

Selected Resources: (1) People's Institute and Beyond (http://www.pisab.org/) in different areas of the United States; (2) Rutgers University Culture Conference (gsappweb.rutgers.edu/conference/); (3) Multicultural Family Institute (www.multiculturalfamily.org); and (4) American Family Therapy Academy (www.afta.org).

Dynamic Sizing

Dynamic sizing is a principal through which the therapist balances general cultural (racial, ethnic) information as a resource with factors that are specifically relevant to an individual's or family's experience (Sue, 2006). Inquiry, guided by a therapeutic hypothesis, helps delineate the relevant specific factors. In this way, more specifically delineated information related to the cultural context of clients can be revealed during the process of therapy.

Skills

Theory. Family therapy approaches need to consider critical race theory and whiteness studies to address the current lacunae in the canon of mental health literature.

Prevention. Clinicians and clinical teachers who incorporate White racial identity into a dimension of instruction and practice may be able to help avert or diminish interpersonal emotional injury in biracial or White families and couples affected by the expectations of White privilege.

Service Provision. Service providers need to examine the intersection of whiteness and marginalized identities. Unexamined biases among service providers about LGBTQI identity in all people, including dominant racial groups, can do harm, particularly to children. Collaboratively identifying the couple's or family's pride story, developing and revising systemic cultural hypotheses, gaining understanding of White families via asking about their migration narratives, and constructing cultural genograms with them are some recommended methods to tailor treatment to White couples and families.

Policy. Requirements for all human services, health/mental health, education and law enforcement professionals should include *initial and periodic* undoing racism or similar training that includes awareness of internalized White privilege. To limit such training to psychotherapists keeps mental health professionals addressing systemic issues as individual or family problems, when the awareness of White privilege reveals that it is structural oppression that creates the very conditions that produce symptoms within individuals, couples, and families.

Research. Further research exploring if there is a correlation between the development of a positive White racial identity and gratifying relationships in couples and families is absent in the family therapy field. Research focused on White racial identity awareness could illuminate factors that may have implications at the individual, family, and societal levels.

Awareness

To address the inevitable societally reinforced institutional and interpersonal racism (that is more expansive and pervasive than individual psychology), undoing racism training or, at the very least, cultural competence training should be institutionalized for all professionals who work with people of diverse social identities.

NOTES

1. The inclusive term "queer" is preferable for many people of LGBTQI orientations rather than binary designations that have marginalizing implications.

2. Cultural humility or cultural attunement is this author's preferred perspective. Cultural humility "incorporates a lifelong commitment to self-evaluation and self-critique, to redressing the power imbalances in the patient-physician dynamic, and to developing mutually beneficial and nonpaternalistic clinical and advocacy partnerships with communities on behalf of individuals and defined population" (Tervalon & Murray-Garcia, 1998, p. 117). Falicov notes, *"Cultural attunement* is most likely the result of both [cultural competence and cultural humility] combined. Professionals must have enough cultural competence to always make room for cultural variables. An inquisitive, open-minded, and humble attitude of not knowing enough about the client should always be maintained rather than resorting to simplistic stereotypes" (Falicov, 2014, p. 176).

3. Fictitious names are used to protect the couple's identity.

REFERENCES

Addison, S.M., & Coolhart, D. (2015). Expanding the therapy paradigm with queer couples: A relational intersectional lens. *Family Process, 54,* 435–453. doi: 10.1111/famp.12171

Alexander, M. (2012). *The new Jim Crow: Mass incarceration in the age of colorblindness.* New York, NY: New Press.

Ali, S.R., Flojo, J.R., Chronister, K.M., Hayashino, D., Smiling, Q.R., Torres, D., & McWhirter, E.H. (2004). When racism is reversed: Therapists of color speak about their experiences with racism from clients, supervisees, and supervisors. In M. Rastogi, & E. Wieling (Eds.), *Voices of color: First-person accounts of ethnic minority therapists* (pp. 117–122). Thousand Oaks, CA: SAGE Publications.

Anderson, H. (2005), Myths about "not-knowing." *Family Process, 44,* 497–504.

Baldwin, J. (1998). The price of the ticket. In T. Morrison (Ed.), *James Baldwin: Collected essays* (pp. 830–42). New York, NY: Literary Classics of the United States.

Bell, D.A. (1995). Who's afraid of critical race theory? *University of Illinois Law Review, 4,* 893–910.

Berthoff, R. (1980). Welsh. In S. Thernstrom (Ed.), *Harvard encyclopedia of American ethnic groups* (pp. 1011–1017). Cambridge, MA: Harvard University Press.

Billigmeier, R.H. (1974). *Americans from Germany: A study in cultural diversity.* Belmont, CA: Wadsworth.

Blitz, L.V. (2006). Owning whiteness: The reinvention of self and practice. *Journal of Emotional Abuse, 6,* 241–263.

Cecchin, G. (1987). Hypothesizing, circularity, and neutrality revisited: An invitation to curiosity. *Family Process, 26,* 405–413. doi: 10.1111/j.1545-5300. 1987.00405.x

Chomsky, A. (2014). *Undocumented: How immigration became illegal.* Boston, CA: Beacon Press.

Coates, T. (2015). *Between the world and me* (1st ed.). New York, NY: Spiegel & Grau.

Conzen, K.N. (1980). The Germans in America. In S. Thernstrom (Ed.), *Harvard encyclopedia of American ethnic groups* (pp. 405–425). Cambridge, MA: Belknap Press of Harvard University.

Coontz, S. (1992). *The way we never were: American families and the nostalgia trap.* New York, NY: Basic Books.

Crenshaw, K. (1991). Mapping the margins: Intersectionality, identity politics, and violence against women of color. *Stanford Law Review, 43,* 1241–1299.

Desilver, D. (2013). *Jewish essentials: For most American Jews, ancestry and culture matter more than religion.* Retrieved from http://www.pewresearch.org/fact-tank/2013/10/01/jewish-essentials-for-most-american-jews-ancestry-and-culture-matter-more-than-religion/

Desilver, D. (2015). *U.S. public seldom has welcomed refugees into country.* Retrieved from http://www.pewresearch.org/fact-tank/2015/11/19/u-s-public-seldom-has-welcomed-refugees-into-country/

Dickerson, V.C. (2010). Positioning oneself within an epistemology: Refining our thinking about integrative approaches. *Family Process, 49,* 349–368.

Du Bois, W.E.B. (2003). *The souls of black folk.* New York, NY: The Modern Library.

Falicov, C.J. (2015). *Latino families in therapy* (2nd ed.). New York, NY: Guilford Press.

Ferber, A.L. (2014). We aren't just color-blind, we are oppression-blind! In A.L. Ferber, & M.S. Kimmel (Eds.), *Privilege: A reader* (3rd ed., pp. 226–240). Boulder, CO: Westview Press.

Freedman, J., & Combs, G. (1996). *Narrative therapy.* New York, NY: W.W. Norton.

Giordano, J., & McGoldrick, M. (2005). Families of European origin: An overview. In M. McGoldrick, J. Giordano, & N. Garcia-Preto (Eds.), *Ethnicity and family therapy* (3rd ed., pp. 501–519). New York, NY: Guilford Press.

Giroux, H.A. (1998). Public pedagogy and rodent politics: Cultural studies and the challenge of Disney. *Arizona Journal of Hispanic Cultural Studies, 2,* 253–266.

Gonzalez-Barrera, A., & Krogstad, M.J. (2014). *U.S. deportations of immigrants reach record high in 2013.* Retrieved from http://www.pewresearch.org/fact-tank/2014/10/02/u-s-deportations-of-immigrants-reach-record-high-in-2013/

Green, R.J. (2008). Gay and lesbian couples: Successful coping with minority stress. In K.V. Hardy, & M. McGoldrick (Eds.), *Re-visioning family therapy: Race, culture, and gender in clinical practice* (2nd. ed., pp. 300–310). New York, NY: Guilford Press.

Guinier, L., & Torres, G. (2002). *The miner's canary: Enlisting race, resisting power, transforming democracy.* Cambridge, MA: Harvard University Press.

Haney-Lopez, I.F. (2013a). The social construction of race. In R. Delgado & J. Stefancic (Eds.), *Critical race theory: The cutting edge* (3rd ed., pp. 238–248). Philadelphia, PA: Temple University Press.

Haney-Lopez, I.F. (2013b). White Latinos. In R. Delgado & J. Stefancic (Eds.), *Critical race theory: The cutting edge* (3rd ed., pp. 801–805). Philadelphia, PA: Temple University Press.

Hardy, K. V. (2008). On becoming a GEMM therapist: Work harder, be smarter, and never discuss race. In K. V. Hardy & M. McGoldrick (Eds.), *Re-visioning family therapy: Race, culture, and gender in clinical practice* (2nd. ed., pp. 461–468). New York, NY: Guilford Press.

Hardy, K. V., & Laszloffy, T. A. (1995). The cultural genogram: Key to training culturally competent family therapists. *Journal of Marital and Family Therapy, 21,* 227–237. doi: 10.1111/j.1752-0606.1995.tb00158.x

Hardy, K. V., & Laszloffy, T. A. (2008). The dynamics of a pro-racist ideology: Implications for family therapists. In K. V. Hardy & M. McGoldrick (Eds.), *Re-visioning family therapy: Race, culture, and gender in clinical practice* (pp. 225–237). New York, NY: Guilford Press.

Hardy, K. V., & McGoldrick, M. (2008). Re-visioning training. In K. V. Hardy & M. McGoldrick (Eds.), *Re-visioning family therapy: Race, culture, and gender in clinical practice* (pp. 442–460). New York, NY: Guilford Press.

Helms, J. E. (1990). *Black and white racial identity: Theory, research, and practice.* Westport, CT: Praeger.

Helms, J. E. (2014). A review of white racial identity theory: The sociopolitical implications of studying white racial identity in psychology. In S. Cooper & K. Ratele (Eds.), *Proceedings of the 30th international congress of psychology* (pp. 12–27). London, England, and New York, NY: Psychology Press.

Hernández, K. L. (2006). The crimes and consequences of illegal immigration: A cross-border examination of Operation Wetback, 1943 to 1954. *The Western Historical Quarterly, 37,* 421–444. doi: 10.2307/25443415

Hernandez, M. (2005). Central American Families. In M. McGoldrick, J. Giordano, & N. Garcia-Preto (Eds.), *Ethnicity and family therapy* (3rd ed., pp. 178–191). New York, NY: Guilford Press.

Heschel, S. (1995). *On being a Jewish feminist: A reader.* New York, NY: Schocken Books.

Hudak, J., & Giammattei, S. V. (2014). Doing family: Decentering heteronormativity in new "marriage" and "family" therapy. In T. Nelson & H. Winawer (Eds.), *Critical topics in family therapy: AFTA monograph series highlights* (pp. 105–115). New York, NY: Springer Science & Business Media.

Hurley, D. L. (2005). Seeing white: Children of color and the Disney fairy tale princess. *The Journal of Negro Education, 74,* 221–232.

Imber-Black, E. (1999). *The secret life of families: Making decisions about secrets: When keeping secrets can harm you, when keeping secrets can heal you—and how to know the difference.* New York, NY: Bantam Books.

Imber-Black, E., Roberts, J., & Whiting, R. A. (2003). *Rituals in families and family therapy.* New York, NY: W.W. Norton.

Kaplan, L. F., & Small, S. (2005). Multiracial recruitment in the field of family therapy: An innovative training program for people of color. *Family Process, 44,* 249–265.

Kliman, J. (2015). Social class and the life cycle. In M. McGoldrick, N. Garcia-Preto, & B. A. Carter (Eds.), *The expanding family life cycle: Individual, family, and social perspectives* (5th ed.). New York, NY: Pearson.

Knudson-Martin, C. (2013). Why power matters: Creating a foundation of mutual support in couple relationships. *Family Process, 52,* 5–18. doi: 10.1111/famp.12011

Kolchin, P. (2002). Whiteness studies: The new history of race in America. *The Journal of American History, 89*, 154–173. doi: 10.2307/2700788

Lipka, M. (2013). *How many Jews are there in the United States?* Retrieved from http://www.pewresearch.org/fact-tank/2013/10/02/how-many-jews-are-there-in-the-united-states/

MacNish, M., & Gold-Peifer, M. (2014). Families in transition: Supporting families of transgender youth. In T. Nelson & H. Winawer (Eds.), *Critical topics in family therapy: AFTA Monograph Series Highlights* (pp. 119–129). Cham, Switzerland: Springer International Publishing.

Madsen, W. C. (2013). *Collaborative therapy with multi-stressed families*. New York, NY: Guilford Press.

Masci, D., & Lipka, M. (2015). Where Christian churches and other religions stand on gay marriage. Pew Research Center. Retrieved from http://www.pewresearch.org/fact-tank/2015/12/21/where-christian-churches-stand-on-gay-marriage/

McDermott, M., & Samson, F. L. (2005). White racial and ethnic identity in the United States. *Annual Review of Sociology, 31*, 245–261.

McEachern, A. G., & Kenny, M. C. (2002). A comparison of family environment characteristics among white (non-Hispanic), Hispanic, and African Caribbean groups. *Journal of Multicultural Counseling and Development, 30*, 40–58. doi: 10.1002/j.2161-1912.2002.tb00476.x

McGill, D. W., & Pearce, J. K. (2005). American families with English ancestors from the colonial era: Anglo Americans. In N. Garcia-Preto, J. Giordano, & M. McGoldrick (Eds.), *Ethnicity and Family Therapy* (3rd ed., pp. 520–533). New York, NY: Guilford Press.

McGoldrick, M. (2011). *The genogram journey: Reconnecting with your family*. New York, NY: W.W. Norton.

McGoldrick, M., Giordano, J., & Garcia-Preto, N. (2005). *Ethnicity and family therapy* (3rd ed.). New York, NY: Guilford Press.

McIntosh, P. (2008). White privilege and male privilege: A personal account of coming to see correspondences through work in women's studies. In M. McGoldrick & K. V. Hardy (Eds.), *Re-visioning family therapy: Race, culture, and gender in clinical practice* (2nd ed., pp. 238–249). New York, NY: Guilford Press.

McNamee, S. J., & Miller, R. K. (2014). *The meritocracy myth*. Lanham, MD: Rowman & Littlefield.

Mirkin, M. P., & Okun, B. F. (2005). Orthodox Jewish families. In N. Garcia-Preto, J. Giordano, & M. McGoldrick (Eds.), *Ethnicity and family therapy* (3rd ed., pp. 689–700). New York, NY: Guilford Press.

Murphy, C. (2016). *Most U.S. Christian groups grow more accepting of homosexuality*. Retrieved from http://www.pewresearch.org/fact-tank/2015/12/18/most-u-s-christian-groups-grow-more-accepting-of-homosexuality/

Nealy, E. (2008). Working with LGBT families. In K. V. Hardy & M. McGoldrick (Eds.), *Re-visioning family therapy: Race, culture, and gender in clinical practice* (2nd ed., pp. 289–299). New York, NY: Guilford Press.

Nir, S. M. (2012). *Daughters of the American Revolution*. Retrieved from http://www.nytimes.com/2012/07/04/nyregion/for-daughters-of-the-american-revolution-more-black-members.html?_r=0

Painter, N. I. (2010). *The history of white people*. New York, NY: W.W. Norton.

Patten, E., & Krogstad, M.J. (2015). *Black child poverty rate holds steady, even as other groups see declines*. Retrieved from http://www.pew research.org/fact-tank/2015/07/14/black-child-poverty-rate-holds-steady-even-as-other-groups-see-declines/

Patterson, O. (1998). *Rituals of blood: Consequences of slavery in two American centuries*. Washington, DC: Basic Civitas Books.

Pew Research Center (2012). Religious groups' official positions on same sex marriage. Retrieved from http://www.pewforum.org/2012/12/07/relig ious-groups-official-positions-on-same-sex-marriage/

Pew Research Center (2013). A portrait of Jewish Americans. Retrieved from http://www.pewforum.org/2013/10/01/jewish-american-beliefs-attitudes-culture-survey/

Potocky-Tripodi, M. (2002). *Best practices for social work with refugees and immigrants*. New York, NY: Columbia University Press.

Roberts, J. (2005). Transparency and self-disclosure in family therapy: Dangers and possibilities. *Family Process, 44*, 45–63. doi: 10.1111/j.1545-5300.2005.00041.x

Roediger, D.R. (2005). *Working toward whiteness: How America's immigrants became white*. Cambridge, MA: Basic Books.

Roediger, D.R. (2007). *The wages of whiteness: Race and the making of the American working class* (Rev. ed.). New York, NY: Verso.

Rosen, E.J., & Weltman, S.F. (2005). Jewish families: An overview. In N. Garcia-Preto, J. Giordano, & M. McGoldrick (Eds.), *Ethnicity and family therapy* (3rd ed., pp. 667–679). New York, NY: Guilford Press.

Ryan, C., Russell, S.T., Huebner, D., Diaz, R., & Sanchez, J. (2010). Family acceptance in adolescence and the health of LGBT young adults. *Journal of Child and Adolescent Psychiatric Nursing, 23*, 205–213.

Sandlin, J.A., O'Malley, M.P., & Burdick, J. (2011). Mapping the complexity of public pedagogy scholarship: 1894–2010. *Review of Educational Research, 81*, 338–375. doi: 10.3102/0034654311413395

Scheinkman, M., & Fishbane, D.M. (2004). The vulnerability cycle: Working with impasses in couple therapy. *Family Process, 43*, 279–299.

Sheinberg, M., & Brewster, M.K. (2014). Thinking and working relationally: Interviewing and constructing hypotheses to create compassionate understanding. *Family Process, 53*, 618–639. doi: 10.1111/famp.12081

Sheinberg, M., & Fraenkel, P. (2001). *The relational trauma of incest: A family-based approach to treatment*. New York, NY: Guilford Press.

Siegel, D.J., & Bryson, T.P. (2011). *The whole-brain child: 12 revolutionary strategies to nurture your child's developing mind*. New York, NY: Delacorte Press.

Sue, S. (2006). Cultural competency: From philosophy to research and practice. *Journal of Community Psychology, 34*, 237–245.

Sue, D.W. (2010). *Microaggressions in everyday life: Race, gender, and sexual orientation*. New York, NY: Wiley.

Sutton, C.T., & Broken Nose, M.A. (2005). American Indian families: An overview. In N. Garcia-Preto, J. Giordano, & M. McGoldrick (Eds.), *Ethnicity and family therapy* (3rd ed., pp. 43–54). New York, NY: Guilford Press.

Tafoya, N., & Del Vecchio, A. (2005). Back to the future: An examination of the Native American Holocaust experience. In N. Garcia-Preto, J. Giordano, & M. McGoldrick (Eds.), *Ethnicity and family therapy* (3rd ed., pp. 55–63). New York, NY: Guilford Press.

Tappan, M. B. (2006). Reframing internalized oppression and internalized domination: From the psychological to the sociocultural. *The Teachers College Record, 108,* 2115–2144.

Tatum, B.D. (1997). *"Why are all the black kids sitting together in the cafeteria?" and other conversations about race.* New York, NY: Basic Books.

Tervalon, M., & Murray-Garcia, J. (1998). Cultural humility versus cultural competence: A critical distinction in defining physician training outcomes in multicultural education. *Journal of Health Care for the Poor and Underserved, 9,* 117–125.

U.S. Census Bureau. (2011). The white population: 2010. Retrieved from http://www.census.gov/prod/cen2010/briefs/c2010br-05.pdf

U.S. Department of Education, Office for Civil Rights. (2014). Dagta snapshot: School Discipline. Retrieved from http://ocrdata.ed.gov/Downloads/CRDC-School-Discipline-Snapshot.pdf

Watts-Jones, D. (1997). Toward an African American genogram. *Family Process, 36,* 375–383.

Watts-Jones, D., Ali, R., Alfaro, J., & Frederick, A. (2007). The role of a mentoring group for family therapy trainees and therapists of color. *Family Process, 46,* 437–450. doi: 10.1111/j.1545-5300.2007.00224.x

Watts-Jones, T. D. (2010). Location of self: Opening the door to dialogue on intersectionality in the therapy process. *Family Process, 49,* 405–420. doi: 10.1111/j.1545-5300.2010.01330.x

Wetzel, N. A., & Winawer, H. with Ashton, D., Lopez-Henriquez, G., Mendelsohn, G., Sutton, C. (2011/2012). Social justice in clinical practice: Family consultations with adolescents in urban schools. *New Jersey Psychologist, 61,* 40–42; *62,* 47–50.

Winawer, H., & Wetzel, N. (2005). German families. In N. Garcia-Preto, J. Giordano, & M. McGoldrick (Eds.), *Ethnicity and family therapy* (3rd ed., pp. 555–572). New York, NY: Guilford Press.

Winawer-Steiner, H. (1979). Getting started in family therapy: A preliminary guide for therapist, supervisor and administrator. In M. Dinoff & D. L. Jacobson (Eds.), *Neglected problems in community mental health* (pp. 154–174). Huntsville: University of Alabama Press.

Young, I. M. (1990). *Justice and the politics of difference.* Princeton, NJ: Princeton University Press.

Zborowski, M., & Herzog, E. (1995). *Life is with people: The culture of the shtetl.* New York, NY: Schocken Books.

Ziv, A. (2005). Israeli families. In N. Garcia-Preto, J. Giordano, & M. McGoldrick (Eds.), *Ethnicity and family therapy* (3rd ed., pp. 680–688). New York, NY: Guilford Press.

PART II

Gender and Sexual Orientation Identities

CHAPTER 6

Gender in Couple and Family Life: Toward Inclusiveness and Equality

Carmen Knudson-Martin

From the moment of birth and across the life span, people categorize themselves and others in relation to a socially created category called gender. This categorization tends to divide people into two groups based on observable biological sex differences. Even though this gender binary does not fit the experience of many people, it sets in motion a whole system of relating that limits interpersonal options and reinforces historical power differences between women and men. Everyone is impacted. In this chapter I will examine gender as an identity system and how gender intersects with other social locations to organize couple and family life in ways that often maintain gendered power disparities. I conclude with a model of relationship equality and illustrate **Socio-Emotional Relationship Therapy (SERT)**, an approach that helps people overcome rigid gender binaries and invites flexibility and equity (e.g., Knudson-Martin, Huenergardt, Lafontant, Bishop, Schaepper, & Wells, 2014; Knudson-Martin & Huenergardt, 2010; Knudson-Martin, Wells, & Samman, 2015).

My analysis takes a critical **social constructionist approach** that examines how larger societal forces and inequities are part of moment-by-moment interactions within families and the issues they face (Knudson-Martin & Huenergardt, 2010; McDowell & Fang, 2007). Four key concepts are involved (Figure 6.1).

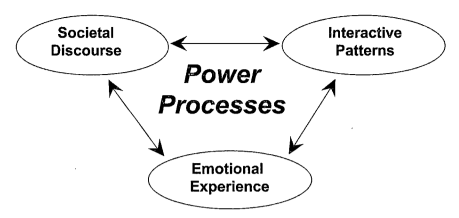

Figure 6.1. Social Construction of the Gender System.
(Adapted from Knudson-Martin, 2013)

SOCIAL CONSTRUCTION OF THE GENDER SYSTEM

Societal Discourse

I use the term *societal discourse* to refer to shared ways of thinking and speaking that give sociocultural meaning to personal experience (Krolokke & Sorensen, 2006). Societal discourses tend to serve the dominant social structure by suggesting appropriate behavior and telling us what to feel (Knudson-Martin & Huenergardt, 2010). Alternative ideas and practices tend to be silenced (Madigan, 2011). In this way, gender identities are socially constructed and maintained. For example, a landmark study found almost no **gender differences** when studying characteristics of individual children; yet, when they engaged with each other, children enacted stereotypic gender patterns (Maccoby & Jacklin, 1974). Though people do not necessarily adhere to the scripts associated with dominant gender discourses, everyone develops their gender identities in context of them and must relate to them in some way.

Emotion

Emotion is a link between society and individuals. Rather than thinking of emotion as something inside a person, a critical social constructionist approach recognizes that emotion arises within a particular social context. The societal gender system has a powerful impact on how people experience themselves and others. For example, societal discourses that say men should not express emotions invite males to feel weak or incompetent if they disclose their feelings (Rabinowitz, 2012). They may encourage a father to feel distant from a son who does not conform to this standard.

A child whose experience does not fit gender stereotypes may feel shame, unsafe, and depressed (Giammettei, 2015).

Interaction

From a critical perspective, interaction patterns are not simply family patterns; they are how the **binary gender system** is enacted or resisted in a particular family or relationship. To understand the meaning of a relational pattern, we needed to attune to the societal messages people have internalized based on gender discourses and other sociocultural contexts (Pandit, Chen-Feng, Kang, Knudson-Martin, & Huenergardt, 2014). For example, ideas that mothers are "naturally" more connected with children encourage fathers to step back from parenting (Cowdery & Knudson-Martin, 2005). Ideas that girls are fragile or sensitive may invite teachers not to challenge them as much as they do boys (Fine, 2010).

Power

Power in relationships is connected to societal power processes. At the interpersonal level, power is the process through which people are able to influence a relationship toward their "own goals, interests, and well-being" (Mahoney & Knudson-Martin, 2009, p. 10). Power imbalances based on the societal gender binary remain surprisingly persistent,

---

WHAT IS THE BALANCE OF POWER?

RELATIVE STATUS
- Whose interests shape what happens in the family?
- To what extent do partners feel equally entitled to express and attain personal goals, needs, and wishes?
- How are low-status tasks like housework handled?

ATTENTION TO OTHER
- To what extent do both partners notice and attend to the other's needs and emotions?
- Does attention go back and forth between partners? Does each give and receive?
- When attention is imbalanced do partners express awareness of this and the need to rebalance?

ACCOMMODATION PATTERNS
- Is one partner more likely to organize his or her daily activities around the other?
- Does accommodation often occur automatically without anything being said?
- Do partners attempt to justify accommodations they make as being "natural" or the result of personality differences?

WELL-BEING
- Does one partner seem to be better off psychologically, emotionally, or physically than the other?
- Does one person's sense of competence, optimism, or well-being seem to come at the expense of the other's physical or emotional health?
- Does the relationship support the economic viability of each partner?

Figure 6.2. Assessment of Relationship Power Positions.
(Knudson-Martin, 2015). Reprinted with permission.

especially among distressed heterosexual couples (Knudson-Martin, 2015; Knudson-Martin & Mahoney, 2009). Invisible and latent powers are embedded in societal norms and expectations in such a way that male needs and interests *automatically* take priority (Komter, 1989). For example, men have latent power when ideas about what constitutes competency are defined in traditionally masculine ways; for example, a good leader demonstrates rational decision-making over ability to express emotion. A man has invisible power if his heterosexual wife automatically plans her career goals around him or the family, while his job takes priority. When power is relatively equal, each notices the feelings, needs, and interests of the other; each feels entitled to express their needs or have them met; and accommodation to the other is reciprocal (Knudson-Martin & Mahoney, 2009). Figure 6.2 provides a useful guide to assessing interpersonal power dynamics.

GENDER AS AN IDENTITY SYSTEM

The U.S. Census Bureau (2013) lists 151,175,000 males and 157,653,000 females. They note that these refer to biological sex. These forced categories tell us little about people's lived experience. Scholars are becoming increasing aware that gender, anatomical sex, and sexuality are considerably more multifaceted than the notion of gender or sexual binaries suggests (Fausto-Sterling, 2012). Persons who experience internal alignment between their assigned biological sex and their gender identities are sometimes referred to as **cisgender**. For example, my body looks female and this fits my internal sense of myself as a woman. However, cisgender persons *express* gender in a variety of ways; they do not necessarily do what is stereotypically considered masculine or feminine (Kimmel, 2011). A woman might assertively express herself in ways often considered masculine, but still very much identify as female.

Transgender, queer, gender questioning, or gender fluid persons also express gender in a variety of ways, but do not internally identify with their physically assigned gender category. While their gender expression, or whether they appear masculine or feminine, is readily visible to the outside world, their *internal inclination* is not (Serano, 2007). Living with this inner dissonance and having to relate to the cisgender world can be extremely stressful, emotionally painful, and stigmatizing (Serano, 2007). **Transsexuals** may actively transition and live as the "other sex," with or without hormone therapy and varying degrees of surgery. Others choose to live outside of society's imposed gender binary categories.

Everyone must repeatedly negotiate societal gender structures and stereotypes. For many cisgender persons, this process is often outside conscious awareness but is expressed in the ways we present ourselves and communicate, and the life choices available to us (Knudson-Martin & Mahoney, 2009; Stone, 2010). Trans persons and those who do not identify within the binary must either "pass" by hiding who they are, or intentionally identify themselves within the predominantly cisgender realm. Those who have lived as both male and female in the eyes of the world give testimony to the power of societal gender categories. According to Serano (2007), who transitioned from male to female, she is the same person that she was before the transition, but now she is "perceived as a woman and treated that way" (p. 63).

Distinguishing Gender and Sexual Orientation

Binary constructions of masculinity and femininity confound biological sex, **gender identity**, gender expression, and sexual orientation; that is, they suggest that if a body looks male, then behavior should demonstrate masculinity and sexual attraction to women. This depiction of gender does not reflect the reality of human experience (Iasenza, 2010). Some "feminine" men and "masculine" women are attracted to same-sex partners; others are not. The range of sexual responses and attractions is highly variable. A person's sex/gender thoughts, feelings, and behaviors may be fluid and multidimensional over time and contexts (Iasenza, 2010).

Hegemonic **gender ideals** tell girls to look and act in ways designed to attract men, and boys learn early on that being masculine requires sexualized dominance over women and repudiation of everything feminine or gay (Kimmel, 2011). An ethnographic study involving observation and interviews over one and a half years illustrates how gender and sexuality identities intersected in a racially diverse high school in a California working class suburban area (Pascoe, 2007). Pascoe found that "boys lay claim to masculine identities by lobbing homophobic epithets at one another" and by "engaging in heterosexist discussion of girls' bodies" (p. 5). She found that girls' popularity depended on masculine approval and their focus on boys' desires rather than their own. In practice, there was actually considerable sex/gender variability; however, school rituals, institutional practices, and interpersonal interactions worked together to support and maintain a hierarchy based on heterosexist masculinity that applied to all genders.

When children's behavior does not conform to the gender binary, parents are often unsure what to do. They know that their children will need to make their way within contexts based on the gender binary (Lev, 2010). Predicting their child's future sex/gender identification is nearly impossible. According to Malpas's (2011) summary of the literature, some gender nonconforming children may become gay and lesbian; some will maintain their cross-gender identification; for others, gender nonconformity will phase out and their sexual orientation will be heterosexual; still others will remain gender nonconforming and be heterosexual. In the meantime, they need affirmation of their current gender expressions and support and safety in what is often an oppressive external environment.

What About Biology?

Scientists are not yet able to explain all the reasons why there is so much sex/gender variability (Fausto-Sterling, 2012). What is becoming increasingly clear is that biology and the social context recursively influence each other. Social experience has considerable impact on how the body is constructed. The meaningful differences at birth between those categorized as male or female are minimal (Eliot, 2010). Eliot, a neurobiologist, points out that studies that show that women tend to have more connections between the two sides of the brain are done on adults and do not take the effect of gendered experience with language into account. Moreover, the differences *among* persons of the same gender are greater than those across genders (Kimmel, 2011). A meta-analysis of 46 studies found males and females statistically equivalent on nearly all the abilities and psychological variables examined (Hyde, 2005).

In her observations of children in middle schools, Thorne (1993) described how she at first saw children primarily enacting stereotypic gender patterns in their style of play and classroom interaction. Then she noticed that a lot of children actually tried to cross the gender boundaries. But the structure of who played where, who got attention in the classroom, and how differences were framed created and maintained a highly gendered social environment. For example, if girls tried to join boys' games they were jeered away with taunts of "cooties"; boys who tried to engage with the girls were teased by the other boys. Teachers often grouped children according to gender and gave most of their attention to a relatively small group of aggressive boys. Like these teachers and children, people often interact in ways that exaggerate and create gender differences. Considerable research shows that when people think an activity is gendered, they perform accordingly. For example, Fine (2010) reports on cross-cultural research that shows that when research participants are told that gender is associated with ability, there is a male advantage in science and math scores. When they are told that girls do well or that there is no gender difference, then girls score as well as boys or better.

HOW DOES GENDER INTERSECT WITH OTHER SOCIAL LOCATIONS?

Gender is not an individual property or a set of personal traits and roles. It is a societal structure of relationships and power experienced and maintained across individual, interactional, and institutional levels (Risman, 1998). The gender system is upheld through the **division of labor**, symbols and images, **communication patterns**, internalized identities, and "objective" criteria for evaluating performance (Kimmel, 2011). However, people are not simply passive recipients of societal gender structures; they also *create* gender each time they perform or enact their identities (Risman,

2009). Each time a female puts a male's interests over hers, the gender system is reenacted. But when a man notices and attends to his female partner's needs, the gender system is resisted. Over time and contexts, gender systems can and do change (Deutsch, 2007).

Across the globe, women do the majority of the household work (Perry-Jenkins, Newkirk, & Ghunney, 2013). "In the United States, gender trumps race, ethnicity, and social class differences, with women across all types of families performing more chores than men" (p. 109). However, inequality is much more than who does the dishes. It is about whose needs and interests take proritiy, who notices and attends to the other, and who organizes around the other (Knudson-Martin, 2013). In any system, those with less power accommodate and attend to those with more. The more powerful group, such as men, typically take their entitlement for granted and may not even notice or be aware of how others accommodate or defer to them. This helps to explain why being feminine is stereotypically equated with other-directed, submissive, nurturing interaction styles while masculinity is associated with assertiveness and **independence** (Jordan, 2009).

Few people have models for how to actually create an **equal relationship**. Gerson (2010) interviewed a diverse group of 120 young adults across the United States. She found that virtually all sought an equal, mutually supportive partner, but they did not have a vision of how to achieve it. Among the heterosexual participants, men described expecting to fall back on traditional gender divisions to make things work, while women reported that they'd need to become independent and go it alone.

When the gender system is in operation, men can work under the illusion that they don't need others while women do the behind-the-scenes work that holds the relationship or family together. Across age and societal contexts, women are less likely to experience heterosexual marriage as beneficial or living up to their expectations (Loscocco & Walzer, 2013). Cross-culturally, the more rigid the division of labor between women and men and the less men are involved in child care, the greater the overall **gender inequality** in the society and the lower the women's status (Kimmel, 2011).

History of the Sex/Gender Binary

The "traditional" division of labor based on a heterosexual male breadwinner and female keeper of the home is actually a relatively new invention (Coontz, 2005). In her history of Euro-American marriage, Coontz notes that in many times and places husbands and wives did not regularly live together. Friendship and intimacy were more likely to be experienced *within* one's gender. As people became involved in the trades and crafts in the 15th century, households in Western Europe began to be organized around a cross-gender married couple as the unit of production (Coontz, 2005). In this business arrangement, husbands were primarily responsible for controlling their wives. The home and domesticity were important to men as well as women, and fathers were typically charged with their children's education and moral upbringing (Coltrane, 1996).

According to Coontz (2005), the notion that male and female "natures" are essentially different evolved along with the idea of love and a personal marriage in the 19th century. In this construction, still popular today, "each sex supplies what the other needs" (Coontz, 2005, p. 187). The male was expected to provide financially and lead through inherent supremacy; women were dependent on men for protection and love. "Only men had sexual desires . . . and women who enjoyed sex reported feeling guilt or shame" (pp. 189–190).

In contrast, family roles among indigenous Americans were often quite fluid and not necessarily determined by sex (Herdt, 1997; Lang, 1998). The relatively equal gender power relations among the Haudenosaunee (also known as Iroquois), in which each woman controlled her own property and women held key political offices, may have provided a model to 19th-century feminists in upstate New York (Wagner, 2001). African American cans have a remarkable history of flexibility in family and work roles (Boyd-Franklin, 2006) and often "actively resisted compliance with family and gender systems that were foreign to their traditions and inconsistent with their status and resources" (Hill, 2005, p. 56). Immigrants also have a legacy of survival through flexibility that may transcend rigid gender prescriptions (Maciel & Van Putten, 2009).

Intersections with Race and Ethnicity

Sexism is sometimes considered a White person's concern. Yet, interaction with the dominant culture and colonizing forces supporting patriarchy and racism have had a major detrimental impact not only across racial lines, but also on how women and men of color interact with each other (Boyd-Frranklin, 2006; Hill, 2005; Rojas, 2009). According to Rojas,

Many Black women are reluctant to report sexual assault because they feel compelled to protect the men in their communities and families. They are wary of an unjust penal system and recognize the potential damage in removing men from their households. However, as women, their dedication to community is often overlooked . . . and illustrate the nature of the violence that surrounds [some] Black women's lives. (p. 46)

The shortage of African American men and effects of racism can be used as justifications to encourage Black women to stay in abusive relationships (Boyd-Franklin, 2006). The "black shadow," or internalized shame at being Black, can cause embarassment and deprecation of self and others, which makes feeling trust and safety in relationships more difficult (Watson, 2013).

Beauty and desire have been racialized so that people of color can never live up to Eurocentric norms. Black women have struggled to control their sexual agency and "the line between agency and exploitation has been blurred" (Rojas, 2009, p. 34). Rojas reports that Native American women are victims of violent crime 2.5 times more often than other ethnic groups and twice as likely to be raped, while Asian American women have the highest rate of suicide of any racial or ethnic group. Continued exposure to racism and misogyny can lead some women of color to link love and abuse (Rojas, 2009). Overcoming these internalized messages of self-hate is critical to personal and relational empowerment (Watson, 2013).

For African Americans, the dynamics of gender and power occur against the backdrop of the struggle for racial justice, in which need for unity can transcend gender divides (Boyd-Franklin, 2006; Cowdery, Scarborough, Lewis, & Seshadri, 2009; Hill, 2005). In response to the denigration of Black men in the larger society, many elevate the role of men in family life. According to Hill, the dominant culture's view of patriarchy perpetuated a myth of the Black matriarch and ignored her lack of power or resources in "virtually every aspect of life" (p. 67).

A qualitative study of gender and power processes among 15 middle-class African American couples found the effects of racial inequity still at play (Cowdery et al., 2009). As in numerous other studies (e.g., Perry-Jenkins et al., 2013), the men shared household labor and child care more than their White counterparts; however, they held invisible power in a variety of ways. Women were sensitive to how societal pressures were affecting men at work and tried to protect them by masking their own power, as illustrated by the example of Henry and Keisha:

Henry: I have to bow down to all sorts of people. Sometimes I have to dummy up for them because they don't want . . . nobody wants a Black man who knows more than they do working for them. (Cowdery et al., 2009, p. 224)

In response, Keisha "dummies down" for her husband to make him feel like he has the power, if not in society, at least in their relationship. These couples also demonstrated a paradox found in the literature on some Black couples (e.g., Furdyna, Tucker, & James, 2008); though they demonstrated considerable behavioral equality, they ascribed to traditional gender ideology. Hill (2005) attributes the focus on traditional gender ideals as an attempt to live up to dominant culture norms that have historically been difficult for Black men to attain.

Gendered dominant culture representations of racial and ethnic minorities tend to be simplistic and denigrating (Falicov, 2010; Rojas, 2009). Falicov describes how her own clinical observations and movies by Latino directors offer more positive and complex alternatives to the narrow dominant culture view of *machismo*:

> Almost invariably, in addition to the Mexican cowboy type who is ruthless, vengeful, and downgrading of women, there are other male characters depicted as honest, humble, and hard working. (Falicov, 2010, p. 311)

Gender inequality is a concern in Latino communities (Rojas, 2009); however, Latino masculinity may be more relationally oriented than Anglo masculinity (Falicov, 2010). For example, it is more permissible for Latino men to "be affectionate, show tender feelings, kiss and hug including male children and close friends" (p. 314).

Intersections with Socioeconomic Status and Work

Women with lower socioeconomic status (SES) always have worked outside the home (Kimmel, 2011). In the United States and many places around the globe, the ability of professional women to be successful in the workplace depends on lower-income women leaving their families to care for others' elderly and children. Increasingly, women from poorer parts of the world migrate to wealthier countries to provide domestic and sex services (Ehrenreich & Hochschild, 2002). This transnational flow of services intersects with gender and economic inequities in important ways. Depending on the situation, women may gain a measure of independence, but little about the structure of the workplace or inequity in the division of labor changes. And the inequities between the "have" countries and the "have not" countries get larger (Ehrenreich & Hochschild, 2002).

When a man's income is limited, he may take on more household labor for pragmatic reasons (Perry-Jenkins et al., 2013). We have seen many such instances in heterosexual couple therapy with low-income couples. Unemployed or underemployed fathers take care of the children while the mother is the primary breadwinner. Though this could give the appearance of gender equality, a closer examination shows that in each of these clinical cases the male partner maintained a power balance through his limited attunement and attention to his female partner's needs and interests such that it was nearly impossible for her to influence him (see Knudson-Martin, 2015). When women make more money than their partners, they seldom hold power in ways that men do, and often both partners compensate to preserve the **male hierarchy** (Esmiol Wilson, Knudson-Martin, & Wilson, 2014; Tichenor, 2005).

Since the 1980s, more mothers of young children in the United States have worked outside the home than not (see Kimmel, 2011, pp. 248–253). Yet there have not been comparative changes in the workplace, such as better access to child care and work standards and schedules more compatible with family life (Jacobs & Gerson, 2004). These environmental challenges reinforce existing gender inequities, making it more likely that women accommodate work to fit family demands than men (Perry-Jenkins, et al., 2013). Solutions vary, but even when men share family tasks, women still typically carry the organizational burden (Zimmerman, Haddock, Ziemba, & Rust, 2001).

Stone (2010) studied highly educated affluent women in the United States who "opted out" of the workplace. These women had already attained considerable career success and invested significant time and resources into preparing for their professions. Stone's qualitative analysis of interviews with 54 women found that they were *not* responding to traditional gender values; rather, their workplaces and marriages were not structured to accommodate integrating work and family responsibilities. The pressures to be the ideal worker and the ideal mother were so great that the women found it impossible to do both. The "choice" to leave work was not so much a personal choice as a reflection of the limited options these women experienced. None of the husbands in this study cut back on their high-powered jobs to facilitate their wives' careers.

Intersections with Culture and Religion

The performance of gender is a major way that cultural ideals are enacted (Silverstein, Bass, Tuttle, Knudson-Martin, & Huenergardt, 2009). For example, in the United States, ideals of independence are culturally prioritized over collectivist cultural ideals that prioritize the group over the person, and ideals of independence also are linked with constructions of masculinity (Loscocco & Walzer, 2013). Women, constructed as emotionally needy and dependent, are held responsible for maintaining the relationship and tending to the emotional needs of their partners and children (Knudson-Martin, 2013; Loscocco & Walzer, 2013). This cultural construction of gender makes it difficult for men to share relational responsibility, even when they say they want relationships and express egalitarian ideals. Moreover, this creates a culturally constructed power imbalance in which women are more focused on men, and male needs and interests end up privileged without conscious intention (Knudson-Martin & Huenergardt, 2010; Knudson-Martin & Mahoney, 2009).

Women also become the "natural" targets for making relational changes suggested by counselors and self-help books (Loscocco & Walzer, 2013). For example, women are often told to "soften" their approach with men. In heterosexual relationships, this tends to leave the responsibility for creating change with the persons with the least power. Relationship satisfaction becomes a gendered issue, with women more likely to be dissatisfied. In a representative national survey, women were more than twice as likely as men to say they wanted their marriages to end (Loscocco & Walzer, 2013).

A gender hierarchy also is embedded deeply in traditional **collectivist cultures** (Triandis, 1995). In this context, gender is part of an elaborate hierarchy also involving family membership, age, and social position and status. Gender is maintained through a clear set of rules and roles that serve to maintain social harmony; for example, the mother may serve as the internal link between father and children, while always deferring to him for major and public decisions (Quek, Knudson-Martin, Rue, & Alibiso, 2010; Silverstein et al., 2009). In collectivist multigenerational cultures, gender relationships are often also less couple focused. Also, while women hold less power relative to men, women may exercise another kind of power hierarchy in how they navigate among other women and in their relationships with sons and other family members (Coontz, 2005).

As collectivist cultures move toward urbanization and women enter the workplace, gender dynamics also change. In our interviews with 20 dual-career heterosexual couples in Singapore, we found that men, as well as women, spoke with a "we-focus" (Quek, 2009; Quek & Knudson-Martin, 2008). While the individualistic focus of men in Western studies tended to create an imbalance in focus on the other, this analysis found that collectivist cultural values of loyalty to the family group rather than the individual could indirectly facilitate more egalitarian practices. Thus when Singapore's government encouraged women to go into the workplace to facilitate national economic goals, men also began to make changes. For example, Meng believed in a traditional division of labor, but automatically took on household responsibilities because he noticed the demands on his wife: "I always do it [household tasks] rather than waiting for her to do it . . . She's got her own busy schedule, so I must understand her" (Quek & Knudson-Martin, 2008, p. 522).

A similar study of Chinese American couples found that many heterosexual partners integrated collectivist ideals with more individualistic values from the dominant culture (Quek et al., 2010). EunJoo and Jai shifted to a more couple-focused *relational* harmony that gave women more voice and viewed expression of each partner's perspective as important to family harmony:

EunJoo: We're both in it together and we are both individuals, we will have different opinions . . . . It's important that you take both perspectives and both expectations into mind.

Jai: She needs to be affirmed as a person . . . that means giving her voice. I think it is good for me, and it's good for her and the whole family. (Quek et al., 2010, p. 371)

There is considerable variation in how people enact gender *within* any particular culture or religion. Any given person or family is always integrating multiple possible values and societal messages (Falicov, 2010; Knudson-Martin & Huenergardt, 2010). Cultures are also always fluid and in the process of transition. It is a mistake to assume that cultural values are inflexible or that how they are constructed is not open to conversation. I saw this most clearly from interviews of Islamic couples in Iran (Moghadam & Knudson-Martin, 2009). Values and social structures supporting male dominance coexisted with ideals of human worth, respect, and dignity and a historical legacy of women's rights. How couples in Iran integrated these various societal values varied considerably. For example, though husband Bahram held the cultural authority to make decisions, both partners agreed that he was attuned to his wife Sima and valued her voice:

Sima: When we are disagreeing then we have to keep talking about it until we make a decision.

Bahram: We end up making the right decisions. This includes business decisions: I give her all the credit because she has a very good business mind. (p. 267)

An example that helps to illustrate the multiple ways gender, culture, and religion may intersect is the Minangkabau of Indonesia. This devoutly Islamic society is based on "maternal" values (Sanday, 2002). Property ownership and lineage pass from mother to daughter but women do not rule *over* men. Rather, power is shared; men hold public roles but cannot take action without the approval of women. The egalitarian organization of this gender system has been relatively untouched by imperialistic conquest, but appears harder to maintain in the face of urbanization (Sanday, 2002).

Intersections with Sexualities

Cross-cultural studies have shown that gender and sex binaries taken for granted in Western societies are not universal (Kimmel, 2011; Lang, 1998; Mead, 2001). There was considerable sex/gender variation and fluidity among indigenous cultures in North America (Lang, 1998). Though multiple genders were sometimes formally recognized in the culture, these gender categories were not necessarily connected to sexual preference and people were not reduced to a sexual category (Herdt, 1997; Jacobs, 1997; Maltz & Archambault, 1995). A person classified as "two spirit" or a Native American person who simultaneously manifests both masculine and feminine traits may or may not have been homosexual. For example, according to Jacobs, strong "warrior women" were not presumed to be masculine or lesbian. One's erotic life was less significant than other social statuses.

Sex and gender intersect in numerous ways everywhere. What this means varies depending on one's social location. On the one hand, efforts to claim a sex/gender identity that actually fits one's personal experience and preference can be personally liberating and important to consciousness-raising and social justice at the societal level (e.g., Serano, 2007). At the same time, categorizing people based on how they respond to or relate to sex/gender can also create new forms of "othering" and narrow people's identities to their sexual attractions (Knudson-Martin & Laughlin, 2005). For example, gay or transsexual persons become an "other" chapter at the end of the book to which couple and family theory and practice can be applied instead of beginning practice models with an inclusive premise.

In order to work with the range of gender experience and facilitate relationships that support and enhance the well-being of everyone, it is important to (a) recognize the influence of the binary societal gender system, (b) counteract the limits and destructive effects of the binary system, and (c) empower people to create more equal, fluid relationship possibilities.

A RELATIONSHIP MODEL BASED ON EQUALITY

Even though most Western people now express egalitarian ideals, they seldom have a picture of what an equal relationship would look like (Gerson, 2010; Knudson-Martin & Mahoney, 2009; Sullivan, 2006). The societal gender system tends to perpetuate itself because gender expectations are taken for granted; they seem so normal that they are invisible to us. When ChenFeng and Galick (2015) studied transcripts of 23 therapy sessions with heterosexual couples, they discovered that even among experienced male and female therapists, gender tended to hijack the therapy; that is, both therapists and clients tended to reinforce male privilege, expect women to accommodate, and protect men from shame at the woman's expense. To counteract this pattern, SERT organizes interventions around a model of equality (Knudson-Martin & Huenergardt, 2010; Knudson-Martin et al., 2014; Knudson-Martin et al., 2015). This model, called the **circle of care** (see Figure 6.3), emphasizes (a) mutual vulnerability, (b) mutual attunement, (c) mutual influence, and (d) shared relational responsibility.

Research shows that mutual responsiveness and a relational focus are keys to a healthy relationship (Beck & Clark, 2010; Nicoleau, Kang, Choau, & Knudson-Martin, 2014). Successful couples can be distinguished by their capacity to notice and respond to each other, tune into emotion, and be open to influence (e.g., Gottman, 2011; Greenberg & Goldman, 2008; Mirgain & Cordova, 2007). On the other hand, power imbalances are destructive. They undermine trust and prevent the shared responsiveness, focus, and investment necessary for relational maintenance (Collett, 2010; Stanley, Rhoades, & Whitten, 2010) and are thus directly tied to relationship distress and dissatisfaction as well as depression and anxiety (DeMaris, 2007; Knudson-Martin, 2013; Steil, 1997). Stereotypic

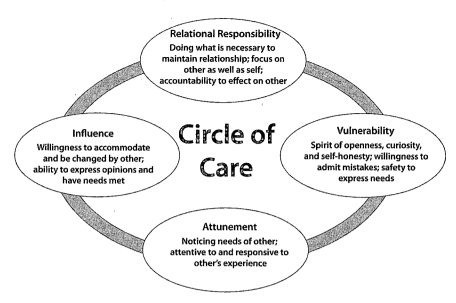

Figure 6.3. The Circle of Care.
(Adapted from Knudson-Martin & Huenergardt, 2015)

gender differences interfere with each aspect of the circle of care, that is, the relational processes needed to sustain **mutual support** and well-being.

The Western binary gender system tells men that they are supposed to be autonomous and invulnerable and that they are supposed to know what to do and how to solve problems. Women learn to focus on others and hide their strength (Jordan, 2009). According to Tannen (1994), a sociolinguist, when women talk they try to avoid hierarchy and preserve equality by minimizing their successes and emphasizing their problems. This disparity in gender socialization and inequalities in how male and female qualities are valued in society means that heterosexual partners typically do not enter a relationship on an equal playing field.

To the extent that people enact stereotypical societal gender constructs, a power difference is created in who attends to the other, who accommodates, and whose interests and well-being take priority. In heterosexual relationships, each partner tends to focus on the male's interests (Knudson-Martin & Mahoney, 2009). Same-sex relationships tend to be more equal (Connolly, 2005; Hardtke, Armstrong, & Johnson, 2010; Shechory & Ziv, 2007), and when power imbalances are present, it appears easier for them to acknowledge the inequities and address them (Jonathan, 2009; Richards, Jonathan, & Kim, 2015).

Viewing relationships through the circle of care not only makes power discrepancies visible; it also provides a positive framework from which to approach couple and family life. Family practitioners and educators can position their work to counteract the taken-for-granted nature of gendered power differences and support equality and mutual support. The goal is to experience new, more flexible ways of relating. For many, this means redefining aspects of masculinity or femininity beyond the constraints of the binary gender system.

PRACTICING SOCIO-EMOTIONAL RELATIONSHIP THERAPY

Socio-Emotional Relationship Therapy (SERT) involves three stages: (1) creating an equitable foundation for change, (2) interrupting the flow of power, and (3) facilitating alternative experience (Knudson-Martin & Huenergardt, 2015).

Phase I: Establish an Equitable Foundation for Therapy

The SERT approach is applicable across diverse populations because reciprocity and mutual support are common societal ideals that transcend gender identities, sexual orientations, and cultural contexts (Richards et al., 2015). In the first session, we tell people we work from the idea that relationships should equally support the health and well-being of each person and ask if they agree. They always do. We use the circle of care (Figure 6.3) to guide the conversation (Knudson-Martin & Huenergardt, 2010, 2015). These ideas bring invisible power processes into the open, so people can be more intentional about the kind of relationships they wish to form. Though the model focuses on couples, the ideas are relevant to work with families, children, adolescents, and individual adults.

As clients share their stories, we seek to attune to each family member, to "get" what it feels like to be in their social context (Pandit et al., 2014). This helps us understand how their sociocultural contexts invite each person's emotional experience and the couple/family interaction patterns. Each feels understood and validated. Understanding their socioemotional experience includes an assessment of their power dynamics.

Phase II: Interrupt the Flow of Power

The second phase involves active persistence on the part of therapists to recognize and interrupt the usual flow of power in the couple and family. In heterosexual couples, this usually means encouraging the male partner to become vulnerable, attune to his partner and family members, and initiate relational connection. Interrupting the usual flow of power helps to create safety so that the most vulnerable partner is not made to carry even more vulnerability and responsibility for the relationship in the therapy. Tracking the relational consequences of the flow of power helps each partner begin to consider alternative ways of relating.

Phase III: Facilitate Alternative Experience

We have learned that it not sufficient to identify gender stereotypes or power imbalances; practitioners must also take the lead in introducing alternative gender discourses by inviting partners to take new actions and in detailing what works when partners break out of gender stereotypes. The circle of care is useful in this phase as partners envision what equality would look like for them and begin to experience something new with each other.

CASE EXAMPLE: BELLE AND JOHN

Belle (36) is a cisgender African American heterosexual woman married to John (38), a cisgender Euro-American. The couple has three children, ages 15, 12, and 8. John is on disability due to chronic pain; Belle works as a teacher even though she also experiences considerable health problems. They sought help for child behavior concerns and marital distress, participating in therapy with a clinical team as part of an ongoing research project focused on gender, power, and cultural issues (Knudson-Martin & Huenergardt, 2010, 2015; Knudson-Martin et al., 2014).

Socio-Emotional Assessment

Assessment was focused on the links between interaction patterns, sociocultural experience, and gender, power, and other societal contexts.

Interaction Patterns

The binary gender system was enacted in this family. In the first session, our team observed that the only time John listened or paid attention was when the therapist focused on him. He appeared to disengage when Belle or the children were speaking. Belle was described as responsible for everything; John was reportedly either angry or focused on his own interests, representing a stereotypical heterosexual gender pattern in the division of labor and communication. The boys, Bobby (15) and Simon (12), vacillated between siding with their mother in her arguments with their father and a power struggle in which they resisted most of the requests she made of them. Jenny (8) appeared anxious and tended to "hide" behind her mother.

Sociocultural Attunement

This case involved the intersection of gender, race, socioeconomic status, and disability with personal identities and relationship processes. Before we could help this family, we had to attune to each family member.

We wondered what John had learned about what was expected of him as a White heterosexual man? What societal messages gave Belle the responsibility for running the household? What had she learned about her place in the world as an African American woman that kept her going to work and engaging with the family even when she was sick or in pain? What beliefs were Bobby, Simon, and Jenny internalizing about what is expected of them and who merits respect? What did it mean to be young men who looked Black but had an angry and disengaged White father?

We discovered that John had internalized the idea that his worth was measured in a paycheck. As a White man raised in a middle-class American family, he also felt deserving of respect, required to provide answers and occupy a position of authority, and entitled to focus on his personal interests and goals. Since he was not employed and family members seldom seemed to respect him, he felt like a failure most of the time. As an African American woman, Belle internalized a very different identity; she learned that no matter what happens, you keep going; you don't necessarily expect respect or to be acknowledged for your contributions; you put the family first. She took pride in her hard work, but frequently felt sad, resentful, and depressed.

Gender and Power

Even though John experienced limited overt power in the family, his needs and interests usually took priority. This happened in part because he felt entitled to express anger when Belle or the children interfered with what he wanted, such as what to watch on television or someone making noise when he wanted to rest. A lot of John's power also came because Belle automatically organized her time around him and encouraged the children to do so. She took on the household tasks she knew John was not interested in and usually only asked him to do things she thought he would be willing to do. Even though he was at home and she went to work during the day, Belle still handled nearly all household responsibilities. When she was not feeling well, he would yell at the children to help their mother. They resisted, saying "why should we when you don't?" It's important to note that John did not *feel* powerful. Like others in powerful positions, he was not aware of how the rest of the family automatically accommodated him (e.g., Kimmel, 2011). John was much more aware that he did not have the power "he should" in the outside world.

As a result of our exploration of the circle of care, John, Belle, and the children agreed that they wanted their family to be more supportive of one another and all agreed that they wanted to lift some of the relationship burdens from Belle and for John to engage in the family, that is, to share relational responsibility and be open to being influenced by and responsive to Belle and the children.

Undoing Gendered Power in Session

In some cases, SERT requires only a few sessions to help a couple or family get on a new track. More commonly therapy lasts 3–4 months. In this case, the issues were complex and therapy included over 40 sessions. Sometimes we met with only Belle and John, other times we met with the whole family, and sometimes we met with the children separately or with various combinations of family members.

Phase I: Establish an Equitable Foundation for Therapy

A challenge in the early sessions was for each person to feel validated without inadvertently appearing to support societal inequities. For example, John spoke with a lot of passion about his limited access to money and how important expenditures for his own needs were to him. We wanted him to "feel felt" (Siegel, 2001); that we "got" how his middle-class White male identity was connected with material accomplishment and possession. At the same time, we needed to help him become aware of where these ideas may have come from and to consider their consequences on his relationships. For example,

Therapist: It must be hard to feel so belittled in the eyes of the world, especially since money meant so much in your family growing up.
John: Yah!! My dad never had to grovel for what he wanted.
Therapist: So it makes sense that sometimes you just want what you want. (pause) I wonder, how do you think it affects Belle when you seem more interested in your own needs than in what the family needs?
John: I know she thinks I'm selfish . . . And I guess I am.
Therapist: How does it work for you when the family sees you spending money in ways that can seem more focused on you than them? (pause) Because I sense that you really do care about them.
John: Yes!! I do!! But it's hard for them to see that.
Therapist: I know. You really want to be part of the family and for them to see you that way.

An important part of this process for John, and many men, was helping him identify his relational needs and interests and affirming them (Englar-Carlson & Kiselica, 2013; Samman & Knudson-Martin, 2015).

Phase II: Interrupt the Flow of Power

In the next phase we had to counteract power imbalances in order to facilitate relational safety and foster mutual attunement. For example, Belle and John were in a heated discussion about how to discipline Bobby for staying out too late. At first Belle was very forceful, but as the debate continued, she began to shut down and quietly agreed with John. It was very important not to simply accept the lack of conflict as success. We recognized this as a sign of accommodation and needed to know more about this power dynamic between them. When we asked Belle what was going on for her that made her stop expressing her point, she voiced hopelessness that John would never listen to her. John had not been aware that his "feisty" wife was actually often afraid to express her views.

Several sessions later, this kind of work enabled Belle for the first time to share with John emotional pain that she had been carrying since the beginning of their relationship. She had felt abandoned when she was raped and John did not stand up for her, but instead seemed to agree with her parents and others that she was wrong to have been partying when he was living in another town. Belle was able to be vulnerable in this way because the therapists actively supported John as someone who *wanted* to know what his wife felt and helped him keep his focus on her. Because of the power imbalance, it was important that John take the initiative in this phase. This then enabled Belle and the children to better understand John without reinforcing the power imbalance and helped everyone experience a side of John that had been hidden by dominant gender discourses.

Phase III: Facilitate Alternative Experience

As John began to demonstrate more attunement to the family, the therapists used a strengths-based approach to identify successes and help the couple and family create a relationship model based on equality. For example, we asked the children to think of a time when their father was more a part of the family. Simon described an instance when his dad sat down with him and joined in a game he was playing. This created an opportunity to identify exceptions to the dominant gender discourse (Dickerson, 2013) and to ask John what it was like for him to feel close to his son, tapping into "engaged father" societal discourses that were meaningful to John but not well developed in their family life. A particularly transformative session was when John met with the two boys and they discussed what it meant to be a father. Belle and John also began to express more empathy for each other and how their different racial and socioeconomic experiences affected their responses to pain and stress.

Rather than the therapists telling them how their family should function, they helped the family detail for themselves what shared relational responsibility looked like for them. In one of the final sessions, eight-year-old Jenny took charge as the family detailed how they demonstrated their care and concern for each other. Her confident voice and the willing cooperation of her older brothers and father in this discussion enabled them to actively perform alternate gender identities. Both Belle and John reported feeling more loved and valued and able to co-parent.

CONCLUSIONS

A critical social constructionist approach to gender makes power differences visible and empowers people to expand beyond narrow gender stereotypes. At the beginning of therapy, this family was among the most distressed we have seen, with individual family members exhibiting multiple symptoms. In the first session, they identified themselves by their disabilities and diagnoses. Our persistent focus on undoing the underlying gendered power imbalance provided a foundation and safe emotional context for addressing the other issues of concern to them (e.g., Wells & Kuhn, 2015). Our attention to the confluence of gender with the effects of socioeconomic status, race, and other inequities helped the family move from a pathological view of themselves to an empowered one (e.g., Watson, 2013) and opened space for them to construct new ways of relating outside binary gender stereotypes.

There is a lot of gender-informed research on the division of labor and how gender inequities are maintained. There is less information about how gender inequities are undone or how mutual support is obtained. Few clinical models explicitly incorporate attention to gender and other larger societal contexts, and thus SERT and other models that incorporate gender need additional testing so that the processes involved in undoing gender for the improved mental health and relational health of all family members can be understood and disseminated. There is also a need to expand the gender lens from a binocular view of "opposites" to a more fluid and multidimensional view that supports relationship equality and is inclusive of the wide range of human experience.

CHAPTER REVIEW

Key Points

1. Gender is a socially created set of binary categories that do not accurately represent the range of human experience.
2. Most people express egalitarian gender ideals but do not have a model for how to implement them.
3. Stereotypic gender differences create power imbalances in who attends to, accommodates to, and influences the other, with negative consequences for all genders.
4. A critical social constructionist approach attends to societal-based power differences and envisions gender as performed, fluid, and open to change.
5. Practitioners can help undo gender inequalities by attuning to the societal context, interrupting the flow of power, and facilitating alternative experiences.

Key Terms

binary gender system, cisgender, collectivist cultures, communication patterns, distinguishing gender, division of labor, emotion, equal relationship, gender and sexual orientation, gender differences, gender ideals, gender identity, gender inequality, independence, male hierarchy, mutual support/circle of care, power, social constructionist approach, Socio-Emotional Relationship Therapy (SERT), transgender, transsexual

Myths and Realities

- It is a myth that gender differences are "natural" or "hard-wired." In reality, gender differences are minimal at birth and tend to be exaggerated through social interaction.
- It is a myth that there are two genders. In reality, there are many ways people experience gender.
- Many people believe that gender equality has been resolved, that everything is different now. In truth, though there have been many changes in gender roles and expectations, societal gender *structures* have changed very little and gendered power differences continue to limit intimacy, communication, relationship satisfaction, and mental health.
- Some people think only women can nurture. This is a myth. Men can and do nurture children and intimate partners, but may step back from trying if they feel incompetent or that women are "natural" caregivers. Like everyone, the more men nurture, the better they get at it. This is similarly true for women as leaders.
- Some educators and practitioners teach people that men and women are from different worlds and simply help people adjust to this. This is a myth that perpetuates gender inequality and limits people's options and flexibility.

Tools and Tips

Knowledge

Fine, C. (2010). *Delusions of gender: How our minds, society, and neurosexism create difference*. New York, NY: W.W. Norton.

Knudson-Martin, C., & Mahoney, A.R. (Eds.). (2009). *Couples, gender, and power: Creating change in intimate relationships*. New York, NY: Springer.

Knudson-Martin, C., Wells, M.A., & Samman, S.K. (2015). *Socio-emotional relationship therapy: Bridging emotion, societal context, and couple interaction*. New York, NY: Springer.

Serano, J. (2007). *Whipping girl: A transsexual woman on sexism and the scapegoating of femininity*. Berkeley, CA: Seal Press.

Tichenor, V.J. (2005). *Earning more and getting less: Why successful wives can't buy equality*. New Brunswick, NJ: Rutgers University Press.

Dynamic Sizing

It is important to take a binocular lens when working with gender issues. One lens views gender as a set of defined patterns and relationships that structure social institutions and family life. This is the context for everyone. The second lens is individual. Every individual experiences gender as it intersects with other societal contexts, personal experience and preference, and biology. The interaction between these two levels is key to analysis and change.

Skills

Theory. Integrating critical and social constructionist theories attends to the societal power dimension as well as offers a framework for studying and addressing the processes of change.

Prevention. Gender non-conforming children need acceptance and help navigating unsupportive or hostile social environments. Well-being for everyone will be promoted with application of an inclusive gender lens and guidance regarding models for equal relationships.

Service Provision. Providers need to position their work to counteract destructive gender binaries. This involves (a) creating an equitable foundation for therapy, (b) interrupting the flow of power, and (c) facilitating alternative experience. If they do not provide this leadership, they may inadvertently reinforce societal gender inequities.

Policy. Policies in schools and workplaces still tend to reinforce inequitable gender structures and disadvantage anyone who actively cares for children or other family members. Changing policies such as how work is rewarded and scheduled and expanded options for child care is critical to advancing an inclusive and equitable society.

Research. Research needs to move beyond a focus on the division of labor or individual gender traits and roles to include a greater focus on interpersonal power processes and communication patterns, as well as the processes through which gender is undone.

Awareness

The assessment tool listed in Figure 6.2 is valuable for raising consciousness. I have students use it to explore their own intimate and family-of-origin relationships as well as apply it to diverse case examples. When using the tool, it is also useful to ask what societal/gender messages invite these relationship patterns. Awareness also can be raised by applying these questions when doing a genogram or family history and by creating a picture or map of all the people and cultural contexts that have given voice to and passed on internalized messages about these gender-related relationship processes.

REFERENCES

Beck, L., & Clark, M.S. (2010). What constitutes a healthy communal marriage and why relationship stage matters. *Journal of Family Theory & Review, 2,* 299–315.

Boyd-Franklin, N. (2006). Black families in America: Understanding the African American experience (2nd ed.). New York, NY: Guilford Press.

ChenFeng, J. L., & Galick, A. (2015). How gender discourses hijack couple therapy—And how to avoid it. In C. Knudson-Martin, M. Wells, & S. K. Samman (Eds.), *Socio-emotional relationship therapy: Bridging emotion, societal context, and couple interaction* (pp. 41–52). New York, NY: Springer.

Collett, J. L. (2010). Integrating theory, enhancing understanding: The potential contributions of recent experimental research in social exchange for studying intimate relationships. *Journal of Family Theory & Review, 2,* 280–298.

Coltrane, S. (1996). *The family man: Fatherhood, housework, and gender equity.* New York, NY: Oxford University Press.

Connolly, C. (2005). A qualitative exploration of resilience in long-term lesbian couples. *Family Journal, 13,* 266–280.

Coontz, S. (2005). *Marriage, a history: From obedience to intimacy or how love conquered marriage.* New York, NY: Viking.

Cowdery, R. S., & Knudson-Martin, C. (2005). Motherhood: Tasks, relational connection, and gender equality. *Family Relations, 54,* 335–346.

Cowdery, R. S., Scarborough, N., Lewis, M. E., & Seshadri, G. (2009). Pulling together: How African American couples manage social inequalities. In C. Knudson-Martin & A. R. Mahoney (Eds.), *Couples, gender, and power: Creating change in intimate relationships* (pp. 215–233). New York, NY: Springer Publishing Company.

DeMaris, A. (2007). The role of relationship inequality in marital disruption. *Journal of Social and Personal Relationships, 24,* 177–195.

Deutsch, F. M. (2007). Undoing gender. *Gender & Society, 21,* 106–127. doi: 10.1177/0891243206293577

Dickerson, V. (2013). Patriarchy, power, and privilege: A narrative/poststructural view of work with couples. *Family Process, 52,* 102–114.

Ehrenreich, B., & Hochschild, A. R. (2002). *Global woman: Nannies, maids, and sex workers in the new economy.* New York, NY: Metropolitan Books.

Eliot, Lise (2010). *Pink brain blue brain: How small differences grow into troublesome gaps.* New York, NY: Mariner Books.

Englar-Carlson, M., & Kiselica, M. S. (2013). Affirming the strengths in men: A positive masculinity approach to assisting male clients. *Journal of Counseling and Development, 91,* 399–409.

Esmiol Wilson, E., Knudson-Martin, C., & Wilson, C. (2014). Gendered power, spirituality, and relational processes: The experience of Christian physician couples: *Journal of Couple and relationship Therapy, 13,* 312–338. doi: 10.1080/15332691.2014.95365

Falicov, C. J. (2010). Changing constructions of machismo for Latino men in therapy: The devil never sleeps. *Family Process, 49,* 309–329.

Fausto-Sterling, A. (2012). *Sex/gender: Biology in a social world.* New York, NY: Routledge.

Fine, C. (2010). *Delusions of gender: How our minds, society, and neurosexism create difference.* New York, NY: W.W. Norton.

Furdyna, H. E., Tucker, M. B., & James, A. D. (2008). Relative spousal earnings and marital happiness among African American and White Women. *Journal of Marriage and Family, 70,* 332–344.

Gerson, K. (2010). *The unfinished revolution: How a new generation is reshaping family, work, and gender in America.* New York, NY: Oxford University Press.

Giammettei, S.V., (2015). Beyond the binary: Trans-negotiations in couple and family life. *Family Process, 54,* 418–434.

Gottman, J.M. (2011). *The science of trust: Emotional attunement for couples.* New York, NY: Guilford Press.

Greenberg, L.S., & Goldman, R.N. (2008). *Emotion-focused couples therapy: The dynamics of emotion, love, and power.* Washington, DC: American Psychological Association.

Hardtke, K.K., Armstrong, M., & Johnson, S. (2010). Emotionally focused couple therapy: A full-treatment model well-suited to the specific needs of lesbian couples. *Journal of Couple & Relationship Therapy, 9,* 312–326.

Herdt, G. (1997). The dilemmas of desire: From Berdache to two spirit. In S. E. Jacobs, W. Thomas, & S. Long (Eds.), *Two-spirit people: Native American gender identity, sexuality, and spirituality* (pp. 278–283). Chicago: IL: University of Illinois Press.

Hill, S.A. (2005). *Black intimacies: A gender perspective on families and relationships.* Walnut Creek, CA: AltaMira Press.

Hyde, J.S. (2005). The gender similarities hypothesis. *American Psychologist, 60,* 581–592.

Iasenza, S. (2010). What is queer about sex?: Expanding sexual frames in theory and practice. *Family Process, 49,* 291–308.

Jacobs, J. A., & Gerson, K. (2004). *The time divide: Work, family, and gender inequality.* Cambridge, MA: Harvard University Press.

Jacobs, S.E. (1997). Is the "North American berdache" merely a phantom in the imagination of Western social scientists? In S. E. Jacobs, W. Thomas, & S. Long (Eds.), *Two-spirit people: Native American gender identity, sexuality, and spirituality* (pp. 21–44). Chicago: IL: University of Illinois Press.

Jonathan, N. (2009). Carrying equal weight: Relational responsibility and attunement among same-sex couples. In C. Knudson-Martin & A.R. Mahoney (Eds.), *Couples, gender and power: Creating change in intimate relationships* (pp. 79–103). New York, NY: Springer Publishing.

Jordan, J. (2009). *Relational-cultural therapy.* Washington, DC: American Psychological Association.

Kimmel, M. (2011). *The gendered society* (4th ed.). New York, NY: Oxford University Press.

Knudson-Martin, C. (2013). Why power matters: Creating a foundation of mutual support in couple relationships. *Family Process, 52,* 5–18.

Knudson-Martin, C. (2015). When therapy challenges patriarchy: Undoing gendered power in heterosexual couple relationships. In C. Knudson-Martin, M. Wells, & S.K. Samman (Eds.), *Socio-emotional relationship therapy: Bridging emotion, societal context, and couple interaction* (pp. 15–26). New York, NY: Springer.

Knudson-Martin, C., & Huenergardt, D. (2010). A socio-emotional approach to couple therapy: Linking social context and couple interaction. *Family Process, 49,* 369–386.

Knudson-Martin, C., & Huenergardt, D. (2015). Bridging emotion, societal discourse, and couple interaction in clinical practice. In C. Knudson-Martin, M. Wells, & S.K. Samman (Eds.), *Socio-emotional relationship therapy: Bridging emotion, societal context, and couple interaction* (pp. 1–13). New York, NY: Springer.

Knudson-Martin, C., Huenergardt, D., Lafontant, K., Bishop, L., Schaepper, J., & Wells, M. (2014). Competencies for addressing gender and power in couple therapy: A socio-emotional approach. *Journal of Marital and Family Therapy, 41*, 205–220. doi: 10.1111/jmft.12068

Knudson-Martin, C., & Laughlin, M. (2005). Gender and sexual orientation in marital and family therapy: A post-gender approach. *Family Relations, 54*, 101–115.

Knudson-Martin, C., & Mahoney, A. R. (Eds.). (2009). *Couples, gender, and power: Creating change in intimate relationships.* New York: Springer.

Knudson-Martin, C., Wells, M. A., & Samman, S. K. (2015). *Socio-emotional relationship therapy: Bridging emotion, societal context, and couple interaction.* New York, NY: Springer.

Komter, A. (1989). Hidden power in marriage. *Gender and Society, 3*, 187–216.

Krolokke, C., & Sorensen, A. S. (2006). *Gender communication theories and analysis: From silence to performance.* Thousand Oaks, CA: Sage Publications.

Lang, S. (1998). *Men as women; women as men: Changing gender in Native American cultures.* Austin, TX: University of Texas Press.

Lev, A. I. (2010). How queer!—The development of gender identity and sexual orientation in LGBTQ-headed households. *Family Process, 49*, 268–290.

Maciel, J. A., & Van Putten, Z. (2009). Pushing the gender line: How immigrant couples reconstruct power. In C. Knudson-Martin & A. R. Mahoney (Eds.), *Couples, gender, and power: Creating change in intimate relationships* (pp. 235–254). New York, NY: Springer Publishing Company

Madigan, S. (2011). *Narrative therapy.* Washington, DC. American Psychological Association.

Maccoby, E. E., & Jacklin, C. N., (1974). *The psychology of sex differences.* Stanford, CA: Stanford University Press.

Mahoney, A. R., & Knudson-Martin, C. (2009). The social context of gendered power. In C. Knudson-Martin & A. Mahoney (Eds.), *Couples, gender, and power: Creating change in intimate relationships* (pp. 17–29). New York, NY: Springer Publishing Company.

Malpas, J. (2011). Between pink and blue: A multi-dimensional family approach to gender nonconforming children and their families. *Family Process, 50*, 453–470.

Maltz, D., & Archambault, J. (1995). Gender and power in native North America. In L. F. Klein & L. A. Ackerman (Eds.), *Women and power in native North America* (pp. 230–250). Norman, OK: University of Oklahoma Press.

McDowell, T. M., & Fang, S. S. (2007). Feminist-informed critical multiculturalism. *Journal of Family Issues, 28*, 549–566.

Mead, M. (2001). *Sex and temperament in three primitive societies.* New York, NY: Harper Perennial. Original work published in 1935, William Morrow and Co.

Mirgain, S. A., & Cordova, J. V. (2007). Emotion skills and marital health: The association between observed and self-reported emotion skills, intimacy, and marital satisfaction. *Journal of Counseling and Clinical Psychology, 26*, 983–1009.

Moghadam, S., & Knudson-Martin, C. (2009). Keeping the peace: Couple relationships in Iran. In C. Knudson-Martin & A. Mahoney (Eds.), *Couples, gender, and power: Creating change in intimate relationships* (pp. 255–274). New York, NY: Springer Publishing Co.

Nicoleau, A., Kang, Y. J., Choau, S. T., & Knudson-Martin, C. (2014). Doing what it takes to make it work: Flexibility, relational focus, and stability among long-term couples with children. *Journal of Family Issues, 37*, 1639–1657. doi: 10.1177/0192513X4543852

Pandit, M. L., Chen-Feng, J., Kang, Y. J., Knudson-Martin, C., & Hunergardt, D. (2014). Practicing socio-cultural attunement: A study of couple therapists. *Contemporary Family Therapy, 36*, 518–528.

Pascoe, C. J. (2007). *Dude, you're a fag: Masculinity and sexuality in high school*. Berkeley, CA: University of California Press.

Perry-Jenkins, M., Newkirk, K., & Ghunney, A. K. (2013). Family work through time and space: An ecological perspective. *Journal of Family Theory & Review, 5*, 105–123.

Quek, K. M. (2009). We-consciousness: Creting equalty iin collectivist culture. In C. Knudson-Martin & A. R. Mahoney (Eds.), *Couples, gender, and power: Creating change in intimate relationships* (pp. 193–214). New York, NY: Springer Publishing Company.

Quek, K. M., & Knudson-Martin, C. (2008). Reshaping marital power: How dual career newlywed couples create equality in Singapore. *Journal of Social and Personal Relationships, 25*, 513–534.

Quek, K. M, & Knudson-Martin, C., Rue, D., & Alabiso, C. (2010). Relational harmony: A new model of collectivism and gender equality among Chinese American couples. *Journal of Family Issues, 31*, 358–380.

Rabinowitz, F. E. (2012). Behind the mask: A primer on understanding the male partner in couples therapy. In D. S. Shepard & M. Harway (Eds.), *Engaging me in couples therapy* (pp. 37–55). New York, NY: Routledge.

Richards, J. C., Jonathan, N., & Kim, L. (2015). Building a circle of care in same-sex couple relationships: A socio-emotional relational approach. In C. Knudson-Martin, M. Wells, & S. K. Samman (Eds.), *Socio-emotional relationship therapy: Bridging emotion, societal context, and couple interaction* (pp. 93–105). New York, NY: Springer.

Risman, B. J. (1998). *Gender virtigo: American families in transition*. New Haven, CT: Yale University Press.

Risman, B. J. (2009). *From doing to undoing: Gender as we know it. Gender & Society, 23*, 81–84. doi: 10.1177/0891243208326874

Rojas, M. (2009). *Women of color and feminism*. Berkeley, CA: Seal Press.

Samman, S. K., & Knudson-Martin, C. (2015). Relational engagement in heterosexual couple therapy: Helping men move from "I" to "We." In C. Knudson-Martin, M. Wells, & S. K. Samman (Eds.), *Socio-emotional relationship therapy: Bridging emotion, societal context, and couple interaction* (pp. 79–91). New York, NY: Springer.

Sanday, P. R. (2002). *Women at the center: Life in a modern matriarchy*. Ithaca, NY: Cornell University Press.

Shechory, M., & Ziv, R. (2007). Relationships between gender role attitudes, role division, and perception of equity among heterosexual, gay and lesbian couples. *Sex Roles, 56*, 629–638.

Serano, J. (2007). *Whipping girl: A transsexual woman on sexism and the scapegoating of femininity*. Berkeley, CA: Seal Press.

Siegel, D. J. (2001). *The developing mind: How relationships and the brain interact to shape who we are*. New York, NY: Guilford.

Silverstein, R., Bass, L. B., Tuttle, A., Knudson-Martin, C., & Huenergardt, D. (2006). What does it mean to be relational? A framework for assessment and practice. *Family Process, 45*, 391–405.

Stanley, S. M., Rhoades, G. K., & Whitton, S. W. (2010). Commitment: Functions, formation, and the securing of romantic attachment. *Journal of Family Theory & Review, 2*, 243–257.

Steil, J. (1997). *Marital equality: Its relationship to the well-being of husbands and wives.* Newbury Park, CA: Sage Publications.

Stone, P. (2010). *Opting out: Why women really quit careers and head home.* Berkeley, CA: University of California Press.

Sullivan, O. (2006). *Changing gender relations, changing families: Tracing the pace of change over time.* Lanham, MD: Rowman & Littlefield.

Tannen, D. (1994). *Gender and discourse.* New York, NY: Oxford University Press.

Thorne, B. (1993). *Gender play: Boys and girls at school.* New Brunswick, NJ: Rutgers University Press.

Tichenor, V. J. (2005). *Earning more and getting less: Why successful wives can't buy equality.* New Brunswick, NJ: Rutgers University Press.

Triandis, H. (1995). *Individualism and collectivism.* Boulder, CO: Westview Press.

U.S. Census Bureau. (2013). Current Population Survey, Annual Social and Economic Supplement, 2012. Internet release date: December 2013. https://www.census.gov/population/age/data/2012comp.html

Wagner, S. R. (2001). *Sisters in spirit: Haudenossaunee (Iroquois) influence on early American feminists.* Summertown, TN: Native Voices Publishing Co.

Watson, M. F. (2013). *Facing the black shadow.* Philadelphia, PA: Author.

Wells, M. E., & Kuhn, V. (2015). Couple therapy with adult survivors of child abuse: Gender, power, and trust. In C. Knudson-Martin, M. Wells, & S. K. Samman (Eds.), *Socio-emotional relationship therapy: Bridging emotion, societal context, and couple interaction* (pp. 107–119). New York, NY: Springer.

Zimmerman, T. S., Haddock, S. A., Ziemba, S., & Rust, A. (2001). Family organizational labor: Who is calling the plays. In T. S. Zimmerman (Ed.), *Balancing family and work: Special considerations in feminist therapy?* (pp. 65–90). New York, NY: Haworth Press.

CHAPTER 7

Sexual Minority Couples and Families: Clinical Considerations

Beverly Greene
Philip B. Spivey

This chapter discusses clinical considerations in psychotherapy with sexual minority couples and families. We use the term **"sexual minority"** to include lesbian, gay, bisexual, and transgender men and women. It can also apply to individuals who do not use these labels for themselves but who are in relationships/partnered with or married to a person of the same sex. For practical purposes in this chapter, the sex of transgender (or trans) individuals is presumed to be represented by their chosen presentation. We recognize that transgender persons who do not undergo surgical reassignment might not be viewed this way by others, including their partners prior to as well as after their transition. For example, a couple presenting as a **cisgender** woman, in that her biological sex aligns with her gender identity, and a trans woman for whom the latter retains male genitalia but adopts a female gender presentation might not universally be considered a same-sex couple. However, in this same example, a cisgender woman who considers herself heterosexual but who remains in the relationship with a formerly male partner but who has transitioned to female may not consider herself lesbian and may or may not view the relationship as a same-sex relationship. It is important that the therapist ask clients questions about how they view or label themselves and not make assumptions (Greene & Boyd-Franklin, 1996). What makes the task of understanding the emergence of "many sexualities" so daunting is that, until recently, none have been afforded expression except in the most obsequious ways.

THE CONTEXT: COMPULSORY
HETERONORMATIVITY

From the founding of the U.S. republic, **patriarchy**, or a male-dominated societal system, was the explicit framework and foundation of American society. It involved **heteronormativity**, or the belief that heterosexuality and traditional male and female roles are the only sexual orientation and gender norms. Among its iterations, sexism gave rise to **misogyny** or denigration and prejudice towards women; misogyny gave rise to child abuse, **heterosexism** or discrimination against homosexuals, **homophobia** or dislike and prejudice against homosexuals, and **transphobia** or dislike and prejudice against transgender people. White supremacy was manifested in institutionalized racism and xenophobia. **Ageism** or discrimination against the elderly, gave rise to **ableism**, or discrimination in favor of able-bodied people. These branches of the patriarchal tree were codified and imbedded in the American social, political, and economic fabric. Developments, particularly in the past 20 years, have yielded radical changes to the way we think about gender identity and sexual orientation. For the purposes of this chapter, we label **same-sex attraction** as a **gender nonconforming** identity or behavior. Same-sex attraction and same-sex relationships flagrantly violate our society's gender norms (Greene, 1994c, 2000). Perhaps the most radical aspect of these developments is that some of our clients will *choose* to self-identify along a spectrum of sexualities that we may have never even considered. They will determine how they are to be addressed. This is very closely related to the ways that ethno-racial, ethnic, language, and national groups have taken back their power to self-identify, rejecting labels that a dominant culture has forced upon them.

What may be troubling to the therapist, apart from our unfamiliarity with this new nomenclature and worldview, is that we can no longer make casual assumptions about what we see or what we have indelibly come to believe. The very person of our clients will challenge our personal worldviews. At this time it is important that clinicians explore their own personal assumptions about gender, sexuality, and relationships and ask themselves a range of questions (Greene, 2000; Greene & Boyd-Franklin, 1996). Why do we need to know a person's gender and what personal meaning does that have for us? What does a discrepancy between a person's biological sex and gender presentation mean to us and why? Why does someone's object of erotic attraction matter to us if it is a consenting adult? Sexual minority clients in the context of our social history have the power to evoke intense feelings in therapists just as they do in other people; however, when therapists lack an awareness of what is being evoked in them and why, they have the capacity to harm clients (Greene, Boyd-Franklin, & Spivey, 2013). The very presence of **gender-variant**, or gender nonconforming, communities compel us to conduct this self-inquiry if we are to provide the kinds of competent services our clients require and deserve.

Conceptualizations of gender have undergone and continue undergoing a rapid evolution. That evolution has moved faster than the field of professional mental health and our attempts to grapple with what these new categories mean and what they do not mean for our patients. It is important to be aware of the potential for a wide range of diversity in how each person and couple conceptualize, label, and manage who they are and what they are doing, what that means to them and to be flexible in our attempts to understand them. Both partners in such couplings may not be in the same place with respect to these categories and their meanings; therefore, it is important to explore them for each person and not assume they are in agreement. As therapists we must resist the temptation to force people into neat, preexisting categories that may not accurately capture the nature of their experience. We continue to struggle with developing language and clinical conceptualizations that more accurately capture this evolution.

Despite changes in the last decade that make same-sex relationships more visible; the elimination in most states of barriers to marriage, adoption, and other legal recognition of those relationships; wider social acceptance than in any other point in our history; and long-standing changes in the diagnostic nomenclature, lesbian, gay, bisexual, and transgender (LGBT) individuals are still stigmatized and continue to face discrimination (Spivey & Greene, 2014). There remain states that do not protect sexual minority clients from discrimination in employment, housing, and services. Discrimination and hostility can range from **microaggressions,** or subtle acts of discrimination (Sue, 2010), to life-threatening violence. This is a central and important factor to consider in the treatment of any sexual minority person. These factors may be in the foreground or background of the client's life, consciousness, and presenting problem; however, they are always there in some fashion. These challenges need not be the central presenting problem, however; how clients navigate these challenges and the contribution they make to other problems in the client's life is a central therapeutic question. Our society remains heteronormative and that condition of heteronormativity creates a hostile social environment for sexual minority persons to negotiate. The need to negotiate that hostility and discrimination is a ubiquitous stressor in their lives and as such affects both their mental and physical health (Greene et al., 2013; Hatzenbuehler, 2009). The stigma of being a sexual minority person remains so potent that many people do not wish to be regarded as LGBT and refuse to acknowledge it in themselves, and some may seek to avoid the label even if they are in same-sex relationships or experience same-sex attraction (Greene, 2000). The latter can also represent **internalized homophobia** (Greene 1994a, 1994b, 2000).

TRADITIONAL GENDER FUNDAMENTALISM

Because gender is such a fundamental category in our society, relationships between two women may differ from those between two men
(Kite, 1994). In each case, gender socialization will influence the overall relationship, as men and women differ in the ways they have been
socialized, the way society regards and treats them, and in their expectations of what relationships should provide. Both lesbians and gay men
face unique forms of discrimination shaped by their gender as well as
the interaction between their gender and a sexual orientation that violates
gender norms. There are long-standing assumptions about lesbian and
gay sexual orientations that are based on their violation of gender norms.
Traditional gender norms presume that women's erotic and sexual attractions should be toward men, and that men's erotic and sexual attractions
should be toward women. Because lesbians are attracted to women, it has
been presumed that they want to be or are more like men, and that gay
men, because they are attracted to men, are more effeminate than men
and are more like women. These assumptions are based on social definitions of what constitutes normal masculinity and femininity (Kite &
Deaux, 1987; Newman, 1989). While these assumptions have often been
embedded in research, they are not the product of any rigorous empirical
research themselves and remain scientifically unsupported. While there is
some evidence that lesbians and gay men may be more likely to observe
nontraditional gender roles and presentations, there is no evidence that
suggests that they do so because they want to be members of the other
sex (Greene, 1995; Kite, 1994). Those categories however represent what a
given society or culture believes are the ideal characteristics for men and
women based on that society's values, not on the reality of how men and
women naturally behave or should behave. These assumptions remain
intact only because the object of sexual attraction is embedded in definitions of normal gender.

All of these factors influence how same-sex couples are responded to
when they present themselves to their families, communities, and the outside world, and that contributes to how they view themselves and their
relationships. There is a legacy of stigma, discrimination, and ill treatment
of sexual minority group members that has extended to their relationships.
It was not until slightly more than 50 years ago that mental health professions removed lesbian and gay sexual orientations from the diagnostic
nomenclature. Until that time LGBT persons were deemed mentally defective and their sexual orientation was presumed to derive from problems
in psychosexual development. Their relationships were deemed defective
when compared to heterosexual relationships and they were considered
psychologically disturbed. They were also considered immoral and deca-
dent and in many places were criminalized. Despite those changes, there
are still small but vocal professional groups who continue to assert that

sexual minority orientations are a result of pathological development. That view however is not supported by any mainstream mental health professional organizations, nor is it supported by research (Greene et al., 2013). It is fair to say that despite enormous progress in their acceptance, sexual minority group members continue to face ill treatment, discrimination, and ignorance, which significantly affects their lives and their relationships. Therefore managing homophobia/heterosexism and its range of incarnations must be considered an important part of the context of their daily lives and is therefore important to assess when we address problems in their relationships. Therapists must be comfortable asking clients about their encounters with discrimination as well as comfortable hearing what may be painful stories about those encounters. Managing stigma and discrimination on an ongoing basis constitutes a chronic stressor in the lives of LBGT men and women. Psychological mechanisms that are intended to assist people in negotiating psychological stress that may work very well in the short term are generally not intended for chronic use and can create their own problems. Furthermore chronic stress has both psychological and physiological correlates that erode optimal mental and physical health (Hatzenbuehler, 2009).

MULTIPLE MINORITY STATUS AND THE DIVERSITY WITHIN

Partners in same-sex couples are also members of other groups, many of which are socially marginalized. It means that in addition to negotiating the stigma and discrimination that accompanies LGBT identity, they must also manage other forms of marginalization (Greene, 1994a, 2000; Hall & Greene, 2002). While traditional explorations of and research on socially marginalized identities tended to view them as if they were separate entities that occurred in isolation, there has been an evolution in those perspectives that views social identities as complex and intersectional. This means that gender, ethno-racial identity, social class, physical ability, sexual orientation, and culture, all interact with one another in dynamic and not static ways across the life span. Some identities may be more salient in certain contexts or during certain developmental junctures than others; however, all exist in interaction with one another.

The privilege or disadvantage associated with any given identity can mitigate or heighten the effects of other identities. Therefore, it is important to consider the effects of multiple minority or marginalized status on clients who are LGBT. On the one hand life presents these individuals with more day-to-day stress (Greene, 1994b; Greene & Boyd Franklin, 1996; Greene et al., 2013; Gutierrez & Dworkin, 1992). On the other hand, people who also have another marginalized identity that they were socialized to manage in healthy ways can use what they have learned to mentally challenge other negative assertions about themselves from the outside world and maintain a healthy identity. Those strategies may prove useful in negotiating social challenges and the potential for internalized homophobia associated with LGBT status. Another challenge for these individuals is that they may belong to multiple minority groups that do not view one another as allies, rather as competitors for social resources or with the same animus toward one another as members of dominant cultural groups have toward them. This can lead to identity conflicts of allegiance and tensions around communities competing for resources or loyalties in ways that leave individuals feeling that they have no place where they can really be their authentic selves (Greene et al., 2013; Gutierrez & Dworkin, 1992; Hall & Greene, 2002). There are many different permutations of intersections between sexual minority identity and other identities; however, they are beyond the scope of this chapter. We will attempt to explore one example of them in a brief discussion of African American same-sex relationships, followed by a special focus on African American gay men.

INTERSECTIONALITY: AFRICAN AMERICAN SEXUAL MINORITIES

African American lesbians and gay men represent a part of the spectrum of diversity among African Americans, men and women and sexual minority group members. As African Americans, women (for lesbians), and sexual minorities, they face double and triple marginalization in American society (Collins, 1990; Greene et al., 2013; Poussaint, 1990). The interaction between race, gender, and sexual orientation is complex in ways that single identity paradigms are unable to capture. African American lesbians' and gay males' cultural positioning is in the nexus of those identities, and the structural inequities associated with those identities can leave them predisposed to psychological vulnerability as well as psychological resilience, depending on other factors in their lives.

The history of African Americans and the gendering of race in the United States have played an important role in shaping perceptions of gender roles and perceptions of what are acceptable forms of sexual expression and sexuality. The diverse family structures and expressions of sexuality among African Americans were initially viewed as pathological when compared to Western models and practices. This was true even when some of those differences were a function of adapting to limited social opportunities that were a direct function of racism and raced sexism. The demonization of African American sexuality and the demonization of same-sex relationships are each based on distortions of African Americans and on sexual minority group members (Greene, 2000; Greene et al., 2013). Those distortions defined these groups as having pathological and immoral sexual predispositions that depicted them as less than human. Just as the diverse family structures of African Americans challenge the normative position of patriarchal family structures, same-sex relationships challenge the rules that frame sex and gender that make them a similar threat to patriarchal domination (Greene, Boyd Franklin, & Spivey, 2013).

African Americans have often needed to defend their humanity when faced with distortions about them usually expressed in degrading sexual stereotypes. Some do so by policing their public sexuality and conduct so that it conforms to the dominant cultural moral order. This is an example of internalized racism. Moore (2011) observes that this public conduct is also "classed" and suggests that more middle- and upper-middle-class African Americans may be even more eager to fit within the social order and therefore more vulnerable to internalizing the dominant cultural values, values that inherently devalue African Americans. The Black middle class sought to distance itself not only from negative racial stereotypes, particularly sexual stereotypes, but also from racialized working-class stereotypes. They did so by developing a posture of "respectability" and conservatism in sexual matters and public behavior. In Moore's analysis, Black lesbians who live openly claim a level of sexual and identity autonomy that places them outside of the normative order of "respectability" that exists for women in the world of the Black middle class struggling to gain acceptance in the mainstream of U.S. society (Hall & Greene, 2002).

Finding healthy intimacy is a challenge for all couples. Some challenges may be rooted in their own psychological and family history and the way those dynamics interact with one another. However, these challenges are exacerbated for African American sexual minority group members and other sexual minority group members of color because there are particular distortions of them that are based on the legacy of racism, internalized racism, heterosexism, and internalized homophobia, which forms the historical and contemporary context in which their relationships take place (Cohen & Jones, 1999; Greene, 1995, 2000; Greene et al., 2013).

In the context of racist ideology, nonconformists among African Americans are often used to reinforce stereotypic beliefs of questionable validity about African Americans in general. Cohen and Jones (1999) observe that an environment is created where African Americans "police" one another to assure that the dominant cultural codes are observed. Because heterosexism institutionalizes patriarchal family structures and rewards heterosexual relationships, it punishes and even demonizes same-sex relationships as well as alternative family structures, establishing them as being outside of the "respectable" and acceptable moral order of the community. It is important to note that there may be a distinction between the way that public and private behaviors are viewed. There is an unspoken, silent "tolerance" of lesbian and gay members of African American communities; however, that tolerance is often predicated on silence. Silence requires an avoidance of any open discussion about one's sexual minority status that is complicated when people are in relationships. The culture of silence that exists even within the group that forms the clients' most loved and trusted figures has clear effects on their relationships with partners. When couples are obliged to protect their relationships from hostility, from a community, and/or from family members, they are challenged in ways that heterosexual couples are not (Greene, 1994c; Greene et al., 2013). Cerbone (personal communication, August 2011) observes that maintaining a cloak of silence and disconnection around their relationships in public spaces, harboring varying degrees of internalized homophobia, does not simply end when the couple is in private. Rather, it lingers on in the relationship, reflected in problems with establishing the trust that is a precursor of intimacy within the relationship, even in relationships whose participants are "out."

Spivey (Greene et al., 2013; Spivey & Greene, 2014) suggests that both internalized homophobia and internalized racism may be responsible for the pattern he observes in Black gay male couples. The pattern he observes is one in which in the early stages of the relationship there is what appears to be a healthy pattern of sexual desire and intimacy. However, as the emotional intimacy intensifies and the relationship deepens, it begins to flounder. A partner expresses the desire to have other sexual partners, has an extramarital affair, or engages in other behaviors that threaten and undermine or end the relationship. When we attempted to discern what this means, we examined the social and historical context of these relationships that includes an examination of the history of sexual violence in our society. Prohibitions against same-sex relationships and interracial relationships prohibit legitimacy in those relationships. These relationships have always taken place despite prohibitions against them, but often took place by force. We assume that male slaves were raped just as female slaves were raped because sexual violence targets both men and women. Gay men are also visible targets of sexual violence from other presumably heterosexual men. While sexual violence is permitted when crossing these forbidden lines, the love that creates healthy bonds of sexual intimacy is not permitted in relationships that are delegitimized (Greene et al., 2013). In Spivey's analysis, when these men find themselves in loving and intimate relationships, they behave as if they find themselves doing or having something they are not supposed to have, which is love. He offers that the men he treats wish for such relationships but they do not necessarily feel deserving of them, nor do they trust one another. Hence they sabotage the relationship from within.

Spivey adds that in his experience, there has been little support even in the gay male community for stable ongoing relationships among its members. He hypothesizes that this may be a function of envy, as many men do not feel deserving of loving relationships and envy those who have them. Members of stable partnerships may be on the receiving end of seductive and envious behavior that seeks to undermine their union. It is important to urge such couples to find arenas that are supportive of their relationship, even if it is among heterosexual peers (Greene et al., 2013).

For a more detailed discussion of this phenomenon and other aspects of therapy with African American gay men that are complicated by internalized, homophobia racism and sexism, see Greene et al. (2013).

Spivey observes that African American gay men face a circuitous stigma in that they are feminized within Black communities and hypermasculinized in the dominant cultural gaze. As men who are both Black and gay, their only locus of power rests in being male in a patriarchal society. This can give rise to competition within their relationships for power and control as a presumed precursor for safety. "Extramarital" affairs may represent a need to be in control and attain power via promiscuity. Value and power are derived by "getting" as many sexual partners as one can. African American lesbians and gay men come from all socioeconomic levels. Stereotypes of them can lead therapists with limited information or contact with group members to viewing them as only coming from impoverished, drug-seeking, street life or poorly educated groups. Therapists are urged to listen nonjudgmentally to these clients' stories about how they have been able to put together the social, professional, and vocational lives they live. It is most helpful to do this from the perspective that often they have been victimized, and while they *have* problems, *they* are not the problem. Being authentic as the therapist is important particularly but not exclusively in therapy with gay Black men because issues of trust are paramount. It is also important to ask questions of the client rather than make assumptions that may be based on attitudes or beliefs of the therapist that may be of questionable validity. Those questions might include how they were treated by parents; what parents' fights or disagreements looked like; what it meant to trust in the family of origin; who was trusted, who was not, and why; what did love look like in the family; who was loved and who was not? What all people seek in their intimate relationships is a sense of personal power and agency, safety, and the realistic potential to get their needs met. Problems enter relationships when manipulation is required to get those needs met. One of the more important questions we ask when treating these couples is what is wrong or dangerous about being authentic. What happens or has happened to the client when they have said what they felt, believed or wanted? If they were punished for any of those things, it becomes no longer safe to ask for them overtly; they must get their needs met by manipulating others, including their romantic partner.

CASE EXAMPLE: INTERSECTIONS OF ETHNO-SEXUAL IDENTITY AND GENDER NONCONFORMITY IN A BLACK MALE CHILD

We use the case of a gender-nonconforming Black male child to exemplify the diverse ways that gender nonconformity is an issue, not only for same-sex parents but also for heterosexual parents who have a gender-nonconforming child. That gender nonconformity, as we have broadly defined it, may be presented as a child with same-sex attraction or a child who has a nontraditional gender presentation or gender identity. We chose this example because we believe that male children and particularly Black male children who are gender nonconforming can elicit the most intense responses from their family members and broader community. We feel that gender-nonconforming children deserve the same love and support of their families as other children but understand how their parents may be at a loss, even when they have the best of intentions, to protect such a child from social ostracism and malevolence (Spivey & Greene, 2014).

Mark

Mark is a 10-year-old who was referred for counseling by his teacher, after he was attacked by a group of boys in his class. An important aspect of this kind of recommendation is that parents seek a counselor or therapist who has credentials, practice, and professional experience in this area. The danger of having someone with only a passing familiarity with working with gender-nonconforming clients is that they will be unable to provide a client, in this case the client's parents, with care based on the latest research and professional judgment on gender nonconformity. The counselor was sensitive enough to see that Mark was heavily burdened by feelings of responsibility for coming to counseling because in his words, "I am the reason we are here, today." First the counselor normalized Mark's behavior with him and, later, separately for his parents. In time, the counselor was able to place the assault Mark experienced from the perspective that the entire family would utilize in their own way: Mark had been a victim of violent social prejudice. He did not provoke nor did he deserve this, nor could he have avoided or prevented it. It was not his nor his parents' fault. He was probably attacked because Mark's gender nonconformity was perceived as vulnerability by these boys who had internalized the social messages that devalue any boy who behaves atypically, especially if that behavior violates gender norms. Part of that vulnerability rests in the knowledge that society permits and sometimes encourages hatred toward gender-nonconforming people, making it permissible to harm them with impunity. They could expect that in all likelihood the authority figures in the boys' homes and in the school, who would have been responsible for punishing and correcting their behavior, shared the boys' attitudes toward Mark and would not protect him. This was a vulnerability that they sought to exploit through violence. In his work with this family, which lasted for three months, the counselor emphasized that parents must attempt to actively shield themselves from the kinds of external values that would threaten the integrity of their own family values. Their family values would include their love and respect for all of their own children. He recounted that, in his experience, he had seen boys harassed and attacked for multiple reasons that included style of dress, coveted sneakers or other clothing, style of jewelry or its monetary value, rejection of experimental drugs, the neighborhood they live in, and, most disturbing, boys who are excelling in school. The counselor concluded that what makes gender-nonconforming behavior for boys so volatile is that, typically, no adults adequately confront the issue or deal with the perpetrators; there is a silence in most communities that can turn deadly. Often these are the same pressures that some parents may feel prompt them to be silent or turn these occurrences into family secrets. Parents are encouraged to reach out to supportive family members as well as competent mental health professionals who can help. Mark and his family were ultimately fortunate in many ways. Three months of meetings with a counselor were enough to mitigate Mark's trauma, normalize his expressive repertoire so that he was no longer as self-conscious and, most importantly, marshal his parents, and eventually his school, to turn their scrutiny away from children like Mark and focus instead on those who bullied and tormented him. All young boys in similar predicaments are not so fortunate. In Mark's school, the children's consciousness had been raised sufficiently so that they then began to scrutinize those individuals, groups and institutions that target children like Mark for differential treatment. Mark and his parents became activists against bullying and all kinds of psychological violence (Spivey & Greene, 2014).

CONCLUSIONS: CHALLENGES TO HEALTHY RELATIONSHIPS FOR SOCIALLY DISAPPROVED COUPLES

Same-sex couples represent a socially disapproved relationship. They share that status with interracial couples, interfaith couples as well as couplings between people who have large social class discrepancies, and people with disabilities. What all of these couples share is social disapproval of their relationship and a lack of appropriate support for the normal range of relational problems. Typically marriage or the formation of stable partnerships, particularly when there are plans to start a family, is met with a sense of welcome and enthusiasm by the community, family, and society in general. Indeed, weddings are often a major focus of family celebration, of celebrating the new union. The formation of stable relationships is viewed as something that stabilizes society and contributes to the health and well-being of partners in these couplings. However, couplings across the lines mentioned can elicit reactions that range from a lack of support to hostility and malevolence. Overall, these pairings violate certain societal norms that are related to the social hierarchy previously discussed and where people are located in that hierarchy.

Marriages and funerals are social rituals that essentially mark the arrival or departure of someone from the family system. For a time, the family's boundaries are in flux. For many people, this is a time of great apprehension because the system they were used to has changed. Conflicts may ensue around the treatment of the new family member who is disapproved of in a wide range of ways. It is important for therapists to remember that in same-sex relationships the family or family members may object to the relationship because it is a same-sex relationship; however, this may also be used to cloak other objections that would not be readily accepted by other family or community members. In some families, there may be a desire to exercise control over highly valued members to keep their personal or tangible resources within the family group. If that individual is part of a couple and has what is now considered his or her own family, whether it is a same-sex or heterosexual relationship, the family or certain family members may feel threatened with the loss of those resources. In families characterized by rigidity, parents may insist on control of their children even after they are emancipated adults. Hence they may feel their child has no right to marry someone or marry at all if they do not approve of that person. There is a range of ways that objections to the same-sex nature of the coupling may be used as the object of family consternation when there are other factors that constitute the problem. Hence the therapist must conduct a careful exploration of the family dynamics and history before blindly accepting that which may seem to be the obvious problem but is not.

Greene et al. (2013) observe that same-sex partners and relationships can be responded to in a wide range of ways that are as diverse as the families we see. Some may be casually or deliberately ignored, banned from family events, treated poorly, and so forth. On the other end of the spectrum, they may be treated just as other family members' spouses. In some families, particularly African American families, there may be a tacit assumption that there is an adult sexual relationship between the two parties where the partner is treated as a family member. However, this assumption may be made without any discussion or overt revelation. When such revelations are made overtly or if there is a decision to marry and formalize the relationship, such news may be responded to as if no one ever considered the reality of the relationship. Clients may report that they are not invited to certain family events at all or that they are invited but their same-sex partner/spouse is not. Others report that when there are problems in the relationship, they are not given the support that would be expected, rather an impending breakup may be greeted with celebration or relief from other family members. When the normal range of challenges presents itself to such couples, they may be treated as though their nontraditional coupling is the problem. It can be seductive for therapists to make such assumptions as well. In the case of same-sex couples, we see homophobia creeping into assumptions the therapist makes about these couples. Such assumptions have at their core the belief that heterosexual relationships are healthier, more stable, and more legitimate than same-sex relationships. It can also be reflected in the therapist viewing such couples as being just like heterosexual couples. While many of the issues same-sex couples and heterosexual couples face are similar, the resources they have access to and the social discrimination they face are not similar. All of the normal and mundane stressors faced by same-sex couples are exacerbated by the hostility their relationships can evoke and particularly the lack of support for their struggles. They may even be blamed by family members for pursuing relationships that are viewed as though they were doomed to fail.

Helping clients determine whom they can seek support from and who will not be supportive is useful as clients sometimes overlook people who are more than willing to be welcoming to them. This means that clients may need to have these conversations with different family members at any given time and avoid relying on information about how a family member would feel from a family member who objects and discourages having these discussions at all. Each person should be dealt with as an individual and every family is different.

Another important aspect of exploration is the nature of the couple's social environment and community. Do they have a community and a network of friends? Community need not necessarily mean LGBT community but one that provides important support and validation for the relationship. It is important to note that same-sex couples who do not have community support of some sort may feel that it is the two of them against the world. When this happens each may look to the other for more support than one person can provide, which can in and of itself lead to challenges in the relationship. Of course all these take place in an environment where same-sex couples have routinely faced structural inequities that heterosexual couples do not have to negotiate. Until the recent Supreme Court decision extending the right to marry to same-sex couples, most same-sex couples could not legally protect their relationship and the rights and status accorded such couplings. Financial, adoption, property, and custody rights that are a routine feature of heterosexual couplings could only be approximated by making very specific and detailed legal arrangements with lawyers privately. For couples who did not have significant income, hiring an attorney and jumping through many extra hoops to derive what marriage provides were elusive. Marriage equality brings sweeping change to this relationship landscape. Still, there are places in the United States where same-sex couples can be subject to challenges from disgruntled local clerks about when and how they obtain a marriage license as well as goods and services needed to conduct a wedding. There are still religious denominations that refuse to permit same-sex couples from marrying within the church or by a church official, despite the significant numbers of those who will permit it. In many states, same-sex couples can be denied apartment rentals, jobs, and the like, in what is still a bastion of legally permitted discrimination. Some states have even attempted to make it a violation of state law to recognize or perform a same-sex marriage within that state. While those battles continue to be fought in the courts, people can face considerable disruption in the business of their lives as well as a homophobic and degrading climate. Ubiquitous public challenges to marriage equality had negative effects on the emotional well-being of LGBT persons. Being subject to public discussions organized around whether or not they should have the same rights as other citizens and some of the animus that people feel toward them is emotionally harmful. While there have been enormous strides over the last 20 years, same-sex couples still do not have full parity with heterosexual couples. All of these challenges can put a strain on relationships that heterosexual couples do not have to confront.

The Supreme Court decision to legalize same-sex marriage has been a major step in the creation of institutional parity for same-sex couples; however, with marriage comes responsibilities that many same-sex couples have not been held legally accountable for until now. In the absence of domestic partnerships and marriage, same-sex couples could make private and abrupt decisions about beginning and ending relationships. Some authors have noted that the absence of legal ties may have resulted in couples aborting relationships that may have been salvaged because there were no rituals, requirements, or legalities to manage in the process of ending them. Those rituals may sometimes give couples time to consider all of the ramifications of ending the relationship that are avoided if partners can simply leave. In the absence of marriage, many same-sex couplings could be invisible in ways that offered them a measure of protection from stigma or family tension. Invisibility brings both advantages and disadvantages. Relationships that are invisible can offer a cloak that conceals the relationship from perhaps a hostile family, employer, and the like. Marriage is a matter of public record and by its very nature is public. For couples who struggle with where, to whom, and how "out" they wish to be, marriage may be viewed as taking that "safety" away. Marriage is a public and institutional event. It formalizes and makes legally binding both benefits and responsibilities in a relationship. This has both benefits and liabilities to same-sex as well as heterosexual couples.

The right to marry for same-sex couples is so recent that we do not have large-scale studies to inform us about whether or not families respond to same-sex couples differently (for better or worse) if they are legally married as opposed to having committed partnerships, or domestic partnerships. Anecdotally we have observed reactions that are as diverse as families can be. In some cases, the families responded with the kind of joy and desire to support and celebrate the marriage as would be appropriate. In other situations, family members expressed concern about who would know and how public it would be and some indicated they would be embarrassed to participate in such an event. Several couples who have been together for over 20 and 30 years reported that one member of the couple was "out" to her family but the other was not. This meant that after a lifetime of being closeted with family members she would have to come out to them before she could invite them to a wedding for a relationship that was theoretically invisible to them. Identity stage theory can be useful in establishing where each partner is with respect to the other in identity stages. It is important to point out that these stages do not follow a linear sequence with everyone, nor do clients move to a certain stage and remain there. People may move to a stage having skipped the one before it and may regress from one stage to another across the life span. However, when each person in the relationship is at a different stage, it can be challenging. If one partner is relatively comfortable with being out and the other is not, it can lead to conflicts about many issues but particularly marriage. Should there be a public event or should they simply go to a justice or licensed person and have a ceremony with no guests? If there is a public event, questions arise about whom to invite, where to hold the event, and so on, that are related to who is out to whom and what it means to be coming out later as opposed to earlier in life. Of course, the nature of the client's relationship with her or his family is an important contextual factor. These events can be fraught with difficulty just as they are with heterosexual couples; however, there is an extra layer of tension in these arrangements for same-sex couples that is not faced by their heterosexual counterparts. As clinicians and therapists, we will be aided in assessing how to best help clients along the gender-nonconforming spectrum by educating ourselves about their personal psychological journey and what this means in their day-to-day life. There is a large first-person literature that is emerging in which individuals chronicle their journeys. However, it is equally important that therapists conduct an exploration of their own identities and assumptions about gender and gender role norms.

CHAPTER REVIEW

Key Points

1. The United States' history of ongoing patriarchy has been followed by a recent rapid evolution in how our society thinks about gender identity and sexual orientation, as well as the emergence of many sexualities that only recently have been afforded expression.
2. It is important to be aware of the potential for a wide range of diversity in how each person and couple conceptualizes, labels, and manages who they are and what they are doing regarding gender and sexual orientation, and to be aware that couple and family members may not be in the same place with respect to these categories and their meanings.
3. Despite greater visibility, legal recognition, and wider social acceptance than in any other point in our history, LGBT individuals are still stigmatized

and continue to face the ubiquitous stress of discrimination, including the lack of some key legal protections in some states.

4. When couples and families are obliged to protect their relationships from hostility from society, a community, and/or from family members, they are delegitimized and challenged in ways that heterosexual couples are not, to the extent that they may lack important supports and experience internalized homophobia. Often they have been victimized, and while they may have problems, they are not the problem.

5. Gender, ethno-racial identity, social class, physical ability, sexual orientation, and culture, all interact with one another in dynamic ways across the life span. The privilege or disadvantage associated with any given identity can mitigate or heighten the effects of other identities. Therefore, it is important to consider the effects of multiple minority or marginalized status on clients who are LGBT.

Key Terms

ableism, ageism, cisgender, gender-nonconforming, gender-variant, heteronormativity, heterosexism, homophobia, internalized homophobia, microaggressions, misogyny, patriarchy, same-sex attraction, sexual minority, transphobia

Myths and Realities

*   It is a myth that sexual minority orientations are a result of pathological development. In reality, that view is not supported by any mainstream mental health professional organizations, nor is it supported by research.
*   It is a myth that because lesbians are attracted to women, they want to be or are more like men, and that because gay men are attracted to men, they are more effeminate than men and are more like women. In reality, gender identity, gender roles, and sexual orientation are different constructs, and people vary on each of those constructs.

Tools and Tips

Knowledge

Greene, B., Boyd-Franklin, N., & Spivey, P. B. (2013). African American lesbians and gay male couples: Threats to intimacy and considerations in couples therapy. In K. Helm & J. Carlson (Eds.), *Love, intimacy and the African American couple*. New York, NY: Routledge.

Spivey, P. B., & Greene, B. (2014). Gender nonconforming Black male children: Endangered, misunderstood and mistreated. In K. C. Vaughans & W. Spielberg (Eds.), *The psychology of Black boys and adolescents* (Vol. 1, pp. 99–105). Santa Barbara, CA: Praeger Publications.

Sue, D. (2010). Sexual orientation microaggressions and heterosexism. In D. Sue (Ed.), *Microaggressions in everyday life* (pp. 184–206). New York, NY: John Wiley and Sons.

Dynamic Sizing

While it is highly likely that sexual minority clients will experience some of the foregoing issues, no one aspect of the foregoing knowledge can be assumed to apply to any individual. Thus therapists need to conduct careful exploration to capture the nature of the experience of each of their sexual minority clients.

Skills

Theory. We continue to struggle with developing language and clinical conceptualizations that more accurately capture the evolution in gender identity and sexual orientation, how clients navigate the challenges of stigma and discrimination, and developing theories of intersectionality that capture the complex interactions between gender, sexual orientation, and other important identities.

Prevention. Society needs psychoeducation about the natural variations in gender and sexual orientation described in this chapter. Institutions and policies are needed to prohibit people from harming gender nonconforming people with impunity. These measures may serve to prevent threats to the well-being of families with members who are sexual minorities.

Service Provision. Service providers must resist the temptation to force people into neat, pre-existing categories that may not accurately capture the nature of their experience, and must learn how to assist clients in managing stigma and discrimination on an ongoing basis.

Policy. In addition to the foregoing prevention policies, it is important to ensure that all states develop adequate legal protections for sexual and other minorities.

Research. Researchers need to recognize and address the fact that studies' definitions of what constitutes normal gender and sexual orientation typically have been embedded with heteronormative assumptions, and find ways to measure intersectionality.

Awareness

Sexual minority clients in the context of our social history have the power to evoke intense feelings in therapists just as they do in other people. Therapists must be aware that when they lack an awareness of what is being evoked in them and why, they have the capacity to harm clients.

The emergence of many sexualities that are socially disapproved of and only recently have been afforded expression makes it important for therapists to explore their own personal assumptions about gender, sexuality, and relationships and ask themselves a range of questions about their own worldviews, reactions, and values about gender and sexual orientation to be able to provide competent service to these clients.

REFERENCES

Cohen, C., & Jones, T. (1999). Fighting homophobia versus challenging hetero-
    sexism: "The failure to transform" revisited. In E. Brandt (Ed.), *Dangerous
    liaisons: Blacks, gays and the struggle for equality* (pp. 80–101). New York, NY:
    New Press.

Collins, P. H. (1990). Homophobia and Black lesbians. In *Black feminist thought:
    Knowledge, consciousness, and the politics of empowerment* (pp. 192–196).
    Boston, MA: Unwin/Hyman.

Greene, B. (1994a). Ethnic-minority lesbians and gay men: Mental health and treat-
    ment issues. *American Psychological Association, 62,* 243–251.

Greene, B. (1994b). Lesbian women of color: Triple jeopardy. In L. Comas-Diaz &
    B. Greene (Eds.), *Women of color: Integrating ethnic and gender identities in
    psychotherapy* (pp. 389–427). New York, NY: Guilford Press.

Greene, B. (1994c). Lesbian and gay sexual orientations: Implications for clinical
    training, practice and research. In B. Greene & G. Herek (Eds.), *Psychological
    perspectives on lesbian and gay issues, Vol. 1: Lesbian and gay psychology: The-
    ory, research, and clinical applications* (pp. 1–24). Thousand Oaks, CA: Sage
    Publications.

Greene, B. (1995). Lesbian couples. In K. Jay (Ed.), *Dyke life: From growing up to
    growing old—A celebration of the lesbian experience.* New York, NY: Basic
    Books.

Greene, B. (2000). African American lesbian and bisexual women in feminist psy-
    chodynamic psychotherapy: Surviving and thriving between a rock and
    a hard place. In L. C. Jackson & B. Greene (Eds.), *Psychotherapy with Afri-
    can American women: Innovations in psychodynamic perspectives and practice*
    (pp. 82–125). New York, NY: Guilford Press.

Greene, B., & Boyd-Franklin, N. (1996). African American lesbians: Issues in couples
    therapy. In J. Laird & R. J. Green (Eds.), *Lesbians and gays in couples and fami-
    lies: A handbook for therapists* (pp. 251–271). San Francisco, CA: Jossey Bass.

Greene, B., Boyd-Franklin, N., & Spivey, P. B. (2013). African American lesbians
    and gay male couples: Threats to intimacy and considerations in couples
    therapy. In K. Helm & J. Carlson (Eds.), *Love, intimacy and the African Ameri-
    can couple.* New York, NY: Routledge.

Gutierrez, F., & Dworkin, S. (1992). Gay, lesbian, and African American: Managing
    the integration of identities. In S. Dworkin & F. Gutierez (Eds.), *Counseling
    gay men and lesbians* (pp. 141–156). Alexandria, VA: American Association
    of Counseling and Developing.

Hall, R. L., & Greene, B. (2002). Not any one thing: The complex legacy of social
    class on African American lesbian relationships. *Journal of Lesbian Studies, 6,*
    65–74.

Hatzenbuehler, M. L. (2009). How does sexual minority stigma "get under the
    skin"? A psychological mediation framework. *Psychological Bulletin, 135,*
    707–730.

Kite, M. (1994). When perceptions meet reality: Individual differences in reactions
    to lesbians and gay men. In B. Greene & G. Herek (Eds.), *Lesbian and gay psy-
    chology: Theory, research and clinical applications.* Thousand Oaks, CA: Sage
    Publications.

Kite, M., & Deaux, K. (1987). Gender belief systems: Homosexuality and the
    implicit inversion theory. *Psychology of Women Quarterly, 11,* 83–96.

Moore, M. (2011). *Invisible families: Gay identities, relationships and motherhood among Black women*. Berkeley, CA: University of California Press.

Newman, B.S. (1989). The relative importance of gender role attitudes toward lesbians. *Sex Roles, 21*, 451–465.

Poussaint, A. (1990, September). An honest look at Black gays and lesbians. *Ebony*, pp. 124, 126, 130–131.

Spivey, P.B., & Greene, B. (2014). Gender nonconforming Black male children: Endangered, misunderstood and mistreated. In K.C. Vaughans & W. Spielberg (Eds.), *The psychology of Black boys and adolescents* (Vol. 1, pp. 99–105). Santa Barbara, CA: Praeger Publications.

Sue, D. (2010). Sexual orientation microaggressions and heterosexism. In D. Sue (Ed.), *Microaggressions in everyday life* (pp. 184–206). New York, NY: John Wiley and Sons.

PART III

Religious and Spiritual Identities

CHAPTER 8

Christian Couples and Families

Suzanne M. Coyle
Christina J. Davis

This chapter presents a multipronged approach to Christian couples and families of different faith perspectives, which includes information on demographics and ethnicity. It analyzes, as an underlying theme, what is unique about Christian families. In what ways do beliefs that are distinctly Christian impact families? How does healthy faith support family cohesion? How does Christian belief affect families? How do therapists make determinations about what is healthy or unhealthy about the role of faith in the family? These questions go to the heart of the relationship between what family members say they believe and what is practiced in everyday life. Counseling Christian couples and families requires that the therapist understand how religious beliefs impact family life. For the therapist, understanding the boundaries between **spirituality** and **religion** is essential. This discussion assists the therapist, Christian or not, in counseling Christian couples and families.

In religious studies, where spirituality and spiritual experiences are seen as first steps in the development of a religion, spirituality is understood as a transcendental experience that leads to a fuller understanding of life's meaning. As soon as that spiritual experience is shared, and others participate in that spirituality, the shared experience becomes a religion. Religion, then, is a shared experience that begins as a deeply felt spirituality. As the religion grows, formal procedures and protocols, such as creeds and rituals, are added. Spirituality can offer meaning and empower individuals in their everyday lives. Healthy Christian religion will have spirituality at its core (Coyle, 2010).

THE HISTORY OF CHRISTIANITY
IN THE UNITED STATES

Grant (2000) has detailed the history of the Roman Catholic Church, its **Protestant** offshoot, and how the Protestant left and right have developed in the United States. This history is presented in brief here to help therapists to understand historical context when a client declares that she is a Christian or he is a **Catholic**. The Christian tradition presents a wide range of religious views and practices that have emerged over the course of a long history; its adherents tend to pick and choose particular elements.

In 1054, during the Great Schism, the Roman Catholic Church claimed papal authority, while the Orthodox Church broke away from Catholicism. Between the 14th and 17th centuries, a series of reform movements took place within the Roman Catholic Church, resulting in a new branch of Christianity called Protestantism. New traditions within the Protestant Church soon emerged: Lutherans, Presbyterians, Baptists, Methodists, and Episcopalians (Ahlstrom & Hall, 2004). In the 17th century, when the Puritans began to flee England, European settlement in what would become the United States was based on religious freedom. But it did not take long for individual colonies to have their own "preferred" religions. Maryland was Catholic, Massachusetts was Puritan, and New Jersey was Presbyterian. Religious intolerance in the colonies prompted Roger Williams, a Baptist, to flee to Rhode Island, where all religions enjoyed equal standing (Grant, 2000).

Early 20th-century U.S. immigration law favored northern European immigrants over southern and eastern Europeans; in other words, Christians over Jews and Muslims (Grant, 2000). This legal context set the stage for Christianity to flourish in the United States in the late 1940s and early 1950s. Postwar economic prosperity benefited growing churches. Baby boomers (born between 1945 and 1964) were the focus of Sunday school and Christian education programs. The Roman Catholic Church established the largest parochial school system, while public education was largely based on Protestant principles. The motto of the era "the family that prays together stays together" reflected a general belief in the importance of uniting faith and family (Grant, 2000).

The term "culture wars" entered the U.S. lexicon in 1991 (Hunter, 1991) to refer to an ideological rift between two Protestant groups: the Christian right and Christian left. Since the 1950s, social conflicts have erupted over issues of integration and rights of African Americans, legalized abortion, feminist rights and equality, federal and state gun control laws, climate change, recreational drug use, gay rights, and illegal immigration. The Christian right, comprised of **evangelical/conservative** churches, emerged in the 1970s to promote cultural values dominant in the 1950s, such as school prayer and intelligent design and the belief in creationism instead of evolution. "Conservative," "evangelical," and "fundamentalist" labels are often used interchangeably to describe this group of Protestants. All fundamentalists are evangelicals. Fundamentalists believe in the literal, inerrant word of God. However, not all evangelicals are fundamentalists, because evangelicals believe in actively converting others to Christianity, whereby individuals become "born again" by inviting Jesus into their hearts as Lord and Savior. Only then can a baptism be conducted. These conservative Protestants tend to adhere closely to values promulgated in the 1950s. In contrast, the Christian left has supported liberation to some extent—such as feminist rights—even though on the left, gay clergy has remained a divisive issue. The terms "liberal," "mainline," and "progressive" are often used interchangeably to describe the Protestant left, which believes in a looser approach to biblical interpretation (Grant, 2000). The Roman Catholic Church and its conservative followers have generally sided with the Protestant right (Browning, Miller-McLemore, Couture, Lyon, & Franklin, 2000; Grant, 2000).

ESSENTIAL CHRISTIAN BELIEFS

Given the diversity of Christian traditions, setting forth what exactly Christians agree on will be helpful, even if there are differences in degree of emphasis and interpretation. Today, 70.6% of the U.S. population identifies as Christian (Pew Research Center, 2015). Christianity's common beliefs are apparent in the **Apostles Creed** (Beck & Haugen, 2013). Admittedly, this creed was only used in the West and was unknown before 390 C.E. Furthermore, evangelical Protestants and some noncreedal mainline Protestants—such as the Christian Church (Disciples of Christ) and American Baptists—do not formally adhere to creeds. Even so, the Apostles Creed summarizes the shared beliefs of most Christians.

God is understood most fully as the Trinity: God, the Father; Jesus Christ; and the Holy Spirit. These relational terms describe God's relationship to humans as the creator parent, the redeemer through Jesus's death and resurrection, and continuing sustenance through the Spirit (Beck & Haugen, 2013). While some Evangelicals prefer a male God, and feminist theologians have suggested more inclusive terminology, such as God the Parent, the point is that God as Creator is beyond gender designations.

Jesus Christ is the Son of God, both fully human and divine. Jesus, through his life, came to understand the experience of human beings. His birth by Mary connected him to humanity. Through his death and resurrection, Jesus took on the sins of humanity, making possible the **forgiveness** of sin for all humanity. The majority of Christians believe that Mary was a virgin at Jesus's conception by the Holy Spirit and Roman Catholicism teaches that Mary was forever a virgin (Beck & Haugen, 2013).

The third person of the Holy Spirit is understood to be the comforter that Jesus sent to his believers. After Jesus arose from the dead, he ascended into heaven to be with God the Father. Believers experience the

Holy Spirit accompanying them on their daily journey of faith. They are strengthened through prayer as they make known their concerns and joys to God (Beck & Haugen, 2013).

Catholic Beliefs, Family Life, and Social Mores

Among Christians in the United States, 20.8 percent are Roman Catholic (Pew Research Center, 2015). Sacraments are central to Catholic identity (McBrien, 1994). A sacrament is "a religious act or ceremony of the Christian church that is regarded as an outward and visible sign of inward spiritual and divine grace" (Livingstone, 2013). The Catholic Church includes seven sacraments: baptism, Eucharist, penance, confirmation, marriage, holy orders, and anointing of the sick. Through marriage, Catholics understand that marital partners see Jesus Christ in the actions of their spouses. Furthermore, marriage partners are drawn closer to God through the marriage covenant.

Catholic marriage is understood to be everlasting, and it parallels the relationship that Christ has with the church (Weisheipl & Larcher, 1980). The Catholic Church provides guidance to couples learning how to live in marriage. One of its most effective programs is Pre-Cana, a formal marriage preparation process. Couples learn about the important aspects of becoming husband and wife while working with a priest and seeking guidance from couples who have stable and solid marriages (Onedera, 2008). Requirements of Catholic marriage are taught as well as communication skills, finances, parenting issues, belief systems, and plans for the wedding ceremony.

Married couples are called to remain faithful to each other just as Christ was faithful to the church. This fidelity is not based on a constant feeling of "wanting" to be faithful. The church assumes that all married couples will go through difficult times. It is at these times that God gives couples grace to withstand challenges to the sanctity of the marital union (Onedera, 2008).

One of the most challenging aspects of Catholicism's understanding of family life is the teaching that every act of intercourse should be open to beginning a new life. While this does not mean that sexual intercourse is only for reproduction, any act of birth control is considered contrary to being open to new life (Onedera, 2008). Many Catholic couples struggle with this dilemma, trying to balance the church's teaching with their decision whether to use birth control.

The Catholic Church also challenges its members on matters of dating and cohabitation. Sexuality is considered a natural part of human life. The Church's teaching is that any form of sexual expression such as intercourse, petting, or masturbation is special and occurs only in a permanent relationship such as marriage. Thus, chastity is expected of all non-married Catholics. Through chastity, humans are understood to gain a sense of self-control and to truly engage in love through interactions with all people (Lawler, Boyle, & May, 1998).

Family roles are included in Catholic teaching. First, children are taught to be respectful to parents and to care for them in old age. Parents are to educate their children in the faith. For families whose children attend private Catholic schools, this education may occur in parochial schools, which are designed to instill a sense of values in children about the differences between material and spiritual yearnings. Catholic parents are supposed to teach children faith so that personal behaviors reflect the gospel, such as being kind to elderly persons. Lastly, parents are to provide for their children's spiritual and physical needs (Catholic Church, 2003).

Divorce is not considered an option in Catholic theology. It is regarded as immoral because it goes against the sacredness of marriage as a sacrament. Thus, remarriage is a serious matter. Remarried couples are living in conflict with God's law. They are not excommunicated from the Church, but these couples cannot receive communion (Catholic Church, 2003). Annulment in the Catholic Church does recognize the fact that some marriages fail. In annulment, all parties agree that the marriage once thought to be Christian was never in fact a Christian marriage. One or both partners must present their situation to the diocesan marriage tribunal. This is often a lengthy process requiring participants to reflect psychologically, emotionally, and spiritually on their lives (Califano, 2004). Divorced Catholics are encouraged to remain close to the Church. The Sacrament of Reconciliation offers a way to a new beginning after divorce, and divorced parents are encouraged to model their faith for their children.

In today's secular culture, social mores are changing. Homosexuality is accepted by 60 percent of the U.S. population (McCarthy, 2016). The Supreme Court's June 2015 ruling legalizing same-sex marriage has broadened the discussion on homosexuality (Wolf, 2015). While the Catholic Church does not approve of same-sex marriage, Pope Francis has recently showed a spirit of compassion toward the LGBT (lesbian, gay, bisexual, and transgender) community, without going against church doctrine (Brekke, 2015).

Another area of changing norms has emerged with today's assisted reproduction technologies. The Catholic Church's official pro-life position usually sets it in opposition to technologies such as in vitro fertilization. But some voices in the Catholic Church are encouraging open dialogue on the matter (Peters, 1996).

Essential Protestant Beliefs

Protestants share four central beliefs: (1) God is sovereign over all creation and purposefully involved in human life and history; (2) human personhood was created "in the image of God," but is fundamentally flawed and distorted because of sin and evil; (3) all humans need divine salvation from sin and evil, which God offers through the life, death, and resurrection of Jesus; and (4) individuals have direct access to God through the Bible as the "word of God" and their faith in Jesus; they do not require the mediation of priests, the church, or sacraments to be in relation to God (Mercer, 2004). Protestants also have many denominations, which vary in methods of practice, but adhere to the basic tenets and beliefs of Protestantism. Some well-known examples of Protestant denominations are Baptists, Lutherans, Methodists, Pentecostals, and Presbyterians, but many others also exist (Hartford Institute for Religion Research, 2015).

Evangelical Conservative Protestant Beliefs, Family Life, and Social Mores

In the United States, 25.4 percent of Christians identify as evangelical or conservative Protestants (Pew Research Center, 2015). In addition, 6.5 percent of Christians identify with historically Black Protestant churches, whose family values correlate with those of Whites, but whose social-political views are more liberal (Pew Research Center, 2009).

Evangelical beliefs center on God as the source of truth, and the Bible as the infallible word of God and the authority for one's faith (Cairns, 2002). Through the Bible and the work of the Holy Spirit, individuals find salvation through forgiveness and regeneration, deriving from personal faith in Jesus Christ (Zink, 2008). This is a unique aspect of evangelical faith, where the relationship to God is made by individual decisions and not through corporate membership in a community of believers. The majority of evangelicals understand the Bible to be the first source for ethical decisions, leading to a process of discernment. This discernment process is connected to the individual believer's understanding of who God is calling him or her to be (Myers, 2006).

While the Evangelical Protestant tradition has a clear perspective on marriage, many men and women do not adhere to every aspect or practice that it includes. Marriage is understood to be a part of God's creation and plan for fellowship between God and humans. "Covenant" describes the notion of marriage where husband and wife "cleave together" in an intimate relationship that affords sexual, emotional, and spiritual bonding (Zink, 2008). Sexual intercourse is understood to be part of God's plan. The decision whether to have children is understood as a choice for the couple, in connection with their discernment of God's will and other considerations, such as the number of children already in the family, physical hardships, and financial considerations (Zink, 2008).

Evangelical Protestants widely accept that individuals who are dating develop increased intimacy and commitment to the relationship to determine whether marriage is appropriate, given the level of commitment and faith values (Phillips & Phillips, 2006). Premarital sex is prohibited in the evangelical faith, as with the Catholic faith. This means that cohabitation is strongly discouraged, because it suggests that couples will engage in sexual intercourse. In reality, surveys show that 80 percent of young evangelical couples engage in premarital sex (Banks, 2012).

Some evangelicals see the roles of husbands and wives as unique, due to inherent gender differences. This perspective can espouse a marriage style in which the husband is the wage earner while the wife is a homemaker. Yet economic realities can dictate a different situation. The U.S. Bureau of Labor statistics indicate that in 53.1 percent of married husband/wife couples, both spouses work outside the home (U.S. Department of Labor, 1999). Accordingly, many Evangelicals base their marriages more on cultural expectations of marital equality than restricted religious belief (Myers, 2006).

One of the scriptures that elicits the most wide-ranging interpretations and concerns the choice of traditional or egalitarian marital roles is Ephesians 5, which includes the term "submission." One interpretation of the passage understands "submission" to refer to the husband having hierarchical rule over his wife while remaining respectful (O'Brien, 1999). Another interpretation means mutual submission rather than subordination, where spouses respect each other, the husband loves the wife as Christ loved the church, and both husband and wife are in submission to Christ. The needs of the marriage are to be balanced with the needs of both individuals (Barth, 1974).

Children are expected to respect their parents, keeping with the commandment "Honor your family and mother." Parents, in turn, are to respect their children. While some very conservative parents could take this to mean punishing children for misbehavior, this interpretation is less common. Churches today emphasize parenting programs and offer advice on how to raise children (Zink, 2008).

Views on divorce vary from evangelical perspectives. Two commonly accepted grounds for divorce are when a marital partner is sexually unfaithful and when one partner deserts the other (Zink, 2008). Some evangelicals argue that a variety of behaviors, such as physical violence or substance abuse, call for divorce. Others contend that the spouse must remain in the marriage and pray for changes in the offending spouse, even amid violence. Still other evangelicals argue that marital incompatibility contributing to unhappiness constitutes grounds for divorce (Barrick, 2008; Zink, 2008). Recent surveys indicate that "born-again" Christians have a 32 percent divorce rate, compared with 33 percent for non–"born-again" persons (Barrick, 2008).

Growing acceptance of homosexuality across much of the United States has elicited opposition from most evangelicals. Bible verses are quoted to condemn homosexuality (Tucci, 2013). Some evangelical colleges have expressed compassion for students who come out as homosexual and some evangelical megachurches condemn homosexuality while encouraging compassion toward members who are homosexuals (Bailey, 2013).

Assisted reproductive technologies have also challenged Christians. Evangelicals agree with Catholics on many issues regarding the use of these technologies, believing that these technologies usurp the role of God. At the same time, members in local churches may differ on the issue, depending on their own personal circumstances (IVF—Global Perspective, 2015).

Liberal Mainline Protestant Beliefs, Family Life, and Social Mores

Liberal mainline Protestants interpret the Bible more loosely than evangelicals (Ottati, 2006), regarding it as a metaphor to apply to marriage and family in light of new knowledge and changing circumstances. Mainline Protestants do not understand marriage to be a sacrament, but a natural state blessed by God, and a context for human companionship, sexual expression, and procreation. For mainline Protestants, no marital roles are normative, and all marriages are understood to have a covenant of spiritual and emotional connection that serves as a safe place for partners. Thus, rigid roles between husband and wife and between parents and children are not encouraged. Spouses are supposed to have equal and mutual roles. However, just as our society is still impacted by sexism, the same is true for liberal Protestant marriages (Haddock, Zimmerman, & Lyness, 2003).

For these reasons, birth control presents no problem for mainline Protestants. Having children is desirable but not required in Christian marriage. Each couple is encouraged to make the decision that seems best for them, given their financial, work, and emotional readiness for the responsibilities of parenthood. Liberal Protestants assume that the relationship between parents and children should be a loving one, and focus on the uniqueness of their children (Everett, 1998). Parents are understood as responsible for raising children and providing for their physical and spiritual needs. At the same time, parents are to create a nurturing home environment based on God's love that will prepare their children to become independent (Post, 1998).

Consistent with the mainline Protestant tendency to apply new knowledge and adapt to changing circumstances, cohabitation and divorce have increased in liberal Protestant homes, mirroring society in general. Whereas dating standards were once conservative, even with liberal parents, now mainline Protestants tend to accept, if not endorse, cohabiting as "that's the way it is." An ethical standard of commitment based on the emotional/spiritual maturity and age of teen and adult children tends to be the norm (Cook, 2008). While theological reverence for marriage discourages divorce, staying in a painful marriage is discouraged. Now pastors regularly refer to competent couple therapists, especially pastoral counselors, who have both extensive theological and clinical training (Doehring, 2015).

Mainline Protestants often share similar social values with political liberals. Liberals, however, may falter as Christians by making sweeping generalizations that derive from secular humanist values (Browning et al., 2000). Protestant liberals may fail to explicitly state how their Christian values inform their social views. They often collaborate on shared causes with politically liberal persons without explicitly stating that their commitment to a social cause is directly linked to their Christian faith. In contrast, conservative denominations and Catholics make clear distinctions between community groups and Christianity on social issues (Browning et al., 2000). Same-sex marriage and homosexuality are generally accepted by liberal Christians (Saad, 2007). Recently, the Supreme Court's ruling in favor of the federal legality of same-sex marriage, *Obergefell v. Hodges*, has prompted discussion in churches (Chappell, 2015). For some congregations, there is a gap between unofficial approval of these marriages and those who perform same-sex marriages (Beredjick, 2014).

Assisted reproductive technologies, such as in vitro fertilization and surrogate mothering, are often seen by liberal Protestants as advances that ease the suffering of many couples. Conflicts exist for some, but not all on this matter (Cohen, 2002).

DEMOGRAPHICS OF CHRISTIAN FAMILIES

Most U.S. Catholics and Protestants emigrated, or their ancestors did, from European countries, the majority from Spain and Germany. A smaller number of Euro-American Catholics have roots in Italy, and these origins are reflected in their beliefs and worship. Lutherans and members of the United Church of Christ have ethnic ties to Scandinavia and Germany. Presbyterians who originated in Scotland are prevalent in Mid-Atlantic states. Baptists predominantly live in the Southern United States. United Methodists and members of other Methodist branches originated in England and are spread across the county (Giordano & McGoldrick, 2005).

Americans of Hispanic origins are largely Catholic, although a growing number of Hispanic Americans are Protestants in Pentecostal denominations. The Pentecostal emphasis on free expression of the Spirit through glossolalia and deeply felt emotion during worship complement the Latino cultural value of emotional expression (Garcia-Preto, 2005; Giordano & McGoldrick, 2005). Three percent of Native Americans identify as Christians (Tundel, 2013).

Americans of Middle Eastern origins are more often linked to the Eastern Orthodox Church, which is organized according to ethnic or geographical origins, such as the Coptic Orthodox Church and the Greek Orthodox Church. Some Middle Eastern Americans are Christians. For example, Lebanese Americans are 50 percent Christian and 50 percent Muslim (Abudabbeh, 2005).

A minority of Asian and Asian-Indian families in the United States profess Christianity. Specifically, 3 percent of Asians are Catholic; 6 percent are evangelical; and 1 percent identify as mainline. Most Asian Americans who are Christians are Korean Americans. In the United States, 70 percent of Koreans are Christian, and the majority of Korean Christians are Presbyterian (Almeida, 2005).

INTERSECTIONALITY WITHIN WHITE, AFRICAN AMERICAN, AND LATINO CHRISTIAN FAMILIES

White Christian Families

Christian religious life in this country has been shaped by Euro-American ethnicity. Whites, or Euro-Americans, include 53 nationalities (Giordano & McGoldrick, 2005). The largest groups in the United States are German Americans and those with English ancestry: British, Welsh, Scottish, and Irish Americans. Irish Catholics and Scottish Presbyterians provide examples of religious groups where ethnicity and religious practice are inextricably linked. Other groups, such as Lutherans, include many ethnicities that define it, such as Finns, Germans, Norwegians, and Swedes. Even faith in the Catholic Church in the United States is expressed differently for Irish Catholics and Italian Catholics, based on the different histories of these countries. The Irish generally show greater obedience to church practices, while Italian Catholics are more mistrusting of the Church. The result was that Italian Catholics relied primarily on the institution of the family to determine their practices (Giordano & McGoldrick, 2005).

Conversely, other White Americans have had generations of intermarriage, and thus are unaware of their ethnic heritage. This unawareness of ethnicity in White families has resulted, in part, in White families assuming that the dominant cultural values in American society are, in essence, "White" values. They carry weight as the normative or "right" way of viewing life. Increasingly, then, the dominant cultural narratives become connected with "White" values (Rappaport, 2000).

Dominant cultural narratives regarding moral and political values derive from White families' Christian faith. Differentiating faith among White Christians thus often falls on class distinctions. In the rural South, poor White families share many basics of faith with African American families, while Christian White families in suburban areas often share upper-middle class values in their faith (Grant, 2000).

Class values can shape the roles of husband and wife in the Christian family. After World War II, women entered the workforce in growing numbers. Educated women were able to secure well-paying jobs;

uneducated women found poorly paying jobs. Due to racial prejudice, African American women competed for the same jobs on an uneven playing field (Grant, 2000).

Ethnicity is an important part of how Christian families view their faith (Deaner, Pechersky, & McFadden, 2008). For White Christian families, the roles of husband, wife, and children are often connected with dominant cultural narratives of the American dream. The result is that these families' faith becomes inextricably linked to their ethnicity, with little differentiation between the two categories (Browning et al., 2000; Grant, 2000).

Among White Christians, worship style derives from ethnicity and socioeconomic status. Generally, mainline Protestants are more reserved in worship style, following their largely northern European values of restraint and thrift. Evangelical Protestants have flourished mainly in Southern states where the expression of emotion is valued. Evangelical worship services are more emotionally expressive and privilege the corporate expression of personal testimony.

African American Christian Families

African Americans are one of the largest predominately Christian non-Euro-American groups. According to a recent Pew poll, 3 percent of Blacks are Catholic, 6 percent evangelical, 3 percent mainline, and 94 percent attend a historically Black Protestant church (Pew Research Center, 2014). The denominations that are included in this last group are National Baptist, Church of God in Christ, African Methodist Episcopal, and Progressive Baptist Convention. No other ethnicity in the United States has such a large segment of its population attending a church with origins dating back to the enforced immigration of slavery. In addition to these formal denominations, nondenominational Black congregations participate in a broader notion of the Black church that transcends denominational boundaries (Wimberly, 1979).

African Americans are considered more religious than any other racial group in the United States, based on levels of religious affiliation, religious service attendance, and frequency of religious practice; 83 percent identify as Christian (Pew Research Center, 2009). There is just as much diversity within groups that identify as Christian as there is within groups that identify as African American. African American Christian families, therefore, cover a wide matrix of values, beliefs, and practices. But all African American families have been shaped by a shared history.

The large number of African Americans identifying as Christian points to the experience of religious de-culturalization of African people that occurred during slavery. Before being taken to the New World, Africans practiced an array of indigenous African traditional spiritual beliefs. These beliefs were so integrated into everyday life that there was no term equivalent to "religion" in their native languages (Boyd-Franklin, 2006). The ubiquity of African religiosity and the sense of isolation from tribal affiliations that followed enslavement set the stage for the acculturation of Africans in the United States. When Africans were taught Christianity by their slave owners, they adopted it as their own (Raboteau, 2004).

African slaves managed, however, to retain some indigenous practices. Slave narratives and autobiographies reveal that African principles could be seen in reinterpretations of Judeo-Christian concepts. For example, the African idea of sin had more to do with broken ties to the gods than offending another human being, a distinction made in many early Black churches (Wilmore, 1998). Enslaved Africans believed in a different form of salvation than what was taught by White Protestants. For Africans, God was received by the affirmation of his presence, through the imparting of God's spirit in song and dance (Wilmore, 1998). There were often differences between what was espoused in the invisible institution—covert African American "church" gatherings—and the obedience-laden doctrine taught by White Protestant slave owners.

Had it not been for their refusal of White spiritual and political despotism, many more enslaved Africans would have experienced disillusionment or nihilism, which could have significantly undermined the cohesion of African American families today (West, 2001). Instead, Black churches have served as sources of survival. Participants have become empowered through solidarity, dignity, and the respect that comes from playing social and economic leadership roles, which were not afforded to them by the larger society. Familial restoration was achieved by adopting surrogate family members. These churches have served as facilitators of resistance and agents of liberation for many African American families (Frederick, 2003; Warnock, 2013).

When responding to African American Christian families in therapy, it is important for therapists to consider this historical backdrop to avoid diminishing the role of religion in family life. African American families continue to attend church in significant numbers. While mainline Protestantism has declined by an estimated five million members since 2007, the number of African Americans within the historically Black Protestant tradition has remained stable (Pew Research Center, 2015).

Given the great importance of religion in African American families, an effective way to include religiosity in family therapy with African American Christians is to employ prayer-focused couples therapy that emphasizes learning how to pray for one's partner. This approach, when added to the Prevention and Relationship Enhancement Program (PREP; Markman, Stanley, & Blumberg, 2001), an empirically supported treatment, aligns with African Americans' religiosity. Moreover, both prayer-focused PREP and a culturally sensitive version of PREP are more efficacious in helping African American couples than an information-only control condition (Beach, Hurt, Fincham, Franklin, & McNair, 2011). With

African American Christian families, culturally aware marriage and family therapy keep historical contexts in the picture and invite religion into therapy as a cultural context and resource for healing and support.

Latino Christian Families

Latinos are a sizable and growing ethnic group and one of the largest predominately Christian non-Euro-American groups. As of July 2014, Latinos are the largest ethnic minority in the country, numbering 55 million, or 17 percent of the U.S. population (U.S. Census Bureau, 2014). The Pew Center 2013 survey of Latinos and religion found that 55 percent of the Latino population identifies as Catholic and 33 percent of all Catholics are Latinos. Additional polling showed that 16 percent of Latinos are evangelical, 5 percent are mainline, and 3 percent belong to other Christian groups.

Immigration to the United States often intersects with race and ethnicity and how Latinos experience and use their Christian faith. Also, immigration is known to increase psychological stress and the incidence of domestic violence. Faith may be used to address these stressors. For example, a review by Austin and Falconier (2013) found two studies in which some churches offer counseling programs and safe houses to victims, in addition to the salvific effects of spirituality on violence. The Catholic Church is active in this area in urban communities (Valentin, 2010). Mexicans, Puerto Ricans, and Cubans continue to be the largest Latino groups in the county (Garcia-Preto, 2005), and Catholicism plays an important role in their lives. Catholicism provides continuity for Mexican Americans who immigrate. Commitment to marriage, fertility, and the sanctity of mothers are particularly important. Catholic values prevail in the Mexican American community when it comes to premarital sex, abortion, contraception, and homosexuality. In large urban areas, the church in the barrio provides public support as well as protection for undocumented workers (Falicov, 2005). For Puerto Ricans, Catholicism has figured prominently, especially in rituals of birth, marriage, and death. Most Puerto Ricans are nominally Catholic, although recent years have witnessed an increase in Protestant denominations as well as Pentecostalism (Fitzpatrick, 1976). Cubans also identify primarily as Catholics, owing in no small part to life-cycle rituals that are important for Cuban Americans.

Meanwhile, a shift in religious identity is occurring for many Latinos in the United States, related to changing social views regarding family life. Most Latino Catholics are at odds with the Church's positions on divorce, contraception, and women's roles. For example, 79 percent of Christian Latinos say that a marriage in which both husband and wife hold jobs and take care of children is preferable to traditional marriage. Furthermore, they favor permitting priests, who want birth control, the freedom to marry, and women as priests (Pew Research Center, 2014). At the same time, Latinos are increasingly open to becoming evangelical and engaging in Pentecostal practice and charismatic experiences, or to becoming religiously unaffiliated. For example, 24 percent of Latinos are former Catholics (Pew Research Center, 2014). This contrast between liberal and conservative religious values remains to be explained.

For Catholic families, the enduring value of liberation theology—and some of the liberal family views that come with it—cannot be overstated. Liberation theology, which emerged in the late 20th century, is concerned with the transformation of social existence as an intrinsically religious pursuit. The first form of liberation theology took root in Latin America (Floyd-Thomas & Pinn, 2010).

SPIRITUAL AND CLINICAL BENCHMARKS FOR CHRISTIAN FAMILIES

The term "Christian couple or family" means the couple or family uses their Christian beliefs to increase cohesion in the home. A 2014 Gallup survey reports that 56 percent of U.S. adults maintain that religion is important in their daily lives, and 86 percent of respondents believe in God (Gallup Poll, 2014). Walsh (2009) reports that spiritual beliefs and practice are important dimensions of healthy family functioning.

One qualitative case study of an evangelical family concluded that family beliefs have an impact when these beliefs are consistent with family behavior (Bailey, 2002). In this study, the Smith family was observed to have positive relationships. The parents used strict guidelines for their children's behaviors. At the same time, in interviews, the children did not express resentment toward their parents as some children might. The Smith parents had a traditional marriage, where the husband played a dominant role and the wife was submissive. Both spouses expressed satisfaction with the way their marital roles complemented each other in the family.

All family members agreed on a conservative interpretation of the Bible and saw their behaviors as consistent with it. Furthermore, the children said that they saw their parents living consistently with their stated beliefs, which likely led to spiritual cohesiveness within the family (Bailey, 2002). Similarly, a progressive liberal Christian family whose members' beliefs match their behaviors could also enjoy spiritual cohesiveness that connects family members. Overall, a deep spirituality based on respect and consistency appears to support cohesive family functioning better than religious beliefs based on doctrine alone (Coyle, 2015).

Practicing Christian faith in everyday family life presents a challenge. On the one hand, a Christian family that attends worship every Sunday but engages in abuse of its members, would not seem to demonstrate Christian beliefs and values. On the other hand, a family that does not regularly attend services but sees itself as Christian might not seem

Christian to others. The "Christian couple or family" of any denomination can be identified by therapists of all faiths through the concepts of **mutuality, justice,** and hospitality (Anderson, 2009; Anderson, Foley, Miller-McLemore, & Shreiter, 2003). From a spiritual perspective, mutuality is understood as a process of give-and-take between individuals that reflects God's care for all of humanity. Clinically, mutuality can be recognized as the ability to listen to and respect others' differences while holding to one's own unique qualities. Humans must also build trust with family members by setting up behavioral boundaries for all persons. Seeking justice in Christian families means focusing on determining and living out what is right and wrong in relationships and working to right the wrongs. Spiritually, Christian justice seeks to lift up the oppressed, which is often in contrast to what society deems most expedient. The passage in Luke 4:18, at the beginning of Jesus's ministry, sets the tone for justice and encourages Christian families to apply it to everyday relationships. Clinically, family members have a sense of what is fair in the family. Their relationships can be evaluated as loyal, or oppressively obligated, to others (Boszormenyi-Nagy & Krasner, 1986).

Another Christian tenet of family life is **hospitality**, which emphasizes welcoming not only new members into the family, but also openness to new ideas from people outside the immediate boundaries of the family (Anderson, 2009). As Christian families practice hospitality, the boundaries of family life extend beyond the nuclear family to include others. Hospitality is a Christian concept that can be seen in the early church, described in Acts. Deacons were established to provide for the financial well-being of widows. Early believers were encouraged to welcome people into their homes (Bruce, 1988). It is believed that by welcoming people unlike themselves, Christians are emulating Christ, who reached out to people outside the confines of organized religion.

Clinical Work with Christian Couples and Families

Therapists will find it helpful to focus on learning spiritual and religious competencies by developing awareness, new skills, and knowledge (Vieten et al., 2013). Clinical work with Christian clients should start with an honest review of the therapist's attitude toward Christianity. Countertransferential issues emerging from one's own negative or positive experiences must be assessed. A liberal Christian therapist can be prejudiced toward an evangelical or fundamentalist client, just as an agnostic or atheist therapist might harbor biases toward a Christian client of any persuasion. Therapists should assess themselves to determine if countertransference negatively affects their work with a Christian couple or family. If so, the therapist should make a referral.

The clinician working with Christian families enables family members to discuss their own spirituality, instead of making an independent assessment. First, the family is encouraged to review their genogram and reflect on what **spiritual narratives** they see in the family. Second, the clinician collaborates with the family to describe their spirituality, and to validate experiences that are newly concretized and labeled. Third, the clinician focuses on the family's spiritual process, rather than on concrete belief, as it relates to everyday life and the pursuit of mutuality, justice, and hospitality.

Competence with Christian couples and families can also come from building knowledge that helps therapists recognize when spirituality forms parts of the clients' concerns and better understand how to work respectfully with the family's Christian faith. Psychiatrists, psychologists, social workers, marriage and family therapists, and mental health counselors now have multiple resources to help them address spirituality and religious matters in treatment. Resources can be obtained from the professional mental health organizations, such as the American Psychological Association, through its Society for Religion and Spirituality, or the Association for Marriage and Family Therapy and its spirituality tracks at conferences. Social workers can gain clinical knowledge about spirituality through the National Christian Social Workers Association. Professional counselors and mental health counselors have resources in the Association for Spiritual, Ethical, and Religious Values in Counseling. These professional organizations mainly attract clinicians coming from a theistic perspective. However, non-Christian clinicians can learn how to better work with Christian clients through these organizations' conferences and publications.

Christian clinicians may want to affiliate with professional organizations that address distinctly Christian beliefs with clinical skills, such as the Christian Association for Psychological Studies and the American Association of Christian Counselors. Another professional organization that has existed for more than 50 years is the American Association of Pastoral Counselors, whose members are Protestant, Catholic, and Jewish. This organization includes individuals who have completed both theological and clinical training with extensive clinical supervision. Its goal is to professionally integrate spirituality and psychotherapy. Historically, it has credentialed individuals as pastoral counselors and seminary counseling programs as training centers (Townsend, 2009).

Beyond general knowledge, there are several ways to build knowledge about the spiritual and religious lives of the specific couples and families that therapists treat. First, some psychotherapists suggest a series of questions to ask spiritually oriented clients to identify religious beliefs (Saunders, Miller, & Bright, 2010). This approach can ensure objectivity, depending on the questions asked, which can counter the dangers of countertransference. Another way to build knowledge about the role of Christianity in the lives of the couple or family is to use paper-and-pencil self-reports as assessment tools (Hodge, 2003). The literature on obtaining knowledge of clients' spirituality and religion is geared toward assessment of individuals (Saunders et al., 2010).

Discover a family's spiritual narrative in the first session by providing a hospitable "home" for clients, using the spiritual genogram. Include a spiritual assessment with the other assessment pieces. The spiritual genogram is an indispensable tool (Hodge, 2001; Willow, Tobin, & Toner, 2009). Interview all family members to discover their family values, spiritual journeys, and worldviews. Working with the family, draw the family genogram on a large newsprint. Go back two generations beyond the current one. Ask the family about the religious beliefs of parents and grandparents. As the conversation unfolds, they may share negative experiences. Be sure to find strength in the ways in which family members have responded to that negativity. Include on the genogram special family rituals attached to their Christian faith during religious holidays such as Christmas and Easter.

Children can be involved by attaching a picture from a Sunday school leaflet, or recalling something important they learned at church. Further discussing the child's belief and how it connects to other family members will be helpful. Encourage the couple or family to take the genogram home and talk about it. Then, at the next session, that discussion will serve as a starting point.

After assessing the family, the next step is identifying how the family spiritual foci of mutuality, justice, and hospitality do or do not appear in the family's spiritual narratives. These ideas might be manifest in narratives in phrases such as "give-and-take," "fair and unfair" (both short- and long-term), "warm or inviting," or "safe or connected" in their family stories.

The therapist asks family members to reflect on their spiritual journey. An adult may have a more richly defined story than a teenager, who may have more questions about faith. A child may simply state who God is and what God does for him or her. Points in the spiritual journey may be represented on a large pad on a chronological timeline. This makes it easy for the therapist to look at the timeline to see what was happening in the family's faith journey during times of joy or loss.

Depending on the family's theological perspective, the therapist might find it helpful to inquire about scripture verses or Bible stories that have been formative in the life of the family. This illumines how the family uses spiritual resources to shape the family narrative. Furthermore, some families may read the Bible together or pray together. Still others might discuss their faith's impact on ethical decision making and current events.

A final consideration for clinical work with Christian couples and families is encouraging them to identify what impact their family spiritual narratives have on their everyday lives. What is the effect of their story on their faith? Are there other stories that are related? Has there been a time when their spiritual narrative has helped them out of a difficult situation?

Case Vignette

Mark and Martha are a White heterosexual couple in their 50s who have been married for four years. They live in a small Midwestern town where Martha is the pastor of a mainline Protestant denomination. Mark is a real estate agent. This is the first marriage for Martha and the second for Mark. His first marriage ended in divorce. He has two adult children: a son and a daughter. Both are married and live in another state. The couple was seen by the first author, Coyle, who is a licensed marriage and family therapist and pastoral counselor. Coyle is theologically moderate and socially liberal and uses narrative therapy to help couples.

In the initial session, the couple said they met in a singles group at a church in a western state before moving to the Midwest. Mark was attracted to Martha because she was dynamic and knew what she wanted. Martha described Mark as someone who was dependable and gentle. Mark's children were supportive of their father's relationship with Martha. His former wife had a long history of mental illness. Mark supported her as long as he could, but the aftermath of their marriage resulted in a deep sense of loneliness and weariness for him. Martha said she struggled to find a man who was not threatened by her feminist views. At the same time, she said she yearned for someone who was soft and calm, unlike her.

Treatment was conducted from a narrative therapy orientation. As the initial sessions progressed, the couple indicated that despite their wish to be close, their personal narratives blocked their potential for closeness and left each feeling isolated. Mark experienced himself as incompetent and worthless. Martha experienced herself as overburdened and overlooked. The closer that Martha moved toward Mark, the more Mark withdrew, fearing emotional intimacy. When Mark did venture out, he said it seemed that Martha pounced on him. Then he retreated to feel safe. The couple also was affected by cultural gender narratives that value the husband as breadwinner and spiritual leader. Mark believed that he was not competent enough to have his job. Conversely, Martha believed that only she could fulfill her congregation's needs. Also, despite Martha being the pastor in a mainline denomination, the role of female pastor is relatively new and conflicts arise with intergenerational values in the congregation. These identity narratives all created distance in the marriage and negatively affected each partner's work situation. The couple had two preferred outcomes. First, they desired for their relationship to be an experience of closeness. Toward that end, they reported the strength of feeling close primarily when Mark leads devotional time with prayer and

Bible reading for the couple at home. Second, they wanted to value Martha's leadership in the family and the church as contributing to Mark's sense of gratitude and worth.

Mark grew up in a large family with six children. He was the middle child. His parents were strict and worked hard on the family farm. The family identified as Protestant but was not religiously active in any church. The family rule was for everyone to take care of themselves. Mark said that he had no one to comfort him. Once, feeling alone and crying in his room, he ran outside onto the wide plains. As he ran, he found a large lone tree and fell down on the ground behind it, exhausted. This tree became his place of safety when he felt scared.

Martha grew up in a family of three. The family was nominally involved in a Protestant congregation. The middle child, she said that she was her father's favorite. But, he had high expectations that she felt she never met. Furthermore, she said that no one comforted her. Martha said she was seen, but "looked over."

The church appealed to Martha. She became involved in a church youth group, whose youth pastor pulled her "out of her shell." There, Martha said she felt that she mattered and was not "looked over." In contrast, while growing up, Mark had no church involvement. God, he said, seemed distant. It was not until he met Martha at church that he began to experience a connection to God.

As we worked through their conflicts, their struggles with faith emerged. The presenting struggle focused on Martha's role as pastor of the church, a position she assumed after the church experienced conflict with the former pastor. She was the first woman called to a pastor at the church. Martha received positive feedback on her sermons and seemed to do well with pastoral care of congregants.

Mark said that he enjoyed being at church and added that Martha just expected too much of herself. Both agreed that the point of friction at church was Martha's getting caught up in conflicts when she micromanaged every minor church event, which led to their negative interaction pattern at home. As they talked, Martha said that, at the core, she yearned to have an "authentic" faith. For Martha, an "authentic" faith would allow her to share her weaknesses and find others who could mutually share their weaknesses. She described her struggle as wanting to express her emotional loneliness through her faith, not fearing the expression of her feelings. Martha admitted that this spiritual yearning was exacerbated because she was a pastor. Yet, she sadly stated that she had always struggled with wanting to have an authentic faith.

Mark said that it would be easy to blame their problems on the church. But he strongly expressed that were Martha a teacher and not a pastor, he would see the faith issue to be largely the same. Like Martha, Mark said that he wanted an authentic faith that offered him room to make mistakes and still feel connected to God. Both indicated that they never felt forgiven in their faith or with each other. As I talked with them, both expressed that connecting to God, each other, and others meant that they must do all the right things. No comfort zone existed, just as there were no comfort zones in their families of origin.

Treatment continued by emphasizing how they could feel forgiven in their faith, each other, and God. This work began by adding spiritual narratives on their genograms. For both Mark and Martha, their families of origin "used" moral religious standards to punish them. Thus, justice in their families was never fully achieved. A cohesive family, with members mutually caring for one another, was missing.

Mark and Martha began to tell their stories over the next few sessions. Then, we began processing the narrative of their coming together and ways in which their individual narratives connected to their narrative as a couple. A turning point in therapy came when Mark and I waited for Martha to arrive at their appointment. Martha arrived 15 minutes late. After a few minutes of heated discussion, Mark blurted out, "I feel I've waited for you my whole life." Martha hotly responded with a flurry of expletives. As I intervened, my focus was on validating Mark's response of being fully present. I asked him if, in similar situations, he felt like that lonely boy hiding behind the large lone tree. This story connected to one of his spiritual narratives of being without God. His eyes filled with tears. Martha's voice softened and she reached for Mark's hand. They held hands and were silent. Martha then shared her story of being in a large family, feeling like just a number. In the church, she said, she felt special.

The remainder of their work focused on that experience of connecting and, in their words, "feeling forgiven." Their Christian faith up to this point had been focused on keeping appearances, closely monitoring angry feelings, and working to earn God's grace. In a parallel fashion, their marital relationship was based on these expectations. Martha's position as pastor was reminiscent of the vocational element of marriage initiated by Luther and the Reformers (Grant, 2000). Both Mark and Martha identified marriage as having a vocational dimension, quite apart from her profession. They focused on establishing mutuality in their relationship. One example was Mark leading devotion for them as a couple, despite Martha being the "professional." Martha came to see her controlling of Mark as a way of her not being able to offer hospitality to her husband.

As they shared created couple narratives, it turned out that justice identified by grace, not legalism, characterized their marriage. Both Mark and Martha's families required that being a family member in good standing meant that one had to have "right" behavior at all times. Fairness and justice in their families of origin had no room for grace. Thus, learning how to co-create couple narratives of justice by grace was a challenge that the therapist helped them to overcome.

CONCLUSIONS

Christian belief includes three major branches of faith, two of which are practiced widely in the United States. The majority of Christians in the United States are Protestants. Among Protestants, one group includes evangelicals and conservatives, while the other includes mainline and liberal Christians. Catholics comprise the country's other significant Christian group.

Christian faith became firmly established in the United States, underpinning political and social life, when the majority of its early settlers emigrated from Europe and established largely Protestant beliefs and practices. Immigrants from Latin America primarily practiced Catholicism; with current trends toward Pentecostals. Asian immigrants brought with them a predominantly syncretistic blend of religions, but the majority of Korean immigrants identify as Protestants. Black Americans who experienced enforced immigration through slavery are primarily Christians, the majority Protestants. All Christians believe in Jesus Christ as the expression of God incarnated. Beliefs vary on the authority of the Bible and the role that church tradition plays in faith. Mainline and/or liberal Protestants believe that the Bible is authoritative but not infallible. Evangelical and other conservative Christians believe that the Bible is infallible. Catholics believe the Bible is God's inspired word, but tend to rely on church traditions and papal encyclicals as a foundation for their faith.

While family life is important for all Christians, vast differences exist in how Christians interpret behaviors in the family. Abortion, cohabiting, birth control, and assisted reproductive technologies all present challenges for faith communities. In many cases, what Christians say they believe differs from what they do. We assert that the key criterion in assessing whether faith has a healthy impact on the family is the degree to which faith forms a cohesive, integrative fabric for everyday family life.

A spiritually sensitive clinical approach that focuses on the couple and family telling their own spiritual stories is presented. Mutuality, justice, and hospitality are theological foci that help the clinician focus on spiritual concerns that are family-focused, rather than individually focused. This spiritual-narrative focus enables the family to tell their own stories. The clinician then discerns through these narratives whether family life is healthy or unhealthy as told by its members.

CHAPTER REVIEW

Key Points

1. While all Christians tend to believe in Jesus Christ as the expression of God incarnated, a wide range of beliefs exist about the authority of the Bible, the role of church tradition in faith, and how faith informs family life.

2. Christian faith can provide healthy family cohesion by creating nurturing bonds between family members, and between the family and the outside world.
3. What Christians say they believe might differ from what they do. A key criterion in assessing if faith has a healthy expression within the family is evaluating the degree to which shared family beliefs align with behavior and form a cohesive fabric for family life.
4. A spiritually sensitive clinical approach focuses on the couple or family members telling their own spiritual stories to provide a window into understanding the ways in which religious norms and values influence family life.
5. Mutuality, justice, and hospitality are theological foci that can help the clinician focus on spiritual concerns that are family-focused, rather than focused on individuals.

Key Terms

Apostles Creed, Catholic, evangelical/conservative, forgiveness, hospitality, justice, liberal mainline Protestants, mutuality, Protestant, religion, spiritual narrative, spirituality

Myths and Realities

- It is a myth that Christianity is a monolithic religion. In reality, there are many expressions of Christian faith, and spirituality and religion are not mutually exclusive. Most religions began with spiritual experiences that once shared and formalized, became religions. Likewise, someone who is religious can continue to have deeply felt spiritual experiences.
- It is a myth that spiritual assessment is only a matter of understanding clients' espoused beliefs. In reality, a spiritually sensitive clinician must also seek to understand clients' practiced beliefs. What couples and families say they believe and what they practice are not always congruent. Some clinicians believe that couples and families will be offended if asked about religion or spirituality and avoid doing so. However, many couples and families welcome the opportunity to bring this aspect of their lives and values into therapy.

Tools and Tips

Knowledge

American Association of Pastoral Counselors, http://www.aapc.org
Association for Spiritual, Ethical, and Religious Values in Counseling of the American Counseling Association, http://www.aservic.org/
Hodge, D. R. (2003). The intrinsic spirituality scale: A new six-item instrument for assessing the salience of spirituality as a motivational construct. *Journal of Social Service Research, 30*, 41–61.
Richards, P. S., & Worthington, E. L., Jr. (2010). The need for evidence-based, spiritually oriented psychotherapies. *Professional Psychology: Research and Practice, 41*, 363.

Rosmarin, D. H., Pirutinsky, S., & Pargament, K. I. (2011). A brief measure of core religious beliefs for use in psychiatric settings. *International Journal of Psychiatry in Medicine, 41,* 253–261.

Saunders, S. M., Miller, M. L., Bright, M. M. (2010). Spiritually conscious psychological care. *Professional Psychology: Research and Practice, 41,* 355–362.

Society for the Psychology of Religion and Spirituality of the American Psychological Association, http://www.apa.org/about/division/div36.aspx

Vieten, C., Scammell, S., Pilato, R., Ammondson, I., Pargament, K. I., Lukoff, D. (2013). Spiritual and religious competencies for psychologists. *Psychology of Religion and Spirituality, 5,* 129–144.

Dynamic Sizing

This chapter outlines broad understandings of Christianity and some of the key variations within the Christian tradition. These understandings can most often be generalized when working with couples and families that identify as Christian; however, with any Christian family, one can assess if family members' espoused beliefs of mutuality, justice, and hospitality are consistent with their practiced behaviors.

Skills

Theory. The expression and experience of mutuality, justice, and hospitality by all family members are key criteria for assessing the health of Christian families. A narrative framework uniquely strengthens the family to identify and deepen their family narratives of these key criteria as a spiritual practice for themselves.

Prevention. Some individuals may have been exposed to teachings that utilize religion to justify staying in abusive or violent family contexts. Premarital counseling with Christian couples is an important opportunity for therapists to offer alternative perspectives as options to prevent detrimental theologies such as these to continue.

Service Provision. First, providers should be aware of their own spiritual and religious countertransference to avoid value-driven judgment calls. Second, providers can take advantage of a number of spiritual assessment tools with clients to assist with objectivity. Finally, using mutuality, justice, and hospitality as theological foci can help focus on spiritual concerns that are family-focused rather than individually focused.

Policy. Policy and religious values are often intermingled in conversations about civil liberties afforded to LBGTQ persons and families. More can be done to disentangle these matters.

Research. More research is needed to address the ways in which individual spiritual beliefs eventually form a family spiritual narrative that contributes negatively or positively to family cohesion.

Awareness

Therapists should honestly review attitudes toward Christianity. Countertransference issues emerging from one's own negative or positive experiences with Christianity must be assessed. A liberal Christian therapist can be as prejudiced toward an evangelical or fundamentalist client as an agnostic or atheistic therapist toward a Christian client of any persuasion. If you assess yourself and discover that your countertransference hinders your work with a Christian client, then it is best to make a referral.

REFERENCES

Abudabbeh, N. (2005). Arab families: An overview. In M. McGoldrick, J. Giordano, & N. Garcia-Preto (Eds.), *Ethnicity and family therapy* (3rd ed., pp. 423–436). New York, NY: Guilford Press.

Almeida, R. (2005). Asian Indian families: An overview. In M. McGoldrick, J. Giordano, & N. Garcia-Preto (Eds.), *Ethnicity and family therapy* (3rd ed., pp. 377–394). New York, NY: Guilford Press.

Ahlstrom, S. E., & Hall, D. D. (2004). *A religious history of the American people* (2nd ed.). New Haven, CT: Yale University Press.

Anderson, H. (2009). A spirituality for family life. In F. Walsh (Ed.), *Spiritual resources: In family therapy* (2nd ed., pp. 194–214). New York, NY: Guilford Press.

Anderson, H., Foley, E., Miller-McLemore, B., & Shreiter, R. (2003). *Mutuality matters: Family, faith, and just love.* Lanham, MD: Rowman & Littlefield.

Austin, J., & Falconier, M. (2013). Spirituality and common dyadic coping: Protective factors from psychological aggression in Latino immigrant couples. *Journal of Family Issues, 34,* 323–346.

Bailey, C. (2002). The effect of spiritual beliefs and practices in family functioning: A qualitative study. In T. Carlson & M. Erickson (Eds.), *Spirituality and family therapy.* (pp. 127–144). New York, NY: Haworth Press.

Bailey, S. P. (2013, March 30). At evangelical colleges, a shifting attitude toward gay students. *CNN.* Retrieved from http://religion.blogs.cnn .com/2013/03/30/at-evangelical-colleges-a-shifting-attitude-toward-gay-students/

Banks, A. M. (2012, April 23). With high premarital sex rates and abortion rates, Evangelicals need frank talk about sex. *HuffPost Religion.* Retrieved from http://www.huffIngtonpost.com/2012/04/23/evanglicals-sex-frank-talk_n_1443062.html

Barth, M. (1974). *Ephesians 4–6.* Garden City, NY: Doubleday.

Barrick, A. (2008, April 4). Study: Christian divorce rate identical to national rate. *The Christian Post.* Retrieved from http://www.christianpost.com/news/study-christian-divorce-rate-identical-to-national-average-31815/.

Beach, S., Hurt, T., Fincham, F., Franklin, K., & McNair, L. (2011). Enhancing marital enrichment through spirituality: efficacy date for prayer focused relationship enhancement. *Psychology of Religion and Spirituality, 3,* 201–216.

Beck, R., & A. Haugen (2013). The Christian religion: A theological and psychological review. In Kenneth I. Pargament (Ed.), *APA handbook of psychology, religion and spirituality. The APA handbooks in psychology.* Washington, DC: American Psychological Association.

Beredjick, C. (2014, March 11). United Methodist bishop says that pastors who perform same-sex marriage ceremonies should not be punished. *Patheos*. Retrieved from http://www.patheos.com/blogs/friendlyathe ist/2014/03/11/united-methodist-bishop-says-that-pastors-who-perform-same-sex-marriage-ceremonies-should-not-be-punished/

Boszormenyi-Nagy, I., & Krasner, B. (1986). *Between give and take: A clinical guide to contextual therapy*. New York, NY: Brunner/Mazel.

Boyd-Franklin, N. (2006). *Black families in therapy: Understanding the African American experience*. New York, NY: Guilford Press.

Brekke, K. (2015, June 1). Why gay marriage poses a "difficult" problem for Pope Francis. *HuffPost Religion*. Retrieved from http://www.huffingtonpost .com/2015/06/01/pope-francis-gay-marriage_n_7484106.html

Browning, D., Miller-McLemore, B., Couture, P., Lyon, R. B., & Franklin, R. (2000). *From culture wars to common ground* (2nd ed.). Louisville, KY: Westminster John Knox Press.

Bruce, F. (1988). *The book of the Acts (New International Commentary on the New Testament)*. Grand Rapids, MI: William B. Eerdmans Publishing.

Cairns, A. (2002). *Dictionary of theological terms*. Greenville, SC: Ambassador Emerald International.

Califano, J. (2004). The annulment: One Catholic's journey of reconciliation. *America, 19*(15), 10–14.

Catholic Church (2003). *Catechism of the Catholic Church* (2nd ed.). New York, NY: Doubleday.

Chappell, B. (2015, June 26). Supreme Court ruling declares same-sex marriage legal in all 50 states. *NPR*. Retrieved from http://www.npr.org/sections/thetwo-way/2015/06/26/417717613/supreme-court-rules-all-states-must-allow-same-sex-marriages

Cohen, C.B. (2002). Protestant perspectives on the uses of the new reproductive technologies. *Fordham Urban Law Journal, 30*, 135–145.

Cook, C. (2008). The practice of marriage and family counseling and liberal Protestant Christianity. In J. Onedera (Ed.), *The role of religion in marriage and family counseling*, (pp. 73–88). New York, NY: Routledge.

Coyle, S. (2015). From systems to narrative family therapy. In F. Kelcourse & B. Lyon (Eds.), *Transforming wisdom: Pastoral psychotherapy in theological perspective*. Eugene, OR: Cascade Books.

Coyle, S. (2010). Spiritual narratives: Hope and healing through stories of faith. In Harold J. Ellens (Ed.), *Healing power of religion: How faith helps humans thrive*. Santa Barbara, CA: Praeger Press.

Deaner, R., Pechersky, K., & McFadden, J. (2008). Ethnicity: Religious practice and marriage and family counseling implications. In J. Onedera (Ed.), *The role of religion in marriage and family counseling* (pp. 37–54). New York, NY: Routledge.

Doehring, C. (2015, revised and expanded). *The practice of pastoral care: A postmodern approach*. Louisville, KY: Westminster John Knox Press.

Everett, W. (1998). Marriage: A Protestant perspective. In H. Anderson, D.S. Browning, I.S. Evison, & M.S. van Leeuwen (Eds.), *The family handbook* (pp. 13–16). Louisville, KY: Westminster John Knox Press.

Falicov, C. (2005). Mexican families. In M. McGoldrick, J. Giordano, & N. Garcia-Preto (Eds.), *Ethnicity and family therapy* (3rd ed., pp. 229–241). New York, NY: Guilford Press.

Fitzpatrick, J. (1976). The Puerto Rican family. In R. W. Habenstein & C. H. Mindel (Eds.), *Ethnic families in America: Patterns and variations* (pp. 192–217). New York, NY: Elsevier.

Floyd-Thomas, S., & Pinn, A. (2010). Introduction. In S. Floyd-Thomas & A. Pinn (Eds.), *Liberation theologies in the United States* (pp. 1–14). New York, NY: New York University Press.

Frederick, M. (2003). *Between Sundays: Black women and everyday struggles of faith.* Berkeley, CA: University of California Press.

Gallup Poll. (2014). Religion. *Gallup.* Retrieved from http://www.gallup.com/poll/1690/religion.aspx

Garcia-Preto, N. (2005). Latino families: An overview. In M. McGoldrick, J. Giordano, & N. Garcia-Preto (Eds.), *Ethnicity and family therapy* (3rd ed., pp. 153–165). New York, NY: Guilford Press.

Giordano, J., & McGoldrick, M. (2005). Families of European origin: An overview. In M. McGoldrick, J. Giordano, & N. Garcia-Preto (Eds.), *Ethnicity and family therapy* (3rd ed., pp. 501–519). New York, NY: Guilford Press.

Grant, B. (2000). *The social structure of Christian families: A historical perspective.* St. Louis, MO: Chalice Press.

Haddock, S., Zimmerman, T., & Lyness, L. (2003). Changing gender norms: Transitional dilemmas. In F. Walsh (Ed.), *Normal family processes: Growing diversity and complexity* (3rd ed., pp. 301–336). New York, NY: Guilford Press.

Hartford Institute for Religion Research. (2015). Official denominational web sites. Retrieved from http://hirr.hartsem.edu/denom/homepages.html

Hodge, D. (2001). Spiritual genograms: A generational approach to assessing spirituality. *Families in Society: The Journal of Contemporary Social Services, 82, 35–48.*

Hodge, D. R. (2003). *Spiritual assessment: A handbook for helping professionals.* Botsford, CT: North American Association of Christians in Social Work.

Hunter, J. D. (1991). *Culture wars: The struggle to define America.* New York, NY: Basic Books.

IVF—Global perspective of religions: Christianity. 2012. Retrieved from http://www.ivf-worldwide.com/education/introduction/ivf-global-perspective-religious/ivf-christianity.html

Lawler, R., Boyle, J., & May, W. (1998). *Catholic sexual ethics: A summary explanation and defense* (2nd ed.). Huntington, IN: Our Sunday Visitor.

Livingstone, E. A. (2013). Sacrament. In E. A. Livingstone (Ed.), *The concise Oxford dictionary of the Christian Church* (p. 496). Oxford, UK: Oxford University Press.

Markman, H. J., Stanley, S. M., & Blumberg, S. L. (2001). *Fighting for your marriage.* San Francisco, CA: Jossey-Bass.

McBrien, R. (1994). *Catholicism* (Rev. ed.). San Francisco, CA: Harper.

McCarthy, J. (2016, January 18). Satisfaction with acceptance of gays in U.S. at new high. *Gallup.* Retrieved from http://www.gallup.com/poll/188657/satisfaction-acceptance-gays-new-high.aspx?g_source=SocialIssues&g_medium=newsfeed&g_campaign=tiles

Mercer, J. (2004). The Protestant child, adolescent and family. *Child and Adolescent Clinics of North America, 13, 161–181.*

Myers, S. (2006). Religious homogamy and marital quality: Historical and generational patterns, 1980–1997. *Journal of Marriage and Family Therapy, 68, 292–304.*

O'Brien, P. (1999). *The letter to the Ephesians.* Grand Rapids, MI: Wm. B. Eerdmans Publishing.

Onedera, J. (2008). The practice of marriage and family counseling and Catholicism. In J. Onedera (Ed.), *The role of religion in marriage and family counseling* (pp. 37–54). New York, NY: Routledge.

Ottati, D. (2006). *Theology for liberal Protestants and other endangered species.* Louisville, KY: Geneva Press.

Peters, T. (1996). *For the love of children: Genetic technology and the future of the family.* Louisville, KY: Westminster John Knox Press.

Pew Research Center. (2009, January 30). A religious portrait of African Americans. Pew Research Center. *Pew Research Center Polling and Analysis.* Retrieved from http://www.pewforum.org/2009/01/30/a-religious-portrait-of-african-americans/

Pew Research Center. (2014, May 7). The shifting religious identity of Latinos in the United States. *Pew Research Center Polling and Analysis.* Retrieved from http://www.pewforum.org/2014/05/07/the-shifting-religious-identity-of-latinos-in-the-united-states/

Pew Research Center. (2015, May 12). America's changing religious landscape: Christians decline sharply as share of population; Unaffiliated and other faiths continue to grow. *Pew Research Center: Religion & Public Life.* Retrieved from http://www.pewforum.org/2015/05/12/americas-changing-religious-landscape/.

Phillips, D., & Phillips, S. (2006). *Holding hands, holding hearts: Recovering a biblical view of Christian dating.* Phillipsburg, NJ: P&R Publishing.

Post, S. (1998). The family: A Protestant perspective. In H. Anderson, D. Browning, I. Evison, & M. Van Leeuwen (Eds.), *The family handbook* (pp. 21–23). Louisville, KY: Westminster John Knox Press.

Raboteau, A. (2004). *Slave religion: The invisible institution in the antebellum south.* New York, NY: Oxford Press.

Rappaport, J. (2000). Community narratives: Tales of terror and joy. *American Journal of Community Psychology, 28*(5), 1–24.

Saad, L. (2007, May 27). Tolerance for gay rights at high-water Mark. *Gallup News Service.* Retrieved from http://www.gallup.com/poll/27694/Tolerance-Gay-Rights-HighWater-Mark.aspx

Saunders, S., Miller, M., & Bright, M. (2010). Spiritually conscious psychological care. *Professional Psychology: Research and Practice, 41,* 355–362.

Townsend, L. (2009). *Introduction to pastoral counseling.* Nashville, TN: Abingdon Press.

Tucci, T. (2013, July 18). Homosexuality in Bible and Christian view. *Bible.org.* Retrieved from https://bible.org/article/homosexuality-biblical-christian-view.

Tundel, Nikki. (2013, November 13). American Indians balance native culture with Christianity. *MPR News.* Retrieved from http://www.mprnews.org/story/2013/11/13/arts/native-spirituality-christianity

U.S. Census Bureau. (2014). Hispanic Americans by the number. *Infoplease.com.* Retrieved from http://www.infoplease.com/spot/hhmcensus1.html

U.S. Department of Labor, Bureau of Labor Statistics. (1999). Both husband and wife work for pay in majority of married couple families. Retrieved from http://www.bls.gov/opub/ted/1999/May/wk4/art03.htm

Valentin, B. (2010). Hispanic/Latino(a) theology. In S. Floyd-Thomas & A. Pinn (Eds.), *Liberation theologies in the United States* (pp. 86–114). New York, NY: New York University Press.

Vieten, C., Scammell, S., Pilato, R., Ammondson, I., Pargament, K., & Lukoff, D. (2013). Spiritual and religious competencies for psychologists. *Psychology of Religion and Spirituality, 5*(3), 129–144.

Walsh, F. (2009). Integrating spiritualty in family therapy: Wellsprings for health, healing, and resilience. In F. Walsh (Ed.), *Spiritual resources in family therapy* (2nd ed., pp. 31–64). New York, NY: Guilford Press.

Warnock, R. (2013). *The divided mind of the black church: Theology, piety, and public witness*. New York, NY: New York University Press.

Weisheipl, J., & Larcher, F. (1980). *Translation of commentary on the gospel of Saint John (St. Thomas Aquinas)*. Albany, NY: Magi Books.

West, C. (2001). *Race matters* (2nd ed.). New York, NY: Vintage Books.

Willow, R., Tobin, D., & Toner, S. (2009). Assessment of the use of spiritual genograms in counselor education. *Counseling and Values, 53*, 214–223.

Wilmore, G. (1998). *Black religion and Black radicalism: An interpretation of the religious history of African Americans*. Maryknoll, NY: Orbis Books.

Wimberly, E. (1979). Pastoral care in the Black church. Nashville, TN: Abingdon Press.

Wolf, R. (2015, January 16). The Supreme Court agrees to rule on gay marriage. *USA Today*. http://www.usatoday.com/story/news/nation/2015/01/16/supreme-court-gay-marriage/21867355/

Zink, D. (2008). The practice of marriage and family counseling and conservative Christianity. In J. Onedera (Ed.), *The role of religion in marriage and family counseling* (pp. 55–72). New York, NY: Routledge.

CHAPTER 9

Socioreligious and Clinical Landscapes of Couplehood and Families in Orthodox Jewish Communities

Isaac Schechter

INTRODUCTION

Judaism and Jewish Identity

When treating couples and families, it is crucial that their dynamics be understood in the context of their culture (Alegria, Atkins, Slaton, & Stelk, 2010; Bernal, Rodriguez, & Jimenez-Chafey, 2009; Bronfenbrenner, 1986). When the Jewish people were exiled from their native land nearly 2,000 years ago, they dispersed throughout world—a process termed "the Diaspora." Such widespread population transfer gave rise to a complex identity encompassing multiple ethnic, cultural, and historical experiences. Judaism is a religion; however, the history of the Jewish people dictates an identity transcending religious beliefs and practices, and incorporates the global nature of a common ancient history and core beliefs, with one that stems from the local culture and context of the current environment (Bronfenbrenner, 1986; Schnitzer, Loots, Escudero, & Schechter, 2009). This "glocal" identity prevalent among the Jewish people has a profound impact on the psychological functioning of the individual, family, and community (Alegria et al., 2010; Alegria & McGuire, 2003), and is a significant component in clinical diagnoses, treatments, and outcomes in the Jewish population (Alegria & McGuire, 2003; Bernal et al., 2009; Kirmayer, 2006). The focus of this chapter is the historically underserved and understudied Orthodox Jewish community.

Jewish history may be seen as a dialectic between tradition and acculturation. Three major branches of Judaism evolved along a continuum of religious observance and identity: Orthodox is the most adherent to tradition, Reform is the most acculturated, and Conservative integrates aspects of both to serve as a midpoint in the continuum (Cohen, Ukeles, & Miller, 2012). Each branch contains additional subgroups differentiated by forms of religious expression and distinct socioreligious markers. Despite a shared history and overlapping areas of identity, stark contrasts exist among the branches of Judaism and members of the Jewish faith.

Orthodox Judaism is distinctive in its strict allegiance to the Torah, translated as "the teaching," and *halacha*, or Jewish law, encompassing both belief and practice. The Torah comprises the Old Testament of the Bible, along with rabbinic teachings found in the *Mishna* and Talmud. The *halacha* emerged from those sources (Maimonides, 1998), and serves as the framework of how to "be Jewish." Although there can be significant variability among individuals and groups in terms of manifestations and levels of observance, all Orthodox life emanates from a strict fidelity to *halacha*.

Orthodox Judaism

Orthodox Judaism comprises various groups, the most prominent of which are the *Chassidic*, Yeshiva Orthodox (*Yeshivish*) and Modern Orthodox streams. These groups may be differentiated by the level of strictness in their adherence to *halacha* and rabbinic authority and their degree of openness to contemporary society, education, and information (Cohen et al., 2012; Schechter, 2011; Schnall, 2006). Concepts applicable to all Orthodox Jews will be offered and illustrations with reference to the streams provided, when relevant. Detailed descriptions of each group, however, will be discussed in the section "Types of Orthodox Jews."

The two most traditional groups, *Chassidic* and *Yeshivish*, comprise the *Chareidi* community, the translation of which is "those who tremble before God." The *Chassidic* community rejects engagement with the outside culture and values purposeful insularity. For example, *Chassidim* have established communities in which all residents belong to a particular *shul* (synagogue). The *Yeshivish* community is organized around the yeshiva (academy of Torah study), its rabbis, Torah study as the focus of family life, and strict observance of Jewish law. It is more open to the larger culture than the *Chassidic* community, yet still imposes significant restrictions on these influences. Modern Orthodox is the most acculturated group, with an open orientation toward cultural exposure to the mainstream, such as movie attendance and internet usage. Unlike the other two streams discussed before, it is not uncommon for the Modern Orthodox Jews to develop careers unrelated to the practice of their faith and to adopt a mode of dress less distinguishable from non-Orthodox individuals.

Orthodox Jewish culture tends to adhere to traditional gender roles. Men are expected to focus on the realm outside of the home, while the role of women is child-rearing and maintaining the family home—even if they work outside of the home. There is slightly more flexibility among the Modern Orthodox, as members of that group often tend to respond to general cultural trends. *Halacha* requires men to spend a great deal of time engaged in religious practice, but women are exempt from such activities as they are expected to devote themselves to meeting the needs of their family and taking care of their home. Within the larger system of traditional roles, significant unique variations exist among the groups comprising Orthodox Judaism, as discussed more fully in the section "Types of Orthodox Jews."

FEATURES OF ORTHODOX LIFE

In Orthodox Judaism, behavior must be conducted in a *halachic* way and emanate from a Torah perspective (Greenberg & Witzum, 2001; Huppert, Siev, & Kushner, 2007). *Halacha* includes *mitzvos* (commandments), both positive and negative in nature, the domains of which encompass virtually every area of life—public, private, interpersonal, intrapersonal, and transpersonal (i.e., between the person and God). Given the widespread nature of the proscriptions and restrictions inherent in *halacha*, it has the power to dramatically shape the nature of experience and identity among Orthodox Jews.

One illustration of a practice rooted in *halacha*, incorporating the duality of both positive and negative commandments, is Sabbath observance. The Sabbath is a 25-hour period from sundown on Friday through Saturday after sundown when all Orthodox Jews are forbidden to engage in work activities. Work is interpreted in an expansive fashion as to incorporate activities unrelated to income production. Thus, cooking, writing, the use of electronics (i.e., phones, computers), listening to music, and driving a car fit within the definition of proscribed work. Those prohibitions are offset by the positive aspects of Sabbath observation—a day set aside, free of distractions, to be with one's family and friends, dress in one's finest clothes, pray, learn Torah, and eat three festive meals.

There are situations, however, in which strict observance of *halacha* is not determinable, often as a result of confronting an issue that has not been addressed previously, where the correct application of *halacha* is unknown, or conflicts exist between salient values. On these occasions, resolution is reached through rabbinic consultation, a formal process in which an individual poses a question (*shailah*) and receives a rabbinic ruling applying *halacha* to this real-life situation. Typical questions concern clarifications of appropriate religious practice, significant medical decisions, and the use of contraception. It is also common to ask for rabbinical rulings with respect to socioreligious areas, such as school choice, child-rearing, and guidance about dating or potential marriage partners, and as the venue for those seeking spiritual guidance and asking for a blessing (Schechter et al., 2015).

Halachic mandates informing Orthodox life necessitate both a social milieu and a comprehensive set of institutions reflective of the emphasis Judaism places on religious practice, community, and the social nature of Jewish religious life (Sublette & Trappler, 2000). Each community must include, at a minimum, a school, synagogue, *mikveh* (ritual bath), burial society, and provisions for kosher food. As driving is prohibited on the Sabbath, these institutions must be within walking distance of community residents.

Rabbinic Authority in Decision Making, and Its Implications for Clinicians

Unlike the secular ethic of valuing individual autonomy, living according to Torah law is considered a noble act rather than a sign of weakness or blind obedience (Shuper, Zeharia, Balter-Seri, Steier, & Minumoi, 2000). The greater the level of adherence, the stronger the significance of rabbinic decisions is over personal autonomy and desire. Clarifying the points of *halacha* by asking *shailahs* is a central feature of both the *Chassidic* and *Yeshivish* communities, particularly among those individuals most committed to acting in accordance with group norms. The practice of asking *shailahs* is less common among the Modern Orthodox Jews as this group tends to grant less power to a centralized rabbinic authority. Research findings have documented a psychological benefit in the *shailah* process: a large segment of the *Chareidi* population reported feeling calmer after receiving a decision or advice from their rabbi (Schechter et al., 2015). Thus, given the reverence for the rabbinic figure and the psychological importance projected upon him, *shailahs* can be appreciated as externalized decision makers and powerful shapers of individual and family experience. Significant tensions may emerge, however, when rabbinic guidance conflicts with clinical recommendations and strong individual desires, or when a couple cannot agree on whom to consult.

Given the great emphasis on detailed religious observance prevalent within the Orthodox Jewish community, concerns exist as to when the model of *shailahs* and *halacha* observance are no longer appropriate manifestations of religious commitment but suggest pathological variants, such as scrupulosity and obsessive compulsive disorder (OCD). In instances of pathology, religious practices, thoughts, and repeated rabbinic *shailahs* may be cultural manifestations of obsessions and compulsions given their significance, social import, and means of achieving resolution (Greenberg & Sheffler, 2008; Huppert et al., 2007). Nonetheless, Orthodox Jews do not have a higher rate of OCD as compared to the general population (Greenberg & Sheffler, 2008), nor does increased religiousness relate to greater obsessive or compulsive thinking (Feiner, Sanderson, & Schechter, 2010).

When determining whether behavior is normative or pathological, it is crucial that clinicians use careful diagnostic and evidence-based treatment, together with cultural sensitivity integrating cultural awareness and clinical judgment (Huppert et al., 2007). In addition, consultation with the patient's rabbi may be indicated before clinicians establish religiously manifest OCD in an Orthodox patient (Greenberg & Sheffler, 2008).

Assuming client consent, there is often great value to bidirectional consultation between the rabbi and the therapist when treating Orthodox clients. Recognition of rabbis' crucial roles in clients' lives and mutual respect between clinicians and clergy are at the heart of effective work with this population. Rabbis may serve as valuable therapeutic adjuncts, building patient trust and providing a culturally congruous voice to the therapeutic process or recommendation. Not only would such collaboration be beneficial to the client, but therapist and rabbi can gain as well. The therapist derives a better understanding of the client's strong and often overriding religious values and contexts (Greenberg & Witzum, 2001; Hoffman, 2014); while the rabbi becomes more familiar with the client's circumstances and/or psychological dynamics, and thus may be able to offer more appropriate and helpful *halachic* guidance. It may also be indicated, on occasion, for the therapist to conduct a joint session with a rabbi or other religious mentor.

Clinicians should be aware that culture and religious practice are not uniform across all Orthodox Jews. Variations in terms of expressed and latent beliefs and practices, as well as the level of observance, are to be expected among individuals, families, and subgroups. Lack of cultural understanding and nuance can create obstacles in treatment, research, or policy (Pirutinsky & Kor, 2013; Schnall, Pelcovitz, & Fox, 2013). Using a point of reference or assumption about Jews in matters of observance, attitudes, or values can be alienating to the Orthodox patient. It is particularly alienating when the therapist—non-Jewish, or Jewish but non-Orthodox—imposes his or her own perspective about issues, such as the strictness of observance or gender roles. Countertransferential reactions are often at play when this occurs (Heilman & Witzum, 1997; Schnall, 2006; Sublette & Trappler, 2000).

Case Vignette

A 35-year-old *Yeshivish* male with six children sought individual therapy for his ongoing conflict with his wife, but ended treatment after two sessions. When asked by his subsequent therapist why he terminated so abruptly, the client reported that he "felt judged," and that he was being given "advice about contraception, without speaking to my rabbi," and "got a sense he was responding to me based on my group—not as me."

In order to address the concerns about making assumptions about clients arising out of their group identity, a multidimensional measure that acknowledges individual diversity within each group was developed (Schechter, 2006). This measure identifies socioreligious affiliation

(Modern Orthodox, *Yeshivish, Chassidic*) and provides a five-point scale to assess client adherence to group cultural norms and ideals (Schechter, 2006, 2013; Schechter et al., 2015). Such particularized assessments help to facilitate clinical and research findings that are meaningful and generalizable.

Couple Relationships and *Halacha*

In general, when both partners in marriage are religious, there is a decreased risk of divorce, improved marital functioning, and better child adjustment (Mahoney, Pargament, Swank, & Tarakeshwar, 2001). Research studies conducted of Orthodox Jewish couples (Kor, Mikulincer, & Pirutinsky, 2012) found that when a married couple experienced conflicts arising out of religion, lower functioning, higher parenting stress, and lower community integration were more likely to result. Preliminary data from a comprehensive divorce survey (Schechter, 2015a) indicated that nearly half of the divorcees reported *halacha* as a divisive factor in their relationship. Interestingly, in this study, significantly higher percentages of *Chassidic* and Modern Orthodox couples reported tension around *halacha* than *Yeshivish* couples.

When tensions in couples arise from issues of *halacha* adherence, the therapist may be able to help the couple improve communication, empathy, and reactivity. In order to resolve the underlying issue, however, the therapist might encourage the couple to consult with an understanding rabbi with whom they feel comfortable. Tensions around *halachic* observance need to be attended to on their manifest level and, when indicated, as a possible cultural expression of underlying pathology or couple/personality dynamic.

Pressure to Conform to Community Norms

Over time, specific customs have taken on the status of *minhag*, which are important traditions particular to a subgroup that are not *halacha* but are observed with reverence. Observance of *minhag* demonstrates allegiance to the community; abandonment of *minhag* may be seen as a rejection of the community. As *minhagim* often are comprised of actions and behaviors visible to the entire community, such as manner of dress, the level of social and internalized psychological pressure to adhere to *minhagim* may be as significant as compliance with religious laws, if not more so.

The stricter streams of Orthodox Judaism value *minhag* as a means of maintaining collective and communal identity (Zalcberg, 2013). To this end, men in the community wear distinctive clothing that sets them apart from prevailing society, that is, long black coats and *shtreimels* (fur hats) worn by *Chassidic* men or black fedoras worn by *Yeshivish* men. Another illustration of *minhag* can be found in rituals surrounding food, such as those prepared for Sabbath dinner. Serving vegetable soup instead of the traditional chicken soup or sushi instead of gefilte fish may appear inconsequential to an outsider but, from an inside perspective, non-adherence carries meaning (Benor, 2012). Deviation from communal norms is strongly frowned upon and risks unofficial condemnation or social consternation, expressed in subtle but powerful social hierarchies. In this way, insular communities maintain their homeostasis and traditional practices in the face of rapidly changing times, as can be illustrated in the following case vignette.

Case Vignette

A *Chassidic* married couple with three children, both 28 years old, entered marital therapy for ongoing conflicts concerning differing degrees of religious adherence, increasing emotional distance, and opposing positions on the exposure of their children to the general culture. After an intervention to enhance the capacity for each to give and receive positive affection and validate perspectives, the couple reported successfully bonding and feeling increasingly positive. Shortly thereafter, the community sent a disapproving letter regarding their children's knowledge of foreign culture, which, together with parental pressure, forced the couple to confront their religious differences. Although enhanced effective communication and mutual respect had allowed the couple to better manage some of their preexisting issues, they remained at an impasse on their next step. The couple contacted a rabbi whom they both respected to ask a *shailah*. At first, the rabbi refused to answer due to his skepticism regarding the couple's deviations from community religious norms. After the psychologist and rabbi conferred, the rabbi better understood the couple's dilemma and was amenable to helping to resolve the situation. He recommended that they move to a neighboring community, with slightly less restrictive standards, that would provide a better fit for them. The couple followed the rabbi's advice, continued working with the psychologist to adjust to their new environment, and made efforts to create a cohesive unit in the face of both of their parents' objections. Through work with the therapist and ongoing consultation with the rabbi, the couple's functioning, marital satisfaction, and even religious identity were increased, as they were able to meet the sociocultural challenges confronted in an insular community.

COUPLEHOOD: FROM COURTSHIP TO MARRIAGE

Understanding couplehood and family in the Orthodox community requires an understanding of its unique gender socialization, courtship, and marriage processes. Although differences in detail exist among the major streams, commonalities prevail.

Gender Socialization

Tznius (modesty), one of the hallmarks of gender separation, is highly valued among *Chareidis* (Ribner, 2003a; Shalev, Baum, & Itzhaki, 2013). *Tznius* has important implications in the treatment process, particularly when female therapists treat *Chareidi* males. Such clients may not be comfortable shaking hands or even fully closing the door in the session, and some *Chassidic* men may not look a female therapist in the eyes. In addition, male clients may be reluctant or unable to freely discuss sexual or other intimate details of marriage.

The *Chassidic* community has the most restrictive customs, with gender separation embedded in the fabric of communal life. *Chassidic* boys and girls are separated when toddlers and educated in separate institutions. In the *Yeshivish* world, children are also separated by gender as early as age 6, and educated in different institutions. Outside of small family events, genders are socialized separately. The Modern Orthodox Jews are closer to prevailing culture, with both gender-separated and coeducational schools (Shalev et al., 2013).

Other than close relatives and family friends, knowledge about and interactions with the opposite gender are minimal in the *Chassidic* and *Yeshivish* communities (Ribner, 2003a; Rockman, 1994; Shalev et al., 2013). Access to the larger culture and media is prohibited and even community media has increasingly limited the availability of images of females. This lack of exposure may increase the discomfort and awkwardness of meeting intended partners when males are given their first opportunity at cross-gender interaction during the dating process (Greenberg, Stravynski, & Bilu, 2004; Milevsky, Niman, Raab, & Gross, 2010); however, such levels of discomfort are mitigated by self-confidence, social skills, and exposure (Milevsky et al., 2010).

Courtship and Marital Decision Making

The typical Western dating experience is usually lengthy and includes physical and sexual contact, if not cohabitation, as an important component of the relationship (Rockman, 1994); however, among the Orthodox population, dating is seen as an activity exclusively for the purpose of marriage (Milevsky et al., 1994; Zalcberg, 2013). This is particularly true for the stricter streams wherein gender mixing is virtually prohibited. Given this vacuum, and the unparalleled value the Orthodox ascribe to marriage, the community employs a matchmaking system called ***shidduchim*** (*shidduch*, singular). Matchmakers may introduce potential marriage partners as a kindness, as a service to the community, or for a fee (Rockman, 1994). While not a matter of *halacha*, most Orthodox Jews utilize some form of *shidduchim* (Schechter, 2015b), which can range from the most traditional and personalized to high-tech, depending on the community (Penkower, 2010).

Sociologically, *shidduchim* serve as a central organizing principle in the Orthodox Jewish community. Getting the best possible match is critically important for the individual, family, and community. In this way, romance is replaced by research into the "fit," focusing on values and interests, between the families and individuals (Ribner, 2003a; Rockman, 1994; Zalcberg, 2013). Although the ideal standard may revolve around the positive trait of character, other qualities often enter the picture, such as height, weight, attractiveness, health, psychological well-being, and familial mental illness, among others, and influence the selection process. For some, scrutiny can be so exacting as to extend to how dishes are stacked on the Sabbath table as an indicator of formality and class.

Therefore, indicators of marriage suitability are not limited to the couple, as is usually the case in the general culture (Birger, 2015; Rosen, Greenberg, Schmeidler, & Sheffler, 2007). In the *Chareidi* communities, consideration extends to the parents and other family members and their place in the community as well. Positive or negative indicators within the family may be attributed to the individual, either conveying a "halo" effect, or prompting his or her elimination as a potential match. Examples of negative indicators are the divorce of parents, mental illness in relatives, and siblings who have lowered standards in religious practice or have left the community altogether.

Such "guilt by association" severely impacts decision making by family members. Choices of schools, camps, vacations, and dress are weighed in terms of their perceived effect on a potential future *shidduch* (Rosen et al., 2007). Parents in nonfunctioning marriages may postpone divorce until all their children are married, lest it ruin a child's chances for a successful *shidduch*; they are fearful of seeking psychotherapy or taking psychotropic medication because of the potential stigma affecting their children's *shidduchim*, though this is less common currently, given the increased acceptability of treatment (Pirutinsky, Rosen, Shapiro, Safran, & Rosmarin, 2010). Also, a recent study indicated that fear of stigma and its effect on *shidduchim* may inhibit women from seeking screening for the BRCA genetic mutation, despite a ten-fold increased risk of Jews carrying those genes as compared with the general population (Schechter, 2015b).

In this way *shidduchim* exert a powerful, ubiquitous, and subtle social force that compels actions and behavior on the part of individuals and shapes the evolving nature of the community, irrespective of marriage possibilities in the foreseeable future. Once a match has been accomplished, however, stress in individuals and friction in marriages may arise when partners and families reveal identities and desires that had been suppressed pre-*shidduch*.

In a recent survey of 539 Orthodox Jewish women regarding the socioreligious determinants of medical decision making (Schechter et al., 2015b), respondents were asked about the use of *shidduchim*. Married women were asked whether they had met their husbands through this service and single women were asked whether they intended to use a matchmaker in the future. In addition, all were asked whether they expected their children to choose this option. The result was noteworthy in that not only the use was prominent across all streams but also the trend was increasing. Not surprisingly, rates were highest in communities with the least gender mixing: For *Chassidim*, virtually 100 percent used *shadduchim* for themselves and intended to or had used this method for their children; *Yeshivish*, 92 percent for themselves, and 96 percent for their children; and Modern Orthodox, 63 percent for themselves, and 83 percent for their children.

There are three primary elements of the *shidduch* process, common to all streams of Orthodox Judaism: (a) the introduction of the potential couple, (b) the couple dating, and (c) the couple making a decision about whether to marry. Prior to making the introduction, the facilitator/matchmaker or *shadchan* (*shadchanim*, plural) sets out to learn about the individuals seeking marital partners, if they are not already known, by reviewing a package of particulars, similar to a résumé, submitted by each party. Photographs may also be included. If the *shadchan* believes the couple to be compatible, permission is sought from both parties before the introduction is arranged. Online *shidduchim* sites, moderated by a group of *shadchanim*, are available for the Modern Orthodox and moderate *Yeshivish* communities (Penkower, 2010). Matchmaking introductions are also often made by friends and/or relatives.

The nature of courtship differs between groups. *Chassidic* and *Yeshivish* communities view dating as a means of assessing compatibility rather than seeking romance (Rockman, 1994; Schnall et al., 2013). These communities perceive the marital relationship as the venue that provides commitment, joint life experiences, mutual support, and vulnerability wherein interest and connection build (Milevsky et al., 2010; Ribner, 2003a). In contrast, among the Modern Orthodox, as with the general culture, the love relationship is expected to be largely formed before marriage. The Modern Orthodox Jews differ from the general culture in that they, like their other Orthodox counterparts, reject physical contact during the dating process, as well as cohabitation, and accord consideration to values and religious directions in decision making (Guterman, 2008; Milevsky et al., 2010; Ribner, 2003a; Shalev et al., 2013). This is consistent with long-standing research findings that religiosity is associated with decreased premarital sexual activity (Guterman, 2008; Hartman & Marmon, 2004).

The prevalence of arranged marriages within the Orthodox Jewish population has important implications for clinicians. Marital therapists will often ask about what drew couples together, and how that initial passion and connection was formed, in order to inspire a couple to return to the positive and ideal state from which the marriage emerged, or use their past connections as a catalyst of change. Since the *shidduch*-based initiation of the dating process was externally driven, that is, recommended by others and not based on attraction, it was transformed from a romantic transaction to a commodities or economic heuristic (Ahuvia & Adelman, 1992; Birger, 2015; Zalcberg, 2013). Thus, a clinical approach that sought to capitalize on a couple's memories of premarital affection, let alone idealized love, would not succeed with a couple whose union relied on the credit of future commitment.

Treatment for couples with the *shidduchim* experience must be more present oriented and skills focused, concentrating on the shared values, expressed connections, and parental support that brought them together. Building communication skills, basic emotional responsiveness, and developing gratitude may be especially important when exposure to the opposite gender and relationships has been limited. In addition, many young couples are developing as emerging adults at the same time as they form their marital relationship. Thus, exploring the basic dynamics of marriage, such as individuality versus couplehood, expectations of self, and expectations of marriage as well as overall values clarification, may be necessary.

Values clarification is a key component of Orthodox Jewish decisions about spousal selection. *Shidduchim*-originated marriage decisions are based on more rational and less emotional factors (Milevsky et al., 2010; Rockman, 1994; Zalcberg, 2013). The single-minded focus of *shidduchim* has been reported as helpful in the dating process (Milevsky et al., 2010; Rockman, 1994), but is also a stressor for both males and females (Ehrenpreis, Perlstein, & Schechter, 2013). Therapists may assist those having difficulty making this decision by asking them to articulate primary values and evaluate whether those factors are present in their prospective match.

Case Vignette

A *Chassidic* couple who had been married for three years was referred by the wife's parents to a local outpatient behavioral clinic. The presenting issue was "We just don't get along." The husband reported lack of interest in, as well as discomfort with, sexual interaction. The wife, who was more exposed to the general culture than her husband, reported similarly, and asked if he had some "anxiety nerves." After clinical assessment, no anxiety disorder was diagnosable, but a clear lack of bonding as a couple was evident. The husband reported not understanding his wife and her interests, and having little patience for her telling him about the local goings on. She thought that sharing everything in her day would automatically lead to a bond. Furthermore, they ate most of their meals together at their respective parents' homes and had shared only five meals alone with each other during their marriage. After facilitating conversations in the session about interests and experiences, the couple increased their conversations at home and began playing board games together. They also created less permeable boundaries with their parents by having supper alone together at their home at least three times a week. Following this, the couple reported doing well and "becoming good friends." At the same time, sexual interest increased and reached normal levels as they reported being more comfortable with each other and better able to talk about sensitive topics.

Marriage and Ritual Purity

As *halacha* dictates even the most intimate details of married life, religious observance has a strong influence on the nature and quality of couplehood. A profound example of this can be found in *taharas hamishpacha* (laws of family purity). According to Torah law, husband and wife are prohibited from having any sexual contact when the wife is a *niddah* (menstruating). The prohibition extends from the first sign of menses until the completion of her bleeding and an additional seven days thereafter, during which no physical contact between husband and wife is permitted, unless it is out of medical or other significant necessity. Several additional measures are taken to facilitate compliance, such sleeping in separate beds, not passing objects from hand to hand when possible, and abstaining from demonstrations of affection. When *niddah* is over, the wife immerses in the *mikveh*, a ritual bath, after which she is deemed ready to resume sexual and intimate contact with her spouse—an act deemed a *mitzvah* (a religious commandment).

Brides and grooms are taught these laws by teachers of the same gender, who are also responsible for instructing the couple on sexuality and intimacy. These teachers serve as important psychological influencers, and couples often maintain a continuing relationship with them to discuss issues related to married life. Research has found that premarriage consultation with these mentors improved the relationship and the quality of the sexual experience between the couple (Pirutinsky, Maybruch, & Pelcovitz, 2014).

Observance of marital purity laws is highly significant for Orthodox couples. It is primarily a symbolic values statement that God takes precedence over sexual and personal desires even in the privacy of the bedroom. This practice, however, may also raise complex emotions for the couple, and for the wife, in particular (Chaya, 2012; Hartman & Marmon, 2004; Ribner, 2003a). In addition, the inability to engage in physical displays of affection for two weeks out of every month results in the need to find alternate ways to maintain closeness and repair relationship ruptures that inevitably occur in marriage.

Women have varied reactions to the experience, from feeling oppressed to empowered (Chaya, 2012; Hartman & Marmon, 2004; Ribner, 2003a). Some women report that this respite allows them independent space without any sexual responsibility toward their husband. This is especially noticeable in couples where the husband requires physical contact to feel a sense of connection. Alternatively, some feel the loss during that time of the human touch their husband provides, unrelated to sexual activity. Similarly, the reactions of many couples vary, with some reporting the separation time as a stressor and others reporting it as more relaxing. The distance and closeness of the couple during this time can be a litmus test of the robustness of the range of the couple's coping, emotional reserves, and bonding.

An interesting finding reported by therapists is that the frequency and enjoyment of sexual engagement between *mikveh*-observant couples is increased, as the periods of separation prevent the possibility of boredom arising out of unfettered sexual access and allow for renewed pleasure in one's partner (Chaya, 2012; Hartman & Marmon, 2004; Ribner, 2003a). This is reflected in an oft-quoted rabbinic teaching: "A woman when she returns in her purity is like a bride on the day of her wedding."

The dynamics of the *niddah* cycle also have important implications for couple therapy, as associating the timing of marital arguments to the cycle can reveal the roles that sexual connection, emotional connection, and physical affection play in the spouses' relationship. Additionally, this cycle may expose a variety of other issues between couples. A salient example often reported by therapists is that a woman's hesitance in going to the *mikveh* may serve as an indicator of her reluctance to resume sexual activity with her husband. This may be attributable to a variety of reasons, among them, sexual discomfort, dysfunction, or aversion; spousal abuse; a history of sexual abuse; trauma; anxiety; or a poor marital relationship.

The *mikveh* also offers a benefit as an environment where mental health and other resources can be made available to women in a safe, comfortable, nonthreatening manner. For example, the international Orthodox Jewish domestic abuse organization, Shalom Task Force, distributes its literature in many *mikvehs*, providing women with information and anonymous hotline numbers. Utilizing this women-only setting for such purpose also highlights the importance of culturally tailored intervention programming.

In one of the only large-scale Orthodox Jewish community studies of marital satisfaction with more than 3,000 respondents, 74 percent of men and women reported that they were mostly or extremely satisfied with their marriage, a figure higher than for the general population sample (Schnall et al., 2013). No assessment of *tahras hamishpacha* (family purity) and satisfaction was performed, although sexual intimacy was reported as a source of conflict. In the large divorce report by this author, sexual difficulty was relatively low on the list of factors cited in divorce (Schechter, 2015a).

Sexuality in Jewish Law and Values

Among Orthodox Jews, sexuality is seen as a private, intimate, and loving encounter between husband and wife. This is supported by several

Talmudic dictates describing it as a sensual and necessarily consensual experience with an intense and loving focus between two committed people. Any form of consensual sexual contact between husband and wife is permitted, although *halacha* generally guides couples to avoid ejaculation outside the vagina. There are some who become so concerned about "spilling seed" that they have difficulty in performing sexually (Ribner, 2003b). This also presents an issue for couples who exhibit sexual dysfunction and require sensate focus and related treatment modalities, where ejaculation outside of the vagina may be likely to occur. Protocols (Ribner, 2003b) have been developed especially for this population, with rabbis often permitting such treatment as resulting in improved relations between the couple and an ability to fulfill their love for each other.

When working with sensitive issues of *halacha* such as these, it is worthwhile for the couple or patient to consult their rabbi and, where appropriate, for the clinician to speak with the rabbi to facilitate the process. Consultation with the rabbi and a conscious nonjudgmental stance by both the rabbi and the therapist are critical when treating very adherent couples, as they are seeking help for a religiously charged, highly intimate topic, which they would generally not speak about, especially with outsiders.

In a small number of adherents, the sex-positive message of sexual intimacy within marriage can be confusing, and potentially conflated with the communal focus on *tznius* (modesty). Allowing oneself pleasure and disinhibition may often be counterintuitive to the prior training of many emerging adults that informs their thinking about sexual experience (Greenberg et al., 2004). Having learned that modesty is greatly valued, those with a propensity toward inhibition, anxiety, and psychological constriction may internalize this as a general discomfort with physical and sensual pleasure.

It is common for many people to present with problems of intimate relationships (sexual or interpersonal) that manifest in increased inhibition and a disconnect from personal experience. The ability to experience natural arousal, even *halachically* sanctioned, may create tension as intimacy and sexuality by definition require psychological and physiological disinhibition and relaxation. Thus, if one is uncomfortable with letting go in mind and body, the capacity for emotional and physical intimacy is significantly diminished. In the extreme, research findings have documented that it is not uncommon for Orthodox couples to report unconsummated marriages despite multiple attempts at sexual intercourse (Ribner & Rosenbaum, 2004).

Indeed, for many, the transition from "stop" (no physical or sexual contact) to "go" (physical and sexual self is good) is significant and requires some adjustment (Ribner & Rosenbaum, 2004; Shalev et al., 2013). As one woman described it: "My whole life boys were off limits, now I am totally intimate with one." Premarital guidance helps to ease that transition and most couples adapt well to the new reality. For those who confront continued challenges in being comfortable with intimacy, the bride and groom mentors, as discussed before, are an excellent resource to frame sexuality in a positive light (Pirutinsky et al., 2014), in addition to seeking guidance from rabbinic or other spiritual mentors.

SOCIOCULTURAL CHARACTERISTICS

Family Structures and Community

In Judaism, the essential link between the parent and the child is the basis of the religious tradition and cherished as a core value. Most of Jewish life revolves around living and teaching the Torah to children, with the family as the central unit entrusted to transmit Torah and *halacha* across generations. Many traditions in Orthodox Judaism illustrate this important value. For example, the focus of the Passover Seder involves parents telling children about the Jewish people's exodus from Egypt (Maimonides, 1998).

Families are generally tightly knit, with the Sabbath and holidays providing opportunities for nuclear and extended families to celebrate together. The amount of preparation required to serve the equivalent of about 150 Thanksgiving dinners annually (two large meals for each Sabbath and holiday) is amplified by the fact that cooking isn't permissible on the Sabbath and similar restrictions exist on holidays.

Jewish holidays engender stress as well as excitement. Elaborate festivities can strain family budgets, tensions may arise when extended family gather together in close quarters, and those without family members with whom they can celebrate may experience great loneliness. It is noteworthy that behavioral health clinics serving the Orthodox Jewish population experience a marked decrease of calls and visits the two weeks preceding major Jewish holidays and increases immediately after Jewish holidays (Schechter, 2013).

Types of Orthodox Jews

Chassidim

Chassidim are the strictest of the three major streams of Orthodox Judaism. Their communities can be characterized by a tight and centrally organized structure with an accompanying collective orientation generally focused on a Grand Rabbi (Rebbe), a strong emphasis on religious authority, and strict observance of Jewish law. Individuals are expected to subordinate themselves to the community, and explicit and implicit pressure is exerted to produce social cohesion. Total gender separation among unmarried individuals is the norm. *Chassidim* generally speak Yiddish, the language of Jews whose origins were in Central and Eastern Europe, both at home and in the community. Secular education is largely absent, other than that which is mandated by law. The gender distinction with regard to knowledge and use of English is noteworthy. Among the *Chasidim*, it is common for women to be fluent and literate in English, while most men speak limited English and have a minimal ability to read the language.

Chassidim have specific practices concerning marital decisions that are stricter than those for the other groups and involve a greater role for the parents. Prior to the introduction, considerable preparation is performed by parents of both sides. Once the parents have decided that a young man and woman are compatible in personality, interests, and general direction in life, and they have negotiated the financial contributions of both sides (Zalcberg, 2013), a meeting, known as the *beshow* (an extremely brief form of courtship), is arranged in one of the parents' homes. The couple is introduced and given privacy to talk to each other for about an hour or so while the parents wait in another room. The couple has the absolute right to refuse the *shidduch*; however, typically the couple agrees, as they have confidence and respect in their parents' choice as well as the Rebbe's guidance. Once such agreement is reached, everyone wishes them a *mazel tov* (congratulations). Marriage is usually within a year of their meeting, prior to which they have limited contact with one another. The *Chassidic* community tends to exemplify traditional gender roles—the overwhelming majority of men work and women largely stay at home to tend to the children and manage the home.

Yeshivish

While more open to the larger culture than the *Chassidic* community, the *Yeshivish* still impose significant restrictions on these influences. Although attendance at movies and listening to popular music are forbidden, filtered internet usage is allowed, the mode of dress is more contemporary within the limits of modesty, and there is slightly less gender separation. Many men prepare for a practical occupational choice, whether through attending some form of college or a vocational training program, usually provided through the *yeshiva* or an affiliated community organization. A significant number of men, however, do not work, and remain in *yeshiva* studying Talmud even after marriage (Berman, 2000; Gonen, 2001).

In the *Yeshivish* community, once the *shidduch* is arranged and the couple meet for an introduction, they dress in their best attire (suit and hat for men and a dressy outfit for women) and typically talk in a public place, such as a park, often having brought with them a quasi-standardized checklist. Formality tends to lessen as dating progresses and the couple is closer to engagement; however, restrictions on expressions of affection remain in place. More open segments of the community encourage couples to have fun and positive experiences (Rockman, 1994).

The *Yeshivish* community offers a contrasting template to the *Chassidic* community in terms of gender roles. Wives, and sometimes the parents of the married couple, are often responsible for the family's financial support (Gonen, 2001; Berman, 2000), while many men continue to study the Torah at *yeshivas* dedicated to married men, known as **kollels.** Despite the increased responsibilities inherent in being the family breadwinner, raising the children, and maintaining the home, "kollel wives" value and support their husband's Torah study. Husbands have become more willing to accept responsibility for the less traditional aspects of home life, most notably grocery shopping, although traditional activities, such as the preparation of Sabbath and holiday meals, remain within the wives' purview.

The distribution of home responsibilities and child care in *kollel* families may cause tension, and this issue is frequently brought up in couples counseling (Shai, 2002). Common themes include the wife feeling underappreciated when her willingness to sacrifice for the value of learning Torah is unacknowledged (Berman, 2000; Gonen, 2001), and the stresses arising out of balancing both traditional and nontraditional roles (Shai, 2002).

A common phenomenon in *Yeshivish* circles is a male remaining in *yeshiva* despite a desire to leave and pursue other interests. Whether to leave *kollel* is often a motivation for *Yeshivish* couples to seek counseling. This event is a major crossroads for a *kollel* couple and usually involves considerable doubts and feelings of failure, inferiority, and fear of the unknown on the part of both partners, as well as relief (Bane, 2015; Berman, 2000; Gonen, 2001; Shai, 2002). In order to facilitate this major lifestyle change and aid in the attendant shifts in identity, lifestyle, couples dynamics, and life demands, a trusted rabbi, mentor, and/or therapist is often consulted. The following case vignette illustrates the tension surrounding this decision.

Case Vignette

A *Yeshivish* couple, who had been married for nearly two years following three months of dating and a three-month engagement, consulted a couples therapist on the recommendation of the husband's rabbi, reporting increased fighting. The wife complained that her husband was invalidating, and that she carried many of responsibilities for the home and their 6-month-old baby. The husband complained that she was overbearing and controlling. After ruling out pathology, it became clear that the conflict was fueled by the husband's unhappiness attending *yeshiva* and his desire to go to college instead. This was very painful to the wife as she felt he misrepresented himself while dating, leaving her feeling "duped." When this issue was explored, the couple was able to discuss their primary concerns arising out of religious commitment and identity, and the emotional implications of an identity shift for each of them. After some open conversation, the couple was able to accept that the husband could leave the *yeshiva* to attend college provided that mutually acceptable religious values were maintained in their home. In a three-month follow-up, the couple reported minimal residual negative interactions, more positive affect and respect between the couple, and increased positive identification with their new identities and roles.

Modern Orthodox

This group is the most acculturated one, with an open orientation toward cultural exposure to the mainstream, such as movie attendance and internet usage. Their manner of dress is modest but, given that, not otherwise identifiable or distinctive. There are less restrictions on extra-communal contact, so that Modern Orthodox often mix freely with those who are not Orthodox Jews and members of other faiths. Although the communal and authority structure exists within this group, it is less significant than with the stricter Orthodox streams. The majority of Modern Orthodox Jews are college-educated, as are their rabbinic and lay leadership (Cohen et al., 2012; Schechter, 2011).

Modern Orthodox *shidduchim* follow less-defined rules, but are governed by a factor that is of most concern to this population, that is, academic or professional achievement, as well as those factors involved in marital decision making for other Orthodox groups, such as internal community status and communal expectation. This is the group most likely to use the online *shidduchim*, and prospective spouses may date for a longer and less-structured period, with the couple dressed in more casual attire and focused on building their relationship.

Orthodox Birth Rate

A striking feature of Orthodox Jewish communities is the large number of children (Cohen et al., 2012). Having and raising children is seen as a primary vehicle of fulfilling God's will by perpetuating Jewish life and teaching. Most couples have children shortly after marriage and have considerably larger families than the general population. Current birth rate estimates range from 3.8 among Modern Orthodox Jews to 7.1 for the *Chareidi* (Freidman, 2014). In the greater New York City area, a recent large-scale survey found that 61 percent of all Jewish children were born to Orthodox Jewish parents (Cohen et al., 2012). For example, the *Chassidic* village of Kiryas Joel, 50 miles northwest of New York City, has the lowest median age (under 12) and the highest household size (almost six) in the nation (Roberts, 2011). Although Talmudic law permits contraceptive use under a variety of circumstances, procreation is strongly encouraged, especially in view of the Holocaust when six million Jews were exterminated. Replacing those lost is a strong communal imperative (Loewenthal & Goldblatt, 1993).

Large family size might suggest an increased burden or stressor on the psychological functioning of parents; however, research conducted with an Orthodox Jewish sample (Pirutinsky, Schechter, Kor, & Rosmarin, 2015) found that the number of children was not associated with psychological stress, pathology, or impaired psychological functioning (Loewenthal & Goldblatt, 1993; Pirutinsky et al., 2015). This finding was replicated in Canada and Israel as well as the United States, which drew Orthodox Jewish subjects from both community and clinical sources. Furthermore, meta-analysis demonstrated no relationship between the number of children and psychological functioning including depression, anxiety, stress, or maladaptive functioning (Pirutinsky et al., 2015).

The lack of association between the number of children and stress can be analyzed in multiple ways, including from an acceptance and commitment therapy (ACT) or values framework (Wilson & Murrell, 2004), in which the profound religious value and sense of mission inherent in having children may minimize or buffer the demands arising from such large families. Similarly, social norms may reinforce the benefits of child-rearing and offer support in times of short-term stress. This has been supported by many studies showing religious coping as a helpful and significant buffer, especially when this is consistent with the shared communal experience (Smith, McCullough, & Poll, 2003).

In addition, ecological adaptations, in the form of older siblings (most typically daughters) serving as "secondary mothers" to the younger children, support the family structure and reduce the burden on parents. This division of labor, buttressed by religious and educational institutions, is consistent with the culture's collective orientation, duty to family, and role definitions (Pirutinsky et al., 2015).

Such findings do not indicate an absence of stress caused by feeling overwhelmed by the demands of family in individual clinical presentations. In fact, this is a common motif, but rather than ascribing stress to the presence of a large number of children, other issues, such as those related to one's family-of-origin communal expectations and cultural or gender identity/role definition, are often indicated.

INTERSECTING IDENTITIES: GAY IDENTITY IN THE ORTHODOX JEWISH COMMUNITY

Homosexuality is prohibited in the Bible, and it is explicitly forbidden for men. Given the primacy of *halacha* and the nature of the socioreligious system in this community, neither is homosexuality recognized as an identity nor are same-sex couples accorded status as a recognized union in the Orthodox community (Rappaport, 2004). Families typically have great difficulty when learning of their child identifying as gay. This is not only due to the inevitable tension that arises when an individual does not conform to expected norms, but because this news is seen as precluding a happy future for the child—dashing their great hopes for the child's ability to lead a healthy life with future children and grandchildren (Rappaport, 2004). The challenges are even more severe in the case of individuals in preexisting heterosexual marriages who felt compelled to comply with community norms, marry, and have children. A later recognition of a gay identity will likely have a divisive, if not rupturing, impact on the lives of many—spouse, children, parents, and extended family—as well as the community.

For gay Orthodox individuals, it is exceedingly difficult to maintain two conflicting identities. The fact that one identity needs to be suppressed out of fear or the actuality concern of a negative communal reaction is taxing and invalidating (Buchanan, Dzelme, Harris, & Hecker, 2001). Often a gay individual distances from the communal identity due to the conflict of values. He or she may move to a very modern and open Orthodox community or a singles community, given that remaining single is more culturally accepted than being gay, or leave observance altogether. Still, observance issues are not often as decisive an issue for emerging adults identifying as gay as sociocultural factors (Rappaport, 2004).

As gay rights and marriage equality become codified into American law and gay identity becomes more open, however, there has been increased discussion, primarily limited to the Modern Orthodox community, about responding in a more supportive manner to individuals who are both Orthodox and gay. Several organizations, focused on addressing the difficulty and developmental pain for someone identifying as gay as well as the alienation and inner turmoil of identity conflict in the gay emerging adult, offer support for Orthodox adherents struggling with or having accepted gay identities. Such organizations have met with varying degrees of communal and rabbinic support, and the tension between support of the individual and support of the gay identity is acute for many Orthodox Jewish mental health practitioners, clergy, and the community (Rappaport, 2004).

Therapists of the community are advised to operate in a supportive fashion, appreciating the difficulty of conflicting identities and aspirations and trying to facilitate familial communication and support. In addition to support, values clarification and realistic decision making in the face of difficult choices are key. Earlier, "reparative" therapies were offered by some therapists; however, this model has been deemed harmful to clients, proved of limited efficacy, and are no longer considered acceptable practice by any professional psychological organization (American Psychological Association, 2015).

CONCLUSIONS

Orthodox Jewish couplehood and family life are greatly impacted by an omnipresent sociocultural milieu, virtually unique among other racial, religious, and ethnic groups in the United States. Successful clinical interventions with this population are possible only when the clinician or researcher understands the cultural and ecological contexts of this community. With sensitivity and an appreciation of cultural nuances, the historically overlooked and insular Orthodox Jewish community can be treated successfully with all effective modern techniques.

CHAPTER REVIEW

Key Points

1. *Halacha* and *minhag* frame Orthodox religious life. Understanding of their distinct contexts and cultural norms is critical to successful treatment of individuals, couples, and families, as well as to research and policy.
2. The Orthodox community has unique gender socialization, courtship, and marriage processes. The system of matchmaking and dating called *shidduchim* is primarily oriented toward creating a good fit between the new couple with limited dating, socialization, and romance.
3. The *shidduchim* model has major consequences for the couple and family life. Early in its development, the couple must learn to transform from relative strangers to a cohesive unit. Later family decisions may be impacted by the fear of stigma adversely impacting children's marriage prospects.
4. Sexuality in marriage, a loving and private intimate encounter, is bound by strict *halachas* dealing with *tznius* (modesty) and *taharas hamishpacha* (laws of family purity; the separation of husband and wife according to her menstrual cycle and culminating in immersion in a *mikveh,* or Jewish ritual bath). Understanding this is necessary to marital or sex therapy with an adherent.
5. There is great value to bidirectional consultation between the rabbi and the therapist. Rabbis can serve as important informants to clarify cultural norms and values, as well as cultural allyies in building trust in the therapeutic process. Therapists can help the rabbi better understand the psychological dynamics of a family so as to enable more accurate, attuned religious guidance and expand therapeutic gains.

Key Terms

halacha (Jewish law), *kollel academy of Torah study for men, mikveh ritual bath, minhag important traditions observed with reverence, shadchan facilitator/ matchmaker, shailah question asked to seek a rabbinic ruling, shidduch (shidduchim* pl.; matchmaking), *taharas hamishpacha* (laws of family purity), *tznius* (modesty)

Myths and Realities

- It is a myth that sex is unholy and only for procreation in traditional Jewish life. In reality, sex in Judaism is seen as enabling bonding, and a positive, important feature of marriage in addition to procreation. Sex, upon the completion of the *niddah* cycle, is a *mitzvah* (and in fact called "the *mitzvah*" in *Chassidic* circles).

- Sex as the "women's obligation" is a myth. In reality, providing sexual satisfaction is a religious obligation of the husband to his wife.
- It is a myth that insular Orthodox Judaism women stay at home. While feminism in the classic sense runs counter to communal values, several features of this community make for a uniquely empowered female population: in many ardently adherent families, women serve as the primary breadwinners, have high levels of education, and engage in significant extracommunal activity.
- It is a myth that large families decrease parental functioning. The very high birthrate present in the Orthodox community shows no evidence of having an overall negative impact on parent functioning, likely because of the strong support networks for Orthodox parents and children.
- It is a myth that matchmaking leads to more divorce. In fact, divorce is significantly lower in the insular Orthodox Jewish community than in the general population.

Tools and Tips

Knowledge

Burshtein, R. (Director). (2013). *Filling the Void* [Motion Picture]. Israel: Sony Pictures.

Greenberg, D., & Witzum, E. (2001). *Sanity and sanctity: Mental health work among the Ultra-Orthodox of Jerusalem.* New York, NY: Yale University Press.

National Resource Center for Healthy Marriage and Family. (2015, May). Working with couples and families in the Orthodox Jewish Community. Retrieved from https://www.healthymarriageandfamilies.org/fostering-cultural-competency

Rosenfeld, J., & Ribner, D. (2011). *The newlywed guide to physical intimacy.* Jerusalem, Israel: Geffen.

Dynamic Sizing

Knowing when to generalize versus individualize diversity about culture is the key to effective clinical treatment in this community. Maintaining the professionalism of clinical assessment and diagnosis needs to be balanced with the humility of knowing one's outsider perspective. Ask questions about communal norms and individual practice without assumptions. Access, as needed, a cultural translator, such as a rabbi or other important collateral of the clients, to clarify.

Skills

Theory. Ecological and sociocultural frameworks are critical to appreciate cultural meaning, assumptions, and forces influencing couples and families and offer robust methods to study their dysfunction, pathology, and treatment.

Prevention. Utilize existing ecological systems, including rabbis, mentors, and cultural structures (i.e., *mikvehs*), to foster early education regarding healthier marriages and to inoculate against stigma emerging from the matchmaking system.

Service Provision. Providers must be attuned to the cultural structures that shape behavior and family life and work toward adjusting evidence-based practices to the cultural realities of couples and families of this community. Also needed are humility and respect for the existing supports/structures indigenous to their system (rabbis, mentors, *halacha*) to improve outcomes and understanding, as well as increasing cultural understanding of mental health needs (rabbis).

Policy. External governmental policies and initiatives, including those related to access of clinical, educational, or other mandated services (e.g., vocational, academic, health or marital), can create change with power beyond the community. However, greatest effectiveness, impact, and sustainability require leveraging existing community structures and values to ensure cultural acceptance and communal assimilation.

Research. There is very limited research on this insular community. For research to be informative and meaningful, it must be community based, move away from general statements about "Jews" or "Orthodox Jews" and instead specify cultural subgroups, and attend to individual practice and experience in this socioreligious context.

Awareness

Using visual media and film (e.g., *Filling the Void*, a cinematic description of the lived experience of *Chassidic* marriage), students can be challenged to understand their assumptions of the "other" and analyze the similarities and differences between cultures and their implications. In addition, readings from *The Newlywed Guide to Physical Intimacy* can further highlight similarities and differences around sexuality and sexual experience.

REFERENCES

Ahuvia, A., & Adelman, M. (1992). Formal intermediaries in the marriage market: A typology and review. *Journal of Marriage and the Family, 54*, 452–463.

Alegria, M., Atkins, M., Slaton, E., & Stelk, W. (2010). One size does not fit all: Taking diversity, culture, and context seriously. *Administration and Policy in Mental Health, 37*, 48–60.

Alegria, M., & McGuire, T. (2003). Rethinking a universalist framework in the psychiatric symptom-disorder relationship. *Journal of Health & Social Behavior, 44*, 257–274.

American Psychological Association. (2015, September 1). *Resolution on appropriate affirmative responses to sexual orientation distress and change efforts.* Retrieved from http://www.apa.org/about/policy/sexual-orientation.aspx

Bane, M. (2015). The ben Torah baal habayis. *Klal Perspectives*. Winter 2015.

Benor, S. B. (2012). *Becoming frum*. New Brunswick, NJ: Rutgers University Press.

Berman, E. (2000). Sect, subsidy and sacrifice: An economist's view of Ultra-Orthodox Jews. *Quarterly Journal of Economics, 115*, 905–953.

Bernal, G., Rodriguez, D. M., & Jimenez-Chafey, M. (2009). Cultural adaptation of treatments: A resource for considering culture in evidence-based practice. *Professional Psychology: Research and Practice, 40*, 361–368.

Birger, J. (2015, August 24). What two religions tell us about the modern dating crisis. *Time Magazine*.

Bronfenbrenner, U. (1986). Ecology of the family as a context for human development. *Developmental Psychology, 22*, 723–742.

Buchanan, M., Dzelme, K., Harris, D., & Hecker, L. (2001). Challenges of being simultaneously gay or lesbian and spiritual and/or religious: A narrative perspective. *The American Journal of Family Therapy, 29*, 435–449.

Burshtein, R. (Director). (2013). *Fill the Void* [Motion Picture]. Sony Pictures Home Entertainment, Israel.

Chaya. (2012, May 22). *What women's media needs to know about Chassidic women*. Retrieved from XOJane: http://www.xojane.com/issues/hasidic-women-sex

Cohen, S. M., Ukeles, J., & Miller, R. (2012). *Jewish community study of New York: 2011 comprehensive report*. New York, NY: UJA—Federation of New York.

Ehrenpreis, K. B., Perlstein, P., & Schechter, I. (2013). *Dating patterns in the Orthodox Jewish community: Gender and explanatory models*. Poster presented at Nefesh International Conference, Hauppague, NY.

Feiner, J., Sanderson, W. C., & Schechter, I. (2010, June). *OCD symptoms and Orthodox Judaism: Are more religious individuals more likely to exhibit symptoms of OCD*. Paper presented at the World Congress of Behavioral and Cognitive Therapies, Boston, MA.

Gonen, A. (2001). *From Yeshiva to work: The American experience and lessons for Israel*. Jerusalem, Israel: The Floersheimer Institute For Policy Studies.

Greenberg, D., & Sheffler, G. (2008). Ultra-Orthodox rabbinic responses to religious obsessive-compulsive disorder. *Israel Journal of Psychiatry and Related Sciences, 45*, 183–192.

Greenberg, D., Stravynski, A., & Bilu, Y. (2004). Social phobia in Ultra-Orthodox Jewish males: Culture-bound syndrome or virtue? *Mental Health, Religion, and Culture, 7*, 289–305.

Greenberg, D., & Witzum, E. (2001). *Sanity and sanctity: mental health work in Ultra-Orthodox Jews in Jerusalem*. New Haven: Yale University Press.

Greenfield, G., Pliskin, J. S., Wientroub, S., & Davidovitch, N. (2012). Orthopedic surgeons' and neurologists' attitudes towards second opinions in the Israeli healthcare system: A qualitative study. *Israel Journal of Health Policy Research, 1*, 30. doi: 10.1186/2045-4015-1-30

Guterman, M. A. (2008). Observance of the laws of family purity in Modern-Orthodox Judaism. *Archives of Sexual Behavior, 37*, 340–345.

Hartman, T., & Marmon, N. (2004). Lived regulations, systemic attributions: Menstrual separation and ritual immersion in the experience of Orthodox Jewish women. *Gender and Society,18*, 389–408.

Heilman, S., & Witzum, E. (1997). Value-sensitive therapy: Learning from Ultra-Orthodox patients. *American Journal of Psychotherapy, 51*, 522–528.

Hoffman, S. (2014). Reflections working at an Ultra-Orthodox mental health clinic. In S. Hoffman (Ed.), *Reader for the Orthodox Jewish psychotherapist: Case studies and contemporary responsa* (pp. 43–51). New York, NY: GoldenSky.

Huppert, J. D., Siev, J., & Kushner, E. S. (2007). When religion and obsessive-compulsive disorder collide: Treating scrupulosity in Ultra-Orthodox Jews. *Journal of Clinical Psychology, 63,* 925–941.

Kaganoff, Y. (2011, September 9). *Singles and a morally oriented Judaism.* Retrieved from http://www.torahmusings.com/2011/09/singles-and-a-morally-oriented-judaism/

Kaplan, A. (1990). *The handbook of Jewish thought.* Brooklyn, NY: Moznaim Publishing.

Kirmayer, L. J. (2006). Beyond the new cross-cultural psychiatry: Cultural biology, discursive psychology, and the ironies of globalization. *Transcultural Psychiatry, 43,* 126–144.

Kor, A., Mikulincer, M., & Pirutinsky, S. (2012). Family functioning among returnees to Judaism in Israel. *Journal of Family Psychology, 26,* 149–158.

Loewenthal, K. M., & Goldblatt, V. (1993). Family size and depressive symptoms in Orthodox Jewish women. *Journal of Psychiatric Research, 27,* 3–10. doi: 10.1016/0022-3956(93)90044-3

Mahoney, A., Pargament, K., Swank, A., & Tarakeshwar, N. (2001). Religion in the home in the 1980s and 1990s: A meta-analytic review and conceptual analysis of links between religion, marriage, and parenting. *Journal of Family Psychology, 15,* 559–596.

Maimonides. (1998). Mishneh Torah. (E. Touger, Trans.) Brooklyn, NY: Moznaim Publishing.

Milevsky, A., Niman, D. S., Rmaab, A., & Gross, R. (2010). A phenomenological examination of dating attitudes in Ultra-Orthodox Jewish emerging adult women. *Mental Health Religion and Culture, 19*(4), 1–12.

National Resource Center for Healthy Marriage and Family. (2015, May). Working with couples and families in the Orthodox Jewish Community. Retrieved from https://www.healthymarriageandfamilies.org/fostering-cultural-competency

Penkower, A. Y. (2010). *The culture of dating and single life in the Modern Orthodox Jewish community* (Doctoral dissertation), Rutgers University, Graduate School of Applied and Professional Psychology.

Phinney, J. (1990). Ethnic identity in adolescents and adults: A review of research. *Psychological Bulletin, 108,* 499–514.

Pirutinsky, S., & Kor, A. (2013). Relevance of the circumplex model to family functioning among Orthodox Jews in Israel. *The New School Psychology Bulletin, 10*(3), 25–38.

Pirutinsky, S., Maybruch, C., & Pelcovitz, D. (2014). Religious premarital education and marital quality in the Orthodox Jewish community. *Journal of Couple and Relationship Therapy, 13,* 365–381.

Pirutinsky, S., Rosen, D. D., Shapiro Safran, R., & Rosmarin, D. H. (2010). Do medical models of mental illness relate to increased or decreased stigmatization of mental illness among Orthodox Jews? *The Journal of nervous and mental disease, 198,* 508–512.

Pirutinsky, S., Schechter, I., Kor, A., & Rosmarin, D. (2015). Family size and psychogical functioning in the Orthodox Jewish community. *Mental Health, Religion, and Culture, 18,* 218–230.

Rappaport, C. (2004). *Judaism and homosexuality: An authentic Orthodox view.* London, England: Vallentine Mitchel.

Ribner, D. (2003a). Determinants of the intimate lives of Haredi (Ultra-Orthodox) Jewish couples. *Sexual and Relationship Therapy, 18,* 53–62.

Ribner, D. (2003b). Modifying sensate focus for use with Haredi (Ultra-Orthodox) Jewish couples. *Journal of Sex and Marital Therapy, 29,* 165–171.

Ribner, D., & Rosenbaum, T. (2004). Evaluation and treatment of unconsummated marriage among Orthodox Jewish couples. *Journal of Sex and Marital Therapy, 31,* 341–353.

Roberts, S. (2011, April 20). A village with the numbers, not the image of the poorest place. The *New York Times,* Retrieved from http://www.nytimes.com/2011/04/21/nyregion/kiryas-joel-a-village-with-the-numbers-not-the-image-of-the-poorest-place.html?_r=0

Rockman, H. (1994). Matchmaker matchmaker make me a match: The art and conventions of Jewish arranged marriages. *Sexual and Relationship Therapy, 9,* 277–284.

Rosen, D., Greenberg, D., Schmeidler, J., & Sheffler, G. (2007). Stigma of mental illness, religious change, and explanatory models of mental illness among Jewish patients at a mental-health clinic in Jerusalem. *Mental Health, Religion, and Culture, 11,* 193–209.

Schechter, I. (2004). Religion and mental health: A theoretical and clinical perspective. In D. Shatz & J. B. Wolowelsky (Eds.), *Mind, body, and Judaism: The interaction of Jewish law with psychology and biology* (pp. 71–80). Jersey City, NJ: Ktav Publishing House.

Schechter, I. (2006). *Multidimensionality in the Jewish religious experience: Results from an ongoing research study.* Paper presented at the Conference of the International Network of Jewish Mental Health Professionals, Baltimore, MD.

Schechter, I. (2011). Sexual abuse in the religious community: Systems, experience and repair. In D. Pelcovitz & D. Mandel (Eds.), *Sexual abuse in the traditional Jewish community* (pp. 304–338). Jersey City, NJ: Ktav Publishing House.

Schechter, I. (2013). *Enough about feeling, let's talk data: How data can transform clinical practice, policy, and real life in the Orthodox Jewish community.* Plenary lecture at NEFESH International Conference, Long Island, NY.

Schechter, I. (2015a, May). Interim report on divorce and marriage in the Orthodox Jewish community. Paper presented at ARCC Community Conference, New York, NY.

Schechter, I. (2015b, June 7). Socioculutral factors in BRCA genetic testing in the Orthodox Jewish community. Paper presentation at *Stakeholder's* conference on *BRCA genetic testing in the Orthodox Jewish community.* New York, NY.

Schechter, I., Respler, L., Liefer, S., Tang, E., David, R., & Crew, K. (2015). *Who are you going to call? Religious factors impacting medical and mental health decision making.* Poster presented at Association for Psychological Science, New York, NY.

Schnall, E. (2006). Multicultural counseling and the Orthodox Jew. *Journal of Counseling and Development, 84,* 276–282.

Schnall, E., Pelcovitz, D., & Fox, D. (2013). Satisfaction and stressors in a religious minority: A national study of Orthodox Jewish marriage. *Journal of Multicultural Counseling and Development, 41,* 4–20.

Schnitzer, G., Loots, G., Escudero, V., & Schechter, I. (2009). Negotiating the pathways into care in a globalizing world: Help-seeking behaviour of Ultra-Orthodox Jewish parents. *International Journal of Social Psychiatry, 57,* 153–165.

Shai, D. (2002). Working women/cloistered men: A family development approach to marriage arrangements among Ultra Orthodox Jews. *Journal of Comparative Family Studies, 33,* 97–114.

Shalev, O., Baum, N., & Itzhaki, H. (2013). "There's a man in my bed": The first experience of sex among Modern-Orthodox newlyweds in Israel. *Journal of Sex & Marital Therapy, 39*(2), 40–55.

Shuper, A., Zeharia, A., Balter-Seri, J., Steier, D., & Minumoi, M. (2000). The paediatrician and the rabbi. *Journal of Medical Ethics, 26,* 441–443.

Smith, T. B., McCullough, M. E., & Poll, J. (2003). Religiousness and depression: Evidence for a main effect and the moderating effects of stressful life events. *Psychological Bulletin, 129,* 614.

Sublette, E., & Trappler, B. (2000). Cultural sensitivity training in mental health: Treatment of Orthodox Jewish psychiatric inpatients. *The International Journal of Social Psychiatry, 46,* 122–134.

Wilson, K. G., & Murrell, A. R. (2004). Values work in acceptance and commitment therapy: Setting a course for behavior therapy. In S. Hayes, V. Follette, & M. Linehan (Eds.), *Mindfulness and acceptance.* New York, NY: Guilford Press.

Zalcberg, S. (2013). The art of the deal: Preferences in spouse selection among parents in a Hasidic community. *Israel Studies Review, 28*(2), 61–82.

CHAPTER 10

Muslim Couples and Families

Karen L. Haboush
Nadia S. Ansary

In Islam, family is considered divinely inspired.

—from Qur'an 4.1

The word "Islam" is derived from the Arabic word *salam*, which means "peace" but also has a supplemental meaning, namely "surrender." According to Smith (2001) the full implication or definition of this termi- nology is "the peace that comes when one's life is surrendered to God" (p. 2). Current estimates suggest that Islam is the second largest religion in the world with approximately 1.2 billion Muslims throughout the world (Council on American-Islamic Relations [CAIR], n.d.). Precise figures for the numbers of Muslims residing in the United States are difficult to obtain, with estimates varying from 1.8 million or 0.8 percent of the total population (Pew Research Center, 2011) to 6–7 million (CAIR, n.d.). Islam is among the fastest growing religions in the world and the fastest grow- ing religion in the United States (Abu-Bader, Tirmazi, & Ross-Sheriff, 2011; CAIR, 2014; Keshavarzi & Haque, 2013) and currently, Muslim Americans comprise approximately 1 percent of the world's Muslim population

---

Tragically, Karen Haboush passed after completing this chapter but before pub- lication of the book. She leaves behind family, friends, colleagues, students, and many clients who will miss her sharp wit, enthusiasm, and caring nature. Karen was an innovator who cultivated a valuable collection of work that has and prom- ises to continue to positively impact psychologists as well as Arab- and Muslim- American communities.

(Pew Research Center, 2011). In terms of projections, it is expected that: (1) the number of Muslims will almost double by 2030, to roughly 1.7 percent of the total population, and (2) the United States will have the second largest population of Muslims worldwide by 2050 (Maslim & Bjorck, 2009). Statistics show that while the majority of Muslim Americans identify as practicing Islam (Pew Research Center, 2011), they are also characterized by considerable variability in terms of the branch of Islam practiced, country of origin, acculturation, and degree of religiosity (Ali, Liu, & Humedian, 2004).

Despite the growth of the Muslim population, anti-Muslim discrimination has been on the rise in the United States in response to the 9/11 attacks and subsequent terrorist acts in the Middle East (Abu-Raiya, Pargament, & Mahoney, 2011; Khan & Ecklund, 2012; Sun, 2015). Since 2014, the rise of ISIS (Islamic State of Iraq and Syria)/Daesh and extensive media coverage of terrorist attacks have further contributed to the misconception that all Muslims are terrorists and a related backlash in terms of greater harassment and intimidation of Muslim Americans (APA, 2015).

Over half of Muslim Americans report that it is more difficult to be a Muslim in the United States since September 11 (Pew Research Center, 2011) and this is likely due to several factors. First, the relatively greater visibility of Muslim Americans heightens the likelihood of being targeted for harassment and discrimination (Khan & Ecklund, 2012). And second, images in the popular media perpetuate negative stereotypes about Islam (Smidt, 2005). Not surprisingly, the most frequent problem cited by Muslim Americans is others' negative views about Islam (Pew Research Center, 2011). As a result, Muslim Americans may be hesitant to identify as such, and therefore, published population estimates vary. In short, for Muslim Americans, all aspects of identity development occur in the context of an acculturation process and societal feedback, which frequently regards Muslims as terrorists and extremists (APA, 2015; Britto, 2008; Peek, 2005; Tindongan, 2011).

The confluence of a growing Muslim American population, negative media images, and increasing discrimination, all suggest the need for more accurate information to inform mental health treatment concerning Muslim individuals, couples, and families. In line with the American Psychological Association's (APA) ethical guidelines (APA, 2010) and the APA's position statement "Living in a World with Diverse Religions" (APA, 2015), this chapter intends to enhance culturally competent practice with Muslim couples and families by equipping readers with knowledge and potential strategies that have been found to be most effective in working with this population. Guidelines provided in this chapter are framed in terms of promoting mental well-being and resilience by emphasizing the role of family and religion, which are central features of the Muslim culture. The application of these tenets to culturally sensitive psychotherapy with a Muslim American family will be illustrated through clinical cases.

OVERVIEW OF ISLAM

Basics of Islam

Islam is a monotheistic faith in which *Allah* is the only God: In fact *Allah*, means "the God" not more broadly "a god among other gods" (Smith, 2001). Though there are many deliverers of God's message, Muslims believe that Prophet Muhammad (peace be upon him or *pbuh*)[1] is the last and most important messenger. As noted earlier, the word "Islam" is the Arabic word for submission or surrender to the will of *Allah*; hence, for many Muslims, Islam is a religion that frames daily life and behavior.

There are six core beliefs that are at the foundation of Islam, namely the belief in: (1) *Allah*; (2) the existence of angels; (3) the prophets and messengers with the Prophet Muhammad being the final prophet; (4) Holy Books meaning that the Bible, Torah, and Qur'an were all divinely inspired; (5) the Day of Judgment when all individuals will be evaluated based on their good and bad deeds; and (6) *Al-Qadr* or that *Allah* has predetermined major events in one's life though the individual has some degree of free will (Haque & Kamil, 2012).

Beyond these six foundational beliefs are five practices that believers are required to undertake, also known as the five pillars of Islam. The five pillars are as follows: (1) the *Shahadah*, the defining declaration by all Muslims that there is no God but *Allah* and Muhammad is His messenger; (2) *salah* or prayer, which is required five times a day; (3) *zakat*, or giving to charity; (4) *sawm* or fast in which believers abstain from food and water from sunrise to sunset during the month of Ramadan; and (5) *haj*, the pilgrimage to the holy city of Mecca (Smith, 2001).

Similarities and Differences between Muslim Subgroups

Sunni and Shi'i Religious Sects

Two major sects within Islam are the Sunni and Shi'i. At the most general level, the division that gave rise to Sunni and Shi'i sects originated after Prophet Muhammad's death (*pbuh*). Those who believed that governance should remain with the Prophet's kin became Shi'i, while those who believed that the Prophet's successor should be elected gave rise to the Sunni sect (Haque & Kamil, 2012; Smith, 2001). Both groups practice prayer, fast, and pilgrimage, yet differences between the groups in how prayer is performed, the rituals surrounding breaking fast, and the pilgrimage exist (Haider, 2014). Moreover, differences between the two sects on views of God and divine justice, legal doctrines, and views of religious authority are also quite different (Haider, 2014). For example, Sunnis reject the Shi'i principle that religious leaders are divinely inspired and should hold both religious and political power (Blanchard, 2005). Sunnis, also known as traditionalists, represent the majority of Muslims comprising 87 percent of Muslims in the world (Smith, 2001), while Shi'i are smaller in number, though they represent the majority in a few countries such as Iran, Iraq, and Bahrain.

There appear to be more commonalities than differences between Sunni and Shi'i sects regarding beliefs surrounding marriage and the family unit. With respect to marriage, both groups view the union as a mutually agreed-upon contract between two individuals and their families. Whereas Shi'i law recognizes temporary marriages as a contract, Sunni law permits similar temporary marriages though these are considered lower forms of the union and are often considered controversial (Waugh, 2015). Another example of nuanced differences between the groups concerns family planning. While family planning in the context of marriage is permissible within both groups, Shi'i scholars have deemed reproductive technologies such as in vitro fertilization permissible, while Sunni scholars prohibit the practice (Bowen, 2015). This difference is largely due to the fact that Shi'i scholars are permitted some flexibility in interpretation of jurisprudence, while Sunni scholars tend to follow established precedents; this is likely why the two groups may differ slightly on contemporary issues (Bowen, 2015).

Divorce is another area concerning couples and families, and here too there are more similarities than differences. Four types of divorce are recognized within both Sunni and Shi'i groups, and these vary based on who initiates the divorce and how permanent the separation will be (Voorhoeve, 2015). According to Islamic law within these two sects, when divorce occurs, custody of young children resides with the mother, though the father must be involved in decisions pertaining to the child. Once a child reaches a permissible age based on the different religious schools of thought, custody is turned over to the father. Shi'i law dictates that this custody shift occurs when boys reach age 2 and girls reach age 7 while Sunni schools of jurisprudence differ in the exact ages (Voorhoeve, 2015).

As can be seen, Islam is not a monolith. Though Sunni and Shi'i sects represent the two largest divisions, within each division are other schools of thought and jurisprudence that govern practices that set the foundation for Muslim couples and families. Thus, while practicing Muslims may be unified by a common set of beliefs and practices, there are within-group differences that can shape relationships between spouses and the broader family unit, and can therefore affect therapeutic outcomes.

Racial and Ethnic Heterogeneity

In addition to different sects, considerable racial diversity and diversity of regional origin exists among Muslims (CAIR, 2014; Pew Research Center, 2007, 2011; Smither & Khorsandi, 2009). In the United States, approximately 30 percent identify as White/Caucasian, 23 percent as Black/African American, 21 percent as Asian, 6 percent as Hispanic, and 19 percent as other or mixed race (Pew Research Center, 2011). Although precise figures regarding immigration are unavailable because the U.S. Census does not collect information about religion, available estimates suggest that the largest group of Muslim American immigrants to the United States (32%) originate from Southeast Asia and the second largest group (26%) from the Middle East and sub-Saharan Africa (Pew Research Center, 2011). Arabic is the language of the Qu'ran; however, not all Arabs are Muslim (Haboush & Barakat, 2014). This misperception has contributed to discrimination against Muslim Americans who are perceived to be Arab (Britto, 2008; Haboush & Barakat, 2014).

Intersectionality: African American Muslims

Among native-born Muslims, the largest subgroup (40%) identifies as Black/African American. They are largely third generation, born in the United States of native-born parents (Pew Research Center, 2011). African American Muslims (46%) report higher levels of religiosity than other native-born Muslims (Pew Research Center, 2011). Also, over 63 percent of African American Muslims are converts to Islam whereas converts, as a whole, comprise only 20 percent of the U.S. population of Muslim Americans (Pew Research Center, 2011).

Muslim African Americans have dual identities and experience oppression based on both race and religion. The first Muslim African Americans were slaves who brought Islam to America (McAdams-Mahmoud, 2005). Though largely prevented from practicing Islam, some traditions were passed down through subsequent generations. By the 20th century, Islam had become closely linked to a political movement involving Black nationalism. This group, the Nation of Islam, led by Elijah Muhammad, Malcolm X, and Louis Farrakhan, offers alternative models of family life and communities based more on Islamic values than on the majority culture's values. Thus, African American Muslims may belong to the Nation of Islam or an orthodox religious sect, such as Sunni Muslims (McAdams-Mahmoud, 2005). Following 9/11, African Americans and other native-born Muslims have been more likely to report being singled out for extra surveillance and discriminatory treatment (Pew Research Center, 2007).

Irrespective of the sect to which they subscribe, for African Americans, the adoption of Islamic customs can alter family life significantly. This is because the commitment to Muslim customs and goals emphasizes "chivalry, marriage, and traditional gender and parent-child roles" (McAdams-Mahmoud, 2005, p. 140). Also, parents often have to work hard to ensure that their children have a large enough peer group that can relate to these customs that do not always fit with the lives of other non-Muslim Americans or African Americans around them (McAdams-Mahmoud, 2005). Regarding the dual discrimination that African American Muslim family members face, spirituality can serve as a buffer against the effects of racism, and couples and family therapy should include exploration as to how faith and spirituality have helped couple and family members cope (Boyd-Franklin, 2010).

COUPLES AND FAMILIES

Islamic Principles Guiding the Family

While we acknowledge that Muslims vary in the degree to which religion dictates daily practices, and we caution practitioners from making assumptions about the extent to which Muslim couples and families incorporate Islam into their lives, there are some foundational principles of the religion that can be an important lens through which to understand Muslim individuals, couples, and families. For example, the Muslim faith places a robust emphasis on family, with the father as head of the household. Given the position of the nuclear and extended family in the lives of Muslims, it is no surprise that "Muslims consider the family the foundation of a good society and marriage its cornerstone" (Smith, 2001, p. 63). This collectivistic orientation is simultaneously the Muslim community's greatest asset as well as its strongest weakness when considering family relations. To illustrate, when one conforms to the values of the family, they likely "add credit to the family reputation and coherence, and may cultivate shame feelings when the individual displays deviance from the family consensus" (Daneshpour, 2012, p. 121).

With respect to gender roles, there is considerable diversity in gender role expectations across Muslim communities. As noted by Daneshpour (2012), "the dynamics of gender relationships may be the product of certain cultural and legal contexts, and are not always consistent with the Islamic ideology where the equality of men and women as human beings has been divinely confirmed and legally protected" (p. 125). The typically seen traditional gender roles in Muslim families, concomitant with negative portrayals in popular culture and media, contribute to the misperception of Muslim women as oppressed, subjugated, and weak (see Abu-Lughod, 2013; Maslim & Bjorck, 2009). While families are patriarchal in the most general sense, the value of women in the family and community cannot be overstated. In fact, one often-cited story of the Prophet (*pbuh*) makes a powerful assertion that the mother should be most highly regarded and valued by her children; three times over that of the father (Smith, 2001).

Marriage

In Islam, marriage is a union in which both consenting parties have responsibilities to one another as well as duties to fulfill (Daneshpour, 2012). In line with the collectivistic cultural orientation, marriage is typically considered a merger between two families and not just a union between two individuals (Ansary & Salloum, 2012). Depending on how traditional the family is, parents and sometimes community members can be heavily involved in the process of spousal selection (Daneshpour, 2012). This investment at the outset is also likely to result in continued involvement and support to assist the couple in marital issues that may arise. Furthermore, just as both parties must consent to the union, in cases of irreconcilable differences, both parties have the power to dissolve the marriage (Daneshpour, 2012). It is important to note that though divorce is not forbidden, it should not be entered into lightly and there are documented steps that must be followed by the couple (Smith, 2001). Thus, both divorce and remarriage are permissible though there may be local cultural variations in terms of the acceptability of these practices.

The issue of polygyny is one that is often misperceived in the West. While Islam allows a man to marry up to four wives, there are strict rules governing this process. For example, the man must provide *equally* for his wives in terms of the following: love, esteem, separate living quarters, and financial support, to name a few (Smith, 2001). Given that a man is unlikely to regard, love, and provide for his wives equitably, the consensus among Islamic jurists is that monogamy is necessarily the only option (Smith, 2001).

Parenting Practices

Honoring the family and respecting parental authority are central expectations for Muslim parents. In terms of parenting style, most Muslim families could be categorized as authoritarian, where family rules should be followed without exception, and respect for authority is paramount. Alternatively, they may be authoritative, where rules are often explained and enforced in a firm, consistent, yet nurturing manner. In traditional families, corporal punishment may be used (Daneshpour, 2012), but this appears to be employed less in more acculturated families.

In terms of expected child behavior, familial rules are often founded on Islamic principles governing behavior, such as abstaining from substance use and any premarital sexual activity. A child's violation of these likely will bring shame to the entire family. Such rules should not be misunderstood to mean that Muslim American youth actually abstain from these activities as emerging evidence suggests that these youth engage in substance use, premarital sex, and other risky behaviors (see Ahmed, 2012). Thus, the challenge for both Muslim American teens and their parents is navigating social norms associated with dating and substance use, and these can often be sources of familial conflict as well as a catalyst for treatment seeking.

IDENTITY DEVELOPMENT: EFFECTS OF POST-9/11 DISCRIMINATION AND RESILIENCE

Identity development for Muslim Americans involves the consolidation of many influences, including culture of origin, race, religious affiliation, degree of religiosity, and gender (Britto, 2008; Peek, 2005). Most theories acknowledge that development involves the interaction of the self and environment (Britto, 2008), and specifically, the view that identity is socially constructed and influenced by multiple systems is well represented by Bronfennbrenner's ecological systems model (Haboush & Barakat, 2014). Consequently, such a theoretical model suggests that experiences of discrimination occurring within these social systems can be a salient force shaping identity development.

The fact that many Americans lack knowledge about Islam (Ali et al., 2004; Khan & Ecklund, 2012; Pew Research Center, 2011) and endorse negative views of Muslims as anti-American and supportive of extremists (Pew Research Center, 2011; Smidt, 2005) means that Muslim American identity development occurs in an environment of mistrust and negative stereotypes. Discrimination is particularly stressful for immigrant Muslims (Abu-Bader et al., 2011) and devout Muslims who can be readily discerned by their appearance (e.g., wearing of headscarf for women and beard for men).

Unfortunately, many Muslim couples and families are confronted by hostility and discrimination as a consequence of 9/11 as well as the rise of the terrorist group ISIS (also referred to as Isil, and Daesh). In the United States, the group has commonly been referred to as ISIS. However, some countries, namely France and the United Kingdom, have begun referring to the group as Daesh, in order to create distance between the group's violent activities, which are in direct opposition to Islamic ideology. In recent years, the rebel group has grown in size, recruiting members from Europe and the Middle East, as well as parts of Africa and Asia (Kalyvas, 2015). According to Kalyvas (2015), the group has (a) grown in strength conquering large territories of Iraq during 2014, and (b) carried out numerous subsequent terrorist attacks around the world and withstood counterattacks by the United States. Because ISIS/Daesh has distorted Islamic principles to justify its activities, Muslims throughout the world are often vulnerable to negative perceptions of them as violent and opposed to Western ideals. Tellingly, 15 percent of Americans believe Muslim extremism is increasing compared to 4 percent of Muslim Americans (Pew Research Center, 2011). It is important to note that according to the Pew Center's (2011) research, 81 percent of Muslim Americans feel extreme violence is never justified to defend Islam. Nevertheless, the rise of ISIS/Daesh and extensive media coverage of acts of terror have further contributed to fear of Islam and intensified misunderstanding and discrimination against Muslim Americans (APA, 2015; Sun, 2015).

In terms of identity, survey data (Pew Research Center, 2011) suggest that nearly half (47%) of Muslims report that they think of themselves as Muslim "first," while 28 percent state they think of themselves as American "first," and 18 percent identify as "both." However, those with a high level of religious commitment (70%), consider themselves to be Muslims first. In contrast, only 28 percent of those with low religious commitment identify as Muslim first and 47 percent see themselves first as American. Thus, religious commitment appears to influence identity development.

In addition to religiosity, degree of acculturation and reasons for immigration also affect identity development (Abu-Bader et al., 2011; Peek, 2005). Acculturation refers to the process of psychological and social adaptation to the dominant culture, which necessarily involves integrating aspects of one's culture of origin and new culture into a cohesive identity (Abu-Bader et al., 2011; Peek, 2005). Identity construction is not a linear process: as part of acculturating, features of both the dominant and Muslim cultures may be alternately accepted and rejected in the process of developing a more cohesive identity. Moreover, during the process of developing a cohesive sense of self, some Muslim Americans may identify with negative media images and stereotypes that can in turn exacerbate psychological distress. This necessarily means that clinicians should be aware of this potential challenge to identity development in their initial and ongoing assessment of Muslim clients (Britto, 2008; Britto & Amer, 2007).

Other forces shaping identity development among Muslim couples and families are the circumstances surrounding immigration. Recent data on refugees, or those displaced from their homes, reveal that the largest percentages of refugees entering the United States are from predominantly Muslim countries such as Iraq, Sudan, and Somalia (Office of Refugee Resettlement, 2012). Since the 1990s, many immigrants have left their homelands due to war. For some refugee families, the acculturation process and relatedly, identity formation have been further complicated since the United States has been at war with their country (Abu-Bader et al., 2011).

Mental Health Treatment

Much of the existing literature on mental health treatment with Muslims and Muslim Americans has emphasized the stigma traditionally associated with mental health problems and help-seeking (Ansary & Salloum, 2012; Ciftci et al., 2012). This sense of shame is related to mental health issues being ascribed to a lack of faith (Ansary & Salloum, 2012; Smither & Khorsandi, 2009), and consequently may translate to a loss of honor for the family. Furthermore, the collectivist emphasis in Muslim societies also means that mental health problems are regarded as a family problem and therefore something to be solved privately (Daneshpour, 2012). Because of strong beliefs in *Allah*'s will, psychological problems may also be viewed as a challenge sent directly from *Allah* in which acceptance of *Allah*'s will is tested (Ciftci et al., 2012). The level of acceptance of deterministic beliefs involving who is cured and who is not may sometimes contribute to a couple's or family's decision not to seek treatment. However, it is important to note that this belief system may also be a source of coping for religiously observant Muslim couples and families who rely on prayer (Ali et al., 2004; Ciftci et al., 2012). Haque and Kamil (2012) note that the *Qur'an* sanctions the use of prayer to aid in dealing with emotional troubles. As such, psychological problems also may be regarded as an attempt by *Allah* to enhance faith.

Concurrent with psychological literature, which recognizes the role of religion and resilience, numerous studies show that the religiously observant turn to faith in order to cope (Abu-Raiya et al., 2011). Furthermore, there is emerging evidence of the role of religiosity in protecting Muslim adolescents from mental illness (Ansary, 2016a), such that youth reporting higher levels of religiosity also reported lower levels of anxiety and depression. Additionally, within a sample of adolescent Palestinian survivors of torture, 99 percent of whom were Muslim, religiosity was found to be the strongest predictor of reduced mental illness (Kira, Alawneh, Aboumediene, & Lewandowski, 2014). High levels of Islamic religiosity have also been found to be associated with character strengths including forgiveness, leadership, and equity among others, within a sample of Muslim adolescents (Ahmed, 2009).

This growing body of evidence regarding religiosity and mental well-being has some important implications for clinicians working with Muslim couples and families. First, while some adhere strictly to the *Qur'an* (Islamic holy book) as well as *Ahadith*, which are the writings depicting the practices and behaviors of Prophet Muhammad *(pbuh)*, others assimilate Islam-prescribed behaviors and practices to varying degrees in their daily lives. Thus, it is important for clinicians to first investigate the degree to which Islam is salient in the life of Muslim couple or family and have this provide some foundation for treatment strategies. A second implication of these findings for clinicians is that individual assessment is recommended but may be challenging because of concerns about privacy. Furthermore, due to stigma, somatic complaints arising from psychological distress occur at a higher rate within this population and may lead to seeking medical treatment, which may be perceived to be a more acceptable avenue for addressing mental health issues (Abu-Bader et al., 2011; Haboush, 2007).

Psychopathology Prevalence Rates

Statistics on the prevalence of mental health issues among Muslim Americans vary due to the numerous methodological and cultural challenges associated with collecting data on Muslim Americans (see Amer & Bagasra, 2013). As such, available figures likely underrepresent the actual prevalence rates, though studies examining adjustment of Muslim Americans following September 11 have helped to shed more light on the issue. Abu-Bader et al. (2011) found that about half of their sample of 70 elderly Muslim immigrants reported feelings of depression on a self-report measure. Acculturative stress was believed to be a salient factor as these clients more strongly identified with their Muslim culture than the majority culture.

In terms of specific disorders, features of post-traumatic stress disorder related to immigration and war have been reported (Ali et al., 2004). Furthermore, disorders such as depression and anxiety may be outcomes related to other problems that Muslim Americans may be hesitant to report, such as domestic violence, alcohol use, and sexual assault (Barkho, Fakhouri, & Arnetz, 2010; Haboush & Alyan, 2013; Rezaeian, 2010). In a related vein, the assessment and treatment of suicidality and alcohol use may be hindered by concerns about religiosity since both are prohibited by Islam, yet both are reported to occur (Ali et al., 2004; Rezaeian, 2010).

Assessment of Muslim Americans may be aided by standardized measures validated for that purpose. The discussion of such measures goes beyond the scope of this chapter but includes considering aspects such as the role of a client's native language and degree of religiosity (see Abu-Raiya & Hill, 2014; Ahmed et al., 2011; Keshavarzi & Haque, 2013). Moreover, assessment of children's social-emotional functioning may be aided by expressive techniques such as drawings as well as standardized behavior checklists such as the Child Behavior Checklist, which has been translated into Arabic and several Asian languages (Ahmed et al., 2011; Haboush, 2007). Measures of Islamophobia, which assess fear-related attitudes toward Muslims, also are available (see Lee et al., 2013).

Barriers and Supports

Barriers to seeking mental health treatment for Muslim couples and families include stigma, shame, fears of being "outed" in the community, limited resources for new immigrants, and fears of clinician's anti-Muslim views (Amri & Bemak, 2013; Ansary & Salloum, 2012; Chapman & Cattaneo, 2013). The role of the collectivist emphasis in limiting disclosure of mental health problems has already been noted. Specifically, disclosing certain problems such as domestic violence, abuse, and sexual matters (Amri & Bemak, 2013; Haboush & Alyan, 2013) has the potential to create further shame if other family members are involved, such as if another family member is an alleged perpetrator of sexual abuse. In these instances, the support of others with power in the community such as *imams* (Islamic religious leaders) can be critical for those making disclosures (Ansary & Salloum, 2012; Haboush & Alyan, 2013).

The establishment of a trusting therapeutic alliance, while critical to any therapeutic relationship, may be especially challenging to create given the larger sociopolitical climate toward Muslims since September 11. Clients may fear that private information divulged during therapy could be passed on to their governments. In particular, clients with a trauma history may be especially wary of sharing personal information (Abu-Bader et al., 2011). Research underscores the importance of clinicians' openness and acceptance of Islam, given the current political context and extent of anti-Muslim prejudice (Ali et al., 2004). Some evidence suggests that some Muslims who have sought mental health services from non-Muslim providers have experienced clinician mistreatment. For instance, Abu-Ras and Abu-Bader (2008) report that nearly all of the 83 participants in their study expressed fear of being stereotyped as violent and abusive by social workers and other mental health practitioners. In fact, several reported that they or others that they knew had been reported to their child's social worker and child protective services based on that stereotype. While a clinician certainly does not have to be Muslim, expressing genuine respect for and interest in Islam is recommended (Ali et al., 2004; Ansary & Salloum, 2012). Given the collectivist emphasis, culturally sensitive therapeutic approaches that support the strengths of family, such as family therapy (Abdullah & Brown, 2011; Haboush, 2007), couples therapy (Chapman & Cattaneo, 2013), and therapy that also recognize the complex role of systems (see Ansary & Salloum, 2012), are recommended. Faith-based approaches to treatment are discussed next.

Islamic Models of Mental Health

Along with the aforementioned therapeutic approaches, approaches to faith-based practices incorporating aspects of Islam exist on a continuum. As noted previously, degrees of religious observance exist along with reliance on religious practices as a means of coping (Ahmed et al., 2011; Ali et al., 2004; Keshavarzi & Haque, 2013). This underscores the critical importance of assessing religiosity before prescribing faith-based interventions such as prayer.

In a related vein, there is increasing discussion in the literature about movements to develop psychology from an Islamic perspective rather than adopting Western models (Ali et al., 2004; Haque & Kamil, 2012; Keshavarzi & Haque, 2004). Although Islam is a religion, and not a theory of personality, it addresses many aspects of human behavior and self-knowledge as described in the *Qur'an* and *Ahadith*. For example, despite a belief in destiny, Islam still recognizes there must be motivation to drive behavior, and individuals are still responsible for their choices (Smither & Khorsandi, 2009). Individual choice may include a desire to experience oneness with God or *tawhid*; indeed, positive mental health can reflect a striving for oneness with God for some Muslims. This active concept might align well with the decision to seek therapy as a means of self-actualizing (Keshavarzi & Haque, 2013). The development of other "aspects of the self" may also align with certain therapeutic goals, including: (1) the "spirited heart" (*qalb*), through which one knows *Allah* and fulfills *tawhid*, (2) the "soul"/"spirit" (*ruh*), which refers to connection with *Allah*, and

(3) *nafs*, which holds different aspects of self, including more negative parts. Interestingly, acknowledgment of the negative parts of oneself is a concept that is also incorporated in certain Western models of personality.

Schools

Clinicians working with Muslim American couples and families may find that school-related stressors constitute a focus of family therapy. Reflecting the population trends noted earlier, the number of Muslim children attending public and private faith-based schools has grown (see Hoot, Szecsi, & Moosa, 2003). In response to increased anti-Muslim bias (Thomas-Brown, 2010; Tindongan, 2011), the number of private Islamic schools has also risen. These schools support the development of an Islamic identity; along with academic subjects, students learn the Qur'an, learn to read Arabic, and observe Muslim practices without fear of discrimination. From an Islamic perspective, academic achievement is valued for *both* boys and girls (Sarroub, 2010).

Muslim families may be impacted by the experiences of their children in school. Clinicians working with Muslim Americans families may find that schools can either support or hinder resilience and positive identity development for children. The right to religious expression and practice of Islamic behaviors in public schools is protected by the First Amendment (CAIR, 2006). Nevertheless, many students face challenges to religious observance in school, especially as teachers frequently report having limited knowledge about Islam (Hoot et al., 2003; Mastrilli, & Sardo-Brown, 2002). Strategies for increasing observance may include: (1) allowing prayer in school in designated prayer areas or semi-private areas such as the nurse's office; (2) offering *halal* dietary selections that enable children to follow acceptable Islamic practices, within school cafeterias as well as during school activities such as birthday celebrations; (3) recognizing major Muslim holidays; (4) adjusting workload such as homework and exams when students are fasting, and (5) allowing modest dress for girls wearing the *hijab* or headscarf and attire that covers the arms and legs for PE. In family therapy, clinicians may encourage greater parental advocacy on behalf of their children's religious practices.

Teachers report scant and potentially inaccurate knowledge about Islam and this may limit a teacher's ability to protect students from discrimination. While some actions, such as pulling the *hijab* off female students (Tindongan, 2011), are readily discernible as discriminatory and require immediate action by school personnel, it is critical for educators to be aware of less obvious forms of microaggressions or small acts of discrimination, such as preferring not to work with a Muslim student or social ostracism during lunch or recess (Brown, 2015). Another subtle but pernicious microaggression lies within academic instruction, involving materials, words, and deeds that promote a climate of negative stereo-types concerning Muslims. Specifically, some textbooks and most films routinely depict Muslims as terrorists and militants, thereby reinforc-ing negative stereotypes (Hoot et al., 2003). Inaccurate and discrimina-tory statements by teachers and students, if left unchecked, can further contribute to misunderstandings (Brown, 2015; Hoot et al., 2003). Class-room climate is a key factor in anchoring students to school, and toler-ance for classroom discourse that espouses negative views about Islam creates an atmosphere of mistrust (Saleem & Thomas, 2011; Thomas-Brown, 2010).

School bullying is a topic that has become part of the national dialogue in the United States as state laws now mandate investigation of alleged incidents. Recent survey data (Ansary, 2016b) on 86 Muslim Ameri-can youth suggest that while reported levels of bullying are similar to non-Muslim youth, those who scored higher on Islamic religiosity also reported significantly higher levels of being bullied on three dimensions: (1) being "threatened or forced to do something," (2) being the victim of "lies or false rumors," and (3) cyberbullying. Furthermore, approximately 50 percent of the sample reported fear of being bullied in the future. Bul-lying rarely affects just the individual but is almost always a source of ongoing stress for the affected family (see Harcourt, Jasperse, & Green, 2014, for a review). Though requiring replication, these preliminary find-ings suggest that observant Muslim youth may be at risk for bias-based bullying and Muslim parents must be vigilant about addressing such inci-dents when they occur.

It is important to remember that alongside these school-based contex-tual variables, academic, religious, social, and other forms of identity development are continuing to coalesce for Muslim American youth. Developmental stages intertwine with religious practices, such as children being expected to fast typically between age 10 and early adolescence and girls being expected to wear the *hijab* upon the onset of puberty. Perceived pressures to acculturate may be especially strong in schools, given that schools are socializing systems. This may be especially salient for Mus-lim American girls, since schools may represent a setting where they can socialize away from parents (Sarroub, 2010; Sheikh, 2009). Muslim youth face numerous challenges associated with different customs from those of the majority culture, such as not attending school dances and having limited contact with the opposite sex. Peer support has been shown to be a protective factor against these stressors; however, female students also report scrutiny regarding their attire and behavior by other students (Sarroub, 2010; Sheikh, 2009; Tindongan, 2011). Thus, Muslim American youth must balance potential tensions associated with shaming their fam-ily with behaving in accordance with peer social norms (Sarroub, 2010; Sheikh, 2009). These generational differences may, in turn, constitute a focus in family therapy cases.

COMMUNITY EMPOWERMENT: APPROACHES TO PREVENTION AND INTERVENTION

Mosques

Imams, Islamic religious leaders, are often the first step in the chain of help-seeking when Muslim individuals, couples, or families are in crisis (Abu-Ras & Abu-Bader, 2008; Abu-Ras, Gheith, & Cournos, 2008; Khan, 2006). However, in focus groups conducted by Abu-Ras and colleagues (2008), in which 83 Arab American community stakeholders were invited to speak about the community impact after 9/11, *imams* voiced concerns about being equipped to treat individuals with varying degrees of mental illness. Importantly, those findings suggest that some *imams* may be open to input from mental health providers, since *imams* in that study generally endorsed the use of psychotropic medication, counseling, and learning about available treatment options (Abu-Ras et al., 2008).

In addition to the unique role of the *imam*, mosques and Muslim-based community centers can be valuable resources that can serve to strengthen the Muslim community. Though there are many Islamic doctrines with application to promoting psychological well-being, three foundational principles in Islam should be exploited by mosques seeking to strengthen the mental wellness of its community: (a) that health, including mental health, is God given and one's responsibility to care for; (b) that the sick, including those suffering from mental illness, deserve care from family and community; and (c) education is valued and knowledge should be passed to family and community (Ansary & Salloum, 2012). Accordingly, these principles can be used to promote mosque-hosted seminars, psychoeducational workshops, and discussions about mental health during the *khutba* after Friday afternoon prayer (a sermon equivalent to Sunday mass in Christianity). Such activities targeting youth and adults separately, as well as joined events that focus on the family, are simple and low-cost means of empowering the Muslim community, which can be done in collaboration with local clinicians. For example, in the second author's experience, the parishes of several mosques were very receptive to seminars aimed at raising awareness on adaptive family functioning and mental health. Such collaboration between mosques and mental health providers can be a powerful source of primary prevention and can ultimately chisel away the stigma associated with mental illness and treatment seeking that many Muslim individuals, couples, and families often experience.

Muslim-Based Community Organizations

Moving beyond the role of the mosque, other Muslim-based organizations have also demonstrated a robust dedication to empowering the community and promoting wellness. For example, the Islamic Society of

North America has hosted conferences, seminars, and youth camps to support and strengthen the Muslim family and community. In a similar vein, and with regard to prevention of discrimination-related distress, CAIR provides information to the Muslim community about Islamophobia and suggestions for response through their "Muslim Community Safety Kit." Another example of an organization that seeks to support the Muslim community is Smile whose mission is to "address sociocultural maladies that occur at every income level including but not limited to hunger, poverty, lack of access to healthcare, lack of awareness of mental health issues and lack of access to the arts." These examples provide a glimpse into ongoing efforts by Muslims to empower their community through social action and the provision of education and services to support a holistic view of wellness.

Evidence Regarding Culturally Adapted Intervention

Given that the evidence is scant with regard to the efficacy of religion-specific interventions, highlighted here is the evidence regarding ethnically sensitive or culturally adapted interventions—a close cousin of religion-specific approaches—addressing the needs of minority populations living in Western countries. Meta-analytic findings suggest a moderate effect size for culturally adapted interventions addressing the mental health needs of minorities (Griner & Smith, 2006). Most importantly, those results suggest that across several studies, clients involved in interventions focused on one ethnic group reported significantly higher positive outcomes than interventions focused on multiple ethnic groups, which, in turn, scored significantly better on the same outcomes than minorities engaged in traditional services (Griner & Smith, 2006). These findings converge with another meta-analysis (Smith, Rodriguez, & Bernal, 2011) as well as the most comprehensive review to date (Huey, Tilley, Jones, & Smith, 2014) in terms of documenting the broad benefits of culturally adapted interventions addressing mental health issues.

Considerable gaps in the literature exist in terms of identifying what factors are the essential ingredients moderating the effects of culturally adapted interventions, or more specifically what mechanisms underlie these associations (Ansary & Salloum, 2016). While the evidence continues to mount, what is known now is that in the real world exists *many* examples of long-standing ethnic specific approaches that have met and continue to meet the mental health and social service needs of unique ethnic groups (Ansary & Salloum, 2016). By extension, we expect that, in general, religion-specific approaches likely best suit the unique needs of Muslim American couples and families seeking mental health treatment. Clinical cases may best illustrate the application of these concepts.

CASE EXAMPLES

The following case examples are included to illustrate integration-ist approaches to couples and family therapy with Muslim Americans. Drawing upon multicultural, systems, cognitive behavioral therapy (CBT), and mindfulness frameworks (Boyd-Franklin, 2010; Daneshpour, 2012; Keshavarzi, & Haque, 2013; McGoldrick, Giordano, & Garcia-Preto, 2005), culturally sensitive interventions were tailored to the level of cli-ents' religiosity. Identifying information has been changed to protect confidentiality.

Case 1: Couples therapy

Amina, a 29-year-old Syrian woman, sought therapy in response to trust and communication problems in her marriage. Amina was born in the United States and self-identified as less religiously observant than her 35-year-old husband Moustapha, who had immigrated from Egypt to attend graduate school. Since the beginning of their six-year marriage, neither Amina nor Moustapha shared private information about their families for fear that "defects" in their respective families—namely dys-functional family patterns and mental illness—would be used against the other during conflicts. Furthermore, in accordance with a collectivist cultural orientation, Moustapha provided financial support to his mother and siblings, many times at the expense of his own family's needs. These factors created mistrust in the relationship that permeated their lives and affected their ability to communicate, as well as their sexual intimacy. Though divorce is permissible in Islam, Amina's family adhered to strong cultural beliefs that divorce is shameful to the individual and family. Thus, Amina sought couples therapy as a last resort.

During their three years of therapy—which was intermittent due to the birth of their second child—the clinician primarily adopted a multicultural approach aimed at incorporating Islamic beliefs and considering issues of acculturation in order to address the couple's needs. Where clinically indicated, CBT and systems interventions were also utilized. Initially, in recognizing Moustapha's reluctance to attend counseling, along with his religiosity, the therapist, adhering to a multicultural approach, chose to affirm the importance of marriage and family as consistent with Islamic tenets. This was a necessary step in the initial establishment of a therapeu-tic alliance between the therapist and the couple. Interestingly, although Amina and Moustapha professed different levels of religiosity, each reported feeling shame at seeking therapy. Also consistent with a multi-cultural approach, the therapist connected with the couple by focusing on their faith, emphasizing the principle that *Allah* is merciful and forgiving as well as the use of prayer as a means to cope in their daily struggles in communicating with one another. It is important to note that the therapist, although Muslim, which she disclosed in order to build trust, was not highly religious, yet utilized religious-based multicultural strategies since these were central to supporting the clients' well-being.

Along with multicultural interventions, several CBT strategies were also incorporated into the couple's treatment to enhance communication. This was especially needed to facilitate sensitive discussions about sexual issues. Role-plays were critical in building skills to improving the couple's communication and enabling them to successfully take risks in trusting the other. The clinician also collaborated with the couple to help them communicate their desires. Addressing their sexual difficulties regarding differences in amount of desire was an obvious challenge, given cultural expectations around modesty and shame. To counter this, the female clinician was careful to handle the couple's discussions about sex with sensitivity and followed these meetings with individual sessions characterized by more candid exploration, primarily with the wife, of the problem and suggestions for solutions. In this manner, the clinician adopted a multicultural approach but tailored it to the couple's needs. Finally, the clinician also reminded Amina and Moustapha that the *Qur'an* sanctions the importance of sex within marriage. This was an example of using both CBT and multicultural strategies to align the couple's core beliefs about sex with Islamic principles.

Addressing acculturation issues was also part of a multicultural therapeutic approach. Differences in acculturation to life in the United States were discussed in order to help Amina and Moustapha understand the impact of these stressors on their marriage and balance Muslim and American cultural values in a satisfactory manner for each. The therapist referenced these issues as a context for helping the couple define boundaries and responsibilities to various family members. Over the course of therapy, Amina became more acculturated to life in the United States and more assertive with her husband about her needs. Over time, Amina mobilized this shift into action, including eventually attending graduate school, which required her to leave her home and community more. This increased Amina's exposure and integration into American society. Moustapha also made certain changes as part of becoming more acculturated to life in the United States, such as caring for the children, which had previously been Amina's sole responsibility. In a similar vein, the therapist worked to address multigenerational issues and utilized a systems framework to encourage Moustapha to establish a firmer boundary with his family abroad. In turn, this helped to reduce Amina's frustration about the importance Moustapha placed upon helping his mother and siblings. Thus, the couple created a stronger coalition between themselves, which helped Moustapha to gently lessen his enmeshment with his family. The couple's marriage remained intact and the progress in their communication, trust, and intimacy issues were at the foundation.

In sum, the case of Moustapha and Amina, while primarily guided by a multicultural approach, also included aspects of CBT and systems interventions. These interventions were guided by a focus on systematically integrating Islamic faith-based practices and beliefs, where appropriate, along with addressing acculturation issues. Furthermore, this case illustrates the manner in which levels of religiosity differ among Muslims and therapeutic interventions must be tailored accordingly.

Case 2: Child and Family

Hoda, an Ethiopian mother of four, sought therapy for her daughter, Shereen, aged 16. At the initial session, Hoda stated that her daughter was unwilling to come to therapy although Shereen's anxiety and obsessive-compulsive behaviors had begun to affect her daily functioning and were also disruptive to the family. Shereen would excessively perform *wudu*, a ritualistic washing that is required before prayer, oftentimes spending hours in the bathroom. Not only was Shereen exhausted by her behavior, but also it caused her to be late for school, and required that Hoda adjust excursions so as not to be outside of the home during prayer time. Hoda also revealed that she was ashamed to share Shereen's problem with her family and felt isolated and overwhelmed.

Treatment with Hoda and Shereen reflected an integrationist approach incorporating features of multicultural, systems, CBT, and mindfulness theories. First and foremost, it was essential to engage Shereen in therapy. Recognizing the need for a flexible approach to engaging Shereen, the therapist was guided by systems theory and conducted a home visit, during which Shereen agreed to attend therapy. Consistent with a systems approach, both individual sessions and sessions with both Hoda and Shereen were subsequently conducted. It became clear that in addition to anxiety over performing *wudu* and prayer properly—so that these would be accepted by *Allah*—she was also overly preoccupied with thoughts of hell. Because religiosity was such a central part of Shereen's presenting issues, the therapist was concerned that her credibility would be lessened with Shereen because she did not wear the *hijab*. Accordingly, and guided by multicultural theory, the therapist asked an *imam* to attend one or two sessions to discuss religious guidelines regarding these principles. The *imam* was receptive to assisting in the therapeutic context and, in session, confirmed to Shereen that *Allah* would accept her *wudu* since her intention was to fulfill her obligation to pray. This multicultural intervention appeared to lessen Shereen's general anxiety and hand-washing behaviors. Importantly, this strategy also afforded the therapist the opportunity to begin utilizing CBT techniques to address Shereen's cognitive distortions regarding religiosity. All-or-none beliefs concerning the appropriate amount of hand washing and catastrophic thinking about the need to wash excessively were among the types of cognitive distortions that

Shereen was successfully challenged to replace. Drawing further upon CBT strategies, and incorporating aspects of mindfulness approaches, Shereen was also helped to substitute replacement behaviors for hand washing, such as focusing on being present.

In addition to faith-based strategies, strength-based techniques were also used with Shereen. These also involved a mix of CBT, mindfulness, systems, and multicultural theories. For instance, the therapist repeatedly pointed out that it was commendable that a young woman her age would have such strong religiosity and that Shereen simply needed to acquire some perspective regarding her religious intention and actions. Furthermore, building upon multicultural theory and mindfulness perspectives, an emphasis on prayer was an important facet of the therapy. Since it is believed that prayers conducted while distracted may not be accepted by *Allah*, the clinician worked with Shereen about being mindful and present when she prayed, which eventually helped to alleviate her anxiety.

In a similar vein, the therapist utilized multicultural and systems frameworks to provide the basis for work with Hoda, Shereen's mother. Hoda assumed a more authoritarian parenting style, characteristic of her culture, in which family information is rarely shared with children. As the resulting ambiguity seemed to raise Shereen's anxiety, Hoda was encouraged to be more open with Shereen about family issues by sharing developmentally appropriate information that concerned her. Guided by systems theory, the therapist encouraged Hoda to outline specific responsibilities for Shereen, such as completing household chores and caring for younger siblings, which also allowed Shereen to develop more autonomy.

In keeping with the systems approach, which includes collaboration between different systems, and because of the impact of Shereen's rituals on school attendance, the therapist collaborated with the school psychologist so that Shereen would not be overly penalized for lateness. Additionally, Shereen was allowed to use the school nurse's bathroom to perform *wudu* before praying in school. As treatment progressed, Shereen began to disclose occasional instances of school bullying related to her wearing the *hijab* and dual identity as an African American Muslim, which was also a source of anxiety for Shereen. As a result of the therapist sharing this information with the school psychologist, the school administration intervened to curtail such bullying. The greater systems-level support provided by the school helped to lessen Shereen's anxiety while in school and improved her concentration.

Having benefited from the application of CBT techniques such as role-plays and communication training, Shereen became more assertive, confident, and better able to cope with daily stressors over the course of treatment. The dysfunctional behaviors she exhibited surrounding prayer improved with CBT response substitution interventions and replacement with mindfulness techniques focused on being present. By the end of therapy, Shereen was attending college and had become engaged to be married. Her relationship with her mother also reflected improved communication and appropriate boundaries.

Case Study Analysis

These two cases demonstrate the complex interplay of forces discussed in this chapter, and illustrate the need for culturally sensitive interventions that require the practitioner to be flexible and design strategies that best fit the clients' individual needs. With regard to cultural factors, both cases are examples of how Muslims' collectivistic cultural orientation, centrality of religion, acculturation challenges, and shame (from *Allah* and family) about seeking therapy can be manifest. In a similar vein, shame surrounding sharing personal information—even between husband and wife as well as mother and daughter—was an issue in both cases.

In terms of therapeutic strategies, both cases reflect an integrationist approach utilizing multicultural, systems, CBT, and mindfulness frameworks. Examples of nontraditional techniques consistent with Islamic principles and degree of client's religiosity were employed. Specific techniques included linking the importance of treatment to the client's valued religious tenets, as well as using faith-based techniques that validated their religiosity as a strength. Other strategies demonstrating flexibility on the part of the therapist included conducting a home visit as well as inviting an *imam* to attend sessions that improved the therapist's credibility and understanding of how the client's issues aligned with their faith. These cases illustrate the importance and potential effectiveness of strength-based culturally sensitive therapy in which the therapist tailored the interventions to the specific religious and cultural needs of each client.

CONCLUSIONS

Muslim Americans represent a highly diverse group unified by a belief in Islam, the fastest growing religion in the United States. Despite the many challenges they have encountered as a result of discrimination following 9/11 and the rise of ISIS/Daesh, as a group they have demonstrated high levels of resilience, rooted in family and faith. Clinicians working with Muslim couples and families should necessarily capitalize on these strengths. Moreover, culturally sensitive mental health treatment entails recognizing the diversity of this group in terms of religiosity, acculturation, and immigration while also employing flexible strength-based treatment approaches. With these tools, mental health practitioners are likely to provide a more tailored treatment approach that optimizes the well-being of their Muslim clients.

CHAPTER REVIEW

Key Points

1. Key considerations for therapist's work with Muslim couples and families includes assessment of acculturation, immigration experiences, levels of religiosity, and post-9/11 discrimination.
2. Though levels of religious observance and sect may differ, therapeutic interventions, which support faith and incorporate a strength-based approach, are recommended.
3. Interventions that enhance the cohesiveness of the family align with the collectivist cultural orientation.
4. Community resources, such as *imams*, can promote the acceptability of mental health treatment.
5. An integrationist approach to treatment—incorporating aspects of multicultural theory, systems theory, CBT, and mindfulness perspectives—allows for the utilization of culturally sensitive interventions.

Key Terms

Ahadith (writings on the Prophet Muhammad [pbuh]), *haj* (pilgrimage to Mecca), *halal* (dietary restrictions), *hijab* (headscarf), *imam* (religious leader), *khutba* (sermon), *nafs* (acknowledgment of negative parts of the self), *pbuh* (peace be upon him), *qalb* (spirited heart), *ruh* (soul or spirit), *salah* (prayer), *salam* (peace, surrender), *sawm* (fast), *Shahadah* (declaration that Allah is the only God and Muhammad [pbuh] is his messenger), *tawhid* (oneness with God), *wudu* (ritualistic washing), *zakat* (giving to charity)

Myths and Realities

• It is a myth that Islam is oppressive to women. In reality, 71 percent of Muslim women and 66 percent of men say that Islam treats both sexes equally well (Pew Research Center, 2011).
• It is a myth that all Muslims support terrorism. In reality, 81 percent of Muslim Americans feel extreme violence is never justified to defend Islam (Pew Research Center, 2011). Twenty-one percent of Muslim Americans say there is "Not much" to "None" in terms of support for extremism and only 1 percent of Muslim Americans say that suicide bombing and other forms of violence against civilian targets are often justified to defend Islam from its enemies (Pew Research Center, 2011).

Tools and Tips

Knowledge

Ahmed, S., & Amer, M. (Eds.). (2012). *Counseling Muslims: Handbook of mental health issues and interventions*. New York, NY: Routledge.
Islamic Society of North America (www.isna.net) hosts conferences and camps to support the Muslim community.

Project Sakinah (http://projectsakinah.org/) is dedicated to addressing domestic violence in Muslim communities. "Take Action" and "Resources and
Tools" tabs offer resources for victims/ families.

Smile, an organization whose mission is to "address . . . hunger, poverty, . . . healthcare . . . mental health" (http://www.smileforcharity.org/about-us/our-
mission).

Dynamic Sizing

The decision to generalize the information in this chapter to any particular Muslim couple or family involves considering the multifaceted nature
of each family member's identity, including important contexts like the
degree of religious commitment, level of acculturation, stance toward
one's country of origin, and the nature or extent of any discrimination
that they experience, as well as their country of origin's relationship to the
United States. These factors and more must be considered in understanding a Muslim person's identity and practices.

Skills

Theory. Integrating multicultural, family systems, and cognitive behavioral frameworks when conducting couples and family therapy attends to
the nuanced features of treating Muslim clients in a culturally competent
manner.

Prevention. Children need assistance navigating unsupportive or hostile
school environments. School initiatives to address bullying are part of the
national landscape. Coordination of services with community organizations and mosques is considered best practice.

Service Provision. CAIR (www.cair.com) provides information about
responding to Islamophobia through their "Muslim Community Safety Kit."

Policy. Harassment, intimidation, and bullying policies are needed in
schools and the workplace to ensure safety for all and consequences for
perpetrators.

Research. Empirical research on the effectiveness of culturally sensitive
therapeutic interventions is lacking; barriers to trust within the Muslim
community need to be addressed in order to conduct adequate research.

Awareness

Islamic Circle of North *America* (www.icna.org) provides information
about family counseling and support for the Muslim community.

NOTE

1. When Muslims mention Prophet Muhammad's name, they typically
promptly state, "Blessings and peace be upon him," or commonly abbreviated as
pbuh, as a sign of reverence and respect.

REFERENCES

Abdullah, T., & Brown, T. L. (2011). Mental illness stigma and ethnocultural beliefs, values, and norms: An integrative review. *Clinical Psychology Review, 31*, 934–948. *Multiculturalism in Education.* Retrieved from http://www.wtamu.edu/webres/File/Journals/MCJ/Volume4/aburumuh.pdf

Abu-Bader, S. H., Tirmazi, M. T., & Ross-Sheriff, F. (2011). The impact of acculturation on depression among older Muslim immigrants in the United States. *Journal of Gerontological Social Work, 54*, 425–448.

Abu-Lughod, L. (2013). *Do Muslim women need saving?* New York, NY: Harvard University Press.

Abu-Raiya, H., & Hill, P. C. (2014). Appraising the state of measurement of Islamic religiousness. *Psychology of Religion and Spirituality, 6*, 22–32.

Abu-Raiya, H., Pargament, K. I., & Mahoney, A. (2011). Examining coping methods with stressful interpersonal events experienced by Muslims living in the United States following the 9/11 attacks. *Psychology of Religion and Spirituality, 3*, 1–14. doi: 10.1037/a0020034

Abu-Ras, W., & Abu-Bader, S. H. (2008). The impact of the September 11, 2001, attacks on the well-being of Arab Americans in New York City. *Journal of Muslim Mental Health, 3*, 217–239.

Abu-Ras, W., Gheith, A., & Cournos, F. (2008). The Imam's role in mental health promotion: A study of 22 mosques in New York City's Muslim community. *Journal of Muslim Mental Health, 3*, 155–176.

Ahmed, S. (2009). Religiosity and presence of character strengths in American Muslim Youth. *Journal of Muslim Mental Health, 4*, 104–123. doi: 10.1080/15564900903245642

Ahmed, S. (2012). Adolescents and emerging adults. In S. Ahmed & M. Amer (Eds.), *Counseling Muslims: Handbook of mental health issues and interventions* (pp. 251–280). New York, NY: Routledge.

Ahmed, S. R., Kia-Keating, M., Tsai, K. H. (2011). A structural model of racial discrimination, acculturative stress, and cultural resources among Arab American adolescents. *American Journal of Community Psychology, 48*(3–4), 181–192.

Ali, S. R., Liu, W. M., & Humedian, M. (2004). Islam 101: Understanding the religion and therapy implications. *Professional Psychology: Research and Practice, 35*, 635–642.

Amer, M. M., & Bagasra, A. (2013). Psychological research with Muslim Americans in the age of Islamaphobia. *American Psychologist, 68*(3), 134–144.

American Psychological Association. (2010). Ethical principles of psychologists and code of conduct, (2002, amended June 1, 2010). Retrieved from http://www.apa.org./ethics/code/index.aspx

American Psychological Association. (2015). Statement of board of directors—Living in a world of diverse religions. Retrieved from http://www.apa.org/news/press/op-ed/diverse-religions

Amri, S., & Bemak, F. (2013). Mental health help-seeking behaviors of Muslim immigrants in the United States: Overcoming social stigma and cultural mistrust. *Journal of Muslim Mental Health, 7*, 43–63. doi: 10.3998/jmmh.10381607.0007.104

Ansary, N. S. (2016a). *Correlates of psychological adjustment among Muslim adolescents: Results of the Muslim Youth Study (MYS)*. Manuscript in preparation.

Ansary, N. S. (2016b). *Bullying and Muslim youth: An exploratory study of prevalence rates and psychological correlates*. Manuscript in preparation.

Ansary, N. S., & Salloum, R. (2012). Community-based prevention and intervention. In S. Ahmed & M. Amer (Eds.), *Counseling Muslims: Handbook of mental health issues and interventions* (pp. 161–180). New York, NY: Routledge.

Ansary, N. S., & Salloum, R. (2016). Community-based programs: Ethnic-specific approaches to optimize mental wellness. In M. Amer & G. Awad (Eds.), *Handbook of Arab American Psychology* (pp. 344–358). New York, NY: Routledge.

Barkho, E., Fakhouri, M., & Arnetz, J. E. (2010). Intimate partner violence among Iraqi immigrant women in metro Detroit: A pilot study. *Journal of Immigrant Mental Health, 13*, 725–731.

Blanchard, C. M. (2005). *Islam: Sunnis and Shiites*. CRS Report for Congress. Congressional Research Service. The Library of Congress. Order Code RS 21745.

Bowen, D. L. (2015). Family planning. In. N. J. Delong-Bas (Ed.), *The Oxford encyclopedia of Islam and Women* (Vol. 1, pp. 291–294). New York, NY: Oxford University Press.

Boyd-Franklin, N. (2010). Incorporating spirituality and religion into the treatment of African American clients. *The Counseling Psychologist, 38*, 976–1000. doi: 10.1177/0011000010374881

Britto, P. R. (2008). Who am I? Ethnic identity formation of Arab Muslim children in contemporary U.S. society. *Journal of the American Academy of Child and Adolescent Psychiatry, 47*, 853–857.

Britto, P. R., & Amer, M. M. (2007). An exploration of cultural identity patterns and the family context among Arab Muslim young adults in America. *Applied Developmental Science, 11*(3), 137–150.

Brown, E. (Dec. 18, 2015). Furor over Arabic assignment leads Virginia school district to close Friday. *Washington Post*. Retrieved from: https://www .washingtonpost.com/news/education/wp/2015/12/17/furor-over-arabic-assignment-leads-virginia-school-district-to-close-friday/?hpid=hp_no-name_ hp-in-the-news%3Apage%2Fin-the-news

Chapman, A. R., & Cattaneo, L. B. (2013). American Muslim marital quality: A preliminary investigation. *Journal of Muslim Mental Health, 7*, 1–24.

Ciftci, A., Jones, N., & Corrigan, P. W. (2012). Mental health stigma in the Muslim community. *Journal of Muslim Mental Health, 7*, 17–32. doi: 10.3998/ jmmh.10381607.0007.102

Council on American-Islamic Relations [CAIR]. (n.d.). *American Muslims*. Retrieved on October 8, 2014, from http://www.cair.com/AboutIslam/IslamBasics .aspx

Council on American-Islamic Relations [CAIR]. (2006). *American public opinion about Islam and Muslims*. Retrieved on June 30, 2016, from https://www.cair .com/images/pdf/american_public_opinion_on_muslims_islam_2006.pdf

Daneshpour, M. (2012). Family systems therapy and postmodern approaches. In S. Ahmed & M. Amer (Eds.), *Counseling Muslims: Handbook of mental health issues and interventions* (pp. 119–134). New York, NY: Routledge.

Griner, D., & Smith, T. B. (2006). Culturally adapted mental health interventions: A meta analytic review. *Psychotherapy: Theory, research, practice, training, 43*, 531–548. doi: 10.1037/0033-3204.43.4.531

Haboush, K. L. (2007). Working with Arab American families: Culturally competent practice for school psychologists. *Psychology in the Schools, 44*, 183–198.

Haboush, K. L., & Alyan, H. (2013). "Who can you tell?" Features of Arab culture that influence conceptualization and treatment of childhood sexual abuse. *Journal of Child Sexual Abuse, 22*, 499–518.

Haboush, K. L., & Barakat, N. (2014). Education and employment among Arab Americans: Pathways to individual identity and community resilience. In S. C. Nassar-McMillan, K. J. Ajrouch, & J. Hakim-Larson (Eds.), *Biopsychosocial perspectives on Arab Americans: Culture, development and health* (pp. 229–255). New York, NY: Springer Publishing.

Haider, N. (2014). *Shi'i Islam: An Introduction.* Cambridge, UK: Cambridge University Press.

Haque, A., & Kamil, N. (2012). Islam, Muslims, and mental health. In S. Ahmed & M. Amer (Eds.), *Counseling Muslims: Handbook of mental health issues and interventions* (pp. 3–14). New York, NY: Routledge.

Harcourt, S., Jasperse, M., & Green, V.A. (2014). "We were sad and we were angry": A systematic review of parents' perspectives on bullying. *Child & Youth Care Forum, 43*, 373–391.

Hoot, J. L., Szecsi, T., & Moosa, S. (2003). What teachers of young children should know about Islam. *Early Childhood Education Journal, 31*(2), 85–90.

Huey, S. J., Jr., Tilley, J. L., Jones, E. O., & Smith, C. A. (2014). The contribution of cultural competence to evidence-based care for ethnically diverse populations. *The Annual Review of Clinical Psychology, 10*, 305–338. doi: 10.1146/annurev-clinpsy-032813-153729

Kalyvas, S. N. (2015). Is ISIS a revolutionary group and if yes, what are the implications? *Perspectives on Terrorism, 9*(4), 42–47.

Keshavarzi, H., & Haque, A. (2013). Outlining a psychotherapy model for enhancing Muslim mental health within an Islamic context. *The International Journal for the Psychology of Religion, 23*, 230–249. doi: 10.1080/10508619.2012.712000

Khan, Z. (2006). Attitudes toward counseling and alternative support among Muslims in Toledo, Ohio. *Journal of Muslim Mental Health, 1*, 21–42.

Khan, M., & Ecklund, K. (2012). Attitudes toward Muslim Americans post-9/11. *Journal of Muslim Mental Health, 7*, 1–15. doi: 10.3998/jmmh.10381607.0007.101

Kira, I. A., Alawneh, A. N., Aboumediene, S., Lewandowski, L., Laddis, A. (2014). Dynamics of oppression and coping from traumatology perspective: The example of Palestinian adolescents. *Peace and Conflict: Journal of Peace Psychology, 20*, 385–411. doi: 10.1037/pac0000053

Lee, S. A., Reid, C. A., Short, S. D., Gibbons, J. A., Yeh, R., & Campbell, M. L. (2013). Fear of Muslims: Psychometric evaluation of the Islamophobia Scale. *Psychology of Religion and Spirituality, 5*, 157–171.

Maslim, A. A., & Bjorck, J. P. (2009). Reasons for conversion to Islam among women in the United States. *Psychology of Religion and Spirituality, 1*, 97–111.

Mastrilli, T., & Sardo-Brown, D. (2002). Pre-service teachers' knowledge about Islam: A snapshot post September 11, 2001. *Journal of Instructional Psychology, 29*(3), 155–161.

McAdams-Mahmoud, V. (2005). African American Muslim families. In M. McGoldrick, J. Giordano, & N. Garcia-Preto (Eds.), *Ethnicity and family therapy* (3rd ed., pp. 138–150). New York, NY: Guilford Press.

McGoldrick, M., Giordano, J., & Garcia-Preto, N. (2005). Overview: Ethnicity and family therapy. In M. McGoldrick, J. Giordano, & N. Garcia-Preto (Eds.), *Ethnicity and family therapy* (3rd ed., pp.1–40). New York, NY: Guilford Press.

Office of Refugee Resettlement. (2012). Fiscal year 2012 refugee arrivals. Retrieved on May 1, 2014, from: http://www.acf.hhs.gov/programs/orr/resource/fiscal-year-2012-refugee-arrivals

Peek, L. (2005). Becoming Muslim: The development of a religious identity. *Sociology of Religion, 66*, 215–242.

Pew Research Center (2007). *Muslim Americans: Middle class and mostly mainstream.* Retrieved on June 30, 2007, from http://www.pewresearch.org/2007/05/22/muslim-americans-middle-class-and-mostly-mainstream/

Pew Research Center (2011). *Muslim Americans: No signs of growth in alienation or support for extremism.* Retrieved on September 5, 2014, from http://www.people-press.org/2011/08/30/section-2-religious-beliefs-and-practices/

Rezaeian, M. (2010). Suicide among young Middle Eastern Muslim females. *Crisis: The Journal of Crisis Intervention and Suicide Prevention, 31*, 36–42.

Saleem, M. M., & Thomas, M. K. (2011). The reporting of the September 11th terrorist attacks in American social studies textbooks: A Muslim perspective. *The High School Journal, 95*, 15–33.

Sarroub, L. K. (2010). Discontinuities and differences among Muslim Arab-Americans: Making it at home and school. In M. L. Dantas & P. C. Manyak (Eds.), *Home-school connections in a multicultural society: Learning from and with multiculturally and linguistically diverse families* (pp. 76–93). New York, NY: Routledge/Taylor & Francis.

Sheikh, M. F. (2009). *An exploratory study of the challenges of living in America as a Muslim adolescent attending public school.* Unpublished doctoral dissertation. GSAPP, Rutgers University, Piscataway, NJ.

Smidt, C. E. (2005). Religion and American attitudes toward Islam and an invasion of Iraq. *Sociology of Religion, 66*, 243–261.

Smith, H., (2001). *Islam: A concise introduction.* New York, NY: HarperCollins.

Smith, T. B., Rodríguez, M. D., & Bernal, G. (2011). Culture. *Journal of Clinical Psychology, 67*, 166–175. doi: 10.1002/jclp.20757

Smither, R., & Khorsandi, A. (2009). The implicit personality theory of Islam. *Psychology of Religion & Spirituality, 1*(2), 81–96.

Sun, L. (December 11, 2015). American Muslim doctors feel greater scrutiny, even patients' suspicions. *Washington Post.* Retrieved from https://www.washingtonpost.com/news/to-your-health/wp/2015/12/11/american-muslim-doctors-feel-greater-scrutiny-even-patients-suspicions/rom

Thomas-Brown, K. (2010). Arab-American and Muslim-American diversity in a Dearborn public high school: A multicultural perspective. *The Journal of Multiculturalism in Education, 5*(1). Retrieved from http://www.wtamu.edu/journal/volume-5-number-1.aspx

Tindongan, C. W. (2011). Negotiating Muslim youth identity in a post- 9/11 world. *The High School Journal, 95*, 72–87.

Voorhoeve, M. (2015). Divorce. In. N.J. Delong-Bas (Ed.), *The Oxford encyclopedia of Islam and women* (Vol. 1, pp. 205–212). New York, NY: Oxford University Press.

Waugh, E.H. (2015). Rites. In. N.J. Delong-Bas (Ed.), *The Oxford encyclopedia of Islam and women* (Vol. 2, pp. 183–194). New York, NY: Oxford University Press.

PART IV

Identity Intersections and Diverse Family Forms

CHAPTER 11

Multiracial Families: Issues for Couples and Children

David L. Brunsma
Monique Porow

INTRODUCTION

In 2008, Edwards and Pedrotti conducted a review of the literature on "multiracial issues" in the top journals in counseling—*Journal of Counseling Psychology, Journal of Counseling & Development, The Counseling Psychologist, Professional Psychology: Research and Practice, Cultural Diversity and Ethnic Minority Psychology,* and *Journal of Multicultural Counseling and Development*—to see the coverage, types of inquiries, and engagement with issues of multiracial people. Their conclusion was quite dire, "considering the growing population of multiracial individuals who are likely to seek counseling ... [the] dearth of published research in counseling journals is concerning" (p. 414). Similar results have been found when the literature on family therapy and counseling for interracial couples is considered (McClurg, 2004). Since this review, only a handful of practitioners and scholars in the disciplines of counseling psychology (Wilt, 2011), social work (Jackson & Samuels, 2011), and family therapy (McDowell, 2015) have begun to remedy this dearth. In this chapter, we focus our inquiries on the realities facing Black/White interracial couples, their **biracial** children, and the **multiracial** families that they compose. Steeped largely in critical sociological analyses of race, **racial identity**, racialization, and racism in the United States, our review of the key issues facing interracial couples and biracial individuals in the 21st century echoes the recent calls of counselors, social workers, and therapists pushing for increased cultural competence within the field of psychology.

Even though the experiences of multiracial individuals and families are not monolithic, it would be quite useful if clinicians themselves were biracial or in an interracial relationship, as it would afford them a degree of social proximity that would enhance the therapeutic relationship. This is simply not the case, as a majority of family therapists do not have such firsthand experience; however, therapists need to be armed with knowledge of the unique issues faced by multiracial families in order to develop the skills they need to effectively work with these families and their biracial offspring. In this vein, our overview covers four basic points we feel are most pertinent for those currently working with multiracial families and biracial individuals: (1) understanding that the lives of multiracial families and children are lived in a society that, confusingly, considers them both a "problem" within the racial landscape of contemporary society and a "promise" for that same society; (2) understanding that the lives of interracial couples, families, and their children are narrated both from without (e.g., from others) and within (e.g., by family members, by self) the realities of their daily lives, and that these two narrations are often in conflict; (3) understanding that the lives of multiracial families and their offspring are centrally lived in a fully intersectional experience of race, gender, sexuality, class, region, ability, language, and so on, and (4) understanding that the lives of interracial couples/families and their multiracial children take place within a culture permeated by contemporary racial ideologies of colorblindness and "post-raciality." One must understand these contours of multiracial reality in a society like the United States in order to even begin crafting therapeutic models and intervention strategies that have a chance of helping these families and individuals to live full and rich lives.

After the 1967 case *Loving v. Virginia*, which struck down the last vestiges of state laws that disallowed interracial marriage, families and their offspring are still asked by others in their communities, whether interpersonally or via mass mediated representations, "Who are you?" "What are you?" "What kind of family is that?" "Are those your kids?" "Your parents?" They are constantly questioned. Such inquiries plunge into the heart of the dilemma of being a "problem" in the contemporary racial landscape. As we will see in this chapter, scholarship on the biracial experience and the realities of interracial families evidence the **microaggressions** or subtle acts of discrimination that are faced on a daily basis in their communities as well as in the culture writ large (Childs, 2005; DaCosta, 2007). It is important that those working with interracial families and multiracial people be aware of such microaggressions as well as its extensive literature (see Wong, Derthick, David, Saw, & Okazaki, 2014, for a review) in developing approaches and methods. This chapter, as well as the bulk of the literature on interracial families and multiracial individuals, remains largely focused on the Black/White binary as one of the central axes upon which other racialized and mixed race experiences turn. However, the families and individuals one works with come from a dizzying array of interracial and multiracial realities that are both problematized and celebrated by our culture.

Life is a set of structured stories and storied structures, and this is also true for biracial individuals and their families (Brunsma 2011). There are Stories (with a capital S) that socially, culturally, and politically narrate our collective understandings (and projections) of what multiracial families and individuals are. There are also stories (with a small s) of those very families and individuals whose experiences within both the institution of family and the institution of race are real. What we have seen in study after study is that these two types of "stories" are often in conflict—with Stories affecting stories, while at the same time, stories alter the larger fabric of Stories in any given society (Rockquemore, Brunsma, & Delgado, 2009). Therapists, counselors, and practitioners would do well to see their clients as fundamentally embedded in *both*, while at the same time attempting to create a third, new understanding with which they might navigate and strategize their walk through this society along their life courses. Finding this new story is a potential outcome for work with multiracial families and individuals.

The history of scholarly and practitioner knowledge production regarding multiraciality has dovetailed with racial ideologies and national struggles at each juncture. When the United States was emerging from the Civil Rights Movement, and striking down the last legal vestiges of overt racism, the approach to counseling families and individuals focused itself on leftovers from the former racial order—with schools, mental health, and other institutional actors trying to fit their clients into the mold of the one-drop rule, in which those with any Black blood were considered to be Black. Then we moved through a multiracial movement, in which family therapists (e.g., Wardle, 1993), counselors (e.g., Kich, 1992), and psychologists (e.g., Root, 1992) were deeply involved. This focus centered on empowerment for multiracial families and individuals struggling, then, to find a meaningful and healthy sense of themselves *as* families and individuals (Renn, 2008). As the century wound down and a new one was born, we saw a stronger focus on the deeply complex individual and family identities, revealing that the racial components of those identities are but one dimension in a much broader matrix. Recognizing that the families and individuals one works with are located at the intersections of race, gender, class, sexuality, region, and others helps us to more effectively understand what they must navigate. Such recognition will provide for better models for "healthy" multiracial families and individuals.

Finally, we end the chapter with an important argument that is one of the central axes of race and racism in contemporary American society. Practitioners must understand that although interracial unions and their biracial offspring have increased since the late 1960s, society is currently steadfast in a color-blind era (Bonilla-Silva, 2013). In *Racism without*

Racists: Color-Blind Racism and the Persistence of Racial Inequality in the United States, Bonilla-Silva (2013) asks: How is it possible to have such tremendous racial inequality in a country where most Whites claim that race is no longer relevant? The answer to this 21st-century question, according to Bonilla-Silva, is **color-blind ideology**. Color-blind ideology explains racial inequality as the outcome of individual shortcomings or conflicts (as opposed to Jim Crow, explicit, in-your-face, racism). This has also been referred to as the "new racism," subtle, institutional, and, according to its proponents, nonracial. Thus, all of the dynamics that are faced in the office or clinic, in the school or church, are woven deeply, ideologically, rhetorically, and narratively with color-blindness. This silences those who wish to call those racial dynamics by name. Therapists and counselors would do well to take great pains to understand this reality, because while the societal attitudes appear to have changed, color-blindness masks real difficulties for interracial families and multiracial children.

To move through these arguments, we draw from an interdisciplinary set of literatures while using results from our own empirical sociological work (Brunsma, 2005, 2006; Porow, 2014; Rockquemore & Brunsma, 2001, 2008) on biracial identities and interracial family processes. One of our goals here is to use the existing literature as well as our own data to challenge readers' assumptions, understandings, and expectations about interracial and biracial couples and families. This chapter will focus on how race is experienced by families, and by individuals within families. Drawing from Rockquemore and Brunsma's collective published results, as well as the innovative recent qualitative study by Porow (2014), we hope to illuminate a research-focused and data-driven overview of multiracial families and the various issues faced by couples and their children. In doing so, we hope to provide readers with inspiration and insight into potential approaches with both interracial couples and their socialization of their children. We specifically draw on interview data from Porow's (2014) study of familial **racial socialization** of Black/White biracial adults to provide illustrations. That study examined the role that parents, extended family members, and siblings play in the process of shaping the racial identity development of biracial people. Data from 22 qualitative, semi-structured interviews with people who have one Black and one White parent were utilized to assess the nature of their relationship with various family members, and the impact of those experiences.

WHEN THE PROMISE IS STILL A PROBLEM

Since the mid-1980s, interracial marriages have more than doubled (Wang, 2012) and have transformed the racial landscape in America. Unfortunately, however, the acceptance of interracial relationships, marriages, and families has been slow. These couples face unique racially based challenges resulting from limited conceptualizations of the family that linger in the American context (Milan & Keiley, 2000; Yancey & Lewis, 2009). The dominant narrative is of the racially homogenous family where children are expected to resemble their parents and parents are expected to be similar in hue and phenotype (Herring, Keith, & Horton, 2004). This expectation sets the stage where such families are perceived as both problem and promise, because their very existence transforms how we perceive racially diverse families (Risman, 2009). The experiences that result can include challenges such as securing housing (Dalmage, 2000), negotiating acceptance and opposition from extended family members (Childs, 2005; Dalmage, 2000), an increased risk of divorce for White women married to Black men (Bratter & King, 2008), and everyday situations that delegitimize one's family ties due to a lack of the expected homogeneity (Crawford & Allagia, 2008; Killian, 2001). These potential issues suggest a growing need for research that is responsive to the experiences of interracial and multiracial families in America today, a result of long historical resistance to multiracial families.

Throughout history, interracial coupling has consistently been framed as "taboo." This persists today, yet it operates more covertly. Although contemporary audiences observe a greater number of interracial couples in various forms of popular media, some with storylines void of racial issues or social stigmas, the fact remains that it is still unlikely to see those same interracial couples get married or exist as part of a family unit with children (Childs, 2005). There is a general lack of representation of multiracial families in the media that are portrayed as "normal" or representative of a "typical" American family. That exclusion perpetuates an understanding of the family that fosters the outright rejection of a legitimate racially diverse family (Collins, 2006). This poses a challenge for people in multiracial families who must construct, develop, and negotiate healthy family identities with few or no positive **representations** in the media. This must also be done while actively rejecting explicit and pervasive framing of the family's existence as taboo. Increasing the representation of racially diverse families in television and films helps to mitigate these challenges, while promoting a framework that does not hinge upon physical or phenotypic similarity. Tapping into the third story that clients are narrating empowers them to narrate past those stories and Stories that have struggled to coexist.

Contemporary societal resistance or intolerance of racially diverse families manifests itself in a plethora of ways. For example, the controversy over a General Mills commercial featuring a multiracial family illustrates this point well. In 2013, the Cheerios brand aired a commercial depicting an interracial couple interacting with their daughter, Gracie. In a seemingly harmless scenario, Gracie, a little girl with light brown, curly hair, asked her White mother about the health benefits of Cheerios for a person's heart. Shortly after, Gracie disappeared, and her father came into view lying on a couch with his chest covered in Cheerios. That man,

Gracie's father, is Black. The commercial immediately ended with the caption "Love" on a blank, yellow screen, showered by a cascade of Cheerios. While many found the Cheerios commercial heartwarming, there was an intense racist backlash, which eventually led General Mills to disable the comment section of the commercial on Youtube.com. The subtle message in this 2013 commercial represents a progressive conceptualization of the multiracial family as promise, paving the way for subsequent media depictions to continue that narrative shift, as did Johnson & Johnson in a bold 2015 ad campaign. As part of a campaign to celebrate diverse families, Tylenol aired a commercial titled "How We Family" in 2015. On the heels of the backlash from the Cheerios ad, this audacious commercial began with the question, "When were you first considered a family?" and displayed a montage that profiled images of diverse families, including interracial couples, same-sex couples, and couples with adopted children. This direct challenge to the limited, dominant narrative of the family draws attention to the reality that many people in diverse families must fight for recognition as a family.

Respondents of Porow's (2014) study of familial racial socialization shared personal accounts of the challenges they faced as members of diverse families. One 24-year-old respondent, Nadine, knew all too well that her family was perceived as a problem when they moved to a predominantly White suburb of Wisconsin at the age of 6. She described her experience growing up in Wisconsin as "crazy," citing the visibility of White supremacist groups in her town, and having experienced her first racially charged incident at the age of 9. According to Nadine, being a multiracial family encouraged social disapproval because her father was a Black man married to a White woman. Recounting the climate she noted, "they still hold Klan rallies in the park across town which is like five blocks away." She recalled many White people echoing similar sentiments about the growing biracial population in their town. If you ask a White person, they'll say, "because all the Black men are coming to get all our women pregnant and leaving them without paying child support. That's what they say." Nadine's family endured extreme opposition and rejection, having harrowing experiences that she described:

In the course of those years our house was spray painted four times with the word "nigger," "leave niggers." Our house was burned down in 1994. The only thing left was the four walls . . . Then we rebuilt the house and our garage got burned down and our fence got burned down. Oh, and throughout the 13 years they'd flood our basement. They'd stick our hose in the window and flood our basement. There would be three or four feet of water. We had a finished basement so it caused a lot of damage.

The overwhelming hatred for interracial unions was a common sentiment among the residents of her town, and her family suffered a great deal as the result of the heightened opposition to unions between Black men and

White women. This is a common challenge for interracial couples consisting of Black men and White women and persists to this day, as evidenced by the reaction to the Cheerios commercial. For Nadine's family, the pressure was more than her parents could bear, ultimately leading to their divorce. From the start, the marriage between Nadine's parents, like many other marriages between White women and Black men, had a far greater chance of ending in divorce (Bratter, 2007; Zhang, 2009). Marriages between White women and Black men are twice as likely to end in divorce by their tenth year compared to marriages between White women and White men (Bratter & King, 2008). Awareness of this unique challenge for those who enter treatment can play a big role in couples processing their experiences within society at large (Fusco, 2010).

FROM RACIALIZED CULTURAL STORIES TO THE STORIES OF MULTIRACIAL EXPERIENCE

Racial meaning-making is always a dynamic, interactive, and multidimensional process for the members of multiracial families. Interracial couples and their biracial children must negotiate their family narratives within an extended familial context, as well as a broader societal context. These interactions, and most notably the ones that convey disapproval and rejection of the multiracial family unit, place a strain on the multiracial family that can be detrimental to the well-being of the unit as a whole (Milan & Keiley, 2000; Rockquemore & Laszloffy, 2005). We have discussed the competing narratives of "promise" and "problem" at the level of the social and cultural structure. Now we wish to turn to the negotiation that occurs between those Stories and the stories of multiracial family and individual experience. One of the central bridges that parents in interracial families have navigated out of utter necessity is racial socialization.

Beginning at a very young age, racial socialization occurs daily through parents' and family members' messages regarding race that shape children's racial self-understandings, their perceptions of racial label availability (Bratter, 2007; Rockquemore & Laszloffy, 2005), and their acknowledgment that they will actively face racialized experiences throughout their lives. Studies of racial socialization emerged in the 1980s and focused on the messages regarding race that were central to the child-rearing practices common within Black families (Boykin & Toms, 1985; Peters, 1985; Phinney & Chavira, 1995). Instilling racial pride, cultivating a healthy self-concept, and preparing a child for racial biases are strategies utilized by Black parents who aim to condition their child for the reality of racism that persists in this country (Boykin & Toms, 1985; Cross, 1971). Though much of the early literature focused on the unique strategies employed by Black parents and family members, there has been an emergence of studies that examine these processes within White and multiracial families.

· Within White families, parental racial socialization often involves messages that are conveyed indirectly when there is a general silence on matters of race. The lack of attention paid to issues regarding race by White parents, or their avoidance of topics pertaining to race, communicates and perpetuates privilege for their children (Hamm, 2001; Rockquemore, Laszloffy, & Noveske, 2006). Often the silence regarding matters of race conveys the notion that "race" refers to non-Whites, indirectly promoting a lack of awareness of oneself as a racialized being. The contrast between racial socialization by parents in White families and parents in Black families (Hamm, 2001) precipitated analyses of racial socialization within multiracial families. Subsequent studies have explored the complexities of that process, and the issues that arise for monoracial parents who are raising biracial children (Fatimilehin, 1999; Rockquemore & Brunsma, 2008).

Parents of biracial children can nurture their child's development of a healthy racial identity that can result in any of a number of identity outcomes. In their COBI (Continuum of Biracial Identity) model, Rockquemore and Laszloffy (2005) outline the diverse ways that biracial individuals racially identify themselves, shifting the assertions of previous models that rigidly place value on specific identity outcomes, such as biracial or Black, as exclusively healthy labels. Instead they assert that a healthy racial identity is achieved through pathways where the individual's self-understanding is, "shaped by cognitive and emotional acceptance of the fact of having one White and one Black parent" (Rockquemore & Laszloffy, 2005, p. 34). Those pathways can lead to a number of healthy **racial identification** outcomes, and parents are integral to this identity-formation process whether they initiate the process or if guidance is solicited by their children. Ultimately, parents influence how biracial children navigate the racial identity options available to them (Bowles, 1993; Kerwin, Ponterotto, Jackson, & Harris, 1993; Kich, 1992; Rockquemore & Laszloffy, 2005; Root, 1992) and the racial ideologies held by parents, irrespective of their race, often dictate the nature of the messages they convey pertaining to race, as well as their views regarding the scope of legitimate racial identity options available for their biracial child (Rockquemore et al. 2006).

Research conducted by Porow (2014), drawing upon data from 22 qualitative, semi-structured interviews with adult Black-White biracial respondents, yielded findings that elucidate the approaches to racial socialization employed by monoracial parents. This study shed light on the nature of parental influence on the biracial identity development process. This analysis uncovered a tendency for parents to assign specific racial labels when ascribing them collaboratively versus independently. Among respondents in Porow's (2014) study, biracial individuals who reported that both of their parents engaged in the process of explicit racial label ascription, also referred to as **dual-parental racial ascription**, often reported that their parents ascribed a blended racial label that incorporated the racial identity of both parents (e.g., biracial, mixed), or their parents deemphasized the importance of racial labels. Among biracial respondents who reported that only one of their parents ascribed a racial label, also referred to as **sole-parental racial ascription**, there was a tendency for a sole White parent to assign a blended racial label, and a tendency for a sole Black parent to ascribe a Black racial label.

Patterns uncovered among respondent narratives reflect the complexity of parental racial influence. Those patterns suggest that the most effective aspect of a parental approach to racial ascription is the collaborative dynamic. Among respondent narratives of accounts of dual-parental racial ascription, many respondents reported adopting the racial labels ascribed by their parents, citing their guidance as the reason, and often maintained those racial identifications into adulthood. This pattern also held among the cases of dual-parental racial ascription involving parents who ascribed a Black identity. For respondents who detailed accounts of sole-parental racial ascription, two patterns emerged. When a mother was reported as the sole-parental racial ascriber, there was a tendency for the respondent to cite her as having influenced their racial identification choices, a pattern that held irrespective of the mother's race. In contrast, Black fathers constituted the majority of the fathers who were identified as sole-parental racial ascribers, and there was a strong tendency for respondents to report aversions to his racial ascription.

These patterns offer a wealth of information for clinicians who seek to better understand healthy racial identity development pathways. Most importantly, it broadens the focus of our analysis, taking into consideration both the parent dynamic involved in the process of parental racial socialization, and making recommendations for collaborative engagement in racial socialization efforts, if possible. Second, it considers the way in which parental influence lies at intersection of race and gender for parents who engage in racial ascription independent of their child's other parent, at least for parents in Black–White interracial relationships. The latter point is of great relevance for professionals who seek to assist the members of single-parent multiracial households, which are predominantly composed of biracial children and their White mothers (Brunsma, 2005). There are many challenges beyond those that arise within the racial socialization process, that uniquely impact multiracial families consisting of biracial children being raised by a single, monoracial parent.

Given the cultural Story of physical similarities within families, what families and their offspring should "look like," biracial children and their monoracial parents often face challenges in their communities and local institutions. In particular, when bystanders observe a parent and a child who appear racially dissimilar, they are often subjected to microaggressions that cast doubt on the legitimacy of the parent–child relationship.

This can occur in various contexts, and as early as a child's infant stages. When an adult and a child are together and appear to be the same race, a parent–child dynamic is often automatically granted, whether or not that is the actual nature of their relationship. However, White and Black parents of biracial children are often questioned about their relationship with/connection to their biracial children, even in contexts where a parenting dynamic is evident. The parents of biracial children are often challenged by others to authenticate their relationship to their child. At times this may be innocuous; at others it may be disconcerting; however, in most cases, the experience is invalidating.

In 2013, a widely reported incident occurred in a Virginia Walmart that illustrates the potential risks and trauma of exclusionary family narratives (Moran, 2013). In 2013, a seemingly concerned customer observed Joseph shopping with his three biracial girls. Unbeknownst to Joseph who is White, that customer alerted Walmart security that the three young girls did not "fit" with the man accompanying them. After completing his purchase, Joseph and his family headed home where he was met by a police officer. Joseph recalls, "He asks us very sincerely, 'Hey, I was sent here by Walmart security. I just need to make sure that the children that you have are your own.'" Joseph continues, "He took my ID and asked my 4-year-old to point out who her mother and father were." The limited, and pervasive, conceptualization of the family in this country results in a common inability to recognize racially and physically dissimilar people as members of the same family. In this case, that limited perspective resulted in an accusation of kidnapping, as well as the criminalization of the parent–child relationship between a White father and his biracial girls.

Multiracial families experience a great deal of societal disapproval that shapes their personal stories; however, they also deal with similar levels of disfavor and rejection within the context of their own extended families. In a study conducted by Pew Research Center (Wang, 2012), in 2010, more than one-third of Americans (35%) reported that a member of their immediate family or a close relative was currently married to someone of a different race, and nearly two-thirds of Americans (63%) said it "would be fine" with them if a member of their own family were to marry someone outside their own racial or ethnic group (Wang, 2012). These findings represent a snapshot of the multiracial family "promise" discussed in the previous section; however, interracial couples and their biracial children still frequently report experiences where their extended family members regard them as the "problem." This is evidenced by respondent Amanda's experience with her father's side of the family (Porow, 2014). Raised in a suburb of California by both her parents, Amanda explains that her racial identity was strongly impacted by her Black mother and her mother's side of the family. She described her relationship with her relatives on her father's side of the family as minimal, attributing that to physical distance and the dynamic established by her White grand-mother. Amanda explained:

We saw her—you know, a decent amount of times, I guess, all things considered, for a woman that lived in another state. But we probably would have seen her more if she had been willing to see my mother, but she wasn't. She would come with [Amanda's mother], but then my grandmother would not let her in the house, So . . . we would go in the house . . . . we would all pack up and drive to Tucson, we'd get to my grandmother's house, Mom would make an excuse and say she wanted to go to the hotel because she was tired, and we would stay with my grandmother and my father, and then mom would come and get us later.

This pattern continued for years. At around the age of 12, Amanda learned of her grandmother's racist exclusion of her Black mother from family visits with her father's extended family:

I was about 12. My mom told me. She said, "Your grandmother is a racist." She was very straightforward. I was like, "Okay." You know? And I said, "Well, why would you say that?" and she told me the whole thing, and I said, "Wow! I didn't know that about Grandma." And you know, then I asked her the obvious question, which was, "Well, then why the heck does she let us in the house?" My mom was like, "I don't know." She was like, "'Cause you guys were her grandchildren. It was different to her."

Amanda explained that her grandmother was always open and receptive to her and her siblings, but when Amanda discovered the reason that her mother never accompanied the rest of the family inside their grandmoth-er's house, her feelings shifted, as did her interest in exerting the effort to maintain her relationship with her grandmother. It remains common for interracial couples and their multiracial children to experience opposition from extended family members, which can range from subtle comments and snubs to outright rejection and severed family ties. Studies of multi-racial families suggest that within White extended families, grandparents, most often grandmothers, are the most commonly cited family members who express disapproval or reject the multiracial family (Childs 2006; DaCosta 2007; Porow, 2014).

MULTIRACIAL LIVES AT THE INTERSECTIONS

Central to the push toward multicultural competence is a challenge to resist clinical conventions that homogenize the experiences of bira-cial people, interracial couples, and multiracial families. The nuances of biracial identity and the multiracial family's experiences require that we scrutinize their multidimensionality, employing a discourse that articu-lates heterogeneity. Many of the essential questions that clinicians should consider must grapple with productive ways to acknowledge and address variation within these various populations. For example, monoracial mothers with biracial children who don't share the same complexion, hair texture, and so on have frequent encounters with people who inquire about their relationship to their child (Kilson & Ladd, 2009; Martin, 2010; Sitt, 2012). Therapeutic consideration of how to cope with/address the common inquiry "Is that your child?" will fall short if there is a failure to address the variation among intragroup experiences (Kilson & Ladd, 2009; Martin, 2010; Sitt, 2012). Not only are these interrogations racialized gender experiences, but they often involve class and region as well. Consequently, failing to attend to the vastly different framing commonly utilized to interrogate White mothers and Black mothers precludes the use of effective therapeutic strategies for those patients. White and Black mothers are often mistakenly assigned roles where they occupy a very different status. When a Black mother's parental status is questioned by others, it is often shrouded in racialized, class-laden assumptions that she is her own child's nanny (Martin, 2010; Sitt, 2012). However, when a White mother's parental status is questioned, other racialized, class-laden assessments are made. White mothers are often mistakenly identified as their biracial child's adoptive parent (Martha, 2013).

The race of both mothers and fathers play a complex role in the racial socialization of biracial youth, as parenting is negotiated in ways that are often race-specific (Brunsma, 2005; Herman, 2004; Miville, Constantine, Baysden, & So-Lloyd, 2005). White fathers who raise biracial sons are particularly relevant to this discussion. Parenting at the intersection of race, gender, and class, in the midst of rising tensions between law enforcement and the general public, can pose a challenge to White fathers. Being male and White provides a level of privilege and protection that isn't granted or extended to a White father's biracial sons. Such privilege also informs how White fathers will approach the racial socialization of their biracial children. Studies have shown that White parents often engage in racial socialization in reactive ways by addressing inquiries and issues when they arise (Katz & Kofkin, 1997). However, parents also generally prepare their children for the bias that they believe their child will encounter (Rockquemore & Laszloffy, 2005). This is indeed a precarious position for many White fathers, some of whom are vigilant of the alarming spike in deaths of unarmed Black people and people of color, and others who may not be aware of the implications for their biracial child, who based on physical appearance, may be perceived as Black.

Mayor Bill de Blasio of New York vocalized his concerns about raising a Black son as a White man in a post-Trayvon Martin society (Durkin, 2014). He and his wife, who is Black, have taken special pains to teach their son how to navigate social space and mediate conflict with those in authority, given his son's Black physical appearance. White parents who raise biracial children must confront race in ways that they have never been required to in the past, or risk having their child navigate society unprepared for the ills of racial injustice and discrimination. While DeBlasio's level of racial awareness as a White man is uncommon, his status as a White father of a biracial son may be more common. In an article titled "Living Color: Fathers Talk to Their Bi-Racial Sons" (Chung, 2015), several White fathers of biracial sons shared their feelings about teaching their sons lessons that they never had to learn. Many fathers addressed the challenge of being explicit about matters of race within a postracial climate that discourages discussions about race and racism. Mark, a White father of a 22-year-old biracial son, described how his social positioning impacts his approach to discussions about race as a White man in a multiracial family. He explains:

It's easier for me to talk to people of color about issues of race than it is to talk to White people about race. It's not something that's on their minds when they get up in the morning. It's on my mind when I get up in the morning, because of the house that I'm living in. I have a Black son, I have a Black wife, I have a Black daughter. I don't have to worry about it, but I have to worry about it for them.

Mark's feelings capture the challenges faced by White parents of biracial children, the intersections at which he experiences race as a White man in a multiracial family, and a concern shared by most parents of children of color who bear the weight of preparing their child to navigate a society where they are more likely to experience differential treatment and discrimination at the hands of law enforcement when compared to their White peers. These unique circumstances challenge White fathers to engage in approaches to racial socialization that are unfamiliar, yet necessary.

While White fathers of biracial sons, like de Blasio and Mark, heed the urgency to discuss matters of race in order to prepare their sons for potentially threatening situations with law enforcement, other White fathers like Thomas are more compelled by their fear of unjust and targeted law enforcement practices that could potentially victimize their sons. Thomas expressed the sentiment that he can best protect his son by removing him from the threatening environment that he cannot control. He explained his feelings about his 8-year-old son, James:

I fear for him, you know, because even as a young man even in England, I was pulled over by police just because I was a young man, you know with maybe the hat on. As a Black young man you get that even more just because you are a young Black man and they are going to assume immediately you're up to no good. And you know it's just doubly dangerous here. And so in the light of recent events, I'm thinking, you know at some point, I just might want to move, you know? The police aren't armed in the UK, he may get pulled over there, but there's not going to be a light trigger finger that I have to worry about. He'll at least come home alive.

Thomas recognized that his biracial son will experience discrimination in the United States as well as in the United Kingdom; however, his heightened fears of raising his son in the United States result from his perception of the potential risks of him navigating a society with increasingly troubling law enforcement practices that are rampant and disproportionately impact people of color. White parents of biracial children are faced with the complex task of preparing them for bias that they have never experienced first-hand. That reality underscores the need for knowledgeable sources of counsel for parents teaching their biracial children how to navigate racial tensions, especially tensions that may pose a physical threat.

CONCLUSIONS

It is significant that the book you now hold in your hands seeks, in a conscientious and concerted way, to bring together a wealth of empirical, theoretical, and methodological approaches, from multiple disciplines, in order to put the best knowledge together in order to inform a 21st-century set of best practices in working with diverse families and their children. From our review here, despite the fact that clinicians, counselors, and therapists who work with both biracial individuals and interracial families most likely do not share the experience of being multiracial in a racist society, we highlight some basic insights that likely would enhance the therapeutic relationship. In order to more effectively work with these families and their biracial offspring, we believe that the literature currently points to four basic points.

First, practitioners would do well to understand that multiracial families and their children are currently interacting within a social and cultural fabric that considers them both a promise and a problem. Acknowledging such a position provides crucial historical context and highlights the everyday variations on this theme that may be faced. Second, and relatedly, the Story of race and being multiracial is continuously being narrated throughout the dominant institutions in our society. Such narratives form the storied, cultural backdrop for the stage where multiracial families and individuals plot their own stories every day. Often, these two stories are at odds with each other. Understanding this reality as we listen to the voices of those navigating their everyday lives, throughout their life course, is also very important.

Third, those who work closely with interracial families as well as multiracial individuals are tasked with yet another difficult, but ever so important, charge, which is to recognize the positional realities of these families and individuals. This is to say that families and individuals both must be seen holistically *as* located in the intersections of race, class, gender, region, and so on in highly complex ways that we are only now beginning to scratch the surface of understanding. While "intersectionality" is the dominant reality, we are often socialized and trained to work on the components of identity one at a time, such as race or gender, thus stripping families and individuals of their complexity. Finally, there is still no doubt that for these same multiracial families and individuals who exist in that complexity, perceptions by others are still rooted in racial ideology. Thus, the current approach is to be color-blind and not see race, or to see America as postracial. Racial ideologies often lay the conceptual groundwork for both therapists and their clients, making racialized experiences seem murky, censored, veiled, and sometimes be silenced. Despite the heralding of contemporary racial ideology, multiracial families and individuals need *more* discussion of race and racism, not less.

CHAPTER REVIEW

Key Points

1. Biracial individuals, interracial couples, and multiracial families experience unique challenges that require therapists to familiarize themselves with the knowledge and skills necessary to address the needs of this population.
2. Because of the history of the United States and the contemporary social and cultural context, multiracial families and their offspring are experientially positioned as both a promise and a problem in American society.
3. The social and cultural story that gives us a narrative with which to understand the multiracial family and the experience of multiracial individuals exists in concert and deep challenge with the experiences of those same families and individuals as they really occur in everyday life.
4. Multiracial families and their children exist within a complicated intersection of race, gender, class, region, and other social locations that serve as crucial lenses through which to understand their lives.
5. The contemporary period in which multiracial families and individuals live, and in which their therapists work, is one characterized by a nonracial lens on clearly racial experiences—color-blindness will not help us work with multiracial clients.

Key Terms

biracial, color-blind ideology, dual-parent racial ascription, intersectionality, microaggressions, multiracial, racial identification, racial identity, racial socialization, representations, sole-parental racial ascription

Myths and Realities

- While it is a myth that therapists who work with multiracial individuals and their families must themselves be multiracial, therapists must be armed with knowledge of the unique issues faced by multiracial families in order to develop the skills they need to effectively work with these families and their biracial offspring.
- Though the dominant ideology of color-blindness encourages individuals and communities to dismiss racism as a thing of the past, the reality is

that racism, racial microaggressions, and racial inequalities still exist in the 21st century. The myth that they do not is part and parcel of the dominant ideology of color-blindness. Pretending that race no longer matters is not the same thing as working to end racism.

- It is a myth that interracial couples and/or their multiracial children are accepted in contemporary society. Indeed, they are "more" accepted than they once were in a different set of racial structures and ideologies; however, if one listens closely to their stories and not only the Story of the larger (read: White) culture of "acceptance," one will begin to understand the reality of their nonacceptance.
- The idea that the experiences of interracial couples and/or multiracial individuals are monolithic is patently a myth—one that has led to misspecifications in our models of intervention. The experiences of interracial couples and multiracial individuals are deeply complex, intimately tied to context, and emerging from an intersectional positionality within the matrix of experience.

Tools and Tips

Knowledge

Bonilla-Silva, E. (2013). *Racism without racists: Colorblind racism and the persistence of racial inequality in the United States.* Lanham, MD: Rowman & Littlefield.

Brunsma, D. (Ed.). 2006. *Mixed messages: Multiracial identities in the "color blind" era.* Boulder, CO: Lynne Rienner.

Childs, E. C. (2005). *Navigating interracial borders: Black-White couples and their social worlds.* Piscataway, NJ: Rutgers University Press.

DaCosta, K. M. (2007). *Making multiracials: State, family, and market in the redrawing of the color line.* Stanford, CA: Stanford University Press.

Kilson, M., & Ladd, F. (2009). *Is that your child? Mothers talk about rearing biracial children.* Lanham, MD: Lexington Books.

Rockquemore, K. A., & Brunsma, D. L. (2008). *Beyond Black: Biracial identity in America* (2nd ed.). Lanham, MD: Rowman & Littlefield.

Rockquemore, K. A., & Laszloffy, T. (2005). *Raising biracial children.* Lanham, MD: Altamira Press.

Dynamic Sizing

Practitioners should work to understand the dynamic relationship between the stories their clients bring to the office and the Stories within which their lives are culturally, socially, and politically embedded. Recognizing that both are critical in their clients' experiences and identities is a central concern when working with these individuals. Listening to and documenting these stories, as well as listening closely to and discussing the third "stories"—those of the everyday navigating between these two—will be a key dynamic in the intervention.

Skills

Theory. To develop theoretical approaches to multiracial individuals and interracial couples requires a combination of critical sociologies and social psychologies of race and ethnicity, feminist understandings of intersectionalities, and work on racial ideologies and racial microaggressions.

Prevention. Multiracial individuals and those in interracial relationships first and foremost need practitioners who understand how to listen *beyond* the contemporary (or even historical) dominant racial ideologies. In lieu of significant others who may be mired in dominant racial ideology, the therapist's room should be a safe place where racial understanding is real and not fully connected to the dominant narratives of the society these individuals live within.

Service Provision. Counselors and family therapists should, when possible, work (or think) together when approaching interracial couples and/or multiracial individuals (who themselves are the offspring of interracial unions), since the individual narratives of multiracial people and the experiences of interracial families are intimately intertwined. Understanding both will be important to provide useful models and interventions for individuals and/or their families.

Policy. The mass media continues to project very limited representations of multiraciality and interracial relationships. Such representations sediment into our daily interactions within our dominant institutions such as schools, churches, the military, and so on. Closer attention to the unequal structures of media ownership and conglomeration that provide these misrepresentations to the populace would go a long way toward altering the realities our clients face on the ground.

Research. Scholarship on the counseling and therapeutic interventions of multiracial people and their interracial families should move quickly beyond the Black/White binary and incorporate the realities of the variability present in multiracial and interracial experiences. Both intersectionality and social context will provide more fruitful models.

Awareness

When dealing with things racial in the United States, in many ways, believing is seeing (not the other way around). What we see is socially and culturally motivated by the dominant racial ideologies of the day. As such, the keenest counselor will be the one who can recognize and be vigilantly aware that color-blind ideology (the idea that race no longer matters) is central to the experiences of multiracials, the ways that interracial couples narrate their experiences, and that recognizing, despite this ideological trapping, that racism is still daily and personally very real for our clients will lead to the strongest, positive outcomes.

REFERENCES

Bonilla-Silva, E. (2013). *Racism without racists: Colorblind racism and the persistence of racial inequality in the United States*. Lanham, MD: Rowman & Littlefield.

Bowles, D. (1993). Bi-racial identity: Children born to African-American and White couples. *Clinical Social Work Journal, 21*, 417–428.

Boykin, A. W., & Toms, F. D. (1985). Black child socialization framework: A conceptual framework. In H. P. McAdoo & J. L. McAdoo (Eds.), *Black children: Social educational and parental environments* (pp. 33–35). Thousand Oaks, CA: Sage Publications.

Bratter, J. (2007). Will "multiracial" survive to the next generation?: The racial classification of children of multiracial parents. *Social Forces, 86*, 821–849.

Bratter, J., & King, R. (2008). But will it last?: Duration of interracial unions compared to similar race relationships. *Family Relations, 57*, 160–171.

Brunsma, D. L. (2005). Interracial families and the racial identification of mixed-race children: Evidence from the early childhood longitudinal study. *Social Forces, 84*, 1129–1155.

Brunsma, D. L. (2006). Public categories, Private identities: Exploring regional differences in the Biracial experience. *Social Science Research, 35*, 555–576.

Brunsma, D. L. (2011). Now you don't see it, now you don't: White lives as covert racism. In Rodney Coates (Ed.), *Covert racism* (pp. 321–332). London, England: Oxford University Press.

Childs, E. C. (2005). *Navigating interracial borders: Black-White couples and their social worlds*. Piscataway, NJ: Rutgers University Press.

Childs, E. C. (2006). Black and White: Family opposition to becoming multiracial. In David Brunsma (Ed.), *Mixed messages: Multiracial identities in the "colorblind" era* (pp. 233–246). Boulder, CO: Lynne Rienner Publishers.

Chung, A. (2015, January 14). *Living color: Fathers talk to their bi-racial sons*. Retrieved from http://www.nbcnews.com/news/nbcblk/living-color-fathers-talk-their-bi-racial-sons-n286386

Collins, P. H. (2006). *From Black power to hip hop: Racism, nationalism, and feminism*. Philadelphia, PA: Temple University Press.

Crawford, S. E., & Allagia, R. (2008). The best of both worlds? Family influences on mixed race youth identity development. *Qualitative Social Work, 7*, 81–98.

Cross, W. (1971). The Negro-to-Black conversion experience: Toward a psychology of Black liberation. *Black World, 20*(9), 13–27.

DaCosta, K. M. (2007). *Making multiracials: State, family, and market in the redrawing of the color line*. Stanford, CA: Stanford University Press.

Dalmage, H. (2000). *Tripping on the color line: Black/White multiracial families in a racially divided world*. Piscataway, NJ: Rutgers University Press.

Durkin, E. (2014, December 7). Bill de Blasio details talk with biracial son about interacting with police: You "train them to be very careful when they have . . . an encounter with a police officer." Retrieved from http://www.nydailynews.com/news/politics/de-blasio-http://www.nydailynews.com/news/politics/de-blasio-details-talk-son-dealing-cops-article-1.2036870

Edwards, L. M., & Pedrotti, J. T. (2008). A content and methodological review of articles concerning multiracial issues in six major counseling journals. *Journal of Counseling Psychology, 55*, 411–418.

Fatimilehin, I. A. (1999). Of jewel heritage: Racial socialization and racial identity attitudes amongst adolescents of mixed African-Caribbean/White parentage. *Journal of Adolescence, 22*, 303–318.

Fusco, R. A. (2010). Intimate partner violence in interracial couples: A comparison to White and ethnic minority monoracial couples. *Journal of Interpersonal Violence, 25*, 1785–1800.

Hamm, J. V. (2001). Barriers and bridges to positive cross-ethnic relations: African American and White parent socialization beliefs and practices. *Youth and Society, 33*, 62–98.

Herman, M. (2004). Forced to choose: some determinants of racial identification in multiracial adolescents. *Child Development, 75*, 730 748.

Herring, C., Keith, V., & Horton, H. D. (Eds.). (2004). *Skin deep: How race and complexion matter in the "color-blind" era.* Champaign, IL: University of Illinois Press.

Jackson, K. F., & Samuels, G. M. (2011). Multiracial competence in social work: Recommendations for culturally attuned work with multiracial people. *Social Work, 56*, 235–245.

Katz, P. A., & Kofkin, J. A. (1997). Race, gender, and young children. In S. S. Luthar, J. A. Burack, D. Cicchetti, & J. R. Weisz (Eds.), *Developmental psychopathology: Perspectives on adjustment, risk, and disorder* (pp. 51–74). New York, NY: Cambridge University Press.

Kerwin, C., Ponterotto, J. G., Jackson, B. L., & Harris, A. (1993). Racial identity in biracial children: A qualitative investigation. *Journal of Counseling Psychology, 40*, 221–231.

Kich, G. (1992). The developmental process of asserting a biracial, bicultural identity. In M. Root (Ed.), *Racially mixed people in America* (pp. 304–317). Thousand Oaks, CA: Sage Publications.

Killian, K. D. (2001). Reconstituting racial histories and identities: The narratives of interracial couples. *Journal of Marital and Family Therapy, 27*, 27–42.

Kilson, M., & Ladd, F. (2009). *Is that your child? Mothers talk about rearing biracial children.* Lanham, MD: Lexington Books.

Martha. (2013, August 20). Talking to my biracial child about why people think she's adopted. [Blog post]. Retrieved from http://www.momsoap.com/2013/08/talking-to-my-biracial-child-about-why-people-think-shes-adopted/

Martin, M. (Narrator). (2010). *No, I am not the nanny.* Washington, DC: National Public Radio.

McClurg, L. (2004). Biracial youth and their parents: Counseling considerations for family therapists. *The Family Journal, 12*, 170–173.

McDowell, T. (2015). *Applying critical social theories to family therapy practice.* New York, NY: Springer.

Milan, S., & Keiley, M. K. (2000). Biracial youth and families in therapy: Issues and interventions. *Journal of Marital and Family Therapy, 26*, 305–366.

Miville, M. L., Constantine, M. G., Baysden, M. F., & So-Lloyd, G. (2005). Chameleon changes: An exploration of racial identity themes of multiracial people. *Journal of Counseling Psychology, 52*, 507–516.

Moran, L. (2013, May 22). *White dad falsely accused of kidnapping own biracial daughters during Wal-Mart shopping trip.* Retrieved from http://www.nydailynews.com/news/national/white-dad-falsely-accused-kidnapping-biracial-daughters-walmart-shopping-trip-article-1.1351429

Peters, M. F. (1985). Racial socialization of young Black children. In H. McAdoo & J. McAdoo (Eds.), *Black children: Social, educational, and parental environments* (pp.159–173). Beverly Hills, CA: Sage Publications.

Phinney, J. S., & Chavira, V. (1995). Parental ethnic socialization and adolescent coping with problems related to ethnicity. *Journal of Research on Adolescence, 5,* 31–53.

Porow, M. (2014). *A comparative study of familial racial socialization and its impact on Black/White biracial siblings* (Doctoral dissertation). Available from ProQuest Dissertations & Theses database. (Accession Order No. AAT 3643340).

Renn, K. A. (2008). Research on biracial and multiracial identity development: Overview and synthesis. *New Directions for Student Services, 2008*(123), 13–21. doi: 10.1002/ss.282

Risman, B. (Ed.). (2009). *Families as they really are.* New York, NY: W. W. Norton.

Rockquemore, K. A., & Brunsma, D. L. (2001). *Beyond Black: Biracial identity in America.* Thousand Oaks, CA: Sage Publications.

Rockquemore, K. A., & Brunsma, D. L. (2008). *Beyond Black: Biracial identity in America* (2nd ed.). Lanham, MD: Rowman & Littlefield.

Rockquemore, K. A., Brunsma, D. L., & Delgado, D. J. (2009). Racing to theory or retheorizing race? Understanding the struggle to build a multiracial identity theory. *Journal of Social Issues, 65,* 13–34. doi: 10.1111/j.1540-4560.2008.01585.x

Rockquemore, K. A., & Laszloffy, T. (2005). *Raising biracial children.* Lanham, MD: Altamira Press.

Rockquemore, K. A., Laszloffy, T., & Noveske, J. (2006). It all starts at home: Racial socialization in multiracial families. In D. Brunsma (Ed.), *Mixed messages: Multiracial identities in the "color blind" era* (pp. 203–216). Boulder, CO: Lynne Rienner.

Root, M. P. (1992). Within, between, and beyond race. In M. Root (Ed.), *Racially mixed people in America* (pp.3–11). Newbury Park, CA: Sage Publications.

Sitt, P. (2012, June 28). No, I'm not the nanny: When you don't look like your kids. *Today Moms,* pp. 1–3.

Wang, W. (2012, February 16). *The rise of intermarriage: Rates, characteristics vary by race and gender.* Retrieved from http://www.pewsocialtrends.org/files/2012/02/SDT-Intermarriage-II.pdf

Wardle, F. (1993, March/April). Inter-racial families and biracial children. *Child Care Information Exchange, 90,* 45–48.

Wilt, J. (2011). Normal families facing unique challenges: The psychosocial functioning of multiracial couples, parents and children. *The New School Psychology Bulletin, 9,* 7–14.

Wong, G., Derthick, A. O., David, E. J. R., Saw, A., & Okazaki, S. (2014). The what, the why, and the how: A review of racial microaggressions research in psychology. *Race and Social Problems, 6,* 181–200. doi: 10.1007/s12552-013-9107-9

Yancey, G. A., & Lewis, R., Jr. (2009). *Interracial families: Current concepts and controversies.* New York, NY: Routledge.

Zhang, Y., & Van Hook, J. (2009). Marital dissolution among interracial couples. *Journal of Marriage and Family, 71,* 95–107.

CHAPTER 12

Intercultural Couples and Families

Traci P. Maynigo

With increased globalization, immigration, and technological advances worldwide, individuals of different cultures and faiths are interacting with one another much more frequently, increasing the probability of the formation of intimate intercultural couple relationships (Bustamante et al., 2011). Despite the national proliferation of these relationships, limited scholarship exists to guide therapists in the treatment of intercultural couples and families (Bustamante et al., 2011; Sullivan & Cottone, 2006). **Intercultural couple** is defined as two people in a committed, intimate relationship who each represent different cultures, including ethnicities, races, faiths, or religions (Perel, 2000). Such a blending of two cultures in this vulnerable context often yields challenges not typically faced by those in same-culture relationships. Successfully navigating these challenges more often than not can be an enriching experience for these couples and families. This chapter provides a review of scholarship to help therapists better understand this growing population, so that they can guide these families toward thriving cross-cultural connections.

HISTORY AND DEMOGRAPHICS

The historical narrative of intercultural relationships in the United States begins with the country's history of racial classification. Since the beginning of slavery, the dominant White racial group has sought to maintain a **racial classification** system with the purpose of giving rights to some and denying rights to others, so that one group can preserve its dominance (Lee & Bean, 2007; Prewitt, 2005). Although the word "race" was initially intended to indicate biological or ancestral transmission of commonality, racial categories are in fact arbitrary social constructs (Brammer, 2004). The arbitrary and transitory nature of racial classification is evident in the frequent changes to these classifications made by the U.S. Census since the category of race was first included in the 1820 census. The number of racial classifications has doubled from 8 in 1890 to 16 in 2000 (Henrikson & Paladino, 2009). **Anti-miscegenation laws** were created to perpetuate these racial categories, maintain racial purity, and justify slavery. By the 1920s, more than half of the United States had enacted anti-miscegenation laws (Henrikson & Paladino, 2009). With the landmark *Loving v. Virginia* (1967) Supreme Court decision came a historical end to anti-miscegenation laws; they were declared unconstitutional, ending marriage restrictions based on race (Henrikson & Paladino, 2009).

Shifts in immigration after World War II also increased the prevalence of intercultural unions. Before 1960, about 80 percent of immigrants entering the United States came from Europe. By the 1990s, more than 80 percent of the more than one million legal immigrants entering the United States each year were non-European, with most coming from Latin America, the Caribbean, and Asia (Crohn, 1998). Many of these immigrants choose to marry partners from other groups. By 1992, 65 percent of the children and grandchildren of the Japanese Americans who were interned during World War II chose European American partners (Crohn, 1998).

The number of intercultural couples has continued to grow rapidly in the United States. Between 2000 and 2010, opposite-sex interracial or intercultural couples grew by 28 percent from 7 percent in 2000 to 10 percent in 2010 (U.S. Census Bureau, 2012). In 2010, about 15 percent of new marriages were intercultural, double from 1980 (Wang, 2012). Additionally, 18 percent of opposite-sex unmarried partners and 21 percent of same-sex unmarried partners were interracial or interethnic, a higher percentage compared to 10 percent of married partners (U.S. Census Bureau, 2012). Currently, 1 in 7 marriages is intercultural, and 1 in 12 marriages is interracial (Falicov, 2014b).

Although intercultural couples have always existed, societal changes have promoted greater acceptance, suggesting that they are likely to increase rapidly in the future. This greater public acceptance is evident in that 43 percent of Americans say that intermarriage is good for society, 11 percent say it is worse, and 44 percent are indifferent (Wang, 2012). In addition, 63 percent of Americans say that they would be accepting if a family member married outside of their own race and ethnicity, a number that is double from the late 1980s (Falicov, 2014b).

CULTURAL COMMONALITIES

Theoretical Frameworks for Understanding Intercultural Couples and Families

Individualism-Collectivism Cultural "Syndrome"

The **individualism-collectivism cultural "syndrome"** has been considered the most significant difference among cultures (Triandis, 2005). While **individualism** values the individual over the in-group, and promotes autonomy, personal responsibility, personal initiative, self-efficiency, and privacy, **collectivism** values the in-group over the individual, and promotes group harmony and loyalty, in-group conformity, and avoidance of in-group conflict (Kellner, 2009; Ting-Toomey, 2009). The individualism-collectivism dimension can be further defined according to four attributes: self, goals, relationship, and determinants of behavior (Triandis, 2005). While collectivism promotes interdependent selves, individualism promotes the independent self. While in collectivistic cultures in-group goals are prioritized, in individualistic cultures personal goals are favored instead. While collectivism encourages relatedness and communal relationships, individualism encourages rationality and interpersonal exchange. Finally, while in collectivistic cultures traditions or norms are considered more important determinants of behavior, in individualistic cultures attitudes are considered more important determinants of behavior. Although individualism-collectivism is best understood as a continuum rather than a dichotomy, American, Australian, Canadian, German, and Scandinavian cultures tend to be more individualistic, while African, Asian, Latin, and Mediterranean cultures tend to be more collectivistic (Kellner, 2009).

These differences in cultural structures impact relationships by influencing connection and autonomy (Ting-Toomey, 2009), particularly when one partner comes from a more individualistic culture and the other comes from a more collectivistic culture. Individualistic couples create a strong boundary between their relationship and the social world to ensure privacy. Individualistic couples also are more likely to confront one another during disagreement, while collectivist couples are more focused on family dynamics, and making their relationship part of the extended family, rather than private (Ting-Toomey, 2009). Given that cultures are mapped along a continuum from individualism to collectivism, this conceptual framework can be used for tracking cultural differences in intercultural couples. Kellner (2009) suggests using a "cultural compass" to help bring differences along this continuum into awareness, with a particular focus on parameters such as emotional expressiveness, continuum of autonomy, gender differentiation, and sexuality.

Ecological Systems Theory

Other scholars have used **ecological systems theory** to understand the development and experiences of intercultural couples. Bronfenbrenner's (1986) ecological model explains couples' entry and adjustment into an intercultural relationship (Silva, Campbell, & Wright, 2012). At the broadest environmental level, the **macrosystem**, individuals from different cultures interact as a result of immigration and globalization, travel, and **acculturation**. Immigrants who have resided longer in a country are more likely to marry interculturally, and such marriages become increasingly more common in later generations as families acculturate (Silva et al., 2012). Also more likely to marry interculturally are individuals whose countries of origin are more accepting of immigrants, who live in major cities near ethnic enclaves, and who have knowledge of and positive contact with those of different cultures (Silva et al., 2012). Intercultural partners tend to come from different macrosystems, making couple conflict harder to manage (Silva et al., 2012). Partners are best able to adjust when they are acculturated to, respectful of, and adopt aspects of each other's cultures (Silva et al., 2012). At the **exosystem** level are the communities in which intercultural couples live. Entry into such relationships is more likely in communities that are accepting and inclusive of different cultures (Silva et al., 2012). Exclusive communities are less likely to nurture entry into such unions, and can also affect couple adjustment to the relationship, putting them at risk for increased marital conflict and divorce. Disapproval by religious and other social institutions can manifest in the form of financial or social estrangement, or even outright hostility, thus influencing how intercultural relationships are viewed by the community (Silva et al., 2012). The **microsystem** level of the family has the greatest influence on entry and adjustment into intercultural relationships (Silva et al., 2012). The more children are exposed to different cultural groups, the more likely they will have friendships and romantic relationships with members of other cultural groups. Families, when accepting, can be a tremendous source of support for intercultural couples. Otherwise, lack of support might lead one or both partners to distance themselves from family and assimilate to their partner's culture, which could lead to increased couple conflict (Silva et al., 2012).

Common Challenges

Intercultural couples are much more likely than intracultural couples to encounter problems because they often hold even more diverse values, beliefs, attitudes, and habits, and such vast differences can increase the potential for misunderstanding (Waldman & Rubalcava, 2005). Each partner is often unaware that his or her assumptions and expectations are culture-bound and therefore may differ from his or her partner's

(Sullivan & Cottone, 2006). The most common challenges and stressors particularly relevant to intercultural couples are discussed next.

Negative Reactions and Discrimination from the Community

Despite increasing prevalence and acceptance, more often than not, intercultural couples differ from most of the other same-culture couples in their surrounding community (Rosenblatt, 2009). For many of these couples, this "differentness" tends to be less concerning within their relationship, and rather more concerning to others outside the relationship (Rosenblatt, 2009). Such unions often lead to negative reactions of varying extremes from the community (Kenney & Kenney, 2009). Most likely to be targets of these negative reactions are interracial couples, especially Black–White couples, and the level of opposition tends to vary depending on the couples' socioeconomic status, level of education, and community of residence (Killian, 2012). Racist and discriminatory actions can include staring, hostility, psychological intimidation, racial epithets or other verbal assaults, violence, or denial of services, and can be perpetrated by individuals, groups, and institutions alike (Killian, 2012; Poulsen, 2003).

A common challenge among many intercultural couples when facing such discrimination are the disparate experiences of each partner, particularly if one partner is White or of the dominant culture, and the other is a person of color or from a minority culture (Killian, 2012). The **cultural or racial "outsider"** might be the primary target of discrimination and as a result experience a great deal of distress, while the **cultural or racial "insider"** might have difficulty empathizing with his or her partner's experience, causing tension between them (Killian, 2012). A similar and equally damaging problem for many intercultural couples is complete denial by one or both partners of the degree of external oppression experienced and the resulting impact on the family (Killian, 2012).

The prevailing **discourse of homogamy**, or the societal assumption that homogamy or the cultural similarity of both partners is the norm and any alternative is pathological, perpetuates a multitude of myths and stereotypes about intercultural relationships, increasing the likelihood of prejudice and discrimination. Intercultural unions are often viewed as inherently dysfunctional, and as a result are assumed to bear children who are troubled, rejected, confused, and destined to a life of challenges (Kenney & Kenney, 2009; Yancey & Yancey, 2002). These couples are also often questioned regarding their motives for entering into the relationship, with common myths suggesting such ulterior motives as racial or cultural self-loathing, inability to attract a mate of one's own race or culture, sexual curiosity, exotic fetishes, rebelling against family or society, seeking upward mobility, needing to feel dominant, or attempting to attain citizenship (Karis, 2003; Yancey & Yancey, 2002).

Negative responses can also come from closer to home—from extended family (Poulsen, 2003). Family members might express concern and fear about the couple's future and future of their children, choose not to provide support and acceptance, or completely reject or alienate them (Poulsen, 2003). Despite often overt prejudice or racism, particularly from older generations, or disapproval of their relationships, many intercultural couples at times feel pressured to preserve cultural traditions in order to maintain family support, or otherwise choose to risk breaking ties with their family for the sake of the relationship (Yahya & Boag, 2014).

Immigration and Acculturation Issues

Another common challenge for many intercultural couples involves immigration and *acculturation*, or the process of adopting the traditions and values of a culture other than one's own. Often one or both partners emigrated to the United States, and the experience of immigration and accompanying acculturative stress can be a harrowing one with great psychosocial impact (Falicov, 2014a). The impact begins prior to immigration, as the events leading up to it are often traumatic, involving, for example, terrorism or dangerous border crossing (D'Urso, Reynaga, & Patterson, 2009; Falicov, 2014a; Mirkin & Kamya, 2008). Immigration often involves limited resources, restricted mobility, isolation, bereavement, and feelings of guilt and shame (D'Urso et al., 2009; Mirkin & Kamya, 2008). Mental health reverberations might span several generations and could manifest in the form of nightmares, somatization, substance abuse, depression, and violence (D'Urso et al., 2009; Falicov, 2014a).

One or both partners' experience of immigration can have a great impact on the relationship and the family, and often the most difficult challenge involves differences in acculturation, particularly if one partner comes from the dominant culture, while the other is from another country. The immigrant partner might not be acculturated to the dominant culture, and both partners might disagree on the extent to which he or she should maintain the values of his or her culture of origin, or otherwise acculturate (Mirkin & Kamya, 2008). This challenge becomes most obvious when raising children, as children often acculturate quickly, leading the immigrant parent(s) to depend on their children, and also causing conflict over the child's and parent's differing values (Mirkin & Kamya, 2008).

Differences in Cultural Values, Beliefs, and Expectations

Another common challenge for many intercultural couples is navigating cultural differences in values, beliefs, and expectations. Not surprisingly, often many cultural norms and beliefs of each partner conflict, a clash that has been referred to as a lack of a shared **cultural code** (Crippen & Brew, 2013). Inability to integrate these differences can cause the couple to maximize their differences and lead separate lives (Falicov, 2014b). Scholarship has identified various culture-related conflicts commonly experienced by intercultural couples, described next. While conflict over these issues arises among intracultural couples as well, cultural differences tend to exacerbate them.

Child-rearing

This is one of the most common areas of conflict, as often the birth of the first child sparks memories of each parent's experiences growing up, leading to specific cultural orientations to child-rearing (Bustamante et al., 2011; Crippen & Brew, 2007). Culture influences various aspects of parenting style, including behavioral expectations, communication style, level of emotional involvement or affection, parental roles, educational style, and disciplinary methods (Bustamante et al., 2011; Crippen & Brew, 2007). These cultural differences can be a significant source of conflict. For example, the couple might disagree on how children should behave at the dinner table, one believing they should be silent while eating and the other believing they should be able to talk. Many intercultural couples have utilized various strategies for reconciling child-rearing differences (Crippen & Brew, 2007). According to the **power rule**, one partner is responsible for all parenting decisions. According to the **sphere of influence rule**, each partner is responsible for different aspects of parenting. According to the **inertia rule**, both parents avoid responsibility over parenting out of deference to the other's culture. This latter strategy, not surprisingly, could have detrimental consequences for children.

Inevitably, many intercultural couples face the challenging and enriching task of parenting *bicultural* children in a *transcultural* family, or a new family culture resulting from their intersecting cultural backgrounds (Crippen & Brew, 2007). This transcultural family "integrates and reflects both partners through a reconstruction of the past and a construction of a new family identity" (p.111). Some conditions promote successful integration of cultural differences in these families, including equal social status of parents, explicit mutual support, different shared traditions, and recognition and resolution of cultural contradictions. When strong, this new **family identity** can be a vindicating force against change, ensuring cultural continuity and cohesion during family life cycle transitions.

Gender Role Expectations

Gender role expectations are another frequent source of conflict, perhaps the most challenging to negotiate, as different cultures often have different expectations regarding the roles of men and women (Bustamante et al., 2011; Rosenblatt, 2009). In one partner's culture, for example, the woman might be considered the caretaker, and the male the breadwinner; while in the other's culture, men and women share these responsibilities equally (Bustamante et al., 2011; Rosenblatt, 2009). Whereas in individualistic cultures men and women tend to be more flexible in their roles, emphasizing equality, power balance, and role diffusion, in collectivistic cultures, gender roles are much more rigid, emphasizing high differentiation and power distribution between women's power in the home and men's power in the public domain (Kellner, 2009). The degree of gender role differentiation in a culture is "a function of the levels of hierarchy or the amount of egalitarianism/ social equality that a culture will tolerate," such that "in a relationship, culturally assigned gender roles define and explain the differences in each partner's attitudes toward work, power, money, and house-related responsibilities" (Kellner, 2009, p. 226).

Interpersonal Relationships, Particularly Extended Family

Cultural difference in interpersonal relationships, particularly with regard to extended family, can be another source of conflict. Often each partner's culture differs on level of respect and hierarchy. Some cultures emphasize hierarchical relationships where respecting authority is of utmost importance, other cultures emphasize cooperative relationships where the needs of the group are more important than the needs of one person, and still others have the individualistic relationship view where each individual is responsible for himself or herself (Kellner, 2009). As such, often one partner is quite influenced by his or her family of origin, while the other is not (Rosenblatt, 2009). If one partner comes from a collectivistic culture, she or he might prioritize the extended family such that it is an extension of the family unit, while another partner comes from an individualistic culture, and thus might place boundaries between the couple and the extended family (Kellner, 2009). These cultural differences often lead to conflict over whether to set boundaries with extended family members, and disagreements over the level of obligation toward them. Thus, it is essential that intercultural couples learn and accept the degree of loyalty each feels toward their extended family in order to negotiate whether each are viewing their marriage as that "between two individuals or two families" (Kellner, 2009, p. 226). A common challenge is that one partner feels excluded from the other partner's family of origin, either because of opposition toward the marriage or competition for or resentment regarding the loss of the partner's time and assistance (Bustamante et al., 2011; Rosenblatt, 2009). Another challenge is that one partner might feel pressure from the other partner's extended family to assimilate to the family culture, by speaking the language, adopting customs or rituals, or raising their children according to the standards of their religion or culture (Rosenblatt, 2009).

Distinct Styles of Emotional Expression

Cross-cultural variations in emotional meaning and expression are a common challenge for many intercultural couples. While emotional miscommunication and misunderstanding are common and vital in any relationship, the possibility for such misunderstanding can be higher for intercultural couples because of different culture-based ways of expressing emotion (Waldman & Rubalcava, 2005). Emotional expressiveness can differ, for example, in levels of intensity, display, and formality. In same-culture relationships, for example, American couples link anger to marital unhappiness, while Israeli couples show no such link because they perceive anger as a normal emotion associated with intimate relationships (Parra-Cardona & Busby, 2006). Also, some Latino couples are influenced by cultural values emphasizing *personalismo*, or a high level of emotional resonance in interpersonal encounters. For some Latino couples, empathy is an important variable, not in soothing, but in shared activities and expressions of affection (Parra-Cardona & Busby, 2006). Japanese and Chinese relationships value social harmony and emphasize that each partner takes equal space in a relationship (Hattori, 2014). As a result, behavioral gestures and somatic activity, such as arm gestures and hand holding, are limited in these relationships; they are seen as taking too much emotional and physical space (Hattori, 2014). In addition, because of this emphasis on social harmony, if a partner directly criticizes, the other partner may assume the relationship is over, whereas in contrast, in Western relationships, direct communication is common and expected (Hattori, 2014). Cross-cultural variation in emotions can have a significant impact on communication and connection in intercultural relationships, particularly if one partner comes from an individualistic or Western culture, while the other comes from a collectivistic or Eastern culture. Complicating this challenge is that these differences in emotional experience and expression impact communication and are often outside of awareness, making it difficult for couples to navigate not only their emotional differences but also other conflicts requiring direct communication.

Coping Strategies

Coping with Cultural Differences

According to Seshadri and Knudson-Martin (2013), many intercultural couples tend to organize their cultural differences according to four types of relationship structures to manage intercultural differences and create strong and meaningful relationships. Integrated couples organize their differences by melding them together and celebrating both cultures. Coexisting couples "agree to disagree" and are able to retain two ways of carrying out their lives. Singularly assimilated couples do not highlight cultural differences; instead, one partner assimilates to the other partner's culture, such that the former's culture becomes nearly invisible. Unresolved couples have not dealt with their differences, and as a result tend to continually conflict around these differences, often leaving them unaddressed and creating tension.

Intercultural couples often use various strategies to cope with stressors related to cultural differences. They often blend values and expectations through **cultural reframing**, creating a "we," or a co-constructed reality that transcends differences (Bustamante et al., 2011; Seshadri & Knudson-Martin, 2013). Couples also cope by being respectful of, appreciative of, and celebrating cultural differences, with one partner often showing cultural deference to another partner (Bustamante et al., 2011; Seshadri & Knudson-Martin, 2013). Another common strategy is **emotional maintenance**, or communicating openly about emotions and insecurities (Seshadri & Knudson-Martin, 2013). These couples also use humor when negotiating differences, as doing so de-emphasizes differences and diffuses stressful situations (Bustamante et al., 2011). Another strategy is the recognition of similarities between each other's cultures, with many finding that, despite differences, their core values remain the same, thereby strengthening the relationship (Bustamante et al., 2011). Another coping strategy involves thoughtful positioning in relation to societal and familial context, or creating boundaries around their relationship to protect themselves from discrimination (Seshadri & Knudson-Martin, 2013). Finally, couples also cope by maintaining flexibility in gender roles, through open and flexible communication and negotiation about expectations (Bustamante et al., 2011).

Coping with Discrimination

Given that intercultural couples, especially interracial couples, are at increased risk of experiencing discrimination, these couples have also developed many of their own strategies for coping with it. Interracial couples often use six "survival" strategies to cope with discrimination (Killian, 2012). Fighting fire with fire might entail reacting to staring by staring back, or even scowling. Making a special effort involves going to lengths to great a good impression, such as by presenting themselves well through dress and behavior. Disassociating from one another might mean sitting separately on public transportation to avoid negative reactions. Restricting itinerary involves avoiding situations or places where negative reactions are likely to occur, and instead only going where they will feel comfortable. Not discussing everyday experiences of discrimination with one's partner is another common survival strategy; this "code of silence" serves a protective function in the relationship. A final common strategy is deprioritizing racial differences, wherein the couple define themselves as altogether unremarkable or unexceptional in order to neutralize distinctions.

Strengths of Intercultural Couples and Families

Despite the many challenges that intercultural couples face, research tends to contradict the common myth that intercultural relationships are dysfunctional, and instead emphasizes a number of strengths. Directly dealing with cultural differences may lead to enhanced intimacy (Troy, Lewis-Smith, & Laurenceau, 2006), and also may promote commitment, intentionality, and secure attachment (Ting-Toomey, 2009; Troy et al., 2006). In addition, despite the commonly held belief that intercultural couples tend to have lower relationship quality, partners in intercultural relationships are found to be more often securely attached than insecurely attached, and report significantly higher relationship satisfaction compared to those in intracultural relationships (Troy et al., 2006). Interestingly, another strength is that interracial couples tend to have more education and higher incomes than their same-race counterparts, with some variations by gender. Rosenfeld (2005) found that 53 percent of interracial couples have at least some graduate education, which may either contribute to or result in increased relationship satisfaction. Regarding income, in 2010, the median income of newlywed White–Asian couples was more than $70,000, compared to about $60,000 for White–White or Asian–Asian couples, with the Asian male–White female couple earning the most (Wang, 2012).

Other major strengths of intercultural couples are byproducts of often having weathered experiences of discrimination. Many of these couples often develop stronger relationships, and are more thoroughly prepared to handle relationship challenges that might pale in comparison to the stigma experienced (Ting-Toomey, 2009). In addition, another powerful strength is greater enrichment of each partner and their children. Each partner experiences greater clarification of values and beliefs, leading to a greater division of self and other, as well as a greater ability to find strength in commonalities (Mahboubi & Mahboubi, 2008; Ting-Toomey, 2009). In addition, in experiencing greater diversity through exposure to different customs, each partner may develop higher tolerance and acceptance, curiosity to explore other cultures, and the ability to develop multiple cultural frames of reference through integrating multiple value systems (Mahboubi & Mahboubi, 2008; Ting-Toomey, 2009). The couple may then pass on these strengths to their bicultural children, who are raised to be open-minded, respectful of all cultures, and able to find a "home" within themselves wherever they are (Mahboubi & Mahboubi, 2008; Ting-Toomey, 2009).

INTERMARRIAGE ACROSS GROUPS AND INTERSECTIONS OF IDENTITIES

While many subgroups exist within the larger group of intercultural couples and families, in the following section, the unique experiences and challenges of three particular groups will be explored: interracial couples and families, interfaith couples and families, and LGBTQ (lesbian, gay, bisexual, transgender, or questioning of their sexual orientation) intercultural couples and families. Exploration of interracial and interfaith couples and families enables an understanding of some similarities and differences among intercultural subgroups. Also, it is important to note that the partners who are in the non-White racial group, the non-Christian religion, and those who are in LGBTQ relationships all experience the intersectionality of multiple oppressions. In short, they experience general societal disapproval of their intercultural union, some other aspect of their identity (e.g., religion, race, sexual orientation), and sometime disapproval of the combination of the two.

Interracial Couples and Families

As a subgroup, interracial unions tend to experience the most distress compared to other intercultural unions, due in large part to the more often visually apparent differences and resulting racist reactions, especially in Black–White unions (Killian, 2012). In a recent study comparing levels of psychological distress among homogamous and interracial couples, distress among interracial marriages was found to vary depending on the interracial combination (Bratter & Eschbach, 2006). Native American men, White women, and Hispanic men and women married to non-White spouses were found to experience more distress than those in homogamous marriages. Higher rates of distress were also found for those married to Native American or African American partners, as well as women married to Hispanic husbands. Interestingly, although Native Americans are the racial group most likely to marry interracially, with 50 percent in interracial marriages, they experience the most psychological distress among both interracial and homogamous relationships (Bratter & Eschbach, 2006). While Whites are the least likely to marry interracially, men experience little to no distress, while women experience higher levels of distress, particularly when married to an African American partner (Bratter & Eschbach, 2006). While lower socioeconomic status contributed to distress in interracial marriages, higher socioeconomic status and acculturation were protective (Bratter & Eschbach, 2006).

Killian (2012) explored the discourses that interracial couples use when negotiating racial differences, and identified four prevailing discourses. The *discourse of homogamy* involves the couple either de-emphasizing their racial-cultural differences and emphasizing their similarities (i.e., "we're just like other couples") or being so hyperaware of their differentness (i.e., "we're different from other couples") that they dissociate from each other or restrict their itinerary to avoid uncomfortable situations. The **discourse of hypersensitivity to persons of color** entails the White partner subscribing to the common myth that persons of color are "paranoid" because of their racial "baggage," resulting in the White partner's lack of awareness of, sensitivity to, and validation of his or her partner's experiences of discrimination. The **discourse of the insignificance of racial and cultural history** involves interracial couples' considering the past as unimportant, particularly when the past includes painful oppressive experiences (i.e., "we leave everything behind when we are together"). This denial of the past can range from simply not discussing these experiences with the partner or family members to choosing not to incorporate their own cultural traditions and rituals in the marriage. Underlying all three of these discourses is the dominant **discourse of "no race talk,"** in which both partners subscribe to the societal notion that discussion about race is transgressive and should be avoided.

Interfaith Couples and Families

Interfaith marriages are rapidly becoming more common in the United States. Religious institutions have traditionally regulated interfaith marriages, citing the difficulties of socialization of children as the primary justification (Lara & Onedera, 2008). Historically, the Catholic Church required dispensation for the validity of an interfaith marriage, while Jewish law prohibited it (Lara & Onedera, 2008). Today, interreligious marriages are more accepted by these institutions, but continue to be discouraged in the service of preserving culture and customs, particularly with those of Jewish faith (Lara & Onedera, 2008). While in the 1960s, 20 percent of married couples were in interfaith unions, between 2000 and 2010, interfaith unions increased to 45 percent (Riley, 2013). In a 2010 You-Gov national survey of nearly 2,500 individuals, interfaith unions were found to be increasing without regard to geography, income, or education level, and age was predictive of interfaith marriage (Riley, 2013). More specifically, 67 percent of people who married between ages 36 and 45 were in interfaith unions, compared to 58 percent of people who married between 26 and 35, and 48 percent of people who married before age 25. In other words, the older one is upon marriage, the more likely one is to marry outside one's faith. One possible explanation for this is that as they age, people are more frequently interacting cross-culturally, increasing the chances of intercultural marriage. Another possible explanation is that as they age, people find intercultural marriage more acceptable, especially once they are beyond childbearing years, and thus need not be concerned about the impact on children.

Interestingly, the changing religious landscape in the United States is the result of more people, particularly young adults, independently shaping their spiritual lives, combining beliefs of various faith approaches (Walsh, 2010). Often they are influenced by their romantic partners to change or combine their beliefs. Some choose a partner from a different faith in order to differentiate from their family of origin's faith, often because they experienced their family's religion as oppressive or abusive in some way. Disapproval and cutoffs from family of origin can be interpreted by parents as a rejection of heritage or a rebellion against parental authority. Such cutoffs can have a deleterious impact on the intercultural couple and their children.

In addition to cutoffs from family of origin, interfaith couples also often face challenges with regard to child-rearing, divorce, and death and loss (Walsh, 2010). Regarding child-rearing, interfaith conflicts typically arise over decisions regarding rituals such as circumcision, christening, or baptism. In the context of divorce, faith differences can have an impact on issues of visitation, particularly when the noncustodial parent has visitation on weekends when worship and religious education often take place. When faced with death and loss, conflicting beliefs about whether to hasten death in the context of medical life support decisions can lead to complicated negotiations. In addition, partners of different faiths might have conflicting beliefs about whether and/or what kind of afterlife exists, as well as the rituals surrounding death, such as burial or cremation.

LGBTQ Intercultural Couples and Families

LGBTQ intercultural couples and families face many unique challenges, given the intersection of sexual orientation minority and another cultural minority such as racial, ethnic, or religious minority. The challenges of such intersectionality have been described using phrases such as "double whammy" (e.g., for queer Latinos), "triple jeopardy" (e.g., for Black lesbians), or "a minority within a minority" (Addison & Coolhart, 2009). Thus, it can be quite distressing for these families of multi-minority status, with one or both partners coping with the reality of life as both sexual and cultural minority, and children navigating the impact of having sexual minority parents along with developing their bicultural identities. Scholars have identified challenges specific to LGBT couples, whether intracultural or intercultural, including coping with homophobia and heterosexism, maintaining a sense of couple identity, creating supportive social networks, and maintaining flexible gender roles (Addison & Coolhart, 2009). Long (2003) identified challenges unique to interracial and intercultural lesbian couples, including managing multiple differences, interracial relationship prejudice, antagonism by the family of origin, adjustment to a new culture, and limited connection to the lesbian community. She also highlighted strengths of these couples, which include heightened awareness of the destructiveness of racism, and cultural expansion, or a deeper understanding of and appreciation for each other's culture. Nazario (2003) described stressors specific to Latino cross-cultural same-sex male relationships. He noted that gay Latino men face the unique challenge of interacting and participating within three conflicting cultures: the Latino community, LGBTQ community, and the dominant culture. The importance of family in Latino families can make it particularly difficult for Latino gay men to negotiate stigma and homophobia within their family circles.

CLINICAL CONSIDERATIONS

Assessment Considerations

Assessment with intercultural couples and families begins with a thorough and comprehensive examination of each partner's cultural background, as well as the cultural background of the clinician. The therapist must acquire cultural knowledge and develop cultural sensitivity so that he or she can model curiosity, understanding, and increased tolerance for each partner's culture. In this way, the therapist serves as a "cultural referee," and may even encourage acceptance by reframing the couple's experience as tourists in a foreign country (Perel, 2000). The clinician might use one or a combination of three methods of assessment: (1) **Falicov's MECA model**, (2) **genograms**, and/or (3) the **Multiple Heritage Couple Questionnaire**.

Falicov's MECA Model

Falicov (1995, 2014a, 2014b) has developed an approach for integrating culture in therapy, a *multidimensional, ecological, comparative approach* (MECA) in which therapists maintain a "both/and" stance to view families in a comparative, sociocultural context through the lenses of cultural diversity and social justice. Therapists utilize four generic ecosystemic domains—(1) migration/acculturation, (2) ecological context, (3) family organization, and (4) family life cycle—to compare three overlapping cultural maps: the therapist's and each partner's (Falicov, 2014a). The migration/acculturation domain, or the **psychology of migration**, explores how, why, and when the individual's family came to migrate, as well as any resulting acculturative stress. The ecological context domain, or the **psychology of coping and healing**, explores where and how the individual lives in relation to the broader environment. The family organization domain, or the **psychology of cultural**

organizational transition, involves an understanding of the individual's family structure and values with regard to family arrangements. The family life cycle domain, or the **psychology of cultural developmental transition**, entails an examination of the cultural patterns of life cycle stages and transitions. By comparing these three overlapping cultural maps, the therapist can then draw attention to similarities and differences across all four dimensions among all three involved, contextualize these differences, and implement culturally attuned interventions with a view toward integrating cultural dimensions and social justice concerns.

Genograms

Genograms can be quite useful as a practical framework for understanding family patterns (McGoldrick, Gerson, & Petry, 2008). Much like a family tree, genograms are a graphic depiction providing information about family members and their relationships over at least three generations, particularly family dynamics and patterns as they have evolved over time. Whereas other forms of assessment tend to be more focused on the individual, genograms help clinicians to think systemically about historical, intergenerational, and cultural influences on the individual, couple, or family, factoring in the extended family, friends, community, society, and culture (McGoldrick et al., 2008). Genograms are particularly useful for intercultural couples and families, as they can become a guide for reconstructing each partner's cultural narrative, helping to contextualize their kinship network in terms of culture, ethnicity, socioeconomic status, race, gender, religion, family process, and migration history. Visual depictions of similarities and differences among family members, particularly intergenerational changes can be illuminating to each partner as well as the therapist. Stories of immigration and resulting cutoffs are also depicted, which can yield further discussions of the impact of such cutoffs. Genograms are most useful when created in collaboration with each partner or family member, and in the presence of the other partner or family members, as such sharing can help aid in increased understanding and empathy with regard to otherwise misunderstood differences.

Multiple Heritage Couple Questionnaire

To help couples identify and describe their different cultural perspectives with regard to the most common areas of conflict such as extended family, child-rearing, and gender roles, Henriksen, Watts, and Bustamante (2011) developed the *Multiple Heritage Couple Questionnaire*. The questionnaire asks about partner and own culture of origin, time orientation, gender roles, family context, religion and spirituality, and child-rearing.

The questionnaire is designed to initiate dialogue about these common issues among intercultural couples, as they are often not part of aware-ness and therefore not openly discussed and negotiated within these relationships.

Treatment Considerations

A Multicultural Approach

Treatment with intercultural couples and families should be collab-orative and characterized by a curious, open, and accepting stance in which the strengths—of the couple and of their respective cultures—are highlighted (Kelly et al., 2013). Nearly all traditional couple and fam-ily therapies have been normed primarily with Caucasian couples, so these treatments have their limitations with diverse couples (Kelly et al., 2013). Therefore, to ensure culturally sensitive treatment, a multicultural approach must be utilized. Kelly, Bhagwat, Maynigo, and Moses (2013) developed a **multicultural approach** to adapting any traditional approach to couple therapy. Utilizing this approach entails conducting treatment as usual, while also enhancing treatment by developing four therapist cultural competencies, and then using these competencies to bridge differences via four mechanisms. The four cultural competencies are: (1) knowledge, (2) dynamic sizing, (3) culturally competent skills and interventions, and (4) self-awareness (Sue & Sue, 2008). Acquiring knowl-edge involves gathering information from several sources, including col-lective observations of therapists about race, ethnicity, and culture, from the couple themselves and from research about risk and protective factors specific to the couple's identity group(s). **Dynamic sizing** emphasizes the idea that individual differences within each group means that there is no one-size-fits-all factor, so it's important for the therapist to consider diver-sity knowledge while testing hypotheses, which determines whether or not emic or etic factors apply to the couple. Developing culturally competent skills and interventions involves using techniques that have been shown to be effective with diverse clients. Self-awareness involves the therapist's developing a deeper understanding about his or her own identity and biases, having an awareness of structural oppression and how it manifests in his or her own beliefs and behavior, and increasing awareness of the importance of and nuances related to his or her own identity so that he or she might foster strengths-based perspective-taking.

Kelly et al. (2013) also discuss four mechanisms by which the four cul-tural competencies may work. The first mechanism, worldview and value differences, involves acknowledging and confronting that the therapist and couple might possess different values and views of the world. The second mechanism, experiences and contexts, involves acknowledg-ing and incorporating differences in experiences and contexts. The third mechanism, power differences between therapist and couple, involves bringing to awareness power differences that may negatively impact treatment if left unacknowledged. The fourth mechanism, felt distance between therapist and couple, involves bringing to awareness a lack of connection possibly caused by unacknowledged cultural differences, or lack of familiarity with treatment, which is common for underserved groups (Kelly et al., 2013).

Culturally Competent Interventions

Seiff-Haron, Hirosaki, and Sonnier (2014) have identified four common injuries or invalidations when working cross-culturally with diverse couples and four interventions to aid in reparation after these invalidations. Although the authors discuss these interventions as repairs to injuries, these interventions can be useful in engaging clients in a culturally competent manner in order to avoid injuries altogether, strengthen rapport, and bridge differences across the four mechanisms described in Kelly's (2013) model. The first injury involves making the client feel like an "other" by referring to him or her as a representative for his or her cultural group. Their recommended repair is a **cultural disclosure**, in which the therapist discloses about his or her own culture with the intention of leveling the playing field, by stating, for example, "In my culture, it's considered disrespectful to express any negative feelings, I wonder if this might be the case for you too?" The second injury involves asking the client about their experience, which can increase feelings of alienation. Their recommended repair is a **collective reflection**, which normalizes the client's experience by introducing the collective experience of a larger group, so that the client does not feel so alone. For example, the therapist might state, "You know, I've heard this before from some of my other Asian clients, that they feel quite ashamed when they've expressed their anger out loud. I wonder if you might have a similar experience?" The third injury involves stereotyping the client such that the client feels unseen. Their recommended repair is a **cultural conjecture**, in which the therapist tentatively names a possible cultural dynamic while reflecting the data that might support it. For example, the therapist might state, "Trisha, you mentioned that it felt 'alien' to you to be asked how you were feeling, while Josh, you said it seemed 'ridiculous' that she wouldn't want to tell you how she is feeling. I wonder if these differences might have to do with your different cultural backgrounds, where in your Italian culture, Josh, being emotionally open was the norm, whereas in your Japanese culture, Trisha, such openness was unheard of. Could this have something to do with what's going on?" The fourth injury involves exploring a client's culture when they themselves are unaware of how their cultural background has impacted them. Their recommended repair is **slicing culture thinner**, which involves slowly exploring a client's narrow windows of experience, through repetition of the client's words, slow pacing, and constant empathy and validation.

Clinical Vignette

Frederich and Irene are married, college educated, and in their late 30s. He is a second-generation half-German and half–Italian American who works in finance, and she is a first-generation Japanese American who works in human resources. They sought treatment after an argument over disciplining their 12-year-old child, Oliver, who had been refusing to go to school since starting at a new private school a month prior, and had become increasingly defiant at home. In the first session, the couple discussed constant disagreements over how to change Oliver's behaviors. During their most recent argument, Irene's mother, who lives in Tokyo, was giving them parenting advice over Skype, which Frederich found intrusive and expressed as much to Irene. Irene found his reaction disrespectful, and stormed out with Oliver. Together they spent the night at Irene's sister's house, and returned home the following day while Frederich was at work. This occurred a week prior to the first session, and the couple had not discussed the argument since. They stated that they had learned from past experience that their arguments tend to go nowhere, as at some point Irene locks herself in their bedroom crying while Frederich tries to talk to her through the door, though ultimately gives up and walks away.

The couple agreed on their issues, but with vastly different perspectives. Frederich felt strongly that Irene's views on parenting were ill-focused, as she did not believe in outright punishment, but rather preferred to remind Oliver of the importance of maintaining his family's reputation. Frederich, on the other hand, felt that Oliver needed to be punished by having privileges taken away, such as video game use. Irene felt that these punishments were pointless, as she preferred that Oliver be motivated to change his behavior due to a desire to represent his family well and keep his parents happy. In addition, Frederich felt that Irene's mother's advice-giving overstepped bounds, and felt strongly that he and Irene should be making parenting decisions on their own. Irene, meanwhile, felt that she needed to respect her mother's wisdom. After all, her mother had experience. Irene also pointed out that Frederich tended to reveal much of their family problems to his own Italian American mother, who called him every other day.

The therapist began assessment by asking questions drawn from Falicov's MECA model and the Multiple Heritage Couple Questionnaire, and collaborated with each partner in constructing each of their family genograms. This comprehensive assessment evinced several important cultural considerations. Irene had emigrated with her parents from Japan when she was a young teenager, a difficult experience for her and her younger sister, as they were close to their extended family. Years later, when she and her sister had established themselves at reputable liberal arts colleges, their parents returned to Tokyo, content that they had given their daughters a brighter future. Irene missed her family, as she had long felt cut off from them, and sought to maintain connections through any means possible, more concretely through Skype, and more abstractly through soliciting and respecting their advice. Aware that a common challenge for couples involves different levels of acculturation, the therapist used a *cultural conjecture* to ask about this. Irene stated that she had adjusted well to American culture upon immigrating, as she had become fluent in English in Japan, and by now felt she had comfortably developed a bicultural identity in which she had negotiated both American and Japanese values and customs.

Further assessment elucidated important differences between Frederich and Irene along the individualism-collectivism continuum. Although Frederich was further removed from the experiences of immigration on both the German and Italian sides of his family, he admitted he could relate to Irene's experience of negotiating a bicultural identity, given the very different cultures of his parents. While he found his German father to be less verbal, less emotional, more private, and more goal-oriented, he found his Italian mother to be much more verbal, more emotional, and desiring to be involved in his personal and family life, such that he tended to speak to her a few times a week, updating her on their family's happenings. Although he tended to prefer more boundaries and a private existence like his father, he also found himself to be much more open and emotionally expressive like his mother. Based on these descriptions, the therapist hypothesized that Frederich's experiences in a bicultural family had led him to adopt values from his mother's more collectivistic Italian culture, as well as his father's more individualistic German culture. In addition, the therapist hypothesized that Irene's experience of her family's Japanese culture fit closer to the collectivism end of the continuum, with its emphasis on in-group cohesion, social harmony, conformity, and avoidance of conflict. Irene stated that unlike Frederich, she preferred not to argue, instead isolating herself when upset, only returning when she was composed, which often necessitated masking her sadness. Although she was close with her family, they did not tend to express negative emotions to each other, as it was considered disrespectful, and she felt the same way about expressing herself to her husband.

The therapist's assessment of each partner's cultural background required the therapist to use the cultural competencies of knowledge and dynamic sizing, and the culturally competent skill of *collective reflection*. The therapist specifically gathered knowledge of the couple's German/Italian and Japanese ethnic identities and values. In using *collective reflection* and dynamic sizing, the therapist was able to determine which individual behaviors fit with their respective ethnic backgrounds and common experiences of immigration, and also where each partner fit along the individualism-collectivism continuum. Prior to this assessment, the couple had not been aware of the impact of Irene's immigration experience on their relationship, nor did they have any understanding of each other's cultural backgrounds. Thus, the assessment itself was an eye-opening intervention that created increased understanding and respect for each other. The therapist noticed a decrease in tension between Frederich and Irene, and a renewed commitment to the relationship following the assessment, a softening that facilitated treatment going forward.

In addition, as part of the assessment, the therapist utilized the cultural competency of self-awareness to explore her own cultural background and any similarities or differences that might impact treatment with this couple, as suggested by the MECA model. As a first-generation Filipina American, she felt she could relate somewhat to Irene's experience of immigration, though she felt much more detached from her Filipino culture than Irene did from her Japanese culture. The therapist also was aware, however, that she was much more individualistic and emotionally expressive, like Frederich, and recognized that this was likely a result of her being quite acculturated to American values. In order to acknowledge differences in experiences and contexts, as well as prevent possible felt distance between herself and either partner, the therapist used the skill of raising diversity factors using a *cultural disclosure*, by discussing these notable similarities and differences. In particular, she asked how each of them felt about being treated by an Asian American therapist, at which point Irene expressed that it somehow made her more comfortable, despite the differing ethnicities. Frederich admitted that he wondered whether the therapist would tend to side with Irene, given that they were both Asian women. The therapist reassured him that their racial match would not affect treatment, and that she in fact felt like she could relate to many aspects of both of their cultural backgrounds, and described these aspects more fully. The couple felt reassured and encouraged that they were free to raise such diversity factors in treatment.

The therapist's formulation was consistent with her integrated emotionally focused therapy and multicultural couple therapy orientation. The couple was feeling disconnected from each other, due in large part to their cultural differences and exacerbated by their lack of awareness of these differences. While Frederich sought connection with his wife through verbal and emotional expression, Irene sought connection with her husband by shielding him from her emotions so as to prioritize his needs. Frederich desired to create a boundary around their immediate family to increase closeness, but Irene's lack of accessibility caused him to welcome his mother's consistent availability—which he otherwise found intrusive. Meanwhile, Irene desired to increase closeness by helping

Frederich to feel included by her larger extended family. These culture-bound attempts at closeness created a strong demand-withdraw pattern in which Frederich's emotionally expressive reaching toward Irene led to her becoming flooded and overwhelmed and pulling away from him in order to protect him from her emotions. Her shutting down then led Frederich to shut down as well.

Through culturally adapted emotionally focused therapy interventions, the therapist first helped the couple to identify their negative cycle, making sure to highlight cultural influences on each partner's attempts to connect. The couple then was helped to access unacknowledged feelings and attachment needs, and to understand the cultural reasons why these feelings remained inaccessible for so long. Frederich was able to describe to Irene that his constant need to talk openly came from his expressive Italian mother, and that he related to her feeling shut out by his private German father. Irene was able to describe to Frederich that her choosing to isolate came from her Japanese family's emphasis on hiding negative emotion so as not to burden or shame him. Frederich was also able to express a desire to feel like he was a priority to Irene over her extended family, such that she would value his opinions over her parents' opinions, and that he often felt lonely when she shut him out. Irene was able to express that she perceived his distancing from her parents as a distancing from her, as she considers them an extension of her, and that when they fought she often felt as though she was failing him as a wife. She expressed that she felt guilty expressing herself to him, instead preferring to connect with him in nonverbal ways, such as through touch. Frederich and Irene were then able to reframe their cycle in attachment terms that incorporated these cultural influences, promote identification and acceptance of each other's needs, and express their unmet needs in ways that felt culturally appropriate for each of them. Frederich learned to reach for Irene in both verbal and nonverbal ways, making sure to notice and titrate when his verbal expressions were becoming overwhelming to her, and Irene learned to reach for Frederich in both verbal and nonverbal ways, making sure to hear Frederich out when he needed to express himself and make more efforts to accompany her nonverbal expressions with verbal ones.

CONCLUSIONS

Despite increased proliferation of intercultural couples and families internationally, little scholarship exists to guide theorists, preventionists, service providers, policy makers, and researchers in understanding the unique needs of this population. This chapter reviewed the literature relevant to intercultural couples and families in order to fill this gap. Overshadowed by a history of racial classification, anti-miscegenation laws, and immigration trauma, these families face challenges often not experienced by same-culture couples, including negative reactions, racism, and discrimination from the community; immigration and acculturation issues; differences in values, beliefs, and expectations; and distinct styles of emotional expression. Despite such challenges, intercultural couples have developed their own strategies for coping, and as a result demonstrate many strengths. These include greater acceptance, curiosity, opportunities for growth and learning; and ability to nurture bicultural children who are open-minded and respectful of all cultures. Intercultural couples can best be understood and helped using ecological and multicultural models, wherein each of their respective cultures are explored and understood.

CHAPTER REVIEW

Key Points

1. Two frameworks that can be utilized to understand cultural differences and entry and adjustment into intercultural relationships are the individualism-collectivism cultural "syndrome" and ecological systems theory.
2. Common challenges faced by intercultural couples include negative reactions and discrimination from the community; immigration and acculturation issues; and differences in values, beliefs, and expectations.
3. Strengths of intercultural couples include greater acceptance and curiosity and the ability to nurture bicultural children who are open-minded and respectful of all cultures.
4. Assessment with intercultural couples and families involves a thorough and comprehensive examination of each partner's and the therapist's cultural backgrounds.
5. Treatment with intercultural couples and families should be collaborative and characterized by a curious, open, and accepting stance, highlighting the strengths of the couple and their cultures.

Key Terms

acculturation, anti-miscegenation laws, collective reflection, collectivism, cultural code/family identity, cultural conjecture, cultural disclosure, cultural or racial "insider," cultural or racial "outsider," discourse of homogamy, cultural reframing, discourse of "no race talk," discourse of hypersensitivity to persons of color, discourse of the insignificance of racial and cultural history, dynamic sizing, ecological systems theory, emotional maintenance, exosystem, Falicov's MECA model, genogram, individualism, individualism-collectivism cultural "syndrome", inertia rule, intercultural couple, macrosystem, microsystem, multicultural approach, Multiple Heritage Couple Questionnaire, power rule, psychology of coping and healing, psychology of cultural developmental transition, psychology of cultural organizational transition, psychology of migration, racial classification, slicing culture thinner, sphere of influence rule

Myths and Realities

- It is a myth that intercultural unions are inherently dysfunctional, and as a result will bear children who are troubled, rejected, confused, and destined to a life of challenges. In reality, intercultural couples have many strengths, as they often have developed stronger relationships, having faced discrimination, and likely are more thoroughly prepared to handle other relationship challenges. Through exposure to cultural differences, many also experience greater clarification of values and beliefs, greater ability to find strength in commonalities, higher tolerance and acceptance, curiosity to explore other cultures, and greater ability to develop multiple cultural frames of reference through integrating multiple value systems. The couple then passes on these strengths to their bicultural children, many of whom are raised to be open-minded, respectful of all cultures, and able to find a "home" within themselves wherever they are.

Tools and Tips

Knowledge

Falicov, C.J. (2014b, October). Loving across differences: Therapy with multicultural couples. *Fall Conference.* Lecture conducted from the Ackerman Institute for the Family, New York City, NY.

Karis, A., & Killian, K. D. (2009). *Intercultural couples: Exploring diversity in intimate relationships.* New York, NY: Taylor & Francis.

Kelly, S., Bhagwat, R., Maynigo, T., & Moses, E. (2013). Couple and marital therapy: The complement and expansion provided by multicultural approaches. In F. Leong, L. Comas-Diaz, V. McLloyd, and J. Trimble (Eds.), *American Psychological Association handbook of multicultural psychology.* (pp. 479–497) Washington, DC: APA.

McGoldrick, M., Gerson, R., & Petry, S. (2008). *Genograms: Assessment and intervention* (3rd ed.). New York, NY: W. W. Norton.

McGoldrick, M., & Hardy K. V. (2008). *Re-visioning family therapy: Race, culture, and gender in clinical practice.* New York, NY: Guilford Press.

Thomas, V., Karis, T. A., & Wetchler, J. L. (2003). *Clinical issues with interracial couples: Theories and research.* New York, NY: Haworth Press.

Dynamic Sizing

Therapists should keep in mind that in particular when working with intercultural couples, one size does not fit all. Not only are there individual differences within each partner's cultural group, but also within the intercultural couple's unique combination of identities. Therapists should therefore test hypotheses by considering diversity knowledge to determine whether or not emic or etic factors apply to each partner and to the couple.

Skills

Theory. Ecological systems theory and multicultural models attend to the many systems that impact intercultural couples and families.

Prevention. Children of intercultural couples need acceptance and help in creating their bicultural identities and navigating discrimination in society.

Service Provision. Providers need to effectively assess cultural differences in treatment by using Falicov's MECA model, genograms, and/or the Multiple Heritage Couple Questionnaire. In treatment, they need to use culturally sensitive models, such as Kelly's multicultural approach to couple therapy. In addition, they need to use culturally competent skills such as cultural conjecture, collective reflection, cultural disclosure, and slicing culture thinner.

Policy. Policies need to promote acceptance of intercultural unions.

Research. Research needs to focus more on the unique challenges faced by intercultural couples and families, impact on children, and treatment methods appropriate for this population.

Awareness

All those working *with* intercultural couples should become intimately aware of their own cultural backgrounds and how those backgrounds fit with and impact those of both partners, which they can explore using Falicov's MECA model, or creating their own family genogram.

REFERENCES

Addison, S., & Coolhart, D. (2009). Integrating socially segregated identities. In M. Rastogi & V. Thomas (Eds.), *Multicultural couple therapy* (pp. 51–75). Thousand Oaks, CA: Sage Publications.

Brammer, R. (2004). *Diversity in counseling.* Belmont, CA: Thomson.

Bratter, J. L., & Eschbach, K. (2006). What about the couple? Interracial marriage and psychological distress. *Social Science Research, 35,* 1025–1047.

Bronfenbrenner, U. (1986). Ecology of the family as a context for human development: Research perspectives. *Developmental Psychology, 22,* 723–744.

Bustamante, R. M., Nelson, J. A., Henriksen, R. C., & Monakes, S. (2011). Intercultural couples: Coping with culture-related stressors. *The Family Journal, 19,* 154–166.

Crippen, C., & Brew, L. (2007). Intercultural parenting and the transcultural family: A literature review. *The Family Journal: Counseling and Therapy for Couples and Families, 15,* 107–115.

Crippen, C., & Brew, L. (2013). Strategies of cultural adaption in intercultural parenting. *The Family Journal, 21,* 263–271.

Crohn, J. (1998). Intercultural couples. In M. McGoldrick (Ed.), *Revisioning family therapy* (pp. 295–308). New York, NY: Guilford Press.

D'Urso, S., Reynaga, S., & Patterson, J.E. (2009). The emotional experience of immigration for couples. In M. Rastogi & V. Thomas (Eds.), *Multicultural couple therapy* (pp. 29–43). Thousand Oaks, CA: Sage Publications.

Falicov, C.J. (1995). Cross-cultural marriages. In N. Jacobson & A. Gurman (Eds.), *Clinical handbook of couple therapy* (pp. 231–246). New York, NY: Guilford Press.

Falicov, C.J. (2014a). *Latino families in therapy* (2nd ed.). New York, NY: Guilford Press.

Falicov, C.J. (2014b, October). Loving across differences: Therapy with multicultural couples. *Fall Conference.* Lecture conducted from the Ackerman Institute for the Family, New York City, NY.

Hattori, K. (2014). *Emotionally focused therapy for Japanese couples: Development and empirical investigation of a culturally-sensitive EFT model.* Saarbrücken, Germany: Scholars' Press.

Henrikson, R.C., & Paladino, D.A. (2009). *Counseling multiple heritage individuals, couples, and families.* Alexandria, VA: American Counseling Association.

Henriksen, R. C., Watts, R. E., & Bustamante, R. (2011). The multiple heritage couple questionnaire. *The Family Journal, 15,* 405–411.

Karis, T.A. (2003). How race matters and does not matter for White women in relationships with Black men. In V. Thomas, T.A. Karis, & J.L. Wetchler (Eds.), *Clinical issues with interracial couples: Theories and research* (pp. 23–40). New York, NY: Haworth Press.

Kellner, J. (2009). Gender perspective in cross-cultural couples. *Clinical Social Work Journal, 37,* 224–229.

Kelly, S., Bhagwat, R., Maynigo, T., & Moses, E. (2013). Couple and marital therapy: The complement and expansion provided by multicultural approaches. In F. Leong, L. Comas-Diaz, V. McLloyd, and J. Trimble (Eds.), *American Psychological Association handbook of multicultural psychology.* Washington, DC: American Psychological Association.

Kenney, K.R., & Kenney, M.E. (2009) Counseling multiple heritage couples and families. In R. C. Henrikson & D. A. Paladino (Eds.), *Counseling multiple heritage individuals, couples, and families* (pp. 111–124). Alexandria, VA: American Counseling Association.

Killian, K.D. (2012). Resisting and complying with homogamy: Interracial couples' narratives about partner differences. *Counselling Psychology Quarterly, 25,* 125–135.

Lara, T.M., & Onedera J.L. (2008). Inter-religion marriages. In J.L. Onedera (Ed.), *The role of religion in marriage and family counseling* (pp. 213–226). New York, NY: Routledge.

Lee, J., & Bean, F.D. (2007). Reinventing the color line: Immigration and America's new racial/ethnic divide. *Social Forces, 86,* 561–586.

Long, J. (2003). Interracial and intercultural lesbian couples: The incredibly true adventures of two women in love. In V. Thomas, T. A. Karis, & J. L. Wetchler (Eds.), *Clinical issues with interracial couples: Theories and research* (pp. 85–102). New York, NY: Haworth Press.

Mahboubi, J., & Mahboubi, N. (2008). *Our Iranian-African American interracial family.* In M. McGoldrick & K. V. Hardy (Eds.), *Re-visioning family therapy: Race, culture, and gender in clinical practice* (pp. 146–154). New York, NY: Guilford Press.

McGoldrick, M., Gerson, R., & Petry, S. (2008). *Genograms: Assessment and intervention* (3rd ed.). New York, NY: W. W. Norton.

Mirkin, M. P., & Kamya, H. (2008). Working with immigrant and refugee families. In M. McGoldrick & K. V. Hardy (Eds.), *Re-visioning family therapy: Race, culture, and gender in clinical practice* (pp. 311–326). New York, NY: Guilford Press.

Nazario, A. (2003). Latino cross-cultural same sex male relationships: Issues of ethnicity, race, and other domains of influence. In V. Thomas, T. A. Karis, & J. L. Wetchler (Eds.), *Clinical issues with interracial couples: Theories and research* (pp. 103–114). New York, NY: Haworth Press.

Parra-Cardona, J. R., & Busby, D. M. (2006). Exploring relationship functioning in premarital Caucasian and Latino/a couples: Recognizing and valuing cultural differences. *Journal of Comparative Family Studies, 37*, 345–361.

Perel, E. (2000). A tourist's view of marriage. In P. Papp (Ed.), *Couples on the fault line* (pp. 178–204). New York, NY: Guilford Press.

Poulsen, S. S. (2003). Therapists' perspectives on working with interracial couples. In V. Thomas, T. A. Karis, & J. L. Wetchler (Eds.), *Clinical issues with interracial couples: Theories and research* (pp. 163–177). New York, NY: Haworth Press.

Prewitt, K. (2005). Racial classification in America: Where do we go from here? *Daedalus, 134*, 5–17.

Riley, N. (2013). Interfaith unions: a mixed blessing. *The New York Times.* Retrieved from http://www.nytimes.com/2013/04/06/opinion/interfaith-marriages-a-mixed-blessing.html?_r=0.

Rosenblatt, P. C. (2009). A systems theory analysis of intercultural couple relationships. In T. A. Karis & K. D. Killian (Eds.), *Intercultural couples: Exploring diversity in intimate relationships* (pp. 3–18). New York, NY: Taylor & Francis.

Rosenfeld, M. J. (2005). A critique of exchange theory in mate selection. American Journal of Sociology, 110, 1284–1325.

Seiff-Haron, J. M., Hirosaki, H., and Sonnier, T. (2014). *Cross-cultural couples therapy.* Lecture conducted from the Arizona Center for Emotionally Focused Therapy, Scottsdale, AZ.

Seshadri, G., & Knudson-Martin, C. (2013). How couples manage interracial and intercultural differences: Implications for clinical practice. *Journal of Marital and Family Therapy, 39*, 43–58.

Silva, L. C., Campbell, K., & Wright, D. W. (2012). Intercultural relationships: Entry, adjustment, and cultural negotiations. *Journal of Comparative Family Studies, 43*, 857–870.

Sue, D. W., & Sue, D. (2008). *Counseling the culturally diverse: Theory and practice* (5th ed.). New York, NY: John Wiley & Sons.

Sullivan, C., & Cottone, R. R. (2006). Culturally based couple therapy and intercultural relationships: A review of the literature. *The Family Journal, 14,* 221–235.

Ting-Toomey, S. (2009) A mindful approach to managing conflict in intercultural intimate couples. In T. A. Karis & K. D. Killian (Eds.), *Intercultural couples: Exploring diversity in intimate relationships* (pp. 31–49). New York, NY: Taylor & Francis.

Triandis, H. C. (2005, March). Issues in individualism and collectivism research. In *Culture and social behavior: The Ontario Symposium* (Vol. 10, pp. 207–225). Mahwah, NJ: Lawrence Erlbaum Associates.

Troy, A. B., Lewis-Smith, J., & Laurenceau, J. P. (2006). Interracial and intraracial romantic relationships: The search for differences in satisfaction, conflict, and attachment style. *Journal of Social and Personal Relationships, 23,* 65–80.

U.S. Census Bureau (2012). *Households and families: 2010, 2010 Census briefs.* Retrieved from https://www.census.gov/prod/cen2010/briefs/c2010br-14.pdf.

Waldman, K., & Rubalcava, L. (2005). Psychotherapy with intercultural couples: A contemporary psychodynamic approach. *American Journal of Psychotherapy, 59,* 227–245.

Walsh, F. (2010). Spiritual diversity: Multifaith perspectives in family therapy. *Family process, 49,* 330–348.

Wang, W. (2012). *The rise of intermarriage: Rates, characteristics vary by race and gender.* Washington, DC: Pew Research Center. Retrieved from http://www.pewsocialtrends.org/2012/02/16/the-rise-of-intermarriage/?src=prc-headline

Yahya, S., & Boag, S. (2014). "My family would crucify me!": The perceived influence of social pressure on cross-cultural and interfaith dating and marriage. *Sexuality & Culture, 18,* 759–772.

Yancey, G. A., & Yancey, S. W. (2002). *Just don't marry one: Interracial dating, marriage, and parenting.* Valley Forge, PA: Judson Press.

CHAPTER 13

Diverse Couple and Family Forms and Universal Family Processes

Brian Mundy
Matt Wofsy

While there have always been diverse families, now more than ever the traditional nuclear family structure of mother, father, and two or three children has been in need of re-consideration. Changes in social policy, migration, increased life expectancy, and multicultural shifts in values have resulted in a refashioning of what is considered "normal" in urban, suburban, and rural families across the United States in the 21st century. In today's complex world, it is not uncommon to encounter families that are blended, are headed by a same-sex couple, have surrogate children and parents, are interracial, have adopted children, or are intergenerational with extended caregiver involvement.

For example, difficult socioeconomic and psychosocial stressors may contribute to family members' need to consolidate their resources and scale down their living environment to one household. Factors such as economic disparity, divorce, chronic illness, poverty, discrimination, and cuts in social policy support, as well as the diversion of traditionally public funds such as Medicaid into privatized silos may contribute to a rise to more intergenerational families in overcrowded apartments and single-parent households. From 2000 to 2010, households with three or more generations rose by 76 percent (Lofquist, 2012). Alternately, such stressors can polarize families, resulting in fragmentation of the family unit. From 2000 to 2010, unmarried partner households rose by 71 percent (Lofquist, 2012). Since 2007, the percentage of mother-only or father-only family groups has increased steadily (Vespa, Lewis, & Krieder, 2013).

The diversification of family structures also continues to expand to include same-sex couples, adoption, and interracial couples and families. The widespread legalization of same-sex marriages has resulted in more and more households with same-sex parents adopting children, and **surrogate families**. Same-sex parent households increased by 80.4 percent from 2000 to 2010 (Lofquist, 2012). It was estimated that 25.3 percent of same-sex couple households had children in 2013 (Roberts & Stark, 2014), and the American Society of Reproductive Medicine (2015) indicates that, from 2000 to 2010, there was a 28 percent increase in gestational carrier cycles, in which a surrogate carries a pregnancy and delivers a child that is created from the egg and/or sperm of the intended parent(s). Families adopted over 7,000 children in 2013, with 32.5 percent of those children coming from China (U.S. Department of State, 2014). Lastly, interracial partnering via marriage rose by 28 percent from 2000 to 2010 (Lofquist, 2012), and in 2011 the multiracial population among children was calculated at 4.2 million, up 50 percent from the year 2000 (Saulny, 2011).

Trends such as these indicate the importance for mental health professionals to engage, understand, and be sensitive to the concerns and needs of members of diverse family structures. First, this chapter will identify and define some of these family structures. Then we will articulate experiences that we as structural family therapists believe are common to all families, paying particular attention to how universal processes are manifest across the myriad intersections of race, class, gender, and other aspects of diversity. Along the way, we explore how family therapy can be adapted to meet the unique needs that stem from diverse family structures. Then we present our key interventions and apply them to a surrogate family case in order to specifically demonstrate both the universal and idiosyncratic dynamics associated with nontraditional families.

SURROGATE FAMILIES

Advances in reproductive medicine have resulted in a rise of children born into families after being conceived using donated sperm or eggs, either through donor insemination or egg donation. In such cases, variations in genetic links between parents and children occur within the family. In the case of donor insemination, where a woman is inseminated with the sperm of a man who is not her husband, the child is genetically related to the mother but not the father who raises the child. Conversely, with egg donation, the child has a genetic link to the father but not the mother (Golombok et al., 2011). In either case, surrogate families must grapple with the same universal developmental challenges characteristic of all healthy family functioning. For example, the ability to form and maintain secure relational attachment supports and optimal emotional and behavioral health throughout the family life cycle is crucial. With surrogate families, there is often concern that the involvement of a third party in the birth of a child may lead to difficulties in parenting and, consequently, psychological problems in the child (Golombok, MacCallum, Murray, Lycett, & Jadva, 2006). In a study examining the quality of the parent–child relationship, and the psychological well-being of the parent and child in families with 2-year-old children, Golombok et al. compared 37 surrogacy families with 48 egg donation families and 68 natural conception families. From this study, it was found that the surrogacy mothers showed more positive parent–child relationships, and the surrogacy fathers reported lower levels of parenting stress than their natural conception counterparts. The surrogacy children did not differ from the natural conception children in terms of socio-emotional or cognitive development (2006). This is significant because it demonstrates that surrogacy does not appear to negatively impact parenting or child development in families with 2-year-old children, and that those surrogacy families can achieve the same level of attachment milestones as traditional families.

Another salient clinical factor associated with healthy family functioning and resiliency is the nature and quality of the communication processes within the family. Froma Walsh (1998) identifies the importance of family members sending clear, consistent messages as well as clarifying ambiguous information as component parts to effective family functioning. Secrecy within families can derail these processes and have negative implications throughout the intergenerational life of the family (Imber-Black 1998). In surrogate families, where the child has a genetic link to only one of the parents, questions about if, when, and how parents communicate with their children about the donation become a challenge. More specifically, surrogate families must grapple with questions such as: Who does the information of the donation belong to: the parents or the child? When is the "right" time to tell the child? What would be the impact on the child if he/she finds out about the donation by accident? To what degree would sharing the information about the donation benefit the child and the parent–child relationship (American Society for Reproductive Medicine, 2014)?

In an effort to investigate the impact of telling children about their donor conception on the mother–child relationship and children's psychological adjustment, Susan Golombok conducted assessments of maternal positivity, maternal negativity, mother–child interaction, and child adjustment on 68 donation and 54 natural conception families with a 7-year-old child and found that nondisclosing donation families showed less positive interaction than mothers in natural conception families. Such a finding supports the potential benefit of surrogate families communicating openly with their child about his or her genetic origin (Golombok et al., 2011).

GRANDPARENT-HEADED FAMILIES

Psychosocial stressors such as parental substance abuse, chronic and persistent medical and mental illness, homelessness, incarceration, child abuse, poverty, teenage pregnancy, and divorce can often result in the need for grandparents to assume custodial guardianship of their grand-children. **Grandparent-headed families** are extremely diverse and cut across socioeconomic and cultural lines. In order for family therapists to better understand and effectively work with grandparents raising grand-children, they must consider the complex interplay of mental health, physical health, and economic issues that are unique to this particular alternative family structure. For example, Henderson and Bailey (2015) note that grandparents raising grandchildren experience significantly more stress and depressive symptoms than grandparents who do not have full-time or part-time care of their grandchildren. They also point to research that shows that grandparent caregivers have poorer physi-cal health and more limitations of physical activity than non-caregiving grandparents. Grandparents also may have limited financial resources, thus putting a strain on their capacity to provide adequate housing, food, and clothing for their grandchildren (American Association for Marriage and Family Therapy, 2015). This is significant because these factors often combine to further complicate the transition process of grandchildren into their grandparents' home.

More specifically, grandchildren needing to live under the custodial care of their grandparents often struggle with developmental, physical, behavioral, emotional, and academic problems such as depression, anxi-ety, attention deficit hyperactivity disorder (ADHD), health problems, learning disabilities, and aggression (AAMFT, 2015). Research suggests that grandchildren exhibiting such problems have grandparents who are more depressed and anxious than grandparents whose grandchildren do not have such challenges. Likewise, mentally healthy grandparents have been shown to more likely have grandchildren with fewer behavioral problems and better adaptation (Henderson & Baily, 2015). In order to foster improved parenting and adaptation between grandparents and the grandchildren under their care, family therapists must consistently assess and respond to the mental health needs of the grandparents, given the foregoing direct correlation between grandparent wellness and the emo-tional health and positive outcomes for the grandchildren.

ADOPTIVE FAMILIES

Adoptive families comprise another example of a diverse family struc-ture where the family must grapple with normative developmental pro-cesses such as attachment, boundary setting, open communication, and identity formation, and simultaneously negotiate the idiosyncratic influ-ences associated with the adoption process. Specifically, adaptation and healthy family functioning for adoptive families correlate with a myriad of complex preadoptive factors (e.g., genetics, prenatal complications), pre-placement adversity (e.g., abuse, neglect, multiple foster care placements, and/or orphanage life), and postadoption factors such as the nature and quality of care provided by adoptive parents (Brodzinsky, 2015). These processes are further complicated by the diverse ways in which adoptive families are formed today, which include domestic private placements, foster care placements, and international adoption. Additionally, the adoption process is often fraught with emotional and systemic barriers, such as infertility issues, medical concerns, mental health needs, and legal involvement. This often results in prospective parents having to simultaneously interact with multiple outside systems, and the various eco-systemic influences and subsystems in which such families are often embedded (Bronfenbrenner, 2005). These family formation and systemic factors may lead to different life experiences and unique challenges, increase their anxiety and uncertainty, and impact their ability to manage adoption related responsibilities in the future (Brodzinsky, 2015; Brodzinsky & Pinderhughes, 2005; Pinderhughes, Matthews, & Zhang, 2015). These adoptive families enjoy the same hopes and dreams and undergo many of the same day-to-day challenges as nonadoptive families. Yet it means that clinicians treating adoptive families must be vigilant for the subtle and nuanced influences of the involvement of outside systems and the preadoptive factors and adversity often associated with this clinically diverse population.

STEPFAMILIES

Changes in marriage, divorce, remarriage, and cohabitation rates have resulted in a re-visioning of family life in the United States over the last few decades. Children and families experiencing a marital transition have become increasingly common, thus making the emergence of stepfamilies no longer a non-normative experience (Hetherington & Jodi, 1994). For instance, it is estimated that up to 25 percent of all children will spend some time in a stepfamily prior to reaching the age of 18 (Visher et al., 1989).

Stepfamilies form when one or both adults in a new couple bring children from a previous relationship. Stepfamilies can be very diverse, where the couple may be gay, straight, or inter-racial. The original parent may have been a single or adoptive parent. Both adults may have been in a previous relationship that ended in divorce or death. The stepfamily may consist of latency or adolescent age-children, or both (AAMFT, 2015). Such diversity in structure and composition can make working with stepfamilies highly nuanced and complex. Family therapists working with **stepfamilies** must be on the lookout for variations and complications in the areas of family cohesiveness, boundary ambiguity, roles, coalitions, and conflicting loyalties (Kheshgi-Genovese et al., 1997). For example, a child who is beginning to form a relationship with a new stepmother may feel as though she is betraying her biological mother. Likewise, a stepfather may feel on the outside looking in at the relationship between his new spouse and her biological children. Threats to family cohesiveness and boundaries may arise in stepfamilies when the stepchild's other biological parent influences the functioning of the stepfamily (American Association for Marriage and Family Therapy, 2015; Kheshgi-Genovese et al., 1997). Thus, in order to facilitate adaptive and healthy family functioning in stepfamilies, family therapists must attempt to support good marital functioning; foster strong, positive bonds between biological parent and child; promote the inclusion of all family members; strengthen the family's capacity to make compromised family decisions; and discourage parent–child coalitions (Anderson & White, 1986).

LGBT FAMILIES

LGBT (lesbian, gay, bisexual, and transgender) families represent another alternative family structure that must contend with the same family life cycle dynamics that all families experience, and simultaneously negotiate the challenges specific to this clinical population (Harway, 1996). For example, similar to heterosexual families, **LGBT families** may seek therapy for issues related to intimacy, family of origin, or child care. However, for LBGT families these dynamics are "complicated by the often stigmatizing social context in which the family is embedded, such as the local community, workplace, and school system" (Grafsky & Nguyen, 2015, p. 204). Additionally, families may seek to embed themselves within a network of intergenerational family support. For LBGT families, this need is often satisfied by creating a surrogate family comprised of friends and people within the community, thus reshaping the notion of family created only through blood, marriage, and adoption (Eeden-Moorefield & Benson, 2015).

When working with LGBT families, family therapists must consider the impact of heteronormativity, or the belief that only heterosexual opposite-sex relationships are normal, as well as other dominant social norms and ideologies of the heterosexual majority. Heteronormativity can result in stigma and internalized homophobia, thus further alienating LGBT families from themselves and others, and placing them more at risk of negative consequences, such as depression and suicide (Eeden-Moorefield & Benson, 2015). Family therapists must also take into account the diversity of LGBT families and the intersectional influences that grow out of such diversity. For example, the impact of heteronormativity will be different for a White working-class woman in a lesbian couple than it would be for a Black middle-class male in a gay partnership, when factoring the different intersections of race, gender, and socioeconomic status (Eeden-Moorefield and Benson, 2015).

Examples such as this illustrate how diverse family structures intersect with and influence normal, universal family developmental processes.

Family therapists must be aware of how universal family processes are colored by the dynamics of diverse family structures and processes. We will now examine some of these universal processes that we have referenced in more detail.

UNIVERSAL FAMILY PROCESSES AND INTERSECTIONALITY

All families, regardless of makeup and/or socioeconomic status, must contend with a myriad of driving pushes and pulls and developmental achievements inherent to the individual family's life cycle (Minuchin, Lee, & Simon, 2006). This concept of **universal family processes** is found in many evidence-based models such as Brief Strategic Family Therapy (Robbins & Gonzalo, 2007), Functional Family Therapy (Sexton & Alexander, 2004), and Multi-Systemic Therapy (Henggeler, Schoenwald, Borduin, Rowland, & Cunningham, 2009), as well as Structural Family Therapy (Minuchin et al., 2006), which Larner (2004) points out has empirical support but is not part of the "evidence-based club" (p. 17). There is not yet a consensus on the family processes deemed universal, and the list we provide next is not exhaustive. It is intended to give the reader a framework for understanding the concept of universal processes, and to show that these processes manifest in different ways. For example, their manifestation may depend on contextual factors such as socioeconomics, varied family structures such as identified earlier, race, and gender.

Consistent with Minuchin and colleagues (2006), and our orientation as structural family therapists, the family processes that we believe are universal include establishing a sense of loyalty; providing mutual nurturance and support; compromising and accommodating around needs; maintaining a commitment to avoid giving pain; tolerating differences; navigating complementarity patterns and circles of causality; establishing boundaries, rules, family roles, and hierarchy; respecting parental influence and healthy child development; and cultivating a sense of belonging and family identity while maintaining individuation.

The way that these universal processes play out is unique to any given family, and clinicians must consider how culture, gender, sexual orientation, class, ethnicity, religion, ability, and identity lend nuance to these processes, especially when working with diverse family structures. The concept of **intersectionality** (Crenshaw, 1991), which contends that the intersection of race, sex, culture, and politics pertaining to a certain group must be examined together rather than as separate entities, helps us to appreciate the way in which these universal processes manifest differently through the prism of gender, sexual orientation, ethnicity, age, and biological and nonbiological association.

Establishing a Sense of Loyalty and Providing Mutual Nurturance and Support

What makes family life so important and ultimately adaptive is the attempt to protect, support, nurture, and defend fellow family members. Family life pulls for a sense of belonging. Minuchin points out that, "young children say quite naturally, 'I belong to mommy and daddy'" (Minuchin, & Nichols, 1993, p. 284). Families identify themselves as "the _____ family," and this statement contains beliefs, history, stories, and love. One can see these processes play out in everyday transactions, such as when 12-year-old Sammy has no interest playing with 9-year-old Louie at home, yet staunchly defends Louie when he is mocked on the playground.

Another example is parents today who are experiencing pressures of raising their children, navigating work life, paying bills, and yet are willing to drop everything and travel to their home of origin to support and advocate for an elderly parent in poor health. Clinicians trained in identifying, drawing out, and mobilizing these natural family processes are less likely to get distracted by discord and tension that families in treatment often present. Interventions that target and elicit families' natural inclinations toward loyalty and support will assist family members with experiencing the family in a different way, and increase hope and optimism while decreasing negativity and blame (Sexton & Alexander, 2004). This is consistent with Walsh's (2003) research on the benefits of tapping into natural resiliencies of families, particularly the relational resilience in families, as opposed to individual resilience. These relational resilience factors fall into three categories: belief systems, organizational patterns, and communication and problem solving (Walsh, 2003).

Through the lens of intersectionality, loyalty can look different based on family composition. For example, in a single-parent household, the older children may dedicate more time to picking up the younger children from school, cooking dinner, or helping with homework, rather than the parents. In another example, loyalty among sibling children of same-sex parents may take on a protective sense of togetherness in an environment where the family is experienced as "other."

Compromising and Accommodating around Needs, Maintaining a Commitment to Avoid Giving Pain, and Tolerating Differences

A strengths-based view of families perceives that a desire for togetherness and interconnectivity lies beneath the strife and discord that sometimes characterizes family relationships (Minuchin et al., 2006). In our experience, family members, when given the opportunity to understand and empathize with kin, will make the necessary adjustments and changes to meet the needs of their loved ones and to maintain a sense of unity and connectedness.

These adjustments include compromise, accommodation, and tolerance of difference, and often entail changes in communication patterns.

In an example related to ability and disability, consider a recently married couple, where the wife has an adult, developmentally disabled sibling who is living with her parents. When discussing future plans around children and buying a residence, the couple assumes the need to accommodate for the eventual caring of this sibling when her parents are no longer equipped to do so.

Lastly, consider a family in which a teenage son comes out to his parents as gay. Saltzburg (2004) posits that parents often experience loss, shame, and fear when a child pronounces a nonheterosexual identity. In addition to these feelings, the father in this family struggles with internalized homophobia. Out of a commitment to maintaining a positive relationship with his son, family togetherness, and a commitment to avoid giving pain, he works hard to confront his beliefs and assumptions and ultimately arrives at a place of tolerance.

Navigating Complementarity Patterns and Circles of Causality

All family members live within transactional patterns of behavior that dictate their sense of self and relationship to others. Thus, in our families, we are simultaneously initiators and responders, involving ourselves in dances of patterned behavior (Minuchin et al., 2006). Family therapists need to understand how family members co-construct one another, and they must see beneath the presenting problem in order to unlock the potential for increased flexibility around cycles of behavior. Clinicians working with families must be on the lookout for patterns that exist beneath the presenting problem on display.

For example, 10-year-old Myron exhibits behaviors often associated with ADHD; he is inattentive in class, talks back to the teacher, fights with peers, and often gets sent to the principal's office. The principal calls the single mom regarding her son's behavior and requests that she come in for a conference. At the meeting, the principal suggests that Myron has ADHD and recommends treatment and medication. When viewed from the perspective of complementarity, a different and more complex understanding of Myron's behavior begins to emerge. For instance, it turns out that every time the principal calls Myron's mother about Myron, it is one of the few times that his mother is activated out of a clinical depression. Additionally, when his mother picks up Myron and takes him home, she calls Myron's father, who is infrequently involved in the family. Myron's behavior can now be understood to have a protective function in the family, in that it mobilizes Myron's mother and serves to reconnect Myron with his absent father. This perspective is inherently strengths-based, in that it de-stigmatizes Myron, brings out the healthy protectiveness amongst family members, and opens up an intervention that is family-based rather than individual-based.

Establishing Boundaries, Rules, Family Roles, and Hierarchy

Every family has a system of hierarchy, established roles, and levels of influence. Clinicians, when assessing family dynamics, must pick up on nonverbal cues that reveal such patterns. For example, if a family of five comes in and the clinician asks what the family would like to discuss, and everyone subsequently looks to the mother, this may illustrate mom's role as a central switchboard of the family.

Take for instance, an intergenerational family comprised of a grandmother, 12-year-old grandson, 9-year-old granddaughter, imprisoned father, and an inconsistently involved, substance-abusing mother. A family such as this will likely be grappling with the universal experiences of establishing a consistent family hierarchy, role definition, and rules and norms. Unique to this intergenerational family is how the adult mother and daughter relationship affects negotiations regarding hierarchy. For example, the grandmother must struggle with maintaining a safe and consistent family environment while also encouraging the mom's natural competency as a parent, which may mean relinquishing control when the mother achieves a relative level of stability. This often unspoken negotiation is strongly influenced by the nature of the parent–child relationship of the grandmother with the mother that colors how they simultaneously care for the little ones. If the clinician is not aware of this subtle interplay regarding hierarchy, he or she can run the risk of overidentifying with the grandmother, or short-circuit the natural pull toward reunification with the mother. The clinician has to celebrate the grandmother while also empowering her to support the mother's recovery and allow room for her adult daughter to take on the role of caregiver when she is ready.

Respecting Parental Influence and Healthy Child Development, and Cultivating a Sense of Belonging and Family Identity While Maintaining Individuation

The attachment literature (Bowlby, 1980) clearly states that we humans have an inborn need for connection and satisfying relationships. Families represent the lifelong vehicle by which these connections are satisfied. The newborn baby comes into the world with a preexisting repertoire of verbal and nonverbal cues to elicit an attachment response from her caregivers. Parents, in turn, are responsive to these cues, thus facilitating bidirectional interconnectivity (Minuchin & Nichols, 1993). This choreography unfolds throughout our lives and is maximized inside family relationships. While family life might be a source of friction, pain, and struggle, it is also potentially our greatest source of healing and nurturance as we navigate the balance of maintaining a sense of belonging and individuating.

Take, for example, a two-parent family with an adopted 11-year-old girl residing in a suburban community outside a large, metropolitan area. This girl's exploration of identity is going to be influenced by her adopted status. She is going to have questions about her identity that the parents may not be able to answer. If the family doesn't navigate this while being sensitive to her need to develop her identity, the potential for rebellion and acting out may be more extreme (Basow et al., 2008). Family therapists working with this family must be sensitive to these undercurrents and the daughter's inclination at some point to contact her biological parent(s). The parents likely will struggle around how much freedom to give their daughter to seek out her biological relatives, and may be rigid in their concern and thus enforce rigid boundaries. They may not understand that flexible boundaries may be more conducive to successful individuation and identity formation due to the daughter's normal desire to find out about her biological roots.

Through the lens of intersectionality, consider now that the daughter was adopted from China and the parents are practicing, conservative Jews. In addition to the child's awareness that she is adopted, she also has to experience looking different from her larger family system and her congregation, including her Hebrew school peers. This child and family might experience microaggressions, such as running into assumptions that the child is not Jewish or questions about why she is attending Hebrew school. This makes identity formation more complicated. For example, how do the parents, who are very attached and committed to Judaism, foster a strong Jewish identity in the child while allowing room for the child to explore questions about her native faith? The parents, if not sensitive to the hidden challenges of individuation and belonging, may feel threatened by natural strivings of their child to establish a cultural identity different from their own and may inadvertently polarize their child by responding rigidly and imposing strict boundaries. Clinicians therefore, must be aware of these hidden dynamics, and work to proactively normalize such feelings. Moreover, they need to create an environment conducive to discussing, exploring, and developing a mutual understanding that, under the umbrella promoting of healthy child development, there are going to be competing needs that do not necessarily have to threaten the integrity of the family.

UNIVERSAL FAMILY PROCESSES EXIST IN DIVERSE FAMILY STRUCTURES

With the increasing likelihood that clinicians in mental health settings across the nation are encountering families of diverse cultures, socioeconomic strata, and structures, it is critical that they are well versed in the above-mentioned universal processes associated with all families, and also are able to broaden their lens to address the hidden subtleties unique to diverse family structures. For example, Smith, Spillane, and Annus (2006) distinguish universal psychological processes, such as the need to be viewed as good, and *cultural instances* of these processes, such as self-sufficiency in the Western world and interdependency found in Eastern cultures. We posit that the universal processes described earlier have varied instantiations, based on family structure, cultural dynamics, and socioeconomic status, as well as the intersection of these dynamics in their countless variations. In other words, clinicians working with families must be able to scaffold their understanding of the universal processes pertinent to each family, and the instantiations of those processes based on family structure, intersectionality, and culture.

Stepfamilies are a good example. Consider a family consisting of a mother with a 14-year-old son with a biological father who lives in a different state, a stepfather, and a biological 4-year-old female daughter of both adults. Pertaining to universal processes, this family will want to promote the healthy development of their children, establish clearly defined roles and boundaries, establish the parents' identity as a couple, and create a sense of family loyalty and connection. Additionally, the mother, son, and stepdad must navigate the inherent challenges of two fathers existing in this boy's life. This might set up conflicts around parenting, loyalty and betrayal, and role confusion. Internal to this system might be challenges around parental control and hierarchy. For example how justified does the stepdad feel in parenting this child? How much room does the mother give the stepfather to exercise control over the son? One must also consider the son's feelings about living in a home where, unlike his sister, he does not have a biological connection to both parents.

Further consideration is needed if this family also happens to be comprised of a Caucasian mother and son, African American stepfather, and a biracial daughter. In this case, societal judgment, biases, and microaggressions or subtle acts of racism (Sue et al., 2007) illustrate the need to identify the unique instances of universal processes as they relate to this family. As an example, society may respond more favorably to a Caucasian mother and Caucasian son than to a Black stepfather and a Caucasian son. This would likely complicate the establishment of parenting roles. Additionally, the parentage of a Black father and biracial daughter would be less likely to be contested in the outside world than a Black stepfather and Caucasian son, which could complicate further the son's sense of belonging in the family and identity formation.

The scenario discussed here illuminates the importance of clinicians being trained in universal family processes while also developing the capacity to identify and work with how family composition and intersectionality involving class, ethnicity, culture, and gender further shape the family's processes and experiences. Clinicians must realize that many varied family formations are not just about one nontraditional, under-served, or misunderstood characteristic or demographic, but multiple ones, such as socioeconomic status (SES), race, and sexuality. What fol-lows is a discussion of several interventions that we deem key in address-ing the myriad forms of diversity that a couple or family may bring, followed by a case vignette involving surrogate parentage that illus-trates this level of complexity. The vignette represents a fictional family, drawn from the authors' composite clinical experiences, that is strug-gling with myriad distinctive factors associated with a diverse family structure.

KEY INTERVENTIONS FOR WORKING WITH DIVERSE FAMILIES

Asking Stance

Especially given the diverse family structures family therapists encounter today, every therapist should assume an "asking stance" (Boyd-Franklin, Cleek, Wofsy, & Mundy, 2013). This stance requires that therapists recog-nize that all families come from a rich tapestry of traditions, rituals, and cultural influences that help define them and that they can draw on dur-ing times of adversity. The focus of the asking stance challenges clinicians to be aware of and work with the various biological and sociological cat-egories such as gender, race, class, sexual orientation, gender expression, and other aspects of identity that influence variance in instances of uni-versal human longings such as a sense of connection, respect for bound-aries, love of children, and loyalty. This requires a clinician's openness to recognizing his or her own cultural, racial, and gender-based learning histories as well.

Identifying Subtle Strengths and Reframing

The therapist in the following vignette links two distinct skills—identifying strengths and reframing—together. Kelly, Bhagwat, Maynigo, and Moses (2014) identify subtle strengths as a core competency for "tai-loring treatment to multicultural factors" (p. 487). This skill is the oppo-site of the problem-focused, deficit approach, and involves openness and appreciation of the inborn, natural competencies of a family system, its individual members, and its resources. Reframing is a technique to help create a different way of experiencing a situation, person, or relation-ship (Nichols & Schwartz, 1998). One way to think about reframing is relating a relationship or behavior to the client or family's best sense of self. When done effectively, reframing offers validation around a behav-ior or relationship that is often experienced as problematic (Sexton & Alexander, 2004).

Establishing a Culturally Relevant Organizational Theme

Similar to reframing, organizing themes describe "problematic patterns of behavior and/or relationships, in a way that suggests they may be motivated by positive . . . intent(s)" (Sexton & Alexander, 2004). Organizing themes often appears akin to, "this is a family struggling with _____, with the intent of achieving _____, and the members attempt to achieve it in _____ ways." It is the authors' contention that, especially when working with diverse family structures, these themes need to be culturally relevant and include dynamics such as oppression, discrimination, and feelings of otherness, all of which are exemplified in the vignette.

Help the Family Identify and Connect with Healthy Community Models

Many couples and family members who are in diverse family structures experience a feeling of otherness that can contribute to reactive cycles in both the public and private arenas. Connecting family members to models composed of others who share common experiences and values can serve to normalize the family's experience (Boyd-Franklin, Kelly, & Durham, 2008).

Therapist Self-Awareness and Making Roles Transparent

Kelly et al. (2014) state that the "goal of increasing one's self-awareness is to understand more about one's identity and biases as well as structural oppression" (p. 487). The dynamics of race, gender, class, privilege, and oppression do not disappear once families step into the therapy office. Therefore, self-awareness becomes a powerful skill when the therapist articulates these dynamics. The purpose of this transparency, which is illustrated in the vignette, is to bridge differences and create a safer and more truthful space for families to share their own experiences.

VIGNETTE

The Watson-Diaz family resided in Arlington, Virginia, with their two sons, Jonathan, 10, and Marcus, 12. They began therapy with Sharon, a family therapist, at a local behavioral health care center. They initiated therapy at the recommendation of the school counselor, due to Marcus presenting with increased oppositional behaviors such as fighting during recess, talking back to adults, and being argumentative in the classroom. Grace and Lizzie, Marcus's mothers, had also been experiencing increasing defiance from Marcus and had been struggling to unite over how to respond to his behavior.

Grace and Lizzie were married, and had been together for 12 years. Grace came from a liberal traditionally White Anglo-Saxon protestant family from Connecticut. Lizzie was from Virginia, and was the daughter of Mexican immigrant parents. Both had advanced degrees, they were from large families, and they both maintained close relationships with their siblings and extended families.

During the first session, Sharon was surprised to learn that Marcus and Jonathan, who were both brown-skinned, were the biological children of Grace, who was White. Grace and Lizzie explained that they chose a Latino male donor, who was a mutual friend but not really involved, for the parentage of their sons. Planning around the pregnancy was very difficult, especially when they learned during the process that Lizzie was unable to bear children. Sharon, utilizing the therapist skill of noticing her own reactions as a way to gain insight into the family's experience, was mindful of her surprise and began to wonder about the family's experiences regarding public response to their family composition. Sharon kept this observation in mind, especially in relation to her own identity as White, heterosexual, and female.

Consistent with family systemic theory and principles, Sharon knew to look beyond the individual presenting problems of Marcus, and to see his behaviors as embedded in a larger familial and social context. She conceptualized the work as family-based, wherein parent alignment regarding discipline, communication processes, particularly around hetero and racial normativity influences, and family resilience must be considered and addressed in the context of treatment. The treatment plan would center on strengthening parental alliance, opening up family communication, and moving the focus of attention away from what happens inside of Marcus to a more systemic familial context, particularly given the diverse family structure.

After a period of initial joining with the family, Sharon became aware of the universal family dynamics at play in this family. For example, there is strong emphasis on healthy child development, respect of adults, and loyalty and support. Additionally, the family struggled to maintain a proper hierarchy, as neither Lizzie nor Grace could agree on how to set limits and expectations for the boys. Sharon sensed that Lizzie tended to be more strict while Grace tended to be more lenient.

An enactment of these dynamics took place after a recent event in which the kids on the school playground were making fun of Marcus for having two moms. Marcus rather disrespectfully protested to his two mothers that "You can't possibly know, so leave me alone!" This prompted Lizzie to get angry and tell Marcus to watch his mouth when speaking with adults. In turn, this statement activated Grace to state that, "this is therapy, and it's important to express feelings here." Sharon saw her own response to this enactment as an opportunity to utilize reframing. She pointed out the differences between Lizzie's disciplinarian approach and Grace's more permissive stance and tone. She identified the potential for these styles to trigger each other, and reframed the different parenting styles as complementary when used in tandem, rather than as a problem. Sharon elicited each parent's love for Marcus by educating Grace and Lizzie the importance of Marcus responding to a unified parental front. She requested that the next session be a couple/parent session that can spend some time on harnessing the potential strength of the two complementary parenting styles.

In the next session, Sharon began by referring back to the enactment, wherein the family's problem dynamic was manifest in the therapy session. She observed how the two parenting styles were mutually reinforced, leading to polarization and a confusing experience for Marcus. To elaborate, she pointed out how in the last session, Lizzie's authoritative response to Marcus activated Grace to be more coddling, which in turn exacerbated Lizzie's strictness. Grace and Lizzie acknowledged that this often happened in the home. Employing the skill of exploring cultural and familial influences on parenting perspectives and approaches, Sharon asked Grace to talk to Lizzie about her experience, which resulted in an organic conversation about each partner's family of origin and the influences on their respective parenting. Both expressed appreciation and respect for each parenting style, and both agreed that these styles in tandem, when unaware of the potential conflict due to difference, caused them to behave in ways that are not helpful and not desirable. In this discussion, Grace shared her belief that the boys do not have to behave as properly as Lizzie mandated. This prompted Lizzie to remark, "You don't know what it's like to be brown, you don't know what it's like to be racially profiled. I'm trying to protect our boys."

Sharon noticed that this last exchange unearthed how skin color further complicated the negative relational cycle being discussed. Based on reading Kelly et al. (2014), Sharon continued to utilize the skill of exploring how experiences of race influence the couple-hood. She began by exploring each partner's feelings about race, and about biracial couple-hood. Grace subsequently came to a place of understanding about how, as the white-skinned person in the family, she felt marginalized, and her desire for a sense of belonging in the family resulted in her leniency in parenting. This prompted Lizzie to express empathy for Grace, and noted that she had never picked up on her marginalized experience. Lizzie related that as a Latina, she too knew what it was like to feel marginalized. She also expressed that she sometimes felt similarly marginalized in the family system, since the boys were not biologically hers. This couple would not have come to appreciate these nuances had the complementary relationship between their parenting styles not been raised as a strength in the first session The identification of strengths, in a reframe, paved the way for discussing their vulnerabilities and different learning histories around parenting without fear that the therapist would not understand.

This exploration caused Sharon to ask specifically about experiences of intersectionality. Sharon took the opportunity to first practice transparency of use of self to empathically share her surprise that the boys were the biological children of Grace. She recognized the response is shaped by her own identity as White, female, and heterosexual. By acknowledging this human response in a culturally nuanced therapeutic relationship, she made it present in the room. Employing the asking stance, she wondered aloud to Grace and Lizzie about their experiences as a lesbian, biracial couple in the outside world. The couple told Sharon about the **microaggressions** they commonly experienced, from the grocery store clerk to the waiter in the restaurant. They often experienced others assuming the boys are the biological children of Lizzie. Toward the end of the discussion, Lizzie pointed out that Marcus's teacher often directed her attention toward Grace as the fellow White person in the room, and she called the teacher a racist. Grace accused Lizzie of reading too deeply into the situation, and Lizzie responded, "The reason you don't pick up on that is because you are White." The session ran out of time, and Sharon chose this as an opportunity to remind them how important it is that these hidden levels of vulnerability and tension be continuously explored. Employing a strength-based perspective, she authentically applauded their hard work during the session and cautioned them to not allow these newly uncovered dynamics lead to the negative relational patterns they had been discussing.

At the third session, Lizzie and Grace came back with Marcus and Jonathan. The couple commented on how, though things had been difficult, the awareness of the complementary and potentially exacerbating parenting styles helped them to form a more united front in parenting the boys. They stated, "It's been hard and painful but the awareness is helping us." This was made evident in session when the family wanted to discuss an incident at school. Marcus claimed that he was being treated unfairly by the teacher, who wouldn't let him go to the bathroom for a second time in the hour. Sharon noted aloud that Marcus was looking directly to Grace, the more lenient parent, in an effort to get her to ally with him around being unfairly treated, and requested Grace to respond to Marcus. Grace was able to respond with some empathy to Marcus, while also stating that rules are rules, and while at school it is expected that he follow the school rules. She also expressed confusion about why he would need to go to the bathroom again anyway. Sharon then asked Lizzie her point of view regarding this dialogue, and Lizzie expressed her agreement with Grace and reinforced the point that rules are rules.

Sharon elicited from Marcus his experience of this interaction. Marcus stated, "no one gets me. My teacher doesn't like me, my parents don't get it. No one knows how hard it is." Sharon chose this moment as an opportunity to elicit the experiences of the family as related to diverse identities. She acknowledged that Marcus was having difficult feelings, perhaps related to a teacher with racial bias. She asked Grace and Lizzie to talk to Marcus about his feelings, leading to Marcus ultimately expressing, "No one in my class has two moms." Jonathan, in what appeared to be an effort to diffuse the tension, responded, "Well I have two moms," to which Marcus replied again, "Yeah but you're not in my class, dumbass." Lizzie displayed a reaction to this, reprimanding Marcus for name-calling.

In this moment, Sharon recognized that a familiar negative pattern was about to emerge and interrupted it by commenting on how this was an opportunity to join together in shared experiences. She established a culturally relevant organizational theme (Sexton & Alexander, 2004) that this was a family struggling with feeling outside of the box. Grace's way of dealing with this was coddling and permissiveness, Lizzie's coping was to be authoritarian, and Marcus dealt with his pain by getting into trouble and challenging authority. Jonathan dealt with this by being the good kid and taking care of everyone. She encouraged the family to come to terms with these feelings in a different way by talking about their experiences with each other and not in ways that can feel alienating to other family members. This resulted in the family tapping into the universal family process of loyalty and support. Sharon challenged the family to join forces and partner to overcome these challenges as a family.

This family was seen over the course of 11 months. They regularly attended both family and couples sessions. In the family sessions, the culturally relevant organizational theme was further developed to be more nuanced, and included experiences as "the other" in terms of culture, ethnicity, and, above all, as a diverse family structure. The reactivity was lessened and members, over time, became increasingly on board with supporting each other and protecting the family and themselves, again linking to the universal family process of loyalty and support. This created a context more conducive for uniting as parents, for improving communication patterns and setting age-appropriate limits for their boys. Lizzie and Grace developed an increased capacity to join their parenting styles and their family-of-origin influences.

With Sharon continuing to deepen the employment of cultural awareness and exploration, the couple's sessions focused on further illuminating the subtle influences of their different backgrounds. Grace and Lizzie continued to refine their understanding of their viewpoints and experiences within a biracial, lesbian couple-hood. With Sharon's encouragement, they began to proactively create more space for themselves as a couple by going on weekly date nights. Over time, they took increased ownership of these date nights, and began more fully enjoying their identity as a lesbian couple. Sharon, using the therapist skill of helping families tap into healthy community resources, encouraged the couple to join a listserv that gave them access to other gay couples within the community. Lizzie and Grace got more involved with that community through meet-ups and events. They also developed a network of biracial couples, with whom they could discuss common challenges. Through ongoing exploration of this process, they began to feel more comfortable inhabiting a confident, multidimensional parenting style.

As the treatment developed, Marcus began behaving in ways consistent with developmental norms and presenting as less angry and preoccupied. His school performance improved. Over time, Marcus was more responsive to Sharon's strength-based attempts to reframe his behavioral struggles as the vehicle that got the family into treatment, rather than as the problem, and examine these subtle, important family dynamics.

CONCLUSIONS

This chapter has sought to illuminate the complex interplay among diverse family structures, universal family dynamics, and intersectional influences. We encourage family therapists to utilize the interventions identified in the vignette, with the understanding that these interventions are underpinned by Sharon's awareness that universal family processes are contextual to family structure, ethnicity, socioeconomic status, and other factors. Our hope is that the information and clinical examples in this chapter serve as guideposts for anybody engaging with the challenging and rewarding work with diverse family structures.

CHAPTER REVIEW

Key Points

1. Diverse family structures are increasingly common.
2. All families grapple with universal processes, regardless of composition.
3. Instances of these processes vary, depending on dynamics such as race, gender, culture, ethnicity, socioeconomic status, biological and nonbiological association, and sexual orientation and expression.
4. Clinicians should engage in cultural competency practices, maintain ongoing curiosity via an asking stance, and be aware of their own biases and judgments.
5. Ask questions, be curious, and tap into felt experience, traditions, and family richness! As Harry Stack Sullivan said, "All of us are much more simply human than otherwise" (2013, p. 61).
6. Understand universal family processes. You may use them as guiding lights to further explore, examine, and make clinical use of the nuanced expression of these processes as influenced by culture, race, ethnicity, SES, gender, and sexual orientation.

Key Terms

grandparent-headed families, intersectionality, LGBT families, microaggressions, stepfamilies, surrogate families, universal family processes

Myths and Realities

- It is a myth that all families should conform to a uniform family structure. In reality, families come in all shapes, sizes, and orientations, and bring unique stories and experiences.
- It is a myth that therapists should be neutral and conservative when working with unfamiliar family structures. In reality, therapists should embrace difference with awareness, compassion, and curiosity.

Tools and Tips

Knowledge

Kelly, S., Bhagwat, R., Maynigo, P., & Moses, E. (2014). Couple and marital therapy: The complement and expansion provided by multicultural approaches. In Frederick T. L. Leong (Ed.), *APA handbook of multicultural psychology* (pp. 479–497). Washington, DC: American Psychological Association.

McDowell, T., & Hernández, P. (2010). Decolonizing academia: Intersectionality, participation, and accountability in family therapy and counseling. *Journal of Feminist Family Therapy*, 22(2), 93–111.

Minuchin, S., Lee, W. Y., & Simon, G. M. (2006). *Mastering family therapy: Journeys of growth and transformation*. Hoboken, NJ: John Wiley & Sons.

Dynamic Sizing

Openness and curiosity are essential to being aware of when it is and when it is not appropriate to apply knowledge of client's culture to a particular client's behavior.

Therapists must also be aware how their own cultural background may affect their experience and interpretation of client behavior.

In multicultural work, clinicians must consistently grapple with the dynamic tension of recognizing clients as individuals while also understanding that all individuals are influenced and shaped by cultural learning histories.

Skills

Theory. The nuanced way that universal family processes transpire in a family system must be examined through the lens of intersectionality—gender identity, culture, ethnicity, class, and sexuality.

Prevention. Workers should be aware of the reality of microaggressions and nonsupportive environments, particularly for children in alternative family structures, and should thus be attentive, open, and accepting of these experiences.

Service Provision. Adopt an asking stance. Identify subtle strengths. Expand family's experiencing of "problems" via reframe. Establish a culturally sensitive organizational theme. Connect families to healthy community models. Make roles transparent.

Policy. Policies in schools regarding acceptance and understanding of alternative family structures are often nonexistent. Cultural competency and teacher awareness should be encouraged, particularly regarding how attitudes impact social and academic development.

Research. Research should seek to understand how attitudes about alternative family structures, including community and school policy, impact children's ability to learn well, live well, and play well.

Awareness

Know yourself. Know your biases and values, and learn about the cultures with which you work.

REFERENCES

American Association for Marriage and Family Therapy. (2015a). *Grandparents raising grandchildren.* Retrieved August 2015 from http://www.aamft.org/imis15/AAMFT/Content/Consumer_Updates/Grandparents_Raising_Grandchildren.aspx

American Association for Marriage and Family Therapy. (2015b). *Stepfamilies.* Retrieved August 2015 from https://www.aamft.org/iMIS15/AAMFT/Content/consumer_updates/stepfamilies.aspx

American Society of Reproductive Medicine. (2015). *Frequently Asked Questions.* Retrieved February 2015 from http://www.reproductivefacts.org/detail.aspx?id=2322

American Society of Reproductive Medicine. (2014). *Fact Sheet.* Retrieved August 2015 from http://www.asrm.org/FACTSHEET-Gamete-Donation-Deciding-Whether-To-Tell/

Anderson, J.Z., & White, G.D. (1986). An empirical investigation of interaction and relationship patterns in functional and dysfunctional nuclear families and stepfamilies. *Family Process, 25,* 407–422.

Basow, S.A., Lilley, E., Bookwala, J., & McGillicuddy-DeLisi, A. (2008). Identity development and psychological well-being in Korean-born adoptees in the US. *American Journal of Orthopsychiatry, 78,* 473.

Bowlby, J. (1980). *Attachment and loss* (Vol. 3). New York, NY: Basic books.

Boyd-Franklin, N., Kelly, S., & Durham, J. (2008). African American couples in therapy. In A. S. Gunnan (Ed.), *Clinical handbook of couples therapy* (4th ed., pp. 681–697). New York, NY: Guilford Press.

Boyd-Franklin, N., Cleek, E. N., Wofsy, M., & Mundy, B. (2013). *Therapy in the real world: Effective treatments for challenging problems.* New York, NY: Guilford Press.

Brodzinsky, D. (2015). Understanding and treating adoptive families. In S. Browning & K. Pasley (Eds.), *Contemporary families: Translating research into practice* (p. 35). London, UK: Routledge.

Brodzinsky, D.M., & Pinderhughes, E. (2005). Parenting and child development in adoptive families. *Handbook of parenting, 1,* 279–313.

Bronfenbrenner, U. (2005). *Making human beings human: Bioecological perspectives on human development.* Los Angeles, CA: Sage Publications.

Crenshaw, K. (1991). Mapping the margins: Intersectionality, identity politics, and violence against women of color. *Stanford law review, 43*, 1241–1299.

Golombok, S., MacCallum, F., Murray, C., Lycett, E., & Jadva, V. (2006). Surrogacy families: parental functioning, parent–child relationships and children's psychological development at age 2. *Journal of Child Psychology and Psychiatry, 47*, 213–222.

Golombok, S., Readings, J., Blake, L., Casey, P., Mellish, L., Marks, A., & Jadva, V. (2011). Children conceived by gamete donation: psychological adjustment and mother-child relationships at age 7. *Journal of Family Psychology, 25*, 230.

Grafsky, E. L., & Nguyen, H. N. (2015). Affirmative therapy with LGBTQ+ families. In S. Browning & K. Pasely (Eds.), *Contemporary families: Translating research into practice* (p. 166). London, UK: Routledge.

Harway, M. (1996). *Treating the changing family: Handling normative and unusual events* (Vol. 1). Hoboken, NJ: John Wiley & Sons.

Henderson, T. L., & Bailey, S. J. (2015). Grandparents rearing grandchildren. In S. Browning & K. Pasely (Eds.), *Contemporary families: Translating research into practice* (pp. 229–265). London, UK: Routledge.

Henggeler, S. W., Schoenwald, S. K., Borduin, C. M., Rowland, M. D., & Cunningham, P. B. (2009). *Multisystemic therapy for antisocial behavior in children and adolescents*. New York, NY: Guilford Press.

Hetherington, E. M., & Jodi, K. M. (1994). Stepfamilies as settings for child development. In A. Booth & J. Dunn (Eds.), *Stepfamilies: Who benefits? Who does not* (pp. 55–79). London, UK: Routledge.

Imber-Black, E. (1998). *The secret life of families: Truth-telling, privacy, and reconciliation in a tell-all society*. New York, NY: Bantam.

Kelly, S., Bhagwat, R., Maynigo, P., & Moses, E. (2014). Couple and marital therapy: The complement and expansion provided by multicultural approaches. In Frederick T. L. Leong (Ed.), *APA handbook of multicultural psychology* (pp. 479–497). Washington DC: American Psychological Association.

Kheshgi-Genovese, Z., & Genovese, T. (1997). Developing the spousal relationship within stepfamilies. *Families in Society: The Journal of Contemporary Social Services, 78*, 255–264.

Larner, G. (2004). Family therapy and the politics of evidence. *Journal of Family Therapy, 26*, 17–39.

Lofquist, D. (2012). *Households and families: 2010*. U.S. Department of Commerce, Economics and Statistics Administration, U.S. Census Bureau.

McDowell, T., & Hernández, P. (2010). Decolonizing academia: Intersectionality, participation, and accountability in family therapy and counseling. *Journal of Feminist Family Therapy, 22*, 93–111.

Minuchin, S., Lee, W. Y., & Simon, G. M. (2006). *Mastering family therapy: Journeys of growth and transformation*. Hoboken, NJ: John Wiley & Sons.

Minuchin, S., & Nichols, M. P. (1993). *Family healing: Tales for hope and renewal*. New York, NY: Free Press.

Nichols, M. P., & Schwartz, R. C. (1998). *Family therapy: Concepts and methods*. Boston, MA: Allyn and Bacon.

Pinderhughes, E. E., Matthews, J. A., & Zhang, X. (2015). Research on adoptive families and their 21st-century challenges. In S. Browning & K. Pasely (Eds.), *Contemporary families: Translating research into practice* (p. 14). London, UK: Routledge.

Robbins, M.S., Szapocznik, J., & Gonzalo, A. (2007). Brief strategic family therapy. In N. Kazantzis & L. LL'Abate (Eds.), *Handbook of Homework Assignments in Psychotherapy* (pp. 133–149). New York, NY: Springer.

Roberts, A., & Stark, C. (2014, October 6). *By the numbers: Same sex marriage. CNN.* Retrieved from http://www.cnn.com/2012/05/11/politics/btn-same-sex-marriage.

Saltzburg, S. (2004). Learning that an adolescent child is gay or lesbian: The parent experience. *Social Work, 49,* 109–118.

Saulny, S. (2011). Census data presents rise in multiracial population of youths. *New York Times,* March 24, 2011.

Sexton, T.L., & Alexander, J.F. (2004). *Functional family therapy clinical training manual.* Baltimore, MD: Annie E. Casey Foundation.

Smith, G.T., Spillane, N.S., & Annus, A.M. (2006). Implications of an emerging integration of universal and culturally specific psychologies. *Perspectives on Psychological Science, 1,* 211–233.

Sue, D.W., Capodilupo, C.M., Torino, G.C., Bucceri, J.M., Holder, A., Nadal, K.L., & Esquilin, M. (2007). Racial microaggressions in everyday life: implications for clinical practice. *American Psychologist, 62,* 271.

Sullivan, H.S. (Ed.). (2013). *The interpersonal theory of psychiatry.* London, UK: Routledge.

U.S. Department of State. (2014, March). *Fiscal year 2013 annual report on adoption.* Retrieved from http://travel.state.gov/content/dam/aa/pdfs/fy2013_annual_report.pdf

van Eeden-Moorefield, B., & Benson, K. (2015). Queers doing family. In S. Browning & K. Pasely (Eds.) *Contemporary families: Translating research into practice* (p. 167). London, UK: Routledge.

Vespa, J., Lewis, J. M., & Kreider, J. M. (2013, August). *America's families and living arrangements: 2012.* U.S. Department of Commerce, Economics and Statistics Administration, U.S. Census Bureau.

Visher, E.B., & Visher, J.S. (1989). Old loyalties, new ties: Therapeutic strategies with stepfamilies. London, UK: Routledge.

Walsh, F. (1998). *Strengthening family resilience.* New York, NY: Guilford Press.

Walsh, F. (2003). Family resilience: A framework for clinical practice. *Family process, 42,* 1–18.

PART V

Identity Models and Structural Systems

CHAPTER 14

Identity Models

Maryam M. Jernigan
Carlton E. Green
Janet E. Helms

Identity development is a function of how an individual comes to view herself or himself and his or her perception of how others view him or her (Erikson, 1968; Marcia, 1966). It is further comprised of a sociodemographic category that refers to how others perceive the person, and a psychosocial **identity** that pertains to how the person perceives one's self (Helms, 1990). Moreover, **collective identity** is a psychological concept that indicates an identity that is shared with others who are perceived as sharing common external characteristics (Ashmore, Deaux, & McLaughlin-Volpe, 2004), but collective identities may not be the same as integrated psychosocial identities. To be relevant to the person's quality of functioning, identities must be personally acknowledged through self-definition, rather than merely being ascribed by a given society. Characteristics of collective and individual identities may include race, ethnicity, gender, class, occupation, or political affiliation (e.g., Deux, 1996), to name a few. Given these complexities, the potential influence of the construction of one's social identity for individuals within couples and/or families is quintessential to understanding and facilitating couple and familial therapeutic interventions.

Historically speaking, many theorists and practitioners have tended to focus on one aspect of identity (e.g., race, gender) to the exclusion of others. However, some scholars and practitioners have made advances in developing identity theories that articulate the multidimensional psychological and social experiences of people from diverse backgrounds (Cross, 1992; Helms, 1990; Phinney, 1992 Sellers, Smith, Shelton, Rowley, & Chavous, 1998). More recently, increasing attention has been given to the need to examine the intersections of identity (Patterson, Cameron &

Lalonde, 1996; Reid, 2004; Shields, 2008). In doing so, one is better able to comprehend how perceived membership in socially constructed categories (e.g., race, gender, class) affects individual and collective life experiences. Although some intersectional models speak to one or more aspects of identity, few discuss and explicitly integrate **racial identity** formation and its importance. As such, there remains a gap in our understanding of the intersections of identity and how to best utilize multidimensional psychosocial identity formation in clinical practice with couple and family systems.

In the current chapter, we highlight the complexity of the intersections of psychosocial identity formation and their potential influences on the interactions between therapists and couples or families. We begin the chapter with an overview of models of racial and **sexual orientation identity**, which are often identified by multicultural scholars and practitioners as important areas of inquiry in counseling. We then present from the scant but burgeoning literature on **intersectionality**. In doing so, we hope to illustrate and provide a model for conceptualizing the multidimensional nature of identity when working with couples and families. We then offer a case illustration focusing on a therapist–couple interaction, recognizing that the couple is a central system that influences larger family dynamics. Couples interact with their families and teach family members to view and think about their own as well as others' social identities (e.g., race, sexual orientation, religion) through the couple members' understanding of their own social identities. As such, a couple's ability to learn to relate to each other and see their mate or partner as either sharing or not sharing a particular social identity may affect their mutual family environment.

RACIAL IDENTITY DEVELOPMENT

Race is a social construct, meaning that, although physical attributes like skin color are inherited, determining which constructs are "racial" is ordained by the power structure (American Anthropological Association, 1998; Spickard, 1992). Throughout history, racial categorization has systematically been used to differentiate individuals identified as belonging to the "superior" sociopolitically dominant White racial group from the "inferior" people of color (POC, i.e., Native Americans, Asian Americans, African Americans, Latino Americans; Helms, 1990). Despite the fact that scholars have consistently proven that there is no evidence of race as biologically determined, the concept of race represents an important psychological reality (Zuckerman, 1990). Views about race are often shaped by early socialization experiences in families of origin and communities, through exposure to messages about racial categorization.

Racial identity development theory provides insight into the way in which racial dynamics and awareness influence understanding of oneself as a racial being (Helms, 1995a). Establishing an understanding of what race is and how it affects one's life is critical to any examination of racial identity formation. The basis for an individual and collective understanding of race is informed by a constantly evolving social, political, and historical context (Saddler, 2005). In other words, the meaning of race changes based on the interaction with time, political climate, and one's local and global environment (Graves, 2001). Thus, how an individual understands race is a result of personal experiences, as well as interactions within the larger society and world. Furthermore, although some commonalities may exist, there is no *single* concept of what it means to be from a specific racial background (e.g., what it means to be Black; Thompson & Carter, 1997).

PEOPLE OF COLOR RACIAL IDENTITY

Racial identity development theory proposes that traditionally racially marginalized individuals (e.g., Blacks, Asians, Pacific Islanders, American Indians, and Latino/as) potentially work through attitudes and beliefs associated with **internalized racism**—the tendency to believe negative racist messages about one's group. As POC develop an active awareness of racism and oppression, they may process and overcome them. In doing so, POC learn to identify, resist, and cope with racism in its many forms (e.g., individual and systemic). The process is informed by a commitment to deliberate ongoing self-examination and acknowledgment of lived experiences (Helms, 1995; Thompson & Carter, 1997). Helms's POC racial identity model (1995b) describes different statuses that reflect attitudes, beliefs, and information-processing strategies an individual may use to make sense of race, including racial encounters (i.e., racial stimuli), which may be useful in understanding the role of racism in family dynamics and reactions to the therapist. For POC, the model includes the conformity, dissonance, immersion-resistance, internalization, and integrative awareness statuses.

Conformity is characterized by attempts to assimilate into society by ignoring, denying, or minimizing racism. The person desires not to be defined by racial terminology (e.g., Black), but instead prefers self-definition by means of more neutral classifications, such as "human being" or ethnicity (e.g., Dominican). This individual may be aware of racial disparities in the larger society, but believes that disparities or perceived mistreatment can be rectified by working harder, ignoring others' bad behavior, or separating oneself from the group of color. Because a conforming family member might be characterized by self-hatred or own-group denigration as expressed through pro-White/anti-POC attitudes, he or she might not be receptive to hearing experiences of family members that contradict his or her assimilationist desires.

Dissonance represents the POC's unwilling capacity to question her or his previous beliefs about race. Self-questioning can sometimes be brought on by a blatant experience of racism, which shatters the previous belief system. Thus, one's former manner of coping is overpowered by this encounter with reality. POC for whom this status is dominant might come to the realization that, despite their attempts to assimilate to White cultural standards, society perceives POC as inferior because of their racial categorization. For example a *dissonant* Asian psychologist who has attempted to be race-neutral in her workplace may experience feelings of anxiety and confusion when clients consistently indicate surprise at her competence as a therapist. In an effort to calm anxiety and confusion, the *dissonance* experience may lead POC to accept their racial identification, allowing access to thoughts and information-processing strategies representative of the immersion-resistance status.

When a person of color is using *immersion-resistance* to cope with racial dynamics, she or he immerses into settings, behaviors, or attitudes that she or he feels represent a newly accepted racial classification. This allows POC to redefine what it means to be from a particular racial group. For example, youths of color attending predominantly White schools often report a transition from having friends from racial backgrounds different from their own to a desire to solely welcome close friendships with their peers whom they perceive as having a similar racial classification (Jernigan, 2007). In doing so, youths of color report a sense of connection through shared racial experiences, which provide feelings of comfort. The therapist, for whom the *immersion-resistance* status is dominant, develops critical and/or hostile thoughts, attitudes, and beliefs toward the majority (e.g., White) racial and cultural groups, while developing a positive attitude about her or his identified racial group.

As development progresses, there is an attempt to strengthen own-group identity and overcome internalized societal stereotypes. The next status, immersion-resistance, encompasses periods of vacillating anger and experimentation with racial definition (e.g., what is and is not Asian) to create a new, self-defined racial group identity. A POC therapist, for whom the immersion-resistance status is dominant, may initially use rigid and stereotypical examples of racial groups to determine and create this new identity definition. Furthermore, the therapist may perceive all clinical interactions solely from a racial perspective at the expense of acknowledging other clinical or identity-related issues.

Resistance is seen as an effort to regain control of one's self-definition and function from a state of positive self-enhancement. Studies that have explored the experiences of POC at work provide examples of attempts to resist oppression within the work environment (Blustein, 2006; Brown, 1995; Fitzgerald & Betz, 1994; Faoud & Bryars-Winston, 2005). Such attempts, however, may result in direct opposition to the environment (e.g., negative social interactions with coworkers or supervisors leading to disciplinary action) or creative expression (e.g., blogs, poetry) about work experiences. A therapist operating from a *resistance* dynamic who has knowledge about the strengths and weaknesses of his or her culture may seek to empower POC clients by enhancing their awareness of what it means to be from a particular racial group. A *resistant* African American female therapist working in a predominantly White academic setting might develop a therapeutic group that promotes the racial and gender identity development, as well as the academic success of POC female students.

As the potential for resisting racism changes, the *internalization* status emerges demonstrating POC's ability to be more secure in their racial classification and appreciate all racial and ethnic groups. The ability to shift between resisting and actualizing perspectives occurs as one gains a sense of racial pride and communalism Helms, 1995a). The POC therapist operating from *internalization* has a commitment to her or his racial group, and is able to use abstract reasoning to analyze complex information to resolve racial dilemmas.

Integrative awareness requires that POC remain aware of racial inequity, as well as other forms of oppression that impact all humans. As a result, *integrative awareness* is represented by an ability to recognize the strengths and weaknesses of all racial groups, including Whites. Meaningful relationships with individuals from all racial backgrounds are established with the goal of engagement and commitment to eradicate social and political manifestations of racism and oppression. The ability to operate from the *integrative awareness* status represents an ideal goal for POC. A few researchers (Langhout, 2005, Morris, 2007) have provided evidence suggesting that the socialization experiences of POC influence their ability to develop, access, and utilize information-processing skills present in *integrative awareness*. The counselor may serve as facilitator of interventions that encourage resistance and allow for continued individual and collective positive racial identity development.

White Racial Identity

As articulated by Helms (1990), **White racial identity** presumes that membership in the White racial group contributes to an individual's belief of racial privilege. White racial identity in the United States, and arguably the world, is closely aligned with the development and progress of racism. Society reinforces environments in which those who identify or are perceived as White are privileged relative to POC. As such, Whites internalize such perceptions, in essence protecting their social status through the denial and distortion of racial information. A healthy identity development for Whites entails the ability to identify and abandon racist or privileged notions of normative racial experiences. The overall developmental task for Whites is the development of a nonracist identity. White racial identity (WRI) consists of six statuses: contact, disintegration, reintegration, pseudo-independence, immersion, emersion, and autonomy (Helms, 1990).

The least sophisticated developmental status of WRI is *contact*, which is represented by denial or obliviousness about race. This individual believes in the notion of "colorblindness" and does not accurately take into account the realities of individual and group racial differences. White trainees may use obliviousness and avoidance of racial information as a means of protection from racial realities, including her or his thoughts regarding race. As an individual is less able to deny the importance and moral dilemmas of race, she or he may begin to recognize race and racism, leading to experiences of anxiety, confusion, or distress.

The *disintegration* status is often represented by discomfort. When *disintegration* is a therapist's dominant status, the therapist may experience guilt and helplessness with POC clients who report microaggressions, which are subtle racist behaviors, or discriminatory interactions at work or school. In an effort to minimize such feelings and overcome a state of ambivalence, White clinicians may begin to operate from the *reintegration* status. *Reintegration* involves a seeming regression back to an adoption of attitudes that idealize the White racial group, minimize the importance of race, and attempt to return to the racial status quo. The *reintegration* status is, however, different, because this therapist is able to see differences with regard to racial dynamics and may justify disparities based on internalized racial stereotypes. A *reintegrative* provider might use statements such as, "If only those people would stop being lazy and work hard like other Americans."

The subsequent rationalization or intellectualized understandings of race characterize the *pseudo-independence* status. Understanding of the complexities of racial dynamics and personal responsibility are minimal, whereas superficial commitment to the group accountability of Whites is demonstrated. *Pseudo-independence* also embodies the notion that POC would benefit by becoming more like Whites to overcome their oppression. A White therapist working with a Latino/a couple, for example, might articulate an intellectual understanding of collectivistic family attitudes while simultaneously suggesting that the couple's relationship can only be healthy if the couple disengages and individuates from their families of origin.

Further maturation is often facilitated by the desire to become more active and humanitarian. *Immersion* involves a re-educating of the self to define whiteness and pursue accurate racial information. The *emersion* status results from an appreciation of a community of similar-minded White individuals focused on self-knowledge. Therapists in both the *immersion* and *emersion* statuses evidence hypervigilance regarding racial dynamics and information, and their anti-racism perspectives may result in rigid, combative race-related opinions. More flexible thinking about race and complex responses to internal and external racial stimuli represents the most sophisticated status of the White racial identity model, *autonomy*. Racial definitions are no longer subjectively arbitrary, but rather flexible (Helms, 1990).

Sexual Orientation Identity Development

The American Psychological Association (2009) has defined sexual orientation as a biologically based pattern of sexual and romantic thoughts, attachments, sentiments, or attractions with members of one's sex (i.e., homosexual), the other sex (i.e., heterosexual), both sexes (i.e., bisexual), or neither sex (i.e., asexual). Conscious awareness, acceptance, and internalization of one's sexual orientation have been defined as sexual orientation identity (Dillon, Worthington, & Moradi, 2011). Cass (1979), who developed the most commonly cited model of homosexual identity development, formulated a six-stage model of identity development that described cognitive, affective, and behavioral characteristics pertaining to integrating sexual orientation identity into one's own self-concept.

Cass's (1979) model suggests that individuals are active participants in the identity process. Thus, a person may choose to foreclose on development at any point and decide not to pursue later stages of development. Development is thought to occur in two related domains—private/personal and public/social—although a person may choose to focus on one domain over the other. For instance, an individual may endorse a private homosexual identity while maintaining a public identity as a heterosexual. Consistency between the private and public identities signifies maturation and integration. Formation of lesbian/gay identity occurs as the person adapts self-perceptions that define one as homosexual, rather than nonhomosexual or heterosexual. Given that society generally presumes heterosexuality for all people at birth, the person will have to work through anti-gay/lesbian attitudes and beliefs. One such belief is in **heterosexism**, a system of bias and discrimination in favor of opposite-sex sexuality and romantic relationships. Herek (1990, 2000) outlined heterosexism as social systems and personal attitudes that oppress, marginalize, or stigmatize homosexuals while simultaneously privileging heterosexual identity, norms, and behaviors.

The first stage in homosexual identity development is *identity confusion*, wherein one becomes aware that social or interpersonal stimuli may have meaning for one's actions. As a result, the person may reflect to himself or herself, "My behavior may be perceived as homosexual." Clients, who have previously assumed a heterosexual identity, may feel confused and begin to wonder "Who am I?" The incongruence may result in foreclosure or acceptance. First, the client may forego exploring this behavior to restore a sense of congruence. Foreclosing may result in inhibiting behaviors that may be perceived as lesbian/gay, avoiding information about lesbians and gays, or developing negative self-perceptions. Conversely, a client may experience a shift in self-perception and search for more information to clarify the personal meaning of the behavior. Remarkably, individuals work through this stage alone unless seeking out the services of helping professional such as a therapist or religious leader. Acceptance of the behavior should move the person into stage 2.

Identity comparison, the second stage, involves a tentative commitment to identifying as lesbian or gay. The primary task is to manage potential social alienation, which may arise from fear of heterosexism. Intersectionality may heighten (e.g., religious group membership) or reduce (e.g., younger generational status) the anxiety related to alienation. Clients who anticipate others' anti-gay attitudes may respond by adopting negative views of the homosexual aspects of themselves, including thoughts, desires, and behaviors. Counseling may be sought to extinguish overt homosexual tendencies. Clients may also alter their self-perceptions to accommodate the behavior. For example, they may say to themselves, "I am only like this with this one special person," "Everybody is a little bisexual," or "This is just a phase." The person may pass as heterosexual while experiencing intense self-hatred.

Pursuing congruence and decreased anxiety may result in acceptance of self and homosexual behaviors. Clients may seek social interaction with others who can assist with feelings of isolation and being "different." Whereas passing as heterosexual may be an option that minimizes the effect of others' perceptions when one doesn't have to care as much about or be as exposed to what others think of him or her due to not knowing about his or her sexual orientation, it also may prevent foreclosure and lead to the next stage.

In the third stage, *identity tolerance*, individuals begin to turn "toward" a homosexual identity (e.g., "I'm probably a lesbian"). Clients may begin acknowledging psychosocial and interpersonal needs related to sexual orientation. Seeking out social engagement with other gays and lesbians may heighten the person's awareness of not being heterosexual. Negative contacts with other homosexuals may stimulate feelings of internalized heterosexism (i.e., internalized anti-gay attitudes) and result in inhibited homosexual behaviors and identity foreclosure. Clients may progress to the next stage of identity formation after experiencing acceptance from other gays and lesbians.

Identity acceptance is the fourth stage. Continued and increased contact with other homosexuals is the hallmark of this stage. Clients may develop more gay/lesbian friendships and demonstrate a preference for settings that validate the homosexual aspects of the person's life. Socializing in environments (e.g., church) that allow for private homosexuality while forbidding public expressions may result in passing as heterosexual, reducing contact with heterosexuals, or selectively disclosing gay/lesbian identity to trusted others. These strategies may result in diminished incongruence and identity foreclosure, which may be an acceptable stage of identity for many. Individuals who strive to integrate a public and private homosexual identity may experience internal distress while beginning to work through heterosexism. Attempts to resolve the existential tension and rejection of social expectations such as conformity to family or religious/racial group standards will facilitate movement into the fifth stage.

The fifth stage, *identity pride*, is characterized by strong pro-homosexual and anti-heterosexual attitudes. Clients may immerse themselves in gay/lesbian culture, nurture a strong group identity, and associate with like-minded individuals. The daily hassles of living in a heterosexual world may foster anger and frustration, which may lead to activism and public disclosure of homosexual identity. Whereas disclosure may signal an alignment of public and private lives, negative reactions may cause the person to selectively reveal his or her homosexuality; foreclosure on identity may occur. Heterosexuals' positive reactions to self-disclosure of gay/lesbian identity may disrupt the inflexible attitudes (e.g., gays are good, heterosexuals are bad) of "proud" homosexuals and lead to the next stage of development.

Identity synthesis, the final stage, involves the recognition that not all heterosexuals are bad and not all gays are good. Incongruence is more easily managed as gays/lesbians develop more flexible attitudes toward those of similar and dissimilar sexual orientations. Furthermore, acceptance of an integrated public–private homosexual identity may complete the identity formation process, as the individual now regards homosexuality as one aspect of his or her personhood (Cass, 1979).

We recognize that identity models beyond the two just presented exist and are relevant (for an overview of these respective identity models, see: Yip, Douglass, & Sellars, 2014—ethnic and racial identity; Reid, 2004—gender; Zea & Nakumura, 2014—sexual orientation). In addition, earlier chapters in the book provide alternate models for consideration. We encourage the reader to further explore and examine additional psychosocial identities and use the framework provided as a model for how to integrate multiple aspects of identity when working with couples and families in the therapeutic encounter.

INTERSECTIONS OF IDENTITY

Many aspects of identity work in concert to influence how an individual feels about her- or himself, as well as others, and we present two great and rare examples of the intersections between or among identities (Settles, 2006; Shorter-Gooden, 2004; Shorter-Gooden & Washington, 1996; Thomas, Hacker, & Hoxha, 2011). Settles's (2006) exploration of an intersectional framework to account for the importance of gender, race, and class collective identities was applied to Black women. The mixed methods study found that, for Black women, the salience of the Black woman identity prevailed over racial identity or gender identity alone. Thomas et al. (2011) subsequently examined the concept **gendered racial identity**, a holistic framework that highlights the importance of gendered racial status as more significant and meaningful than race or gender alone, especially for Black women. Findings indicated that Black women more often prefer to articulate gendered racial experiences in which both race and gender influenced self-perception, making this social identity a unique identity. Nevertheless, which identity is salient may depend on the context or the extent to which the person is permitted to self-define. Thus, it is important to assess all relevant key aspects of couple and family members' identities at the outset to work effectively with them in treatment.

INITIAL ASSESSMENT OF IDENTITIES

Many practitioners agree that gathering background sociodemographic information is essential to the assessment and treatment process. How such assessment occurs, however, is discussed much less often. As a consequence, trainees may report a lack of confidence and skills that allow them to explore collective identity experiences such as those associated with race, ethnicity, and/or sexual orientation or corresponding psychosocial identities. The ability to explore such factors begins prior to the actual clinical encounter. Careful attention should be paid to the types of questions asked of clients to gather background information and presenting concerns either via phone or on paperwork prior to a first appointment. Therapists should take care to use nonbiased language and refrain from making assumptions about clients' sociodemographic backgrounds. For example, referrals for couples or family therapy should not presume heterosexual couples or families. When speaking to a woman-identified client, rather than asking if her male partner/husband will attend therapy with her, inquire about important individuals to be included in the treatment process, allowing the client to identify and define those individuals.

Clinical intake forms are another mechanism to collect a wealth of client information. Many forms ask clients about their address, age, gender, or personal information, such as insurance provider. Some health providers collect information regarding sociodemographic backgrounds, but they use standard methodologies, such as the U.S. Census categorical checkboxes to gather such information. An alternative, used by one of the authors of this chapter in clinical practice, is represented next because it primes clients to begin the process of race, gender, and sexual orientation self-identification, and allows for the therapist to further explore related issues in the clinical encounter.

SAMPLE
ADULT CLIENT INTAKE FORM

BACKGROUND INFORMATION

Date: _____

Name: _____

Gender: _____ Preferred Pronoun(s): _____

Sexual Orientation: _____

NOTE: Often people are asked to choose their race and/or ethnicity from a list. I recognize that this method may not reflect how people would actually identify their own race and ethnicity.

Race: _____

Ethnicity: What best describes your ethnic background?
(Haitian, Dominican, Italian, Chinese, etc.) _____

Date of Birth: _____

Place of Birth: _____

USING IDENTITY MODELS IN THERAPY: SOCIAL INTERACTION MODEL

Based on the aforementioned research, continued exploration of collective and intersectional frameworks is needed to fully comprehend the experiences of individuals, couples, and families. Such articulation will lead to the ability to inform and provide practical recommendations for couples and family therapy. A potential translational framework with practical implications for clinicians can be found in the **Social Interaction Model** (SIM; Helms, 1990). The SIM is designed to assess the influence of psychosocial identities and social power within relational interactions to determine the likelihood for growth-fostering versus barrier-laden relationships. Given the essential nature of relational interactions within couple and family therapy, the SIM framework can be applied in treatment to strengthen couples and families.

The relationship between the therapist and the couple and family members is a vital aspect of the treatment process. A therapist's ability to engage and join with a couple or family in an effort to assess presenting concerns, gain background information, explore relational patterns, and define treatment goals will depend upon the nature of interactions during the therapeutic process. When couples and families seek counseling, it is crucial for the therapist to acknowledge the effects of her/his inherent social power within the counseling relationship, as well as to be attuned to which of her/his collective and psychosocial identities are activated by the family's dynamics. The therapist's ability to remain self-aware and recognize the complexities of interactions influenced by the multiple identities present in the counseling encounter, including his or her own and the clients' identities, may determine the quality of the interactions between all involved.

Helms's SIM was initially articulated to assess race-related interactions influenced by racial identity and relational power dynamics in therapy and therapy supervision (Helms, 1995a 1990; Helms & Cook, 1999; Jernigan, Green, Helms, Henze, & Perez-Gualdron, 2010). The SIM provides a helpful explanatory framework for understanding and illuminating how power can shape multidimensional psychosocial dynamics in therapeutic relationships, as well as social interactions more generally, including interactions within couples and families.

Importantly, whereas Helms's theoretical conceptualization has focused primarily on racial identity interactions (1984), here we also propose to include relational power dynamics that may pertain to sexual orientation, and we note that this conceptualization also can apply to the other individual and collective identities. Given the sociopolitical underpinnings of sexual orientation and the individual differences associated with sexual orientation identity development, it is possible that power dynamics associated with heterosexism may influence between-group (e.g., heterosexual therapist–lesbian couple) and within-group (e.g., same-sex couple) relationships. As initially outlined by Helms (1984, 1990, 1995), there are four potential relationship types in social interactions: *progressive, parallel, regressive, and crossed*, which are defined from the perspective of the person(s) with least social power in a given context.

Progressive interactions occur when the development of the person with the "most power in the relationship is more advanced than that of the other person" (Helms & Cook, 1999, p. 282). Those whose power in the relational context and predominant identity statuses is more advanced than their client (in therapy) or partner (in couples) have the ability to model sociodemographic responsiveness, depending on which aspect of identity is salient. Modeling alternative perspectives may guide others toward more developed understanding of the intersections of sociodemographic factors as they relate to the dynamics of therapy and the couple or family (Helms, 1990). For example, an African American father with *internalized* perspectives (i.e., nuanced attitudes about identity) may be able to empathically assist his partner, an *immersive-resistant* African American mother, who is struggling with her gay son's sexual orientation and cross-racial dating. Progressive dyads are ideal, growth promoting, and encourage persons to address racial, ethnic, and other relevant psychosocial identity issues in their relationship(s).

Parallel dyads are those in which the therapist and client(s) or two or more family members share congruent psychosocial identity statuses. For example, with respect to racial identity development, *parallel* relationships occur when more than one party's dominant racial identity status is less developed (e.g., *conformity*—POC racial identity and *contact*—White racial identity). In this example, both parties are operating from similar statuses and worldviews, characterized by denial or minimization of race, but *parallel* events or interactions can involve virtually any racial identity schemas. *Parallel* relationships, therefore, are often identified as agreeable, but not necessarily healing or growth-fostering interactions, particularly if the therapist forms a coalition with one of the couple or family member that excludes or antagonizes another family member, or if family members form parallel coalitions that disempower the therapist. For instance, a White clinician–Black gay couple therapeutic interaction, in which all participants operate from early racial identity statuses may avoid discussions about race-related dynamics that could affect the couples' presenting concerns. These might include coping with anti-gay attitudes in a Black church setting or anti-Black sentiment in predominantly White settings.

The *regressive* relationship type exists when psychosocial identity status of the individual with *less* power in the relationship (e.g., client, family member) is at least one status more advanced than that of the person with more social power. This power differential can apply to the client's status relative to the therapist or within the couple or family system. *Regressive* relationships are characterized by direct opposition, anger, and psychological and social withdrawal. The range of responses often depends on the degree of disparity in identity development between those with more or less power and whether leaving the relationship (e.g., premature termination, divorce) or psychologically withdrawing (e.g., unwillingness to communicate) is most feasible for the vulnerable person. When the therapist senses that conflict is the major theme of the interaction, she or he should seek to assess the types of identity statuses in play, which includes self-assessment. For instance, contention and anguish might typify a Latina lesbian couple's discussion of the race of a potential adoptive child. Whereas the immersive-resistant (i.e., pro-Latino/a) partner might prefer to only adopt a Latino/a child, the dissonant partner may express race-neutral attitudes concerning the race of the child.

Crossed interactions transpire when the therapist and clients' understanding of relevant collective identity factors are in complete opposition and they are using incompatible aspects of their psychosocial identities. In *crossed* dyads, difficulties with communication are a direct result of a lack of shared framework with which to reference psychosocial identity. The implications for couple or family therapy depend on the therapist–client

interaction. If the dyad represents one in which the individual with power
(e.g., therapist and/or less powerful family member) exhibits a less
sophisticated understanding of psychosocial identity issues than the other
person, such relationships are often unsatisfactory and conflictual because
they are defined by opposing worldviews. Alternately, if the *crossed* interaction is one in which the individual with more power when compared
to those with less social power exhibits a more sophisticated understanding of the intersections of psychosocial identities than those with less
social power, this can lead to the client couple's or family's increased self-
exploration and empathy for others' development. The therapist may be
more competent in working with the family system if the therapist or the
more developed client does not rush the other person's developmental
processes.

It is also necessary to take into consideration the role of the socioecological context for the couple or family. Extended family members, colleagues,
or friends of persons in therapy may offer different outlooks or views on
psychosocial factors that influence the client family or couple's dynamics, particularly if the client couple or family has formed coalitions with
extended family members or friends that conflict with immediate family
members. If the person with less power in the couple or family brings an
alternate worldview into the therapy interaction, the person may be perceived as challenging the worldview of the therapist and/or the family
member with more perceived relational power in the system. Thus, the
therapist should be attuned to instances in which the mood of interactions shifts from harmonious to contentious. This involves the potential
to interpret cultural information in a potentially biased manner due to its
consistency with the therapist's worldview (Helms, 1990). In other words,
the therapist is likely to interpret cultural information in a manner consistent with her or his own social identity status beliefs. When the therapist
holds a view consistent with one member of a couple/family, the therapist will likely privilege the perspective of the individual with whom she
or he holds a similar worldview within the treatment session.

THE SOCIAL INTERACTION MODEL IN THERAPY: TREATMENT GOALS AND INTERVENTIONS

Goals of the therapist in family and couples counseling should be to
(a) foster progressive relationships or parallel-advanced-status therapy
climates and (b) model analogous behaviors and perspective taking for the
client couple or family. Helms and Cook (1999) identified several characteristics of social interaction dyads that likely promote high parallel
(i.e., all persons operate from advanced racial identity statuses) or progressive relationships. Among those noted are: (a) creation of a climate
that encourages exploration of a client's experiences, attitudes, and values of racial and cultural issues; (b) motivation to process and articulate

one's own racial and cultural perspectives; (c) awareness of the influence of the sociopolitical histories of the sociodemographic identities (e.g., race, sexual orientation) of those socially categorized or represented by the client and therapist; and (d) encouragement of in-depth discussion of psychosocial dynamics relative to how such factors are impacting the therapy alliance and the couple or family interactions. In creating therapeutic climates, the therapist does not necessarily need to abandon her or his normal therapy theoretical orientation, although implementation of Helms and Cook's therapeutic social interaction criteria might be experienced as easier to implement in some orientations than others. Yet most theoretical approaches require the therapist to be sensitive to the client's dynamics; SIM provides structure for the sensitivity.

In an effort to demonstrate how a therapist might approach treatment with a couple using a multidimensional framework, we use the SIM involving both racial identity and sexual orientation, two important collective identities. Ashmore and colleagues (Ashmore et al., 2004) have detailed the core elements of collective identities (Organizing Framework for Collective Identity; Ashmore, et al., 2004). These are self-categorization, evaluation, importance, attachment and a sense of **interdependence**, social embeddedness, behavioral involvement, and content and meaning. Next, a couple therapy case will illustrate how therapists can apply the SIM to elicit and address the core elements of these collective identities, thereby enhancing the multidimensional relationship between a couple that presents for therapy.

CASE ILLUSTRATION

Background Information

Daniela and Skylar presented for therapy to facilitate communication and reduce verbal arguments in their relationship. The couple reported that they began dating 10 years back and married 1 year prior to seeking couples counseling. The couple reported that they do not feel as though they are in crisis per se, but want to avoid current patterns of engaging, which they believe will lead to increased problems in the relationship. At the outset, Daniela and Skylar's presenting concerns seemed straightforward; a focus on better communication could be the considered the primary goal of counseling. Further exploration helps to highlight how collective identity, including differences in racial identity, may affect their relational functioning.

Self-Identification

Key information, including quotes from clients (see Tables 14.1 to 14.4), can help to illuminate the exploration of factors related to self-identification, or articulation of the aspects of identity that are most salient to both parties. Making note of and comparing information gathered from each person within a couple or family can highlight important differences between ascribed identities, which are identities often assumed by a given society based on phenotypic characteristics, versus self-identification. Through such exploration, the therapist is able to assist couples and families in better understanding what shapes their worldviews and how differences in perceptions can lead to misunderstanding.

Both Daniela and Skylar's phenotypic skin tones are a dark-brown hue. They reported that many ascribe to them a racial classification of Black/African American. Although this is in line with Skylar's self-identification with regard to racial and perhaps ethnic identity, such is not the case for Daniela. She reported on her intake documents and in the therapeutic encounter that she identifies racially as Black and ethnically as Dominican. She also refers to herself as "Afro-Latina." Potential differences in the partners' racial and ethnic cultural psychosocial identities may account for racial and cultural issues that have emerged for the couple over the course of their relationship. Daniela spoke about the importance of immigration and how it has affected her worldview, career goals, and aspirations to pursue a college education. Daniela reported that conversely, higher education was seen by her family as distraction from the need to work to support family members. Daniela also discussed *how* her family immigrated to the United States, often leaving family members behind and waiting years to be united. Familial immigration patterns have resulted in a collectivist worldview in which she prioritizes Dominican familial needs and support. Thus, she appears to be *immersed* with respect to ethnic identity and *conforming* with respect to racial identity.

Skylar on the other hand, is very attuned to race and racism as a self-identified Black woman. In discussing her family of origin she speaks about the legacy of slavery and civil rights, which she refers to as "her history." Skylar talks about the forced immigration of her ancestors due to the trans-Atlantic slave trade. As such, Skylar asserts that she is unaware of her true "ethnic identity" origins in Africa and is only able to reference "what began in the United States with slavery." She expresses an inability to articulate a connection to a specific ethnic or national background, such as Ethiopian. Thus, with regard to racial identity, she appears to be *immersed* and *conforming* with respect to ethnic identity.

With regard to sexual orientation, Daniela and Skylar also identify differently. Daniela described her sexual orientation as lesbian, whereas Skylar discussed the importance of a bisexual identity, a point of contention in the relationship. When asked how they describe their current relationship, both agreed that they are in a lesbian relationship. Daniela described a consistent attraction to girls in childhood and subsequently women as an adult. As a self-proclaimed Afro-Latina, her perception is that persons of Dominican descent and POC are historically less accepting of the lesbian and gay community. During sessions she often described the intersections of the importance of being a woman and a woman of color, as well as a lesbian. Such experiences she perceived as leading to multiple forms of discrimination in her immediate ethnic community of Dominicans, as well as in society, but also she seemed unaware of how her psychosocial identity statuses may have interacted with others' responses to her.

Skylar's self-identification as a bisexual woman is one that led to challenges within her family, across her lifespan. As an adolescent and young adult, Skylar stated that she has always been attracted to women and men. However, she more often engaged in intimate relationships with men, which was seen as acceptable by her family members. She considers the current relationship with Daniela as her first "official" relationship with a woman. Skylar maintains a commitment to her relationship, but also stated that she equally could be in a committed relationship with a man. She contends that her capacity to form intimate relationships with women and men does not negate her love or dedication to Daniela, but also she does not acknowledge the extent to which such freedom of choice gives her sexual power relative to Daniela.

The two women have struggled with discussions regarding their experiences coming out to family members. For example, Daniela reported that, for many years, she feared what her family, friends, and community might think of her lesbian identity. Skylar, on the other hand, reported that she did not have such experiences growing up and although she faced some challenges when coming out to her family and discussing her relationship with Daniela, she largely feels supported by her immediate family. Skylar also spoke at length about her experience as a "Black woman" in a lesbian relationship in the United States. Although she exhibited a strong sense of pride in her racial and ethnic identity, she was self-aware of society's view and negative treatment of Black women and even more so about the mistreatment of POC within the LGBT community stating, "You would think that other people who have been marginalized would stand together, but racism still exists in the gay community."

Identity Evaluation

Asking members of a couple or family to demographically self-identify is an initial step in the therapy process. The therapist should make sense of this information by using relevant identity models (e.g., racial, gender, sexual orientation) to better understand how such factors are understood by each person in the couple or familial relationship. It is essential to make note of personal perceptions relative to those that each person may perceive as a societal or global belief, given the importance of the distinction between private self-regard, or one's personal evaluation of one's racial identity and public self-regard, or one's perceptions of how society views one's racial groups. Healthy identity representation can be interpreted as one in which self-concept is intact alongside recognition that societal views may not coincide with personal beliefs.

Table 14.1
Self-Representative Assessment of Identity: Self-Identification

Placing Self in Social Category
Categorizing self in terms of a particular social grouping.

Construct	Daniela	Skylar
Racial collectivist racial identity	Black	Black
Racial psychosocial identity	Conforming	Immersion
Ethnic self-identity	Dominican Afro-Latina	African American
Sexual orientation	Lesbian	Bisexual

Perceived Similarity
Subjective assessment of the degree to which individual is a prototypical member of the group.

	Daniela	Skylar
	My parents immigrated from the DR. I grew up in the states but the island is in my blood. Some people assume I am Black, like African American Black because of my skin color. They obviously do not realize that Dominicans come in all shades. It depends on where I am.	My parents taught me a lot about the history of racism and Black people in the United States. African American culture was something we had to learn outside of school.

Perceived Certainty of Self-Identification
Degree of certainty with which a person categorizes self in a particular social grouping.

	Daniela	Skylar
	It is interesting growing up in the United States and being connected here, but also being connected to the DR. That feels like home.	I know exactly who I am and I am proud of it. I was taught that early on.

Both Daniela and Skylar state that they are proud of their racial and ethnic identities. They are also aware that the sociopolitical histories of Black, African American, Latina, bilingual Spanish-speaking individuals, who also identify as sexual minorities in the United States, have traditionally

Table 14.2
Assessment of Identity: Evaluation

Private Regard
Favorability judgments made by people about their own identities.

Construct	Daniela	Skylar
Self-esteem	I think I am a pretty proud Latina.	I would never change being a Black woman for anyone or anything else.
Racial identity	I am still learning to figure this out. It is like, I see myself as Black. That is how people treat me regardless of where I go. I think of myself as Dominican first and foremost.	I am pretty happy with who I am. I would not change my identity for anything. It does not mean I don't have challenges at work or when I was in school, but I would not want to be any other race.
Sexual orientation	Yea . . . I think my people are very homophobic at times. The more time progresses, the more lesbians and gay people are accepted but nobody really talks about it. They just kind of say . . . oh that her "friend." They know what it is.	I was once in a relationship with a man. This is an issue for us. I think Daniela thinks this makes me less of a female partner to her now or that somehow I am not able to be in relationship with her at this time. To add that to that, I think my family had a hard time dealing with my sexuality but I can't change that. I am not going to change that.

Public Regard
Favorability judgments that one perceives others, such as society, to hold about one's social category.

Public acceptance and regard	Black women get treated like shit. People with an accent, especially a Spanish accent get treated even worse. I have a little of both. I mean I can turn off my accent so to speak but I do not feel I should have to.	Black women have in many ways been invisible for a long time. They have and are expected to play the role of nurturer, quiet, giving, yet also strong. Anything outside of that and people do not know what to do with you. They either react negatively or ignore you.

been one of marginalization and oppression. Such awareness on behalf of the therapist is necessary to avoid social interactions that are *regressive*, leading to increased tension in the therapeutic relationship(s). It is also important for the therapist to make note of the differences in how Daniela and Skylar evaluate their identities in similar or different ways based on who has perceived power with the relationship. This will help the couple avoid conflict based on potentially *regressive* interactions.

Identity Importance, Attachment, and Interdependence

The importance of identity and sense of interdependence for Daniela and Skylar further illustrate their ability to build upon positive identity factors as individuals, in relation to those they identity with collectively, and with one another as a couple. Having a sense of consciousness about the significance of their respective collective identity factors allows for a basis of exploring the construction of values and experiences. Such discussion will assist with their primary therapeutic goal of increased positive communication. It is often the case that couples experience difficulty with communication because their own experiences facilitate how they perceive and interact with others. For example, how Daniela or Skylar perceive social interactions with one another or others in their community or society will be based their own socialization experiences. If such socialization experiences differ or are nonexistent, this may lead to interpersonal conflict. Increased awareness however, can facilitate their ability to collectively examine their beliefs and attitudes, which leads to a growth-promoting experience.

The therapist's explicit goal of asking Daniela and Skylar to discuss how they identify and the significance of their identity, as shaped by their personal experiences, allows them to better understand what may lead to the other's perception or misperceptions. This further allows the couple to develop empathy and deepen their sense of attachment to one another. In other words, a couple's or family member's ability to fully understand another's perspective and what has shaped such attitudes and beliefs facilitates connection, which may reduce unnecessary conflict.

During sessions that followed the initial assessment and discussion, the therapist worked with the couple to attend to specific issues presented at the outset of therapy and reframe conflict to identify a reasonable solution. Such an intervention was successful because having a better understanding allowed Daniela and Skylar to reduce their tendency to make assumptions when communicating and further explore what may have led to the disruption. For Skylar, this meant understanding the importance of the legacy of the value of assisting family members rather than operating from the belief that Daniela lacked family boundaries. Daniela, in turn, was able to accept that Skylar's worldview as a woman of color may embody some notions of collectivism. Her identity as a young African American adult, however, means that she was raised in a Westernized society that also promotes individuation and separation, especially for younger generations reared following the Civil Rights Movement of the 1960s. As opposed to reenacting society's tendency to ascribe characteristics based on assumptions about identity, such as how each should behave as women of color, Daniela and Skylar were able to begin to explore how their respective cultural and collective identity factors influenced their relational patterns in a nuanced manner, and see how it often had caused them to misperceive aspects of communication when interacting.

Case Review

Identity formation begins early in life. Daniela and Skylar defined their individual psychosocial identities internally and their group identities in relation to others by comparing and contrasting perceptions of their respective group membership across their lifespan. As with many couples and/or families engaging in social identity comparisons, this may lead to complex subjective experiences of reciprocity, superiority, or inferiority. It is imperative to understand such experiences in order to assist couples

Table 14.3
Assessment of Identity: Importance

Explicit Importance (Significance, Strength, Importance)
Subjective appraisal of the degree to which a collective identity is important to overall sense of self

Daniela	Skylar
Being the daughter of Dominican immigrants makes me who I am. I watched my parents work hard to make a life for us. They came here with nothing.	If I am not confident about who I am the world would eat me alive. I think that the stories I have heard my entire life are what makes being a woman of color, being a Black woman even more important. I do not walk out of my house one day a woman and one day Black. Both matter.

Implicit Importance (Salience, Elevation, Importance)
Placement of a particular group membership in the person's hierarchically organized self-system.

I think about who I am on an everyday basis. I mean, how can I not? I am constantly reminded of how people see me when I interact with them. In some ways it shapes how I interact with others. Do I speak Spanish or nah? What do I reveal about myself?	We live in a society that reminds a section of people that they are POC and that they should somehow be less than as a result. No decision is made in my day without thinking about who I am. On any given day, I have to leave my house. Heck, when we are at home, if we turn on the TV there are plenty of examples of how society sees us as Blacks or lesbians.

Table 14.4

Assessment of Identity: Attachment and Sense of Interdependence

Construct	Assessment	
	Daniela	*Skylar*
Interdependence *Perception of the commonalities in how group members are treated in society*	I used to think it was not a big deal. Now, being Black and being Latina is important. A lot of people tend to deny the importance of race sometimes. Both matter in terms of how people see me and treat me and how I think about myself.	When people see me, they see and make judgments about many things, my gender, my race, perhaps they wonder about nationality. All of that matters.
Affective commitment *Sense of emotional involvement with or affiliative orientation toward group*	I think it is important. I have a proud Dominican family. I could probably know more about my culture, like the history of the DR but we are proud.	It is important to me and for me to have a sense of who I am who I am and how the world may see me.
Interconnection of self and others *Degree to which people merge their sense of self and the group*	Family is first. Period. It is never "I." I was always raised to think about "we." This is important for survival. You don't survive immigration to the states and not rely on others including family and friends that you can trust. I think Dominicans respect and look out for each other. There is a shared history and sense of family there.	What is crazy is that the sense of community has changed with each generation. Black people did not survive without coming together and helping to support one another in history. I do not see that as much now. I see it when I visit relatives who are older. They are always searching to make a connection. I think it is lost on younger generations. That is hard for me. I see my parents one way and I feel like I was raised different. Although I have roots that talk about the importance of "I am because, we are," there are times when I feel like I have taken on the individual values of the United States. It is complicated.

and families in recognizing how interpersonal dynamics may impact a presenting problem in therapy. As such, a primary goal of the initial phase of treatment was to engage with Daniela and Skylar to better assess and understand how identified concerns related to communication fit within a broader systemic context, such as between couples and their respective environments. While it is not presented in this chapter, the therapist also elicited and addressed aspects of the couple's social embeddedness, behavioral involvement, and content and meaning regarding their racial and sexual orientation identities.

The role of the therapist as the identified person with social power in the therapeutic relationship is to remain aware of such nuanced experiences and assist clients in understanding how their social identities may affect relational communication and connection. In the case illustration, the therapist used a *progressive* social interaction style to gather information from each member of the couple during the initial phase of therapy. Attending to psychosocial identity statements that clients do or do not offer is an essential component of the assessment process. Statements from clients should be elicited to help highlight what aspects of social identity are important (e.g., "I am a Latina woman"), as well as what positive or negative associations may be related to such factors (e.g., "I am a proud Christian woman"). Further exploration helped Daniela and Skylar identify important socialization experiences that informed significant aspects of their psychosocial identity development.

The therapist's knowledge of individual and collective psychosocial identity models allowed for increased understanding of Daniela's and Skylar's development relative to salient aspects of their identity (e.g., race, sexual orientation). This allowed the therapist to create awareness of the intersections of collective identity and how Daniela's and Skylar's experiences of their own, as well as the other's identity, affected the relationship. Daniela and Skylar were able to improve their communication skills by working with the therapist to explore the ways in which their respective psychosocial identities influenced their perceived experiences in their individual (e.g., work) and shared (e.g., home) environments. Thus, the couple was able to begin to develop and maintain positive individual and collective psychosocial identity associations. Additional strategies were used to model active listening and responsible communication and emphasize the positive strengths offered by each person. At the conclusion of therapy, Daniela and Skylar were able to reduce conflict, increase empathic responses, and engage in active problem solving when issues arose in their relationship.

CONCLUSIONS

Scholar-practitioners must continue to advocate for multidimensional identity models that help inform assessment and treatment with couples and families. Doing so allows for the illumination of the complex ways in which people may define themselves individually and collectively, subsequently affecting relationships with other members of the immediate couple or family, as well as their respective environment. Although some models have alluded to the importance of moving beyond singular exploration of identity (e.g., gender and sexual orientation) to highlight the relevance of intersections of identity (e.g., gendered sexual orientation), few models have translated theoretical propositions to clinical practice.

Increased attention to developmental models that target multidimensional aspects of psychosocial identity will inevitably allow for more training experiences and clinical practice that reflects this approach. In doing so, therapists will likely feel better equipped to engage in practice that encourages couples and families to examine how their development of various psychosocial identities influences their relationship. Such attention and practice will inevitably also influence policy advancement. Researchers and scholars will be encouraged to alter collection of demographic information that allows for self-identification (versus ascribed categories) and better exploration of how collective psychosocial identity factors shape individuals, social interactions, and communities.

CHAPTER REVIEW

Key Points

1. Individual identity models are a basis for understanding how couples and families may construct how they define and see themselves individually and collectively.
2. People define themselves in various ways. How a member of a couple or family determines the salience of certain aspects of psychosocial identity is often related to situation and context.
3. It is essential to understand how multiple aspects of identity intersect.
4. Social interactions represent how the collective identities, for all persons involved, interact to produce either growth-promoting or regressive interactions within the couple or family and treatment relationships.
5. Practitioners must remain aware of their own thoughts and beliefs about the multidimensional nature of social identity. Knowledge through self-exploration is a necessary initial step. In doing so, therapists can avoid negatively influencing the therapy relationship and learn to balance insights related to their own identity with the insights of those they are working with in a couple or family.

Key Terms

affective commitment, collective identity, explicit importance, gendered racial identity, heterosexism, identity, implicit importance, interconnection of self and others, interdependence, internalized racism, intersectionality, people of color racial identity, perceived certainty of self-identification, perceived similarity, private regard, public regard, racial identity, sexual orientation identity, Social Interaction Model, White racial identity

Myths and Realities

- It is a myth that race is biologically determined. The reality is that race is a social construct.
- It is a myth that individuals define themselves based on how others may define them with respect to race, gender, or sexual orientation. In reality, many learn to use predetermined systems and categories for demographic information. If given the opportunity, they will articulate a different reality, and show how these identities play huge roles in their couple and family relationships, such as with parental socialization and relationship choices.
- It is a myth that individuals think that the most important aspects of their identity are related to what others are able to observe and/or perceive. In reality, the way to determine identity salience is to inquire. The therapist should not make assumptions about the ways in which clients identify without explicitly asking.

Tools and Tips

Knowledge

Carter, R. T. (Ed). (2005). *Handbook of racial-cultural psychology and counseling: Theory and research* (Vols. 1–2). New York, NY: Wiley.

Graves, J. L., Jr. (2001). *The emperor's new clothes: Biological theories of race at the millennium.* New Brunswick, NJ: Rutgers University Press.

Helms, J. E. (1992). *A race is a nice thing to have.* Topeka, KA: Content Communications.

Jenson, R. (2005). *The heart of whiteness: Confronting race, racism, and white privilege.* San Francisco, CA: City Lights.

Sue, D. W. (2003). *Overcoming our racism: The journey to liberation.* San Francisco, CA: Jossey-Bass.

Dynamic Sizing

In order to know what knowledge of the group pertains to our clients, we must ask them about themselves. Use intakes that prime clients to begin the process of self-identification regarding their sociodemographic backgrounds and enable therapists to further explore these backgrounds, use nonbiased language, refrain from making assumptions, and continue to explore collective and intersectional identities by eliciting the clients' articulation and processing of their own identities and worldviews.

Skills

Theory. Integrate notions of multidimensional and collective identity factors, as well as their intersections, when conceptualizing the experiences of individuals, couples, and families.

Prevention. More opportunities to encourage individuals to think about identity and social interactions are needed. Rather than continue to use one-dimensional and antiquated categorical systems to classify persons, more organizations (e.g., schools, workplace) should encourage and explore self-identification.

Service Provision. Do not make assumptions about the personal information of clients, especially with regard to race, ethnicity, sexual orientation, and the like. Providers need to review their intake documents and how they assess relevant and important demographic information. Allow for open-ended responses and follow-up in the therapeutic setting with exploration of such responses.

Policy. Researchers and scholars often set the tone for policy advancement. A shift in recommendations about how to collect demographic information, as well as encouragement of exploration of multidimensional aspects of self-identity, will affect how individuals begin to think about themselves and how they may be viewed in a larger societal context. As such, policies in schools and workplaces can begin to reduce the reinforcement of traditional methods for classifying individuals based on differences, rather than exploring how collective identity factors shape experiences.

Research. Research needs to move beyond an individual identity models and begin to qualitatively and quantitatively examine collective identity factors, multidimensionality, and intersectionality. How one self-identifies and which aspects of identity are more or less salient, may change across one's lifespan or in a given situational context (e.g., family, school, work). Researchers should examine variables within models that are more complex, rather than reductionist, to better understand individual experiences, as well as their couple and family relationships and social interactions.

Awareness

The following activity can be used with clients to facilitate identity awareness for the therapist and clients being served. The current chapter highlights how to explore identity with clients in a couple or a family. It is important to note that such exploration should begin with the individual therapist prior to working with clients. This allows for insight into how the therapist may also perceive information shared with and by clients in an effort to guide the therapeutic process.

IDENTITY EXERCISE

OBJECTIVES

- Reflect on the various aspects of identity.
- Notice similarities and differences within couple or family members.
- Understand the anxiety that accompanies entering a therapeutic relationship.
- Consider asking the couple or family member to engage in a warm-up discussion to allow them to gain comfort with the activity. Choose one of the examples below for members to complete.

- The origin or history of their full name
- Their three personal s/heroes and the values gained from those persons
- Their greatest accomplishment in life
- Their fondest childhood memory
- The last book they read and/or their favorite authors

- Introduce the identity wheel as an opportunity for reflection to share their identities with others.

NOTE: It might be useful to establish some ground rules (i.e., shared expectations for group participation and sharing)

IDENTITY WHEEL

- Pass out paper and markers, and explain the exercise.
- Have clients think about the aspects of their identity that are most important to them.
- After doing so, they should draw a circle with eight "spokes" (i.e., lines) out from the middle of the circle. On each "spoke," write something that is important to their identity.
- The spokes do not have to be equidistant from each other. Encourage clients to allot more space for larger parts of their identity that feel more important than other aspects of their identity.
- Have clients share directly from the Identity Wheel or have them respond to the following questions:

  - Share the thing you are most proud of or happy about right now.
  - Share the thing that is most controversial for you or that you are struggling with right now.
  - Share the thing that you put down that surprised you.
  - Share 2–3 other things you want others to know about you.

- Give all persons the opportunity to share without being interrupted. After all have spoken, you may lead a discussion. Here are some sample questions that could be useful:

  - What was this exercise like for you? What thoughts and feelings did you have?
  - Were you surprised by any of the words you chose for yourself?
  - Are there words that your friends or family might use that you did not use?
  - Why is it that others see us differently that we see ourselves?
  - Describe the importance of race/ethnicity as important factors for members of this group.
  - How about gender? Sexual orientation? Age? Class? Family upbringing?
  - What did you notice as common factors in the couple/family?

> ## OTHER RECOMMENDATIONS
> ## FOR REFLECTION
>
> Please reflect on the process of creating the identity wheel activ-
> ity using the following questions:
>
> - What types of thoughts and feelings did you have while deciding
>   what to share with the group?
> - Were there parts of your identity that were easier to share than
>   others? If so, why?
>
> ## SUGGESTED READINGS FOR THERAPISTS
>
> Black, L.L., & Stone, D. (2005). Expanding the definition of privilege: The
>   concept of social privilege. *Journal of Multicultural Counseling and
>   Development, 33*, 243–255. (Can be found in Appendix A under
>   "Becoming a Counselor: Popular Notions, Evolving Notions.")
> Hays, P.A. (2008). Evaluating cultural identity and biases. *Addressing
>   cultural complexities in practice: Assessment, diagnosis, and therapy*
>   (2nd ed., pp. 15–34). Washington, DC: American Psychological
>   Association.

REFERENCES

American Anthropological Association. (1998). *AAA statement on race.* Arlington,
     VA: APA. Retrieved from http://www.americananthro.org/ConnectWith
     AAA/Content.aspx?ItemNumber=2583
American Psychological Association. (2008). *Answers to your questions: For a bet-
     ter understanding of sexual orientation and homosexuality.* Washington, DC:
     American Psychological Association. Retrieved from www.apa.org/topics/
     lgbt/orientation.pdf
APA Task Force on Appropriate Therapeutic Responses to Sexual Orientation.
     (2009). *Report of the Task Force on Appropriate Therapeutic Responses to Sexual
     Orientation.* Washington, DC: American Psychological Association.
Ashmore, R. D., Deaux, K., & McLaughlin-Volpe, T. (2004). An organizing frame-
     work for collective identity: Articulation, significance, and multidimen-
     sionality. *Psychological Bulletin, 130,* 80–114. doi: 10.037/0033-2909.130.1.80
Blustein, D. L. (2006). *The psychology of working: A new perspective for career develop-
     ment, counseling, and public policy.* Mahwah, NJ: Erlbaum.
Brown, M.T. (1995). The career development of African Americans: Theoretical
     and empirical issues. In F. T. L. Leong (Ed.), *Career development and vocational
     behavior of racial and ethnic minorities* (pp. 7–36). Hillsdale, NJ: Erlbaum.
Carter, R.T. (Ed.). (2005). *Handbook of racial-cultural psychology and counseling: The-
     ory and research* (Vols. 1–2). New York, NY: Wiley.
Cass V. C. (1979). Homosexual identity formation: a theoretical model. *Journal of
     Homosexuality, 4,* 219–235.

Cross, W. E. (1992). *Shades of black: Diversity in African American identity*. Philadelphia, PA: Temple University Press.

Deaux, K. (1996). Social identification. In E. T. Higgins & A. W. Kruglanski (Eds.), *Social psychology: Handbook of basic principles* (pp. 777–798). New York: Guilford Press.

Dillon, F. R., Worthington, R. L., & Moradi, B. (2011). Sexual identity as a universal process. In S. J. Schwartz, K. Luyckx, & V. Vignoles (Eds.), *Handbook of identity theory and research* (pp. 649–670). New York, NY: Springer. doi: 10.1007/978-1-4419-7988-9_27

Erikson, E. H. (1968). *Identity: Youth and crisis*. New York, NY: W. W. Norton.

Fitzgerald, L. F., & Betz, N. E. (1994). Career development in cultural context: The role of gender, race, class, and sexual orientation. In M. L. Savickas & R. W. Lent (Eds.), *Convergence in career development theories: Implications for science and practice* (pp. 103–117). Palo Alto, CA: Counseling Psychologists Press.

Graves, J. L., Jr. (2001). *The emperor's new clothes: Biological theories of race at the millennium*. New Brunswick, NJ: Rutgers University Press.

Helms, J. E. (1989). Considering some methodological issues in racial identity counseling research. *The Counseling Psychologist, 17*, 227–252.

Helms, J. (1990). *Black and White racial identity: Theory and research*. Westport, CT: Greenwood.

Helms, J. E. (1992). *A race is a nice thing to have*. Topeka, KA: Content Communications.

Helms, J. E. (1995a). An update of Helms' White and People of Color racial identity models. In J. G. Potterotto, J. M. Casas, L. A. Suzuki & C. M. Alexander (Eds.), *Handbook of multicultural counseling*. Thousand Oaks, CA: Sage Publications.

Helms, J. E. (1995b). *The people of Color (POC) racial identity attitude scale*. Unpublished manuscript, University of Maryland, College Park.

Herek, G. M. (1990). The context of anti-gay violence: Notes on cultural and psychological heterosexism. *Journal of Interpersonal Violence, 5*, 316–333. doi: 10.1177/088626090005003006

Herek, G. M. (2000). The psychology of sexual prejudice. *Current Directions in Psychological Science, 9*, 19–22. doi: 10.1111/1467-8721.00051

Jenson, R. (2005). *The heart of whiteness: Confronting race, racism, and white privilege*. San Francisco, CA: City Lights.

Jernigan, M. M. (2007, December). Managing race and culture in schools. Presented at the Annual Metco Director's Association Conference, Norwood, MA.

Jernigan, M. M., Green, C. G., Helms, J. E., Henze, K., & Perez-Gualdron, L. (2010). An examination of people of color supervision dyads: Racial identity matters as much as race. *Training & Education in Professional Psychology, 4*, 62–73.

Langhout, R. D. (2005). Acts of resistance: Student (in)visibility. *Culture & Psychology, 11*, 123–158.

Marcia, J. E., (1966). Development and validation of ego identity status. *Journal of Personality and Social Psychology, 3*, 551–558.

Morris, E. W. (2007). "Ladies" or "Loudies"?: Perceptions and experience of Black girls in classrooms. *Youth and Society, 38*, 490–515.

Patterson, L. A., Cameron, J. E., & Lalonde, R. N. (1996). The intersection of race and gender. Examining the politics of identity in women's studies. *Canadian Journal of Behavioral Science, 28*, 229–239.

Phinney, J.S. (1992). The multigroup ethnic identity measure: A new scale for use with diverse groups. A new scale for use with diverse groups. *Journal of Adolescent Research, 7*, 156–176.

Reid, P. T. (2004). A postscript for research on Black women: New populations, new directions. *Journal of Black Psychology, 30*, 443–446.

Saddler, C. (2005). The impact of Brown on African American students: A critical race theoretical perspective. *Educational Studies: Journal of the American Educational Studies Association. Special Issue: The Contradiction of the Legacy of Brown v Board of Education, Topeka, 37*, 41–55.

Sellars, R. M., Smith, M. A., Shelton, J. N., Rowley, S. A. J., & Chavous, T. M. (1998). Multidimensional model of racial identity: A reconceptualization of African American racial identity. *Personality and Social Psychology Review, 2*, 18–39.

Settles, I. H. (2006). Use of an intersectional framework to understand Black women's racial and gender identities. *Sex Roles, 54*, 589–601.

Shorter-Gooden, K. (2004). Multiple resistance strategies: How African American women cope with racism and sexism. *Journal of Black Psychology, 30*, 406–425.

Shorter-Gooden, K., & Washington, N. C. (1996). Young, black, and female: The challenge of weaving an identity. *Journal of Adolescence, 19*, 465–475.

Shields, S. (2008). Gender: An intersectionality perspective. *Sex Roles, 59*, 301–311.

Spickard, P. R. (1992). The illogic of American racial categories. In M. P. P. Root (Ed.), *Racially mixed people in America*. Thousand Oaks, CA: Sage Publications.

Sue, D. W. (2003). *Overcoming our racism: The journey to liberation*. San Francisco, CA: Jossey-Bass.

Thomas, A. T., Hacker, J. D., & Hoxha, D. (2011). Gendered racial identity of young women. *Sex Roles, 64*, 530–542.

Thompson, C. E., & Carter, R. T. (1997). *Racial Identity Theory*. Mahwah, NJ: Erlbaum.

Yip, T., Douglass, S., & Sellers, R. (2014). Ethnic and racial identity. In F. Leong, L. Comas-Diaz, G. Hall & J. Trimble (Eds.), *APA handbook of multicultural psychology, Volume I: Theory and research* (pp. 179–206). Washington, DC: American Psychological Association.

Zea, M. C., & Nakamura, N. (2014). In F. Leong, L. Comas-Diaz, G. Hall & J. Trimble (Eds.), *APA handbook of multicultural psychology, Volume I: Theory and research* (pp. 395–410). Washington, DC: American Psychological Association.

Zuckerman, M. (1990). Some dubious premises in research and theory on racial differences: Scientific, social, and ethical issues. *American Psychologist, 45*, 1297–1303.

CHAPTER 15

Disparities in Mental Health Care and Homeownership for African Americans and Latinos in the United States

Kiara C. Wesley

Structural disparities, or conditions of large-scale inequalities wherein categories of people are attributed an unequal status to others (e.g., Rimal, Limaye, Roberts, Brown, & Mkandawire, 2013), exist between Whites and ethnic minority groups in the United States. They arose from historical inequity, segregation, and discrimination, resulting in disproportionate burdens on ethnic minority groups that negatively impact overall well-being and health. Of the many ethnic groups in the United States, African Americans and Latinos represent the two largest ethnic minority groups, comprising approximately 13 percent and 16 percent of the American population, respectively (Lopez, Barrio, Kopelowicz, & Vega, 2012). As African Americans and Latinos together make up roughly 29 percent of the population, the nature and impact of such disparities are particularly important to understand. This chapter highlights a body of literature showing the complex ways in which structural disparities manifest, important areas for potential intervention, and the persistent gaps that remain in the literature.

One way to conceptualize the role of structural factors in lives of African American and Latino families is using the **Process-Person-Context-Time (PPCT) Model** of Bronfenbrenner's bioecological theory (Tudge, Mokrova, Hatfield, & Karnik, 2009). The PPCT Model proposes a system of reciprocal interactions, or processes, between people and their environment, or context, which occur over time and impact well-being (Tudge et al., 2009). Bronfenbrenner further explicates *context*, outlining four inter-related systems (Tudge et al., 2009). Contexts where individuals spend most of their time, such as home or school, comprise the **microsystem**. Microsystems interact with each other as people develop, comprising the **mesosystemic** level. Next, the **exosystemic** level involves contexts that individuals do not interact directly with, but nonetheless have an impact on their well-being. Tudge and colleagues (2009) discussed a mother experiencing work-related stress, which negatively impacts her interactions with her child once she gets home. As a result, the child is indirectly affected by his mother's work. Finally, the **macrosystem** comprises systems that encompass larger groups wherein the members of that group share characteristics and/or experiences (Tudge et al., 2009). Thus, structural disparities can impact families at any of these levels, directly or indirectly.

The large structural forces of persistent racial and ethnic disparities in health care and homeownership are well documented (e.g., Lopez et al., 2012; Rugh & Massey, 2010; Snowden, 2012). Given the impact of quality health care and the benefits of homeownership on quality of life, disparities between Whites and both African Americans and Latinos have significant implications for the well-being of families. Furthermore, understanding the nature of disparities may explicate interventions that can increase positive outcomes and reduce risk and burden in such areas. Homeownership and health may be linked in important ways, as homeowners report better mental health even after controlling for demographic factors. Also, this relationship is mediated by, or operates through, psychological factors such as perceived control (Manturuk, 2012). Thus, this chapter focuses on the current literature regarding disparities for African Americans and Latinos in mental health care and homeownership.

INTERSECTIONALITY

Intersectionality refers to the intersections between two or more identities, and is inherently discussed throughout this chapter. This chapter focuses on intersectionality reflecting dual oppression: oppression of African American and Latinos as racial/ethnic groups and the oppression that results in the disparities that many of them experience as patients in the mental health care system and as homeowners or renters. In addition, it is important to note that these two disparities represent only two examples of many structural disparities that exist between many minority groups (e.g., persons of color, sexual minorities, women) and their dominant group counterparts (e.g., White heterosexual men). Two other well-documented examples are racial/ethnic disparities in education (e.g., Gregory, Skiba, & Noguera, 2010) and the justice system (e.g., Higgins, Ricketts, Griffith, & Jirard, 2013; Nicosia, MacDonald, & Arkes, 2013). Together, each of these disparities combine to adversely affect the health, mortality, achievement, overall quality of life, and couple and family relationships of African Americans and Latinos as compared to their White counterparts.

RACIAL AND ETHNIC DISPARITIES
IN HEALTH CARE

A History of Health Care Disparities

Health disparities are health-related differences between social groups, such that disadvantaged groups experience worse health outcomes and or more health risks than more advantaged groups (Braveman, 2006). Reports from the U.S. Department of Health and Human Services highlight significant physical and mental health disparities at a national level in the United States between ethnic minorities and Whites (U.S. Department of Health and Human Services, 1985, 2000, 2001). Such disparities are not fully explained by patient-level factors such as demographics, preferences, the appropriateness of interventions, or access to care, although disparities also may exist at those levels (Penner, Albrecht, Coleman, & Norton, 2007). In fact, such patient-level disparities are seen as reflective of larger, systemic factors rooted in persistent experiences of disadvantage or discrimination (Braveman, 2006; Penner et al., 2007).

The Institute of Medicine was charged with evaluating disparities in the quality of health care, and it found not one root cause, but a complex interaction of historic inequality and disparities at multiple levels of health care (Smedley, Stith, & Nelson, 2003; Snowden, 2012). It concluded that disparities exist at such a high level that it constitutes a public health issue. For example, African Americans had higher rates of cardiovascular disease than White Americans, even when illness severity, income, and insurance were accounted for in analyses (e.g., Smedley et al., 2003). Data further suggest that disparities are persistent, or long-lasting, as between 2000–2001 and 2003–2004 disparities in access to treatment between African Americans and Whites and Latinos and Whites increased (Cook, McGuire, & Miranda, 2007). Research also indicates that African Americans and Latinos, as compared to their White counterparts, were less likely to utilize mental health services, were less likely to receive evidence-based treatments when services are utilized, and were at a greater risk for premature dropout from treatment (Smedley et al., 2003; Snowden, 2012).

Differences in health outcomes may in part be attributed to a lower likelihood of receiving quality care. Data indicate that African American patients were significantly more likely than White patients to receive an inappropriate and poorer quality health care procedure across a number of health conditions (Smedley et al., 2003). For example, in a study on cardiovascular health within a sample of 12,402 patients (10.3% African American) with coronary disease, African Americans were 13 percent less likely than Whites to receive an angioplasty and 32 percent less likely to receive bypass surgery (Peterson et al., 1997). Such findings were significant after adjusting for severity, and held even in cases when such procedures would be medically recommended based on severity and survival benefit. In addition, African American patients were more likely to be diagnosed as psychotic, but less likely to receive antipsychotic medication (Smedley et al., 2003). Taken together, the body of research and reviews of reports compiled at the request of the federal government indicate unequivocally significant disparities between ethnic minorities and Whites, which occur from initial access to care to treatment outcomes.

Disparities in the Prevalence of Mental Illness and Mental Health Outcomes

While data indicate a clear pattern of disparities in health care overall, closer scrutiny reveals a complex picture. Data from large sample survey studies indicate a **race paradox,** as across studies African Americans and Latinos had lower rates of psychiatric disorders than Whites, findings that are counterintuitive given historic disparities between ethnic minority groups and their White counterparts (Lopez et al., 2012; Mouzon, 2013). Furthermore, data comparing native-born ethnic groups with their immigrant counterparts indicate an **immigrant paradox,** wherein first-generation immigrants tend to have better mental health than their second-generation or later counterparts born in the United States (Alegría et al., 2008; Earl, Williams, & Anglade, 2011). Each paradox suggests that there are significant strengths of each group that may initially protect them against mental illness, such as the central role of the family and strong ethnic identity (e.g., Boyd-Franklin, 2003; Lopez et al., 2012). Consider this case example: Rondall came to the United States from Jamaica to increase his life opportunities. He stayed with his cousin, who frequently complained of racism. While Rondall did notice occasional episodes of racism, he largely dismissed them, happy that the United States gave him a better job to send significant money home to his family until he could make enough to bring them to the United States permanently.

While researchers struggle to account for the immigrant paradox, research on the race paradox reveals lower rates of mental illnesses for ethnic minorities, which mask key disparities once disorder is present. For example, in a study using a nationally representative sample of 5,657 Latinos (9%), non-Latino Blacks (12%), and non-Latino Whites (78%), lifetime **prevalence,** or overall likelihood of suffering from a particular illness, and persistence of mood, anxiety, and substance use disorders were examined. Findings indicated that African Americans and Latinos had a lower lifetime prevalence rate of psychiatric disorders (Breslau, Kendler, Su, Gaxiola-Aguilar, & Kessler, 2005). However, when examining the prevalence of lifetime cases that persisted for 12 months, Latinos had a higher prevalence of mood, anxiety, and any disorder overall as compared to their White counterparts (Breslau et al., 2005). Black participants had higher levels of anxiety disorders and any disorder overall, coupled with a lower prevalence of substance use disorders than their White counterparts (Breslau et al., 2005).

Research also supports disparities once illness is present at severe levels requiring hospitalization. In a sample of 925 individuals hospitalized for severe mental illness, follow-up data during the year after hospitalization indicated that African Americans experienced significantly less improvement in a number of domains, including global functioning, activation, and likelihood of returning to work, than their White counterparts (Eack & Newhill, 2012). These findings are notable given similarities between the African American and White participants in **baseline** symptomatology, or symptoms present at the start of treatment. Outcome disparities remained significant even after adjusting for sociodemographic factors and diagnosis, although a trend-level interaction indicated that disparities in reemployment after hospitalization were exacerbated for Africans Americans of low socioeconomic status (SES; Eack & Newhill, 2012). Together, findings indicate that ethnic minority groups are less likely to have mental health problems; however, once mental illness is present, ethnic minority groups disproportionately experience worse duration of illness and poorer treatment outcomes.

Unique Considerations for Black Americans

A Model Unique to African Americans

Once present, African Americans' mental illnesses may be more persistent and severe due to lower treatment rates, poorer quality treatment once diagnosed, and greater exposure to adverse life circumstances. The chronicity and severity of mental illness are theorized to result in a greater "mental illness-induced disease burden" (Snowden, 2012; p. 527), wherein mental illness serves as a significant contributor to the overall global burden of disease. Notably, current data support the presence of such burden particularly for African Americans as compared to other racial and ethnic groups (Snowden, 2012). This pathway is an important framework for continued future research, as it accounts for disparities observed in mental health once disorder is present.

Subgroup Differences

The heterogeneity of groups representing the African diaspora in the United States is frequently overlooked in research, with African Americans, Caribbean Black Americans, Africans and other Black immigrant groups often categorized as one homogenous group (Earl et al., 2011). Notably, 6 percent of all Black Americans are foreign born and 10 percent of Black Americans are second-generation immigrants with parents born in other countries (Jackson et al., 2004). Furthermore, disparities in mental health may disproportionately impact certain ethnic subgroups of Black Americans (Earl et al., 2011), as Caribbean Black Americans tend to utilize mental health care services at lower rates than African Americans (Neighbors et al., 2007). When considering gender, research indicated that Black Caribbean men had higher psychiatric disorder prevalence rates than African American men, whereas Black Caribbean women exhibited lower rates than African American women (Williams et al., 2007). Thus, while research comparing African Americans to their White counterparts provides important data, comprehensive analysis of various subgroups of the African diaspora can deepen our understanding of disparities. As Earl and colleagues (2011) note, such nuanced analyses are critical toward parsing out the complex ways in which mental health care disparities impact Black Americans.

Research also indicates that the immigrant paradox in mental health may operate in a unique way for Caribbean Blacks. While research indicates that second and later generations of Asians and Latinos experienced worse mental health than their first-generation counterparts, this decline in mental health appeared to be greater for Caribbean Blacks. This is notable given that Caribbean Blacks represent the largest Black immigrant group in the United States (Williams et al., 2007). This, coupled with aforementioned findings regarding differences between African Americans and Black Caribbean Americans, indicates a need to attend to the intersectionality of immigration status and ethnic subgroup of origin in research on disparities.

Unique Considerations for Latino Americans

Many studies also treat Latino Americans as one homogenous group in analyses, which ignores the diversity between Latino ethnic subgroups. A study that utilized two major national surveys of U.S. born Latinos, non-Latino Whites, as well as their immigrant counterparts (Alegría et al., 2008) indicated that Latinos, regardless of nativity, reported lower lifetime prevalence rates in the majority of mental illnesses as compared to their White counterparts. This overall finding masked the significant differences in each individual disorder except depression that occurred for at least two of the Latino ethnic subgroups (Alegría et al., 2008). Most striking, Puerto Ricans had significantly higher prevalence rates for any disorder at 37.4 percent, followed by Mexicans (30%) and Cubans (28%).

Alegría and colleagues (2008) further examined evidence of the immigrant paradox within the sample. Specifically, the paradox was consistently supported for Mexican participants whereas no evidence of the paradox was observed among Puerto Rican participants. Also, the paradox appeared to be evident only for other ethnic Latino subgroups when examining the lifetime prevalence rates of substance use disorders (Alegría et al., 2008). Given that Puerto Ricans in the sample were more likely than other ethnic subgroups to be born in America, it appears that larger environmental, cultural, and systemic conditions that seem to uniquely operate in the United States are driving such disparities (Alegría et al., 2008). Thus, these findings indicate the importance of examining not only nativity, but also nuanced ethnic identity in order to adequately address disparities in health for Latinos in the United States.

The following case vignette highlights how serious mental illness can impact the family, particularly for ethnic minority clients who may experience barriers to treatment related to language, cost, or stigma. In addition, cultural values around the importance of family for many ethnic minority groups can place strain on caregivers within the family, who may feel overburdened but ultimately responsible for caring for family members.

Case Vignette

A second-generation 23-year-old Mexican American woman was referred to mental health treatment by a primary care doctor for an alcohol use assessment. The client reported significant conflict with her family, as she currently lived at home. In addition, she was the primary caregiver of her mother who suffered from schizophrenia, and felt torn between going to school out of state or staying with her family. She noted the difficulty in getting her mother treatment, as she went for years without a formal diagnosis due to both the extended family and doctors dismissing her symptoms and a lack of health care coverage. In addition, the client stated that she was the only person to make sure her mother regularly took her medications, and she accompanied her to the doctor as a translator, as most of her family did not speak English. As a result, she acknowledged that she drank to manage feelings of stress and guilt.

RACIAL AND ETHNIC DISPARITIES IN HOMEOWNERSHIP

A History of Disparities in Housing and Homeownership

Homeownership plays a central role in defining success in the United States, and a legacy of neighborhood- and policy-level segregation and discrimination against ethnic minorities in the United States has led to current disparities in homeownership. The literature has primarily focused on African Americans, as this ethnic minority group appears particularly vulnerable to disparities in housing. While Jim Crow laws legally sanctioned segregation in neighborhoods after the abolition of slavery, segregation was maintained after the Jim Crow era through **redlining,** where mortgages were limited or denied to certain neighborhoods based on racial or ethnic composition, irrespective of resident qualifications or creditworthiness. This practice, operating legally from 1934 to 1968, forced ethnic minorities to purchase homes through predatory lenders who were not backed by the Federal Housing Administration. Lenders also refused loans to minority families who desired to move into predominately White neighborhoods that often had greater access to resources (Friedman & Squires, 2005). Thus, a historical dearth in access to mortgage credit fostered segregated neighborhoods. The Fair Housing Act officially outlawed redlining in 1968 (Friedman & Squires, 2005); however, its legacy remains through ongoing and persistent disparities in homeownership. For example, during the housing market bubble and subsequent crash in the 2000s, ethnic minority families were much more likely to receive a subprime loan and disproportionately experience foreclosure as compared to White families (e.g., Rugh & Massey, 2010).

Census data indicate that 74 percent of White heads of households own their homes compared to 45 percent of African Americans (U.S. Census Bureau, 2013). Socioeconomic differences alone do not fully explain disparities between African Americans and Whites in homeownership, as significant differences persist even among households with similar SES resources (Alba & Logan, 1992; Rosenbaum, 1996). Dawkins (2005) examined rental tenure duration, or the duration from renting to first-time homeownership, from 1978 to 1987. Findings indicated that equality across household characteristics, such as income, eliminated much, but not all, of the racial gap in the transition to homeownership. For example, if the income of African Americans were equated to that of their White counterparts, the gap in rental tenure duration would be reduced by more than 20 percent (Dawkins, 2005).

It is notable that the foregoing factors do not completely explain the racial gap in the transition to homeownership. In Dawkins's (2005) study, unlike with African Americans, loan volume, or the amount of credit that they could access to buy a home, increased the pace at which White renters transitioned to homeowners. This finding is consistent with the fact that many African Americans have faced mortgage market discrimination, as African Americans were more likely to be denied loans before the housing boom, and then disproportionately marketed subprime loans during the housing boom in the early 2000s (e.g., Rugh & Massey, 2010). Dawkins (2005) asserts that housing market discrimination hinders African Americans' efforts to take advantage of credit, and as a result, loan volume does not impact the transition to homeownership for this group.

Research indicates that African American households also are disadvantaged through the burden of providing support to more economically vulnerable family members, and disadvantaged in access to parental and extended family wealth (Hall & Crowder, 2011). Using longitudinal data from 8,217 householders and controlling for sociodemographic characteristics such as age, sex, and educational level, the national Panel Study of Income Dynamics from 1985 to 2005 found that household income explained only 47 percent of the variance in the household racial wealth gap. It also found that African Americans had a significant wealth disadvantage at both the household and extended family level compared to Whites (Hall & Crowder, 2011). When extended family wealth and extended family poverty were included in the model, the racial gap in wealth reduced further by a fifth. Thus, disparities between African American and White households in household wealth are in part due to household income, and in part due to the fact that White households are situated within families that have greater economic resources overall and lower rates of poverty (Hall & Crowder, 2011).

This disadvantage in wealth adversely impacts the transition to home-ownership, as African Americans were less likely than Whites to transition from renters to homeowners over a two-year observation period. In addition, such differences remained significant even when examining African American and White households with similar sociodemographic characteristics *and* resources in the extended family (Hall & Crowder, 2011). In fact, analyses revealed that the extended family wealth gap was so large that an African American extended family would need an average of $500,000 more in wealth to order to meet the probability of homeown-ership for White households. Yet even extended family wealth did not provide the full picture, because in models in which wealth and poverty levels of extended families are held constant, racial disparities in wealth still existed (Hall & Crowder, 2011).

In addition to disparities in overall wealth, research indicates that sub-prime lending plays a role in residential segregation and subsequent disparities in homeownership. Rugh and Massey's (2010) review of the literature examined the period before the housing bubble burst in 2007 and the subsequent foreclosure crisis. During that period, an increase in subprime lending occurred, defined as loans where the "interest rate at origination exceeded that for a comparable U.S. Treasury security, such as 30-year bond, by three percent or more" (Rugh & Massey, 2010; p. 636). Subprime lending practices altered the view of minority borrowers who historically were considered undesirable, as lenders began to seek out Black and Latino communities to explicitly market predatory subprime loans (Rugh & Massey, 2010). Findings indicated that African Ameri-cans were more likely than their White counterparts to receive subprime loans during this period, even when comparing African Americans and Whites with similar credit histories, down payment ratios, residential locations, and demographic characteristics (Avery, Brevoort, & Canner, 2007). In another study, Avery, Brevoort, and Canner (2008) obtained data from mortgage lenders who went bankrupt in 2007, finding that ethnic minority borrowers who received loans in 2006 were much more likely to receive a subprime loan. Seventy-four percent of Black borrowers and 63 percent of Latino borrowers received a subprime loan, whereas only 43 percent of White borrowers received a subprime loan (Avery, Brevoort, & Canner, 2008). In contrast, Avery and colleagues (2008) found that among mortgage lenders who did not go bankrupt in 2007, Black borrowers were just as likely to receive a subprime loan as a prime one.

Residential segregation influences foreclosures, with subprime lending as the mechanism, even when controlling for SES, borrowers' creditworthiness, and other economic causes of foreclosure (Rugh & Massey, 2010). Rugh and Massey (2010) hypothesized that racial segregation facilitates racially targeted subprime mortgages, which are disproportionately offered in ethnic minority neighborhoods, thus resulting in a concentration of foreclosures within minority neighborhoods during the foreclosure crisis. Findings indicated that segregation was indeed a significant predictor of the number and rate of foreclosures, but only for segregated neighborhoods with a high concentration of African Americans, whereas segregated Latino neighborhoods only predicted foreclosures for one measure of segregation, namely isolation (Rugh & Massey, 2010). Together, these findings indicate that segregation intensified the impact of the foreclosure crisis along racial lines, with its effects disproportionately falling on African American and Latino neighborhoods. The following case vignette shows how aspects of the foregoing housing disparities can affect family life.

Case Vignette

An African American family sought treatment for their teen son's declining grades and frequent angry outbursts in school. The parents reported difficulty in addressing their son's issues in school; he "shut down" at home and would not talk to them. Exploration revealed that the family experienced significant financial strain over the past year and the foreclosure of their home during the housing market crisis. Thus, the family was forced to move in with the wife's parents, and their son had to attend a school in a predominately White district away from his African American school friends. The son reported frequently seeing his parents fight over money, and that he often did not want to come home after school.

The foregoing brief case vignette highlights how significant housing issues and the accompanying economic stress leads to increased emotional and behavior difficulties for family members. Furthermore, moving from their segregated neighborhood to a predominately White one with extended family significantly disrupted their daily lives and routine. Such housing disruptions are common for ethnic minority families facing chronic economic stress.

Unique Considerations for the Latino Community

Similar to other ethnic minority groups, only 45 percent of Latino households own their house (U.S. Census Bureau, 2013). However, further research highlights important differences in housing inequality for subgroups of the Latino community. Homeownership rates for Mexican Americans and other Latinos appear to be accounted for by factors such as linguistic isolation, SES, and duration in the United States, resulting in rates lower than their White counterparts (Desilva & Elmelech, 2012). Puerto Rican communities are influenced by many of the same factors, but in contrast, their disadvantage in homeownership more closely resembled that of African Americans, a group that is consistently observed as particularly disadvantaged (Desilva & Elmelech, 2012). Research indicates that demographic factors accounted for a large proportion of the disparity in homeownership for Puerto Ricans. Yet the inclusion of all available variables in the model, such as socioeconomic, demographic, and immigration factors, did not fully account for the gap between Puerto Ricans and Whites in homeownership (Desilva & Elmelech, 2012). These findings suggest that discrimination may continue to play a role in the housing gap, and that such experiences may disproportionately impact Puerto Ricans as compared to other subgroups of the Latino community. Continued research on factors that impact Latino homeownership, while attending to variations by ethnic subgroup, is critical.

STRESS AND STIGMA ACROSS DISPARITIES FOR COUPLES, FAMILIES, AND COMMUNITIES

Although there are many ways in which structural disparities impact the lives of African American and Latino families and communities directly, experiences of stress that arise from such disparities exacerbate the direct effects of such disparities. As a result, researchers theorized potential pathways in which stress impacted functioning and led to disparities in health outcomes. Specifically, theory suggests that members of marginalized groups in society, such as members of racial and ethnic minority groups, experience differential exposure to stressors that can be acute and or chronic (Schetter et al., 2013). Responses to those stressors may or may not vary as a result of their social status, and a greater volume of stressors depletes healthy coping responses over time. This process is theorized to then result in differential health outcomes for marginalized groups as compared to their higher-SES White counterparts (Schetter et al., 2013).

Current research provides support for the stress pathway to health disparities, and suggests that stress maybe related to other structural disparities. In a study of 2,448 mothers and 1,383 fathers who recently had a child, stress experienced by the parents was examined from the birth of the child and over the two years following birth. Results indicated that being poor or near the federal poverty level was associated with higher levels of chronic life stress with moderate effect sizes across racial and ethnic groups (Schetter et al., 2013). However, associations between factors known to buffer against poorer stress outcomes, such as greater income or educational attainment, were weaker with ethnic minority families. For example, greater educational attainment was associated with lower levels of various forms of stress; however, this association was weaker for African American and Latino families as compared to White families (Schetter et al., 2013). Given the impact of economic strain on families, and that African American and Latino families are at greater risk for experiencing such strain, such experiences interact in critical ways with housing, and opportunities for homeownership for both groups.

Theory also indicates that chronic experiences of economic hardship negatively impact couple and family relationships and the well-being of children, described within a **"Family Stress Model"** (e.g., Conger, Conger, & Martin, 2010). The Family Stress Model posits that economic hardship fosters economic pressures that tax and deteriorate romantic relationships over time, thus impacting the lives of families. In particular, economic hardships give rise to economic pressure, defined as the increasing economic demands that come with negative financial experiences such as the inability to pay bills (Conger et al., 2010). As a result, the romantic relationship is impacted, as the psychological effects of economic pressure increase risk for mental health problems. Such mental health problems include an increased risk for emotional distress, depression, and substance use, thus deteriorating positive coping of each partner. Emotional and behavior problems in the relationship also deteriorate positive interactions, as partners withdraw supportive behaviors, distance themselves from each other, and increase hostile behaviors within the relationship (Conger et al., 2010). Thus, the cumulative effect of such negative behaviors and interactions over time erodes relationship quality and stability. The development of children within the family is then subsequently impacted through negative interactions between parent and child, which can result in poorer mental health and behavioral problems for the child (Conger et al., 2010).

Current research supports the Family Stress Model and its progression for couples, as well as its impact on the family system across a number of racial and ethnic groups (Conger et al., 2010). In a study on African American families (Conger et al., 2002), economic hardship predicted economic pressure, and economic pressure then predicted conflict at the couple level. Conflicts at the couple level then predicted problematic parenting behaviors, such as uninvolved and inconsistent rearing practices, which in turn predicted child maladjustment, such as externalizing behaviors. The foregoing pathway was supported with Mexican American families as well (Parke et al., 2004); however, interparental conflict directly predicted child maladjustment for this ethnic group instead of operating through problematic parenting.

In conjunction with stress, stigma often accompanies many disparities faced by African American and Latino families. For example, a qualitative study on the impact of infant mortality in an African American community indicated that many families in the community knew that African American families disproportionately experienced infant mortality (Baffour &

Chonody, 2009). Participants noted negative views of this disparity and victim blaming that occurred as a result (Baffour & Chonody, 2009). In another study utilizing a community sample of 275 participants (34% African American, 37% White, and 29% Latino), parents of adolescent children rated the extent to which stigma-related, logistical, and socioeconomic concerns served as barriers to treatment (Young & Rabiner, 2015). Findings indicated that parents reported more socioeconomic and stigma-related barriers to mental health care than physical health care. In addition, Latino parents reported such barriers as more inhibiting to their likelihood to receive treatment than their African American counterparts (Young & Rabiner, 2015). Taken together, families and communities often experience the stigma associated with health care and negative perceptions that others may hold regarding the source of such disparities. This may impact a family's willingness to seek treatment, and interact with other barriers to adequate health care.

POLICY AND PREVENTION CONSIDERATIONS FOR REDUCING DISPARITIES

Policy and Prevention Considerations for Disparities in Mental Health Care

In a comprehensive review of current developments related to mental health disparities experienced by African Americans, Snowden (2012) outlined key considerations for future policy and research endeavors in this area. Snowden (2012) noted that the controversial view that differences in treatment *preferences* may lead to mental health treatment disparities does not account for social factors that may inform or create treatment preference. Stigma associated with mental illness may result in the rejection of mental health treatment by African Americans, and Snowden (2012) called for efforts to reduce and address stigma. Research supports Snowden's (2012) call, as qualitative studies with African American samples indicated stigma was a treatment barrier (e.g., Thompson, Bazile, & Akbar, 2004), and quantitative studies cited stigma-based beliefs as a contributor, in part, to observed disparities in the use of mental health services between ethnic groups (e.g., Ojeda & McGuire, 2006). Thus, stigma-related research may help identify ways to prevent some of the barriers in access to treatment for African Americans, and likely many other ethnic minority groups. Given that explicit policy fosters comprehensive reviews of disparities in health care at a federal level, policy that also privileges rigorous study of stigma-related barriers would be a critical step in supporting such work.

Preliminary prevention research indicates that psychoeducational programs to address stigma that are tailored to cultural factors can be effective. In a study of 42 African American clients referred for outpatient treatment, participants were randomly assigned to receive standard brochures about services or a psychoeducational booklet (Alvidrez, Snowden, Rao, & Boccellari, 2009). The psychoeducational booklet outlined common stigma-based experiences faced by Black mental health consumers, such as barriers to attending treatment (e.g., wanting to avoid social judgments). Results indicated no significant differences in treatment attendance at three-month follow-up between individuals assigned to either group; however, greater stigma reduction was observed in participants with a greater perceived treatment need or greater uncertainty about treatment (Alvidrez et al., 2009). These findings suggest that more attention and research are needed on the impact of stigma in treatment, and that effective preventive interventions can be implemented to target experiences of stigma for African Americans.

Snowden (2012) also discussed how policy changes, specifically the Affordable Care Act (ACA), were related to health disparities. Data indicated that in 2009, 21 percent of African Americans lacked health insurance coverage as compared to 15.8 percent of White Americans (DeNavas-Walt, Proctor, & Smith, 2010). Furthermore African Americans were disproportionately more likely to rely on Medicaid (27.1%), compared to White Americans (10.7%). As the ACA includes expansions to Medicare, such programs would greatly increase access for poorer African American families who are at the greatest risk for health disparities (Snowden, 2012). However, as the Supreme Court ruled that the implementation of Medicare expansion provisions could not be mandatory, states are not required to expand their Medicare program but instead are offered strong incentive programs to do so (Snowden, 2012). Thus, unless all states fully implement these expansions, there will be many African Americans who likely will remain uninsured.

In addition, barriers to "uptake," or the rate at which individuals participate in programs that are offered, are a concern. African Americans do not take advantage of health insurance benefits when offered as much as their White counterparts (Snowden, 2012), and it is unknown exactly what barriers exist that impact the uptake of insurance programs. As the ACA requires uptake by administering penalties to those who do not purchase insurance, African Americans will likely be disproportionately penalized. Such penalties could widened the gap in disparities related to coverage and access rather than close it (Snowden, 2012). Research and policy efforts should critically examine barriers that prevent African Americans from taking advantage of health services. While Snowden (2012) focused on African Americans, he noted that such issues related to insurance are likely relevant for many ethnic minority and poor Americans.

In a similar review documenting current research on mental health care disparities for Latinos, Lopez and colleagues (2012) highlighted potential approaches to reducing and eliminating disparities for Latinos. They drew from Rogler and Cortes's (1993) pathways to mental health care framework, which states that there is a sequence of contact between individuals and organizations. This sequence of contact is the pathway that leads to help seeking and care, and occurs from the moment of initial distress, to illness onset, and to the arrival of the patient into treatment. This sequence also includes interactions with social networks, such as family members, and the health care system itself (Lopez et al., 2012). Thus disparities should be addressed at all levels of this pathway. Starting with illness onset, Lopez and colleagues (2012) noted that psychoeducational interventions tailored to Latino culture could be used to increase knowledge about mental health conditions, and increase help seeking. For example, in one study researchers developed and piloted a Spanish language program to help 95 Spanish speakers identify symptoms of psychosis in others using a culturally relevant mnemonic device and videos. Assessed using hypothetical vignettes, participants exhibited significant increases in their ability to identify symptoms of psychosis, as well as significant increases in their recommendations for help seeking after completing the program (Lopez et al., 2009).

Consistent with the Rogler and Cortes (1993) pathway model, for many Latinos the family plays a central role in the care of those with mental illness (Snowden, 2007). In addition families can function as a source of support or conflict related to mental health treatment (Lopez et al., 2012). For example, while data have shown the importance of a family's expressed emotion in relapse rates for those suffering from schizophrenia across ethnic groups (e.g., Kavanagh, 1992; King & Dixon, 1999), data suggest that there may be unique factors that matter for Latino families. Specific to Mexican American families, research indicates that emotional overinvolvement between family members played a greater role than expressed emotion in symptom relapse for those suffering with schizophrenia (e.g., Aguilera, Lopez, Breitborde, Kopelowicz, & Zarate, 2010). Such findings suggest that family processes can and do impact treatment outcomes, and may vary in important ways for different ethnic groups.

Lastly, Lopez and colleagues (2012) noted that while cultural adaptations are important, one should use caution in applying such treatments solely based on ethnicity, as there is vast heterogeneity within any one ethnicity. Thus, in order to avoid stereotyping, explicit assessment of the specific needs the family and factors that may impact decisions regarding treatment interventions is critical (Lopez et al., 2012). Taken together, Snowden (2012) and Lopez et al. (2012) outline current research relevant to mental health disparities for African Americans and Latinos, respectively. Their comprehensive reviews provide important areas for future study related to policy and the prevention of mental health disparities.

Policy and Prevention Considerations for Disparities in Homeownership

Legislation such as the **Community Reinvestment Act** (CRA) serves to eliminate and prevent discriminatory practices in the housing market, and increase access to mortgage credit for ethnic minority groups. The CRA requires monitoring of lenders and the degree to which they lend to low- and moderate-income borrowers and low- and moderate-income neighborhoods (Friedman & Squires, 2005). In some areas, lenders sign CRA agreements with community groups to more explicitly increase lending to traditionally underserved neighborhoods. Data show that the CRA has improved access, with African Americans and Latinos more likely to purchase homes in predominantly White neighborhoods that have more loans from CRA lenders, even after controlling for socioeconomic characteristics (Friedman & Squires, 2005). Thus, the enforcement and extension of policies designed to counteract the impacts of redlining and racial discrimination in lending play an important role in addressing homeownership disparities.

Homeownership is impacted by the interplay of a number of individual, household, and environmental factors; thus policy and prevention interventions must occur at many contextual levels to effectively eliminate disparities. Given that most of the gap between ethnic groups in the transition to homeownership could be eliminated by addressing racial differences in income and poverty (Dawkins, 2005), policies that improve access to affordable housing and reduce gaps in family income would be critical toward reducing disparities in homeownership.

CASE CONSIDERATIONS

Therapists must give special attention to the ways in which structural disparities impact couples and families in order to effectively tailor their interventions to the family's needs. A multicultural framework guides therapists in applying cultural knowledge, skills, and awareness to tailor treatment (Kelly, Bhagwat, Maynigo, & Moses, 2014). This approach includes understanding culturally based worldview and value differences, key experiences and contexts for the family, power differences in treatment, and felt distance between the therapist and family, in order to successfully bridge differences that would otherwise hinder treatment.

In order to honor the worldview and values of diverse clients, incorporating a strengths-based approach is an important component of treatment (Kelly et al., 2014). Thus, therapists should assess for the strengths of the couple or family early on in treatment, as well as their goals and preferences for treatment. Mobilizing strengths within the family normalizes and validates common cultural views, empowering families to draw on such strengths in times of hardship. The therapist's awareness of his or her own biases is also important, as biases can hinder our ability to recognize culture-based strengths in diverse couples and families (Kelly et al., 2014).

Perhaps the most central component in addressing structural disparities in treatment involves understanding the experiences and contexts of diverse couples and families. Therapists draw on knowledge of the historic, cultural experiences of the group, as well as the various contexts within which families operate (Kelly et al., 2014). Consistent with Bronfenbrenner's PPCT Model (Tudge et al., 2009), structural disparities related to economic resources and housing, as well as mental health care, represent key contexts that may impact the therapeutic process and overall well-being for families. Thus, it is important to assess for potential treatment barriers related to transportation to sessions, employment status, living arrangements, and other practical aspects of the lives of couples and families. Structural disparities in such areas often require therapists to serve as an advocate for their clients within their agencies or institutions, as well as within the larger community (e.g., Boyd-Franklin, 2003). This may include requesting a fee reduction for services on behalf of the family, or role-playing with clients as to what questions to ask their primary care doctor about a health concern. Over time, empowering clients to be their own advocate within these systems allows the clients to leave treatment with a road map for addressing future barriers as they arise (e.g., Boyd-Franklin, 2003). Empowering couples and families involves drawing on their strengths, teaching couples and families how to identify and access positive role models and resources in their communities, and strengthening problem-solving skills.

Structural disparities can require interventions to decrease stigma, as they are a byproduct of long-standing, historical discrimination for ethnic minority families. Stigma can impact treatment through the manifestation of power differences and or felt distance between the therapist and family in treatment. As a result of stigma, diverse families may lack experience with treatment, or may have had negative past experiences with service providers. Thus, orienting clients to treatment, providing a rationale for treatment, and discussing treatment goals, are important interventions toward engaging families in therapy (Kelly et al., 2014). Using a cultural **genogram** to map the family tree, family history, and the nature of relationships between family members is another tool to engage clients, while also gaining important cultural knowledge about the family (Kelly et al., 2014).

Given the structural nature of disparities, some couples and families have difficulty recognizing the impact of such forces in their daily lives. As a result, couples and families may attribute their difficulties to specific interpersonal problems within the family or with family members, without acknowledging structural stressors exerted on the family. The therapist's role involves explicitly labeling these disparities, and working to de-stigmatize their impact by validating and normalizing the family's response to such stressors (Kelly et al., 2014). For example, psychoeducation on how financial strain negatively impacts families can help clients see their own reactions as understandable responses to such stress.

The following case example highlights the intersectionality of mental health and housing-related issues with an interracial, unmarried, cohabitating couple. In conjunction with a cognitive behavioral approach to treatment, a multicultural framework was utilized that emphasized cultural knowledge, awareness of the impact of large societal and cultural influences and potential differences between the therapist and couple, and the use of interventions from a culturally sensitive framework tailored to the couple (Kelly et al., 2014).

CASE EXAMPLE

Beth, a 38-year-old White female, and Matt, a 35-year-old African American male, sought couples treatment because of significant fighting at home. Their arguments frequently revolved around commitment to the relationship and finances. Beth and Matt described their relationship as "on again off again," as Matt struggled to commit to Beth, and Beth wanted to get married. In addition, Beth, who suffered from bipolar disorder, would often have periods of medication noncompliance, particularly around periods of turbulence in the home.

Both partners suffered from significant financial strain, and experienced conflict around the allocation of their limited financial resources. Sources of financial strain included a multitude of areas reflective of disparities directly experienced by the couple. The couple lost their first home together due to a subprime loan and subsequent foreclosure. In addition, Matt was previously incarcerated, negatively impacting his ability to secure stable employment opportunities. Beth's excessive spending during periods of mania, coupled with overall symptom severity and a history of medication noncompliance, often prevented her from maintaining employment. Thus, although she was compliant with her medication for a number of months at the start of treatment, Beth was not employed. These cumulative experiences throughout the course of their relationship created chronic financial hardships that eroded their relationship quality.

To begin treatment, the therapist worked to decrease the felt distance between the therapist and the couple, and understand the specific concerns of the couple. A number of pressing issues related to SES and housing were identified through the exploration of the circumstances that triggered fights for the couple. At the start of treatment, Matt had recently lost a job. Although Matt was scheduled to start a new part-time job soon, due to failure to make rent payments the couple faced eviction from their apartment. Thus, the therapist worked collaboratively with the couple to identify affordable housing options, including housing provided by a local church that the therapist knew about from her own network, and together they outlined a plan for the couple to follow up on those options as a team.

The couple frequently experienced difficulty getting to sessions weekly, due to both a reliance on public transportation and the inability to pay for sessions every week. Through a systematic exploration of challenges related to attending treatment, the therapist and the couple agreed to a biweekly meeting schedule. The therapist also advocated on the couple's behalf with her institution to get a lower fee schedule, reducing the financial burden of attending sessions. All of the aforementioned interventions were necessary to reduce barriers that would impact the couple's ability to attend and fully engage in treatment.

Next, the therapist used cultural genograms to map each partner's family of origin. The genogram revealed key cultural factors that impacted the relationship. For example, Matt grew up in an impoverished community and reported no positive models of romantic relationships. As a result, while he strived for connection with others, he had an aversive view of relationships. He also strived to be financially settled before committing to marriage, in order to overcome the financial strain he experienced growing up. Conversely, Beth was raised in a financially stable two-parent home. However, she experienced significant conflict with her family, as they did not support her interracial relationship and cut her off from the family once the couple moved in together. Taken together, these different cultural contexts and experiences created distance and misunderstandings between the couple around their presenting concerns. One of the couple's strengths included their ability to successfully navigate the lack of acceptance from Beth's family as an interracial couple. Furthermore, in their daily lives their racial differences did not hinder their ability to connect emotionally. Lastly, through the genogram, church and religion arose as consistent sources of strength and financial assistance for the couple.

Once barriers to treatment were identified and addressed, and family backgrounds were explored, treatment focused on addressing the problematic fights between Beth and Matt. Using a multicultural framework, the therapist worked to de-stigmatize the couple's relationship difficulties, by highlighting how financial strain negatively impacts relationship quality for many couples. To make this psychoeducational component more concrete for the couple, the therapist collaboratively mapped out with the couple when fights occurred over the month, noting patterns. This intervention allowed Beth and Matt to notice that they fought more near the end of the month when they were more financially strained. In addition, the therapist worked with the couple to identify the most problematic behaviors that occurred during their fights, such as name calling. In doing so, the therapist was able to teach the couple alternative methods for communication, such as using "I" statements and not talking about issues until they could keep their voices calm. Such skills gave the couple tools to more effectively communicate, and reduce their fights based on the behaviors they identified as most problematic.

In order to address the financial strain that often fueled their fighting, the therapist helped the couple to create a budget each month. As a couple, they were to outline together the money to allocate for bills, and how much extra money was available to spend for the month. Before going to any event that required money, they worked collaboratively to identify how much they each wanted to spend. This empowered them to increase the predictability of their finances, and to face this significant burden together as a team. As a result, Beth and Matt began to see their new ability to navigate financial strain as proof of their resilience as a couple.

To address commitment issues, the therapist worked to bridge cultural differences between Beth and Matt. This involved engaging each partner in explicit sharing around their upbringing, its emotional impact, and how such experiences affected their own views of romantic relationships. For example, Matt strived to be financially settled before committing to marriage, whereas Beth saw marriage as an important step toward combining resources and achieving financial stability as a couple. Both of these views stemmed directly from the different types of romantic relationships each partner witnessed growing up. The therapist explicitly labeled such experiences as culture and family upbringing, thus normalizing the origin of these beliefs and validating their experiences. This helped Beth and Matt understand each other's different views of marriage, and positively reframed their behaviors as a normal response to the contexts in which they were raised. By bridging such differences, Beth and Matt were then able to utilize problem-solving skills to identify strategies to increase intimacy in ways that were congruent with cultural preferences and their goals.

Lastly, it was critical throughout treatment to draw on the strengths of Beth and Matt as a couple. From the start of treatment, it was evident that they shared many similar interests. Thus, they were encouraged to make time together special by explicitly labeling this time as a "date." The therapist also worked with the couple to identify joint activities that did not cost money, such as going for a walk together, thus minimizing the impact of finances on their positive time together. To further support their faith, the therapist and couple collaboratively outlined a "mini church service" they could have at home in the event that finances and or transportation prevented them from attending church. Beth and Matt also decided to pray together more at home, particularly if they were feeling stressed regarding money. Lastly, the couple was encouraged to get more involved in their church, thus increasing their social network.

Overall, the therapist's interventions were tailored to the unique needs of the couple. Significant financial, housing, and mental health strains negatively impacted their relationship, and decreased the likelihood that

Beth would take her psychotropic medication. By addressing their external stressors as much as possible within the dyadic context, Beth and Matt were able to significantly reduce their fighting and face these structural burdens as a team.

CONCLUSIONS

Current data indicate significant disparities for African American and Latino families in mental health care and housing that impact overall well-being. This chapter focused on health and housing disparities for African Americans and Latinos as compared to their White counterparts. Yet disparities exist between many ethnic minorities and their White counterparts in physical health (e.g., Smedley et al., 2003), poverty (e.g., Schetter et al., 2013) criminal justice (e.g., Higgins et al., 2013; Nicosia et al., 2013), and education (e.g., Gregory et al., 2010). Each has a detrimental impact, not only on African Americans and Latinos, but on many minority groups. These disparities converge to provide an increase in structural disadvantage that affects many families, warranting further study. This chapter serves as an important framework for considering these influences on couples and families within a broader, structural context.

CHAPTER REVIEW

Key Points

1. Current structural disparities between ethnic minority groups and their White counterparts in the United States arose from historical inequity, segregation, and discrimination, resulting in disproportionate burdens on ethnic minority groups that negatively impact overall well-being and health.
2. Data indicate unequivocally that significant disparities between African American, Latino, and their White counterparts occur at all of levels of the mental health care system, from initial access to care to treatment outcomes.
3. Data indicate that significant disparities between African American, Latinos, and their White counterparts occur at multiple levels of the home-buying process, from available income to purchasing a home to disparities in lending practices.
4. While this chapter focuses on mental health and housing disparities for African Americans and Latinos, these merely serve as examples of the many structural disparities that exist in physical health, poverty levels, education, and the criminal justice system. Together, such disparities result in significant burdens faced by ethnic minority couples and families that are significantly less likely to be present for their White counterparts.

Key Terms

baseline, Community Reinvestment Act, exosystemic, Family Stress Model, genogram, health disparities, immigrant paradox, intersectionality, macrosystem, mesosystemic, microsystem, prevalence, Process-Person-Context-Time (PPCT) Model, race paradox, redlining, structural disparities, uptake

Myths and Realities

- It is a myth that disparities in mental health care between ethnic minorities and their White counterparts do not really exist, and easily can be accounted for by demographic differences between ethnic groups. In reality, disparities in mental health care that exist beyond the impact of demographics are well documented. Data indicate that disparities in mental health care have no one root cause, but are a result of a complex interaction of historic inequality and disparities at multiple levels of health care.
- It is a myth that disparities in housing between ethnic minorities and their White counterparts can be accounted for by individual differences such as income, creditworthiness, and/or SES. In reality, disparities in housing cannot be fully accounted for by sociodemographic factors, including creditworthiness, and are evident in studies even when such factors are statistically accounted for in analyses. Historic and ongoing segregation and discrimination at multiple levels create and maintain these disparities.

Tools and Tips

Knowledge

Coates, T. (2014, June). The case for reparations. *The Atlantic*. Retrieved from http://www.theatlantic.com/magazine/archive/2014/06/the-case-for-reparations/361631/

Madrigal, A. C. (2014, May 22). The racist housing policy that made your neighborhood. *The Atlantic*. Retrieved from http://www.theatlantic.com/business/archive/2014/05/the-racist-housing-policy-that-made-your-neighborhood/371439/

Rugh, J. S., & Massey, D. S. (2010). Racial segregation and the American foreclosure crisis. *American Sociological Review, 75*, 629–651. doi: 10.1177/00031224103 80868

Smedley, B. D., Stith, A. Y., & Nelson, A. R. (Eds.). (2003). *Unequal treatment: Confronting racial and ethnic disparities in health care*. Washington, DC: National Academies Press.

The Editorial Board. (2015, September 15). How segregation destroys Black wealth. *The New York Times*. Retrieved from http://www.nytimes.com/2015/09/15/opinion/how-segregation-destroys-black-wealth.html?smid=tw-nytopinion&smtyp=cur&_r=0

Dynamic Sizing

Although cultural adaptations and considerations are important, one should use caution in applying any treatment or intervention solely based on ethnicity, given the heterogeneity within any one ethnicity. In order to avoid stereotyping, it is important to assess the specific needs of each individual or family, and factors that may impact decisions regarding interventions appropriate for the family.

Skills

Theory and Prevention. Theorists and prevention scientists should work to create community-based programs and psychoeducational materials to reduce stigma and increase mental health knowledge in a culturally sensitive manner.

Service Provision. Therapists can take a collaborative and validating stance while exploring and destigmatizing couple and family challenges related to structural disparities, such as financial and housing issues. Also, therapists can help couples and families to address the impact of disparities in their lives, as well as advocate outside of sessions, such as requesting reduced fees within their agencies and finding assistance within the clients' communities.

Policy. Policy makers should attend to policies that increase access to affordable health care, and programs designed to connect potential homebuyers with prime loans.

Research. Researchers should continue to critically examine the nature of structural disparities, with greater attention to the unique needs of ethnic identity subgroups, and intersectionality between identities.

Awareness

Given the significant and disproportionate burden faced by ethnic minorities due to structural disparities, attention to and awareness of potential differences in the lived experiences of various ethnic minority groups and their couple and family relationships are important. These include clinicians' awareness of their own cultural identification, SES, and personal views related to perceived sources of such disparities.

REFERENCES

Aguilera, A., Lopez, S. R., Breitborde, N. J. K., Kopelowicz, A., & Zarate, R. (2010). Expressed emotion, sociocultural context and the course of schizophrenia. *Journal of Abnormal Psychology, 119*, 875–885. doi: 10.1037/a0020908

Alba, R. D., & Logan, J. R. (1992). Assimilation and stratification in the homeownership patterns of racial and ethnic groups. *International Migration Review, 26*, 1314–1341. Retrieved from http://dx.doi.org/10.2307/2546885

Alegría, M., Canino, G., Shrout, P. E., Woo, M., Duan, N., Vila, D., . . . & Meng, X. (2008). Prevalence of mental illness in immigrant and non-immigrant U.S. Latino groups. *American Journal of Psychiatry, 165*, 359–369. doi: 10.1176/appi.ajp.2007.07040704

Alvidrez, J., Snowden, L. R., Rao, S. M., & Boccellari, A. (2009). Psychoeducation to address stigma in Black adults referred for mental health treatment: A randomized pilot study. *Community Mental Health Journal, 45*, 127–136. doi: 10.1007/s10597-008-9169-0

Avery, R. B., Brevoort, K. P., & Canner, G. B. (2007). The 2006 HMDA Data. *Federal Reserve Bulletin, 93*, 73–109.

Avery, R. B., Brevoort, K. P., & Canner, G. B. (2008). The 2007 HMDA Data. *Federal Reserve Bulletin, 94*, 107–146.

Baffour, T. D., & Chonody, J. M. (2009). African American women's conceptualizations of health disparities: A community-based participatory research approach. *American Journal of Community Psychology, 44*, 374–381. doi: 10.1007/s10464-009-9260-x

Boyd-Franklin, N. (2003). *Black families in therapy: Understanding the African American experience*. New York, NY: Guilford Press.

Braveman, P. (2006). Health disparities and health equity: Concepts and measurement. *Annual Review of Public Health, 27*, 167–194. Retrieved from http://dx.doi.org/10.1146/annurev. publhealth.27.021405.102103

Breslau, J., Kendler, K. S., Su, M., Gaxiola-Aguilar, S., & Kessler, R. C. (2005). Lifetime risk and persistence of psychiatric disorders across ethnic groups in the United States. *Psychological Medicine, 35*, 317–327. Retrieved from http://dx.doi.org/10.1017/S0033291704003514

Conger, R. D., Conger, K. J., & Martin, M. J. (2010). Socioeconomic status, family processes, and individual development. *Journal and Marriage and Family, 72*, 685–704. doi: 10.1111/j.1741-3737.2010.00725.x

Conger, R. D., Wallace, L. E., Sun, Y., Simons, R. L., McLoyd, V. C., & Brody, G. (2002). Economic pressure in African American families: A replication and extension of the family stress model. *Developmental Psychology, 38*, 179–193. doi: 10.1037//0012-1649.38.2.179

Cook, B. L., McGuire, T., & Miranda, J. (2007). Measuring trends in mental health care disparities, 2000–2004. *Psychiatric Services, 58*, 1533–1540. doi: 10.1176/appi.ps.58.12.1533

Dawkins, C. J. (2005). Racial gaps in the transition to first-time homeownership: The role of residential location. *Journal of Urban Economics, 58*, 537–554. doi: 10.1016/j.jue.2005.08.004

DeNavas-Walt, C., Proctor, B. D., & Smith, J. C. (2010). *Income, poverty, and health insurance coverage in the United States: 2009*. Washington, DC: U.S. Census Bureau.

Desilva, S., & Elmelech, Y. (2012). Housing inequality in the United States: Explaining the White-minority disparities in homeownership. *Housing Studies, 27*, 1–26. Retrieved from http://dx.doi.org/10.1080/02673037.2012.628641

Eack, S. M., & Newhill, C. E. (2012). Racial disparities in mental health outcomes after psychiatric hospital discharge among individuals with severe mental illness. *Social Work Research, 36*, 41–52. doi: 10.1093/swr/svs014

Earl, T., Williams, D., & Anglade, S. (2011). An update on the mental health of Black Americans: Puzzling dilemmas and needed research. *Journal of Black Psychology, 37*, 485–498. doi: 10.1177/0095798410396077

Friedman, S., & Squires, G. D. (2005). Does the Community Reinvestment Act help minorities access traditionally inaccessible neighborhoods? *Social Problems, 52*, 209–231. doi: 10.1525/sp.2005.52.2.209

Gregory, A., Skiba, R. J., & Noguera, P. A. (2010). The achievement gap and the discipline gap: Two sides of the same coin? *Educational Researcher, 39,* 59–68. doi: 10.3102/0 013189X09357621

Hall, M., & Crowder, K. (2011). Extended-family resources and racial inequality in the transition to homeownership. *Social Science Research, 40,* 1534–1546. doi: 10.1016/j.ssresearch.2011.07.002

Higgins, G. E., Ricketts, M. L., Griffith, J. D., & Jirad, S. A. (2013). Race and juvenile incarceration: A propensity score matching examination. *American Journal of Criminal Justice, 38,* 1–12. doi: 10.1007/s12103-012-9162-6

Jackson, J. S., Torres, M., Caldwell, C., Neighbors, H., Nesse, R., Taylor, R., . . . & Williams, D. R. (2004). The national survey of American life: A study of racial, ethnic and cultural influences on mental disorders and mental health. *International Journal of Methods in Psychiatric Research, 13,* 196–207.

Kavanagh, D. J. (1992). Recent developments in expressed emotion and schizophrenia. *British Journal of Psychiatry, 160,* 601–620. doi: 10.1192/bjp.160.5.601

Kelly, S., Bhagwat, R., Maynigo, P., & Moses, E. (2014). Couple and marital therapy: The complement and expansion provided by multicultural approaches. In F. Leong, L. Comas-Diaz, V. McLloyd, and J. Trimble (Eds.), *American Psychological Association handbook of multicultural psychology.* Washington, DC: APA.

King, S., & Dixon, M. J. (1999). Expressed emotion and relapse in youth schizophrenia outpatients. *Schizophrenia Bulletin, 25,* 377–386. doi: 10.1093/oxford journals. schbul.a033385

Lopez, S. R., Barrio, C., Kopelowicz, A., & Vega, W. A. (2012). From documenting to eliminating disparities in mental health care for Latinos. *American Psychologist, 67,* 511–523. doi: 10.1037/a0029737

Lopez, S. R., Lara Mdel C., Kopelowicz, A., Solano, S., Foncerrada, H., & Aguilera, A. (2009). La CLAve to increase psychosis literacy of Spanish-speaking community residents and family caregivers. *Journal of Consulting and Clinical Psychology, 77,* 763–774. doi: 10.1037/a0016031

Manturuk, K. R. (2012). Urban homeownership and mental health: Mediating effect of perceived sense of control. *City & Community, 11,* 409–430. doi: 10. 1111/j.1540-6040.2012.01415.x

Mouzon, D. M. (2013). Can family relationships explain the race paradox in mental health? *Journal of Marriage and Family, 75,* 470–485. doi: 10.1111/jomf.12006

Neighbors, H., Caldwell, C., Williams, D., Nesse, R., Taylor, R., Bullard, K., . . . & Jackson, J. S. (2007). Race, ethnicity, and the use of services for mental disorders: Results from the National Survey of American Life. *Archives of General Psychiatry, 64,* 485–494. doi: 10.1001/archpsyc.64.4.485.

Nicosia, N., MacDonald, J. M., & Arkes, J. (2013). Disparities in criminal court referrals to drug treatment and prison for minority men. *American Journal of Public Health, 103,* e77–e84. doi: 10.2105/AJPH.2013.301222

Ojeda, V. D., & McGuire, T. G. (2006). Gender and racial/ethnic differences in use of outpatient mental health and substance use services by depressed adults. *Psychiatric Quarterly, 77,* 211–222. doi: 10.1007/s11126-006-9008-9

Parke, R. D., Coltrane, S., Duffy, S., Buriel, R., Dennis, J., Powers, J., . . . & Widaman, K. F. (2004). Economic stress, parenting, and child adjustment in Mexican American and European American families. *Child Development, 75,* 1632–1656. Retrieved from http://dx.doi.org/10.1111/j.1467-8624.2004.00807.x

Penner, L. A., Albrecht, T. L., Coleman, D. K., & Norton, W. E. (2007). Interpersonal perspectives on Black-White health disparities: Social policy implications. *Social Issues and Policy Review, 1,* 63–98. Retrieved from http://dx.doi.org/10.1111/j.1751-2409.2007.00004.x

Peterson, E. D., Shaw, L. K., DeLong, E. R., Pryor, D. B., Califf, R. M., & Mark, D. B. (1997). Racial variation in the use of coronary-revascularization procedures: Are the differences real? Do they matter? *New England Journal of Medicine, 336,* 480–486. doi: 10.1056/NEJM199702133360706

Rimal, R. N., Limaye, R. J., Roberts, P., Brown, J., & Mkandawire, G. (2013). The role of interpersonal communication in reducing structural disparities and psychosocial deficiencies: Experience from the Malawai BRIDGE project. *Journal of Communication, 63,* 51–71. doi: 10.1111/jcom.12000

Rogler, L. H., & Cortes, D. E. (1993). Help-seeking pathways: A unifying concept in mental health care. *American Journal of Psychiatry, 150,* 554–561.

Rosenbaum, E. (1996). Racial/ethnic differences in home ownership and housing quality, 1991. *Social Problems, 43,* 403–426. Retrieved from http://dx.doi.org/10.2307/3096952

Rugh, J. S., & Massey, D. S. (2010). Racial segregation and the American foreclosure crisis. *American Sociological Review, 75,* 629–651. doi: 10.1177/0003122410380868

Schetter, C. D., Schafer, P., Lanzi, R. G., Clark-Kauffman, E., Raju, T. N. K., Hillemeier, M. M., & the Community Child Health Network. (2013). Shedding light on the mechanisms underlying health disparities through community participatory methods: The stress pathway. *Perspectives on Psychological Science, 83,* 613–633. doi: 10.1177/1745691613506016

Smedley, B. D., Stith, A. Y., & Nelson, A. R. (Eds.). (2003). *Unequal treatment: Confronting racial and ethnic disparities in health care.* Washington, DC: National Academies Press.

Snowden, L. R. (2007). Explaining mental health treatment disparities: Ethnic and cultural differences in family involvement. *Culture, Medicine and Psychiatry, 31,* 389–402. doi: 10.1007/s11013-007-9057-z

Snowden, L. R. (2012). Health and mental health policies' role in better understanding and closing African American-White American disparities in treatment access and quality of care. *American Psychologist, 67,* 524–531. doi: 10.1037/a0030054

Tudge, J. R. H., Mokrova, I., Hatfield, B. E., & Karnik, R. B. (2009). Uses and misuse of Bronfenbrenner's bioecological theory of human development. *Journal of Family Theory and Review, 1,* 198–210. doi: 10.1111/j.1756-2589.2009.00026.x

Thompson, V. L. S., Bazile, A., & Akbar, M. (2004). African Americans' perceptions of psychotherapy and psychotherapists. *Professional Psychology: Research and Practice, 35,* 19–26. doi: 10.1037/0735-7028.35.1.19

U.S. Census Bureau. (2013). *Residential vacancies and homeownership in the fourth quarter 2012.* Retrieved from: http://www.census.gov/housing/hvs/files/qtr412/q412press.pdf

U.S. Department of Health and Human Services. (1985). *Report of the Secretary's Task Force on black & minority health.* Washington, DC: U.S. Government Printing Office.

U.S. Department of Health and Human Services. (2000). *Healthy people 2010: Understanding and improving health* (2nd ed.). Washington, DC: U.S. Government Printing Office.

U.S. Department of Health and Human Services. (2001). *Mental health: Culture, race, and ethnicity: A supplement to Mental Health: A report of the Surgeon General*. Rockville, MD: Author. Retrieved from http://www.surgeongeneral.gov/library/reports

Williams, D. R., Haile, R., Gonzalez, H. M., Neighbors, H., Baser, R., & Jackson, J. S. (2007). The mental health of Black Caribbean immigrants: Results from the National Survey of American Life. *American Journal of Public Health, 97,* 52–59. doi: 10.2105/AJPH.2006. 088211

Young, A. S., & Rabiner, D. (2015). Racial/ethnic differences in parent-reported barriers to accessing children's health services. *Psychological Services, 12,* 267–273. doi: 10.1037/a0038701

PART VI

Cross-Cultural Assessment, Research, and Practice on Health and Pathology

CHAPTER 16

Cross-Cultural Assessment and Research

Sumie Okazaki
Ariane Ling
Stephanie N. Wong
Ming-Che Tu

The history of research and assessment with ethnic minorities in the United States is replete with critiques of Eurocentric bias (Dana, 2013; S. Sue, 1999). Responding to the critique of ethnic minority and cross-cultural research as insufficiently rigorous, Sue (1999) asked whether scientific psychology is biased against ethnic minority psychology. Sue pointed to discipline-wide bias that privileges internal validity over external validity, in which the studies' ability to make causal inferences through tightly controlled experimental studies is valued more than the generalizability of study findings to populations beyond those sampled in the study. Additionally, although studies involving diverse populations are often critiqued for not being able to make causal inferences about sources of group differences, studies with White middle-class American participants are rarely questioned about the generalizability of findings to diverse populations. More recently, Henrich, Heine, and Norenzayan (2010) argued that the majority of claims about human psychology are based on research with individuals from Western, educated, industrialized, rich, and democratic (WEIRD) societies but that research evidence suggests that the behavioral science findings from WEIRD societies are in fact the outliers in the realm of global human experience.

With respect to clinical assessment, documented differences between various ethnic minority groups and White American group performance on a wide range of psychological and cognitive instruments tended to pathologize those who deviated from the White American norms. For example, Malgady, Rogler, and Constantino (1987) discussed various types of bias in mental health evaluations of Hispanic individuals, including the appropriateness of the populations on which tests are normed, differential reliability and **validity of tests**, and biases introduced by inadequate **translation and interpretation of instruments** and interviews. Concerns of interpretability of group differences on psychological measures have long plagued cross-cultural research as well (Okazaki & Sue, 1995; Van de Vijver & Poortinga, 1997).

Taken together, there is a growing chorus for the field of psychology to become more attuned to the diversity of human experience. In this chapter, we provide an overview of the major issues in research and assessment with culturally diverse couples and families in the United States in an effort to echo the broader call for diversification. Entire books and series have been devoted to the topic of multicultural assessment and research; as such, a thorough discussion of all relevant instruments and topics are beyond the scope of this chapter. Interested readers are referred to recent handbooks that provide more in-depth coverage of various topics (e.g., Paniagua & Yamada, 2013; Suzuki & Ponterotto, 2008). Our aim is to consider how the broad discussion in multicultural psychology applies to assessment and research with couples and families, with a particular attention to how clinicians and researchers may contend with the thorny issues concerning bias in assessment and research methodology. And because principles and practices of multicultural training cut across both research and practice, we start with a discussion of broad considerations in training.

TRAINING CONSIDERATIONS FOR RESEARCHERS AND CLINICIANS

Building multicultural competence into couple and family research and assessment is imperative as the United States continues to become more racially and ethnically diverse (Cooper, 2012). The challenge of building multicultural competence and sensitivity into research and therapeutic assessment lies in the understanding of culture as a "broad-based, multidimensional concept" that cannot be reduced to any one dimension, such as race or ethnicity (Hardy & Laszloffy, 2002, p. 569). Therefore, building multicultural competence necessitates a departure from either-or thinking and an immersion into both-and thinking to enable mental health practitioners to fully appreciate the complexity of how culture impacts couple and family systems (Hardy & Laszloffy, 2002). Sue et al. (1998) advocate for adapting an idiographic systems approach to implement multicultural competence across three levels: personal, professional, and organizational. Extant work on multicultural competence generally focuses on the personal level; however, D. W. Sue and Sue (2012) assert that it is of little use to train culturally competent mental health professionals if the working environments that employ them still operate under a monocultural, Eurocentric perspective. Therefore, in the realm of couple and family assessment, it is important to emphasize not only self-awareness of personal biases, values, and assumptions, but also the policies, practices, and structures within which clinicians operate. The challenge for practitioners arises in attempting to understand the couple-in-context or the family-in-context during assessment. How can practitioners extend their multicultural competence into *all* the systems in which a couple or a family lives?

Self-Awareness of One's Own Biases and Cultural Norms

Adapting the idiographic systems approach (Sue et al., 1998) can help elucidate how to conduct research and clinical assessment that are respectful of the layered identities within which the couple or family system operates. McGoldrick, Giordano, and Garcia-Preto (2005) identify "respectful clinical work" as "helping people clarify their cultural identity and self-identity in relation to family, community, and their history, while also adapting to changing circumstances as they move through life" (p. 37). Starting with building personal multicultural competence, the practical takeaway for researchers and practitioners lies not in compiling a comprehensive list of helpful and unhelpful questions to target all contexts in which a couple or family live, but rather to emphasize that the integration of multicultural competence in assessment is a matter of attitude (Nichols, 2013, p. 77). A "multiculturally competent attitude" is one that includes remaining curious and open to understanding the clients' worldview while asking questions that ideally enable dyadic and family systems to work more effectively.

Evaluating Multicultural Competency

In addition to building multicultural competence, building models of psychological research and assessment that focus on preemptive action is important to consider because they provide recommendations for ensuring that professional psychology programs are graduating mental health professionals who already possess the necessary knowledge and skills to conduct respectful, multiculturally competent research and clinical work with couples and families. Krishnamurty et al. (2004) identify the **knowledge, skills, abilities, and other characteristics (KSAO) framework** in enabling professional psychology programs to evaluate multicultural competency in the same manner. In standardizing an evaluation framework, these programs can more effectively serve their gatekeeper function in ensuring that their graduates will have educational and clinical training experiences that aid in sustained competency development. The three central principles of the KSAO framework are: (a) there should be a focus on an integrated array of psychological assessment activities, including but not limited to conducting the initial interview and implementing culturally appropriate intervention strategies; (b) program content areas should reflect and be evaluated on core competencies in line with the objectives of multicultural competence (Sue et al., 1998), and (c) individualized evaluation for professionals in training should provide thorough and meaningful feedback. Therefore, not only will professionals have a firm knowledge base in psychological research and assessment, but they will also possess the skills to critically evaluate the impact of intersecting roles, contexts, and relationships within which their clients function on assessment activities.

Attending to Intersectionality

Much of the cultural validation effort in research to adapt existing measures for family and couples represents a cross-cultural paradigm in which the presumed differences between the two groups (e.g., White mother–child dyad versus Mexican American mother–child dyad) are attributable to a broad but singular conception of culture (e.g., American versus Mexican culture). Researchers and practitioners are expected to be well-versed on the existing literature that examines the psychometric properties of a measure when applied to specific populations. However, the discourse in psychology around culture have been criticized as reifying "culture" as separable from individuals and essentializing it into holistic dichotomies such as East versus West (Gjerde, 2004), ignoring the complex **intersectionality** of multiple cultural identities and obscuring the impact of structural factors such as institutional support for inequalities (Viruell-Fuentes, Miranda, & Abdulrahim, 2012).

MAJOR ISSUES IN CROSS-CULTURAL RESEARCH

Sue and Sue (2012) discussed several reasons why there continues to be a lack of adequate research on ethnic minorities and culturally different populations, including the small sample size of many minority populations, lack of culturally valid measures and theories, and inadequate funding and support for research. In addition, collecting data from diverse couples and families adds another layer of challenge when members do not speak the same language or hold same cultural identities. In this section, we will discuss methodological challenges in sampling and measurement across cultures.

Sampling Small or "Difficult to Locate" Populations

One of the challenges of conducting research with ethnic minorities, according to Sue and Sue (2012), is the relatively small size of ethnic minority populations that often makes it difficult for researchers to locate representative samples of adequate size. This is especially true for researchers interested in particular ethnic groups (e.g., Haitian Americans, Nepali

Americans, Native American tribes) or those who risk safety, stigma, or discrimination if they were to openly identify themselves (e.g., LGBT population). Recruiting a representative sample of **sexual minority** populations is difficult because some are not out to others in the community or only selectively to a trusted network, whereas some may reject the dominant society's categories of their sexual orientation or gender identities (Savin-Williams, 2001). In addition, past abuses of minority communities in research have led to mistrust of researchers among some ethnic minority communities (Yancey, Ortega, & Kumanyika, 2006). **Immigrants** from countries where voluntary participation in research studies may be an unfamiliar concept may present a different type of challenge for recruitment. For example, Brugge, Kole, Lu, and Must (2005) compared responses to hypothetical scenarios of research recruitment between immigrant Asian elderly and nonimmigrant non-Asian elderly community residents. The researchers found that immigrant Asian older adults were reportedly more susceptible to coercion to participate in research when their son/daughter, landlord, physician, or advertisement made requests and that these immigrant elders may require additional layers of protection to ensure informed consent.

There are several strategies that are frequently employed to recruit minority populations of interest. Convenience sampling, without a particular regard to representativeness of the community, is the most widely used method in small studies. Larger epidemiologic studies that aim to collect data representative of the population require more complex methods such as stratified random sampling, with oversampling in geographic areas highly concentrated with specific ethnic groups, and applying statistical weights to correct for various sampling biases (Alegria et al., 2004). However, population-based methods have proven to be extremely costly and time-consuming (Yancy et al., 2006). Community involvement that includes the use of lay outreach workers from the community, partnering with community-based organizations, and including "cultural insider" investigators on the research team are also common approaches to build trust and to reduce barriers to retention (Yancey et al., 2006).

In order to recruit a more diverse sample of bisexual men rather than those who were already connected to LGBT support groups or those who had been seen in counseling, two effective methods were used recently. McCormack, Adams, and Anderson (2012) described an effective recruitment method in which the researchers made themselves highly visible by wearing cowboy hats and bright clipboards. They also loudly called out "bisexual men, forty dollars for academic research" every 20 seconds, in heavily congested pedestrian streets in New York, London, and Los Angeles. Concerned that most research with LGBT individuals recruit from highly urban locations, Warren, Smalley, and Barefoot (2015) explored the efficacy of recruiting LGBT participants online via listservs and Craigslist; these researchers were able to recruit diverse participants from all 50 states, 30 percent of whom reported living in rural areas.

In principle, the sampling caveats and strategies for recruiting specific minority individual research participants apply to couples and families. However, there are recruitment and sampling issues specific to research with diverse couples and families. For example, Rogge, Cobb, Story, Johnson, Lawerence, Rothman, and Bradbury (2006) examined how recruitment strategies and selection criteria alter the demographic composition of couples who participate in preventive intervention research. For example, African American couples dropped out more than their White counterparts due to the burden of assessment measures at the start of the study. Of particular note was the finding that couples from at-risk demographic groups, such as African American couples, couples lacking a high school education, and couples with children at the time of marriage were excluded from the selection criteria for marital research but in fact were more interested in participating in preventive intervention. Requiring couples to be childless in order to participate in marital research also tended to reduce the frequency of African American couples but increased the proportion of Asian American couples.

Measurement: Issues of Cultural Equivalence and Bias

Issues of **cross-cultural equivalence,** or absence of bias, are critical for researchers because a measure that is not similarly reliable and valid across cultural groups makes findings uninterpretable. Clinicians depend on empirical research to decide how and when to use measures with known or unknown reliability and validity with diverse couples and families. Scholars have used the prevailing psychometric approaches as well as qualitative approaches in efforts to establish cross-cultural reliability and validity of a number of couple and family scales (Van Widenfelt, Treffers, De Beurs, Siebelink, & Koudijs, 2005).

An important methodological issue with respect to equivalence concerns the translation of measures across two or more languages. The majority of family and couples research measures are originally developed in English; thus researchers working in non-English-speaking nations tend to undertake translation and cultural adaptation of an English-language measure. Van Widenfelt et al. (2005) discussed some of the most common errors involved in the translation of psychological measures in child and family psychology, such as translation of items that is too literal or simply mistranslated, and insufficient attention to translation of instructions and response options. Poor translation problems may result in phrases that do not make sense or lose the original meaning of the item.

Erkut, Alarcón, Coll, Tropp, and García. (1999) proposed a dual-focused methodology for creating bilingual measures with the following components: (1) a horizontal collaboration between researchers from indigenous cultures as full and equal members of the research team, and (2) achievement of conceptual and linguistic equivalence of the measures guided by a conceptual approach, rather than a translation-driven approach. The dual-focused method addresses the common challenge of translation in which an English concept is relevant to another culture and has a strong correspondence in the English-speaking and the other language community, yet the specific words for the concept in the two languages may not be functionally comparable in effect, word frequency, and clarity. As an example, Matías-Carrelo et al. (2003) described a process of translating the Burden Assessment Scale—a measure of caregiver burden for families of individuals with mental illness—into Spanish. In an item that asked if the caregiver had ever become "embarrassed because of [relative's] behavior," the English word "embarrassed" was initially translated into the Spanish word *vergüenza* (ashamed), but the Spanish word's negative connotation was judged to go beyond the item's intent and meaning. The focus group arrived at the word *incómodo* (uncomfortable) instead. Having a team that includes bilingual researchers a well as monolingual informants with lived experiences in the language community ensures that the translation effort attends to subtle cultural and linguistic nuances.

Nair, White, Knight, and Roosa (2009) argued that careful translations are necessary but not sufficient for ascertaining cross-language measurement equivalence. Earlier, Hui and Triandis (1985) had argued that multiple-language versions of a measure must demonstrate measurement equivalent at the item, functional, and scalar levels. Item equivalence exists when individual items have the same meaning, and researchers such as Matías-Carrelo et al. (2003) have discussed the painstaking effort involving bilingual experts and community members to achieve this level of equivalence. Functional equivalence refers to the construct having similar antecedents, precursors, and consequences across groups, whereas scalar equivalence refers to the scale scores across multiple measures having the same degree, intensity, and magnitude of the construct across groups. In their effort to ascertain cross-language measurement equivalence of English-to-Spanish translated parenting measures commonly used in research with Mexican American mothers and children, Nair et al. (2009) found that each of the four parenting measures in their study had similar factor structures across English and Spanish for both mothers and children, and construct validity tests indicated similar slope relationship between the parenting measures and outcomes across two languages and for mothers and children. These findings suggest that the translated measures have achieved functional equivalence. However, equivalence in intercepts was only demonstrated for some outcome variables, and it was unclear whether the mean-level differences between language groups were reflective of true differences in the underlying parenting dimensions or due to measurement artifacts associated with translation process. These results suggest that although the Spanish and English versions of the measures can be used in research with Mexican American families, interpretation of differences in the levels of reported results between the two language versions cannot be meaningfully interpreted without further research.

Another example of an ambitious effort to ascertain psychometric properties of a measure used in marriage and family research was reported by Straus (2004). A collaborative study across 17 nations examined the psychometric properties of the revised Conflict Tactics Scale (CTS2; Straus, Hamby, Boney-McCoy, & Sugarman, 1996), a scale of intimate relationship violence, among university student dating couples. The list of 17 nations with information derived from 33 universities across Europe, Asia, Middle East, and North and South America yielded a total sample of over 7,000 university students who had been in a dating relationship for at least the past 12 months. Straus reported that the alpha coefficients were generally high, and there was evidence of construct validity across cultural contexts based on partial correlations and scatterplots of the 33 university sites among subscales of the CTS2. However, some research challenges arose in carrying out a study of cross-national equivalence across 17 nations. For example, some university sites such as in India had low number of students who were in dating relationship, raising the question of the comparability of dating couples across nations. Furthermore, university students around the world are a rather selective subset of each nation's population, and may be more similar to each other than to less educated, non-middle-class individuals from their own countries.

This last point about socioeconomic class as an important source of cultural variations is worth noting, particularly in family research contexts. In the seminal qualitative sociological study of families of Black and White 10-year-old children from middle-class, working-class, and poor backgrounds, Lareau (2003) demonstrated that the parenting strategies of both Black and White middle-class families were more closely aligned with the value and standards of the dominant culture than the strategies of working-class and poor families. Middle-class children, regardless of race, spent most of their time in activities and settings structured and supervised by adults whereas less-affluent children spent most of their non-school time in unstructured leisure activities with family. Not only did the daily ecology of the children from middle-class and poor families look very different, but Lareau also found vast divergences in life outcomes of the children when she returned some 20 years later to interview them as young adults (Lareau, 2015). Other sociological works have shown that family structures reproduce and magnify socioeconomic inequalities, such as with the socioeconomic differences of married two-parent households versus single-parent households (McLanahan & Percheski, 2008). Thus, it is critical for research with diverse families and couples to consider socioeconomic class and its intersection with other major cultural determinants and to ensure that selection criteria do not inadvertently marginalize subpopulations of couples and families with respect to race/ethnicity, sexual orientation, socioeconomic status, and so on.

Methodological Approaches

The foregoing discussion on cultural equivalence in measurement centers on quantitative and nomothetic approaches to assessment research on diverse couples and families. **Nomothetic research** and assessment seek to uncover general patterns of behavior that have a normative base, with the goal of providing prediction and explanation for behavior (Ponterotto, 2005). An alternative approach is idiographic assessment and research that focus on understanding the individual, the couple, or the family as unique and complex (Ponterotto, 2005), typically through qualitative methods. Various authors have made a case for how qualitative inquiry can advance not only general psychology in general, but also multicultural psychology research in particular. For example, Ponterotto (2010) argued that constructivist qualitative researchers aim to understand the worldview of participants through deep engagement, attending to and intently listening to marginalized voices, and respecting the minority individuals' voices and interpretation of life events. In addition, the constructivist–interpretivist stance in qualitative inquiry calls for researchers to acknowledge and describe their own "lived experiences" and values that impact the researcher–participant interaction and the research process (Ponterotto, 2005). Such attention to the impact of researcher biases and values, as well as to the unequal power between the researcher and the participant, is especially valuable in research with minority individuals, couples, and families.

Recent research used a qualitative method to understand what constitutes culturally sensitive practice in cross-cultural family therapy. Pakes and Roy-Chowdhury (2007) used a discourse analysis to examine conversations around "culture" in family therapy sessions between a Sudanese immigrant family in the United Kingdom and a White therapist from the United Kingdom. In the analysis, the researchers uncovered themes of cultural assumptions and biases that played out in the cross-cultural family therapy case. For example, the therapist praised the family for open and direct communication and conflict resolution, which was a value held by the White therapist as well as built into the structure and aim of family therapy. The analyses of both the therapist's talk about "culture" and the family members' mirroring of the therapist's talk also revealed reification of culture into a simplistic, essentialized entity, when the therapist initiated a discussion asking them about "your culture." This discursive act tended to limit the family's expression of their desires or dilemmas that could not be easily dichotomized as "British culture" or "Sudanese culture." This example points to the distinctive contribution that qualitative

approaches make not just to culturally sensitive therapy but also to culturally sensitive research with couples and families.

MAJOR ISSUES IN CROSS-CULTURAL ASSESSMENT
WITH COUPLES AND FAMILIES

Psychological assessment is, by nature, a complex process. As Ridley,
Tracy, Pruitt-Stephens, Wimsatt, and Beard (2008) put it, "the critical
challenge in assessment is to simultaneously account for both the ecology
of the client and the client's subjective experience, but clinicians must do
so without overemphasizing or under-emphasizing either consideration"
(p. 27). Assessment of families and couples is further complicated by having to account for multiple individuals' subjective experiences within a
family system that is embedded in multiple social ecologies of individual
family members. These ecologies may overlap to varying degrees such
as across schools, workplace, peers, colleagues, and extended families,
as well as the shared social ecology of the neighborhood and community
in which the couple or family is embedded. Despite numerous measures
regarding assessment and clinical intervention within diverse systems,
the field lacks a unified theory of family and couples functioning and
instead has varying definitions of healthy and dysfunctional relationships
(Bray, 1995).

In this section, we will provide a review of common issues seen in family and couple assessment, including **normative population** concerns and
issues with interpretation and translation in assessment. With these considerations in mind, we then shift focus to conducting family and couple
assessments, including conceptual considerations, models of assessment,
clinical tools, and case studies to illustrate culturally informed assessment
procedures.

Common Issues

Normative Population

Assessment results in a raw score form must be compared against a
specific criterion or a population norm to be interpretively meaningful.
However, a majority of psychological tests have been conceptualized,
standardized, and validated with White, heterosexual, middle-class,
English-speaking individuals (Van de Vijver & Leung, 2000). In response
to critiques that validation samples did not accurately reflect the diversity of the U.S. population, widely used personality and cognitive
tests now include subgroups stratified by gender and ethnicity that
aim to approximate their relative representation in the U.S. population. However, it is not always clear if a proportionate representation
of ethnic minorities in the standardization pool improves the validity

of assessment results for ethnic minorities (Okazaki & Sue, 1995). For example, American Indians and Alaska Natives (AI/NAs) make up about 2 percent of the total population of the United States. Even if a test's standardization sample includes a proportionate representation of AI/NAs (i.e., 2% of the normative sample), the overall sample norm comprising 98 percent non-AI/NAs may not necessarily be valid for an individual AI/NA client. Moreover, the sample of AI/NAs in the standardization pool, if they represent only 2 percent of the sample, may be too small to constitute a meaningful norm against which individual AI/NA client's scores can be compared. In other words, if a standardization sample is 1,000 individuals, only 20 AI/NAs (or 2 percent of 1,000) would be included. This sample size of 20 is not sufficient to create an AI/NA-specific norm.

The establishment of separate norms for diverse groups is a thorny issue. In an effort to examine the utility of establishing separate norms for older African American adults for neuropsychological tests, the Mayo Older African Americans Normative Study successfully demonstrated improvement in diagnostic accuracy for older African Americans (Manly, 2005). At the same time, the study acknowledged that separate racial norms may promote misunderstandings and dangerous biological and genetic interpretations. Moreover, racial/ethnic classifications used to recruit participants for standardization samples are imprecise and unscientific proxies for the behavioral, attitudinal, experiential, or psychological variables thought to be responsible for group differences on psychological tests (Manly, 2005). Too often, it is unfeasible to develop separate norms for populations with intersecting cultural identities (e.g., Mandarin-speaking Chinese immigrants of lower socioeconomic status in the United States; Okazaki & Sue, 1995). Thus the clinician is left to contend—often without much guidance—with the decision surrounding how to best interpret a cultural minority individual's assessment results against population norms established with theoretically multicultural, albeit still relatively homogeneous, samples.

Similar concerns are present in couple and family research used for assessments. Most of the existing research on couple and family assessment has been conducted from a White, middle-class family perspective with heterosexual married couples with biological children (Wegar, 2000). Costigan and Cox (2001) noted that mothers tend to participate more frequently than fathers in family research and that fathers who do participate in research are not representative of the general population. Fathers with less education, later-born children, more ambivalent marriages, and partners having traditional child-rearing beliefs were found underrepresented in family research (Costigan & Cox, 2001). This was also true for ethnic minority and working-class families, as well as those with less optimal parenting environments, infants who were unplanned, had more difficult temperaments, and were less healthy.

Issues with Translation and Interpretation in Assessment

When monolingual English-speaking clinicians are tasked with assessing couples and families with limited English proficiency and a bilingual clinician is not available, interpreters are often enlisted either formally or informally to assist with the evaluation. Problems with the use of informal or insufficiently trained interpreters are well known, but research has shown that trained interpreters in hospital settings also make significant number of interpretation errors (Searight & Searight, 2009). There are many potential sources of interpreter-related biases, such as inadequate linguistic or translation skills of the interpreter; the interpreter's lack of knowledge about mental health and psychological assessment; the interpreter's own ideas about the family or couple, the clinician, and the community; and the interpreter over-identifying with the client and minimizing pathology (Malgady et al., 1987; Searight & Searight, 2009). The lack of uncertainty regarding the quality of interpretation service presents particular ethical challenges for psychologists, as poor or erroneous interpretation may greatly compromise the quality of assessment and intervention (Wright, 2014).

There are also numerous problems associated with asking children or other members of the family to serve as impromptu interpreters, or "language brokers" in family or couple assessment (Searight & Searight, 2009). In a family assessment session, when the bilingual child or adolescent speaks directly with the clinician in the common language while the parent must rely on interpreters, parental authority may be undermined and the youth may be placed in a parentified role (Björn, 2005).

Conversely, research findings regarding the impact of language brokering on family dynamics and mental health are mixed. Recent research with nearly 700 Mexican American adolescent language brokers (Kam, 2011) found that translating for immigrant parents had both positive and negative psychological impacts on the adolescents. Language-brokering frequency was indirectly related to higher levels of alcohol abuse but lower levels of other risky behaviors, with the adolescents' positive or negative feelings toward brokering being key factors in predicting their psychological outcomes. A study of 256 Chinese American adolescents (Wu & Kim, 2009) also found that whether the adolescents experienced language brokering as a sense of efficacy or burden varied according to the extent of identification with Chinese values and family obligation. Results showed that Chinese oriented adolescents had a stronger sense of family obligation and were more likely to perceive language brokering with a sense of efficacy. In contrast, adolescents who were less oriented to Chinese culture had a weaker sense of family obligation and were more likely to feel a sense of alienation from their parents. Also, a sense of parental alienation was associated with a sense of burden as a language broker. However, Hua and Costigan (2012) found that more frequent language brokering among Chinese Canadian adolescents was associated with poorer mental health for those who held strong family obligation values or perceived their parents as highly controlling. Given the potential for increased negative family outcomes as well as inaccurate translation or interpretation, clinicians are discouraged from relying on family members as language brokers in assessment.

Issues of translation and interpretation also apply to couples and families of deaf or hard-of-hearing individuals. Some individuals and families who use American Sign Language or ASL as their primary mode of communication may identify as culturally Deaf, and clinicians' knowledge of the Deaf culture is critical to working successfully with families and couples where a member identifies with the Deaf culture (Williams & Abeles, 2004). There are professional standards and certifications for interpreters in ASL and Visually Coded English, and clinicians are encouraged to enlist fully certified interpreters in their work with couples and families whose members communicate using ASL (Fellinger, Holzinger, & Pollard, 2012; Steinberg & Silverberg, 1986). It is also important for clinicians to know that individuals who communicate primarily in ASL may not have the same level of fluency in written English as hearing individuals, and assessment considerations for non-native English speakers also apply to ASL users (Mason, 2005).

Assessing Families

The most common forms of assessment in family therapy rely on self-report measures and behavioral observation of family dynamics and interaction. Observational methods of family functioning may include qualitative measures, such as narrative descriptions of family relationships that are most commonly employed by clinicians, as well as quantitative approaches such as specific coding of interactions that are more commonly employed in research settings (Bray & Stanton, 2009). Bray (1995, 2009) noted that despite the complexity and diversity of family relationships, practitioners tend to focus on four major areas of assessment related to family functioning. The first area is *family composition*, which includes factors such as membership, children, and understanding the structure of the family, such as if they are a stepfamily, are a divorced family, have grandparent caretakers, and the like. *Family process* factors include behaviors, interactions, conflicts, and the way family members communicate, solve problems, and assert control. The third component of family functioning is *family affect*, and family affect factors assess how members express emotion and how this influences communication within the system. Lastly, *family organization* factors refer to the roles, or hierarchy in which the family functions. These also include family rules, expectations for behavior, and boundaries. In this section, we first introduce a case study, followed by the descriptions of various models of family assessment and application of each model to the case study.

Family Assessment Case Study

Jin is a 14-year-old boy born in the Yanbian Korean Autonomous Prefecture in northern China. His mother and father were both born in Korea and identify culturally as Korean even though they had spent the majority of their adult lives in China. When Jin was an infant, his parents immigrated to the United States to seek better job opportunities. His maternal grandparents who also resided in Yanbian raised Jin. Jin's primary language is Mandarin Chinese but he can also hold simple conversations in Korean. When Jin was 10 years old, his parents arranged for him to immigrate to the United States, and Jin has been living with them since. The family currently lives in low-income urban housing. Jin attends a bilingual public school, Jin's mother works as a nail salon technician, and his father works at a Korean supermarket. Jin's father makes all financial decisions for the household. Jin's mother sought help from a community mental health agency due to concerns about Jin's rebellious attitude toward his parents. She kept her help-seeking behavior secret from her husband, who believes that asking for help outside the immediate family is shameful. Jin presented as sullen and withdrawn. He reported having a few close friends with whom he spends time playing video games or watching Chinese language dramas on the internet. When his parents tell Jin that he must stop wasting time and study harder, Jin typically ignores them or tells them that he doesn't have to listen to them because "this is America and it's a free country." Jin and his parents have difficulty communicating because Jin speaks primarily Mandarin Chinese and English whereas his parents speak primarily Korean.

Bowen's Family System Model

Bowen's family systems therapy represents one of the foundational models in family assessment and relies on the therapist's informal observation of the family process while incorporating a structured assessment protocol that seeks to understand conflict, symptoms, and patterns of over- and underfunctioning in the family (see Bowen, 1966, 1976; or Kerr & Bowen, 1988, for a full explication of this model). A family systems perspective such as the Bowenian approach is important to take in family assessment because of its emphasis on understanding the holistic functioning of a family.

Later work by Gushue and Sicalides (1997) combined Bowen's family systems perspective with racial identity theory (Helms, 1990) to create more culturally competent family interventions that can be adapted in family assessment with racially diverse family systems. Gushue (1993) applied Helms's racial identity theory to family assessment and treatment through the creation of a racial-cultural map that identifies racial identity statuses of family members and the therapist. This map could help the therapist predict interactions within the family as well as between the family and the therapist. In doing so, the therapist is better able to understand the family system while maintaining flexible and clear boundaries (for a detailed case study, see Gushue & Sicalides, 1997). The value of this type of assessment can be understood when applied to the case study of Jin. Intergenerational conflicts between Jin and his parents are important to recognize, as Jin's parents both have very different career-related beliefs and opportunities than he does in America due to their upbringing in China. Further, it could be helpful for this family to complete a racial-cultural map with the therapist to fully explore how their racial identity statuses might impact their view of the presenting issue. Their racial identity statuses may be very different from Jin due to the parents' strong Korean identity and the fact that Jin is ethnically Korean but spent the first 10 years of his life immersed in Chinese culture and 4 years in American culture. As such, racial identity status differences that emerge from the racial-cultural map would also enable the therapist to assess for acculturative family distancing, defined as "a problematic that occurs between immigrant parents and children that is a consequence of differences in acculturative processes and cultural changes that become more salient over time" (Hwang, 2006, p. 398).

Circumplex Model of Marital and Family Systems

One of the most widely researched family models is the **Circumplex Model of Marital and Family Systems** and its related assessment scales, the Family Adaptability and Cohesion Evaluation Scales and the Clinical Rating Scale (Olson & Gorall, 2003). This model has been applied to diverse couple and family systems on several levels, including ethnicity/ race, marital status, family structure, family life cycle stage, socioeconomic level, and sexual orientation. The Circumplex Model focuses on the relational system, integrating three dimensions that have been shown throughout family theory models to be highly relevant. The three dimensions of family cohesion, adaptability/flexibility, and communication are understood in a five-level approach that illustrates a spectrum of unbalanced to balanced behaviors. *Family cohesion* can be defined "as the emotional bonding that couple and family members have toward one another" (Olson & Gorall, 2003, p. 516). *Family flexibility* refers to how much change occurs in the family's leadership, role relationships, and relationship rules. *Communication* is identified as a critical component to facilitate family cohesion and family flexibility and is measured by assessing the family's listening and speaking skills, self-disclosure, clarity, respect and regard for each member, and continuity tracking.

In the case study of Jin, family cohesion might be presumed to be unbalanced and disengaged due to the emotional separateness of family members, as evidenced by Jin's emotional withdrawal and his mother's secret-keeping behavior. In the family flexibility dimension, Jin's family system might be viewed as rigid or inflexible due to the parents' role as unquestioned authority figures and their expectation of Jin to respect their authority despite their 10-year separation. Communication skills are likely to be low in this family system; however, in assessing these skills, it is important for clinicians to recognize that a Eurocentric viewpoint is often adopted when defining which skills are "healthy." For instance, a low level of self-disclosure might be considered maladaptive in a Eurocentric perspective, but could be viewed as adaptive from Jin's parents' Chinese culture that emphasizes maintaining privacy surrounding personal matters (Hwang, 2006).

Grieger and Ponterotto Model

Grieger and Ponterotto (1995; 2008) developed a conceptual framework to guide culturally based conceptualization, and paid particular attention to the family context. The **Cultural Assessment Interview Protocol** (CAIP; Grieger & Ponterotto, 2008) is a qualitative assessment tool that guides clinicians to incorporate the client's cultural context and to assist in more accurate diagnosis and treatment planning. The current CAIP contains 11 areas: (1) problem conceptualization and attitudes toward helping, (2) cultural identity, (3) level of acculturation, (4) family structure and expectations, (5) level of racial/cultural identity development, (6) experience with bias, (7) immigration issues, (8) existential/spiritual issues, (9) counselor characteristics and behaviors, (10) implications of cultural factors between the counselor and the client, and (11) summary of cultural factors and implications for diagnosis, case conceptualization, and treatment. Cultural and clinically relevant data within the first nine categories are collected during the clinical interview or intake/assessment phase. Categories (9) and (10) call for the clinician to engage in a process of continued self-appraisal and awareness of one's own level of racial/identity development and knowledge of multicultural issues. The last consideration of the framework allows for the practitioner to summarize cultural factors of the client, presenting problem, and clinician's personal awareness that is most relevant for diagnosis, case conceptualization, and treatment planning.

In relation to the case of Jin, the CAIP assessment seems to comprehensively cover areas of interest related to his presenting problem. First, it is possible to conceptualize his problem as stemming from intergenerational conflict due to his acculturation to American values and the lack of emotional attachment to his parents that misalign with his parents' Korean family role expectations and strong desire for their son to succeed in schooling. Further, attitudes toward help-seeking clearly differ between Jin's mother and father, which may be important to consider in treatment planning. It may additionally be important to understand the racial and cultural identity development of this family system, considering their complex ethnic and cultural heritage with roots in Korea, China, and America. For further reading on racial and cultural identity development, we refer readers to Chapter 14.

Tools

Diagrammatic models of assessment have been widely used and have been shown to be multiculturally useful (Sciarra, 2001). Genograms are pictures of a family across three generations and are used to understand how individual members are part of system embedded in patterns of living and relating (Hartman, 1995). Specific to working with issues of diversity, **culture genogram**s seek to uncover hidden values, expectations, and assumptions of members in a family system. The major contribution of culture genograms is to examine the impact of race, immigration, multiple ethnicities, class, religion, beliefs about health, holidays, and acculturation upon members of the family (DeMaria, Weeks, & Hof, 2013). Culture genograms can be used to examine both cultural differences between the family and the clinician, and also among members within the family system. Questions to create a culture genogram can focus on both in-group experiences and norms as well as out-of-group biases and prejudices. For instance, a genogram used with Jin and his parents might reveal unspoken expectations of his mother about Jin's academic future that are based on her own thwarted academic and career aspirations and fueling her concern for him. Further, as assessed by the racial identity status differences that emerged Gushue's (1993) racial-cultural map, it could be very helpful for Jin and his parents to examine the impact that immigration and acculturation have had on each member of the family.

Assessment for Couples

Previous assessment and treatment models for couples have relied heavily upon culturally prescriptive methods that are limited in scope and biased toward a Eurocentric and heteronormative worldview. We return to Ridley and colleagues' (2008) assertion that cultural assessment must account for both the couple's unique perspective as well as the ecological context in which the couple and therapist are embedded. One cannot be emphasized over the other, but rather both must be understood thoroughly through the immersion of the therapist in the couple's world and the awareness of surrounding sociocultural issues.

Similar to family assessment, the approaches to couple assessment presented in this section emphasize the use of idiographic criteria and the awareness that the clinician becomes another moving piece in the relational dynamics. The careful balance between accounting for the couple's unique perspective and sociocultural context can be found only when complemented by the clinician's exploration and development of his or her own cultural competence (S. Sue, 1998). Couple assessment and treatment not only work toward differentiation within the couple subsystem between individuals, but also differentiation between the couple subsystem and the therapist.

Snyder, Heyman, and Haynes (2005) described a conceptual framework for couples-based assessment strategies that are grounded in empirically documented relationships between couple distress and individual and relationship dynamics. Their evidence-based approach outlined various domains that are subject to assessment such as relationship behaviors, affect, and broader aspects of a couple's socioecological system. Importantly, Snyder and colleagues (2005) note that there has been little attention paid to developing measures that assess domains of relationship functioning at the cultural level, such as cultural standards or norms for emotional expressiveness, balance of decision making in relationships, boundaries around interaction of couples and extended families, and so on. While the influence of culture among diverse couples has largely been unexamined (Johnson & Lebow, 2000), in current section, we refer to a couple case study and identify interview approaches and tools that have been developed to address diversity in couples assessment and therapy. As with the previous section on family assessment, the case study is presented first, followed by a discussion of couple assessment approaches and their application to the case example.

Couple Assessment Case Study

Guillermo and Ryan are a same-sex couple and have been married for two years. They presented to counseling reporting low levels of marital satisfaction and high frequency of conflicts regarding Ryan's desire to adopt a child. Guillermo, 45 years old, was raised in an upper middle-class home in South America and moved to the United States to attend business school. Guillermo has a high-stress job and is the primary financial provider in the relationship. He admitted he had never expected to become a parent. Ryan, 30 years old, grew up in a small rural town in the Southwest of the United States. He enlisted in the military at the age of 18 and served two tours of service before being honorably discharged. After returning from active duty, Ryan had difficulty keeping his job for more than a few weeks at a time. At the suggestion of Guillermo, Ryan entered therapy for symptoms of posttraumatic stress disorder and difficulties adjusting to civilian life. Through his work in individual counseling, he developed healthier coping strategies and discovered his desire to become a father.

Given the individual needs of each person, a clinician working with Guillermo and Ryan might experience difficulties assessing the needs of the couple as a system and developing a culturally informed case formulation. Hardy and Laszloffy (2002) offer basic questions that are considered integral to conducting informal assessments of couples' health and functioning. The questions include: (1) How do partners make meaning in their lives? (2) What are the areas of incongruence between the couple's stated beliefs and the partner's actual practices or behavior? (3) How does the couple negotiate differences? (4) What are culturally based pride–shame issues prevalent in the relationship, and how are these negotiated? (5) What are the "invisible wounds of oppression" such as learned voicelessness, psychological homelessness, and rage, and how do they shape the couple dynamics? (6) What are the cultural legacies and loyalties that each partner brings to the relationship, and how do these inform their couple dynamics? For Guillermo and Ryan, these questions may open a discussion regarding values and how their cultural backgrounds have influenced their expression of emotions and beliefs about their roles in the relationship.

These questions offered by Hardy and Laszlioffy (2002) also emphasize how intrapsychic and interactional processes must be considered in a broader sociocultural context. Relational dynamics are paramount in culturally competent assessment, both at the interpersonal and sociocultural levels; each of these questions seeks to enable the mental health professional to immerse him- or herself in the dynamics of the individual relationship within the broader sociocultural context. Guillermo endorsed a strong sense of machismo and was accustomed to making decisions within their relationship. But he also expressed fear of becoming a father so late in life; he was worried about discrimination in the adoption process as a gay couple and his ability so close to retirement to support a family. As the younger partner, Ryan felt he had less power in the relationship and expressed feeling silenced, similar to how he was forced to hide his sexual orientation in the military.

A careful assessment of individual and interpersonal dynamics should not lose sight of the presenting issue and how the couple views the problem from their cultural perspective. For our case example, this would include a detailed inquiry about parenting beliefs, the adoption process, and goals for therapy. It may be helpful to ask both partners about their roles within the home and within their extended families, and each person's family of origin. Clinicians may find themselves needing to balance a wide range of norms found in the literature and comparing standards and norms with the couple with whom they are working. In addition to questions about culture and the presenting problem, other areas of assessment should include issues regarding the customary age for men/women to marry within the cultural group, expectations regarding roles, responsibilities of each partner, conceptualization of the sexual relationship, and expectations of therapy (Bhugra & De Silva, 2000). For same-sex couples, assessing minority stress or discrimination due to their sexual orientation and the impact of minority stress on relationship quality is important (Rostosky, Riggle, Gray, & Hatton, 2007). The multiculturally competent practitioner considers the therapeutic goal of developing a holistic understanding of the clients' subjective reality, challenging segregated either-or thinking, respectfully identifying and healing wounds of oppression and domination, and promoting intimacy through embracing differences.

Tools

In addition to these general questions for assessment, there have been a number of standardized measures of relationship quality that are worth noting because of their widespread use and cultural adaptation efforts. For example, the **Dyadic Adjustment Scale** (DAS; Spanier, 1976, 1989) was designed to measure the strength of relationships. The original scale contains 32 self-report items rated on a Likert scale, from 0 = never or always disagree to 5 = all the time or always agree. The DAS consists of four subscales: *dyadic satisfaction* ("How often do you discuss or have you considered divorce, separation, or termination of your relationship?"), *dyadic consensus* on matters of importance to relationship functioning ("How much do you and your partner agree regarding aims, goals, and things believed important?"), *dyadic cohesion* ("Do you and your mate engage in outside interests together?"), and *affective expression* ("How much do you and your partner agree regarding the demonstration of affection?").

The Revised DAS (R-DAS; Busby, Christensen, Crane, & Larson, 1995) contains 14 items and 3 subscales: (1) consensus regarding decision making, values, and affection, (2) satisfaction measured by stability and conflict, and (3) cohesion reflecting shared activities and how often the couple engages in discussion. Both the DAS and R-DAS have been used in studies assessing the health of diverse relationships including gay couples (Greene & Britton, 2015; Tornello & Patterson, 2012), lesbian couples (Klostermann, Kelley, Milletich, & Mignone, 2011), intercultural relationships (Silva, Campbell, & Wright, 2012), and immigrant Latino couples (Falconier, 2013; Falconier, Nussbeck, & Bodenmann, 2013).

Another measure that has seen a number of cultural adaptations is the **Kansas Marital Satisfaction Scale (KMSS**; Schumm et al., 1986). A number of studies across various cultural backgrounds and languages have been conducted using the KMSS, including a Korean version with Korean American wives in interracial marriages (Jeong & Schumm, 1990), Chinese parents in Hong Kong (Shek, 1995), and Chinese parents of children with special needs (Shek & Tsang, 1993). Its original English version has also been explored in research with Arab immigrants to the United States (Faragallah, Schumm, & Webb, 1997), and with gay and lesbian couples (Kurdek, 1994), Overall, the internal consistency reliability and factor structure of the measure appear to be have been maintained across these diverse samples. Clinical measures such as the R-DAS and KMSS can be administered as a one-time assessment of relationship quality and can also be utilized as a progress-monitoring tool to track relational satisfaction and emotion expression over the course of treatment.

Additionally, the **Relationship Evaluation Questionnaire** (RELATE; Busby, Holman, & Taniguchi, 2001) is a relationship evaluation instrument that includes extensive measures of characteristics and behavioral exchanges between individuals, family background, culture, and values. RELATE is rooted in the systemic model that trait-like characteristics of individuals and behavioral exchanges in relationships are developed and maintained within a series of contexts or subsystems (Fincham & Bradbury, 1987). There are many contexts in which couples are embedded; the most relevant for couple assessment are individual, familial, cultural, and couple contexts (Busby et al., 2001). RELATE asks each member of the couple to rate him- or herself and his or her partner on several characteristics in each context. After each person completed the ratings, results from each person would be presented side by side in a graphic form. The inventory is designed to encourage discussion between partners' perceptions regarding their relationship and multiple contexts. For Guillermo and Ryan, recognizing similarities and differences in areas such as flexibility may provide an understanding of each other's views regarding the adoption process and may promote acceptance and empathy of their shared differences.

CONCLUSIONS

As we have detailed in this chapter, there is a sufficient body of knowledge within the psychology of diverse populations to suggest important cultural variations in couple and family processes that cannot be overlooked when conducting assessment or research. However, our review has also revealed rather stark gaps in knowledge about specific assessment tools and instruments that are culturally relevant to various groups. Importantly, there is increasing fluidity in the identities of American families, where not everyone in the family shares the same set of cultural influences. For instance, there are more families that are interracial or interethnic through marriage or adoption, or where sexual orientation differs between parents and children, or where members of the family diverge in their religious affiliations and practices (Rosenfeld, 2007). Thus, it is not practical to aim for a development and validation of assessment tools assuming monolithic cultural groups. And given the complex interaction of identities that make for contemporary couples and families (e.g., a White American woman who marries a Korean American partner and adopts a child from China), a broader framework for conducting culturally attuned assessment is appropriate.

As an alternative, we encourage assessment strategies that attend to the intersectionality of identities rather than to focus solely on cross-cultural comparative approaches. Szapocznik and Kurtines (1993) first pointed to the movement in the field of psychology toward keen considerations of contextual issues in terms of the individual in the contexts of both family and culture even though these two contexts had developed separately. To marry two distinctive bodies of literatures, they proposed the concept of embeddedness, where the individual became situated within the context of the family and within the context of culture.

CHAPTER REVIEW

Key Points

1. Research and assessment with minority groups in the United States are replete with Eurocentric, middle-class, heterosexist biases, and clinicians and researchers must strive to understand the impact of these biases in their work and to become more attuned to the diversity of human experiences.
2. Some of the major issues in cross-cultural research and assessment involve the underrepresentation of minority groups. This is in part attributed to the nature of many minority groups as being difficult to recruit. More importantly, a range of methodical shortcomings have also contributed to this disparity, such as the measurement norming biases, inadequate linguistic adaptation, and tendency to privilege nomothetic and quantitative research over idiographic and qualitative research.
3. Similar issues of misrepresentation of normative sampling and inadequate translation or interpretation also plague research and assessment with families and couples.
4. Multicultural competence in couple and family research and assessment demands appreciation of the complexity inherent in the multidimensional cultural contexts that shape the lived experiences of couples and families. Researchers and clinicians are therefore challenged to remain vigilant on one's own biases and become able to consider the intricacies of intersectional identities.
5. Assessment and research with nontraditional families and couples require understanding that what is considered a standard practice for one couple, family, or culture may be considered abnormal in another and vice versa.

Key Terms

Bowen's Family System Model, Circumplex Model of Marital and Family Systems, cross-cultural equivalence, Cultural Assessment Interview Protocol (CAIP), culture genogram, Dyadic Adjustment Scale (DAS), immigrants, intersectionality, Kansas Marital Satisfaction Scale (KMSS), knowledge, skills, abilities, and other characteristics (KSAO) framework, nomothetic research, normative population, Relationship Evaluation Questionnaire (RELATE), sexual minority, validity of tests, translation and interpretation of instruments

Myths and Realities

- It is a myth that standardized norms always accurately reflect a population when in reality instruments are normed typically on White, middle-class, heterosexual, English-speaking individuals, couples, and families, resulting in overpathologizing of minority groups.
- It is a myth that research with minority groups lacks internal validity and thus cannot make causal inferences, when in reality such critiques fail to acknowledge the methodological challenges involved in research with culturally diverse populations. Furthermore, studies with White middle-class American participants are rarely questioned about the generalizability of findings to diverse groups.
- It is a myth that the children of non-English speakers should translate for them. In reality, although enlisting children or adolescents as language broker for their non-English-speaking parents provides convenience, the practice has also been associated with negative psychological outcomes and places children or adolescents in a parentified role.
- It is a myth that multicultural competence entails developing an exhaustive protocol to address all aspects of cultural identities among couples or families. In reality, it is vital for clinicians and researchers to hold an attitude that strives to be curious and open to understanding the perspective of one's clients.

Tools and Tips

Knowledge

Krishnamurthy, R., VandeCreek, L., Kaslow, N. J., Tazeau, Y. N., Miville, M. L., Kerns, R., . . . Benton, S. A. (2004). Achieving competency in psychological assessment: Directions for education and training. *Journal of Clinical Psychology, 60,* 725–739.

Paniagua, F. A., & Yamada, A.-M. (2013). *Handbook of multicultural mental health: Assessment and treatment of diverse populations,* 2nd ed. Cambridge, MA: Academic Press.

Sue, D. W., & Sue, D. (2012). *Counseling the culturally diverse: Theory and practice.* Hoboken, NJ: John Wiley & Sons.

Suzuki, L. A., & Ponterotto, J. G. (2008). *Handbook of multicultural assessment: Clinical, psychological, and educational applications.* Hoboken, NJ: John Wiley & Sons.

Dynamic Sizing

Clinical assessment that considers clients' intersectionality and their embeddedness within the contexts of family and culture aid in dynamic sizing by increasing our accuracy in knowing which cultural factors apply to each couple or family and what roles those cultural factors play in each of their lives. Tools such as racial-cultural maps, cultural assessment interview protocols, and cultural genograms are useful aids in this process.

Skills

Theory. Developing theoretical frameworks for both couples and families that adequately incorporate multicultural considerations by recognizing the layered embeddedness of couples and families within a larger cultural context is crucial.

Prevention and Policy. Policies in professional psychology programs and within all service-provision organizations need to ensure that mental health professionals are imparted with knowledge and skills to conduct respectful, multiculturally competent clinical work with couples and families to prevent culturally insensitive treatment provision.

Service Provision. Providers aspire to develop a holistic understanding of the clients' subjective reality, challenging segregated either-or thinking, respectfully identifying and healing wounds of oppression and domination, and promoting intimacy through embracing differences.

Research. Research needs to shift its preference of quantitative and nomothetic approaches to integrate the unique advantages of qualitative and idiographic perspectives, particularly in multicultural research with couples and families, remain mindful of the sampling biases in normative population, and endeavor to achieve cross-cultural equivalence with all measures used.

Awareness

The KSAO framework provides ways for service providers and researchers to self-evaluate multicultural competence to explore their own potential blind spots and biases. In addition, they are also encouraged to self-administer assessment tools with both families and couples, including cultural genograms, R-DAS, and RELATE, to empathize with individuals, couples, and families they are working with and to raise researchers' and practitioners' own multicultural and relational self-awareness.

REFERENCES

Alegria, M., Takeuchi, D., Canino, G., Duan, N., Shrout, P., Meng, X.-L., . . . Woo, M. (2004). Considering context, place, and culture: The National Latino and Asian American study. *International Journal of Methods in Psychiatric Research, 13,* 208.

Bhugra, D., & De Silva, P. (2000). Couple therapy across cultures. *Sexual and Relationship Therapy, 15,* 183–192.

Björn, G.J. (2005). Ethics and interpreting in psychotherapy with refugee children and families. *Nordic Journal of Psychiatry, 59,* 516–521.

Bowen, M. (1966). The use of family theory in clinical practice. *Comprehensive Psychiatry, 7,* 345–374.

Bowen, M. (1976). Theory in the practice of psychotherapy. *Family Therapy: Theory and Practice, 4,* 2–90.

Bray, J.H. (1995). Family assessment: Current issues in evaluating families. *Family Relations, 44,* 469–477.

Bray, J. H., & Stanton, M. (Eds.) (2009). *The Wiley-Blackwell handbook of family psychology*. Chichester, West Sussex: Wiley-Blackwell.

Brugge, D., Kole, A., Lu, W., & Must, A. (2005). Susceptibility of elderly Asian immigrants to persuasion with respect to participation in research. *Journal of Immigrant Health, 7*, 93–101.

Busby, D. M., Christensen, C., Crane, D. R., & Larson, J. H. (1995). A revision of the Dyadic Adjustment Scale for use with distressed and nondistressed couples: Construct hierarchy and multidimensional scales. *Journal of Marital and Family Therapy, 21*, 289.

Busby, D. M., Holman, T. B., & Taniguchi, N. (2001). RELATE: Relationship evaluation of the individual, family, cultural, and couple contexts. *Family Relations, 50*, 308–316.

Cooper, M. (2012, December 12). U.S. will have no ethnic majority, Census finds. *The New York Times*. Retrieved from http://www.nytimes.com/2012/12/13/us/us-will-have-no-ethnic-majority-census-finds.html

Costigan, C. L., & Cox, M. J. (2001). Fathers' participation in family research: Is there a self-selection bias? *Journal of Family Psychology, 15*, 706.

Dana, R. H. (2013). Personality assessment and the cultural self: Emic and etic contexts as learning resources. In L. Handler & M. J. Hilsenroth (Eds.), *Teaching and learning personality assessment* (pp. 325–346). London, England: Routledge.

DeMaria, R., Weeks, G., & Hof, L. (2013). *Focused genograms: Intergenerational assessment of individuals, couples, and families*. London, England: Routledge.

Erkut, S., Alarcón, O., Coll, C. G., Tropp, L. R., & García, H. A. V. (1999). The dual-focus approach to creating bilingual measures. *Journal of Cross-Cultural Psychology, 30*, 206–218.

Falconier, M. K. (2013). Traditional gender role orientation and dyadic coping in immigrant Latino couples: Effects on couple functioning. *Family Relations, 62*, 269–283.

Falconier, M. K., Nussbeck, F., & Bodenmann, G. (2013). Dyadic coping in Latino couples: Validity of the Spanish version of the Dyadic Coping Inventory. *Anxiety, Stress & Coping, 26*, 447–466.

Faragallah, M. H., Schumm, W. R., & Webb, F. J. (1997). Acculturation of Arab-American immigrants: An exploratory study. *Journal of Comparative Family Studies*, 182–203.

Fellinger, J., Holzinger, D., & Pollard, R. (2012). Mental health of deaf people. *The Lancet, 379*(9820), 1037–1044.

Fincham, F. D., & Bradbury, T. N. (1987). The assessment of marital quality: A reevaluation. *Journal of Marriage and the Family, 49*, 797–809.

Gjerde, P. F. (2004). Culture, power, and experience: Toward a person-centered cultural psychology. *Human Development, 47*, 138–157.

Greene, D. C., & Britton, P. J. (2015). Predicting relationship commitment in gay men: Contributions of vicarious shame and internalized homophobia to the investment model. *Psychology of Men & Masculinity, 16*, 78.

Grieger, I., & Ponterotto, J. G. (1995). A framework for assessment in multicultural counseling. In J. G. Ponterotto, J. M. Casas, L. A. Suzuki, & C. M. Alexander (Eds.), *Handbook of multicultural counseling* (pp. 357–374). Thousand Oaks, CA: Sage Publications.

Gushue, G. V. (1993). Cultural-identity development and family assessment: An interaction model. *The Counseling Psychologist, 21*, 487–513.

Gushue, G. V., & Sicalides, E. I. (1997). Helms' racial identity theory and Bowen's family systems model: A case study. In C. E. Thompson & R. T. Carter (Eds.), *Racial identity theory: Applications to individual, group, and organizational interventions* (pp. 127–145). Mahwah, NJ: Erlbaum.

Hardy, K. V., & Laszloffy, T. A. (2002). Couple therapy using a multicultural perspective. In A. S. Gurman (Ed.), *Clinical Handbook of Couple Therapy*, 3rd ed. (pp. 569–593). New York, NY: Guilford Press.

Hartman, A. (1995). Diagrammatic assessment of family relationships. *Families in Society, 76*, 111.

Helms, J. E. (1990). *Black and White racial identity: Theory, research, and practice.* Santa Barbara, CA: Greenwood.

Henrich, J., Heine, S. J., & Norenzayan, A. (2010). The weirdest people in the world? *Behavioral and Brain Sciences, 33*, 61–83.

Hua, J. M., & Costigan, C. L. (2012). The familial context of adolescent language brokering within immigrant Chinese families in Canada. *Journal of Youth and Adolescence, 41*, 894–906.

Hui, C. H., & Triandis, H. C. (1985). Measurement in cross-cultural psychology a review and comparison of strategies. *Journal of Cross-Cultural Psychology, 16*, 131–152.

Hwang, W. C. (2006). The psychotherapy adaptation and modification framework: Application to Asian Americans. *American Psychologist, 61*, 702.

Jeong, G. J., & Schumm, W. R. (1990). Family satisfaction in Korean/American marriages: An exploratory study of the perceptions of Korean wives. *Journal of Comparative Family Studies, 21*, 325–336.

Johnson, S. M., & Lebow, J. (2000). The "Coming of Age" of couple therapy. *Journal of Marital and Family Therapy, 26*, 25–58.

Kam, J. A. (2011). The effects of language brokering frequency and feelings on Mexican-heritage youth's mental health and risky behaviors. *Journal of Communication, 61*, 455–475.

Kerr, M. E., & Bowen, M. (1988). *Family evaluation.* New York, NY: W. W. Norton.

Klostermann, K., Kelley, M. L., Milletich, R. J., & Mignone, T. (2011). Alcoholism and partner aggression among gay and lesbian couples. *Aggression and Violent Behavior, 16*, 115–119.

Krishnamurthy, R., VandeCreek, L., Kaslow, N. J., Tazeau, Y. N., Miville, M. L., Kerns, R., . . .Benton, S. A. (2004). Achieving competency in psychological assessment: Directions for education and training. *Journal of Clinical Psychology, 60*, 725–739.

Kurdek, L. A. (1994). Areas of conflict for gay, lesbian, and heterosexual couples: What couples argue about influences relationship satisfaction. *Journal of Marriage and the Family, 56*, 923–934.

Lareau, A. (2003). *Unequal childhoods: Class, race, and family life.* Oakland, CA: University of California Press.

Lareau, A. (2015). Cultural knowledge and social inequality. *American Sociological Review, 80*, 1–27. doi: 10.1177/0003122414565814

Malgady, R. G., Rogler, L. H., & Costantino, G. (1987). Ethnocultural and linguistic bias in mental health evaluation of Hispanics. *American Psychologist, 42*, 228–234.

Manly, J. J. (2005). Advantages and disadvantages of separate norms for African Americans. *The Clinical Neuropsychologist, 19*, 270–275.

Mason, T. C. (2005). Cross-cultural instrument translation: Assessment, translation, and statistical applications. *American Annals of the Deaf, 150,* 67–72.

Matías-Carrelo, L. E., Chávez, L. M., Negrón, G., Canino, G., Aguilar-Gaxiola, S., & Hoppe, S. (2003). The Spanish translation and cultural adaptation of five mental health outcome measures. *Culture, Medicine and Psychiatry, 27,* 291–313.

McCormack, M., Adams, A., & Anderson, E. (2012). Taking to the streets: The benefits of spontaneous methodological innovation in participant recruitment. *Qualitative Research, 13,* 228–241. doi: 10.1177/1468794112451038.

McGoldrick, M., Giordano, J., & Garcia-Preto, N. (2005). *Ethnicity and family therapy.* New York, NY: Guilford Press.

McLanahan, S., & Percheski, C. (2008). Family structure and the reproduction of inequalities. *Annual Review of Sociology, 34,* 257–276.

Nair, R. L., White, R. M. B., Knight, G. P., & Roosa, M. W. (2009). Cross-language measurement equivalence of parenting measures for use with Mexican American populations. *Journal of Family Psychology, 23,* 680–689. Retrieved from http://doi.org/10.1037/a0016142

Nichols, E. (2013). A case study: Exploring cultural competency in faculty at an institution of higher education. (Doctoral dissertation). Retrieved from ProQuest. (Order No. 3630492).

Okazaki, S., & Sue, S. (1995). Methodological issues in assessment research with ethnic minorities. *Psychological Assessment, 7,* 367.

Olson, D. H., & Gorall, D. M. (2003). Circumplex model of marital and family systems. In F. Walsh (Ed.), *Normal family processes: Growing diversity and complexity* (3rd ed., pp. 514–548). New York, NY: Guilford Press.

Pakes, K., & Roy-Chowdhury, S. (2007). Culturally sensitive therapy? Examining the practice of cross-cultural family therapy. *Journal of Family Therapy, 29,* 267–283.

Paniagua, F. A., & Yamada, A.-M. (2013). *Handbook of multicultural mental health: Assessment and treatment of diverse populations.* Cambridge, MA: Academic Press.

Ponterotto, J. G. (2005). Qualitative research in counseling psychology: A primer on research paradigms and philosophy of science. *Journal of Counseling Psychology, 52,* 126.

Ponterotto, J. G. (2010). Qualitative research in multicultural psychology: Philosophical underpinnings, popular approaches, and ethical considerations. *Cultural Diversity and Ethnic Minority Psychology, 16,* 581.

Ponterotto, J. G., & Grieger, I. (2008). Guidelines and competencies for cross-cultural counseling research. In P. B. Pedersen, J. G. Draguns, W. J. Lonner, & J. E. Trimble (Eds.), *Counseling across cultures,* 6th ed., (pp. 57–72). Thousand Oaks, CA: Sage.

Ridley, C. R., Tracy, M. L., Pruitt-Stephens, L., Wimsatt, M. K., & Beard, J. (2008). Multicultural assessment validity: The preeminent ethical issue in psychological assessment. In L. A. Suzuki & J. G. Ponterotto (Eds.), *Handbook of multicultural assessment: Clinical, psychological, and educational applications* (pp. 22–33). Hoboken, NJ: John Wiley & Sons.

Rogge, R. D., Cobb, R. J., Story, L. B., Johnson, M. D., Lawrence, E. E., Rothman, A. D., & Bradbury, T. N. (2006). Recruitment and selection of couples for intervention research: Achieving developmental homogeneity at the cost of demographic diversity. *Journal of Consulting and Clinical Psychology, 74,* 777–784.

Rosenfeld, M.J. (2007). *The age of independence: Interracial unions, same-sex unions, and the changing American family.* Boston, MA: Harvard University Press.

Rostosky, S.S., Riggle, E.D., Gray, B.E., & Hatton, R.L. (2007). Minority stress experiences in committed same-sex couple relationships. *Professional Psychology: Research and Practice, 38,* 392.

Savin-Williams, R.C. (2001). A critique of research on sexual-minority youths. *Journal of Adolescence, 24,* 5–13.

Schumm, W.R., Paff-Bergen, L.A., Hatch, R.C., Obiorah, F.C., Copeland, J.M., Meens, L.D., & Bugaighis, M.A. (1986). Concurrent and discriminant validity of the Kansas Marital Satisfaction Scale. *Journal of Marriage and the Family, 48,* 381–387.

Sciarra, D.T. (2001). School counseling in a multicultural society. In J.G. Ponterotto, J.M. Casas, L.A. Suzuki, & C.M. Alexander, (Eds). *Handbook of multicultural counseling,* 2nd ed., (pp. 701–728). Thousand Oaks, CA, US: Sage Publications.

Searight, H.R., & Searight, B.K. (2009). Working with foreign language interpreters: Recommendations for psychological practice. *Professional Psychology: Research and Practice, 40,* 444.

Shek, D.T. (1995). Gender differences in marital quality and well-being in Chinese married adults. *Sex Roles, 32,* 699–715.

Shek, D.T., & Tsang, S.K. (1993). The Chinese version of the Kansas Marital Satisfaction Scale: Some psychometric and normative data. *Social Behavior and Personality: An International Journal, 21,* 205–214.

Silva, L.C., Campbell, K., & Wright, D.W. (2012). Intercultural relationships: Entry, adjustment, and cultural negotiations. *Journal of Comparative Family Studies, 43,* 857–870.

Snyder, D.K., Heyman, R.E., & Haynes, S.N. (2005). Evidence-based approaches to assessing couple distress. *Psychological Assessment, 17,* 288.

Spanier, G.B. (1976). Measuring dyadic adjustment: New scales for assessing the quality of marriage and similar dyads. *Journal of Marriage and the Family, 38,* 15–28.

Spanier, G.B. (1989). *Dyadic Adjustment Scale (DAS): Manual.* North Tonawanda, NY: Multi-Health Systems.

Steinberg, L., & Silverberg, S.B. (1986). The vicissitudes of autonomy in early adolescence. *Child Development, 57,* 841–851.

Straus, M.A. (2004). Cross-cultural reliability and validity of the Revised Conflict Tactics Scales: A study of university student dating couples in 17 nations. *Cross-Cultural Research, 38,* 407–432.

Straus, M.A., Hamby, S.L., Boney-McCoy, S., & Sugarman, D.B. (1996). The revised conflict tactics scales (CTS2) development and preliminary psychometric data. *Journal of Family Issues, 17,* 283–316.

Sue, S. (1998). In search of cultural competence in psychotherapy and counseling. *American Psychologist, 53,* 440.

Sue, S. (1999). Science, ethnicity, and bias: Where have we gone wrong? *American Psychologist, 54,* 1070.

Sue, D.W., & Sue, D. (2012). *Counseling the culturally diverse: Theory and practice.* Hoboken, NJ: John Wiley & Sons.

Suzuki, L.A., & Ponterotto, J.G. (2008). *Handbook of multicultural assessment: Clinical, psychological, and educational applications.* Hoboken, NJ: John Wiley & Sons.

Szapocznik, J., & Kurtines, W. M. (1993). Family psychology and cultural diversity: Opportunities for theory, research, and application. *American Psychologist, 48,* 400.

Tornello, S. L., & Patterson, C. J. (2012). Age, life pathways, and experiences of gay fathers: Life course perspective. Unpublished Manuscript, Department of Psychology, University of Virginia, Charlottesville, Virginia.

Van de Vijver, F. J., & Leung, K. (2000). Methodological issues in psychological research on culture. *Journal of Cross-Cultural Psychology, 31,* 33–51.

Van de Vijver, F. J., & Poortinga, Y. H. (1997). Towards an integrated analysis of bias in cross-cultural assessment. *European Journal of Psychological Assessment, 13,* 29.

Van Widenfelt, B. M., Treffers, P. D., De Beurs, E., Siebelink, B. M., & Koudijs, E. (2005). Translation and cross-cultural adaptation of assessment instruments used in psychological research with children and families. *Clinical Child and Family Psychology Review, 8,* 135–147.

Viruell-Fuentes, E. A., Miranda, P. Y., & Abdulrahim, S. (2012). More than culture: structural racism, intersectionality theory, and immigrant health. *Social Science & Medicine, 75,* 2099–2106.

Warren, J. C., Smalley, K. B., & Barefoot, K. N. (2015). Recruiting rural and urban LGBT populations online: differences in participant characteristics between email and Craigslist approaches. *Health and Technology, 5,* 103–114.

Wegar, K. (2000). Adoption, family ideology, and social stigma: Bias in community attitudes, adoption research, and practice. *Family Relations, 49,* 363–369.

Williams, C. R., & Abeles, N. (2004). Issues and implications of Deaf culture in therapy. *Professional Psychology: Research & Practice, 35,* 643–648.

Wright, C. L. (2014). Ethical issues and potential solutions surrounding the use of spoken language interpreters in psychology. *Ethics & Behavior, 24,* 215–228. Retrieved from http://doi.org/10.1080/10508422.2013.845532

Wu, N. H., & Kim, S. Y. (2009). Chinese American adolescents' perceptions of the language brokering experience as a sense of burden and sense of efficacy. *Journal of Youth and Adolescence, 38,* 703–718.

Yancey, A. K., Ortega, A. N., & Kumanyika, S. K. (2006). Effective recruitment and retention of minority research participants. *Annual Review of Public Health, 27,* 1–28.

CHAPTER 17

Conclusions Drawn from the Experts on Tailoring Treatment to Diverse Couples and Families

Shalonda Kelly

In this volume, I have amassed the expertise of those who are part of this field and also work with diverse couples and families to supply the field with knowledge of how to tailor their treatment, assessment, and research to the complexities found in most families. The diversity represented in this book is wide-ranging in its breadth and depth, and provides compelling rationales for professionals to learn about and tailor treatment to these populations. But it also presents a daunting challenge for each professional in being able to address the complexities without becoming overwhelmed. Many scholars and clinicians note the importance of theoretical models or frameworks to organize vast flows of information, as well as the need for cultural competence in addressing the issues and concerns of diverse couples and families (e.g., Sue, Zane, Hall, & Berger, 2009). Thus, the purpose of this chapter is to share a model of the mechanisms by which cultural competence enhances work with diverse couples and families, and evaluate it based upon the wisdom of the expert contributors to this book. I provide examples and a summary of final recommendations for working with diverse couples and families, as well as an overview of the overarching strengths, issues, and future implications resulting from this work.

There are compelling reasons to learn more about these diverse couples and families. Readers of this book have learned that Latinos are the largest minority and foreign-born group, that they often face racism and bicultural stress, and that they will double in size by 2050. Whites are the majority group that also is impacted by racial oppression, yet clinicians are challenged to negotiate uncomfortable emotions in raising its impactful role in their lives. Jews have both a religion and a cultural identity, and the omnipresent sociocultural milieu of Orthodox Jewish couples and families is little understood by many therapists. The binary way of viewing gender does not match many experiences, yet it promotes a system of relating that impacts everyone and reinforces gendered power differences in families. Clinicians increasingly will encounter families that are blended, intergenerational, or interracial, headed by a same-sex couple, or have surrogate or adopted children and parents. Many couples and families face large-scale inequalities perpetuated by social norms and institutions that frequently are misunderstood and overlooked, despite the life constraints imposed and the impacts on their physical and mental health. Knowledge of diverse couples and families often is inadequate, due to assessment issues such as test norms, interpretation, and translation, as well as research that lacks diversity yet tends to generalize its findings to all. The recent combination of the 2015 Supreme Court ruling legalizing same-sex marriage and the 2016 tragedy of the largest mass shooting in the United States that targeted attendees of a gay nightclub in Florida reveal controversies in accepting this community. Most importantly, these realities underscore the need to understand diverse couples and families as normal, integral contributors to society, and in need of support, advocacy, and culturally competent treatment.

INTRODUCTION TO THE MODEL BY WHICH CULTURAL COMPETENCE BRIDGES DIFFERENCES

Background

Sue, Zane, Hall, and Berger (2009) identify three approaches to and multiple definitions of cultural competence. With the **type of person approach to cultural competence**, some consider cultural competence to be related to the kind of person the clinician is, and the most widely accepted definition, incorporated into the American Psychological Association multicultural guidelines, falls under the person approach to cultural competence. In this approach, the therapist has **knowledge** of the client's culture, worldview, and expectations for treatment. The therapist also has the **skills** to treat clients in a culturally relevant and sensitive way. In addition, the therapist has cultural **awareness** that involves understanding how her or his biases and values impact treatment. Alternatively, the **skills or tactics approach to cultural competence** focuses on having the therapist choose the appropriate strategies under the appropriate circumstances for each client, and this approach is considered to be the only one that is fairly amenable to the specification and operationalization needed to conduct research on it. The **process approach to cultural competence** focuses on the interactional processes between the therapist and clients. Within this approach, Stanley Sue has identified three characteristics of cultural competence. There is **scientific mindedness** involving cultural hypothesis testing. **Dynamic sizing** involves the ability to be flexible in individualizing knowledge of a client (such as from the client's own idiosyncratic life history) or generalizing culture-specific knowledge to a particular client (such as applying the common worldviews of the group to the specific client). Finally, **culture-specific resources** involve the cultural knowledge and skills used in response to different clients.

Key Definitions and the Model

Kelly, Bhagwat, Maynigo, and Moses (2014) developed a composite definition of cultural competence including widely accepted concepts, as well as aspects of the person, skills, and process approaches. They define **cultural competence** as being comprised of **knowledge, dynamic sizing, skills,** and **awareness**. Three aspects of knowledge should be gathered about clients, including knowledge derived from therapist experience with clients of the family's background, from the family itself, and from data on risk and protective factors relevant to the family. Kelly et al. (2014) adapted dynamic sizing to incorporate the concept of hypothesis testing inherent in scientific mindedness, as therapists can use indicators to test the hypothesis that they should generalize cultural information to a couple or family, or reject it and individualize how they addresses client concerns. For example, if an immigrant lives in an ethnic enclave, it can be an indicator that the hypothesis that immigrant issues matter for that client is supported. Skills can involve specific behaviors, as well as the stance of the therapist, and awareness should include self-awareness of the role of one's own cultural background and identities, as well as awareness of the biases and limitations of the profession.

Kelly and colleagues (2014) also devised a theoretical model to explain how cultural competence works. They assert that there are four mechanisms by which cultural competence enhances treatment, which are through its ability to build bridges across differences among the therapist and family members related to: (1) worldviews, such as those derived from religion and important values; (2) experiences and contexts, such as the experience of immigration and the context of structural oppression; (3) power, such as the marginalization of many clients due to racism, sexism, heteronormativity, or the therapist's influence over her or his clients, and (4) the felt distance between people within the therapy room as a result of the first three differences, such as clients' disengagement and suspicion or therapist perceptions that he or she cannot help them. It is important to be clear that these four mechanisms overlap significantly, but each is presented separately due to their non-overlapping heuristic value. For example, knowledge about structural oppression faced by a couple or family involves both their experiences and contexts, such as living in the inner city, being poor, and the context of violence in the community, and it involves knowledge of their lack of power that is intertwined within those experiences. Yet failure to consider either experiences or power would overlook key differences that need to be bridged by using cultural competence in treatment. See Kelly et al. (2014) for examples of every aspect of the model.

EVALUATION OF THE MODEL BY WHICH CULTURAL COMPETENCE BRIDGES DIFFERENCES

Given that the theoretical model was based upon my expertise, for this chapter, it was important to evaluate the model in light of the extensive and varied expertise of the authors who have contributed to this book. Given the operational difficulties in empirically testing the person and process approaches to cultural competence (Sue et al., 2009), the evaluation was analytic and rational, rather than empirical. I analyzed the degree to which the aspects of cultural competence focused upon by the authors of the chapters in this book are consistent with the model. Most significantly, I found that across all the chapters in this book, the authors' expertise clearly is consistent with all aspects of the model. I also developed summary recommendations based upon the expertise of the many chapter authors. Table 17.1 presents the recommendations about the therapist's cultural competencies that can be used to bridge differences, based upon the expertise of the authors of all 16 chapters. Next, I will provide representative points and recommendations of authors from every chapter to show that every aspect of the model is being utilized by a range of experts, to show how they are useful, and to substantiate the overarching recommendations provided.

Mechanism One: Worldviews and Values

The top left statement in Table 17.1 presents my first recommendation regarding knowledge of diverse worldviews and values, derived from the recorded wisdom of the chapter authors in this book. I recommend that those who work with diverse couples and families should know about the common worldviews, identities, and values that clients are socialized into, as well as common cultural variations in how health and psychopathology are manifest. For example, it is important to know that couples and families from Asian American and Latino cultures, as well as from the Muslim religion, may present with somatic symptoms as a culturally sanctioned way of expressing distress (Haboush & Ansary, Chapter 10; Marano & Roman, Chapter 3; Suzuki, Wong, Mori, & Toyama, Chapter 2, this volume). In the Muslim community, the need for mental health services commonly is stigmatized as a lack of faith and loss of honor to the family, but it also helps to know aspects of the faith that support therapeutic goals (Haboush & Ansary, Chapter 10, this volume). Also, therapists should know how universal family processes are manifest across diverse family structures, including surrogate families, grandparent-headed families, and step-families (Mundy & Wofsy, Chapter 13, this volume).

In regard to dynamic sizing regarding when to apply worldviews and values to a specific family, I recommend that therapists use intakes and questionnaires, ask couple and family members about their identities using genograms, and consider the family members' experiences to determine their levels of acculturation. Jernigan, Green, and Helms (Chapter 14, this volume) specify the importance of therapists *asking* their clients about their identities, beginning with intake forms modified to capture all relevant identities, followed up by more questions. Notably, genograms, or family trees, were by far the most frequently recommended tool suggested by most authors, likely due to their flexibility in being able to capture almost every aspect of diversity. For some families, there are specific models or parameters that can indicate the types of worldviews and values espoused by couples and families. For example, Christian families can be interviewed to determine if their espoused beliefs of mutuality, justice, and hospitality are consistent with their practiced behaviors (Coyle & Davis, Chapter 8, this volume). Intercultural couples and families can be interviewed to determine if they discuss themselves as more interdependent than independent, espouse goals of the in-group more than individual goals, value relatedness more than rationality and exchange, and traditions over attitudes, as indicators that they are more collectivist or individualistic (Maynigo, Chapter 12, this volume). For Asian Americans and Muslims (Haboush & Ansary, Chapter 10; Suzuki et al., Chapter 2, this volume), questions regarding the importance of their religion, immigration generation, and discrimination experiences can indicate the degree that acculturation factors into their worldviews and values.

I recommend that the skill set used to address worldview and value differences involves using cultural norms and resources, intervening in ways consistent with the culture, and validating and fostering positive identity development. For example, with Native Americans and Latinos, it may be helpful to involve tribal or family supports, respectively, and use culturally appropriate ways of healing (Marano & Roman, Chapter 3; Robbins, Ryland-Neal, Murphy, & Geis, Chapter 4, this volume). With many Orthodox Jewish couples and families, it can help to consult with a rabbi regarding issues of adherence to halachas, or Jewish laws, and for the therapist to help with values clarification regarding shidduchim or matchmaking issues (Schechter, Chapter 9, this volume). In working with individual Latinos, therapists can transform treatment into a family intervention to bolster cultural congruence with the value of familismo, or the importance of the family, and work within the couple's preferred gender roles (Marano & Roman, Chapter 3, this volume). In working with clients having a variety of sociocultural identities, such as race or sexual orientation, therapists can help the family members to develop an identity wheel to aid in discussion of important impactful identities, and they can model and foster interactions among family members that aid in the development positive identities, as well as model perspective taking (Jernigan et al., Chapter 14, this volume).

To develop their awareness in regard to worldviews and values, I recommend that therapists consult with experts and in-group members and use explicit frameworks to evaluate their own multicultural competence and explore their own blind spots and biases. For example, Coyle and Davis (Chapter 8, this volume) recommend that therapists explore their own countertransference. Also, they note that awareness regarding Christianity can be cultivated from divisions within professional organizations such as the American Psychological Association's Division 36, as well as from Christian-based organizations that also teach clinical skills, like the American Association of Pastoral Counselors. Greene and Spivey (Chapter 7, this volume) recommend that therapists ask themselves a series of questions to reveal and correct their gender assumptions regarding LGBT (lesbian, gay, bisexual, transgender) couples and families. For awareness regarding assessment issues, Okazaki, Ling, Wong, and (Chapter 16, this volume) recommend use of the knowledge, skills, abilities, and other characteristics framework that focuses on a variety of assessment activities, content that reflects multicultural competencies, and individualized evaluation and feedback.

Mechanism Two: Experiences and Contexts

The second row of Table 17. 1 presents the cultural competencies used to address differences among the therapist and family members in their experiences and contexts. I recommend that therapists know each group's unique experiences, as well as the experiences that present barriers to the American dream at multiple contextual levels. As an example of uniqueness, therapists need to know that Orthodox Jews tend to live in insular communities supported by many nearby community institutions to support their religion and lifestyle. Many experiences and contexts also present barriers at many contextual levels, resulting in five chapters citing Bronfenbrenner's ecological model as a framework to encompass systems and contexts ranging from the macro culture to the local environment (e.g., Kelly & Hudson, Chapter 1; Mundy & Wofsy, Chapter 13; Wesley, Chapter 15, this volume). Therapists need to know that society has phenotypic expectations of couples and families, such that the violation of those expectations may lead to nonacceptance or de-legitimization of multiracial families (Brunsma & Porow, Chapter 11, this volume). Even for Whites, the majority group, one needs to know the history of their aspiring to 1950s' nuclear family models with strict gender roles that ignored identity intersections of ethnicity, socioeconomic status (SES), and sexual orientation that sometimes result in a loss of the privilege to which they may be accustomed. Knowledge of experiences and contexts regarding research barriers includes factors that result in small sample sizes, lack of culturally valid measures and theories, and inadequate funding and support for research on diverse populations (Okazaki et al., chapter 16, this volume).

To facilitate dynamic sizing, I recommend that therapists use a genogram and a framework for hypothesis testing about experiences and contexts impacting lives and couple and family relationships. For example, genograms can be used to gather a family's spiritual narrative that can indicate where the family's religious and spiritual issues lie (Coyle & Davis, Chapter 8, this volume). Winawer (Chapter 5, this volume) advocates the use of a systemic cultural hypothesis that combines interactional and contextual factors to facilitate inquiry and further revision to clarify how they relate to family problems and problematic interactions within the family. Maynigo (Chapter 12, this volume) identifies within-family differences on aspects of their experiences of childrearing, gender, or family relationships, or degree of expressiveness as indicators of inter cultural clashes within the family. Regarding gender and multiracial families, experts consider and contrast larger societal stories and definitions regarding gender and race with clients' lived experiences (Brunsma & Porow, Chapter 11; Knudson-Martin, Chapter 15, this volume).

I recommend linking couples and families to community supports, exploring how experiences differ and impact relationships, being a cultural broker, and utilizing "both/and" thinking and positive framing as core skills that enhance work with diverse couples and families. Authors on the chapters covering the three major religions and Asian Americans all suggest that therapists can enhance treatment by linking couples and families to community supports and resources. These can be resources obtained by the therapist (e.g., Coyle & Davis, Chapter 8, this volume), and those supports can be brought into the therapy session (e.g., Schechter, Chapter 9, this volume), accessed for bolstering a sense of belonging (Suzuki et al., Chapter 2, this volume), or to reach out to partner with those communities toward raising mental health awareness (e.g., Haboush & Ansary, Chapter 10, this volume). Jernigan et al. (Chapter 14, this volume) and Wesley (Chapter 15, this volume) both suggest creating a climate that encourages family members to explore their experiences, attitudes, and values, and assist them in understanding how their experiences and identities affect their perspectives of relationships and their interactions. Other experts additionally advocate that the therapist serve as a cultural referee who models curiosity, tolerance, and understanding of cultural differences in families (Maynigo, Chapter 12, this volume), or as a cultural broker in helping family members to negotiate cultural differences between them (Kelly & Hudson, Chapter 1, this volume), such as in bridging their acculturation differences (Haboush & Ansary, Chapter 10, this volume). Okazaki et al. (Chapter 16, this volume) encourages therapists to counter either-or thinking with both/and thinking to better help the therapist and family to grasp cultural complexity. Mundy and Wofsy (Chapter 13, this volume) suggest the use of a cultural organizing theme that both frames family members' differences in relationship to their problems and implies positive intent, similar to the reframing of an intercultural couple's experience as tourists in a foreign country (Maynigo, Chapter 12, this volume).

I recommend that therapists be aware that many diverse family members may experience dominant perspectives, measures that do not apply to their specific group, and exclusionary gatekeeping. Experts emphasize the dominance of color-blind or postracial narratives that multiracial families tend to experience (Brunsma & Porow, Chapter 11, this volume), and the internalized dominance of White perspectives that White families tend to experience (Winawer, Chapter 5, this volume). They note that such views do not end racism, and instead they imply that whiteness is the standard and is superior. Those assessing families whose first language is not English must be aware of the need for multiple language versions of measures to demonstrate equivalence (Okazaki et al., Chapter 16, this volume), and therapists, assessors, and researchers all need awareness of the gatekeeper function of programs, institutions, and professions, which can deny access to diverse populations.

Mechanism Three: Power Differences

I recommend that those working with diverse couples and families know about inferior portrayals, the push to assimilate groups, and their linkage to structural oppression, as well as their strengths derived from diversity. It helps to know about sociopolitical identities created to portray groups as inferior (Jernigan et al., Chapter 14; Winawer, Chapter 5, this volume), and particularly about how those portrayals and forced assimilation facilitate the intergenerational pain and trauma of structural racism and oppression (Kelly & Hudson, Chapter 1; Robbins, et al., Chapter 4, this volume). Also, these oppressions can be due to gender (Knudson-Martin, Chapter 15, this volume) and many life areas such as mental and physical health and homeownership for African American and Latino families (Wesley, Chapter 15, this volume). Greene and Spivey (Chapter 7, this volume) highlight knowledge of internalized oppression at the intersection of race, sexual orientation, and class, such that some middle-class African Americans may distance themselves from all three identities in policing one another toward only presenting respectable behaviors to the larger society. Knowledge of the vast array of strengths within diverse couples and families that may get overlooked with the preponderance of deficit perspectives ensures that these strengths can be utilized to enhance treatment (e.g., Kelly & Hudson, Chapter 1; Robbins et al., Chapter 4, this volume).

Again I highly recommend the use of genograms and a framework or concepts to assist hypothesis testing toward dynamic sizing for the mechanism of power imbalances, as these tools can indicate where power imbalances lie so that they can be addressed. Genograms may indicate the presence of oppressive discourses, and internalized oppression within couples and families, reflecting the lack of power held by one or more of them. For example, Maynigo (Chapter 12, this volume) cites Killian's (2012) identification of four discourses used by interracial couples, involving de-emphasis of their cultural differences or hyperawareness of their differentness as a couple, the White partner's views of the partner of color as being hypersensitive about race, their shared perspective that race and culture do not matter, or their tacit agreement not to discuss race at all. Kelly and Hudson (Chapter 1, this volume) note that sometimes internalized oppression can be indicated by negative statements about the group revealed in genograms and interviews, such as family members' race-based criticisms of each other. Wesley (Chapter 15, this volume) highlights how power imbalances related to the intersection of SES and race can be indicated by treatment barriers such as transportation issues, employment status, living arrangements, and other practical SES-related aspects of clients' lives. Knudson-Martin (Chapter 15, this volume) presents her useful "circle of care" framework to assess gendered power imbalances based upon a lack of mutual vulnerability, attunement, influence, or shared relational responsibility.

I recommend that those who work with couples and families identify and decrease support for "isms," validate, support, and use strengths, and empower and advocate for their clients. Robbins et al. (Chapter 4, this volume) uses de-colonializing conversations that help Native American couples and families to remove adverse colonial influence and support their place-focused values, and they also seek to foster bicultural competence. With White couples and families, Winawer (Chapter 5, this volume) suggests practicing cultural humility, sharing her own social location and asking about theirs, which suggests that therapists be mindful that majority group members also need empowerment and safety in therapy. Kelly and Hudson (Chapter 1, this volume) and Wesley (Chapter 15, this volume) emphasize the importance of labeling the "isms" and providing education about their presence and role in African American and Latino couples and families' lives, thus reducing self-blame. In addition, they work with these clients to reduce stigma, by normalizing their coping responses and supporting the positive ones, including the decision to seek treatment. Regarding gendered power imbalances, Knudson-Martin (Chapter 15, this volume) has developed a treatment approach that recognizes influences of the binary societal gender system, counteracts it, and empowers more equal, fluid relationship possibilities.

Chapter authors' expertise also leads me to recommend that those who work with diverse couples and families become aware of deficit models, disparities, the therapist's power in treatment, and assessment and research biases and exclusions. Many chapter authors highlight issues of privilege, deficit models, and structural disparities (Kelly & Hudson,

Chapter 1; Maynigo, Chapter 12; Wesley, Chapter 15; Winawer, Chapter 5, this volume). Jernigan et al. (Chapter 14, this volume) recommends that therapists be aware of their own social power in treatment, as well as the impact of their natural tendency to interpret information through the lenses of their own social identities. Regarding assessment and research, Okazaki et al. (Chapter 16, this volume) identifies how common assessment and recruitment practices affect norms, such that diverse couples and families are un-empowered in being judged by White norms, less likely to be recruited into studies, and suffer from the fact that internal validity gets privileged over external validity that could contribute more about their communities.

Mechanism Four: Felt Distance among Therapist and Family Members

I recommend that those who work with diverse couples and families gain knowledge of common injuries, invalidations, and ways to build rapport to bridge felt distance. For example, Marano and Roman (Chapter 3, this volume) identify knowledge of Latinos' history, beliefs, and values that can be used to positively impact rapport-building. Also, Maynigo (Chapter 12, this volume) outlines knowledge of common injuries and invalidations made by therapists, such as when they alienate clients by referring to them as representatives for their cultural group, or by asking about their experiences in ways that may make them feel that they do not fit with the norm.

I recommend that client's questions and negative reactions be used as dynamic sizing indicators of felt distance in the therapy room. For example, Robbins et al. (Chapter 4, this volume) note that it is not uncommon for members of Native American couples and families to question therapists' tribal knowledge or connections.

I recommend that therapists use skills of role induction, use an open, warm, curious, validating stance and tentative and useful conjectures to decrease felt distance. Many authors use some form of role induction with diverse couples and families, as these explanations make therapist and client roles clear and transparent (Kelly & Hudson, Chapter 1; Mundy & Wofsy, Chapter 13; Suzuki et al., Chapter 2; Wesley, Chapter 15, this volume). Maynigo (Chapter 12, this volume) highlights Seiff-Haron, Sasaki, and Sonnier's (2014) four key cultural interventions, two of which are cultural disclosure, wherein therapists seek to balance power with clients by sharing aspects of their own culture, and collective reflection, which normalizes client experiences by linking it to the collective experience of their larger group, to help the client to feel normal and not alone. Jernigan et al. (Chapter 14, this volume) seek to have discussions with diverse couples and families regarding how their identities impact the therapeutic alliance and family interactions. Okazaki et al. (Chapter 16, this volume) also remind us to embrace differences, be curious and open, and ask questions that facilitate effective family functioning.

Finally, I recommend that therapists decrease felt distance with awareness of their own assumptions and impositions, as well as ways they serve to increase or decrease safety and cultural honesty of diverse couples and families. For example, Schechter (Chapter 9, this volume) notes that assumptions and the imposition of therapists' own perspectives can be alienating to clients. Moreover, Mundy and Wofsy (Chapter 13, this volume) assert that transparency around identity dynamics promotes safety and cultural honesty.

Overarching Strengths, Issues, Implications

There are many strengths of the combined wisdom of the authors. A major strength is that many of the chapters provide frameworks or useful concepts or heuristics regarding what to assess and how to address it with diverse couples and families. Thus, those who work with diverse couples and families are helped to determine what is important with each diverse family. Some of the chapters provide guidelines or examples for clinicians to determine what is healthy or not within families that may be unfamiliar to clinicians (e.g., Mundy & Wofsy, Chapter 13; Schechter, Chapter 9, this volume). Others emphasize that the therapist should look to diverse families' communities to determine if values or behaviors are deemed appropriate by healthy community members. Both approaches help therapists to avoid automatically pathologizing differences. Many chapters specifically seek to empower clients to compensate for oppression. Others may use positive reframes and work with client strengths. Both are helpful, and the latter implies that contrary to deficit models wherein diverse groups are judged according to White, heterosexual, male, middle-class, and Christian norms, diverse couples and families have factors within their cultures that enhance their relationships and society as a whole.

One big issue that continues to deserve attention is that many chapters reveal ongoing legally sanctioned oppression of various racial, ethnic, and religious groups. African Americans have suffered from housing discrimination (Wesley, Chapter 15, this volume). Winawer (Chapter 5, this volume) notes how immigration laws have been variable and unequal throughout the history of the United States, and have included or excluded many groups due to economic needs as well as public opposition and xenophobia, resulting in burdens for non-White groups. For example, unlike other groups, refugees from war-torn countries in Central America were denied U.S. entry, and the 1954 "Operation wetback" initiative deported over a million Mexicans from the United States (Winawer, Chapter 5, this volume). Puerto Rico's status as a territory prevents its citizens from voting for the president of the United States (Marano & Roman, Chapter 3, this volume). In the 1960s, the government stopped being the officiant to determine who is considered to be Native American. Yet no efforts were made to redress the community-wide losses of rituals and support systems and devastations of the prior laws less than one generation ago (Robbins et al., Chapter 4, this volume). Currently, over half of Muslims in America report that it is more difficult to be a Muslim since 9/11 and the rise of ISIS; others' negative views of Islam is one of their most frequently reported problems (Haboush & Ansary, Chapter 10, this volume). In 2016, there has been a national debate about banning transgender people from using bathrooms consistent with their transition status, and banning all Muslims entry into the United States. This includes banning refugees from many countries due to the perceived chance that some may be Muslims. While these factors occur outside of treatment, they underscore that oppression is not a thing of the past, and that it still often has legal backing.

Another issue relates to the models of cultural competence. The wisdom of the experts in this book support the therapist as a person approach to cultural competence, as every expert provided knowledge, skills, and awareness factors. The skills or tactics approach to cultural competence was partially supported, in that in being asked to provide concrete skills, each expert was able to do so, and it appears that many of the skills provided can be operationalized so that future research may evaluate their usefulness. Moreover, there seems to be a common set of skills that often are recommended, such as role induction, cultural reframes, use of a genogram to ask about relevant identities, linking families to their own positive community supports, consulting as needed, labeling diversity-related differences and helping family members to negotiate them, normalizing responses to and educating clients about the impact of the oppressions they face, noticing and using strengths, intervening in ways that are consistent with their values, and advocating within institutions regarding SES and other barriers. Each should be the priority for future research. The reason that the skills approach was only partially supported is that a significant but smaller subset of authors explicitly discussed the importance of the therapist's stance, and process-related recommendations such as what factors to attend to and contingently respond to in treatment. For example, several experts explicitly stated that stances such as being curious, open, and understanding are most important (e.g., Okazaki et al., Chapter 16, this volume). Thus, the process approach also was partially supported. Notably, the experts had the least to say in the area of dynamic sizing, or hypothesis testing, either as originally defined by Sue, or as combined by Kelly et al. (2014). Clearly, this aspect of cultural competence may not have been included by the majority of authors if they had not been asked to identify it. This may be because many knowledge factors were indicators of when to generalize the group's culture to the particular family, such that therapists may not separate mentally the fact of knowing something like immigration status/generation from its use as an indicator to address particular immigration experiences.

The volume of the experts' recommendations differed significantly regarding the particular mechanisms of difference to bridge. They had much to say about bridging differences in worldviews and values, and experiences and contexts. This may relate to the data suggesting that not only does tailoring treatment to diversity enhance effect sizes, but also tailoring treatment even more specifically to bridge worldviews increases effect sizes (Benish, Quintana, & Wampold, 2011). It also may relate to data on risk and resilience factors that are widely known to be important for every specific group, and which themselves can be categorized under experiences and contexts. Conversely, the experts had considerably less to recommend about the potential mechanisms of bridging differences in power and felt distance in the therapy room. Still, there were consistent recommendations provided in these areas, such as psychoeducation and discussions designed to reduce stigma and the "isms," and role induction to build rapport and transparency with couples and families.

In sum, these experts' chapters suggest much about the models and mechanisms of cultural competence. Future research is needed to evaluate the implications of their wisdom.

REFERENCES

Benish, S., Quintana, S., & Wampold, B. (2011). Culturally adapted psychotherapy and the legitimacy of myth: A direct-comparison meta-analysis. *Journal of Counseling Psychology, 58*, 279–289. doi: 10.1037/a0023626

Brunsma, D. L., & Porow, M. (this volume). Multiracial families: Issues for couples and children. In S. Kelly (Ed.), *Diversity in couple and family therapy: Ethnicities, sexualities, and socioeconomics* (pp. 289–308). Santa Barbara, CA: Praeger.

Coyle, S. M., & Davis, C. J. (this volume). Christian couples and families. In S. Kelly (Ed.), *Diversity in couple and family therapy: Ethnicities, sexualities, and socioeconomics* (pp. 203–230). Santa Barbara, CA: Praeger.

Greene, B., & Spivey, P. (this volume). Sexual minority couples and families: Clinical considerations. In S. Kelly (Ed.), *Diversity in couple and family therapy: Ethnicities, sexualities, and socioeconomics* (pp. 181–199). Santa Barbara, CA: Praeger.

Haboush, K. L., & Ansary, N. S. (this volume). Muslim couples and families. In S. Kelly (Ed.), *Diversity in couple and family therapy: Ethnicities, sexualities, and socioeconomics* (pp. 259–285). Santa Barbara, CA: Praeger.

Jernigan, M. M., Green, C. E., & Helms, J. E. (this volume). Identity models. In S. Kelly (Ed.), *Diversity in couple and family therapy: Ethnicities, sexualities, and socioeconomics* (pp. 363–392). Santa Barbara, CA: Praeger.

Kelly, S., & Hudson, B. (this volume). African American couples and families and the context of structural oppression. In S. Kelly (Ed.), *Diversity in couple and family therapy: Ethnicities, sexualities, and socioeconomics* (pp. 3–32). Santa Barbara, CA: Praeger.

Kelly, S., Bhagwat, R., Maynigo, P., & Moses, E. (2014). Couple and marital therapy: The complement and expansion provided by multicultural approaches. In F. Leong, L. Comas-Diaz, V. McLloyd, & J. Trimble (Eds.), *American Psychological Association handbook of multicultural psychology*. Washington, DC: APA.

Killian, K. D. (2012). Resisting and complying with homogamy: Interracial couples' narratives about partner differences. *Counselling Psychology Quarterly*, 25, 125–135.

Knudson-Martin, C. (this volume). Gender in couple and family life: Toward inclusiveness and equality. In S. Kelly (Ed.), *Diversity in couple and family therapy: Ethnicities, sexualities, and socioeconomics* (pp. 153–180). Santa Barbara, CA: Praeger.

Marano, M. R., & Roman, E. (this volume). Latino couples and families. In S. Kelly (Ed.), *Diversity in couple and family therapy: Ethnicities, sexualities, and socioeconomics* (pp. 63–89). Santa Barbara, CA: Praeger.

Maynigo, T. P. (this volume). Intercultural couples and families. In S. Kelly (Ed.), *Diversity in couple and family therapy: Ethnicities, sexualities, and socioeconomics* (pp. 309–336). Santa Barbara, CA: Praeger.

Mundy, B., & Wofsy, M. (this volume). Diverse couple and family forms and universal family processes. In S. Kelly (Ed.), *Diversity in couple and family therapy: Ethnicities, sexualities, and socioeconomics* (pp. 337–359). Santa Barbara, CA: Praeger.

Okazaki, S., Ling, A., Wong, S. N., & Tu, M. (this volume). Cross-cultural assessment and research. In S. Kelly (Ed.), *Diversity in couple and family therapy: Ethnicities, sexualities, and socioeconomics* (pp. 423–451). Santa Barbara, CA: Praeger.

Robbins, R., Ryland-Neal, T., Murphy, S., & Geis, C. (this volume). Challenges faced by Native American couples and families and a place-focused approach to treatment. In S. Kelly (Ed.), *Diversity in couple and family therapy: Ethnicities, sexualities, and socioeconomics* (pp. 91–119). Santa Barbara, CA: Praeger.

Schechter, I. (this volume). Socioreligious and clinical landscapes of couplehood and families in orthodox Jewish communities. In S. Kelly (Ed.), *Diversity in couple and family therapy: Ethnicities, sexualities, and socioeconomics* (pp. 231–257). Santa Barbara, CA: Praeger.

Seiff-Haron, J. M., Hirosaki, H., and Sonnier, T. (2014). Cross-cultural couples therapy. Lecture conducted from the Arizona Center for Emotionally Focused Therapy, Scottsdale, AZ.

Sue, S., Zane, N., Hall, G. C. N., & Berger, L. K. (2009). The case for cultural competency in psychotherapeutic interventions. *Annual Review of Psychology*, 60, 525–548.

Suzuki, L. A., Wong, G., Mori, M., & Toyama, K. (this volume). Asian American couples and families. In S. Kelly (Ed.), *Diversity in couple and family therapy: Ethnicities, sexualities, and socioeconomics* (pp. 33–62). Santa Barbara, CA: Praeger.

Wesley, K. (this volume). Disparities in mental health care and homeownership for African Americans and Latinos in the United States. In S. Kelly (Ed.), *Diversity in couple and family therapy: Ethnicities, sexualities, and socioeconomics* (pp. 393–419). Santa Barbara, CA: Praeger.

Winawer, H. (this volume). White racial identity in therapy with couples and families. In S. Kelly (Ed.), *Diversity in couple and family therapy: Ethnicities, sexualities, and socioeconomics* (pp. 121–150). Santa Barbara, CA: Praeger.

About the Editor and Contributors

SHALONDA KELLY, PhD, is a clinical psychologist and associate professor. For 18 years at the Graduate School of Applied & Professional Psychology at Rutgers University, Kelly has trained doctoral students and published manuscripts on addressing race, ethnicity, and culture in individual, couple, and family therapy. Kelly's research examines racial and cultural perspectives and related behaviors and individual and couple functioning, particularly with African American couples. In private practice, she sees diverse clients. She received a diversity award from the National Council of Schools and Programs of Professional Psychology and was named a Leader in Diversity at Rutgers.

NADIA S. ANSARY, PhD, is Associate Professor of Psychology at Rider University. She has several research interests exploring: (1) Muslim youth and young adult mental well-being and community-based outreach, (2) bullying (particularly bias-based) and school-based prevention programming, and (3) the association between problem behaviors and achievement particularly focusing on affluent youth. Her research also includes a focus on cross-cultural issues including ethnic identity as well as acculturative stress.

DAVID L. BRUNSMA, PhD, is Professor of Sociology at Virginia Tech. He is the author/coauthor of 12 books including *Beyond Black: Biracial Identity in America* (now in its second edition) and *Mixed Messages: Multiracial Identities in the "Color-Blind" Era*. He is founding coeditor of *Sociology of Race and Ethnicity* and the executive officer of the Southern Sociological Society.

SUZANNE M. COYLE, PhD, is Associate Professor of Pastoral Theology and Marriage and Family Therapy at Christian Theological Seminary, Indianapolis, Indiana. She is also executive director of the CTS Counseling Center and program director of the MAMFT program, as well as a licensed marriage and family therapist and licensed pastoral counselor. She is the author of *Re-storying Your Faith and Uncovering Spiritual Narratives: Using Story in Pastoral Care and Ministry*, and her work is highlighted at www.spiritualnarratives.com. She was named a 2014–15 Tutu Fellow by the Desmond Tutu Center for Peace, Reconciliation, and Global Justice.

CHRISTINA J. DAVIS, ThD, LMFT, is Clinic Director and Assistant Professor of Pastoral Care and Counseling at Christian Theological Seminary in Indianapolis, Indiana. Her research and professional interests include spiritually integrated counseling, relational psychoanalytical approaches to therapy, and culturally appropriate counseling interventions. Dr. Davis is an ordained minister in the Progressive National Baptist Church.

CHRIS GEIS, BA, is a graduate student in the professional counseling program at the University of Oklahoma and has interests in working with Native Americans.

BEVERLY GREENE, PhD, ABPP, is a Professor of Psychology at St. John's University. She specializes in the context of psychotherapy, including the role of institutionalized oppressive ideologies, psychological resilience, social privilege, marginalization, and multiple identity paradigms. She has interests in the use of psychotherapy and psychological science to facilitate social justice. She has received more than 32 national awards for distinguished professional contributions. She has published more than 100 articles, book chapters, and commentaries and maintains a private practice in New York City.

CARLTON E. GREEN, PhD, is a staff psychologist in the Counseling Center at the University of Maryland (College Park). His scholarship focuses on providing mental health practitioners and trainees with tools for effectively navigating racial and cultural issues in practice settings. He is Co-Chair of the Committee on Racial and Ethnic Diversity for the Society for the Psychological Study of Lesbian, Gay, Bisexual and Transgender Issues (Division 44).

KAREN L. HABOUSH, PsyD (deceased), was Clinical Associate Professor and School Psychology Internship Coordinator at the Graduate School of Applied and Professional Psychology, Rutgers, the State University of New Jersey. She has authored numerous articles on culturally competent practice with Arab American and Muslim families.

JANET E. HELMS, PhD, is the Founding Director of the Institute for the Study and Promotion of Race and Culture, the Augustus Long Professor of Testing and Assessment at Boston College, and a licensed psychologist. Her more than 80 published works explore race and culture influences on measurement, counseling, and psychotherapy interventions, as well as cultural barriers in testing and assessment. She received the 2011 Elizabeth Hurlock Beckman Award for Inspirational Mentoring, the 2007 Association of Black Psychologists' Distinguished Psychologist Award, and the 2008 American Psychological Association's Award for Distinguished Contributions to Research in Public Policy. Her self-help book, *A Race Is a Nice Thing to Have*, is a popular teaching resource.

BRITTANI N. HUDSON, MA, is a PsyD student in Clinical Psychology at the Graduate School of Applied and Professional Psychology at Rutgers, the State University of New Jersey. Her research and clinical interests include cultural minority couples and African American women's relationship formation.

MARYAM M. JERNIGAN, PhD, is an Assistant Professor of Clinical Psychology at the University of Saint Joseph and Assistant Clinical Professor at Yale University School of Medicine. Dr. Jernigan also maintains a private practice dedicated to individual and couples therapy. She has published in peer-reviewed journals and given numerous presentations on the racial and cultural factors that influence mental and physical health outcomes for children, adolescents, and their families with an emphasis on health equity.

CARMEN KNUDSON-MARTIN, PhD, LMFT, is Professor and Director of the Marital, Couple, and Family Therapy Program at Lewis & Clark College. She has published over 70 articles and book chapters on the larger sociocultural context in couple and family relationships and the political and ethical implications of therapist actions on marital equality, relational development, and couple therapy. She is coeditor of *Socio-Emotional Relationship Therapy: Bridging Emotion, Societal Context, and Couple Interaction* and *Couple, Gender, and Power: Creating Change in Intimate Relationships*. She is a past president of the American Association for Marital and Family Therapy, California Division.

ARIANE LING is a doctoral candidate in Counseling Psychology at New York University. Her research interests broadly include multicultural counseling and the study of Asian and Asian American mental health.

MELISSA RIVERA MARANO, PsyD, is a practicing licensed psychologist in Freehold, New Jersey. Her clinical practice serves children through adults. She is on the medical staff at Monmouth Medical Center working with the Regional Newborn Extension Program. She also currently serves as a Board Trustee on NAMI NJ.

TRACI P. MAYNIGO, PsyD, MEd, is a clinical psychologist at Montefiore Medical Center, the University Hospital for Albert Einstein College of

Medicine of Yeshiva University. She has expertise in the cross-cultural treatment of diverse youth, adults, couples, and families, as well as in the areas of reproductive psychology and sexual trauma. She has published on issues related to cross-cultural treatment of diverse couples and families, and she is also the author of *A Girl's Guide to College: Making the Most of the Best Four Years of Your Life* (2011).

MASAKO MORI, PhD, is a visiting associate professor of clinical psychology at Kobe College, Kobe, Japan when she wrote the chapter. She treats Japanese children and their families with issues including acculturative stress, ethnic identity confusion, and intergenerational cultural conflicts at the Japan Education Center in Rye, New York. She has numerous publications and coauthored the book, *Kaigaidesodatsukodomono shinri to kyoiku* ("Psychology and education of children living abroad").

BRIAN MUNDY, LCSW-R, practices individual, couples, and family behavioral therapy in private practice. He is a coauthor of the book, *Therapy in the Real World: Effective Treatments for Challenging Problems*, and publishes on trauma, family therapy, and Acceptance and Commitment Therapy (ACT). He is a professional trainer and consultant for Sound Behavioral Health, and an adjunct professor at New York University School of Social Work.

SHANNON MURPHY, BA, is a graduate student in the professional counseling program at the University of Oklahoma, and has interests in working with Native Americans.

SUMIE OKAZAKI, PhD, is Professor of Applied Psychology in the Steinhardt School of Culture, Education, and Human Development at New York University and the past president of the Asian American Psychological Association. She conducts research on the impact of immigration and race on Asian and Asian American adolescents and emerging adults within local and transnational contexts. She is the recipient of W. T. Grant Foundation Distinguished Fellowship to examine research–policy–practice partnership in education research.

MONIQUE POROW, PhD, is a lecturer in the Department of Sociology at Rutgers, the State University of New Jersey. Her research examines racial socialization within multiracial families and the integral role that parents, extended family members, and siblings play in that process.

ROCKEY ROBBINS, PhD (Cherokee/Choctaw), is a Professor in the Professional Counseling Program at the University of Oklahoma. He has published over 50 articles and his research areas include re-norming psychological instruments for use with American Indians, means of coping for Indian students in boarding schools, needs of therapists who work with Indian clients, studies that focus on American Indian family resiliency, and American Indian spirituality as it is related to psychological health.

EMILY ROMAN, BA, is a PhD candidate in Clinical Psychology at Rutgers, the State University of New Jersey. She specializes in helping couples and families cope with the psychological and neuropsychological effects of severe or chronic illness.

TAHEREH RYLAND-NEAL, BA, is a graduate student in the professional counseling program at the University of Oklahoma, and has interests in working with Native Americans.

ISAAC SCHECHTER, PhD, is a clinical psychologist and Director of the Center for Applied Psychology at Bikur Cholim in Monsey, New York. He launched the Institute for Applied Research and Community Collaboration. Dr. Schechter lectures internationally and has published articles about psychology and the religious community.

PHILIP B. SPIVEY, PhD, is a clinician in independent practice in New York City where he specializes in chemical dependency recovery, people of color and gay and lesbian mental health, and cultivating psychological structures for spiritual well-being and resilience. He coauthored chapters on the psychology of Black male youth and African American gay and lesbian couple relationships.

LISA A. SUZUKI, PhD, is an Associate Professor in the Counseling Psychology Program in the Department of Applied Psychology at New York University. She is senior editor of the *Handbook of Multicultural Assessment* (Suzuki & Ponterotto, 2008) and a coeditor of the *Handbook of Multicultural Counseling* (Casas, Suzuki, Alexander, & Jackson, in progress) and *Qualitative Strategies for Ethnocultural Research* (Nagata, Kohn-Wood, & Suzuki, 2012). She is coauthor of *Intelligence Testing and Minority Students* (Valencia & Suzuki, 2001). Suzuki received the Distinguished Contribution Award from the Asian American Psychological Association (2006) and Visionary Leadership Award from the National Multicultural Conference and Summit (2007).

KYOKO M. TOYAMA, PhD, is an Associate Professor of Counseling at LaGuardia Community College of City University of New York, where she teaches and counsels students in the College Discovery Program. She is author of *The Peer-Partner-In-Learning: Integrating the Practice of Reflection into the New Student Seminar in In Transit.*

MING-CHE TU, MA, is a doctoral fellow in Counseling Psychology in the Department of Applied Psychology at New York University. His research interest focuses primarily on Asian American mental health, specifically among the immigrant population.

KIARA C. WESLEY, MS, is a PhD candidate in the Clinical Psychology program at Rutgers, the State University of New Jersey. Her research focuses on the impact of sociocultural factors on romantic relationships, particularly for African American couples.

HINDA WINAWER, MSW, LCSW, is Executive Director of the Center for Family, Community, & Social Justice, Inc., Princeton, New Jersey. She is a faculty member at the Ackerman Institute for the Family, New York, and maintains a private practice in Princeton, New Jersey. She is coeditor of *Critical Topics in Family Therapy*, and the 2010 corecipient of the AFTA Distinguished Contribution to Social Justice award. She is also a former president of the American Family Therapy Academy.

MATT WOFSY, LCSW, is Adjunct Professor at the New York University Silver School of Social Work and maintains a private practice in New York City. He is the former director of Evidence-Based Treatment and Practice Innovation at the Institute for Community Living. He is the coauthor of *Therapy in the Real World: Effective Treatments for Challenging Problems*. He received the 2011 Mid-Career Social Work Leader Award from the NYC chapter of the National Association of Social Workers.

GRACE WONG, PhD, is a Clinical Psychologist on staff at South Beach Psychiatric Center and an Adjunct Professor at the New York University. At the hospital, she specializes in monolingual Chinese-speaking patients and patients from other diverse cultural backgrounds. She maintains a private practice in Manhattan.

STEPHANIE N. WONG, MA, EdM, is a doctoral fellow in the Counseling Psychology Program in the Department of Applied Psychology at New York University. Her research primarily focuses on Asian and Asian American mental health.

Index